Dictionary of
Social Work

Dictionary of Social Work

John Pierson and Martin Thomas

Mc Graw Hill

Open University Press

Open University Press
McGraw-Hill Education
McGraw-Hill House
Shoppenhangers Road
Maidenhead
Berkshire
England
SL6 2QL

email: enquiries@openup.co.uk
world wide web: www.openup.co.uk

and Two Penn Plaza, New York, NY 10121-2289, USA

First published 2010

A catalogue record of this book is available from the British Library

ISBN-13: 978-0-33-523881-1 (pb),   978-0-33-523882-8 (hb)
ISBN-10: 0335238815 (pb),   0335238823 (hb)

Library of Congress Cataloging-in-Publication Data
CIP data applied for

Typeset by RefineCatch Limited, Bungay, Suffolk
Printed in the UK by Bell and Bain Ltd, Glasgow

Fictitious names of companies, products, people, characters and/or data that may be used herein (in case studies or in examples) are not intended to represent any real individual, company, product or event.

Mixed Sources
Product group from well-managed forests and other controlled sources
www.fsc.org Cert no. TT-COC-002769
© 1996 Forest Stewardship Council

*The **McGraw·Hill** Companies*

General Editors
John Pierson, Staffordshire University
Martin Thomas, University of Manchester

Contributing Editors:
Helen Barnes, University of Manchester
Rhoda Castle, Staffordshire University
Michael Cavadino, University of Central Lancashire
Jim Radcliffe, Staffordshire University

Contributors:
Ju Blencowe, Wolverhampton University
Jane Boylan, University of Keele
Jane Dalrymple, University of the West of England
Santokh Gill, University of Huddersfield
Sue Jenkinson, Staffordshire University
Keith Puttick, Staffordshire University
Adrian Randall, Birmingham City Council
Helen Robson, Staffordshire University
Keith Savage, Stockport College
Mark Savage, Staffordshire University
Paul Stepney, Wolverhampton University
Ben Whitney, Wolverhampton City Council
Claire Worley, Manchester Metropolitan University

Using the dictionary

This edition of the *Dictionary of Social Work* reflects the enormous changes that have dominated social work since 2002. The separation of children and adult services has contributed significantly to this. Our emphasis is, as previously, on terms and concepts that arise from, or impact directly on, social work practice. But practice is more policy-driven than ever and the entries here also define and illuminate the many new concepts in relation to children and adults services that have emerged over the past 8 years.

The aim of this dictionary is to provide both social work practitioners and students, and those in allied fields, with a single, ready source of information, definition and clarification of the critical terms that now dominate practice. But the entire team of contributors firmly believe that practitioners and students should be constantly reflecting on their work and its consequences and we intend that the book be a source of thought and reflection about contemporary practice. We want practitioners to have accurate understanding of the concepts, terms and policies they work with and under but also to have the capacity to think through the consequences of their actions. We hope the dictionary contributes to that process.

To make the vast range of social work terminology accessible for all readers, we have defined and explained each entry in as straightforward and concise a way as possible. Each entry is defined so as to stand on its own. We have, however, included within many entries one or more cross-references. The reader is encouraged to follow these through in order to reach a full understanding of the subject under discussion. Wherever appropriate, we have discussed implications for social work and social care practice under the individual entry. Thus readers will not find a separate entry 'social work with older people' but will find that information under older people. Finally, readers will find all entries to do with welfare benefits under the series of welfare rights entries. This enables the important links among benefits to be made more easily than if they were individually found in their alphabetical order.

Where appropriate, we have given suggestions for further reading underneath each entry.

John Pierson
Martin Thomas
General editors

Dedications

In memory of my lovely son Carl; much loved and much missed.

Martin Thomas

For Sally Katrina Sharp.

John Pierson

Acknowledgements

The editors wish to thank Miriam Sharp Pierson for her work in helping to prepare the dictionary for publication. They would also like to thank Marilyn Brookfield of Cheshire West and Chester Library based at the Bishop Heber High School for her help in obtaining needed books and articles.

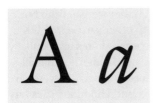

A a

able-bodiedism the assumption that the bodily characteristics of non-disabled people are superior to those of disabled people, who should accept an inferior social status as a result.

Disabled people may have physical, sensory or psychological attributes that differ from what is most common in the general population. The definition of certain attributes as 'normal', however, suggests that they are not only the most common but also the most desirable. This approach is associated with systems of classification for people who deviate from the norm in particular ways. Some of these have resulted in pejorative labels such as 'cripple' and 'spastic'. Although these terms are no longer socially acceptable, assumptions about bodily inferiority affect the way non-disabled people interact with disabled people. Sometimes this takes the form of pity or fear. Able-bodiedism is also associated with a tendency to attribute any difficulties experienced by disabled people to bodily inferiority and to design social and physical environments to suit non-disabled people.

abortion the premature ending of a pregnancy when the foetus is lost because of miscarriage or removed by surgical means from the womb before a baby can survive independently.

The Abortion Act 1967 (amended by the Human Fertilisation and Embryology Act 1990) specifies that in Britain abortion is legal up to the 24th week of pregnancy. However, if there are foetal abnormalities or there is a substantial risk to the woman's life, there is no time limit for an abortion. The issue of risk to the mother's life had already been raised in the earlier Infant Life Preservation Act 1929. 'Foetal abnormalities' in this instance is interpreted to mean that where there are likely to be serious physical or intellectual disabilities or significant genetic problems which are likely to result in an 'unacceptable quality of life'. To comply with the Act, two doctors must be convinced that the pregnancy is likely to be a risk to the physical or **mental health** of the woman or to her children.

The 1967 Act does not apply to Northern Ireland where abortion is still illegal. Cultural and religious attitudes in the UK and in other societies vary enormously although there can be significant differences between formal beliefs and actual behaviour. For example, abortion is illegal in Northern Ireland and the Irish Republic but women from both societies do have abortions often by travelling to other parts of the UK. This is also the case for societies where Catholicism is dominant. Similarly Islamic, Buddhist and Hindu beliefs are mostly against abortion but all think it is permissible in certain circumstances including, generally, to save the life of a mother. In practice Islamic, Buddhist and Hindu societies vary significantly in the incidence of abortion. Their policies regarding the number of weeks by which an abortion must take place generally prescribe much shorter periods than the 24 weeks allowed under UK law, although most abortions in the UK are actually carried out within the first 12 weeks of pregnancy. A large proportion of terminations are carried out in **NHS** facilities but over half are dealt with by private, usually non-profit-making, clinics. Should a young woman under the age of 16 seek an abortion, legally doctors should consult her parents although they do have considerable discretion in this regard. If they think that the young woman is sufficiently mature, has a clear understanding of the key issues and prefers her parents not to be involved then doctors will often accept the young woman's wishes.

Some groups oppose abortion on moral grounds. Disability advocates feel that the justification for an abortion on grounds of 'foetal abnormality' clearly devalues disabled people. Pro-life groups tend to argue that a foetus is a human being from conception, that killing human beings is immoral and that, by implication, abortion has to be wrong. Many would add that the right of the foetus to life outweighs the mother's right to control her own body apart from, exceptionally, to save her own life. Some take the view that a foetus becomes a human being at a particular point in an attempt to answer the question 'when does life begin?' More pragmatically abortion laws in many societies tend to specify a number of weeks in foetal development after which an abortion is normally not legal (except where a mother's health/life is at stake) based upon notions of when a foetus is likely to be 'viable'. Developments in medical care have enabled younger foetuses to survive, but this has not led to changes in UK law despite pressures to do so.

Although there will be many individual and different views, the range of reasons cited by pro-choice groups to justify the woman's right to choose are wide ranging. The frequently cited reasons include where pregnancy was the result of rape; the failure of contraception and, by implication, the child was not planned or wanted; the pregnancy was caused by not knowing that sexual intercourse brings about pregnancy (this might include very young people and those lacking mental capacity); that a pregnancy would prevent the mother achieving some particular objective in her life; that the mother could not look after the child or an additional child; that the family could not afford to have another child; the child is not going to be of a preferred gender or, finally, that the child's disability would place too much stress on a family or disadvantage other children in the family.

Some have argued that the father of a child should have a part to play in decisions about whether a pregnancy should be terminated. Most societies do not accept that a father has any right to insist that a woman does or does not have an abortion, although the Chinese have given men and women equal rights to argue for or against an abortion. Paradoxically some societies have it that men should be financially responsible for a child even though he may not have been consciously party to the conception.

The **social work** or counselling tasks in relation to pregnant women who are unsure about whether to have a child or not are wide ranging depending upon the circumstances. Key issues include whether the pregnancy was planned (clearly with incidents of rape or where the possible repercussions of sexual intercourse are not understood, it will not have been planned); feelings about having a child; whether the father/ relationship will be supportive; whether there are other sources of support should the mother 'go it alone'; and likely feelings about having an abortion. Should a woman decide to have an abortion there may be issues around coming to terms with the decision. Person centred practice should mean that social workers will support women regardless of their decision.

absolute discharge see **discharge**

abuse intentional, purposeful acts or acts of omission leading to a person being hurt, injured or killed.

Attention has focused mainly on **child abuse**, more recently on **adult abuse**, including abuse of people with **mental health problems** or disabilities, such as learning disabilities. 'Spouse abuse' is more commonly referred to as **domestic violence**. Particular environments can be abusing (for example, to be a child in any society where there is violent conflict or extreme **poverty**). In most industrialized societies, however, abuse is thought of as a non-accidental act perpetrated by an individual, family or group, or as something that an individual, family or group fails to prevent. Individuals are therefore held to be responsible, although mitigating circumstances related to abusive environments may be accepted. While most accounts now distinguish between physical, emotional and **sexual abuse**, different forms of abuse may overlap or interact with each other. Physical abuse is likely to be accompanied by **emotional abuse**; sexual abuse is likely also to involve emotional abuse; emotional abuse can occur independently of the other two forms. Historically, physical abuse was the first to be recognized. **Social work** services and public awareness have focused on this form of abuse for some decades. The 'discovery' of **sexual abuse** is relatively recent in Britain, but it has attracted considerable attention in the last two decades. Emotional abuse is the most likely form to pass unrecognized unless associated with other forms of abuse.

Definitions of abuse are value-laden, and for this reason attempts to define abuse are usually couched in fairly general terms. In relation to physical abuse, for example, when does the physical chastisement of a child constitute abuse? Or in relation to neglect (acts of omission), to what extent must a child's development be impaired for the situation to be considered unsatisfactory and to warrant intervention? Some cultures would hold that young children forced to sleep alone is a form of emotional abuse – while others strongly encourage emotional self-control in children at an early age. Sexual abuse is frequently couched in terms of an adult or older young person in some sense exploiting a dependent and developmentally immature person in a sexual act that the immature person perhaps does not fully understand and could not give informed consent to. How understanding and informed consent are to be interpreted are clearly matters of delicacy. Some societies have the age of sexual consent as low as 12, others as high as 18.

Definitions of abuse may simply utilize a medical model, listing injuries or deficits in relation to behaviour that cannot be explained by natural events or accidents. Or they may emphasize the circumstances in which care and protection outside the family will be required. Some definitions take a more general approach, seeking to describe the difference between the optimal development of children and their actual achievement. Others try to give shape to the needs they believe all children have and then ask what it is about a particular child that prevents the fulfilment of those needs. These attempts at definitions have helped to establish a substantial consensus that appears to 'fit' most children in most circumstances, but for many children in certain situations the problem of interpretation will be difficult.

Abusive relationships between adults are usually characterized by the misuse of **power** against a vulnerable person. Difficulties can arise in trying to label any behaviour as abusive if the abused person's experience of life suggests that such behaviours are 'normal'. The same issues arise in structurally unequal societies that may be patriarchal or dictatorial. The search for predictors of abusive behaviour has been long and, so far, inconclusive. Research has concentrated both on groups of factors (explanations rooted in environmental issues, in family dysfunction, in parental characteristics and in the children themselves) and on combinations of what might be precipitating factors. No single explanation or apparent combination of explanations has to date revealed reliable predictors of who will and who will not abuse others. Clearly there are combinations of factors whereby the incidence of abuse increases. For example, a **couple** living in **poverty**, with debt, who are poorly housed, are inexperienced parents, have a poor marital relationship and have a demanding child to look after are more likely to abuse their child than a couple who do not experience these difficulties. But not all couples in these adverse circumstances will abuse their children; indeed, most will not.

Abuse in all its forms is to be found in most societies where research has been completed and in all social classes. As to its incidence, there have been widely varying estimates of the extent of sexual and physical abuse. Sources of information are confined to current cases of substantiated abuse and adult survivors who are willing to reveal their experiences. The former source overlooks undetected abuse and the latter those unwilling to share their histories with researchers; both are probably substantial groups.

access the extent to which disabled people can use the services and public amenities enjoyed by non-disabled people.

Access to public buildings, workplaces, educational establishments, public transport and leisure facilities is necessary if disabled people are to be included within the mainstream of society. The **Chronically Sick and Disabled Persons Act 1970** first made it a requirement for new public buildings to be accessible, but there are many older public buildings to which disabled people have limited access. This can also limit their access to services. Since the Disability Discrimination Act 1995, access to public buildings and services has been improved, but disabled people can still be disadvantaged by the physical environment as well as by other forms of indirect discrimination which limit eligibility to participate in activities and utilize services.

accommodation a family support service in which a child is cared for away from home for 24 hours or more by mutual agreement between parents and a local authority.

Accommodation is part of the wider range of services that a local authority may offer to families and parents. In using it, parents do not lose their **parental responsibility**, nor are they placing their child 'in care'. The use of accommodation should not be taken as a sign of parental inadequacy. Under section 20 of the **Children Act 1989**, the local authority has a duty to provide accommodation to any child in need who appears to require it, either because the child is lost or abandoned, or there is no one with parental responsibility or because the person who has been caring for the child is prevented for any reason from providing suitable accommodation or care. As a service to families, accommodation can be used flexibly to include short-term and respite care or longer periods when a child has to live away from home for whatever reason. Even where a child is abused, social workers should explore the possibility of accommodating that child on a voluntary basis.

Parents (or others with parental responsibility) retain control over the use of this service. A local authority may not provide accommodation for a child if a person holding parental responsibility (usually a parent) objects and is at the same time willing and able to provide accommodation or to arrange to have it provided. The only occasion when this power of 'veto' does not apply is if a person (usually a parent) with a **residence order** for the child agrees to the child being accommodated. In this case, the parent without the residence order cannot veto the child's being accommodated. Any person with parental responsibility may remove the child at any time; the Act does not require notice of any kind – although how and when a child is to be removed from accommodation would be covered in the **written agreement** that must accompany any placement. The Act also requires prior consultation with the child. A young person 16 years and over may consent to accommodation against parental wishes. (See **looked after**.)

accountability   the principle and process of ensuring that public-sector officials and elected representatives are responsible for their actions.

Liberal democracies must ensure that civil servants and other appointed officials are accountable to the people whose interests they are intended to serve. Accountability is the idea that office-holders must not abuse their positions for corrupt or irresponsible purposes. Accountability is also meant to guarantee that decisions and policies made on behalf of the public by its elected representatives are in the public interest and are actually carried out. Traditionally this has meant that most bureaucracies are based on a rigid hierarchy, with rules and regulations to ensure that officials comply with policy decisions and that their actions are recorded in detail. Accountability flows upwards, to ministers in central government and to the full council at local government level, and this results in a tendency for decision-making also to flow upwards. Some would argue that this form of accountability also includes working in accordance with the law. Others have held that **social work** organizations might not always honour their legal mandate or that the legal mandate can be variously interpreted in relation to 'powers' (things that **local authorities** might do) but also sometimes in relation to 'duties' (things that local authorities have to do). Hence it is probably worth distinguishing bureaucratic accountability from legal accountability, although they should more or less coincide.

In the case of social workers and other professional officers, accountability operates in two additional ways. First, it may flow downwards to the client or user of the service. Officials may therefore see their actions as determined by their relationship with and responsibility to the individual client, since they are advocates for that person's interests. As a result, they may sometimes find themselves in conflict with the more traditional form of accountability, which operates upwards in the **social services department** within which they are employed. Second, social workers and other professionals may identify a further form of accountability towards their profession: the need to behave in an acceptable professional manner, particularly in their relationship with other **social work** colleagues and in relation to other professional groups, such as the **probation service** and the **police**. Finally, some have it that professionals or, indeed, any worker can be accountable to his or her own principles and moral precepts, including religious convictions. Such convictions could have a profound effect upon how social workers advise **service user**s on, say, issues such as **abortion**, marital problems or family obligations. This fivefold process of accountability creates a permanent source of tension for social workers as well as a framework for understanding their roles in their work.

Recent incidents have also highlighted the problem of how accountability and the related issue of responsibility can cause problems for social work. The **Baby Peter** case resulted in the Director of the Children's Services involved to be held responsible as well as accountable and this resulted in her sacking along with the resignation of the leader of the council and other councillors and officials. The debate over who was responsible and the impact of media scrutiny is telling in the way it places the issue of accountability in **social care** at the centre of debate over professional standards and behaviour.

Banks, S. (2003) *Ethics, Accountability and the Social Professions.* Houndmills: Palgrave Macmillan.

action plan order a **sentence** for young offenders introduced by the **Crime and Disorder Act 1998** that imposed requirements to be carried out by the young person under the **supervision** of a member of a **youth offending team**. The action plan order is now replaced by the **youth rehabilitation order**.

activity requirement a requirement which may be included in a **community order, youth rehabilitation order** or **suspended sentence order**, obliging the offender to participate in specified activities for up to 60 days. Activities could include day centre activities, education or training, or **reparation** to **victims** or the **community** affected by the crime. An activity requirement is normally combined with a **supervision requirement**.

additional educational needs a broader term than **special educational needs,** which identifies those children who require extra educational attention because of a variety of factors that may affect their learning. This group approximately equates to those seen as **children in need** or 'vulnerable' children under the **Children Act 1989** and are a key focus for the duties of **local authorities** (LAs) and schools in promoting **educational inclusion**. It includes children, for example, whose family life is disrupted, who are young **carers**, or at risk of sexual exploitation, **travellers** and the **victims** of **abuse** as well as those with an identified **learning difficulty** and those whose attendance at school is poor. See also **inclusion, educational inclusion** and **social inclusion**.

adolescent support team a multi-disciplinary **team** that diverts young people from the care system and works to keep adolescents at home in families with high levels of conflict.

Adolescent support teams provide a short-term intensive service that helps families defuse problems in relationships that might otherwise lead to a young person leaving home prematurely, with the risk of **homelessness**.

Most of the families that such teams work with are characterized by a high degree of conflict, parental **mental health problems** or **domestic violence**. Such problems are frequently intertwined with the behaviour problems of the adolescent. As many as half the young people such teams work with have suffered abuse, neglect, placement in care or social services involvement. A **team** typically will include social workers, education support workers, **Connexions**' personal advisers and a family therapist. Their wide brief reflects its multi-disciplinary make-up: to improve skills of parents of adolescents particularly in conflict resolution, to tackle problematic behaviour of the young person, and to offer support to troubled or disaffected adolescents through anger management and work on self-esteem.

adoption the process by which the legal relationship between a child and his or her birth parents is severed and a new legal relationship established with adoptive parents. Adoption was introduced into English law in 1926 to clarify the position of children brought up by adults other than their own parents, in particular to ease concerns that such children would be taken back by their parents. Until that year it was impossible to transfer parental rights permanently, although in practice *de facto* adoptions did occur. Adoption creates a new legal relationship nearly identical to that between a child and his or her natural parents. When a child is adopted, all the powers, duties and rights of the natural parents in relation to the child cease and are transferred to the adopting parents; this is the traditional transplant model of adoption. Social workers' views on adoption were traditionally dominated by the intention of creating a completely new family for the adopted child, with no ties to the old one. The objective was to provide a permanent, secure and loving home for children whose parents were unable or unwilling to look after them. The common image of an adoption involved placing an infant with a childless couple who were complete strangers to the child's parents. The natural parents did not know the identity of the adopters and lost all right to see the child. To avoid **stigma** for the child, and to protect mothers of non-marital children, secrecy concerning the child's origins was strictly maintained throughout **childhood** and beyond.

In this view, adoption was supposed to provide permanent security for children in public care who otherwise might have drifted from one foster home or **children's home** to another. It also met the needs of the adults, rather than prioritizing the child's welfare.

This perspective changed from the 1980s on. Studies confirmed that the secrecy surrounding adoption often led to confusion and unhappiness for adopted people. Lack of information about their natural parents and the mystery surrounding their family background frequently produced distrust and bitterness as the adopted child grew older. Consequently, adoption law was changed, making it possible for adopted people aged 18 and over to obtain access to their birth records and to search for their natural parents if they wished. Moreover, the value of continuing contact between natural parents and the adopted child was recognized as helping to dispel confusion over identity and to stabilize the adoption placement. Courts can in fact make a **contact order**, for direct or indirect **contact** under section 8 of the Children Act, in favour of the natural parents at the same time as making an **adoption order**. The old view was also modified because, with the advent of widespread birth control and less social disapproval of 'illegitimacy', the number of babies placed for adoption fell dramatically (now less than fifty babies a year). Now adoption is increasingly used to secure a family for older children with **special educational needs** who may require considerable care that their natural parents are unable or unwilling to provide. **Local authorities** may pay adoption allowances in such cases. Step-parents have also used adoption in greater numbers to secure parental responsibility for a child of their new partner.

Who can adopt? In an effort to increase adoptions the 2002 Act relaxes the limitations on who can adopt: now anyone can become an adopter who is at least 21 years old; couples must be married, in a civil **partnership** or 'living as part of an enduring relationship'. Single people may adopt. Adopters must fit the habitual residence requirements and not have been convicted of a specified offence. The Adoption Agency Regulations 2005 lists the grounds local authorities should consider when deciding potential adopters' suitability.

Who can be adopted? Under the **Adoption and Children Act 2002** any child under 18 can be adopted but must be at least 19 weeks old and have been placed with prospective adopters for a continuous period of at least 13 weeks before an adoption order is made. Under the Act the child's wishes should be ascertained by the **children's guardian** or reporting officer as well as reported on by the social worker from the **adoption agency** giving the child's opinion a more formal footing in the adoption process than before.

Social workers have a number of tasks during the adoption process. They must obtain consent from the child's natural parents, explaining to them the effect of the adoption on their parental rights and responsibilities. They must also explain what each stage of the process involves. Such work may be extremely fraught, since parents of a child to be adopted may change their mind several times. Sometimes when parents refuse permission and the local authority concludes that adoption is the only long-term arrangement able to promote the welfare of a child in its care, the social worker has to persuade the court to dispense with parental consent (see **adoption hearing**). Since the 2002 Act the consent issue must be dealt with early on, at the stage of placement. Local authorities have a delicate balancing act to protect children's best interests and decisions about adoption can run concurrently with rehabilitation attempts, a process known as 'twin tracking'.

Social workers must also gather information and write detailed reports. Because a child may be placed for adoption only by an adoption agency after a properly constituted **adoption panel** has met to consider the decision, a social worker has to provide the adoption panel with a report covering a range of information concerning the natural parents, the child and the adopting parents. Such reports involve considerable skill in the presentation of information, based on lengthy interviews on often sensitive topics – for example, about when the prospective adopters would propose to reveal to the child the fact of their adoption. Other tasks include **supervision** of the child placed for adoption but not yet adopted and going to court on behalf of the adoption agency to explain why this irrevocable step needs to be taken.

Continuing professional support for adoptions has become critical. In the past virtually all adoptions were of 'relinquished infants'; now most adopted children have spent substantial time within the care system with experiences of frequent moves and perhaps **abuse** or neglect in their histories. Many prospective adopters are unaware of the range of circumstances that may compromise a child's health and development; according to the British Agencies for Adoption and Fostering, some 40 per cent of children placed for adoption in 1999 had developmental or learning difficulties or medical problems. In this context adoption should be seen as a lifelong service to children, with the need for close support from health, education and psychological services. There is also a historical division between fostering and adoption that may now be obsolete. Recent evidence from the USA shows that **foster care**r **adoption**s have increased dramatically, as have kinship **adoption**s, accounting in all for some 80 per cent of adoptions from care.

Perhaps the most recent development for practitioners is the increased emphasis on making adoption a child-centred process, proceeding strictly along the line of what is in the child's welfare and to make the child's own wishes and feelings paramount. Some children's advocates are urging that children over 12 be given the right to consent or object to their own adoptions. Both the process and function of adoption have been under constant review since the passage of the Children Act in 1989, and adoption remains a controversial and sensitive area of policy and practice. Because it requires terminating the rights, responsibilities and relationships of birth parents and transferring them to a new set of parents it links with other powerful issues around fairness, social inequalities, religion, '**race**' and gender. These matters are potentially important at the 'matching' stage of the process. The Labour government elected in 1997 placed adoption high on its agenda as a solution for children who, for whatever reason, cannot return to their parents. To make adoption somewhat easier it attempted to loosen some of the adoption regulations – making it easier for a wider range of would-be adoptive parents to contemplate adopting a child.

Douglas, A. and Philpot, T. (1999) *Adoption: changing families, changing times.* London: Routledge.

adoption agency an organization approved by the Secretary of State at the **Department of Health** to undertake **adoption** services.

Local authorities and diocesan adoption societies are both examples of adoption agencies. One of the main tasks of an adoption agency is to oversee arrangements for the adoption of children. This includes selecting prospective adoptive parents, placing and supervising children for adoption and providing post-**adoption** services such as counselling for birth parents who have had children adopted. The **Adoption and Children Act 2002** formal acknowledgement of the value of same sex relationships is problematic for some agencies. Increasingly, local authorities as adoption agencies are being encouraged by central government to compare the quality of their service to those in the independent sector.

Adoption and Children Act 2002 legislation that introduced both significant changes to the **adoption** process and greater legal oversight for the way **local authorities** implement their care plans for individual children. This legislation modernized the existing legal framework for domestic and inter-country adoption to make the child's welfare the paramount consideration in all decisions concerning the adoption of a child, thus bringing it into line with the **Children Act 1989**, and introduces a **welfare checklist** of matters that the court and **adoption agency** must consider closely. These include the child's wishes and feelings regarding the adoption, the effect on the child throughout her or his life, the relationship the child has with relatives as well as any harm that the child may have suffered. Adoption agencies must also have regard for the child's religious persuasion, racial origin and cultural background. Another major change requires that adoption agencies place a child for adoption only where the parents of the child have given their consent or a *placement order* has been obtained. The grounds for dispensing with parental consent now are: if the parent cannot be found or is incapable of giving consent; or if the welfare of the child requires that consent be dispensed with. In other words, dispensing with parental consent is to be judged only in the light of what is in the child's interest. This is a shift from previous adoption law, which allowed a parent's consent to be dispensed with by the test of 'unreasonableness', that is, that the parent was acting unreasonably in withholding consent. This was sometimes invoked by the court after a prolonged period in care (for whatever reason) and was a source of dispute – and often considerable **grief** – for the parents of the child. The Act formally recognizes same sex and cohabiting **couple**s as possible adopters. Notably for the first time it is now possible for a child to have two mothers or two fathers, but never more than two legal parents. Finally, a special form of guardianship is introduced for those children for whom **adoption** is not suitable but who cannot return to their birth families. Under the national standards for adoption launched in association with the Act, looked after children are entitled to have adoption considered as a means to give them a secure and permanent home. Under these standards, within six months after a child has been defined to be 'continuously **looked after**' a decision regarding a permanent home should be made. If adoption is the plan, a decision in principle should be made within six weeks with suitable prospective adopters identified within six months. National standards also require that looked after children be well prepared before joining a new family while the prospective adoptive family should reflect the child's birth heritage as long as this does not introduce undue delay. The Act also puts the implementation of local authority care plans for individual children under greater official scrutiny. It does this by establishing the role of *independent reviewing officer*, who will carry out review meetings on the progress of individual care plans for children looked after by the local authority. Where the local authority has failed to carry out key parts of the plan, the reviewing officer will be able to take the case to the children and family court advisory service.

adoption contact register a national register of names of people adopted as children and willing to be **contact**ed by their birth parents or other relatives. The register also lists the names of parents and relatives wishing to **contact** children who were adopted and who have reached 18 years of age. The Register is provided by the National Organisation for Counselling Adoptees and Parents. The function of the register is to facilitate **contact** between both sides of the original family. The setting up of the register is further recognition that the secrecy that used to surround **adoption** and the finality of the separation that occurred between adopted children and their birth parents often caused distress to both sides, and, in the case of the children, could lead to confusion as to their identity and background.

adoption hearing the proceedings in court that determine whether a child is to be adopted. Applications by prospective parents for an **adoption order** are heard in **magistrates' court**s but more usually in county courts and are always in private. Information placed before the courts at an adoption hearing is strictly confidential. If the natural parents of the child have not given their consent to the **adoption**, the hearing is usually in two parts. First, the court considers whether grounds exist for overriding the requirement for each parent to agree to the **adoption**. Under the **Adoption and Children Act 2002** it is required that the making of an order is in the child's welfare following the **welfare checklist** in section 1(4) which includes consideration of the child's wishes and feelings, also that the birth parent have consented or their consent has been dispensed with. The legal representatives of the agency, the **children's guardian** and the child's parents are represented and place their arguments before the court; the prospective adopting parents are not in court at this stage. The second stage follows if the court decides to dispense with parents' consent. (Alternatively, if both parents have given their consent, the hearing starts at this point.) In this second stage the court focuses on the merits of the application and whether the adoption is in the child's best interests. The would-be adoptive parents are usually in court at this stage and the natural parents are not. If the child has been in the care of a local authority and adoption is seen as the best way to secure a permanent home for him or her, social workers may be called to give evidence in support of the application at either stage of an adoption hearing. Social workers' evidence is often crucial to the outcome, so command of the facts and circumstances of the case, and the reasoning behind the application, is essential.

In reaching any decision, the court's first consideration is the need to safeguard and promote the welfare of the child throughout **childhood**, that is, until the child reaches 18. Social workers' arguments to the court must bear this long-term perspective in mind. The court will also take into account the wishes and feelings of the child if it is practical to do so. Under the Adoption and Children Act 2002 the freeing order (under the Adoption Act 1976) is replaced by a *placement order*, which can be made only if the child is subject to a care order or the court is convinced that the conditions for a care order are met. The placement order also requires parental consent unless the court is satisfied that their consent should be dispensed with.

adoption order a court order that transfers legal responsibility for a child from his or her birth family to the adoptive family. Following an adoption order, all the rights, duties and responsibilities of the natural parents in relation to the child cease and are assumed by the adoptive parents. Occasionally courts will also order that some form of **contact** between the child and the birth parents should continue. More usually, the adoptive parents agree to afford contact to members of the birth family and the need for a **contact order** is avoided.

adoption panel the panel constituted by each **adoption agency** that authorizes the decision to place a child for **adoption** by that agency. In deciding whether a child should be placed for **adoption**, the panel considers whether the **adoption** is in that child's best interests and whether a particular child should be placed with particular adoptive parents. Panels also decide whether individual applicants should be approved as prospective adoptive parents. Would-be adopters may include single people or a gay or lesbian **couple** since the **Adoption and Children Act 2002** was passed. The panel is made up of lay members, such as doctors, local councillors and parents, and is usually chaired by a senior member of the adoption agency. The panel officially makes only advisory judgments, with final decisions left to the agency, but its decisions are almost always respected in practice.

adult abuse the abuse of adults by people who are more powerful than less powerful and vulnerable adults. Such abuse may serve self-interests or group interests of abusers. There is an extra component of betrayal by those having a duty of care, or 'care contract' towards the person, whether the perpetrator is a relative, or a paid carer.

These definitions of abuse thus highlight the misuse of **power**, betrayal of trust, and harmful consequences for the person. Children are at risk of encountering these experiences because they are routinely in a relatively powerless position in relation to adults. Significantly, however, there is also a greater risk for adults who receive health and **social care** services in contrast with the general adult population. These adults include **older people**, physically and sensorily disabled people, learning disabled people, people with **mental health problems**, people with long-term health conditions and people with serious **substance abuse** concerns.

Since 2000, policy for adult **service user**s has recognized and responded to this concern. Initially this took place in the **No Secrets** multi-agency policy for adult abuse, currently being revised to take account of **personalization** principles. Then in 2005, the Association of Directors of Social Services (ADSS) published standards for **No Secrets** policy (see **adult safeguarding** for the legal and policy response to adult abuse).

No Secrets understood adult service users to be at greater risk of abuse because their disabilities and **impairment**s rendered them less capable. They were viewed as dependent vulnerable adults, potentially unable to protect themselves against **significant harm** or exploitation. The concept of **safeguarding adults**, however, significantly changed the nature of practice, reflecting greater emphasis on **empowerment**, **citizenship**, social inclusion and prevention amongst adult **service user**s. This highlighted the importance of countering adult abuse because it threatened basic rights of independence, **wellbeing** and quality of life. This understanding is encapsulated in provisions of **Fair Access to Care** eligibility criteria for service provision. In this context, they viewed adult **service user**s' greater vulnerability to abuse as a matter of their not being able to access the support needed to live safer lives.

The policy concern with the risk of abuse to adult **service user**s formed a response to the **Human Rights Act 1998** which placed duties on public bodies to protect the human rights of their **service user**s. Examples of these rights include the right to protection against torture and degrading and inhuman treatment (Article 3), and the right to liberty (Article 5). Thus No Secrets defines abuse as 'a violation of an individual's human and civil rights by any other person or persons' (2.5), and *Safeguarding Adults* states that adult **service user**s 'have the right to live a life free from violence and abuse'. The specific concern regarding adult service users relates to the above policy beliefs that these service users would be at greater risk of abuse, together with the requirement from Article 14 of the Human Rights Act which prescribes there must be no **discrimination** against any group of people in upholding human rights.

The forms of abuse identified as those requiring a response within No Secrets policy and *Safeguarding Adults* are physical, sexual, psychological, financial or material, neglect and acts of omission and discriminatory abuse. Importantly, these include criminal offences, such as theft or assault. Thus responses to **adult abuse** include use of the criminal justice system – a principle prioritized in adult safeguarding policy.

Some of the other forms of abuse constitute **breach**es of professional codes of ethics, and others can be understood as institutional abuse, involving poor care which breaches legislation for the regulation of care provision – for example, the **Care Standards Act 2000**. Importantly too, discriminatory abuse relates to the **Race Relations (Amendment) Act 2000**, and the **Disability Discrimination Acts of 1995, and 2005**, which place duties upon public agencies to promote equality and to take positive steps to counter **discrimination** – although in no small number of cases, discriminatory abuse has involved criminal acts of violence and murder.

Surveys have demonstrated the high rates of abuse experienced by adult service users: for example, up to 80 per cent of learning disabled service users; 6 per cent or 342,000 older people living in private households, and 47 per cent disabled people report abuse experiences. Nearly a third of care workers have observed physical abuse of older people in residential care. As No Secrets also points out, anyone can be a perpetrator – informal carers, paid care workers, **volunteer**s and professionals, family members, neighbours, friends, associates, strangers, and other service users.

Understandings of how adult service users come to be at greater risk of abuse are very important in promoting effective prevention and response. Policy understandings as we have seen, focus on the impact of disability and health conditions upon the person's capacity to protect him- or herself and to access sources of assistance. Current policy also focuses upon the social **stigma** attached to adult **service user**s which renders low standards throughout society and the services acceptable – for example the National Care Standards for Older People 2001 **direct payments** legislation, and the **Mental Capacity Act 2005** stipulate that services should not respond on the basis of discriminatory assumptions regarding the person's age, disability or health condition.

In addition, understandings from the **social model of disability** draw attention to the sources of abuse in the structural inequalities faced by adult service users who are more likely than the adult population generally to experience **poverty** and to lack social influence and resources. They are also the subjects of negative social beliefs, expectations and **stereotype**s. These inequalities together have far-reaching consequences. On the one hand, devaluing stereotypes can result in the motivation to abuse, and on the other, lack of resources and options, and low self-worth, internalized from society, can present insuperable obstacles to adult service users exerting control over the situation. Their limited resources, any difficulties which may arise from a health condition or **impairment** such as **dementia**, and stereotypes construing them as totally incapable also make for many difficulties in their accessing justice.

Further factors in the lives of adult service users that can make abuse more likely can be found in the circumstances of informal **carers**, and the high expectations placed upon them by policy. The **service user** is often isolated from society and in close and frequent **contact** with carers, and as observed in a report by the Disability Rights Unit in 2005 there is insufficient provision of services which can support the person's greater independence and thus less vulnerability to abuse. Informal carers are also likely to face a range of difficulties such as poverty, unemployment or balancing work with caring quite aside from the physical and emotional implications of caring. It used to be thought that the stress created by the 'burden' presented by the **service user** was the main reason for abuse by carers, but now it is recognized that this will more often be connected to emotional problems, **substance misuse** or poor coping on the part of the carer him- or herself, linked in many cases to the whole range of stressors that they face.

This can also be true of paid carers who work in a context of **low pay** and poor conditions in the **mixed economy of care**. Staff shortages, poorly qualified staff, and cost-cutting practices, all contribute to poor quality care within which abuse then occurs. Institutional abuse involves actions motivated by negative social constructs of adult service users ingrained in an organization's practices. In addition, there are criminally-motivated people across the range of carers and others that the adult service user encounters – people who can take advantage of the service user's relative powerlessness – and perpetrators who, like perpetrators of **child abuse**, gain satisfaction from the act of abuse itself.

Crucial in making an adequate response to the adult **service user** who has been abused, is an understanding of how abuse affects people. Post-traumatic stress is a likely response to the experience, whatever the type or severity of abuse, and this can have a major impact on the person's mental capacity and social functioning. It also creates unbearable distress. This can result in the person experiencing 'dissociation' and perhaps flashbacks – states in which the person is not at all in control. All these difficulties can mean serious risk, and also, significantly, will affect the person's capacity to problem-solve and make empowering decisions. Fear of retribution, or a loyalty to the perpetrator can also place powerful restraints on the person's ability to act in her or his own best interests.

These considerations have implications for assessment, and for interventions. **Assessment** understandings of abuse and its impact, skills, and use of research findings – e.g. indicators for different types of abuse – are essential to an empathic and sensitive engagement with the service user, and to an anti-discriminatory appreciation of unusual reactions as possibly connected to abuse rather than simply as signs, perhaps of mental disturbance. With regard to interventions, service users' experiences of trauma suggest a very important need for a therapeutic response alongside the range of other provisions that may be required to promote prevention of further abuse, protection and **empowerment** in a care plan. Awareness of the social barriers to independence and prevention of abuse suggests too that longer-term provisions should include the **social care** services which can fully support the person in living the life they choose.

adult autism strategy long-term planning for meeting the needs of adults with **autistic spectrum conditions**.

The Autism Act 2009 requires the government to publish by 2010 a strategy to improve relevant services provided by **local authorities** and the **NHS** for adults with **autistic spectrum conditions**. The strategy will have to be prepared in consultation with interested parties and revised regularly. NHS bodies and local authorities will have to implement guidance issued by the Secretary of State in connection with the Strategy. The guidance will include the provision of diagnostic services; the identification of adults with autistic spectrum conditions; the **assessment** of need; service planning and staff training.

The introduction of the strategy follows campaigns by voluntary organizations, relatives and potential **service users** emphasizing the support needs of adults with autistic spectrum disorders, the shortage of appropriate service provision and the exclusionary effect of the current eligibility criteria for access to **social care** services. A recent report by the National Audit Office identified a range of issues requiring attention, in particular the lack of support for those with 'high functioning' autism, who are often ineligible for services. The **Department of Health** has launched a consultation process to help shape the first adult autism strategy:

Department of Health (2009) *A Better Future: a consultation on a future strategy for adults with autistic spectrum conditions.* London: DH.

adult protection see **safeguarding adults**

adult training centres see **day services**

advance directive a written, signed and dated **statement** by an individual indicating the kind of medical treatment he or she would like to receive in the event that they are incapacitated, but may take the form of witnessed verbal instructions.

In general, advance directives, sometimes known as 'living wills' or 'advance decisions', are used to indicate the wish to refuse all or some forms of medical treatment should the person lose mental capacity in the future. The most common is the request to not be resuscitated if stricken by particular conditions such as a severe stroke. Under the **Mental Capacity Act 2005,** the statute governing advance directives, they cannot be used to ask that the person's life be ended nor can it force doctors to act against their professional judgement. They cannot compel a particular treatment be administered or nominate a person to decide about treatment on one's behalf.

advice   the process by which people with subject knowledge, or with considerable experience of a problem and its potential solutions, indicate how a problem might be solved or eased. Advisers are found in many guises. They include advice centre workers, local authority workers, solicitors, social workers, **charity** workers, youth workers, **probation officers**, and specialists working in particular fields, such as AIDS counsellors, trading standards officers, consumer advisers and child guidance workers.

In many instances **advice** workers continue to be **volunteers**. In addition, advice can be offered by people who themselves have experience of a certain problem. In this context, **self-help** can be the method of advice work among those who have the same difficulties, with professional advisers expressly excluded from the process.

Since the late 1990s attempts have been made to give the 'advice-giving industry' more coherence in relation to both service provision and the education and training of advice workers. The government established the **Community Legal Services Commission** and gave this body the responsibility for creating a quality assurance framework for all advice services and agencies with Quality Marks given for high standards of specific legal service providers. The standards are designed to ensure that a service is well run and has its own quality control mechanisms, receiving either a General Quality Mark (GQM) or a Specialist Quality Mark (SQM).

The General Quality Mark is split into two sections:

General Help – The Quality Mark defines general help as services that provide the following: diagnosing clients' problems; giving information and explaining options identifying further action the client can take; generally accomplished in one **interview** although there may be some follow-up work.

General Help with Casework – covers a **casework** service, i.e. taking action on behalf of clients in order to advance their interests. This may include negotiation and **advocacy** on the client's behalf to third parties on the telephone, by letter or face-to-face. By definition, most cases will involve follow up and cannot be accomplished in a single interview.

The Specialist Quality Mark covers services that: supply complex legal help in specific areas of law; provide the full range of legal services, including representation in court (where necessary and permitted) by formally trained professionals; wish to receive **Legal Services Commission** funding; are well run and provide good client care. The education and training of **advice** workers is covered by the National Occupational Standards developed for legal **advice** in 2004, in consultation with representatives from the **advice** sector. These standards seek to unify and rationalize differing standards across the sector and provide a consistent approach to service delivery. The development of the standards has also resulted in a framework for the development of **National Vocational Qualification**s and Scottish vocational qualifications and for foundation degrees in legal advice. Higher education has also taken an interest in this 'industry' both in terms of entry level qualifications, continuing personal development, undergraduate and postgraduate awards in Advice Studies.

advocacy speaking up, or being helped to speak up. In **social work advocacy** involves making sure that the views and wishes of **service user**s are heard and understood.

Advocacy is best understood in the formal context of legal services where the role of an advocate in court (i.e. a solicitor or barrister) is to represent the interests of someone by speaking up on their behalf and protecting their rights. Within **social work** various forms of non-legal advocacy have become established as an accepted way of working with people who need support to put forward their wishes and feelings. It has developed in this context to challenge inequality and oppression and social workers are expected to take on an advocacy role in their work with **service user**s and carers. Where social workers find that they are unable to do this independent advocacy services may be required. Advocacy may refer to work with individuals or small groups such as families (often referred to as *issue-based* or *case advocacy*) or have a wider sphere of activity in terms of promoting structural changes in relation to legislation, policy or practice (often referred to as *cause* or *systemic advocacy*).

People requiring advocacy have been disempowered by the systems and processes that impact on their lives. They either need someone to speak or act on their behalf or support to enable them to advocate for themselves (*self-advocacy*). A number of forms of advocacy have developed to support service users in various settings and situations. *Citizen advocacy* involves a long-term relationship between a person and an advocate; a *peer advocate* is someone who has had similar experiences to the person they are supporting; a *professional advocate* is trained and paid and often supports people in a task-centred way to help resolve particular situations or enable **participation** in decision-making; *non-directed advocacy* is sometimes needed when an advocate supports a person whose form of **communication** is difficult to interpret or who lacks capacity. (See also **self-advocacy**.)

Boylan, J. and Dalrymple, J. (2009) *Understanding Advocacy for Children and Young People*. Maidenhead: Open University Press.

age appropriateness the notion that people with learning disabilities should dress, behave, take part in activities and be treated in ways suitable to their chronological age.

This notion is often associated with normalization. The principle of age appropriateness suggests, for example, that adults with **learning disability** should not **play** with children's toys, even if the toys might be apparently suited to their developmental level. The rationale for this approach is that such behaviour is at odds with social norms, is undignified and is unlikely to gain respect from other people.

Concerns about age appropriateness also focus on the tendency for non-disabled people to treat adults with learning disabilities as if they were childlike. Similar concerns have been raised about this 'infantilization' of **older people** in some service settings.

ageism the discriminatory behaviour towards **older people** stemming from the socially constructed attitudes and beliefs that growing old is accompanied by loss of competence and intellectual deterioration.

Underlying ageism is the fear of growing older with the inevitable link to mortality; those who are younger seek to distance themselves by creating a distinct 'otherness'. Ageism encompasses a set of attitudes that assume and maintain powerlessness in old people. It is used to legitimate the 'rearranging' of **power** relationships between people who are young and old, which results in **older people** being alienated from other social groups. **Ageism** is apparent in the 'splitting' of images of older people – for example, perceiving them as a 'burden' contrasted with images of 'kindly' grandparents.

Substantial differences exist in the attitudes to **older people** from one society to another, some clearly venerating and valuing old people while others perceive them as economically unproductive and thus as a burden. **Anti-discriminatory practice** includes countering ageist attitudes. Ageism is now included as a form of **discrimination** recognized by the **Equalities and Human Rights Commission in England and Wales**, the Scottish Commission for Human Rights and the Equality Commission in Northern Ireland.

age of criminal responsibility the age at which it becomes possible to prosecute an offender in the **criminal courts** – 10 in England and Wales, 12 in Scotland. In the UK the age of criminal responsibility is lower than in many European countries prompting periodic debates between those who advocate raising it and those who argue for retaining it as is.

aids and home adaptations equipment and alterations to the home that enable disabled people to live more comfortably and independently.

The provision of aids and adaptations is primarily the responsibility of local authority **social care** services, although some equipment is also supplied by the **NHS**. It is also possible for disabled people to buy their own equipment privately. Aids include kitchen utensils, **mobility** aids, handrails, bath seats and hoists to assist with lifting. Equipment can also be provided to meet the requirements of people with sensory **impairment**s. Adaptations to the home may include the provision of ramps for wheelchair users, structural alterations to allow access to bathrooms and toilets, the extension of homes to provide more ground floor living space, the installation of stair lifts and the refitting of kitchens so that equipment is at a suitable height.

Under Section 2 of the **Chronically Sick and Disabled Persons Act 1970, local authorities** have a duty to provide aids and adaptations where there is a need. Need is established through a specialist assessment, usually carried out by an occupational therapist. At first, aids and adaptations were provided free, although limited budgets meant that disabled people often had to wait. Now there is usually a charge, and service users are means-tested by local authorities. Housing adaptations are most often provided through local authority housing departments, under Part 1 of the Housing Grants, Construction and Regeneration Act 1996. Disabled people may apply for a Disabled Facilities Grant to cover the costs of the adaptations they need. Housing departments consult with an occupational therapist from the **social services department** on whether the adaptations are 'necessary and appropriate'. Grants for some purposes are discretionary rather than mandatory. For example, adaptations to provide a safe **play** space for a disabled child attract only a discretionary grant. Disabled Facilities Grants are means-tested on the basis of the size of the loan that the applicant can afford to repay from her or his weekly income. Recent research has highlighted the effectiveness of well-planned adaptations in promoting the capacity of disabled people to gain control over their own daily lives.

The system for the provision of aids and adaptations has been criticized by disabled people because of delays and resource constraints that reduce its effectiveness. However, commentators have also referred to injustices in the 'structure of aiding', whereby the equipment needed by non-disabled people is easily accessible at reasonable cost while disabled people are subject to gate keeping processes, including means testing, professional **assessment** and administrative delay.

Local authorities and **NHS** trusts have been encouraged to pool their resources for **community** equipment and run an integrated service under the flexibilities allowed by the Health Act 1999. Since 2003, certain funding from central government has only been available to areas running an integrated service. In order to improve Community Equipment Services in England, the government has introduced a Transforming Community Equipment Programme which aims to provide the simpler aids to daily living through the retail sector, thus avoiding problems with backlogs in local authority provision and delivery. Following an assessment, a **service user** would be given a 'prescription' for the aids they needed. This could then be taken to a retail supplier. This would not change the current arrangements about charging, and simple aids and equipment would still be provided free to the user. However, the government believes that the new system will stimulate the supply and availability of aids in normal retail outlets and increase **service user** choice.

Heywood, F. (2001) *Money Well Spent, the Effectiveness and Value of Housing Adaptation*. Bristol: Policy Press/Joseph Rowntree Foundation.

alcohol abuse see **drug and alcohol dependency**

alcohol treatment requirement a requirement which may be included in a **community order** or **suspended sentence order**, obliging the offender to attend a treatment programme with the aim of reducing drink dependency. The requirement can last between six months and three years, and can only be included in an order if the offender expresses willingness to comply with the requirement. See also **intoxicating substance requirement**.

allocation the process whereby tasks are distributed among workers within a **social work** team. This process is undertaken sometimes within **team** meetings, sometimes with individual **team** members on an *ad hoc* basis and sometimes by a combination of both practices. Allocation within team meetings has the advantage of conveying to all workers what each is undertaking in relation to the quantity and range of cases and to other kinds of work. Such a system may help build or develop teams by giving members information about how the **team** is functioning. Knowledge of colleagues' work can facilitate the sharing of tasks. Clearly some work, such as dealing with emergencies, must be allocated quickly by team managers. Allocation should be closely related to **workload management** and **supervision** to determine that work is being done well and that workers are not overwhelmed by the quantity and the demands of their tasks.

alternative dispute resolution (ADR) usually referred to as ADR, the collective term for the ways that parties can settle civil disputes, with the help of an independent third party and without the need for a formal court hearing.

Interest in alternative dispute resolution has been growing steadily among the judiciary and legal profession over the last decade. A significant push came from Lord Woolf's 1986 report *Access to Justice*, that identified the need for fair, speedy and proportionate resolution of disputes. Those principles lay at the heart of the Civil Procedure Rules, which came into force in April 1999. The civil procedure rules included references to ADR in rules of court and introduced pre-action protocols, with their emphasis on settlement, even before court proceedings are issued. ADR has begun to feature strongly in a wide range of areas, including separation and **divorce**, neighbourhood disputes, and industrial and employment disputes. ADR is also found in educational settings where peer **mediation** is used to help students of all ages to resolve difficulties.

Fundamental to the process is a third party whose role is to help those in dispute – to explore their difficulties in a safe environment and then to work together towards a mutually acceptable solution. Several methods are used in this work. Mediation places the emphasis and responsibility upon the disputants to arrive at mutually acceptable solutions. Arbitration puts the onus upon the third party to decide the outcome, and in conciliation an impartial third party helps people in dispute by hearing both sides and then offering an opinion on settlement.

There is strong encouragement coming from government to make wider use of ADR in order to reduce the pressures on the court system and to help people in dispute to 'own' the resolution process more effectively.

Doyle, M. (2000) *Advising on ADR: The essential guide to appropriate dispute resolution.* London: Advice Services Alliance.

alternative educational provision the provision which may be made by schools either individually or in **partnership** or by **local authorities** for children to receive part or all of their education away from the school site itself, often in response to disaffection or **unauthorized absence**.

Most children will remain on the roll of a school, wherever they are actually receiving their education, unless they have been subject to a permanent **exclusion from school**. But education does not have to be delivered only at a school. Provision may include extended work experience, special vocational and other programmes and courses in colleges of further education. Providers are now expected to be closely monitored and have their services approved by the local authority, including ensuring that appropriate **safeguarding** and **safer recruitment** procedures are in place. There is also an increasing emphasis on ensuring quality measurable **outcomes** which the young person can use to evidence their learning. For those children and young people not also registered at a school, provision may be only part-time but there must be a full-time offer for certain specified groups such as those who are subject to exclusion from school, those subject to certain youth offending services or who are **looked after**. See also **pupil referral unit**.

Alzheimer's disease an organic age-associated disorder typified by progressive brain degeneration, named after the neurologist Alois Alzheimer who first described it in 1907.

It affects around 500,000 people in the UK and is the most common **dementia** illness, characterized by 'plaques' and 'tangles' that develop in the structure of the brain, leading to **loss** of brain cells. No single factor has been identified as causing Alzheimer's disease since it is likely to stem from a combination of factors such as age, genetic inheritance, environmental factors, diet and general health. However, age is the greatest risk factor for dementia, which affects one in 20 over the age of 65 and one in five over the age of 85. Fewer than 10 per cent of people with Alzheimer's are under the age of 65. People with Down's syndrome are more at risk of early onset because of their chromosomal make-up, and in fewer than 5 per cent of all cases, there is a form of Alzheimer's known to be entirely inherited.

The disease affects a broad range of mental and physical functions; memory **loss** and recall difficulties occur, and learning, perception, attention and recognition are all impaired. Rapid forgetting is evident. Disorientation and confusion are usually present, combined with aphasia (**loss** of words) and agnosia (**loss** of recognition of objects). Other characteristics include mood swings, irritability, over-activity and repetitive movements. **Depression**, apathy and lethargy may also be observed.

There is no cure for Alzheimer's although there are a number of drug treatments available that can delay the onset of symptoms for some people in the early to middle stages. Good **social care** practice aims to maintain a person centred approach when working with people with Alzheimer's in order that the person does not become lost behind the condition. The goal for rehabilitation is that of helping an individual to adapt to the difference between his or her desired role and what is achievable. In spite of maintaining physical independence, such as walking or climbing stairs, many people with Alzheimer's become physically inactive because of poor social engagement. Crucial to good practice are clear agency risk management policies that ensure practitioners have an informed conceptual understanding of 'risk', the balance between rights and 'risks' and an awareness of the value of 'risk-taking'. Practitioners also need to take account of the needs of carers and to mediate any conflict of interest between the rights and needs of an individual and those of the carer. See also **dementia**, **risk assessment**.

anti-discriminatory practice a perspective in which practitioners seek to reduce individual and institutional **discrimination** particularly on the grounds of race or ethnic origin, gender, disability, social class, age, sexual orientation, gender reassignment, and religion or belief.

Anti-discriminatory practice refers to **social work** that is specifically aimed at challenging the unfair, discriminatory treatment experienced by specific groups in society. It is a key part of **social work** education, policy and practice.

In the current context, anti-discriminatory practice is governed by a series of legislation, including the **Human Rights Act 1998**. This new framework of anti-discrimination legislation has been implemented following demands for recognition from various social movements (e.g. feminists and disabled activists) since the late 1960s who sought to both highlight and challenge the nature of inequality, **discrimination** and oppression for particular groups within society.

Anti-discriminatory practice has sometimes been mistakenly characterized as an aspect of 'political correctness' and sometimes this has resulted in an overly simplistic approach to what are undoubtedly complex issues (Thompson 2006). Anti-discriminatory **social work** aims to support individual users and to assist them to tackle discrimination in their own lives a well as to challenge discrimination when found in the media, in local communities and in public **stereotype**s. Such a practice places demands on both social work agencies and individual practitioners.

Anti-discriminatory practice is often used interchangeably with **anti-oppressive practice**, the latter has tended to subsume and replace the former. Some distinction, however, is still evident. The former addresses those areas where users face **discrimination** as well as challenging public stereotypes and prejudices experienced by specific groups. Anti-oppressive practice, on the other hand, focuses on the extreme differences in power between service users and those in dominant positions in service provision and decision-making about services. It therefore has a broader, but perhaps less focused, set of objectives.

More recent approaches to anti-discriminatory practice can be seen as being part of a wider 'diversity approach', but these may be guilty of 'celebrating' diversity and difference without proper attention to the realities of discrimination and oppression.

Thompson, N. (2006) *Anti-Discriminatory Practice*. Basingstoke: Palgrave Macmillan.

anti-oppressive practice **social work** practice that aims to counter the sources of oppression in society, whether public **stereotype**s, **discrimination**, social and economic disadvantage or unequal distribution of **power**.

Social work moved from concepts of **anti-discriminatory practice** to anti-oppressive practice principally because it unified the different forms of **discrimination** within a single theory embracing **patriarchy, racism, able-bodiedism, ageism** and many other forms of oppression. Anti-oppressive practice begins with the recognition that individuals' lives are enmeshed in social relationships shaped by structures and attitudes that are embedded in society at large. This recognition marks the beginning of the capacity to change both those same social structures *and* individual lives. Making this connection between their personal condition and wider social forces enables a critical understanding – to define the oppression and to tackle its causes.

Anti-oppressive practice asks that the social worker encourage this process of users' self-understanding as well as challenging the forms of oppression that face the users they work with. Stimulating people to define their own oppression, to look at the sources of their own disadvantage, unemployment or prejudice that they face, is a starting point. Sharing a commitment to change those circumstances, to make links between personal, social and political structures, is fundamental. Part of any **social work assessment** should uncover the sources of oppression that disempower particular users and lay the basis for challenging those barriers that restrict **service users**' freedom to act.

Challenging the many forms of oppression is difficult because of the somewhat limited tools at social work's disposal. Society is skilful at hiding its oppressive ways as the dominant groups – adults (over children), the able-bodied, men, white people, straight people – with their leverage in the media, thus setting public attitudes, succeed in creating universal definitions of normality that only confirm their advantages. One aspect of practice has been to challenge the language (and hence the stereotypes) that are routinely used. Language itself is never neutral but reflects dominant interests. Some words are derogatory and insulting, others exclude in more subtle ways. Anti-oppressive practice attempts to reshape the discourse around the specific oppressed groups that social workers and other professionals work with. Using the law to break down discriminatory barriers is another feature of anti-oppressive practice, and, where effective legislation does not exist, to campaign in favour of such statutes. Proponents of anti-oppressive practice have noted that the law has slowly been reflecting an enhanced role for users in decision-making and combating discrimination in their lives, so mastery of particular statutes and the specific uses to which they can be put is essential.

There are criticisms of anti-oppressive practice. First, it often pays scant attention to **poverty**, the **power** of social class and the means for improving income. Second, anti-oppressive practice is suspicious of notions of neighbourhood and **community** because it regards them as masking difference and therefore as sources of oppression. But 'neighbourhood' is precisely where many initiatives to tackle **social exclusion** are unfolding. Third, anti-oppressive practice places a premium on language as the medium through which oppressive ideologies are cemented in place, and the **social work** practice it promotes requires close examination of language to reveal the extent of oppression. See also **empowerment**.

anti-poverty strategy addresses specifically and systematically the **poverty** of **service user**s, whether through local campaigns or maximizing their income through benefits or **advice** on employment and training or by assisting them to participate in society through a variety of other tactics.

Social work practitioners' awareness of how **poverty** increases stress and stress-related difficulties historically has not been well developed. Yet the common thread in so many users' lives is the fact that they are poor. An anti-poverty strategy should be central to any social worker's practice; a practice that will include a concern for income maximization; for help with the management and minimization of debt; for help in accessing social work/welfare services at little or no cost; of helping service users to secure at least an acceptable standard of living in relation to housing and fuel usage; and of helping socially marginal service users find ways to participate fully in society in order to achieve equality of opportunity in relation to 'life chances'.

Any competent social worker should either have the knowledge to help service users directly themselves in relation to the key elements of the anti-poverty strategy outlined above or have a clear understanding of relevant agencies to whom they can refer service users that will offer direct practical support. Only a minority of **local authorities** have developed anti-poverty strategies for their 'locality' to be implemented by all departments. Where such strategies are absent social workers might usefully press for the development of such overarching strategies in order to encourage 'joined up thinking'.

anti-racism an attempt to confront and eradicate any view that encourages a belief that one ethnic or racial group is biologically superior to another ethnic group. See also **racism**.

Since the mid-1960s, there have been several pieces of legislation designed to challenge **racism** in different arenas, for example in the context of accessing housing or employment, with the most recent amendment in 2001 (see **Race Relations (Amendment) Act**). The 1970s and 1980s also saw a highly politicized anti-racist movement in the UK which was instrumental in bringing about changes and reform to race relations policies and practices. Progress has been made in some areas of society. However, this has been very uneven, and in some areas, patterns of **discrimination** have remained remarkably persistent. Some would argue that there has also been a resurgence of racism in recent years, with racist views being directed towards new migrant communities arriving in the UK, including those of 'white' ethnicities.

In the context of **social work** and social welfare, policies and practices need to work to challenge racism at both the personal and institutional level. Challenging racism is not the responsibility of those from Black and minority ethnic groups, and recent years have seen increased attention being given to the need for a deconstruction of **whiteness** as a racialized identity. This should not be approached in any crude way, but rather, requires a sophisticated approach that is supported by policy and in practice. Racist acts by staff should be clearly denoted as serious matters for both disciplinary and grievance procedures. Comprehensive training programmes accompanied by induction packages for new staff should convey to employees the commitment of the organization to the eradication of racism in staff relationships and employment practices. In relation to issues of service delivery, particular policies may need to be developed to ensure anti-racist practice. This might include ethnic monitoring of all the critical decision-making processes, the inclusion of minority ethnic groups in shaping policy and practice, and many other possibilities.

In other circumstances, it is the under-use of **social work** and social welfare facilities that has been notable in relation to minority ethnic groups. Examples include the use of facilities by people with learning disabilities and **older people**. In these circumstances, dialogue with minority ethnic communities about their needs, explanations of the functions of particular services, the provision of good information for minority ethnic groups in appropriate languages and the employment of workers from under-represented minority ethnic communities can all be part of a committed anti-racist strategy.

In sum, anti-racism starts from an assumption that processes of racialization continue to structure and shape British society and while this may not be always overt, forms of **racism** need to be challenged at all levels. Any **social work** practice must therefore be rooted in a recognition and acceptance of the persistence of **racism** in all its complexity. Such recognition is the first necessary step towards an effective anti-racist approach. Policies that confront both employment practices and issues of service delivery can then be developed. (See also **anti-discriminatory practice, equal opportunities policies, ethnically sensitive practice, Race Relations Act 1976, trans-racial adoption, community cohesion**).

Dominelli, L. (2008) *Anti-Racist Social work*, 3rd edition. Houndmills: Palgrave Macmillan.

anti-sexism see sexism

anti-social behaviour a wide and rather vague term applied to a range of activities such as young people hanging around in groups in public places, verbal intimidation of others, fighting, public drunkenness, vandalism and creating high levels of noise. Although the concept has been particularly associated with young people, it is also applied to adults, including 'nuisance neighbours'. Many **local authorities** now expel from their council housing tenants who engage persistently in anti-social behaviour towards neighbours. From 1997 onwards, the Labour government introduced a number of initiatives to control such behaviour, especially in relation to young people. (See also **curfew, anti-social behaviour order**.) Following the general election of 2005 the campaign against **anti-social behaviour** was central to the Labour government's **Respect Agenda**.

Anti-social behaviour can be distressing for residents of a particular area to the point that the quality of life is severely curtailed. 'Nuisance neighbours' who play loud music in the middle of the night or adolescents with menacing behaviour have a disruptive and frightening impact on local residents such as **older people** or young children. Many local authorities now expel from their council housing any tenants who engage persistently in anti-social behaviour towards neighbours.

To tackle anti-social **behaviour** in social housing, **registered social landlords**, including **local authorities**, can apply for possession of the property, **anti-social behaviour orders**, **injunctions**, **parenting orders** and contracts, and acceptable behaviour contracts. They can also apply to 'demote' the tenancy, which means the tenant loses their security for a period of time. Local authority landlords can additionally extend an Introductory tenancy, suspend the Right to Buy scheme, and refuse mutual exchange applications.

Anti-social Behaviour Act 2003 legislation concerned to strengthen provision in relation to **anti-social behaviour**.

Following the government's report *Respect and Responsibility* published in 2003, this piece of legislation gave more agencies **power** to intervene in the event of **anti-social behaviour** and widened the scope of instruments that might be used in relation to 'low level criminality and nuisance crime'. The new provision allows social landlords, **local** authorities and the British Transport Police to apply for and monitor **anti-social behaviour order**s (**ASBO**s). The **police** were also given new powers to order young people under the age of 16 after 9 p.m. to return home if they were indulging in unruly behaviour. Other provision included the creation of 'Closure Orders' enabling the police to close down premises thought to be associated with the supply, use or production of class A drugs; such orders could apply for a period of up to 6 months and potentially, on-the-spot **fine**s for noisy behaviour, **truancy** and minor criminal damage to property in the form of, for example, graffiti. More controversially '**dispersal order**s' were introduced enabling the police and **police community** support officers to disperse two or more people if their behaviour was thought to be causing **harassment** or distress; failure to leave the area or to return later would in both instances be regarded as a criminal offence. Agencies such as Liberty argued that such provision compromised the human rights associated with 'Freedom of Assembly' and, moreover, blurred criminal law with civil law – the latter with a lower threshold for proving an offence, but with criminal penalties if **breach**ed.

anti-social behaviour order ('ASBO') an order introduced by the **Crime and Disorder Act 1998**, which prohibits a person from engaging in any kind of **anti-social behaviour** specified in the order for a period of at least two years. **ASBO**s are made by a **magistrates' court** in England and Wales or by a sheriff in Scotland, and may be issued against a person aged 10 or over who has acted 'in an anti-social manner', defined as behaviour 'that caused or was likely to cause **harassment**, alarm or distress to one of more persons not of the same household'.

ASBOs are technically civil orders, but **breaches** are a criminal offence punishable by **fine**s or a **custodial sentence**. Originally they could only be made in **civil proceedings** at the request of the **police** or a **local authority**, but they can now also be made by a **criminal court** following a conviction. All ASBO applications in **civil proceedings** are heard in the adult magistrates' court, regardless of the age of the person against whom it is sought. When a court makes an ASBO on a young person under 18, it must also make an **individual support order** if satisfied that this would be desirable in the interests of preventing further anti-social behaviour. Approximately half of all ASBOs are made on young people under 18; approximately half are breached; and approximately half of those proceeded against for **breach** receive a custodial sentence.

ASBOs have been praised as an effective method for dealing with a wide range of nuisance behaviour, but have also been criticized for criminalizing conduct which should be dealt with by less formal means, **stigma**tizing young people and increasing the numbers of young people in **custody**. Research has suggested that they can be counter-productive, with many offending teenagers regarding an **ASBO** as a 'badge of honour'.

Youth Justice Board (2006) *Anti-social behaviour orders*. London: Youth Justice Board.

anxiety a high level of fear, tension and sense of imminent danger in direct response to an experience felt to be threatening.

This can be an understandable response to a situation which would generally be regarded in the person's culture as threatening, but it can also be viewed as a **mental health problem** or a **mental illness** if the reactions appear too prolonged, or too extreme, in relation to the person's circumstances. As many as 10 per cent of the population at any one time may be experiencing **anxiety** to a level where it would be diagnosed as a mental health problem. **Anxiety** involves a range of subjective feelings and bodily reactions that are uncomfortable and distressing. Subjective experiences include fear, dread, apprehension, panic, and physically the person can experience palpitations, gastric upsets, headaches, lack of concentration and faintness. It is also the case that some physical conditions, for example an overactive thyroid, asthma or heart problems, can produce the same symptoms of anxiety, and therefore **assessment** of both physical and **mental health** forms a crucial part of an effective response to the person. People with serious mental health problems such as Schizophrenia can also often experience anxiety alongside their other symptoms.

As with all mental health problems and symptoms linked to **mental illness**, the experiences of anxiety can have serious implications for roles such as parenting or work, relationships, and coping: they can also result in risk – for example lack of concentration can lead to accidents, and discrimination reaches into every aspect of people's lives. Again too, as with all mental health problems, social factors such as financial difficulties, life events such as bereavement, and perhaps **childhood sexual abuse** are of major importance in the development of anxiety, and positive help with social stressors can help promote recovery. People are responded to mainly in primary care, but if the difficulties are severe and prolonged they may be referred to mental health services (see **mental health policy**). In either setting, social workers have much to contribute to integrated health and **social care** working with people experiencing these concerns.

Golightley, M. (2008) *Social Work and Mental Health*, 3rd edition. Exeter: Learning Matters.

appeal the process by which an administrative or judicial decision can be contested in a tribunal or court. If it has full powers the tribunal or court can then make the decision it believes should have been made. For example, a First Tier Tribunal in a benefits or tax credits case can usually allow the appeal and then make an award of benefits; or a county court hearing a **homelessness** case can allow the appeal, determine the claimant's eligibility for housing, and then require the housing authority to house the appellant. In some areas, including **community care**, **appeal** opportunities are more limited, and it may be necessary to make a **judicial review** claim (usually only after other avenues of redress, including a complaint under the local authority **complaints procedure**, have been pursued). In criminal cases appeals against conviction or **sentence** in a **magistrates' court** are heard in a **Crown Court**. Appeals from the Crown Court lies to the Court of Appeal (Criminal Division), with opportunities for further appeal to higher courts. In civil cases, depending on the particular jurisdiction, appeals may be dealt with by a tribunal, the county court, or the **High Court**. Opportunities are then provided for further appeals to higher tribunals or courts, usually subject to leave to **appeal** being granted. The highest appellate court in the UK for both criminal and civil appeals is now the **Supreme Court** of the United Kingdom, formerly the Appellate Committee of the House of Lords. See also **civil proceedings**, **family proceedings** and **judicial review**.

appeal tribunal an independent judicial body that can hear appeals against decisions in a variety of jurisdictions, including those dealing with benefits, tax credits, special needs and disability of children, **child support**, and immigration and asylum. A large part of the tribunal system was reformed by the Tribunals, Courts and Enforcement Act 2007. The Act and implementing regulations modified appeals procedures so that appeals are now generally heard under a system that operates at two 'tiers'. In most cases appeals go, initially, to a First Tier Tribunal, which can hear evidence and determine 'facts' as well as 'law'. This tribunal can either reject the appeal, or allow the **appeal** and overturn decisions. If this is appropriate it generally has the **power** to substitute its own decision for that of a decision-maker. Parties who are dissatisfied with the tribunal's decision may, with leave, **appeal** on a point of law to the **Upper Tribunal** (formerly the Social Security and Child Support Commissioners). The Upper Tribunal can overturn the lower tribunal's decision and either send the matter back to be determined by that tribunal (or a new tribunal), with directions as to how the matter is to be dealt with; or it may make the decision that it believes should be made, if it has sufficient evidence and 'facts' that enable it to avoid referring the matter back for further consideration. The Upper Tribunal now has **judicial review** powers so that, in appropriate cases, it may review a decision or action, and assess its legality, procedural propriety, rationality, and compatibility with human rights requirements. The process is undertaken in a similar way to review proceedings in the Administrative Court. See **appeal** and **judicial review**.

appropriate adult a person appointed to safeguard the interests of vulnerable people while they are detained and questioned by the **police**. According to Code of Practice C issued under the **Police and Criminal Evidence Act 1984**, in the case of every suspect under the age of 17 and every suspect with **learning difficulties** or **mental health problems** the police must inform an appropriate adult that they are being detained for questioning and ask that adult to attend the police station. Appropriate adults may be parents, guardians, social workers, **mental health** workers or any other responsible adult not employed by the police. Their role is to help the person being interviewed to understand the process, assist **communication** between the police and the suspect, and ensure that the suspect's rights are protected. In most areas of England and Wales, **local authorities** train appropriate adults and maintain a rota so that the service is available around the clock. In the case of young people, the appropriate adult service may be organized by the local **youth offending team**.

approved premises see **bail hostel**

Arnstein's ladder a way of mapping out the different degrees of **participation** by local residents and users in the services or **community** projects that affect them.

The tool literally uses the shape of a ladder with the highest degree of participation on the top rung and the lowest degree at the bottom rung. At the higher end of the ladder citizens exert maximum **power** and control over a project or service. At the lower end are forms of participation that are manipulative and something of a sham. From the highest rung in descending order are citizen control, delegated power, **partnership**, placation, consultation, informing, therapy and manipulation. Because **social work** is committed to **empowerment** in principle, practitioners may be tempted to think that in their work they automatically should aim for the levels of participation at the top of the ladder. But other legal obligations and the dictates of the social work agencies' policies might point otherwise. Each project or service should be looked at carefully to determine what level of participation is both desirable and realistic.

ASBO see **anti-social behaviour order**

Asian in the UK, the term is applied to those who originate from what is geographically known as the Indian Subcontinent; this includes India, Pakistan, Bangladesh and Sri Lanka. The category also includes East African Asians who settled in Britain in the 1970s.

As with most forms of ethnic categorization, the term has been subject to much academic discussion and debate. In the United States and

Canada, it is usually applied to those from South East and North East Asia countries (e.g. China, Vietnam and Japan), with the term 'South Asian' being applied to those from the Indian Subcontinent. In the British context, the terms 'Asian' and 'South Asian' are both apparent. In the British census, the category 'Asian' is used as an umbrella ethnic label, which is further sub-divided into country of origin and more recently, religious affiliation. Indeed there is much diversity present amongst those categorized as 'South Asian' or 'Asian', including difference of religion, caste, language, cultural practices and traditions, experience and time of migration, as well as place of origin. There are also clear differences in terms of educational attainment, employment and wealth between 'Asians', with Muslims, Bangladeshis and Muripuri Pakistani Muslims generally facing harsher levels of unemployment than those from Indian origin, such as Sikhs and Hindus. However, there remains a commonality of experience derived through being **'Asian'** evident in shared cultural practices but particularly in racial and cultural **discrimination**.

Rai, R. and Reeves, P. (eds) (2009) *The South Asian Diaspora: transnational networks and changing identities.* London: Routledge.

Puwar, N. and Raghuram, P. (eds) (2003) *South Asian Women in the Diaspora.* Oxford: Berg.

Asperger's Syndrome see **autism**

assertive outreach a highly user focused approach for people with **mental health problems** that maintains intensive **contact** with them in their own environment. Assertive outreach teams are multi-disciplinary comprising social workers, **community** psychiatric nurses, psychiatrists, counsellors and support staff.

First developed in the USA, assertive outreach attempts to ensure that those who require medication or support services receive it no matter where they are – at home or on the street. **Assertive outreach** workers offer a broad range of services, from **advice** to help with shopping. They maintain frequent **contact**, perhaps four times per week, and are committed to the long term. Their aim is to prevent crisis situations from developing, such as hospital admissions, evictions or offending. The National Service Framework for Mental Health included a commitment to establish **assertive outreach** teams in England and Wales by 2003. In practice, **assertive outreach** teams have been developed unevenly across the UK. There is debate, however, around how fully such teams are reflecting the objectives of outreach. Two models of practice seem to be emerging. One focuses on keeping in **contact** with people, ensuring compliance with medication and reducing hospital admissions. The other focuses on a person's network – on quality of life, social interactions, leisure and occupation. There is every reason to think that these two approaches might usefully be combined to offer a more comprehensive service.

assessment to judge the importance, quality or significance of something or the process for determining a **service user**'s eligibility for a benefit or service.

In **social work**, assessment is a key skill used to evaluate situations, functioning and standards in relation to some agreed or defined measures usually underpinned by law or statutory guidance. Assessment is a dynamic and continuous process that takes account of changes in behaviour, circumstances and relationships as well as new evidence or changes in the weighting given to evidence. Social work assessments tend to focus upon social problems that have been found to be widespread in society. For example, in childcare assessment might be about parenting capacity, the development of a child or an evaluation of the effects of **domestic violence** on a child. In **mental health** work the issues might be about mental capacity, perceptions of reality and whether a **service user** is a danger to himself or others. With older and disabled people **assessment** might focus on the ability to live independently while for a young offender the issue might be about self-control or a sense of right and wrong.

Specialist teams dealing with children and families, adults or young offenders tend to use prepared assessment formats that require social workers to explore key issues that research has shown to be crucial in understanding problems associated with each of these client groups. In relation to children and adults there are common assessment frameworks now in place, a single 'front door' so to speak for all professionals working in those areas.

Social workers have in the past regarded assessment as their exclusive professional task, akin to a medical or psychiatric diagnosis. The wide scope of social work assessments involves too many complex variables for diagnostic certainty to be achievable. Moreover, the emphasis on users' **participation** in their own assessment (and recognition of the need to consult groups like partners, family members, and other professionals like GPs) means that assessment is no longer under exclusive professional control.

Two models are still influential in relation to the social worker–**service user** relationship underpinning assessment. In the *questioning model* of assessment, the practitioner gathers information from the user and others such as carers and family members before reaching a judgement or 'assessment' on what his or her needs or problems are and the solution to them. The practitioner's conduct is based on asking questions, processing the answers and using the responses to make a decision about the level and nature of care to be offered. It is a model that reflects the agency's objectives, which links service user need to pre-set categories and budgets within the agency. The *exchange model* takes a different approach. It focuses on the exchange of information between practitioner and all others involved. The objective is to engage family members and other significant members of a network. Perceptions of a situation, the inherent strengths and weaknesses of key players, the definition of problems and their possible solution derive as much from the user and his or her family as from the practitioner. In this model the social worker is a resource, an enabler, not a conductor of the outcome. **Communication** across ethnic, racial, class and gender boundaries is also made easier because preconceived agency categories and solutions are not subtly framing the interaction.

Recent court cases have shown that the courts are not slow to quash care plans and other support arrangements, and order **assessment** processes to be re-run. A key consideration, among others, is the importance of following the requirements of 'guidance', and taking account of the input made by other professional groups, agencies, and family members. In some cases these groups' rights are now reinforced by primary legislation.

A key issue in relation to assessments is the problem of making decisions about what constitutes good evidence to underpin sound judgements. This raises two important problems. First, there is the issue of what evidence is relevant; and second, there is the issue of whether some threshold has been crossed that helps social workers to decide, for example, whether any parenting is 'good enough', or an elder has sufficient mental capacity to make responsible decisions or whether a carer is close to breaking point and needs substantial support or, perhaps, some respite from the 'cared for' person. Household standards are sometimes cited as evidence of a concern about a family with dependent children or an elder living alone. The questions to be asked will be about whether, for example, a lack of hygiene, or the lack of safeguards to protect a child from an open fire or from falling down the stairs are both relevant and sufficiently concerning to warrant intervention. Social workers often have to operate in circumstances which are neither 'Black nor white' but of various degrees of grey.

There will be differences of opinion sometimes between professionals even when they agree on what is relevant evidence but perhaps disagree about its significance. This is where individual **values** may be important in understanding how professionals sometimes disagree. A currently contentious area of work, which sometimes divides social workers, concerns drug using parents. Social workers have to make judgements about whether a lifestyle is sufficiently chaotic, because of drug use, to warrant some kind of intervention. There are many areas of **social work** where these kinds of judgements and dilemmas have to be faced. Other **values** may also affect what evidence is to be given serious attention in assessments. A 'pro-life' stance in relation to **abortion** on the part of a social worker may predispose him/her to give particular attention to any positive expressions by a woman about having a baby and to overlook or 'downgrade' any doubts the prospective mother may be expressing.

In an entirely different context it is possible that one social worker might perceive some problems between neighbours as racist and another as an understandable complaint about the noise that one family routinely makes late into the night when the other family wants to sleep.

Social workers should be prepared to re-evaluate evidence in the light of new information or, perhaps, where more weight needs to be given to a problem that was thought to be minor but is actually of greater significance. For example, it is possible that a service user was thought to be 'a little low' but because they had failed to complete some tasks that were clearly in their interests a social worker might hypothesize that the service user was actually clinically depressed. In another scenario a woman's reluctance to speak about her concerns was initially thought to be a reflection of personal reticence rather than, as was later revealed, the result of being in an abusive relationship. Social workers have to be prepared to be 'light on their feet' and to avoid taking referral information or earlier assessments for granted. Being willing to be **reflective practitioners** is crucial in competent social work practice. See also **needs-led assessment, framework for assessment of children in need, common assessment framework** and **common assessment framework for adults**.

Association of Directors of Adult Social Services an umbrella organization that brings together the directors of all the **social services departments** in England, Wales and Northern Ireland.

Membership of the association is strictly limited to directors of adult social services in accordance with the **Children Act 2004**. Its major role is to act as a forum for heads of departments to exchange ideas and to develop policy initiatives at a national level. The association's other roles include: consultation with civil servants, ministers and Opposition spokespersons on social services issues; to meet regularly with other professional and managerial groups to discuss common issues of concern; to provide information to members and facilitate research initiatives; to give evidence to relevant parliamentary select committees; and to provide information to the press and other media.

Association of Directors of Children's Services With the creation of the Association of Directors of Adult Services a parallel association representing children's services was set up. This association involved the merger of directorates of education in local government as a result of the ending of separate education departments and the creation of new children's services departments. This was a statutory requirement following the implementation of the **Children Act 2004** and the Change for Children programme. This brings together the delivery of educational services for children with local government's responsibility for their safety and protection.

Association of Directors of Social Work an organization representing the directors of **social work** departments in Scotland. The association's activities are comparable with those of the association of directors of adult and children's social services in England. However, the social work departments of the unitary authorities in Scotland also have responsibilities associated with probation, court services and **parole**. This gives directors of **social work** a wider area of concerns than that of their English, Welsh and Northern Ireland counterparts.

asylum seekers and refugees an asylum seeker is a person who has applied for refugee status in the UK and is still awaiting a decision. A refugee is a person given leave to remain in the UK. Since 2007 refugees are only given 5 years leave to remain and after that will have to apply for further leave.

Many asylum seekers are destitute when they arrive in the UK so they need to apply for accommodation and support from the UK Border Agency. Accommodation is provided on a no-choice basis and asylum seekers are dispersed around the UK in order to reduce the burden experienced by **local authorities** and other service providers in the south-east.

Under the terms of the UN Convention on Refugee Status 1951, a person will qualify as a refugee if he or she is unable or unwilling to return to his or her country of nationality because of a well-founded fear of persecution for reasons of race, religion, nationality, social group or political opinion. A person accepted as a refugee in the UK is entitled to benefits and social housing, like any member of the indigenous population, and can also apply to bring dependants over under family reunion. Each year between 10 per cent and 20 per cent of people applying for asylum are given refugee status (3,700 in 2008) but others are given limited leave to remain by way of '**humanitarian protection**' or 'discretionary leave'.

Asylum seeking has been a long-standing social phenomenon in many parts of the world for centuries, driven often by the persecution of minority religious and ethnic groups. Anti-Semitism in Germany and Russia in the 20th century (leading to Jews settling in the UK and the

USA) and the persecution of Puritans in England in the 18th century (migrating to what became the USA) are well-known historical examples. In the last years of the 20th century and the first years of the 21st century the 'problems' of asylum seekers and refugees have again achieved a high political profile as international migration, fuelled by conflicts and the dissolution of empires, has gained momentum. A significant amount of this migration, although not all, has been from relatively poor countries to comparatively affluent democracies. These democracies have varied in their responses to both asylum seekers and refugees, many containing factions who are unsympathetic to the claims of those wishing or needing to start new lives in a new country.

Unsympathetic groups claim that asylum seekers are often in fact economic migrants seeking a more affluent lifestyle, that the difficulties in the asylum seekers' countries of origin are much exaggerated, that the host society lacks the jobs, accommodation or the capacity to absorb alien peoples, or that other countries are better placed to take more asylum seekers. At the other end of the continuum are factions who are more inclined to accept the asylum seekers' accounts of their problems and are thus predisposed to offer meaningful support in a more trusting manner.

The tasks for workers supporting asylum seekers and refugees are wide ranging. First, there are issues about securing a 'fair hearing' for applicants for asylum, both in relation to initial applications and to appeals. In this context there can be complications around the issue of whether people present themselves as asylum seekers at the point of entry to the UK (as official policy requires) or whether they gain entry in some other way before declaring themselves to be asylum seekers. Regardless of where a claim for asylum is registered, there is equivocal evidence about how 'just' the vetting processes are. There can be major difficulties for asylum seekers in proving persecution when they have left countries where official records are unlikely to support their allegations. These problems can be compounded when claims are being made through interpreters, when asylum seekers are disoriented because of stressful and sometimes life-threatening experiences and do not understand the host country's systems and processes. Second, if asylum is granted there is the issue of helping people to settle in a strange land. The characteristic problems are those of income, accommodation, reunion with family members who may still be in danger in the country of origin, education and/or employment, as well as personal and social support in communities that may be hostile to strangers or even overtly racist. The dispersal policy has created problems for some because of inappropriate placements, a lack of support, and poor quality housing in depressed communities because these areas are the places where accommodation is more easily available to the contractors who provide these services for the Border Agency. Accommodation and support is 'terminated' 21/28 days after the final decision on an asylum application unless a person has dependent children when they can be supported until they are deported. Others may be eligible for continuing support under Section 4 (of the **Immigration and Asylum Act 1999**) if it is not possible for them to return to their country of origin. Unaccompanied asylum seeking children are supported by local authority children's services.

attachment a long-lasting emotional bond between two individuals, involving their seeking proximity to each other and having pleasure in each other's company. Typically, **attachment** is developed by infants towards their principal care-givers, but it may also characterize feelings between other people, or between a person and some object.

While in adults the term 'love' would be appropriate, 'attachment' is usually reserved for the bond between infants – human and animal – and their care-givers or parents. Close proximity of infant and care-giver ensures that the former's biological needs are met and that both partners build up trust and satisfaction through a close social relationship. Such is the importance of an early relationship of this kind that biologists have suggested that the conditions for its formation must be innate. For example, newly hatched ducklings will follow the first moving object to which they are exposed – a phenomenon called 'imprinting'. Some child psychiatrists have suggested that the responses of a baby to its mother, such as smiling, are human examples of imprinting. Both psychologists and psychiatrists have modified their viewpoints in recent years, taking into account evidence that some mutual instrumental learning is also involved in mother–infant interaction. Care-givers 'reinforce' the behaviours that they enjoy from their babies, and these behaviours, in turn, reinforce their care-giving.

Whatever the relative importance of innate and learned factors in the development of attachment, its significance is universally acknowledged. Infants who are securely attached are more confident in exploring their environment, using their care-givers as a base. They are also more confident in responding to the overtures of strangers, again using their mothers as a secure base. It has been suggested that babies who have not built up secure attachments in early life are more at risk of emotional disorders in later life than securely attached infants; also that parents who have not had an opportunity to form strong attachments to their children are more likely to abuse them.

Social workers must be careful not to interpret **attachment** as something that happens once and for all to newborn babies. Such an interpretation has been used to justify the permanent removal of children from families where separation between infant and care-giver (usually the mother) took place, for example as a result of that person's hospitalization or where the infant's care-giver did not form a close relationship with the infant in the first weeks of life. This narrow conception of **attachment** viewed children as unable to form attachments either later in their **childhood** or to more than one person. Such was the importance that social workers placed on attachment that rating scales were devised to help them judge the quality of attachments formed between particular children and their care-givers. Recent research conducted by psychologists now suggests that attachment is a continuous process that passes through different phases, so that if there is disruption, even early on in the relationship between mother and child, this does not mean that attachment will not take place at all. Social workers have also learned to use the concept more flexibly, as one of many aspects they consider when forming a view of the strength of a relationship between a child and its parents.

Howe, D. (1995) *Attachment Theory for Social workers*. Houndmills: Palgrave Macmillan.

attendance centre a centre for young offenders, who may be ordered by a court to attend the centre for specified periods of up to 36 hours (24 for offenders under 16) and take part in activities as instructed. Most centres are run by **police** officers, usually at weekends, and the activities include physical exercise and work. Attendance centres are often used for young people convicted of vandalism and hooliganism at sporting events. They were previously only available for offenders up to the age of 21 until the age limit was raised to 25 by the **Criminal Justice Act 2003**. Offenders can be required to attend a centre under a requirement included in a **youth rehabilitation order** or (for those over 18) a **community order** or a **suspended sentence order**.

audit the annual examination of the financial accounts of an organization aimed at independently establishing the probity of its records and expenditure. Audit is particularly important in public-sector organizations, where expenditure involves the use of public money; it is therefore related to the public accountability of such organizations.

In local government, annual audits are performed by auditors contracted by or working directly for the **Audit Commission**. This is an independent organization established by the government to examine the accounts of local government and, more recently, the **National Health Service**, to establish whether these bodies have spent money economically and efficiently. The accounts of the authorities have to be published in annual reports, and auditors can refuse to sign the accounts if they believe these do not reflect the true situation or if there are doubts concerning particular areas of expenditure. More recently, the government has expanded the role of the audit to cover the effectiveness of local government spending. This has brought the Audit Commission and the role of the audit into a more sensitive area of study. The concern with 'value for money' has led the commission to expand the role of the audit to include the identification of ways in which **local authorities** can make policy implementation more effective. There have been doubts, however, as to whether this is an appropriate role for the audit, given that there may be several political perspectives on what constitutes effectiveness.

Audit Commission a central government agency whose task is to **audit** the activities of **local authorities** and the **National Health Service** on the basis of economy, efficiency and effectiveness. Established under the Local Government Finance Act 1982 and operational in 1983, the commission took over from the District Audit Service responsibility for approving the accounts of local authorities for their annual reports. At first its remit was concerned with ensuring that the accounts had been appropriately drawn up, that there was evidence of probity in financial dealings and that spending was in line with statute. In addition, it was to provide **advice** on economy and efficiency. More recently the Audit Commission has joined with other independent watchdogs to assess the achievements of local authorities through the **Comprehensive Area Assessment** (CAA). By bringing together the **Care Quality Commission**, HM Inspectorates of Constabulary, **prison**s, Probation, and **Ofsted** the aims of the CAA and the role of the Audit Commission has developed to enhance the way local services are evaluated in an integrated way. This is a new development emerging out of the Local Government and Public Involvement Act 2007 and is yet to show how it will benefit **service user**s in the way it evaluates the quality of local government services.

authorized absence **(from school)** absence from school that has been allowed by the head teacher acting in accordance with the school's policy.

All such absences are supposed to be either 'unavoidable', (such as due to illness), or as 'leave' granted by the school, e.g. for a family holiday or some other special circumstance. In law it is schools, not parents, who authorize children's absence. Such absences are not then an offence by the parent, unlike **unauthorized absence**. Both kinds of absence are totalled together and published annually for each school as part of the performance tables, alongside the level of **persistent absence**.

The status of each absence from school needs to be understood against a wide range of potential explanations, only some of which will be legitimate. The potential response depends entirely on the definition placed on the absence by the school, not by the parent. A parent may feel that the absence was for a legitimate reason, such as an illness, but it is the school that determines whether or not to accept the explanation, if, for example, staff feel the absence was excessive or unnecessary. There is no requirement to authorize an absence because the parent has provided a note. Parents do not generally have any right to question these decisions, but should the case result in **prosecution**, they may argue in their defence that the school has acted unreasonably.

Other authorized absences may be initiated by the school (such as an **exclusion from school**), when the parent feels the child should have been allowed to attend. School staff should operate according to standard criteria, ideally agreed across a locality, to ensure consistency, but this does not always happen. Absences may be authorized where the family is in crisis or in special circumstances, or during study leave. These decisions may, in practice, be made by the person entering the data into the registration system, but they should be operating on criteria managed by senior staff according to a written policy. There is otherwise a danger that different judgements may be applied to different children and a risk that the decisions could be seen as discriminatory or unfair.

Whitney, B. (2008) *A Guide to School Attendance*. London: David Fulton/Routledge Falmer.

autistic spectrum conditions a spectrum of related neurological conditions that typically involve **impairment**s in social **communication**, social interaction and imagination.

Autism was once thought to be categorical, or, as Simon Baron-Cohen puts it, 'You either have it or you don't'. More recently it has been recognized that autism is a spectrum condition in which people are affected to different degrees and in different ways. Intelligence and language skills can vary widely. People with 'classic autism' will have experienced delayed/limited language development and may have below average intelligence. However, the spectrum approach to autism owes a lot to the recognition of Asperger's Syndrome and 'higher functioning autism'. Hans Asperger identified a group of children who displayed pronounced autistic traits but also well-developed language and at least average intelligence. The two groups tend to share difficulties with social **communication**, narrow interests and a tendency towards repetitive actions.

Individuals with autistic spectrum conditions (ASCs) typically have difficulties in using and understanding verbal and non-verbal **communication**. For example, common figures of speech may be taken literally and facial expressions misinterpreted. There can also be difficulties in making sense of what is going on around them. This can involve limited capacity to understand and predict other people's behaviour. When this is combined with the heightened sensory sensitivity experienced by some people with autistic spectrum conditions, the social and physical environment can be unpredictable and alarming. This may account for a preference for fixed routines, difficulties in adjusting to change and, in some cases, **challenging behaviour.**

The recognition of 'higher functioning' autism and Asperger's Syndrome has led to higher prevalence figures for ASCs. Although there is a lack of reliable national data, a prevalence rate of 1 per cent was found in a recent regional study. ASCs are significantly more common in men than women. The number of children diagnosed with autism has risen dramatically in recent years across the developed world – with many possible causes suggested including most prominently toxins in the environment which affects the foetus at early stages. The government recently committed itself to commissioning a national prevalence study as a step toward identifying possible causes.

Although attention has been given to improving services for children, services for adults with ASCs was until very recently a neglected area. Those with 'classic autism' tend to use general **learning disability** services, while those with Asperger's Syndrome or 'higher functioning autism' are often unable to access any service whatsoever. Due to their 'normal' intelligence, they may be refused access to learning disability services. As autism is not a **mental illness**, they may also have difficulties accessing **mental health** services. However, **mental health problems**, particularly **anxiety** and **depression**, are relatively common in adults with ASCs. Recent research carried out by the National Autistic Society found that 45 per cent of local authorities had no provision for supporting adults with autism who do not have a learning disability or a mental health problem. Adults with 'higher functioning autism' may experience social isolation and require ongoing support from their families in order to achieve **independent living**. The draft adult autism strategy acknowledges and sets out to tackle some of these problems.

Caring for an autistic child can have a significant impact on family life, and the pressures on parents and siblings can sometimes be underestimated when the child's **impairment** is not immediately visible. There has also been a history of attributing autism to poor parenting, a theory which has now been discredited. However, families need support with a range of issues, including access to specialist **advice** on handling behavioural problems, which, if not addressed, can lead to families becoming isolated. Parents may also need access to short breaks (previously known as respite) in order to 'recharge their batteries' and spend time with their other children. Some parents have experienced difficulties in accessing appropriate education for children with ASCs, as indicated in evidence given to a recent Parliamentary Select Committee and also in reports published by the National Autistic Society, which recently ran a campaign called Make School Make Sense. In particular, children with Asperger's Syndrome may experience difficulties in mainstream education if their needs are not properly understood, while 'special' provision tends to be targeted on children of lower intelligence. Although progress has been made in recent years, parents and others have expressed concerns about the lack of understanding of ASCs among some teachers and social workers.

It is now recognized in the draft adult autism strategy issued by the government that the diagnosis of ASCs is important in order to gain a full understanding of an individual's behaviour and needs. However, there has at times been disagreement between those who stress the importance of diagnosis and others who maintain that this is no more than pejorative '**labelling**' which discourages professionals from acknowledging the individuality of the person. As such diagnostic 'labels' have been historically associated with **stigma** and segregation, it is not surprising that some people advocating **inclusion** (for example, in education) have opposed their use. It has been argued, for example, that Asperger's Syndrome is a social construction, and involves the inappropriate application of medical discourse to children whose behaviour is perceived as problematic. However, the autobiographical accounts of people diagnosed in adulthood indicate that diagnosis has enabled them to make sense of the difficulties they had earlier in life and can be experienced as something of a relief.

An approach which may reconcile the two sides of this argument is that of Simon Baron-Cohen and others, who argue that Asperger's Syndrome and 'higher functioning autism' are differences rather than deficits. This is not the same as saying that these differences do not exist outside of medical discourse, but does indicate that they should be interpreted more positively. Qualities which are particularly characteristic of 'higher functioning autism', such as attention to detail, can be seen as assets which may be valuable to employers. This approach has some common features with neuro-diversity, a term first developed by Judy Singer and deployed by autistic self-advocates.

Baron-Cohen, S. (2008) *Autism and Asperger Syndrome: facts.* Oxford: Oxford University Press.

B b

Baby Peter/Baby 'P' the 17-month-old boy, Peter Connelly, who died in August 2007 after sustaining more than 50 injuries at his home in the London borough of Haringey despite having been seen regularly by a range of professionals including social services. His death triggered an outcry in much of the media which accused the borough's social services of having too casual an attitude toward **children in need** of protection. This view was shared to some extent by the then Secretary of State for Children, Schools and Families who intervened in the borough to ensure that the head of children's services was sacked. A country-wide review of child protective services was rapidly undertaken and highlighted weaknesses in six other authorities including Birmingham.

The child's death placed children's services in all areas on the defensive with resources diverted away from family support and toward pre-emptive interventions in families with children at risk of abuse. In the year following his death the percentage of children being removed from their families and placed in care rose sharply, by as much as a third in some areas.

bail the release of a suspected offender pending trial or further investigation. Suspects may be granted bail by the **police** following arrest. This may be 'street bail' (introduced by the **Criminal Justice Act 2003**), whereby the **police** release arrested suspects without taking them to a **police** station; or bail granted either before or after any charge is brought. If **police** bail is not granted, bail may be given by the court pending trial as an alternative to **remand** of the defendant in **custody**. Bail may be subject to conditions such as specified residence (for example in a **bail hostel**) or the provision of a surety to be forfeited if the suspect fails to appear for trial (although this is a comparative rarety). It is an offence to commit further offences while on bail. The Bail Act 1976 requires bail normally to be granted unless there is reason to believe that the alleged offender will fail to appear for trial or will reoffend or interfere with witnesses. Bail hostels enable homeless offenders to be given bail rather than be held in custody while awaiting trial. (See also **remand**.)

For some courts the **probation service** or **youth offending team** run bail information or remand management schemes to assist defendants in obtaining bail. A bail information scheme collects verified, factual information about defendants to assist courts in making decisions about whether to grant bail, and research shows that this can prevent large numbers of unnecessary custodial remands. Remand management goes further, supplementing bail information with bail support for individuals and interagency negotiations to prevent unnecessary remands. Bail support involves regular **supervision** of (usually young) defendants and help to ensure that they meet bail conditions and attend further court appearances.

bail hostel an unofficial (and highly inaccurate) term commonly applied to what are officially 'approved premises', which succeeded probation **hostel**s (for offenders on **probation** or **supervision requirements**) and bail hostels (for defendants on **bail**). **Hostel**s are provided by the **probation service** and some organizations in the voluntary sector. They now house relatively few bailees; their primary function is to provide enhanced **supervision** for convicted offenders upon their **early release** from **prison**.

baseline data or information the record of behaviour or frequency of a social problem at the start of a service intervention or project against which comparisons are later made within a set time-frame to judge whether the intervention or project has had a positive impact.

The concept of baseline data was originally developed within behavioural **assessment** linked to **behaviour modification** programmes. There it provided a record of the frequency in which an individual engages in a particular kind of behaviour before any programme of help begins. Obtaining this record usually depends on some form of direct observation – such as reports from the client, from other family members or by the general practitioner – in which the results have been recorded at timed intervals. Keeping track of the number of tantrums a child has during a week is an example. Such a record is used to help measure subsequent progress after intervention begins and almost always forms part of a behavioural assessment.

A baseline, or start point data as it is often now called, is also widely used in programmes seeking to bring about specific social changes, such as improving the educational attainments of children **looked after** by the local authority, or efforts to reduce **anti-social behaviour** by **youth offending team**s. Such data describes a set of social conditions or problems prior to the project starting its work, for example by logging the

rate of GCSE passes by young people looked after in a given local
authority area. Such programmes invariably set targets that improve on
the baseline rate over time, in this instance improving the GSCE pass rates
of looked-after young people.

bed and breakfast a form of temporary accommodation for families
considered to be homeless by **local authorities**.

Under the Housing Act 1996, local authority housing departments
are responsible for **homelessness** in relation to 'priority groups'
(see **homelessness**). This includes families with dependent children,
pregnant women, women experiencing **domestic violence** and others
considered to be vulnerable. The term 'vulnerable' is not defined, which
has meant that services to other people considered to be vulnerable across
the country have been very uneven. The 1996 Housing Act allowed
local authorities to discharge their duty by the use of temporary
accommodation (mostly in the private sector), and although the
Homelessness Act 2002 has repealed these clauses, there is still
widespread use of temporary accommodation across the country,
especially in urban areas. In 2007/8 the government (see Social Trends,
39, 2009 edition) estimated that around 3,000 households had recourse
to emergency bed and breakfast accommodation. Refugees figured
prominently in this group. So bed and breakfast is still used as a form of
temporary accommodation, although the Homelessness (Suitability of
Accommodation – England) Order 2003 states that bed and breakfast
accommodation should not be used for families or pregnant women
unless there is no other accommodation available, and then only for a
maximum of 6 weeks (there is a similar Order for Wales).

The problems associated with living in bed and breakfast hotels and
boarding houses are numerous. There is often overcrowding, with a
single family expected to share a bedroom. Kitchen, toilet and bathroom
facilities are likely to be shared. Such multi-occupied dwellings are
frequently in poor condition, sometimes with structural damp and
inadequate heating. Not surprisingly, people living in these conditions are
vulnerable to **depression** and other mental distress. There is compelling
evidence to show that accessing schools, health services and other key
services, including housing and welfare benefits, can be difficult, especially
if families are mobile. There is a strong association between being housed
in such temporary conditions and poor school performance and
non-attendance at school. Success in securing employment for this group
is also poor. To date people living in bed and breakfast facilities have been
less visible than rough sleepers. The Homelessness Act 2002, however,
requires local authorities to develop a coherent strategy to deal with and
prevent homelessness in **partnership** with other housing providers. In

relation to this duty, Shelter, an **advocacy** organization, has proposed that **local authorities** should seek to increase the supply of good-quality temporary housing, including the long- and medium-term leasing of private sector housing to local authorities or other social landlords and to improve financial support for temporary housing by improved housing benefit processes and improved financing of short-life temporary housing to make them habitable for the short and medium term.

Currently there is no clear mechanism for **social work** departments to be informed about the presence of homeless families living in bed and breakfast accommodation in their area. Yet the children of such families are clearly '**children in need**', although the evidence seems to suggest that statutory childcare authorities rarely get involved unless a child protection issue comes to light.

Fitzpatrick, S., Quilgars, D. and Preece, N. (2009) *Homelessness in the UK*. London: Chartered Institute of Housing.

behavioural, emotional and social difficulties/disorder (BESD) a defined category of **special educational needs** (SEN) or **learning difficulty** in which children's educational development is significantly impaired as a result of emotional and social factors. This may be in addition to issues affecting cognitive or sensory development. Not all children who misbehave or who are subject to **exclusion from school** have necessarily been identified beforehand as having 'behavioural needs' under SEN procedures. Where problems persist, schools should take action under the **Special Educational Needs Code of Practice**, as either **school action** or **school action plus**. The child's **individual education plan** should address his or her behavioural needs in addition to any other learning difficulties.

behaviour modification a method of training people to change their behaviour by the systematic use of reinforcements and, infrequently, low level forms of punishment. It is based on **learning theory**.

In general, behaviour modification programmes aim to reduce unwanted behaviour – such as tantrums, acts of self-mutilation or dependency on alcohol – and to increase positive or socially appropriate behaviour in its place. Several points are fundamental to behaviour modification: all behaviour, even extreme problem-behaviour, is viewed as serving a purpose for the individual who engages in it; strong emphasis is placed on defining problems in terms of behaviour that can be observed rather than looking for psychological roots of a problem in the person's past; the person is capable of learning other, more effective behaviours; the behaviour to be reduced, along with the behaviour to be increased, must be measurable, since measurement is the best indicator of the extent to which a problem is being resolved.

The simplest way to increase particular behaviours, according to **learning theory**, is to reward, or reinforce, the person engaging in that behaviour. A reinforcer can be something tangible, such as toys, trips, preferred activities or preferred foods, or intangible, such as attention, praise, a hug, personal satisfaction or increased effectiveness in completing a task. A reinforcer is particular to an individual, however, and may not resemble a typical reward; one cannot assume that what acts as a reinforcer for one person will do so for another. For example, for some children a reprimand acts as a reinforcement rather than a punishment and increases rather than decreases the possibility that the behaviour that caused the reprimand will happen again. So behaviourists define a reinforcer as anything that increases the likelihood that the behaviour in question will be performed again.

Part of any effective behaviour modification programme relies on discovering what it is that acts as a reinforcer for each individual. Once identified, any reinforcement should be made immediately after the selected behaviour occurred and should be applied consistently and with conviction. The approach can be particularly effective in working with children with behaviour problems. For example, the parents and teachers of a 7-year-old boy report that he is unable to sit still for more than a few seconds. Because of this it has been impossible to teach him to read, to sit for meals or to use the toilet. They agree that teaching him to sit still is the target behaviour, since other activities will follow from that. They further agree to teach the boy to sit still for 1 minute and listen to instructions. Reinforcers are chosen that are attractive enough to override the boy's continuous motion. In a room free of other distractions, the boy is asked to sit down and is then held and seated on a chair. Immediately he is praised and given a crisp and a cuddle. The process continues in short sessions of no more than 10 minutes with some ten to twenty attempts at the task, each similarly reinforced.

Behaviourists have also used punishments following unwanted behaviour. These have tended to fall into one of four categories: physical punishments, reprimands, time out, and 'response costs' whereby the person who engages in unwanted behaviour loses a specified reinforcer. Punishments are used less and less, however, as behaviourists realize that they present considerable ethical dilemmas and are much less effective than reinforcement. Only time out is used with any frequency, particularly in work with children. In behaviourist language, it means 'time out from positive reinforcement' and involves removal of the child to a neutral space for no more than 2 to 3 minutes where he or she receives no stimulation or reinforcement, social or otherwise, but can still be kept in view. Parents of children with behaviour problems are often taught how to administer time out rather than to use physical punishment or shouted verbal reprimands.

The use of reinforcers and punishers has attracted much criticism from non-behaviourists, since their use seems to imply a mechanical and crude view of human nature. Bestowing reinforcers creates an imbalance of **power** that can be used for ends other than changing behaviour. For example, in the 1950s and 1960s token economies were introduced into wards in mental hospitals. This system allowed patients to 'earn' tokens for specified behaviours, the tokens being redeemable in terms of specific goods or privileges. In fact, token economies often encouraged psychiatric nurses to act as behavioural engineers and had more to do with controlling the patient population than with teaching more effective behaviour to individuals. Behaviourists now acknowledge that the techniques were often employed by under-trained staff and used for purposes other than what they were designed for. The use of punishments, such as electric shocks, ammonia vapours and prolonged tickling deployed in some of the early behaviour regimes of the 1950s, has left a legacy that behaviour modification has found hard to live down. Virtually all punishment used in programmes today are called 'negative punishment', that is not allowing a person to engage in activities that they would enjoy. A common example of negative punishment is a 'timeout' for children following an act of unwanted behaviour in which the child spends a set period of time away from peers.

Behaviour modification has proved effective in certain circumstances with people with severe learning disabilities, with children with conduct disorders. In the main such programmes rely on positive reinforcement – praise or engagement in joint activities – of behaviours to be encouraged. Parenting classes often teach parents how to use such responses when dealing with the difficult behaviour of the children. **Cognitive behavioural therapy** is a major offshoot from behavioural programmes and relies on using some of its principles to help individuals manage their thoughts about themselves and their world.

Macdonald, G. (2007) Cognitive behavioural social work, in J. Lishman (ed.) *Handbook for Practice Learning in Social work and Social care*. London: Jessica Kingsley Publishers.

bereavement and grief the **loss** of a close relative or friend and the feelings associated with such **loss**es.

Bereavement is often a profound experience for people when they lose someone who is very important to them. It can lead to feelings of loneliness, acute sadness and a generalized disorientation and malaise. It can also be quite a different experience if, for example, the 'lost' relationship was both emotionally close and yet oppressive; in these circumstances **loss** might be tempered with relief and liberation for the survivor. In other circumstances the death of a loved one might trigger very negative thoughts to the point of contemplating **suicide** or feelings of **depression**. The degree of loss and grief experienced is likely to reflect closeness with the deceased and their importance in the emotional and social functioning of the severed relationship. For some there will be questions about the meaning of life, their future without the deceased and often very real and practical issues concerned possibly with continued parenting, reconfigured family relationships, economic matters and even issues of where people might live.

While some people may find solace in a faith others might have their beliefs seriously challenged when they feel the **loss** to be unexpected and maybe unjust in some regard. Even those whose beliefs include some notion of 'life after death' can be bewildered and unsettled by a loss. It is possible that being able to express grief is therapeutic for some people and in this regard cultural and gendered expectations about the behaviour of the bereaved may be more or less helpful. An Irish Catholic wake, for example, will usually have the corpse in a prominent position with mourners encouraged to participate in an open and expressive way. Communal grief typifies many Muslim funerals and openly flamboyant funerals in African-Caribbean communities; and cultural expectations of men in white Anglo-Saxon communities seem to encourage restraint and a disinclination to be seen to be openly grieving. Eurocentric models of bereavement and grief must not distract social workers from trying to understand that other cultures do things differently and many cultures are now clearly visible in a multi-faith and multi-cultural Britain. There may also be other circumstances where it is difficult to grieve – in gay and lesbian relationships where such relationships are regarded negatively by both a wider society and perhaps immediate family. The death of a person in a covert relationship or a 'disappeared' person or a probable death of a loved one in another country where there is a civil war are all examples of a grief that is difficult to express or to be publicly acknowledged. In essence grief is an intensely personal and individual experience and social workers will need to listen closely to be able to begin to understand the very particular meaning of any loss.

It has been argued by some theorists that **grief**, like **loss**, proceeds through some quite well-defined stages for many people. The first stage involves experiencing the loss very acutely; a further stage of adjusting to the loss and a final stage of 'devising a new life'. Such thinking can be useful but movement through these stages need not be linear in any simple sense. Stages might be experienced simultaneously and it is possible that some people might get 'stuck' and not achieve any kind of positive resolution of grief and personal growth. Social workers and counsellors sometimes have the task of trying to identify where people have got to in any process of adjustment to a bereavement. Social workers need to know that bereavement can be experienced in a wide variety of ways and that a loss can outwardly be borne with stoicism and yet be as distressing as it is for someone seemingly disabled by a death. For some the process of 'getting on with life' is a defence mechanism and their distress may come later with their grief expressed in solitude. The **social work** tasks might include encouraging the bereaved person to express their feelings, to encourage them to re-engage with the world if their response to grief has been to withdraw, to address issues about their health (grief can affect both physical health and **mental health** leading to people feeling very low) and to support them in dealing with practical problems associated with income, housing, debt and sometimes a wide range of resultant and residual difficulties.

See also **death**, **dying** and **loss**.

Humphrey, G. and Zimpfer, D. (2007) *Counselling for Grief and Bereavement*. London: Sage.

bipolar disorder   defined in **psychiatry** as a **psychosis**, involving the experience of extreme moods and emotions and formerly referred to as manic **depression**.

The experiences connected with this diagnosis have traditionally been understood as symptoms of **mental illness**. Extreme mood swings are the central experience of bipolar disorder. Involved in these swings are elation and depression, and either may be predominant for some time. Elation can lead the person to experience powerful 'flights of ideas', vigorous activity – perhaps involving excessive drinking, spending money, or sexual activity. Depression involves overwhelming feelings of pessimism and hopelessness, sadness, guilt and low self-esteem, and carries a risk of **suicide**.

As with all **mental health problems**, these experiences can result in many serious difficulties and risks for the person and others, and medical interventions play a significant part in the response. But at the same time, many changes are taking place in **mental health policy** and in the services' responses to mental health problems. These include a greater appreciation of how social discrimination adds to the problems experienced; more recognition of how social and personal factors can affect the course of the illness and recovery; a concern that the person has a right to be supported in living an ordinary life and accessing social inclusion; and importantly, promotion of a fully integrated health and social care response in place of the traditional primacy accorded to medical approaches. Within the context of mental health services, which for more serious mental health problems such as bipolar disorder, will include the **care programme approach**, social work has much to offer. Workers have a major statutory role in relation to people with these experiences, and have much to contribute to their greater **wellbeing** and control over their lives.

Golightley, M. (2008) *Social Work and Mental Health*, 3rd edition. Exeter: Learning Matters.

Black a contested term, which has a number of different social, political and cultural interpretations and meanings.

As a political label, it first gained prominence within the Black **Power** movement in the United States in the late 1960s and early 1970s, and was tied to African American identities. In the British context, the term 'Black' has a different meaning, and came to represent those from non-white groups, especially post-war migrants and their children, with shared experiences of **racism** and marginalization. The term thus became a focus for mobilization against racial and ethnic inequalities and **discrimination**, alongside enabling political organization, reflected in organizations such as the Southall Black Sisters who continue to work with Black women around the issue of domestic/familial violence.

The term 'Black' as a political label lost some currency during the 1980s, a period which saw an increased emphasis on the diversity and differences between those who had previously assumed a 'Black' identity. For example, as writers such as Tariq Modood (1998) highlighted, those from **Asian** and South Asian groups did not always easily identify with the label Black, which was more readily associated, at least in the public consciousness, with the experiences of those of African and African-Caribbean origin.

Nevertheless, despite this apparent dismantling of the term, alongside an ever-increasing emphasis on ethnic and religious distinctions, there remain organizations and individuals who continue to employ it as a means of mobilization, representation and identification.

Modood, T. (1998) 'Black' racial equality and Asian identity. *New Community*, 14(3).

blind and partially sighted registration **local authorities** keep a register of blind and partially sighted people living in their areas or ensure that this is done on their behalf.

The registration of people with **visual impairment** is voluntary. The main purpose of registration is to assist in service planning. While registration may still be required in order to access services from some local voluntary groups, to participate in some employment training schemes and to gain some financial concessions, most services and benefits are available without registration. However, registration as severely sight impaired (blind) can ease access to some entitlements, such as the blind persons' personal income tax allowance and other benefits targeted at disabled people in general.

The registration of blind people predates local authority registration of disabled people generally and was originally intended to identify potential claimants of financial benefits. Only people who have been examined by a consultant ophthalmologist (eye specialist) and certified as blind or partially sighted can be registered. The **National Assistance Act 1948** defines blindness as 'being so blind that they cannot do any work for which eyesight is essential'. However, a person need not be completely without sight to be registered blind. Generally, registration as blind is considered if a person can see at 3 metres what a 'normally' sighted person can see at 60 metres. This is referred to a 3/60 vision. Registration may also be considered for people with 6/60 vision if they have a restricted field of vision.

Partially sighted people are defined for registration purposes as 'substantially and permanently handicapped by defective vision, caused by congenital defect or illness or injury'. Registration as partially sighted is considered for people with a visual acuity between 3/60 and 6/60 with a full field of vision, but higher levels of visual acuity will qualify if the field of vision is more limited.

On receipt of the certification form, known as a BD8, from a consultant ophthalmologist, the local authority should make **contact** to find out whether the person would like to be included on the register and whether services are required. However, **service user**s have reported long delays between certification and the **assessment** of their needs, and shortcomings in the services that are eventually offered. The experience of sight **loss**, medical diagnosis and certification can raise significant anxieties about the future, so prompt provision of support, information and services is crucial.

Improving Lives Coalition (2001) *Improving Lives: priorities in health and social care for blind and partially sighted people.* London: RNIB.

Bliss symbol communication system   a system of symbols that facilitates **communication** for people with limited speech and physical **impairment**s. **Bliss** symbols provide a means for people with multiple impairments to make their wishes known to care staff and informal carers. They are designed to be quick and easy to draw, and can be set out on conveniently placed communication boards. They do not rely on reading skills, but words can be added to the symbols so that they are easily understood by any staff who are not familiar with the system. People need to be able to indicate a symbol, but this can be done in a range of ways including eye gaze.

Bliss symbols were originally created in 1949 by Charles Bliss, who believed that the development of a common world language would improve international understanding and make war less likely in the future. The language was first developed for disabled people in Canada in the 1970s. Although it has been associated with people with communication, language and learning disabilities, it allows for varying levels of abstraction and can be appropriate for people with a range of intellectual abilities. More applications for Bliss symbols have been devised as computer technology has developed. They have been used with speech synthesizers and incorporated within computer software. The latter has been particularly important since the development of the internet, which has facilitated the use of Bliss symbols in international communication in line with the original aims of Charles Bliss. The advocates of Bliss symbols believe that disabled users are in a position to assist speaking persons to discover the benefits of communication between people who use different languages.

Braille a system of raised dots embossed onto paper which allows visually impaired people to use their fingers to read script; named after Louis Braille, who invented the system.

There are two levels of Braille. One spells out each word fully and the other uses abbreviations for recurring groups of letters or words. However, Braille texts tend to be bulky, which restricts the volume of material which it is practical to produce. Many visually impaired people prefer other means of reading text. About 19,000 visually impaired people use Braille, which is a minority of those registered as blind. Braille texts are usually produced by a transcription agency, but it is now possible to obtain computer software to convert word processing files into Braille.

breach a term used to refer to the breaking of requirements of a legally binding order and also to the procedures ('breach proceedings') whereby sanctions can be brought against those who break such requirements. For example, breach of the requirements of a **community order** can lead to breach proceedings in the **magistrates' court** as a result of which the offender may be warned, **fine**d, ordered to perform more **unpaid work** or re-sentenced for the original offence (including **imprisonment**). The **responsible officer** for the **community order** is required by Schedule 8 of the **Criminal Justice Act 2003** to either issue a **warning** or initiate proceedings for any breach without a reasonable excuse, and to return the offender to court for any such second **breach** within 12 months of a **warning** being given.

British Association of Social Workers (BASW) the main professional body representing the interests of social workers in Britain.

The British Association of Social workers, founded in 1970, emerged as the result of a fairly long period of discussion between various social services associations under the auspices of the Standing Conference of Social workers, established in 1963. Before 1970 social workers were organized in associations based on client or functionally related areas. Its role is now to represent all social workers whether working in the state sector or as independent social workers. It identifies itself as the largest organization representing social workers in the UK and as a professional body aims to ensure that members operate within its professional Code of Ethics. Due to the national differences in the organization of **social work** within the UK the BASW is also organized into national branches to support its membership as well as having regional branches within England.

British Crime Survey (BCS) a national survey carried out annually by **Home Office** researchers **interviewing** a large sample of people about their experiences as **victims** of crime.

Until recently the BCS did not cover crime against children, but since January 2009 those aged 10–15 have been included in the survey. Its findings are detailed each year, along with statistics of crimes recorded by the **police**, in *Crime in England and Wales*, published by the **Home Office**. Victim surveys of this kind invariably show that crime is under-reported to the **police** (and sometimes under-recorded by the **police** even when they are reported) and that particular kinds of crime are especially unlikely to be reported. The BCS normally uses face-to-face interviews to gather its data, but in recent years BCS researchers have also used computer-assisted **interviewing** techniques in an attempt to encourage discussion of sensitive offences, and extra samples of members of minority groups have been used to improve understanding of their experiences as **victims**.

British Sign Language (BSL) a visual language which is indigenous to the UK and used by members of the deaf **community**.

British Sign Language is one of the languages used by **deaf** people. It is usually associated with movements of the hands, but also comprises a range of gestures involving the arms, head and body and also facial expression. BSL is not based on English spelling or grammar, and therefore has its own structure. It is estimated that BSL is the first or preferred language for 70,000 people. It is considered to be a crucial component of Deaf culture. Organizations of **deaf** people have sought official recognition of BSL in order to promote the rights of the deaf community, and in 2003 it was recognized as an official UK language. If BSL is a deaf person's preferred means of **communication**, there may be a duty under the **Disability Discrimination Act 1995** to provide a BSL interpreter. This will depend on the circumstances, the availability of other people whose BSL skills are sufficient to meet the need, and the appropriateness of providing information by other means, such as in writing.

bullying harassment, threats, intimidation or physical violence toward a person by one or more other persons, in school, the workplace or elsewhere. Bullying can include name-calling, text-messaging, **communication** via the internet and social **networking** sites, racist and sexually motivated abuse, aggression and extortion of money or property, as well as actual violence.

Surveys suggest that large numbers of children are subjected to various forms of bullying at both primary and secondary schools. All schools should have policies and procedures designed to combat bullying and for dealing with incidents. There is often a strong association between bullying and other educational issues such as **special educational needs** and **unauthorized absence** from school. All **local authorities** should have advisers to assist schools in developing appropriate responses. These may include classroom work and involving pupils through initiatives such as school councils and 'circle time' as part of the **citizenship** curriculum or through assertiveness training and personal, social and health education. Some schools may make use of techniques of restorative justice, conflict resolution and other 'no blame' approaches, in addition to the appropriate use of sanctions and punishments and the involvement of parents. Schools should report incidents of bullying to their local authority, (many use the Sentinel system) and analyse the data to develop appropriate strategies to combat, for example, racist or homophobic bullying where these are identified. Organizations such as ChildLine provide helpful **advice** and support for children, parents and professionals.

Tackling bullying in a school is also closely related to the **social and emotional aspects of learning (SEAL)** agenda, and not only about resolving individual incidents. All schools should be working with their pupils to promote mutual respect and emotional health and **wellbeing**. Developing appropriate relationships, both with peers and with adults, is an essential element in a school's ethos. This is also linked to the **safeguarding** duty in order to provide an environment in which children and young people feel safe and able to report their concerns with confidence. No school should now be expected to adopt an approach that they do not have a bullying problem and therefore do not need to be doing anything to address it.

Bullying is now recognized as an important feature of adult lives in the workplace, in care homes and in adult familial/caring relationships. Many workplaces now have explicit anti-bullying policies linked to disciplinary and grievance procedures. Bullying is also associated with **domestic violence** and **elder abuse**.

Department for Children, Schools and Families (2007) *Safe to Learn: embedding anti-bullying work in schools, guidance for schools.* London: DCSF.

Cc

capabilities approach an approach to disadvantage and inequality based on opportunities to choose and achieve valued 'functionings', which may be states of being or activities, including **participation** in society.

This approach has recently been adopted by the UK government as a means of defining and measuring inequality, and has also been applied to disability issues in the academic literature. Income distribution has often been used as an indicator of equality/inequality, but Amartya Sen, the best-known theorist of the capabilities approach, has argued that this is not the best indicator of social justice. Different people may need different levels of income in order to achieve the same **outcomes**. For example, it is well documented that there are additional costs associated with living with **impairment** or illness. However, the amount of this additional cost does not depend only on individual factors but also on the accessibility of the social and physical environment.

The capabilities approach aims to overcome the drawbacks of other approaches to equality of opportunity by emphasizing substantive freedom. The approach is about 'real' opportunities, which may be dependent on resources and on tackling systemic barriers. It allows for differences in preference – not everybody will want to achieve the same 'functionings'. With some capabilities, these preferences could lead to differences in outcome between groups. However, what is important is which functionings people have the capability to achieve if they so choose. In **social care** terms, this is one of the issues which have caused debate in policy-making. The UK government recently carried out an Equalities Review which included consideration of how equality should be defined and measured. The Interim Report, which was circulated for consultation, argued for the capabilities approach. Several organizations which responded to the consultation were critical of the Interim Report. Criticism focused not so much on the capabilities approach itself but on the way it had been interpreted. One response asserted that the Report was too ready to attribute persistent inequalities to choice and culture as opposed to systemic **discrimination**. Others argued that in some sections of the Report capabilities had been discussed in terms of individuals' personal qualities – intrinsic capabilities – rather than societal barriers. While the language of the capabilities approach at times is inconsistent with the **social model of disability**, there are some clear parallels. Both focus on substantive freedom and on tackling the barriers which may limit this.

Burchardt, T. (2004) Capabilities and disability: the capabilities framework and the social model of disability. *Disability and Society*, 19(7): 735–51.

care order a court order under section 31 of the **Children Act 1989** directing a local authority to take into care the child named in the order. Only the local authority or the National Society for the Prevention of Cruelty to Children, as an 'authorized person', may apply for a care order.

For a care order to be made, the applicant must convince the court that the child is suffering, or likely to suffer, **significant harm**, and that this harm can be attributed to a standard of care falling below what a parent could be reasonably expected to provide or to the child's being beyond parental control. The applicant must also show the court how the care order will benefit the child, by outlining a plan for the child and showing why other alternatives, such as providing support services to the family, will not work. Once an order is obtained, the local authority acquires **parental responsibility** for the child, who then passes into its care, although the necessity continues for parents and the local authority to work in **partnership** since parents retain parental responsibility. A care order lasts until the child is 18, unless a court has previously discharged the order. An order cannot be made on a young person who is 17 or who is 16 and married. Applying for a care order is an extremely serious step that should be taken only after other alternatives such as support services have failed.

The court reserves the care order for the most serious cases where the probability of significant harm to the child's health or development is high and the willingness of parents to cooperate is low. Such an order does not give the local authority the power to do whatever it likes with the child, and parents do not lose their parental responsibility. The authority may restrict the parents' exercise of their responsibility only when it is satisfied that this is necessary to safeguard or promote the child's welfare. Indeed it is often sharp disagreement between parents and the local authority over the exercise of parental responsibility that determines whether the authority seeks a care order or not. If there is no evidence of an unwillingness on the part of the parents to meet their parental responsibilities in the way advised by the local authority the courts are unlikely to grant an application.

Other sections of the **Children Act 1989** require joint planning and decision-making with parents, as well as consultation with the child before a placement is made with **foster care**rs or in a **children's home**. Throughout the duration of a care order the child's circumstances must be regularly reviewed to evaluate whether the plan for the child is working. The parents and others important to the child should be able to visit at reasonable intervals or have other forms of **contact** with the child. Parents, the child or the local authority may **appeal** against a decision to the **High Court** or apply for a **discharge** of a care order.

The courts have made it clear that the local authority's **care plan** for the child for whom it is seeking a care order will be subject to close scrutiny during any care proceedings. Where detail is available for parts of the plan, such as the proposed foster parents for the placement of the child, evidence about those specific foster parents should be presented to the court. The courts have established that it is entirely consistent practice to obtain a care order, rather than a **supervision order**, on a child yet allow the child to continue to live at home. Such a plan allows the authority to remove the child should that prove necessary without further judicial sanction and, further, allows the authority to make long-term plans for the child, including placing them elsewhere on a long-term basis without further reference to the courts.

Department of Health (1991) *Guidance to the Children Act. Vol. 1, Court Orders.* London: HMSO.

care plan   a written **statement** specifying the objectives for the future, agreed by practitioners and users and their carers or family, outlining the means by which those objectives are to be met.

The **Department of Health** requires **local authorities** to draw up substantial plans for adults who receive their services under **community care** arrangements and for children who are being **looked after** by the authority. For adults such a plan would usually begin with a **statement** of what the person's needs are, following **assessment**. In **care proceedings** the local authority's proposed care plan for the child receives close scrutiny. Where detail is available, for example the identified foster parents with whom the authority proposes to place the child, it should be included in the plan. A properly constructed plan is essential to enable the court to make its decision on the application. It should be put together in consultation with parents and other interested parties; where it is appropriate the child or children should be involved.

care proceedings   legal proceedings by the local authority to bring a child into its care under section 31 of the **Children Act 1989**. Such proceedings may result in a **care order** or an **interim care order** or a **supervision order** under that Act. Best practice guidance, issued by the **Ministry of Justice** in 2008, requires that social workers, prior to proceedings, should explore fully the voluntary arrangements as well as carers other than the local authority. A planning meeting should also be held before instituting proceedings in which the local authority seeks legal **advice** about the particular case. During this meeting social workers should set out what work has been undertaken with the family. The ultimate question is whether the **threshold criteria** are met and whether court proceedings are necessary. If so, in most instances (but not all) a letter should be written to the parents of the child in question informing them that an application for a care order will shortly be made and that they should seek legal advice. This letter – in fact a lengthy document called 'Letter before Proceedings' – will state the cause of concern, the existing care plan and why proceedings are being instituted. It should also include the date and time of a pre-proceedings meeting. The latter is **social work**-led, and not adversarial in nature in which the facts, issues and legal position of the authority is discussed and made clear.

Care Quality Commission the regulatory agency for health and adult social services in England. This organization replaced the Healthcare Commission and the Commission for **Social Care Inspection** in 2009. As such it carried out the **inspection** of all health and adult **social care** providers in England and is the formal registration body for statutory, private and voluntary providers to ensure common standards across the sectors. They will also continue the work of the previous organizations in publishing their reports and providing significant levels of **advice** on best practice to all the organizations in its remit. They also have the necessary powers to levy **fines** or provide public **warnings** if standards are not met.

Care Standards Act 2000 legislation that brings together government proposals for improvement in **social care**. Essentially the Act is concerned with **social care** standards both in the workforce and in statutory, private and voluntary sector provision.

In relation to improving workforce standards, the Act set up a new body in October 2001, namely the **General Social Care Council** (GSCC). This has responsibility for regulating the **social care** workforce by setting high standards for education and training, registering the trained workforce and setting codes of conduct and standards of practice. It also deals with matters of serious misconduct. Other main provisions of the Act are to ensure that there are systems in place to monitor standards of care in **children's home**s and homes for vulnerable adults, in both the public and private sector. This remit also applies to non-**NHS** hospitals.

Standards for domiciliary care to people living in their own homes and arrangements for fostering and **adoption** are also subject to monitoring. To support these developments a National Care Standards Commission has been set up whose key aim is to establish and maintain similar standards throughout the UK, and a new **power** for ministers allows statutory guidance to be issued on charges for residential care. The Act also passed local authority responsibility for the regulation of child-minding and **day care** for under-5s to the Early Years Directorate, a new branch of **Ofsted** (Office for Standards in Education).

carer a person – often but not always a relative – responsible for looking after another person who cannot look after himself or herself in some or all respects. The care provided is likely to take place in domestic settings and to be largely without monetary reward.

The term describes a range of relationships whereby one person cares for another, sometimes solely, sometimes in conjunction with others. The level of dependence of the cared-for person varies enormously, from people largely able to look after themselves – except for, say, shopping – to others requiring almost constant attendance. The more demanding caring role is likely to be with people with conditions such as **dementia**, enduring and serious **mental health problems** and people with multiple disabilities. Care involves a wide range of physically and emotionally tiring activities: bathing, assistance with basic bodily functions, help with personal hygiene, feeding, containment, home nursing, the management of personal finances, and organizing or liaising with health and social services. The care given may or may not be supplemented by domiciliary and **day care** services provided by social welfare and health agencies. It is difficult to estimate the exact number of carers since it is not clear-cut the point at which informal 'helping' becomes caring. Analysis of the 2001 Census indicated that there are around 6 million carers in the UK of which 58 per cent are women and 42 per cent men. Approximately 175,000 carers are under the age of 18. Of all carers 1.9 million people care for more than 20 hours a week and from this group 1.25 million people care for more than 50 hours a week.

Caring often imposes a financial cost for items such as extra heating, lighting and laundry. A limited number of carers are able to claim welfare benefits in recognition of their caring duties, but most are ineligible for help from the state. To care for someone means, in many instances, giving up the chance of paid employment, and such 'opportunity costs' are incalculable. Sadly, the government's National Carers Strategy, launched in 1999, simply did not address this issue. Carers are characterized as wanting to promote the **wellbeing** of the person they are caring for but also to have a life of their own. They want to be able to have confidence in services and a say in how services are provided. On the issue of income, the strategy had little to offer and fell significantly short of acknowledging the **poverty** that many carers face. The welfare benefits that can be claimed by most carers continue to be significantly less than 'wage replacement' benefits such as Job Seekers Allowance.

The **National Health Service and Community Care Act 1990** brought the first official recognition of the needs of carers. The White Paper preceding the Act, the Act itself and subsequent government guidelines made it clear that statutory service providers should do everything reasonably possible to assist and support carers. Further, there was an understanding that the needs of cared-for people and of carers may differ or even conflict; in these circumstances separate **assessment** of need was perceived as a requirement, and this was subsequently legislated for by the **Carers (Recognition and Services) Act 1995**. This Act gave two new duties to **local authorities**: first, to assess the needs of carers if they (the local authority) were also undertaking an assessment of the needs of the cared-for person and, second, to take account of the carer's assessed needs when making decisions about the services that may be offered to the person cared for. The Act did not permit a separate assessment of a carer's needs if the cared-for person did not want any services from **social services department**s. As a result, and because there was mounting evidence of relatively few carers in fact having their needs assessed (research conducted by the Carers National Association), pressure mounted for some more comprehensive legislation, culminating in the **Carers and Disabled Children Act 2000**. This Act now permits carers to have an independent assessment of their needs irrespective of the wishes or needs of the cared-for person.

The most recent piece of legislation, the **Carers (Equal Opportunities) Act 2004**, has emphasized the importance of carers in work, training and education being offered the same rights as non-carers. This legislation is consistent with the government's commitment to *flexible working* that is designed to improve work–life balance. In sum, employers are supposed to give serious consideration to any employee's request to work flexibly if they can still fulfil their duties in a manner that will satisfy the employer.

There are difficulties with the words 'care' and 'carer'. Both assume or imply that the domestic environment is a place of warm or loving reciprocal relationships between kin. Such connotations can disguise the feelings of duty and obligation that may be involved as well as the considerable levels of stressful work. Carers usually provide care because of a pre-existing relationship with the cared-for person; such relationships may contain a range of emotions, from hostility (including elder abuse) to affection, and from satisfaction to guilt. Feminist arguments indicate that assumptions about the loving nature of caring may be exploitative of carers in general and coercive in relation to people who are reluctant to undertake the task. It is suggested that a distinction can usefully be made between 'caring for' and 'caring about', the former implying the labour involved and the latter acknowledging the love or affection. Other criticisms of the term come from **service user**s, particularly in the disability movement, who argue that it can diminish the reciprocity of relationships even where there is a need for physical care. Those who are cared for can also be care-givers, giving emotional support to partners and friends, and those who are carers have other dimensions to their lives that can be overlooked. Some assert the right to be cared for by people with whom they are not in a relationship, thus challenging the current policy emphasis on informal familial care. The report, *Without Us*, published by the **charity** Carers UK, claims that to replace existing carers with paid staff would cost the country the equivalent of a second **NHS**.

A key anti-oppressive task for social and health service workers is to create a climate in which it is possible for potential carers to reveal feelings about the extent to which they are willing, if at all, to undertake caring tasks and responsibilities.

Carers' support groups have burgeoned in the past few decades. Sometimes such groups are supported directly by social workers and by financial help from statutory sources; other such groups are organized on a **self-help** basis. There is no doubt that current statutory provision for vulnerable people rests upon the assumption that families and relatives will undertake the bulk of caring activities. The relief provided to carers under considerable stress is often negligible. Local authority assessments of carers' needs are heavily influenced by available resources, such as day-care centres, respite services, counselling, carer support groups and occasional modest monetary grants rather than by the actual needs of the individual carer. With more women working and with the increasing **divorce** rate – hence a potential **loss** of the daughter-in-law as carer – the assumptions held by the statutory services will have to be adjusted if current provision is to be maintained, if not improved. The experience of **Asian** and African-Caribbean carers appears to be broadly similar to those of white British carers, except that there is generalized evidence that ethnic minority families use social services less than white British people (such as **respite services**), are even less likely to have their needs as carers assessed, experience greater **poverty** and, more likely in the case of **Asian** carers, spend more time in the caring role.

Some **local authorities** have their adults services teams deal with carers' assessments, others subcontract the service to specialist voluntary sector agencies. These agencies can be generic, where all carers are catered for; others may organize their services to support particular client groups such as carers of people with serious **mental health problems** or perhaps young carers. The needs of young carers in particular have only recently been recognized although the extent of the pressures upon them have yet to be rigorously researched. It is plain however that many have seriously compromised their own futures because of the often considerable duties they have to shoulder.

Carers and Disabled Children Act 2000 legislation that strengthens the right of carers to an **assessment** of their needs and extends the groups to which **local authorities** may make **direct payments** for **community care** services.

Under previous legislation, an informal carer could request an **assessment** of her or his own needs only if the person cared for had agreed to being assessed for community care services. In some cases, this led to carers having no access to support services. The Act entitles people aged over 16 who are providing substantial and regular care for someone over 18 to request an **assessment** in his or her own right irrespective of whether the person 'cared for' has been assessed. The Act gives the local authority the **power** (rather than the duty) to provide services to assist the carer. Services can be provided directly to the carer, and this can be done in the form of direct payments. These direct payments or services must concern the carer's needs, but can involve services delivered to the cared-for person (for example, to meet the carer's need for a break) if both parties agree to this. However, this would not normally include 'intimate care'. Carers can be charged for services provided for themselves rather than for the cared-for person.

The Act also applies to parent-carers of disabled children. The Act amends the **Children Act 1989** so that local authorities can make direct payments to parent-carers as an alternative to providing services to the *child*. To encourage independence during the transition period, the Act extends direct payments to young disabled people aged 16 and 17 in lieu of all or some of the services they may need. However, parent-carers and young people are not normally allowed to use the direct payments in order to purchase services from relatives living in the same house. The Act also provides a system of vouchers that carers and disabled people who are assessed as in need can use in order to 'purchase' short-term respite breaks. It is envisaged that this will provide more flexibility as to when and where these breaks are taken.

The previous legislation, the **Carers (Recognition and Services) Act 1995**, covers carers of all ages, including adult carers caring for adults, parent-carers of disabled children and young carers under the age of 18.

This has not been repealed. However, the Act does *enhance* the right to assessment of any **carer** aged under 16 or of parent-carers of disabled children. Organizations representing the interests of carers have been critical of this and have argued that reliance on the **Children Act 1989** is likely to lead to insufficient emphasis on the needs of carers.

This is a complex area of law which requires an understanding of the interaction between carers' legislation and assessment under the Children Act 1989. Important changes strengthening the rights of carers have been introduced by the **Carers' (Equal Opportunities) Act 2004**. As a result, in 2005 the government introduced policy guidance covering both the 2004 legislation and the Carers and Disabled Children Act 2000.

Clements, L. (2009) *Carers and their Rights: the law relating to carers*, 3rd edition. London: Carers UK.

Carers (Equal Opportunities) Act 2004 legislation which builds upon existing statute for **carers** with a predominant focus upon equality of opportunity in relation to carers' own needs especially in relation to employment, education and training.

Three principal changes feature in the Act building upon the earlier legislation for carers. The first placed a duty upon **local authorities** to develop comprehensive information strategies to inform carers of all of their rights, especially their right to an **assessment** of their needs and to identify 'hidden carers'. The second change was to recognize the needs of carers, as individuals and independent of the caring role. *The Equity Principle* in this context sought to ensure that people who care have access to the same opportunities that non-carers have, especially with regard to work or preparation for work. The third ingredient in the Act was to facilitate improved cooperation between agencies dealing with carers in order to provide a seamless service, which would take into account the religious, cultural and ethnic needs of carers. All of these changes were designed to enhance and achieve positive **outcomes** for individual carers. Although many commentators have welcomed this Act's aspirations, the reality is that social workers continue, implicitly, to expect carers to continue with the caring role. Given the continuing stringent interpretation of **Fair Access to Care** eligibility criteria, rather than the innovative and creative approaches advocated for carers within this Act, carers will continue to receive very limited support from statutory agencies.

Prior to the Carers (Equal Opportunities) Act 2004, legislation had addressed the carer role as a means of recognizing and ensuring the continuation and sustainability of existing, practical and emotional support to the cared-for person already in receipt of **community care** services (see the **Carers (Recognition and Services) Act 1995**. The later National Carer's Strategy: *Caring about Carers* (1999) highlighted the need for carers to have an **assessment** of their needs irrespective of whether a cared-for person had their needs assessed or not and the **Carer and Disabled Children Act 2000** implemented this proposal. With this legislation came the **power** to provide services directly to carers, to charge for these services and to offer some limited direct payments to carers in support of their own needs. The strategy concerning carers in the White Paper *Our Health, Our Care, Our Say* (2006) revised the 1999 strategy to include a nationwide consultation process described by Gordon Brown as: 'the most far reaching national consultation ever on the future of carers'. The Social Policy Research Unit's analysis of this first consultation (2007) identified carers' principal hopes and aspirations as increased control over their own lives and identity, improved emotional and physical **wellbeing**, adequate resources, support for family life for all family members, improved relationships with professionals and enhanced 'quality time' with the cared-for person.

Department of Health (2006) *Our Health, Our Care, Our Say.* London: DH.

Social Policy Research Unit (2007) *Outcomes for Carers of Disabled or Older Adults.* York: Social Policy Research Unit.

Carers (Recognition and Services) Act 1995 an Act that provides carers with a statutory right to an **assessment** of their needs by the local authority.

In reforming the arrangements for **community care** provision in the early 1990s, the government recognized the substantial contribution made by unpaid carers to the care of those with needs arising from age, disability or illness. Following sustained **advocacy** by carers' organizations, there was formal recognition that such care was often provided at considerable personal cost and that carers' needs should be taken into account. The Act provides that when an **assessment** of need of the cared-for person is taking place under section 47 of the **National Health Service and Community Care Act**, anyone providing a substantial amount of care for the **service user** on a regular basis (excluding professional, paid carers) is eligible for a carer's assessment. The carer must request the assessment. This provision gives carers a statutory right to an assessment of *their* needs, and those needs must be taken into account when making decisions about what services might be offered to the **service user**. However, it placed no obligation on the local authority to provide services. The legal mandate for services to carers is found in the **Carers and Disabled Children Act 2000**, which also allows a carer's **assessment** to take place in the absence of a **community care** assessment. The needs of carers of disabled people are also covered by section 8 of the **Disabled Persons (Services, Consultation and**

Representation) Act 1986, which requires a carer's ability and willingness to care to be taken into account when deciding on service provision for the disabled person under section 4. The duty arises whether or not the carer has requested such consideration.

Department of Health (1989) *Caring For People: community care in the next decade and beyond*. London: HMSO.

case history a historical account of a person and his or her family, emphasizing significant events or factors that appear to 'explain' the individual's or family's problems.

Some social welfare agencies prefer the term 'social history'. Health authorities use the term 'medical case records'. Trends in relation to the **recording** of case records have sometimes stressed full case histories, at other times brief notes on the individual and the family background. The consensus until the late 1960s, influenced by therapeutic models of **social work** practice, was to keep full case histories. Since then **recording** has become relatively brief, focused and involving critical incidents and events. Research sponsored by the **Department of Health**, however, has been critical of the lack of family background information in relation to children in care. For long-term cases at least, the current practice is to keep fuller accounts of case histories. Major practice dilemmas concern the keeping of records and the issue of access. Regarding the former, the concern is whether records should be kept for each individual in a family and whether there should be a family file or both. With the latter the issue is who should have access to the records and what information, if any, might be kept confidential. Although they have a different purpose there is some overlap with **life story books** for children and young people and, more recently, elders.

casework an approach to working with individuals and families based on relationship and ethical principles such as unconditional regard for the user. Casework originated as a method in the work of the Charity Organisation Society in the last quarter of the nineteenth and early twentieth centuries in which the social worker attempted to familiarize themselves with all aspects of a family's life and to build a supportive relationship that offered guidance and, occasionally, some material assistance. The relationship was unequal in many respects with caseworkers often of middle class origins and the families they worked with on low income, even subsistence living. The ever-present threat of having to go to the workhouse for relief of **poverty** was a powerful incentive for families to oblige the worker.

From the 1920s to the 1960s casework was dominated by the **psychodynamic** perspective which tended to focus on family relationships, on the quality of the relationship with the social worker and on users' own **childhood**s. The term was widely used among social workers in the 1950s and 1960s, when all casework was thought to entail the giving of support to the person or 'ego' and/or seeking to help him or her achieve insight into their problems and effect permanent change. Through it **social work** was cast as a therapeutic endeavour that could be undertaken in families or with individuals. The problems experienced by the person or family were considered amenable to the influence of the social worker (therapist), and external factors (such as poor housing or debts) were regarded as less important in unravelling a person's difficulties.

The realization that **poverty** was still endemic in Britain in the later 1960s and 1970s undermined older models of casework as social workers gave greater prominence to social and structural origins of what appeared to be personal and family based problems. Casework came to involve a greater range of tasks such as liaising with other organizations with whom the **service user** had a problem, acting as advocate in the interests of the user and providing advice on welfare benefits, although it still relied on the personal relationship with individuals and families.

By the 1970s casework was regarded as only one **social work** approach among many, including **group work** and **community work**, and had adopted more solution-focused formats such as **task centred work**. Problems could now be solved or eased by non-therapeutic methods or combinations of methods. The radical social work movement of the 1970s was critical of the casework method, which it regarded as rooted in the belief that problems were to be explained by personal or individual failure rather than by wider social causes, such as unemployment, poor housing and poverty. Casework, with its emphasis on users coming to terms with their problems through the relationship with the worker, was thought to actively inhibit users from understanding the structural origins of their problems. However, it is possible to envisage a radical form of casework in some circumstances, such as feminist counselling in relation to **domestic violence** or rape, as a means of understanding wider social issues.

Mayer, J. and Timms, N. (2009) *Client and Agency: working class responses to casework*. London: Aldine Transactions.

caution   a formal disposal of a criminal case, consisting of a **warning** administered to an offender by a **police** officer. The measure is an alternative to prosecution and a means of **diversion** out of the criminal justice system. It should only be used when the offender has admitted guilt. Cautions may be cited in court in the same way as previous convictions. Since the **Crime and Disorder Act 1998** cautions have been replaced for offenders under the age of 18 by a new system comprising a single **reprimand**, followed by a **warning** (or ('**final warning**') and then prosecution. Around 40 per cent of all detected indictable offences are dealt with by cautions (including reprimands and **final warning**s). See also **conditional caution**.

centile chart measures to track the growth of children from birth to 4 years of age. A child's weight, length or height, head circumference and body mass index (BMI) are all measured at regular intervals, plotted and compared with national averages.

Children tend to grow at a regular rate, albeit within broad variations, and this simple fact is used to assist in recognizing when a child has suffered some disturbance. Depending on weight and height at birth, a child should proceed to grow along a recognized curve, or centile, which is simply the average for a child of similar height and weight at birth. But a child may stop growing in some way when emotionally upset over a long period of time or inadequately fed or ill. An unexplained change in the rate of growth can be a sign of the child's **failure to thrive**. To be of use, the charts require regular measurement of the child in question. Young infants are usually measured by health visitors at specific intervals. School-age children for whom there might be concern can be monitored by the school doctor. Social workers often use this information to help them to decide whether a child is being neglected or not. New charts – developed by the Royal College of Paediatrics and Child Health – were introduced in 2009 based on the assumption that breastfeeding (rather than formula milk) is the norm. It is hoped that these charts will promote breastfeeding of the newborn and infants and that in turn will reduce the incidence of obesity. The charts are intended to be 'parent-friendly' so that mothers and fathers can monitor their child's growth. The principle behind the use of these growth charts is that children grow and gain weight at established and predictable rates and that divergence from these norms may indicate illness or inadequate diet. So, for example, a child's BMI should be between the 25th and 75th centile if her weight is average for her height. Social workers may take account of information from the use of growth charts to help them to decide whether a child is being abused or neglected.

chaining a method of teaching a person a new skill or activity by breaking it down into small steps or behaviours and reinforcing the mastery of each part until the entire chain is learned and the skill or activity can be performed. Chaining is frequently used in work with people with learning disabilities who need to learn ordinary skills of day-to-day living, such as dressing themselves, eating with utensils, shopping or using public transport.

challenging behaviour a broad spectrum of behaviours that can be experienced as aggressive or unpleasant and can adversely affect the health and safety of those who engage in it and their carers.

Challenging behaviour includes self-injury, destructiveness, verbal threats, screaming and tantrums, inappropriate sexual conduct and physical aggression such as biting or pinching. The term originally referred to behaviour displayed by some young people and adults with **learning disability** that was dangerous to themselves or other people, or was sufficiently unacceptable to limit significantly their opportunities for living in the **community** or going out into public places. More recently the term has been used in relation to behaviour by other groups of **service users** including young offenders and young people who are in secure accommodation, adults with **mental health problems** and confused **older people**.

In each case the behaviour poses dilemmas for **social work** and **social care** professionals. How far, for example, can the actions be tolerated of an older confused male resident who repeatedly throws his dinner at residential staff? How often can a young male with mental health problems living in a small **group home** be allowed to verbally abuse others living in the same home or in the neighbourhood? The key issues for social workers are the same across all users who engage in challenging behaviour: the degree to which the person's behaviour is a threat to himself or herself or others and how far other people are willing to put up with that behaviour, which can be extremely disruptive.

In relation to severe learning disabilities, challenging behaviour is thought to be associated with limited **communication** and social skills. This makes it difficult for the person to communicate what he or she wants in more socially acceptable ways. Challenging behaviour may also be a means of escaping from demands (for instance at school or in the home) with which she or he is unable to cope. It may be that the methods of control that most people use are not available. However, challenging behaviour can be a response to pain or discomfort. Attention should be paid to changes in behaviour as these may be the key to understanding what a person is trying to communicate.

It is generally recognized that prevention and early intervention are preferable to allowing challenging behaviour to escalate. Challenging behaviour can be exhausting and emotionally draining for carers, but they may be able to prevent some incidents by ensuring that needs are met promptly and encouraging skills which might enable the person to communicate their needs in more acceptable ways. It is also useful to keep records of what happens, when it occurs, what has been done to try and deal with it, and the result of this. If professional help is sought, it is important to first check out any health reasons for the behaviour. If a psychologist is consulted, she or he will probably want to carry out a 'functional analysis'. This may draw on information carers have already recorded about the circumstances in which the behaviour occurs, and help to identify which needs are being met through the challenging behaviour. Information that is useful for a functional analysis is sometimes referred to as an 'ABC' analysis, meaning antecedents, behaviour and consequences.

Physical intervention and restraint raises significant ethical problems, and should be avoided whenever possible. Learning to recognize early signs of agitation and to defuse these is important. It has been pointed out that although there is much concern about physical restraint, the use of medication to suppress **challenging behaviour** has in fact been more common. It is now considered that routine use of medication alone is inappropriate, and that it should only be used following a detailed **assessment** of the social, psychological and biological factors that may have contributed to the behaviour.

The British Institute of Learning Disabilities has produced policy guidelines to improve practice, and the **Department of Health** has published best practice guidance in the form of the 2007 (revised second edition) of the 'Mansell Report'. This acknowledges that although there has been progress in **learning disability** services, provision for those with challenging behaviour has not kept pace with services for other groups. Unfortunately this is borne out by recent cases of abusive treatment in institutional settings for people with severe learning disabilities.

Mansell, J. (2007) *Services for People with Learning Disabilities and Challenging Behaviour or Mental Health Needs*, revised edition. London: DH.

charity a non-profit-making organization registered with the Charities Commission that seeks to dispense services and sometimes grants to people in need. Charities in the UK have to be able to demonstrate that they are of 'benefit to the public or a section of the public'.

Charities have different practices and different terms of reference. Some deal directly with potential recipients/**service user**s of their services and/or grants; others deal with intermediaries such as social workers; yet others work only through other organizations. Some charities are extremely modest, with very specific objectives within perhaps a very small area. Others are comparatively wealthy, with wide terms of reference and perhaps serving an area as large as the whole of Britain. Many voluntary or '**third sector**' organizations are also charities; well-known examples include Barnardos, Action for Children, the Children's Society, Scope, Age Concern and Mind.

The Charities Act 1993, amended by the Charities Act 2006, provides the legislative framework for agencies to be registered as charities. The established categories of charitable objectives are the relief of **poverty** (and the associated relief of unemployment), the advancement of religion, the advancement of education, and other activities beneficial to the **community** (including urban and rural regeneration). Many **social work** and social welfare agencies in the voluntary sector are charities. In fact, their legal status can vary substantially, from unincorporated associations to companies limited by guarantee and other legal entities. The advantages of charitable status include tax relief of various kinds; the disadvantages for some will be the restriction on political activity since charities cannot be involved in party political activity. They can, however, be involved with politics in order to further their own agency's objectives or to provide information to groups and parties explicitly involved in politics (such as parliamentary briefings).

The Charity Commission initiated a fundamental review, in 2008–9, to consult all stakeholders regarding the criterion of 'public benefit' that all charities have to satisfy. A number of key debates had brought about the review. The Commission clearly felt the need to establish a consensus around questions such as 'can some agencies such as public schools continue to be charities when their claim to offering a public benefit may be tenuous?' and 'should charities be permitted to charge fees and, if so, in what circumstances?', and 'can some faith based organizations, with what might be regarded as factional interests, also argue a public interest?'. Given the considerable tax advantages offered to charities in the UK and their access to funds that other agencies are denied, the Charity Commission felt the need to look again at charitable rules.

Social workers make appeals to charities on behalf of **service user**s in need. Many workers feel uneasy about this practice, especially if the need arises from poverty or disability. This unease rests upon the view that, first, the state ought to meet these basic needs and, second, the kinds of account of **service user**s' difficulties that charities find persuasive smack of the 'deserving poor'. Some also make the point that the use of charitable funds or services inhibits the realization of a more just society because ideas of **charity** and of discretion obscure the need for basic rights in relation to, for example, an adequate income for all or the ability of a disabled person to participate in society on equal terms with able-bodied people. Workers prepared to **appeal** to charities on behalf of people in need argue that present problems need present solutions and that they wish to deal with a problem immediately in order to enhance people's life chances.

child abuse physical or psychological harm done to a child through a deliberate act or neglect.

Social workers work with several forms of child abuse. *Physical abuse* is the intentional use of physical force to hurt, injure or kill a child. Social workers are not expected to diagnose with certainty whether a child has been physically abused or not, but they are expected to be alert to suspected cases of abuse so that they can initiate an investigation to safeguard the child. To do this, they require some familiarity with injuries that might have been deliberately inflicted on a child. Some knowledge of the difference between accidental bruising and inflicted injury assists in this recognition. The former usually occurs where bone is close to the skin, such as the forehead, shins or knees. The latter is more frequently present on soft parts of the body, such as the cheeks, buttocks, upper legs and mouth. Bruises caused by an adult slapping or grabbing a child often leave a distinctive mark, such as several finger bruises. Burns, particularly cigarette burns and scalds from hot liquids, and frequent fractures are other injuries deliberately inflicted.

Social workers also encounter children harmed through *neglect*: the persistent lack of attention paid to the child's needs by his or her parents or carers. Pre-school children are most vulnerable to neglect, which can take the form of injury in repeated accidents, for example burning a hand in an unguarded fire, weight **loss** or abnormally slow growth rates (see **failure to thrive**). Social workers also work with children who have been *sexually abused*. Child **sexual abuse** can take several forms: exposure, such as the viewing of sexual acts, pornography and exhibitionism; molestation, that is, the fondling of genitals, either the child's or the adult's; sexual intercourse – oral, vaginal or anal – without the use of force and over a period of time; and rape, that is, intercourse achieved by use of force.

Although injuries to an abused child can be extreme, detection of abuse is rarely easy and is usually achieved only by the pooling of knowledge and expertise by both professionals and lay people. Health visitors, pre-school playgroup assistants, teachers, general practitioners and medical staff at hospital emergency units as well as paediatricians, social workers and **police** all play important roles in this task. Often the children's own willingness to speak to someone confidentially about the abuse happening to them or the observations of non-abusing parents are critical to detection. The social worker's task is to assemble all the information and opinion. Frequently a safeguarding conference, attended by professionals and others who work with the child, as well as by the child's parents, will be held to appraise precisely the nature of the abuse that has taken place.

There are risk factors or indicators that, when present in a child's life, might suggest an increased likelihood of abuse of that child. Such indicators usually include a young (teenage) mother without support, an infant who was premature or of low birth weight, a previous history of violence in the family, alcoholism, and one parent who was abused as a child. Such indicators have been criticized by feminist practitioners as apparently laying the responsibility for abuse with the mothering of the child and ignoring the fact that the great majority of abusers, particularly child sex abusers, are male. Others have argued that heavy emphasis on safeguarding children has skewed the nature of **social work**, which has become excessively cautious as a result, relying more on compulsory legal action than on the development of preventive and support services for families. It is important to underscore that the incidence of child murders has fallen dramatically in the United Kingdom since 1973, with the biggest drop being among infants. For all the publicized failures of **social services department**s to protect certain children, children are relatively more protected now than they were twenty years ago.

HM Government (2010) *Working Together to Safeguard Children. A guide to inter-agency working to safeguard and promote the welfare of children.* London: HSMO.

child and adolescent mental health services (CAMHS) a multi-disciplinary agency with responsibility for supporting children and young people with emotional, behavioural, psychological and **mental health problems**.

The Departments of Health and Children, Schools and Families (DCSF) have established CAMHS replacing the former Child Guidance clinics. CAMHS teams usually comprise clinical and **educational psychologist**s, psychiatrists, social workers, counsellors and ancillary workers. The terms of reference for CAMHS teams is to deal with troubled children and young people and their families or carers. Referrals to CAMHS teams may come from social services children and families teams, schools, **education welfare service**s, GPs, **youth offending team**s and others.

child assessment order an order under section 43 of the Children Act requiring any person in a position to do so to produce the child named in the order for assessment. To obtain a child assessment order, the applicant, which may be the local authority or the NSPCC, must have reasonable cause to suspect that the child is suffering or is likely to suffer **significant harm**, that **assessment** of the child's health and development is necessary in order to establish whether that harm has occurred or is likely to occur and that the **assessment** would be unlikely to take place without the order being made.

If the court grants the order, it can also direct where, when and how the assessment will take place; it imposes a duty on any person in a position to produce the child to do so and to comply with any directions relating to the assessment included in the order. The maximum duration of the order is 7 days from the date specified in the order although court orders have indicated that it is possible to spread the 7 days over a period of time. The child can refuse to undergo the arranged assessment, since the **Children**

Act 1989 allows children of sufficient age and understanding to refuse medical or psychiatric examination although the court can, and has, overruled the child's refusal. The **children's guardian** will advise the court on whether the child is of sufficient understanding to refuse to submit to the examination or assessment. The child assessment order is implemented under close control of the court and the applicant must specify the type of assessment, who will carry it out and where, and the number of days it will take. Only rarely will the **assessment** involve the child in an overnight stay away from home but if it should the court will issue a direction as to the extent of **contact** with parents and others.

Childcare Act 2006 focuses primarily on children from birth to 5 and the services that should be provided for them. It is the first piece of legislation of its kind in the UK.

The definition of 'childcare' provided in the Act is broad and includes most forms of care, outside of family or **foster care**, and education, outside of school hours, for children up to 14 (or up to the age of 18 for children with disabilities). The Act outlines a number of duties for **local authorities** in England and Wales and requires them to work with partners in providing services. The **children's centre** model of integrated, holistic care is endorsed and the **Every Child Matters** agenda is reinforced. Local authorities are required to have regard to the views of young children in planning and organizing services – partly in recognition of the UN Convention on the Rights of the Child. They have a statutory duty to ensure that there is sufficient childcare provision for those wanting it – though this provision can be delivered by the private, voluntary or independent sectors. Local authorities are not required however to make direct provision themselves. Childcare provision – from 8 a.m. to 6 p.m. is seen as vital by the government to support working parents and help them escape **poverty**. The Act establishes new registration procedures for those offering services. Those working with children under 5 must deliver the **early years foundation stage** – a **play**-based learning and **assessment** framework.

childhood defined in a number of ways – by reference to law, to physical and emotional development or to how people are viewed by others. Any definition is likely to have been provided by an 'adult' and imposed on the 'child'.

In UK and English law there are ambiguities about what it is to be a child. The **Children Act 1989** considers a person's 18th birthday to be the decisive landmark yet it is possible to work full-time, marry and have sex legally at 16. At the age of 10 – in England – a child is regarded as responsible for his or her actions and may be dealt with according to criminal law. Physically many young people are capable of reproduction at the age of 12 – but few would argue that becoming a parent at that age is a good idea. This implies that the transition from childhood to adulthood involves more than physical growth – that the emotional and social skills required to live independently are part of what is understood in becoming adult. Professionals who work with children and young people bring different constructions of 'childhood' to their work. **Early years** professionals are trained to see infancy and childhood as periods of development, growth and opportunity – when anything is possible. For social workers their encounters with children may well be associated with family breakdown, violence, neglect or substance abuse and 'childhood' is akin to a battleground.

Conflicting views of childhood can be traced back over several hundreds of years in Western thinking and elements of these different ways of thinking about children and **childhood** survive in policy-making, childcare and education today. There is one view that sees the child as essentially selfish, pleasure seeking and in want of discipline. There is a quite different tradition, which sees the child as pure, innocent and looks at childhood in a sentimental way – because of what is lost on the way to adulthood. As psychologists and educationalists have studied children and childhood, views of what distinguishes the child from the adult and what drives children towards adulthood have developed. Though Freud and Piaget had quite different approaches and concerns both argued that there is something within the child that drives her to progress from an emotional or intellectual state of underdevelopment through to stages of relative maturity. It is these ideas – that **childhood** is about development, progress and dependency – that inform much of early 21st-century policy-making in Britain when it comes to early education and care. These ideas give legitimacy to the target-setting and **assessment** regimes of the **early years foundation stage**. Equally much of the **Children and Young People's Plan** is motivated by an ambition to 'narrow the gap in **outcomes**' between children at the top and bottom of the social and educational ladders. The premise that children are vulnerable and passive also accounts, in part, for the raft of measures aimed at shielding and protecting children.

Some critics have argued that the risk averse culture that has developed means that children are denied the sorts of practical experiences needed to evaluate the dangers inherent in any situation. This policy approach might also be explained by a fear that those caring for children have of putting their own careers at risk in the event of accidents. Current academic and philosophical thinking tends to be dominated by the view of children and childhood as something that is socially constructed – that there is no single, ideal experience of what we can call childhood. Rather we should understand that an individual's experiences are shaped by a number of other constructs such as gender, class or ethnicity. This understanding also allows for children to be agents in their lives and experience.

Child Maintenance and Enforcement Commission the agency that replaced the **Child Support Agency**. It was set up by the Child Maintenance and Other Payments Act 2008, and has a wide-ranging remit to encourage and facilitate voluntary arrangements for the payment of child maintenance. It can also assess non-resident parents' liability to pay maintenance using a formula that was revised in 2008 (see **child support**).

childminders people who look after children under the age of 8 on domestic premises, usually in the childminder's own home, for reward, usually money.

Childminders need to be registered and inspected by the Office for Standards in Education, Children's Services and Skills (Ofsted); they are also subject to **Criminal Records Bureau** (CRB) and health checks. The National Childminding Association (NCMA) aims to support and train childminders and nannies, and ensure that the occupation is seen as professional. Childminders are required to meet the standards set out in the **early years foundation stage** (EYFS) framework when it comes to the care and education of children. With increasing regulation the number of registered childminders has dropped sharply. Childminders are required, therefore, to work in **partnership** with parents and carers in providing a safe, stimulating, caring, learning environment. The EYFS framework requires that childminders record a child's development and achievements using the Foundation Stage Profile (FSP) and this record is to be shared with parents. NCMA childminders and nannies are expected to manage children's behaviour in a positive manner – and not to hit or humiliate children. The NCMA also expects that equality of opportunity be recognized and promoted, that children develop a sense of their own identity and culture. Childminders – as skilled, trained, professionals – are expected to manage their business accordingly. Some parents may be reluctant to recognize that as self-employed professionals childminders need to set terms and conditions for their services, and that contracts should be respected by both parties.

child poverty the specific ways in which **poverty** (see **poverty**) impacts upon children's lives, for example in terms of education, health, and **wellbeing**.

According to the Campaign to End Child **poverty** (CPAG 2009), the proportion of children living in **poverty** grew significantly during the period 1979–1998. In 1999 **New Labour** made a historic and ambitious pledge to halve child poverty by 2010 and eradicate child **poverty** by

2020. They have implemented a series of measures designed to challenge child poverty (such as the Sure Start programme and increased per-child payments such as child tax credit and child benefit), alongside placing an increased emphasis on the value of paid employment ('work for those who can'), a theme which cuts across much of **New Labour** policy (CPAG 2009). However, at the time of writing 4 million children in the UK (one in three) are defined to be living in poverty. This is one of the highest rates of child poverty in advanced industrialized countries. Forty per cent of poor children live in a household headed by a lone parent. The majority of poor children (57 per cent) live in a household headed by a **couple**. There is also a relationship between child poverty and **wellbeing**. Some campaigners have argued that in order to end child poverty, there needs to be more emphasis on challenging income inequality through redistribution.

Child poverty Action Group (2009) *Ending Child poverty: a manifesto for success*. London: CPAG.

Children Act 1989 the single most important piece of legislation concerning children, providing a wide-ranging framework of responsibilities and duties for parents, courts and **local authorities** for safeguarding and promoting the welfare of children.

The Act, which came into effect in October 1991 with the support of all the major political parties, marked a significant break from the principles and laws that had governed childcare for most of the 20th century. Its central principle is that children are best **looked after** by their own family, with both parents playing a full part. The concept of **parental responsibility**, which replaces the notion of parental rights over children, reflects this. Both parents whether married or not have **parental responsibility** for their child, and both retain that responsibility should they separate or **divorce**. They also retain parental responsibility even if the local authority looks after their child for a period of time.

The Act places a primary duty on the local authority to promote the upbringing of **children in need** by their families as long as this is consistent with the children's welfare. **Children in need** are defined as those who are disabled or whose development and health would be impaired if they *did not* receive certain services. To carry out this duty, the authority must identify children in need in their area and offer a range of support services to them, including care and education for children under 5, the provision of family aides, and accommodation either in a **children's home** or in **foster care** for those children who need to be **looked after** away from home. Other services include financial help in exceptional circumstances, guidance and counselling, making holiday arrangements, and cultural or educational activities.

The local authority is not expected to provide all such services itself and may assist voluntary sector organizations in providing them. Other family members may be the recipients of these support services as long as it can be established that provision of the service will assist the child in need to remain with his or her family. For example, an adolescent who shoulders a large role in caring for a younger sibling with a severe **physical disability** may be supported in this through regular leisure opportunities arranged by the authority.

The Act established a vital principle: that for parents to ask for such services is *not* a sign of parental inadequacy but a reasonable decision to seek support when and where it is available. In doing so it overturned a long-established, if hidden, view that parents who ask for help are of limited competence and need to be watched all the more closely. The provision of services should be agreed on the basis of a **partnership** between parents, the local authority and any voluntary organization involved. Local authority services, including **accommodation** for a child away from home, are provided only after negotiation and agreement with parents in order to help them meet their responsibilities towards their children rather than as a substitute for them. The family's racial origin and cultural and linguistic background are considerations that the authority must take into account when making plans with parents for their children.

The Act recognizes, however, that support services are not always enough to protect the child from harm. For instance, parents may be uncooperative and refuse services, or the child may be subject to **abuse** by a parent or another person in the household. In such cases the local authority can apply to the courts to take further action under one of several orders. A **child assessment order** requires the parents to cooperate in the **assessment** of their child. Alternatively, the local education authority may apply for an **education supervision order** to help ensure school attendance. In more extreme cases the local authority may apply for a **care order** or a **supervision order**. To obtain either, it must convince the court that the child is suffering, or is likely to suffer, **significant harm** because of a lack of reasonable standard of parental care or because the child is beyond control. In addition, the authority must demonstrate to the court that making an order will be better for the child than not making it (the 'no order' principle), by explaining the plans it has in mind for the child in question.

Although the grounds for a care order are exactly the same as for a supervision order, the courts will in practice grant a care order only in the most serious circumstances, where other alternatives have been tried and have failed to safeguard the child from **significant harm**. A care order lasts until the child is 18 years of age, unless **discharge**d earlier, and, more importantly, gives the local authority parental responsibility and, with it, decision-making powers over the plan for the child.

Not only does the Act govern court proceedings between local authority and parents ('public law'), it also introduces new orders for use in disputes between parents over their children when the local authority is not involved ('private law'). The Act does not use the concept of **custody** of the child but provides four orders that take their name from the section of the Act in which they appear: section 8 orders. Each of the four orders in that section is intended to resolve disputes over practical arrangements concerning the child of parents who are separating or divorcing, such as **contact** with the child for the non-resident parent and where the child is to reside. The spirit of the orders is clearly to encourage both parents of the child to work out these arrangements between them. The two most important of the section 8 orders are the **residence order**, which designates with whom the child is to live, and the **contact order**, which establishes the frequency of **contact** between the child and parents or others in the family (see also **prohibited steps order, specific issue order**).

The courts have great flexibility in using these orders in both matrimonial and care proceedings. For a child subject to care proceedings, the court may decide to combine a residence order, to a grandparent for instance, with a **supervision order** to the local authority instead of granting a care order. Older adolescents who wish to separate from one or both of their parents are also able to apply for these orders but have only occasionally succeeded in court.

When a child is involved in any **family proceedings**, that is, proceedings for care or supervision order or matrimonial proceedings, the Act stipulates that the **child's welfare** is the court's paramount consideration. To underscore this, the **welfare checklist** lists a number of factors that the court must bear in mind when making a decision on the case before it. Whether a child is accommodated with the agreement of the parents or subject to a care order made by the courts, the Act considers that child as looked after by the local authority, which then has the responsibility of placing the child in foster care or in a children's home. The authority must try to place the accommodated child as near to home as possible and to consult the child about the placement decision. If the child is accommodated by agreement with the parents, the arrangements must be covered by a **written agreement** covering such matters as the continuing role of the parents in the life of the accommodated child and when the placement will end.

Following a care order through which the local authority obtains parental responsibility for the child the authority must still attempt to work in partnership with the child's parents, who also retain parental responsibility. It is recognized, however, that after contested care proceedings parents may continue to dispute the local authority's plans for their child. In exceptional circumstances the local authority may limit the parents' exercise of parental responsibility in relation to their child as long as that child is subject to a care order. Detailed regulations covering plans, written agreements and reviews for children looked after by the authority are covered in the *Arrangements for Placement of Children Regulations* accompanying the Act.

The Act also sets out how the local authority, the **police** or the National Society for the Prevention of Cruelty to Children should respond when they believe that a child may need emergency protection. Where the local authority has reasonable cause to suspect that a child is suffering from **significant harm**, it has a duty to investigate the child's circumstances. The objective of that inquiry is to enable the authority to decide whether it should apply for an **emergency protection order** or take any other action under the Act, such as offering support services to the family in question. The emergency protection order should be made only in extremely urgent cases, where the child's safety is under immediate threat. The order allows the authority either to remove the child from home or other place of danger, or to retain the child in a safe place, such as a hospital, for a maximum of 8 days, with a possible extension of up to another 7 days in exceptional circumstances.

Taken together, the major reforms initiated by the Children Act 1989 marked a sharp break with earlier childcare law and practice that had been heavily weighted against parents and largely excluded the child's own opinions. The Act seeks to avoid bringing children before the courts if at all possible, but should this happen, it ensures that the child's voice is heard in proceedings involving the local authority and that parents have an opportunity to be represented at every stage. It also underpins the importance of the parents' point of view in planning for children in need with the local authority. Making this partnership work, often in difficult and stressful circumstances, is the most important challenge the Act presents for **social work** professionals.

Department of Health (1989) *An Introduction to the Children Act.* London: HMSO.

Children Act 2004 the principle legal basis for the overhaul of children's services as outlined in the Green Paper *Every Child Matters* which emphasized multi-disciplinary and **community**-based provision as part of a strategy to tackle fragmentation and long-standing lack of accountability in children's services. The restructuring of children's services contained in the Act now dominates procedural and organizational approaches to services for children.

The Act requires in each area an integrated strategy of joint assessments of local needs of children, young people and their parents, and the delivery of integrated frontline services to improve **outcomes** for children. It also created a **Children's Commissioner** in England to represent the views and interests of children and young people and placed a duty on **local authorities** to make arrangements to promote cooperation between agencies and other appropriate bodies in order to improve children's **wellbeing**. It further placed a duty on key partners, including **primary care trust**s and **NHS** trusts, to take part in these collaborative arrangements.

In addition it placed a duty on all key agencies to safeguard and promote the welfare of children and for the local authority to set up local safeguarding boards to oversee children at risk. The Act also established the legal basis for the **Integrated Children's System** containing basic information about children and young people to enable better sharing of information. Other requirements imposed on local areas include that a **Children and Young People's Plan** be drawn up by each local authority, the creation of an integrated **inspection** framework, and the conduct of Joint Area Reviews to assess local areas' progress in improving **outcomes** and in provisions relating to **foster care**, private fostering and the education of children in care.

Children and Family Court Advisory and Support Service (CAFCASS) a service which looks after the interests of children involved in **family proceedings**. CAFCASS was created by the Criminal Justice and Court Services Act 2000, bringing together the family court services previously provided by the Family Court Welfare Service, the Guardian ad Litem Service and the Children's Division of the Official Solicitor's Office. The single, national service covering England and Wales reports to courts on children's views in contested **divorce** cases, in applications for a care order sought by the local authority and supports parents who are in dispute over finances or arrangements for children. Since the rise in the number of applications for a care order following the death of **Baby Peter** CAFCASS has been under significant pressure to supply sufficient guardians and to provide timely investigations into family circumstances of vulnerable children.

Children and Young People's Plan (CYPP) the overarching, strategic plan for all services that impact on the lives of children and young people in a given area indicating how all such services, working in **partnership**, will integrate their provision to improve child **wellbeing**.

The plan is the defining **statement** as to how **children's trust**s will deliver measurable improvements across all five of the **Every Child Matters** (ECM) **outcomes**. Non-statutory guidance on the development of the CYPP, published in January 2009, brought together earlier regulations on the formation of plans and introduced performance management arrangements to improve quality. Each plan should include: **assessment** of needs using the ECM outcomes as standards; what key actions will be taken to achieve progress toward those outcomes; a **statement** on how budgets will be used; and the **partnership** arrangements for joint working in pursuit of that progress.

While originally a local authority plan under newly strengthened **children's trusts**, CYPP's become the legal responsibility of the local children's trust board who are responsible for preparing and monitoring the plan in a given area and must be developed as part of a wider local strategy involving all partners in the Local Strategic Partnership and within the Local Area Agreement. All areas are now expected to have arrangements in place for preventative work, early identification and early intervention to improve **outcomes** for all children. Plans should be developed on the basis of wide consultation – with children, young people, families, schools, voluntary organizations working with children, the **Local Safeguarding Children Board** among others.

Department for Children, Schools and Families (2009) *Children and Young People's Plan Guidance*. London: DCSF.

Children and Young Persons Act 1933 (section 53) gave the **Crown Court power** to pass a long-term **sentence** of **detention** on a young offender convicted of one of a limited number of 'grave crimes'. This provision has since been replaced by sections 90 and 91 of the Powers of the **Criminal court**s (Sentencing) Act 2000 but practitioners continue to refer to 'section 53'. If the offence is murder then indefinite detention 'during Her Majesty's pleasure', the equivalent of a **life imprisonment sentence**, is the **mandatory sentence**. For other crimes a period of detention up to the maximum period of imprisonment normally allowable for an adult offender is possible. Young offenders subject to these sentences are allocated to **prison** or to institutions within the **secure estate** appropriate to their age.

children in need a central concept in the **Children Act 1989** on the basis of which **local authorities** are able to offer family support services.

According to section 17 of the Act, a child is 'in need' if he or she is unlikely to achieve or maintain a reasonable standard of health or development without support services from the local authority. Should the child fall sufficiently below this 'reasonable standard', in either health or in developmental progress, or if the child's development is impaired to the point that services are required, that child is defined as 'in need' in contrast to children who attain a reasonable standard of health and development. Since the passage of the Children Act 1989, there has been a gradual broadening of the factors that social workers should take into account when trying to determine whether a child is in need. These include looking at how the whole family may be struggling to cope on its own, particularly with low income or other factors to do with **social exclusion** that place parents under strain. (See also **framework for assessment of children in need, Every Child Matters, child poverty**.)

Children (Leaving Care) Act 2000 stipulates the responsibilities and tasks that a local authority has to undertake in preparing a child or young person for leaving its care. The Act lays important duties on the local authority in relation to young people leaving its care. These include the duty:

- to assess and meet the needs of eligible people aged 16 and 17 who are in care or are care leavers and to remain in touch with all care leavers until they are 21 regardless of where they live;
- to have a clear 'pathway' plan mapping out a route to independence for every eligible young person when he or she turns 16 for whom **local authorities** must provide the personal and practical support;
- to provide each care leaver with an adviser who will coordinate provision of support, with particular emphasis on education, training and employment;
- to introduce new more straightforward financial arrangements that offer comprehensive support, especially with education and employment, up to the age 21 and beyond if necessary.

Young people in public care have historically been well below average in educational attainment, in acquiring basic skills and in health or social relationships, and yet their ability ranges match national averages. The under-achievement at school goes hand in hand with higher rates of **truancy** and exclusion. The effects of this experience take their toll in later life: a higher than average level of **looked after** children are unemployed and homeless, and engage in criminal and abusive behaviour. Among homeless young people, young offenders and the **prison** population, the proportion of those who were in care is extremely high: roughly some 30–40 per cent of each population.

In assisting in the transition to adulthood of a young person in care, there are a number of matters that have to be dealt with. Accommodation may involve initial moves to interim forms of housing, such as **hostels**, lodgings or staying with friends, which are often followed up by moves to independent tenancies in the public, voluntary or private sectors. Life skills include budgeting, negotiating with officials, landlords and employers, and practical skills such as self-care and domestic skills such as cooking, laundry and cleaning. Social networks, relationships and identity are other facets of leaving care that both the young person and practitioner have to come to grips with. Even if family links had not been positive, retaining them was important and lent symbolic certainty to their lives. Those that did not have even this lacked self-esteem, were less confident and less assertive.

The object of the Act is to achieve what has been so elusive for **local authorities**: effective 'corporate parenting' in which the local authority continue involvement with a young person after leaving their care as a parent would for their young person who has left home. A 'pathway plan' for each care leaver should be based on the extensive involvement of the young person and should look ahead at least to his or her 21st birthday. It should pick up and extend the dimensions covered in the **framework for assessment of children in need**. The young person's health needs, future education such as college or university and supporting family relationships are all elements of a plan. Accommodation needs should be carefully looked at before young people leave care and arrangements made for joint **assessment** between social services and **housing authorities**. Sources of income and avenues to employment must also be considered.

children missing education children in a local authority area who are not engaged in education, either by being registered at a school or through **elective home education**.

This has become a much higher profile issue in recent years following a number of cases in which children were subject to **child abuse** but were not known to any school. There has also been concern that significant numbers of children are effectively lost to systems at times of school transfer or when they change address, including **asylum seekers**, **refugees** and those at risk of sexual exploitation. All members of the children's workforce, not only those in education services, have a duty to assist in the identification of any such children. It was hoped that the electronic database Contact Point would facilitate this process though it is now clear that some of the most vulnerable children still do not appear on official records.

All **local authorities** must have a designated officer for **children missing education,** usually located in either the education admissions service or the **education welfare service**. Government guidance sets out a range of standards and expectations about arrangements for tracking children who may move schools or whose parents may not ensure that they are engaging in education. Schools have a duty to place children's details onto the Lost Pupils **database**, a secure website at the DCSF, where they are unable to transfer information to a new school through normal procedures. This enables a receiving school or local authority to download their details once they have been identified. Here as in other areas of promoting children's welfare, sharing information is essential.

See also Department for Children, Schools and Families (2009) *Revised Statutory Guidance for Local authorities to Identify Children not Receiving a Suitable Education.* London: DCSF.

children's centres service hubs where children under the age of 5 and their families can receive seamless integrated services and information.

Part of central government's drive to deal with **child poverty** and **social exclusion** in England is through **Sure Start** policies and programmes established in the most disadvantaged neighbourhoods. (These apply in England; in Scotland, Wales and Northern Ireland the devolved administrations have their own responsibility for early education and childcare.) The government has set out a strategy in the **Children and Young Persons' Plan** with the aim of ensuring that every child and young person has the chance to fulfil their potential with a particular focus on early child development.

Sure Start **children's centre**s provide integrated services for children under the age of 5 and their families through a **team** of professionals from social services, education and health. This is achieved by bringing together childcare, early education, health and family support services from service providers in the statutory, voluntary and private sectors as well as **community** organizations. The aim is to ensure that services are based on the needs of children **Working Together** with parents, carers and children in order to improve **outcomes** for all children. Children's centres are a key element of a ten-year government childcare strategy.

Children's centres are funded through local authorities with guidance issued by the Department for Education and Skills. Local authorities have the responsibility for service delivery and meeting the aims of the Sure Start programme. Services are individual to each centre in order to meet the needs of the local community but must provide core services which comprise integrated early education and childcare, support for parents, child and family health services and helping parents into work.

Children's Commissioner an office, independent of government, dedicated to giving voice to all children and young people in Britain, particularly the vulnerable and the disadvantaged. Each of the four nations of the UK has its own Children's Commissioner. Wales was the first of the four nations to appoint a Children's Commissioner in 2001. The Commissioners' functions include reviewing and monitoring arrangements made by care providers in the voluntary, statutory, private and independent sector in relation to complaint, **advocacy** and whistle-blowing. The Welsh Commissioner must exercise his/her functions with regard to the **United Nations Convention on the Rights of the Child** (UNCRC) 1989. The Northern Ireland Commissioner was appointed in 2003 and has a remit that includes safeguarding and promoting the rights and best interests of children, and promoting an awareness of **children's rights**. The Northern Ireland Commissioner for Children and Young People also has a function similar to the Welsh Commissioner in relation to monitoring, reviewing and whistleblowing, and must exercise his or her functions with regard to the UNCRC.

The Scottish Children's Commissioner was appointed in 2004, the Commissioner's functions include promoting and safeguarding children's rights and reviewing policy and legislation relating to children's rights. Unlike the Welsh and Northern Ireland Commissioner, the Scottish Commissioner does not have the power to investigate the circumstances of individual children, but must exercise his or her functions with regard to the UNCRC. The Children's Commissioner for England was the last of the four nations to appoint a Commissioner for Children in 2005. The functions of the Commissioner are set out in the Children Act 2004 and include promoting awareness of the interests and views of children, and ensuring children's views inform policy. The Children's Commissioner of England is obliged to have consideration of the interests of children.

children's guardian a trained social worker selected from a local panel to provide an independent **social work** opinion to a court about what is best for a child's welfare during proceedings for an **adoption order**, a care order, an **emergency protection order** or a **supervision order**. The children's guardian makes a full **assessment** of each case by **interviewing** the child and his or her family, as well as any professionals such as health visitors and teachers who are involved with the child. The guardian also has access to records kept about the child. On the basis of this assessment, the guardian reaches a decision about what he or she thinks best serves the child's welfare. At all times the guardian represents the child and, if necessary, instructs a solicitor on the child's behalf. The management of children's guardians is administered by the **Children and Family Court Advisory and Support Service** (CAFCASS).

children's home a residential unit that provides 24-hour care for children and young people.

The **Department of Health** guidance on the **Children Act 1989** refers to several different types of children's home:

- community homes maintained, controlled and assisted by the local authority;
- homes run by voluntary sector organizations;
- registered children's homes run by private organizations;
- independent schools accommodating between four and 50 boarding pupils and not approved under the Education Act 1981.

The Act further defines a children's home as a place providing care and accommodation for more than three children. Each home must register under the Act and issue a **statement** of purpose and function describing what the home sets out to do for children and the manner in which care is provided. There is a diversity of services offered by children's homes, including emergency placement, short-term or respite placement, bridging placements (for example, between a child's own home and a foster placement), secure accommodation and long-term placements that may incorporate some therapeutic provision. Increasingly, children's homes are aiming to meet specific needs of children at particular phases of their lives, such as preparing children for long-term **foster care** or helping young people to prepare for living on their own.

It is legally possible for some voluntary children's homes or registered children's homes to apply to the Secretary of State for Health for a certificate that allows them to provide a refuge for children who appear to be at risk of harm. This exempts the home from offences under the Children Act, such as harbouring or abducting children. The significance of such status lies in the fact that it recognizes that some young people do require a legitimate breathing space where refuge workers can help them return to parents or local authority care or to sort out some other arrangements if appropriate.

Following the **Care Standards Act 2000**, the **Department of Health** introduced National Minimum Standards and Regulations in respect of children's homes, published in March 2002. These regulations and accompanying guidance aim to eliminate the institutional **abuse** that has been evident in a number of children's homes throughout England and Wales over the past 20 years.

children's rights   claims to treatment, benefits or protection made by, or on behalf of, children on the basis of law, code of practice or declaration.

Children's rights broadly refer to the human rights of children. Human rights apply to all human beings, both adults and children, and are based on respect for the dignity and worth of each person, regardless of race, gender, language, religion, opinions, wealth or ability. The full range of human rights include civil, cultural, economic, political and social rights. Generally a child is defined as a human being under the age of 18.

The **United Nations Convention on the Rights of the Child** (UNCRC), adopted by the United Nations General Assembly in 1989, incorporates specific children's rights in international law. The rights in the Convention define universal principles and standards for the status and treatment of children and can broadly be categorized into three areas:

- Provision – children have the right to an adequate standard of living, health care, education and services and to **play**;

- Protection – children have the right to be protected from abuse, neglect, exploitation and **discrimination**;
- **Participation** – children have the right to participate in communities.

The key provisions of the Convention stipulate that all rights apply to all children without exception or **discrimination** (set out in Article 2); that the best interests of the child must be the primary consideration in all actions concerning them (Article 3); that states have an obligation to ensure the survival and development of every child (Article 6); and that the view of children must be taken into account in all matters that affect them (Article 12).

The Convention has been ratified by all but two countries in the world (The USA and Somalia). When a country signs up to the Convention it becomes a 'State Party' to the Convention and agrees to review its national law to ensure that it complies with the articles of the convention. The Committee on the Rights of the Child, based in Geneva, monitors compliance to the Convention.

children's rights officer   an advocate and sometimes **mentor** for children and young people in the care system.

Children's rights officers seek to give voice to children's rights, especially those who are '**looked after**' by the local authority. Often located in the voluntary sector officers aim to support and advocate for and with children and young people. They can explain what rights a child or young person may have in certain situations and often will support them in making a complaint to a local authority or in preparing for reviews or other set pieces where support is needed. They are also able to identify other specialist sources of support where, for example, a disability is an issue or a young person is experiencing difficulties about their sexuality. Sometimes officers will also work with groups of children and young people in the care system where group support and solidarity may benefit the 'looked after child'.

children's trusts   local **partnership**s that bring together services for children and young people in a given area. Usually they are led by the directors of children's services within the local authority but include other local services that are by law included within the trust such as strategic health authorities, **primary care trust**s, **police**, **probation board**s, **youth offending team**s, **Connexions partnership**s and skills councils. Other organizations are also brought into the trust although their **participation** is not required by law such as schools, colleges, adult **social care** services and housing. The term 'children's trust' covers the entire collaborative system but it is not in itself a separate organization; each of the participating agencies retain control over their particular responsibilities. Nevertheless trusts set the broad objectives and coordinate front-line services across all work with children. Trusts' priorities include:

- identifying children and young people with high need or at risk of harm and intervene early in their lives;
- narrowing the gap in educational attainment between vulnerable children and young people and the average levels of achievement and reducing **child poverty**.

In meeting these priorities they are to elicit the views of children and young people and their parents and carers on the kinds of services they value. They are also to promote joint working, ensure effective commissioning of services to meet area needs and promote smooth sharing of information. Trusts play an influential role within local area agreements (LAAs) particularly in helping to implement a key LAA target – increasing young people's **participation** in positive activities. The key priorities for any trust, adapted to local conditions, should be reflected in a **Children and Young Persons' Plan**.

Department for Children, Schools and Families (2008) *Children's trusts: statutory guidance on inter-agency cooperation*. London: DCSF.

child safety order   a court order introduced by the **Crime and Disorder Act 1998** made in respect of a child under 10 who is at risk of becoming involved in crime or is behaving in a criminal or anti-social manner. The order places the child under the **supervision** of a **responsible officer** and requires the child to comply with arrangements aimed at ensuring that he or she receives appropriate care, protection and support and is subject to proper control.

child support   the system which provides for the **assessment** of a non-resident parent's financial contribution to the cost of bringing up his or her child. Payments, when assessed, are made to either the parent with care or, in some cases, the young person. The principle that parents are responsible for meeting, or helping to meet, the cost of their child's upbringing is set out in the 'duty to maintain' in the Child Support Act 1991. This continues after relationship breakdown, and as it states in section 1(2) 'a non-resident parent shall be taken to have met his responsibility to maintain any qualifying child of his by making periodical payments of maintenance with respect to the child of such amount, and at such intervals, as may be determined . . .'

Although reforms to the system, particularly since the Child Maintenance and Other Payments Act 2008, now give parents more options for making their own arrangements, assisted by guidance and support from the new agency responsible for child maintenance, the **Child Maintenance and Enforcement Commission**, there is still a standard formula to assess how much the non-resident parent should pay. The commission has powers to assess, collect and enforce these payments if this is what the parent with care wishes. Since late 2008 a parent with care is no longer obliged to stay in the child support system. She or he can make their own arrangements, assisted by **advice** on voluntary arrangements provided by the Commission or other advisers. A parent with care is entitled to help in the form of a calculation based on the statutory formula. The Commission has a wide range of powers to assess, collect, and enforce child maintenance, both for parents on benefits and others. Among the sanctions available against a non-resident parent who does not pay **child support** is **attachment** of wages, and **curfew order**s. The commission may also make an administrative decision, without reference to a court, disqualifying him (or her) from holding a travel authorization or driving **licence** if he (or she) fails to pay child maintenance due under the Child Support Act 1991.

As with the **Child Support Agency**, the Commission still has to rely on the parent with care providing information to help trace the non-resident parent. To encourage cooperation in cases where the parent with care is in receipt of benefit, a proportion of maintenance received in any week is disregarded in the **assessment** of 'income' (currently up to £20) – and in the case of a parent with care receiving tax credits all maintenance is disregarded. From April 2010, however, it is planned that all maintenance received will be disregarded when income is assessed for the purposes of determining benefits eligibility. Until these changes were made, for the majority of **lone parent families**, particularly those on income support, there was no gain in the arrangements.

Child Support Agency the agency responsible for assessing and collecting **child support** since 1992. It is replaced by the **Child Maintenance and Enforcement Commission**, but has residual powers pending abolition in 2010. See also **child support**.

choice-based letting Choice-based letting schemes were introduced in the Housing Green Paper 'Quality and Choice: A Decent Home for all' (2002). The aim was for all **local authorities** to manage the allocation of properties by a choice-based letting scheme. Priority is given on the basis of need, but eligible applicants can bid for a home from a range of properties on offer. The main problem is that demand exceeds supply, so there is no real choice for many applicants. Some schemes have failed to provide for those in priority need and have been proved unlawful when challenged in the courts.

Chronically Sick and Disabled Persons Act 1970 legislation which sets out the duties of **local authorities** in respect of providing the support necessary for disabled people to live in the **community**.

This is one of several Acts of Parliament under which **community care** services are provided. It relates solely to disabled people who fall within the definition of disability provided in section 29 of the **National**

Assistance Act 1948. Because of the link with this definition, it falls within the definition of **community care** services in section 46 of the **National Health Service and Community Care Act 1990**, but it is important to note that the Act applies equally to disabled children.

The Act requires **local authorities** to maintain a register of disabled people, and also specifies services which should be provided for disabled people where need has been established. There has been disappointment about the impact of the Act in practice, but it did considerably strengthen the existing responsibilities of **local authorities** to provide support for disabled people in their own homes. The Act is still the basis for the provision many aids, adaptations and services for older and disabled people.

This was the first **social care** legislation to focus on disabled people specifically. However, disability is age related, and the Act has therefore also proved significant for **older people**. It differs from previous legislation, which focused primarily on making provision for residential services, by laying out the duties of local authorities in respect of supporting disabled people in the **community**. The Act imposes a duty on the local authority to inform itself of the number and needs of 'handicapped' people in its area, and to publicize available services. Section 2 lists the services which local authorities should provide to those whose need for them has been established by an assessment. These include practical assistance in the home, recreational facilities, travel, adaptations and 'special' equipment, holidays and the provision of meals.

Although the **NHS and Community Care Act 1990** brought about changes in the way that needs are assessed and social welfare services delivered, the duty of local authorities to provide these particular services to those in need still stems from the Chronically Sick and Disabled Persons Act. Initially the passing of this Act led to optimism about future provision, and some commentators described it as 'a charter for the disabled'. Its focus on entitlement to services in the home was thought to exemplify an acceptance of the social rights of disabled people and a changed attitude to their presence in the community. However, the Act did not live up to these expectations, with many local authorities being inadequately funded to fully comply with it. Assessments were often delayed, as authorities could then claim ignorance of the needs they were failing to meet. It was not until the **Disabled Persons (Services, Consultation and Representation) Act 1986** that the duty of local authorities to carry out an assessment when requested to do so by a disabled person was clarified. The extent to which local authorities had a duty to provide services irrespective of resource constraints has been unclear. In 1990, the NHS and Community Care Act stipulated that all community care services must be provided within budgetary limits. However, there have been a number of legal test cases since in which the courts have supported local authorities' right to restrict access to services for budgetary reasons. Current **Department of Health** Guidance, *Fairness in Access to Care Services 2002*, stresses that resources can be taken into account. The Chronically Sick and Disabled Persons Act has also been criticized for its lack of potential for choice and **service user** self-determination. However, it remains a landmark in that it acknowledges a collective responsibility for the support which disabled people need in order to live in the community.

Oliver, M. and Sapey, B. (2006) *Social Work with Disabled People*, 3rd edition. Houndmills: Palgrave Macmillan.

citizenship legal, social and political status conferred by a state on individuals in which certain rights, duties and obligations are placed on both the state and the citizen. Citizenship also forms a key part of the national curriculum and has seen revived debate and discussion in recent years. In effect, citizenship is legal membership in a nation state. It emerged as a concept in the 17th and 18th centuries with the consolidation of strong centralized state authorities in Europe and in the wake of the English, French and American revolutions, which called into question the limits of that authority in relation to individuals. Citizenship was underpinned by the idea that states should be founded on the will of the people, involving a contract of mutual rights and responsibilities. One of the most influential interpretations of citizenship has been that of T. H. Marshall, who broadly linked citizenship with the acquisition of rights over the last three or four hundred years: legal rights, such as the right to property and freedom from arbitrary arrest; political rights, such as the right to assembly and to vote; and social rights, such as health care and welfare benefits. In Marshall's view, citizenship in our own time has come to include economic welfare and security for each citizen as well as the right to live life according to the client standards prevailing in the society.

A number of factors have undermined Marshall's progressive concept of citizenship. Much of it was based on the presumed permanence of a thriving **welfare state** providing a range of entitlements and a safety net for the poorest. Financial limits placed on welfare spending and the widespread retrenchment of the **welfare state** have called into question the inevitability of this concept of citizenship. The political philosophy of the new right, which emphasizes responsibilities rather than rights and believes in the market as a way of allocating services, has also introduced new elements into discussions of citizenship.

Feminism contests such an understanding of citizenship and its gender neutrality, and challenges the inherently male precepts of citizenship.

Feminists argue that such a concept is defined by male interests and concerns, and needs transformation to include the development of feminist political and social theory.

It is being increasingly recognized that citizenship may also contain negative connotations and include restrictive citizenship, as defined within the UK immigration laws and restrictive practices within the European Union.

There has also been debate regarding citizenship, partly in response to a perceived decline in democratic participation and calls for increased citizenship education. This has been evident in **New Labour** policies around the concept of 'active citizenship'. This relates to a broad range of issues including active involvement in public life and wider social/moral behaviour; participating in the democratic process; empowering communities and encouraging meaningful participation in community life; and knowledge and awareness. There remains considerable debate (and sometimes conflict) regarding the terms of citizenship, and what should constitute the grounds for citizenship in an increasingly diverse, multi-ethnic and multi-faith society.

Lister, R. (2003) *Citizenship: a feminist perspective*. London: Macmillan.

Dwyer, P. (2004) *Understanding Social Citizenship: themes and perspectives for policy and practice*. Bristol: Policy Press.

Civil Partnership Act 2004 allows same sex **couples** to form a civil **partnership** entailing a formal, legal commitment to each other. The two people have to be over the age of 18 or be able to provide evidence of parental (or equivalent) consent if aged 16 or 17.

Before the Act was implemented same sex relationships had virtually no way of securing legal recognition of their relationship as a **couple**. Civil partnerships entail new and important rights. Provisions in the Act include:

- equal treatment (in comparison with heterosexual **couples**) for purposes of tax including inheritance tax and inheritance of a housing tenancy agreement; life insurance; benefits in relation to employment and pensions; and **assessment** for **child support**;
- an obligation to provide reasonable maintenance for any children of a family and civil partners;
- recognition for purposes of nationality and immigration; new rights in relation to the death of a partner including recognition of a partner in relation to intestacy rules; access to **compensation** in the event of a fatal accident; and the right to register a partner's death.

civil proceedings court proceedings that are concerned with civil rather than criminal matters. The **High Court** deals with many aspects of civil law in England and Wales, but the civil proceedings most relevant to social workers and **probation officers** are those relating to **family proceedings** under the **Children Act 1989** and those relating to **domestic violence**. Most civil proceedings start in a **Magistrate's** Court (notably the Family Court), County Court, or tribunals. **Magistrates** have a number of important jurisdictions, including powers to deal with applications relating to **domestic violence** (at least where they do not involve disputed questions as to parties' entitlement to occupy property by virtue of property interests and contractual rights to remain in occupation); and to make orders requiring maintenance to be paid by one spouse to another, or to children (including a 'child of the family' – at least while the parties are still living together). The County Court has an important family jurisdiction, dealing with a range of matters such as **divorce**, court-based maintenance, and **adoption**. In some cases a case that starts in the County Court may be transferred to the High Court. County Court and High Court cases may be appealed to the Court of **Appeal** (Civil Division) on appeal. (See also **children** and **family court advisory support service** and **appeal**).

cognitive behavioural therapy an approach to group and individual therapy that aims to change the ways in which people think about themselves and their environment and change their behaviour as a consequence.

The approach, which grew out of behaviour therapy, stresses that thought patterns are crucial to the ways in which a person views his or her own behaviour. Changing such thought patterns can be important in the resolution of problems such as **depression** and in anger management. People are taught to monitor their 'self-talk' for entrenched lines of thought, interrupting these destructive ways of thinking and replacing them with strategies ('thinking skills') taught as part of the therapy. Successful experiments with these new strategies are reinforced by more positive responses from other people, thus maintaining the changed approach. If one learns to handle anger effectively, for example, one gets a better reaction from other people, which may reinforce one's use of the new skills.

Since the 1990s, cognitive behavioural work has become extremely popular among practitioners and counsellors in their work with a range of groups. These include those with low self-esteem, compulsive disorders or **depression**. Ubiquitous anger management classes working with aggressive or anti-social young people or adults are essentially based on cognitive behavioural theory.

This approach concentrates upon helping individuals to face up to the consequences of their actions for themselves and others, to understand their own motives and to develop new ways of controlling their behaviour. Cognitive behavioural methods are often successfully combined with other approaches such as social skills training, for example in the case of **group work** with **sex offenders**. Cognitive behavioural therapy has been found to be helpful with many other 'conditions' such as **anxiety** states, panic attacks, **phobias** and low level depression.

Grant, A., Towend, M., Mills, J. and Cox, A. (2009) *Assessment and Case Formulation in Cognitive behavioural therapy.* London: Sage.

cohabitation   a term commonly used to describe two adults living together in the same domestic unit, particularly in the benefits and social welfare context. The **couple** may be in a heterosexual or a homosexual relationship. The term is often used to describe two parties who are not married, or who are not civil partners and who are in a relationship and sharing the same accommodation. Cohabitation is widespread, with one quarter of all children born to cohabiting **couple**s. Reasons for cohabiting differ considerably. For some **couple**s it is not the result of a clear decision but a gradual process that in the end has the partners living together. But research also indicates that a sizeable majority of those cohabiting view cohabitation as an equivalent to **marriage**, requiring a commitment to the relationship over a lengthy period of time. Formal ties, sanctioned by the state, are viewed as a relic of a more religious and even oppressive past. In some important areas cohabiting individuals, even when they are in a long-term, stable relationship, may still have different rights from those of married **couple**s or civil partners – for example, in relation to tenancies, **injunctions** and welfare benefits.

For the purposes of welfare benefits, including 'living together' rules, the **Civil Partnership Act 2004** now defines a '**couple**' as encompassing *four* types of relationship, namely:

(a) a man and woman who are married to each other and are members of the same household;

(b) a man and woman who are not married to each other but are living together as husband and wife;

(c) two people of the same sex who are civil partners of each other and are members of the same household; or

(d) two people of the same sex who are not civil partners of each other but are living together as if they were civil partners.

In practice, category (d) can still be problematic in its application. There remain concerns in the gay **community** that the living together rules can operate unfairly, particularly when they are deployed in respect of short-term relationships – and particularly if they do not necessarily have the characteristics of longer-term, stable relationships that living together rules envisage. For that reason, and partly in response to representations by gay and lesbian advocates, the original legislation was modified to try to ensure that same sex **couple**s who have not registered as civil partners are treated in a similar way to unmarried, opposite sex **couple**s. A compromise was, eventually, enacted as an integral part of the revised definition in the following terms: 'Two people of the same sex are to be regarded as living together as if they were civil partners if, but only if, they would be regarded as living together as husband and wife were they instead two people of the opposite sex.'

Similar definitions of 'couple' are provided for the purposes of tax credits, **child support**, and other social welfare legislation.

The relationship of cohabiting couples is approximately four times more likely to break down than that of married couples, according to contemporary statistics. As with married men after separation, cohabiting fathers' **contact** with their children drops dramatically even when they had been the child's primary care-giver. See **marriage**.

Commission for Racial Equality see **Equality and Human Rights Commission**

commissioning the process of purchasing, arranging or otherwise procuring services to meet health care or social care needs of individuals, families, or groups of people in a given area.

Commissioning is the systematic process of specifying, securing and monitoring services to meet identified needs. Within children's services, guidance issued under the **Children Act 2004** requires local authorities to set up a joint commissioning framework bringing together all service agencies, private, public and voluntary to i.) address specific needs ii.) how best to use funding and personnel to secure services and iii.) agree contractual and monitoring arrangements across public, private and voluntary services to ensure effective delivery. A similar process governs social care services for adults.

While the very word 'commissioning' implies a proactive role in purchasing services of highest quality with the funding available, a number of constraints undermine this such as a tendency to award multi-year contracts to dominant third sector organisations and a well documented absence of users' voice and influence in the commissioning process. (See also **market**.)

common assessment framework (CAF) a single, combined **assessment** process shared by the principal organizations within children's services for those children who may be in need.

It encourages a move away from exclusive focus on short-term targets to develop a longer-term view of how services should be deployed across the whole life of the child. It presses these services to identify how the absence of a particular service – for example support for parents on managing their child's behaviour or pre-school care and education – can lead to difficult, more costly problems later on.

The CAF strives to find a language and format that all agencies can use to assess the complex interaction between children's development and their environment and how to decide when services should intervene to improve **outcomes**. The need for the CAF arose from the realization that earlier arrangements for identifying and responding to the needs of children were not sufficiently outcome based. This earlier culture of assessment tended to assess particular aspects of a child's welfare while overlooking other dimensions of a child's life and needs. It also tended to ignore previous assessments of the child. But perhaps the biggest fault of the old approach was to use it simply as a way of making a decision as to whether a child met or did not meet the threshold for a service offered by the assessing agency. In short the assessment objectives were about outputs (whether or not a child qualified for a particular service) and not about outcomes (the child's **wellbeing**).

The CAF is intended for use when there is an early sign of difficulty in a child's life, to identify further supports should these be needed. The assessment takes place within a universal setting such as nursery or primary school or a care and education pre-school. A multi-agency approach is likely to be required so that information can be shared between agencies. It is intended as a 'front end' to the assessment process, a mechanism through which any practitioner working with a child or young person can conduct a good-quality, but relatively non-specialized, assessment. Above all, parents and children where at all possible should be involved in it and be able to understand the process at every step. It is specifically non-bureaucratic and looks at the whole child in the ecological sense. Should a more specialized service be required, the CAF helps ensure that the referral is made.

The framework should provide:

- a common set of processes for practitioners to follow if they think a child or young person would benefit from a common assessment;
- a common method for assessing the needs of children and young people based on models of successful children's development and concepts of **wellbeing**;
- supporting guidance to help practitioners record their findings, including gaining appropriate consent;
- requirements and guidance as to the roles and responsibilities of agencies and practitioners.

The CAF developed locally should reflect local patterns of service delivery and priorities. Particularly significant is the size of the network to be trained in using the CAF. Central government guidance makes it clear that *all* practitioners in an area who provide services for children should know about the CAF and how to complete it. The reach of the CAF is also wider than the **assessment** framework for **children in need**. It is triggered when a practitioner from any setting judges that a child or young person may have additional needs which are not then being met but which have to be met if the child is to achieve his or her potential in relation to the five **outcomes** of **Every Child Matters**.

However, critics have noted that the CAF has become part of a larger first response system to rapidly escalating overall referral rates which have overwhelmed many teams. Untrained 'gatekeepers' will make critical decisions concerning **allocation** while initial assessments involve time-consuming completion of standardized records. These require workers to comment on many aspects of children's lives which they have not had time to complete and are compelled to leave blank. White and colleagues found that CAFs were completed in ways that guidance did not suggest with social workers paying less attention to the detail of strengths and weaknesses of a child's circumstances and more to general worries and concerns with strong pleas for action framed by language that draws on their personal authority. They argue that in effect there are 'two CAFs': one has positive policy goals that are hard to disagree with and the other bogs social workers down in time-consuming requirements for routinized information which acts as a barrier between practitioners and the family they work with.

White, S., Hall, C. and Peckover, S. (2009) The descriptive tyranny of the common assessment framework: technologies of categorization and professional practice in child welfare. *British Journal of Social Work*, 39(7): 1197–217.

communication the giving or exchange of information, opinions, decisions, explanations and viewpoints through a variety of means.

Communicating with people is the bedrock of **social work** practice. How a social worker communicates, what objectives they have in mind and what situations they are having to communicate within are all critical factors for practitioners to consider. In discussions of **social work**, skills communication is often combined with 'interviewing' as if there were a set of techniques to follow. In general interviews are conversations initiated by the social worker for a specific purpose, for example assessment, providing advice, gathering information or explaining to users a particular statute or agency policy.

But a great deal of social work communication is multi-purpose aiming to enhance strengths and capabilities of users. In this dialogical form social workers have to be good listeners as well as expressive communicators, and be able to absorb and respond to what users and their families are saying. Often listening is part of a therapeutic endeavour, reflecting back to the user what the practitioner has heard so that the person can evaluate their own views. A key objective of this work entails gathering users' experiences and information. Listening to users' accounts of their lives helps make links between what may appear to be individual problems and their root in wider social conditions; it also provides insights into users' strengths and resources but also the obstructions and hardships that a person or family has encountered.

Social work and social welfare agencies rely on good, clear, accurate communication to achieve certain purposes. First, all organizations should provide accurate and accessible information about the services that they offer. This often involves communicating in the range of languages relevant to their local community but also in web-based, **Braille** and perhaps taped formats. Second, all staff need to develop appropriate communication skills both for face-to-face and for written communications. The ability to avoid jargon and to communicate in good clear English is of paramount importance. When using other languages, it is equally important that the clear meaning is fully communicated. Staff need to consider the context in which they are required to speak and to write, and to ensure that they develop a style that is appropriate and relevant for their audience. Third, some people have very specific communication needs. People who take pride in belonging to the deaf **community**, for example, need to be offered trained competent **British Sign Language** (BSL) interpreters so that they can communicate clearly in their first language. Some people who have serious communication problems as a result of disability may require specialist support for communication (see **Braille, low vision aids, Moon**). Fourth, agencies that are closely collaborating on projects, working in **partnership**s or negotiating service level agreements need to develop effective channels for communication in order to enhance collaboration. Fifth, with the developing emphasis upon a research culture in social welfare, workers need to be able to communicate clearly with funders, research colleagues and research participants in order to produce stipulated **outcomes** and be able to disseminate their findings clearly and imaginatively in order to improve practice.

community a contested term used to refer to a group of individuals with associated interests and/or common goals; the concept also describes social relationships within groups or territorial boundaries.

Many writers in the social sciences have sought to analyse the concept of community, offering numerous definitions. It has been suggested that attempts to make sense of the concept fall broadly into three groups: community as geographical locality; community as a collection of related interests; and community as a network of relationships. Geographical proximity, interests and relationships may coincide, and often do, but there is no necessary overlap between them.

Community defined by geography may appear to be easily identified (for example, a parliamentary ward, an inner city housing estate or a village). However, the assumption of consensus, of common goals even of relationships cannot be made in these examples. Communities can be relatively anonymous. Even where people live in close proximity, it cannot be assumed that they have similar interests or that they will have any kind of meaningful relationship. When an issue or common cause arises, however, then the 'community' may begin to self-identify, to campaign together to achieve an improvement, for example, in poor quality housing, or to prevent chemical waste being disposed of the locality. Thus the geographical community is transformed into a community of interest(s), the second meaning of community. If common cause has facilitated the development of personal and/or social relationships, then community becomes, in part, an expression of relationship or the achievement of a particular quality of relationship, the third meaning of 'community'.

There is perhaps an implied notion in the way that the idea of community is used in discourse. There appears to be an assumption that to have community is better than not to have it. Yet some have argued that rural communities, for example, can give rise to parochial, conservative and confining relationships. Urban settings, by contrast, because they can be more anonymous and contractual, have the potential to be liberating because they could potentially reflect what people have become rather than the limitations and constraints of birth or origin.

Community or neighbourhood can also be the unit of analysis and thus the unit of intervention for some social welfare work. **Community work** certainly takes the view that communities can have a major impact upon the experience of individuals, families and **peer group**s in important ways and that communities can be mobilized to bring about improvements in the quality of life for residents. In addition, it is used as a way of characterizing some statutory services, such as **community care** services, community health services or community policing, where services are organized around a designated area. Since 1997, there has been an increased focus on the idea of 'community', with 'community' and community **participation** becoming a key aspect of **New Labour** policy-making, reflected in area-based regeneration programmes such as New Deal for Communities and Sure Start.

Community can also describe services delivered by members of a community (as in community support or network) in contrast to those offered by professional agencies. Finally, community could also describe services delivered to people in their own homes (in effect, domiciliary services) or to community facilities within a locality by contrast with services delivered in residential or institutional setting. In sum, the word community is capable of many shades of meaning.

Crow, G. and Allan, G. (1994) *A Community Life: an introduction to local social relations.* Hemel Hempstead: Harvester Wheatsheaf.

community care the provision of **social care** services for people living in the **community**, usually in their own homes but with outreach services and domiciliary visits as part of the support system.

The range of services under the banner of community care is extensive but has a single aim: to support adults with disability or those who have some incapacity or other vulnerability to continue to live 'in the community'. Usually this phrase means that people live in their own homes, but it can also mean that they live in a house or flat shared by others and overseen by care staff. The objective of providing such services is to enable a person to continue to live in familiar surroundings rather than in an institution such as a hospital or residential home. Indeed the phrase was first defined by what it was not: large institutional care.

The domiciliary services most commonly associated with community care, particularly with frail **older people**, are assistance with dressing, meal provision and health care but they could also include the work of **personal assistant**s in the direct employ of, for example, an adult with **physical disability**. Services provided nearby and outside the home, such as at **day care centres**, or **supported employment** options can also be defined community care. Other services linked to community care are those that enable a person to develop social, leisure or educational interest. Still other services focus on the needs of carers, such as arranging for cared-for people to spend a few days in residential care so that the carers have time to themselves.

The term 'community care' was first used in the 1960s to describe the policy of relocating people from psychiatric hospitals into less institutionalized surroundings. The term became a major policy focus with the **NHS and Community Care Act 1990**, in the context of large-scale de-institutionalization in relation to people with **mental health problems** and people with learning disabilities. In this sense the term is now used very loosely to describe any policy or service designed to help people stay out of institutional care, including residential homes and hospitals. To some degree it has been subsumed if not actually replaced by the concept of **social care**, that refers to a vast range of services both residential, day and domiciliary. It also is less used as a phrase as constituent elements of community care have increasingly become central in their own right – **independent living** strategy for disabled people, carers' strategy and the **personalization** agenda.

'Community Care' is a contested term and encompasses debates about the relationship between the individual citizen and the state and the responsibility for care. At the heart of such debates are concerns about whether, as a society, we endorse collective responsibility for providing care or whether responsibility lies with individuals and families. Many of the same criticisms of the concepts of care and **social care** apply to community care also – namely that it relies on women supplying most of the labour, some of it paid, much of it not. See also **care management**, **domiciliary services**, **intermediate care**, **National Health Service**.

Community Care (Delayed Discharges) Act 2003 legislation requiring **local authorities** to make payments to **National Health Service** trusts, **primary care trust**s and health service hospitals in cases where the **discharge** of patients is delayed for reasons relating to the provision of **community care** services or services for carers.

When a person is in hospital they are under the care of the health service until it is defined by the medical **team** and chiefly the consultant that the patient is clinically ready to be **discharge**d, therefore no longer in need of acute hospital care. This is often referred to as 'Ready for **Discharge**'. When a vulnerable person is admitted to hospital and it is thought likely that the patient will need some form of **community care** service following **discharge**, the hospital will inform the local authority of the admission in anticipation of an **assessment** of the **service user**'s likely needs (section 47 of the **NHS and Community Care Act 1990**) when the patient is considered well enough to be discharged. This is what is known as a Section 2 notice. A Section 5 notice is then sent to the local authority within a minimum of 3 days informing of the imminent intended **discharge** from hospital. If there is a delay beyond this anticipated date due to a failure to set provision in place, charges to the local authority are incurred.

The **discharge** process should involve a multi-disciplinary approach and embrace the choices, wishes and individual circumstances of the person involved. This includes exploring social issues, carer circumstances and ongoing health needs. Delays can occur when people live alone and may not have significant others to advocate on their behalf or where they do not have capacity to be able to make an informed decision for themselves. Historically studies have also highlighted barriers to effective, smooth discharge from hospital, which may include the absence of a carer, entry to nursing and residential homes and a shortfall in assessment staff. Lengthy assessment processes, seeking clarity on who will fund the service and nursing or residential home waiting lists may also impact upon timescales for discharge. This Act was defined a controversial piece of legislation because of its emphasis upon rapid hospital **discharge** in order to prevent 'bed blocking' and its resulting reflection within health sector performance indicators, rather than upon qualitative consideration of the long-term impact of 'hurried' decision-making upon vulnerable people. It can be argued that this piece of legislation has a predominant focus upon risk rather than of person centred practice (McDonald and Taylor 2006). Recent reports have highlighted the long-term impact of rapid decision-making upon the lives of individual vulnerable people, particularly older adults. Few older people return home if discharged into residential care and rehabilitative strategies are called for in order to maximize options for increased autonomy and choice (CSCI 2005).

Commission for Social Care Inspection (2005) *Leaving Hospital*, Revised. London: CSCI.

McDonald, A. and Taylor, T. (2006) *Older People and the Law*. Bristol: Policy Press.

community care plan a 3-year plan produced by **social services departments**, providing details of proposed **social care** service provision in the area over that period.

Community care plans were a requirement under section 46 of the **NHS and Community Care Act 1990**, with the aim of increasing the public accountability of **local authorities**. In drawing up the plans, social services were required to involve other agencies involved in **community care**, including health authorities, **housing authorities**, and the voluntary and private sectors, to ensure consistency and coherence of service provision. The requirement for these was repealed in 2002, due to a greater policy emphasis on joint health and **social care** collaboration.

Now, separate plans are created for different user groups – those with **mental health problems**, **older people**, those with drug and alcohol dependency, for example – and as a consequence the community care plan for a locality provides an overview of service and an information base rather than planning the service itself. A wide range of partners now contribute to the plan – local authority **social care**, health services, voluntary sector organizations, registered social landlords as well as users and carers. Often included in this overview are: the local structures and factors that shape community care in the area; a summary of the specific services for each user group and links, often electronic, to information about community care. Thus plans act as a repository for policies, national standards and other information that the public may utilize as needed.

Individual users, particularly those with **mental health problems**, will also have individual care plans to coordinate community health services. See **care programme approach**.

community cohesion a policy framework which aims to encourage and enable different groups of people to get on well together.

The term emerged following the widespread civil disorder which occurred in various northern England towns and cities (including Bradford, officially classified as a riot; Oldham; and Burnley) during the summer of 2001. The conflict involved young men of **Asian** origin, the **police** and far right groups.

A series of reports which sought to examine the causes for the disorder identified several instrumental factors, with the government-commissioned report of the Independent Review **Team** chaired by Ted Cantle (commonly referred to as 'the Cantle report') identifying that communities in these towns and cities, whilst living side by side, were often living segregated lives. The phrase 'parallel lives' was used to indicate that this segregation was not just about geographical location, but also extended much deeper and to wider aspects of everyday life, including schooling, employment and leisure. Cantle, and others, believed that this was a fundamental factor leading to the civil disorder which had taken place. This was a very different conclusion from that of Lord Scarman's inquiry into the 'race riots' of the early 1980s between sections of the African-Caribbean community and the **police**. Indeed, Scarman suggested that political and economic exclusion and methods of policing Black communities were key factors.

Whilst the **New Labour** government also recognized structural inequalities, one of the key focuses was now to be formulating policy and practice which could challenge the apparent segregation of particular communities, with a particular, even if unsaid, focus on Muslim communities (see for example, Worley, 2005 for a fuller discussion of this). Since then, subsequent policy documents have sought to develop and define what this means in practice, and the current working definition of 'community cohesion' is rather different from its early incarnation. According to the Department for Communities and Local Government (2008: 10) community cohesion is considered to be based on three foundations: 'people from different backgrounds having similar life opportunities; people knowing their rights and responsibilities; and people trusting one another and trusting local institutions to act fairly'. This is seen as being underpinned by three ways of living together: 'a shared future vision and sense of belonging; a focus on what new and existing communities have in common, alongside a recognition of the value of diversity; strong and positive relationships between people from different backgrounds' (Department for Communities and Local Government, 2008, p.10).

Nevertheless, it is without doubt that the civil disorder of 2001 was a catalyst in shifting government policy, from policies advocating multi-culturalism to policies promoting community cohesion. This shift has been subject to intense critique. Some question the very idea of segregated communities existing in England, whilst others have suggested that this new approach to race relations has similarities with earlier policies of assimilation, especially because of the emphasis being placed on processes of integration.

Worley, C. (2005) 'it's not about race. It's about the community': New Labour and 'community cohesion'. *Critical Social Policy*, 25(4).

Department for Communities and Local Government (2008) *The Government's Response to the Commission on Integration and Cohesion*. London: DCLG.

Community Legal Service (CLS) a legal service that provides publicly funded information, **advice** and legal representation for those who cannot afford legal costs. The CLS was set up by the Access to Justice Act 1999 and replaced the previous system of civil legal aid. It is run by the **Legal Services Commission** and works through local **partnership**s that include solicitors, law centres and Citizens Advice Bureaux. All publicly funded legal assistance in civil matters is now provided by the CLS. Its priorities include cases of child protection, **domestic violence** and abuses of human rights.

community order a court order, introduced by the **Criminal Justice Act 2003**, which may be passed on a convicted offender and which may contain one or any combination of 12 different requirements: **unpaid work, supervision, curfew** and **exclusion requirements** enforced by **electronic monitoring, activity, prohibited activity, programme, residence, mental health treatment, drug rehabilitation**, and **alcohol treatment requirements**. The community order replaced ten separate **community sentences**, including the **community rehabilitation order** (formerly the **probation order**), the **community punishment order** (formerly the **community service order**) and the **curfew order**. A community order can only be imposed for an offence punishable with imprisonment, or on a persistent offender who has previously been fined, and only if the court deems the offence serious enough to warrant such a **sentence** (although there is an exception for less serious but sufficiently **persistent offenders**). Community orders can last for a maximum of 3 years, although some of the requirements have shorter time limits.

Community Payback the name given by the government to **unpaid work** by offenders since 2006. It is not a statutory term. The phrase is ambiguous, suggesting both retributive punishment (the **community** 'pays back' to offenders the punishment they deserve for having committed the offence) and **reparation** (the offender makes amends by 'paying back' something to the community).

community profile   a systematic and comprehensive description of the needs of a particular local area defining itself as a **community** and the local resources available for tackling any problems identified.

Essentially the profile is a catalogue, or audit, of the needs of the local area as experienced by residents. Such needs may be numerous, whether overcrowding in housing, poor housing infrastructure, not enough activities for young people, insufficient transport links, local shops that overcharge. But they also may be reported in ways that do not simply echo existing services but express the difficulties that residents have in living their everyday lives. Reports of feeling endangered on the streets may be a generalized fear built on the fact that shops have closed down, there are no **police** patrols on foot or gangs of young people are simply hanging about. A community profile will also include the resources at hand to deal with social problems – whether the level of skills, the strength of local institutions such as churches or mosques or the effectiveness of local networks. In addition, a community profile is carried out, with local residents playing an active part from the beginning in the range of activities required to complete the profile and also involved from the beginning in putting together an action plan – how to overcome the problems uncovered with the resources available.

Profiling can be time-consuming to plan and carry out, can absorb a group's attention and divert time and energy from other main tasks, produce poor-quality information that in the end is unusable and perhaps raise expectations that the findings on their own will lead to change. Forming a steering group with high levels of resident **participation** and developing a management structure are essential first steps. At this stage there are key questions that any profiling effort should answer before starting to collect information: What is the purpose of the profile? How will the information be used? Will it be used to lobby within your own or other service organizations to improve the level of provision? Present to the media or use at a public meeting in order to raise public awareness or support? Develop better relations with neighbourhood residents and activists who want to move on some issues?

Gathering data may involve different forms of information-gathering, such as observation, description of existing services, case studies or public opinion surveys. Data and information may be quite technical and will certainly be comprehensive. In general, there are important categories of data to pursue: land use, the condition of public spaces, the environment and degrees of pollution, population statistics, types and quality of housing, the state of the local economy, including employment, the availability and quality of local services, the **communication networks** and media, and the local **power** structure.

In drawing up plans for data-gathering there are a few rules to remember amidst the complexity: try to keep it simple – a lengthy questionnaire will put residents off. It must be easily understood by all who come in **contact** with it; collect all relevant information, especially that which might run counter to what you expect or want to get out of it; use sound research methods that cannot be easily dismissed when used to back up the action plan for improvement. The Office of National Statistics website also provides comprehensive data on the social conditions in specific neighbourhoods.

Hawtin, M. and Percy-Smith, J. (2007) *Community Profiling: auditing social needs*. Buckingham: Open University.

community punishment order the official name for a **community sentence** requiring the offender to perform **unpaid work** between 2001 and 2005. The name was changed from **community service order** by the Criminal Justice and Court Services Act 2000, emphasizing the punitive aspects of such orders as opposed to any elements of **rehabilitation or reparation**. The orders have now been replaced by **community orders** with **unpaid work** requirements.

community rehabilitation order the official name for a **probation order** between 2001 and 2005. The name was changed from '**probation order**' by the Criminal Justice and Court Services Act 2000. The orders have now been replaced by **community orders** with **supervision requirements**.

community safety plan a programme with the objectives for **local authorities** to devise, implement and regularly review measures designed to reduce crime and create a safer environment. The **Crime and Disorder Act 1998** (amended by the **Police and Justice Act 2006**) places a duty on **local authorities** to establish community safety **partnerships**, sometimes called local **crime and disorder partnerships**, comprising key justice, social welfare and voluntary sector agencies to coordinate efforts around **community** safety.

The government currently has six key objectives underpinning the community safety plan. These are – making communities stronger and more effective; reducing crime and **anti-social behaviour** and building a culture of respect; preventing extremism and countering terrorism; creating a safer environment; protecting the public and building confidence; and finally, improving peoples' lives so they are less likely to commit offences or re-offend. Each of these key objectives have sub-components that can vary in emphasis depending upon the profile of any **community**, although there tend to be major continuities concerning problems such as **domestic violence**, drugs and substance abuse, and juvenile offending in all or most communities.

Community safety plans have substantial discretion to support particular initiatives or give priority to specific problems. Thus, it would be possible, for example, to encourage the establishment and support of **domestic violence forums** as well as local initiatives that encourage collaboration between community groups and justice and welfare agencies. These mechanisms are crucial if communities are to be **police**d with the consent of people and there is substantial **participation** of communities in the implementation of policies that reflect community needs.

community sentence a category of **sentence**s which includes the **community order**, the **youth rehabilitation order** and the **reparation order**. A court must not pass a **community sentence** unless it believes that the offence was serious enough to warrant such a **sentence**. The term may also be used more widely to include any non-**custodial sentence** including **fine**s.

community service, community service order the original name for a **sentence** that required **unpaid work** in the locality. The name of the court order was changed to **community punishment order** in 2001, and the order was replaced by the **community order** with an **unpaid work** requirement by the **Criminal Justice Act 2003**.

community work/community development a wide-ranging set of practices designed to improve the quality of life for individuals within designated areas, geographical localities or communities.

Community work can entail work with individuals, groups and communities, but the key indicator of success for community work activity appears to be whether conditions, social relationships and social capital in a locality are improved. Enhanced 'social inclusion' of people previously marginalized could also be regarded as a key objective.

Recent years have seen increased attention given to the role of 'communities' in addressing social issues and social problems. **New Labour** policy has placed a clear emphasis on community involvement, **empowerment** and **participation**, **partnership** work between service providers and communities, and active citizenship reflected in initiatives such as **Sure Start** and New Deal for Communities. These provide a great opportunity for **social work** interactions and practice, but it is also increasingly recognized that **social work** practice is now often more about managing risks and resources than supporting and developing 'communities'.

Historically, community work has been construed as an alternative or additional form of social work. Such work can focus upon individuals, families, groups or larger collectives within an area. Work with individuals is regarded as important in its own right, but such work can also contribute to **community** goals. Experiments during the 1970s and 1980s in Britain witnessed various attempts to solve individual and family problems through collective work, rather than the individual or family **casework** approaches that had previously dominated **social work** activity. Instead of being treated as separate cases, with sometimes an implied suggestion that the individual or family was to blame for their malaise, individual families were invited to join **community** groups designed to address problems experienced by many people within a locality. Such an approach was thought to be appropriate for apparently personal problems like **domestic violence**, alcohol dependence or confidence building as well as problems construed as external to individuals or families, such as housing conditions, refuse clearance or the absence of a community nursery.

In this context, community work can be grouped into three broad groups of activity or theoretical perspectives, namely community development, community action and community service delivery. In practice, it is often difficult to distinguish the perspectives from each other, and many community workers are eclectic in their working practices. There are, however some discernible differences or emphases.

Community development has its roots in a broadly based movement to try to encourage better living standards in colonial societies especially after the Second World War, when literacy schemes to promote **citizenship** were prominent, especially in countries where there were different ethnic groups trying to develop ways of existing peacefully. Since then community development, at a basic level, has been loosely applied to activities promoting the generation of community **contact**s where there are none or where they are poorly developed, such as in new towns or in localities where people do not linger, like 'hard to let' or 'sink' estates.

Later, with the **Home Office**'s ambitious Community Development Programme (CDPs), community development acquired more ambitious operational objectives. These projects entailed a series of well-funded experiments designed to tackle areas of multiple deprivation in both inner-city areas and areas of rural **poverty**. **Home Office** funding was used to improve infrastructure, such as renovating housing stock and community facilities, enhanced staff–pupil ratios in primary schools (in order to try to help children to compensate for the negative impact of their depressed communities on their school performance) and the provision of resource centres to assist people in relation to welfare benefits advice and job creation. The central focus of the Home Office's conception of community development, however, appeared to be to determine how much communities could mobilize to help themselves.

Researchers evaluating the CDPs found virtues in locally based initiatives but considered that improvements to neighbourhoods and communities would always be seriously constrained by wider economic and political forces, such as industrial decline, rising unemployment or a decrease in the value of state benefits. As some commentators pointed out, if General Motors or Ford (based in the USA) sneezed, then areas where there are car production plants in the UK would catch colds or even pneumonia. Similar arguments have been cited in relation to the closure of coal mines or shipyards. The final CDP reports were critical of government policies that sought to tackle **poverty** solely through local activity. The Home Office abandoned the schemes in the mid-1970s. Nevertheless, similar approaches have been taken by a number of both government and voluntary initiatives across the country since that time, particularly in the context of urban regeneration programmes such as New Deal for Communities.

The term *community action* has been used rather more specifically to describe attempts to secure additional resources for a locality, to achieve a measure of political participation for marginalized groups or perhaps to defeat some proposal thought to be against the interests of those living within the locality. Hence, groups have campaigned to have high-rise blocks demolished because they were damp, expensive to heat and inappropriate for young families. Others have worked collectively to prevent, say, the building of a highway through a neighbourhood. The achievement of change or, paradoxically, its prevention, are usually the focus of community action. There is also a sense in which community action implies that campaigners will use rigorous if not combative methods to try to achieve their goals. The activities of eco-warriors in relation to the Newbury bypass in Berkshire and the second runway at Manchester Airport are examples of this kind. The various professional and qualifying bodies representing community workers have always dissociated themselves from any activities that involve violence, but aggressive 'civil disobedience' has always been regarded as a legitimate tactic. Other less combative forms of community action have involved petitioning demonstrations, rent strikes, the use of the media and lobbying political institutions, either locally or nationally. The latter raises interesting issues about identifying appropriate targets for campaigners. Sometimes activists have to decide whether the target is to be local government, for example when regarding some local facility, or whether to try to influence central government if it is construed as a problem of national government starving local government of much needed resources.

The third perspective, community service delivery, focuses on the provision of community services. It aims to restructure the delivery of services to make them more responsive to community needs. In this respect it is argued that real community involvement is fundamental. A further element of this perspective is a requirement that all services that have a stake in a problem should seek to collaborate effectively, again taking into account a community's views of its needs. While mostly a 'top-down' approach that seeks to encourage community consultation and **participation** in developing responsive services, the community service delivery model has been adapted by community workers to try to develop a more 'bottom-up' approach, an approach that can challenge the 'professional-bureaucratic ethos'. The model takes the view that those in need of services are most able to identify that need. In this view the role of the community worker is to assist communities in articulating their needs. Partnership between communities and the service providers is also perceived as key. An example of good practice is perhaps **Women's Aid**, an organization that has a strong track record of involving **service users** in management committees and of employing previous service users. The organization has also played a major role in bringing relevant agencies together and in supporting women in violent relationships so that they can shape the very services that are supposed to help them. Difficulties can arise if agencies bring hidden agendas and competing aspirations to consultations with service users. In these circumstances, it is the task of the community worker to facilitate **mediation** and negotiation between service users and relevant agencies to effect agreements in the service users' interests. However, this is an immensely complex and multilayered process, which can involve debate regarding **power** and conflict between different stakeholders.

Community work does not imply a particular political perspective, although in practice many community workers tend to be 'left of centre'. More significantly, there is usually a connection between a community worker's analysis of the origins of social problems and the community work methods adopted by a worker. Thus, there can be community workers who stress individual responsibility for behaviour or personal difficulties, thereby emphasizing the importance of responsibilities as well as rights. Others will take the view that articulating community needs and interests and mobilizing problem solving are the two key dimensions of the role. Significant difficulties can arise when there are fundamental differences between what a community wants and the beliefs and **values** of the community worker. For example, a community may not wish to have a facility to support refugees sited nearby while the community worker has considerable sympathy for this vulnerable group.

In the contemporary context, community based approaches have become far more mainstream and central to much of central government policy, with a revived interest in the possibilities of 'community work' and especially collaborative partnerships. However, these 'new' ways of working with communities also operate within a policy framework which is framed by increased regulation (for example through targets) and risk assessments. On the one hand, there is an emphasis on support and inclusion, whilst on the other, there is an emphasis on regulation and control; creating something of a policy paradox (Stepney and Popple 2008). See also **community social work**.

Pierson, J. (2008) *Going Local: working in communities and neighbourhoods.* London: Routledge.

Stepney, P. and Popple, K. (2008) *Social Work and the Community: a critical context for practice.* Basingstoke: Palgrave Macmillan.

compensation a financial payment made to a **victim** of crime by either the offender, a **criminal court** or the Criminal Injuries Compensation Scheme as reparation for injury, **loss** or damage or to recognize it symbolically. A court compensation order requires the offender to make a payment which is passed on to the **victim**. Courts are required to consider making a compensation order in relevant cases and to give reasons if they do not. Courts should give compensation priority over **fines** and court costs, but it may nevertheless be paid in small amounts over a long period if the offender does not have the means to pay outright. Criminal injuries compensation is paid only to victims of violent crime (and the relatives of murder and manslaughter victims).

complaint and complaints procedure a grievance or accusation and a formal mechanism for hearing the complaint and making recommendations. Both the **Children Act 1989** and the **National Health Service and Community Care Act 1990** (Chapter 6 of the policy guidance on **community care**) require **local authorities** to establish complaints procedures. For example, section 26 of the Children Act enables representations and complaints to be made in relation to **looked after** children and **children in need** and gives rights to make representations and complaints to parents of such children and those with **parental responsibility**. This now includes, since the Welfare Reform Act 2009, a father named by the child's mother on the birth registration; any local authority foster parent; and any person the authority considers has a sufficient interest in the child's welfare to warrant representations being considered about the **discharge** by the authority of any of their qualifying functions in relation to the child.

The Health and Social Care (Community Health and Standards) Act 2003 requires a general complaints procedure to operate. Specific requirements are in the Local Authority Social Services and **National**

Health Service Complaints (England) Regulations 2009/309. Social services procedures were made following consultations on proposals in 2002. The procedure is a highly formalized one, and among other things provide for an initial discussion with the complainant as to how the complaint is to be handled, and the likely period for investigating the complaint and responding. Investigative procedures must comply with minimum standards and guidance; and social services and other responsible bodies must ensure that complaints arrangements are publicized. Oversight is provided by the **Care Quality Commission**.

Details are in the regulations and guidance, but procedures for dealing with complaints must now possess a number of key features, including designation of managers responsible for compliance, and a complaints manager for handling the procedure. Complainants are entitled, within limits, to disclosure of information to facilitate their complaint; and there are time limits governing the process.

Another possible channel for complaints is to use the local government ombudsman system. Complainants have direct access to the local system (unlike complaints to Parliamentary and Health Service Commissioner for Administration which requires complaints to be supported by a member of Parliament. The local **ombudsman** can investigate complaints of injustice caused by maladministration, for example in relation to most local authority services including **social care** and housing. Investigators have similar powers to those of the **High Court** in requiring documents to be disclosed, and requiring witnesses to give evidence. Joint investigations by both the Parliamentary and local ombudsman can be carried out where the complaint straddles local authority and **NHS** services. Remedies include **compensation**; requirements to take action or make a decision that should have been taken; reconsideration of decisions; reports identifying procedural or other failures, with conclusions that expect the authority or other body to improve its procedures so that similar problems do not happen again. Further details of the local government ombudsman service is available at their website. There are other ombudsmen systems in operation, and with similar powers, for example the Housing Ombudsman Service (dealing with complaints about registered housing providers, including **housing association**s and other landlords, managers, and agents. The **police** are also subject to investigation. As well as their own internal mechanisms for dealing with complaints by the public, including by people in **custody**, there is the Independent Police Complaints Commission.

Department of Health (2002) *Learning from Complaints: consultation on changes to the social services complaints procedure for adults.* London: DH.

Comprehensive Area Assessment (CAA) This is a new approach to the **assessment** of the performance of local government services in England and is aimed at identifying the way in which services are improving or in need of improvement across local government. It is argued that increasingly services are **Working Together** in an increasingly joined up way and the new process aims to encourage these developments through independent **assessment** of performance. This process brings together the **Audit Commission** and five other **inspection** agencies: the **Care Quality Commission**, HM Inspectorates of Constabulary, **Prisons**, and Probation, and Ofsted. While a key aim is to reform the **inspection** process it is also aimed at providing further guidance for local government as well as an independent source of transparency for **service users** and the public as a whole. This will not replace the role of the different **inspection** units, but will aim to provide further sources of quality assurance where services work together. It is as yet unclear what the impact will be and whether this will create a regime which results in overlap between **inspections** without adding to the overall quality of services provision. A single website will be developed and will be hosted by the **Audit Commission**.

compulsory school age the ages of children within which parents are required by law to ensure that they receive full-time education, either at a school or 'otherwise' under sections 7 and 8 of the **Education Act 1996**.

The period begins at the start of the term following a child's fifth birthday, though most children will start at school on a voluntary basis before that date. It ends, for all children, on the last Friday in June in the school year in which the child becomes 16 (to be raised to 17 in 2013). It does not end on the child's actual 16th birthday, which may be several months earlier. There is an increasing expectation, under the 14–19 Reform Agenda, that young people should remain in some form of education or training, at least on a part time basis, until the age of 19, with some element of compulsion on the young person themselves, but this is not a further raising of school leaving age as has happened previously or an extension of the legal duty on parents. The definition of compulsory school age affects all other definitions used in education, for example those relating to the **employment of children**. In this context, the term 'young person' is applicable only to those who have completed compulsory education. A parent does not have to send their child to a school to meet the legal requirement. Education can take place in other ways, such as tuition at home by a parent or private tutor, a further education college or a **self-help** group. **Elective home education** as a full-time alternative to sending a child to a school is subject to limited

inspection by officers of the local authority but must continue until the same age as if the child were registered at a school.

Whitney, B. (2008) *A Guide to School Attendance*. London: David Fulton/Routledge Falmer.

conditional caution a **caution** combined with additional specific conditions for an offender aged 18 or over. It is up to the **Crown Prosecution Service** to decide whether a conditional **caution** is appropriate, and in most cases the **police** who administer it. Conditional **caution**s were given a statutory basis by the **Criminal Justice Act 2003**. Currently, conditions can be for the purpose of rehabilitating the offender or for ensuring **reparation**. Provisions in the **Police and Justice Act 2006** (not yet implemented) would also allow conditions for the purpose of punishing the offender, including the possibility of a financial penalty (maximum £250). See also **youth conditional cautions**.

conditional discharge see **discharge**

confidentiality the safeguarding of privacy in relation to information about **service user**s. There are several key issues about access to information about **service user**s that concern social welfare agencies. First, service users are concerned that information about them is not freely and irresponsibly shared with third parties. Second, workers may wish to protect the identity of people who help to reveal, say, **child abuse** or some other criminal offence. Third, there may be information on **social work** or other files to which access by the service user is denied. Fourth, information divulged to a worker by a service user may not, and perhaps should not, in some circumstances be kept confidential.

Many of the issues surrounding confidentiality are complex in practice. Information about a service user is habitually shared with other agencies with welfare or safeguarding issues as the justification. Thus a case of alleged **child abuse** may involve a social worker in inquiries with the family doctor or health visitor or at the child's school. Some argue that such inquiries should be initiated only with parental permission (which may be withheld). Others argue that the interests of a possibly abused child or vulnerable adult should be sufficient to override such concerns.

There are often confidential sections on social work files to which the service user has no access, justified because such information may be upsetting to them or involve sensitive material about third parties. In these circumstances social workers might at least indicate whether there was confidential material in any file and provide information about the kinds of information held in such files in order that the service user or client might challenge a decision not to allow him or her access to such material. Finally, can a social worker ever guarantee confidentiality when such information may concern his or her statutory duties? British law takes the view that confidentiality must be **breach**ed when crimes have been committed and where vulnerable adults' and children's welfare is at stake. (See also **databases**.)

Connexions the chief advisory service for young people that provides personal advisers for all young people to assist them in the transition from school and adolescence to employment and adulthood. The focus of services is upon young people aged 13–19 and from 13–25 for young people with significant disabilities. In many areas local youth services are now managed by Connexions.

Connexions advisers focus much of their attention on helping young people still in school or after they have left school to access careers guidance, to apply for advertised jobs or to secure appropriate training which may be about general preparation for work or about targeted training for a particular occupation. They undertake outreach work in schools, colleges and pupil referral groups; they also undertake visits to the homes of young people; and offer **advice** in duty sessions in Connexions offices. Connexions have the task of dealing with a high proportion of 'hard to reach', disaffected young people with few or modest qualifications. This is the group often described as NEET's (**not in employment, education or training**).

Connexions has close working relationships with agencies offering pre-employment training although some offices do offer some training of this kind too. Help offered by these agencies as well as Connexions advisers might focus upon issues such as a young persons' interests and aspirations, identifying suitable jobs, applying for jobs, CV preparation and role plays to prepare for telephone enquiries and interviews. A small number of agencies dealing with NEET's specialize in work with disabled young people. Personal advisers have a wider brief advising young people who are homeless or threatened with **homelessness**, have personal and relationship problems including pregnancy and sexual health, benefit problems and issues concerned with offending. Advisers routinely attend area meetings, often given the label of 'early intervention forums', where representatives of social services, probation, **youth offending team**s, education, youth services, housing agencies and the **police** share information about young people experiencing significant difficulties with the objective of providing comprehensive and 'joined up' support for troubled young people.

contact the different means by which a child keeps in touch with family members when away from home. A child living away from home, for example in local authority care, or not living with one of his or her parents following separation or **divorce**, can maintain links with people such as parents, siblings and grandparents in a variety of ways, including visits and overnight stays, telephone calls, cards, email, photos, letters and gifts. Maintaining contact for a child being **looked after** by the local authority and his or her family is a matter of great importance to social workers. Research has shown that the consistency and degree of contact between a child in care and his or her parents or grandparents contributes significantly to the child's **wellbeing**, is associated with fewer placement breakdowns and is one of the best indicators as to whether the child will return home successfully or not. Because of this key finding, the **Children Act 1989** pays a great deal of attention to contact.

Section 34 of the Act requires that children subject to a care order have 'reasonable contact' with their parents or other member(s) of the family as long as this is in the welfare of the child. The Act does not define what is 'reasonable' but leaves this to the parties concerned to work out, including the child, if old enough, the parents and other important family members. The Act also lays a general duty on social workers to promote contact with parents, relations and others whenever a child is accommodated by the local authority 'unless it is not reasonably practicable or consistent with the child's welfare' to quote Schedule 2, paragraph 15 (1) of the Act. In making arrangements social workers should give due consideration to the wishes and feelings of the child concerned but is not bound by them. Promoting contact can include covering travel expenses for parents and others to enable contact to happen if such expenses would cause undue hardship. Facilitating contact is not always easy. Difficulties in the parent–child relationship, distance from the child's placement and resistance of the child's **foster care**rs are all factors that can adversely affect the frequency of contact. Nevertheless, social workers are expected to commit considerable resources to ensure that contact comes about. The frequency of contact and how it will be undertaken form an essential part of any care plan for a child. Only if the welfare of the child is jeopardized may the local authority ask the court for a **contact direction**, restricting contact or even terminating it altogether. Similarly, parents may ask the court for such a direction for increasing contact (see **contact order**).

Contact between a child and his or her non-residential parent can be among the most contentious issues facing parents who have separated or **divorce**d. Where conflicts over the extent of **contact** or the nature of that contact occur family **mediation** is often a first step toward resolution. Where that conflict continues one parent or the other may seek a **contact order** under section 8 of the **Children Act 1989**. Such an order can secure a court judgment on the nature and frequency of contact for a particular family. It may be that a social worker would oppose contact by one parent or the other perhaps on the grounds that the specific contact would expose the child to risk of abuse, physical or emotional. If that is the case it is important that the practitioner explain very clearly the reasons why this is in the child's best interest to all family members, and particularly to the parent who is having their **contact** ended or curtailed.

Some women-centred researchers have uncovered the less positive side of presuming contact between a non-resident father and his child when violence and **abuse** have characterized the relationship of the child's parents. Contact between father and child, they argue, offers only further opportunity for the violent father to continue his intimidating, controlling and abusive behaviour. In fraught situations many **local authorities** have opened **contact** centres where supervised contact can take place and support for all parties is provided. (See also **contact order, reunification, feminist social work**).

Bullock, R., Gooch, D. and Little, M. (1998) *Children Going Home: the reunification of families.* Aldershot: Ashgate.

contact direction   stipulation by a court regarding the degree of **contact** to take place between a child in the care of the local authority and other members of the family. Under section 34 of the **Children Act 1989**, the court making a care order may also specify the degree of **contact** that the child may have with those who have **parental responsibility** for him or her, or any other person the court deems relevant, such as siblings. It may do this at the time the care order is made or at any time afterwards. Any party to the proceedings may ask the court for such a direction. This includes a local authority that wishes to terminate all **contact** between a child in its care and his or her parents, or a parent of a child in care who wishes to visit his or her child more frequently. If no such direction is made, the Children Act assumes that 'reasonable contact' will take place between the child in care and the parents.

contact order   a court order under section 8 of the **Children Act 1989** determining the frequency and kind of **contact** that a child will have with a parent or others with **parental responsibility** for the child in private law proceedings.

Contact orders are generally used to settle differences of opinion as to how often the child should see one or the other of the parents in matrimonial disputes. An order can also be used in relation to a child who goes to live with other members of the family, such as grandparents, including a child who might otherwise have come into local authority care. The **Children And Adoption Act 2006** gives the courts more flexible powers to enforce **contact order**s under section 8 of the **Children Act 1989** and to help find solutions in cases where there is serious conflict between the parties. These powers enable the court to direct parties to attend specific activities or events such as parenting classes that are designed to promote **contact** with the child concerned or award financial **compensation** from one party to another (for example to repay the cost of a lost holiday).

A contact order is a private law order and should not be confused with a **contact direction**, made by a court to regulate **contact** between a child in local authority care and the parents or other family members.

councils of voluntary service (CVS)   the major coordinating bodies for voluntary sector organizations within particular geographical areas, usually coterminous with **local authorities**.

Some rural areas are able to sustain a CVS, but predominantly they are located in large towns and cities. Most councils receive their primary funding from local authorities. Their functions include the development of voluntary activity in the locality, often through the provision of **volunteer** bureaux to recruit volunteers to affiliated organizations; the provision of information about local conditions and needs; **advice** on fund-raising – usually with access to a **database** of fund and grant giving bodies/trusts; the coordination of effort and policy among voluntary bodies; and sometimes the direct delivery of services to the public and to voluntary organizations (for example, printing and distribution of newsletters, or training of volunteers including management committee members). Councils of voluntary service have in recent years been active in opposing cuts in public expenditure. Given that many voluntary organizations work with vulnerable and marginalized groups, the councils are in a unique position to offer opinions about how such groups are faring in relation to government policy. The councils have also been particularly active in promoting harmonious race relations through **Race Equality Councils**.

couple   in the context of a relationship between two adults, a 'couple' is legally defined for a number of purposes including the determination of eligibility for benefits and **assessment** of the income and capital resources which the parties concerned share, or are defined in law to share. The application of the concept is problematic, however, especially when decisions are made that two people are living together as a couple, and are therefore subject to the rule that their resources should be aggregated and treated as available to both of them – and for other eligibility purposes. Not surprisingly, appeals against decisions by welfare agencies that two people have 'couple' status, even when evidenced by the characteristics of 'living together' recognized by the law (shared accommodation, responsibility for finances and childcare, and 'stability', etc.) are characterized by a high success rate. See also **cohabitation and Civil Partnership Act 2004**.

credit union   a group of people, with a common bond, who save money together in order to build up sufficient funds to make low-interest loans available to participants in the union. Credit unions in Britain are governed by the Credit Union Act 1979. The credit union movement is long established and international. Popular and successful unions exist, for example, in Ireland, the Caribbean, Canada, Japan and many other countries. Poor people often do not have access to 'mainstream' credit facilities because credit agencies, such as banks and loan and insurance companies, will not lend to them. Facilities that are available to them, such as local money lenders, invariably charge very high rates of interest or operate other constraints, such as the requirement that goods are purchased from certain stores. Credit unions must comprise people who have a 'common bond' – for example, people who all live in the same neighbourhood, belong to the same church or work for the same company. Members save and, once a personal target and a collective target have been reached, can borrow. Loans are usually modest and rates of interest low. In Britain, interest rates must not exceed 1 per cent per month (annual percentage rate 12.6). Credit unions have grown significantly over the past ten years, although some smaller unions have not been able survive. Some attribute this to the growing burden of bureaucracy now that credit unions are accountable to the Financial Services Authority (FSA) and they have to pay for an annual audit as well as fees to the Financial **Ombudsman**, the FSA and to the Association of British Credit unions for various protective and regulatory purposes.

crime and deviance (theories of) the collective term for the various explanations offered for social rule-breaking in general and criminal lawbreaking in particular.

Theories of crime and deviance vary in the extent to which they emphasize personal, cultural, social or structural factors. They assist us in understanding why people commit crime, but they do not necessarily provide prescriptions for what should be done about crime. Although there are links between theories of crime and **principles of sentencing**, it is usually argued that solutions to crime reside in the attitudes and conditions in society as a whole rather than in the policies and practices of the criminal justice system. The earliest systematic attempt to provide an explanation of crime emerged in the late 18th and early 19th centuries as a response to earlier barbaric, repressive and arbitrary legal practices. The *classical school of criminology* was based on a number of key beliefs about human nature and society, drawn from the philosophical movement known as the Enlightenment. All individuals were believed to be self-seeking and greedy by nature and therefore liable to commit crime. Nevertheless, there was believed to be a consensus in society as to the desirability of protecting private property and personal welfare. In order to prevent a 'war of all against all', individuals freely entered into a social contract with the state to preserve the peace within the terms of this consensus. All individuals are rational and equal in the eyes of the law. The individual has free will and is responsible for his or her actions; mitigating circumstances or excuses are therefore inadmissible. (Closely allied to these beliefs were the sentencing principles of proportionality and deterrence.) Crime was therefore viewed as a matter of choice – a deliberate attempt to undermine the social contract.

Classical criminology, however, was subject to some fairly obvious criticisms. Because of differing mental capacities, not all people could be held to be equally responsible before the law. Some allowance had to be made for the very young, the 'feeble-minded' and the insane. It was also apparent that material inequalities existed in society that meant, first, that the impact and effects of punishment would differ and, second, that crime might be a rational response to inequality or **poverty**. Neoclassical explanations of crime, therefore, began to take account of the personal circumstances and characteristics of the criminal. Many people believe that neoclassicism is still the predominant view in the criminal justice system today.

With the development of medical science during the 19th century, there was increasing interest in the possible existence of a 'criminal **personality**' that could be identified by biological or mental abnormalities. This school of thought was known as *positivist criminology*. Its basic tenets were that crime was induced or determined by factors of birth or environment; and that these could be studied scientifically, so that crime could be predicted and prevented by the treatment rather than the punishment of criminals. Some of the best-known positivist theories of crime include the apparent discovery of physical stigmata on criminals and the apparent preponderance among criminals of particular body builds or types, particular chromosomal make-ups, low intelligence and extrovert personalities susceptible to poor conditioning. Such theories led to the ascendancy of rehabilitation as a sentencing principle. They have been widely criticized, however, on technical grounds (that the so-called scientific findings are unreliable), on sociological grounds (that they provide a very narrow explanation of crime that ignores issues of **power** and inequality) and on political grounds (that the 'treatment' required to 'cure' a criminal **personality** may be out of all proportion to the seriousness of the offence, thus infringing civil liberties and notions of '**just deserts**').

Despite this, the belief that criminal activity is learned, or a matter of conditioning that can be unlearned, has enjoyed a revival over the past decade with the cognitive and behavioural approaches adopted by the **probation service**. These have involved offenders (often in groups) analysing their offending behaviour, identifying factors that trigger criminal responses and expanding their social skills to handle situations in more socially acceptable ways.

Psychodynamic theories of crime focus on the early emotional experiences of offenders. Criminal activity is seen as an attempt to compensate for **childhood** (especially maternal) deprivation and for an inability to resolve – as a healthy person would – the internal emotional conflicts of growing up. Crime is viewed as disturbed, attention-seeking behaviour that requires an individual psychotherapeutic response. In the mid-20th century such theories were seen as particularly relevant in understanding juvenile crime, but their influence has declined with a return to **just deserts**.

Social organization theories developed in the United States from the 1920s onwards and were the first attempt to provide sociological explanations of crime. Theories of 'social space' were concerned with the influence of what would now be called town planning or building development on the attitudes and behaviour of city dwellers. The constraints of poor housing and decaying inner-city residential areas were highlighted as contributory factors to the development of a socio-economic 'pecking order' and subcultures that condoned the commission of crime. Closely related to the 'social space' theories were those concerned with 'social (lack of) opportunity'. With increased affluence in society, people trapped at the bottom of the social structure are frustrated by the vision of success and wealth alongside the absence of legitimate opportunity for them to achieve those goals. The response to this may be the development of delinquent subcultures or a proclivity to 'drift' in and out of crime.

Social reaction and social control theories are less concerned with why people commit crime in the first place than with how criminal behaviour is perpetuated as a result of social responses to the criminal. Social reaction theory argues that official responses to crime (such as heavy policing and severe sentencing) serve to label and stigmatize criminals and thus make it more difficult for them to reintegrate into the **community** as law-abiding citizens. Consequently, criminals are likely to seek the company of other criminals and fulfil the negative predictions made about them. In this way, deviance is amplified, and there is a danger of moral panics being constructed by the media, which reinforce stereotypical reactions and play on public fears about the escalation of crime. Social control theories develop this idea further (and also hark back to classical criminology) by arguing that, if it were not for the strength of our socialization and our fear of getting caught, most people would commit crime at some point in their lives. Whether or not we commit crime depends on the extent to which we feel we have an investment in remaining law-abiding; the strength of this feeling may vary over time and in different situations. Being labelled and stigmatized as a criminal may be a decisive factor in continuing rather than discontinuing a life of crime.

The major criticism of all these theories is that they fail to take account of the **power** structure and conflicts in society. *Conflict theories* argue that it is impossible to separate individual criminals (or even local environments and responses) from the way the criminal law and the criminal justice system have been constructed and are maintained to serve the interests of powerful groups in society. Defendants are overwhelmingly drawn from the ranks of working-class and unemployed people, but some of the most serious crime (particularly financial crime) is committed by the rich and powerful. Serious class and racial conflicts are dealt with as matters of narrow criminal justice rather than as issues of broad social justice. Similarly, *feminist explanations* of crime have underlined the fact that both crime and criminal justice are overwhelmingly male enterprises and that this requires analysis of gender **power** relations within society.

Theories of crime and deviance provide different levels of explanation, and many people feel that they are not all necessarily mutually exclusive. Professionals working with offenders frequently adopt an 'eclectic' approach that combines elements of structural, cultural and biographical explanation. Most **probation officer**s and **youth offending team** members would probably describe their own approaches as eclectic, but there is increasing agreement about the relevance of the research on risk and effectiveness and its implications for practice with offenders. Specifically, these theories have led to increased use of cognitive behavioural methods, particularly with groups of offenders, and a decline in one-to-one work. This is paralleled by a distrust of counselling and a greater emphasis upon criminogenic need.

Walker, N. (1993) *Why Punish?* Oxford: Oxford University Press.

Crime and Disorder Act 1998 an Act which made sweeping changes to the law relating to **sentences** and measures to deal with crime and offenders, especially regarding **youth justice**, and can be seen as heralding the **new youth justice**. It stated that the principal aim of the **youth justice** system is to prevent offending by children and young persons, implying that young offenders were to be seen as offenders first and as **children in need** second, although the provisions of the **Children Act 1989** remain applicable to young offenders, and **criminal courts** remain bound by section 44(1) of the **Children and Young Persons Act 1933** to 'have regard to the welfare of the child. (See also **Crime and Immigration Act 2008**.)

The Act introduced a range of new orders including the **anti-social behaviour order, parenting order, child safety order, action plan order, reparation order**, and the **detention and training order**. It also introduced local child **curfews**, replaced the **caution** for young offenders with the **reprimand** and **final warning**, and abolished the *doli incapax* rule. Most importantly, it established the national **Youth Justice Board** and required **local authorities** to set up multi-agency **youth offending teams**. For adult offenders, the Act's innovations included **sex offender orders, racially aggravated offences** (see **hate crime**) and **early release** from **prison** on **home detention curfew**. It also required the creation of local **crime and disorder partnerships**. The **Sentencing Advisory Panel** was created, to assist (originally) the Court of **Appeal** and (following the **Criminal Justice Act 2003**) the **Sentencing Guidelines Council** in framing **sentencing guidelines**.

crime and disorder partnership partnerships that give **local authorities** a responsibility to coordinate the preparation and implementation of strategies to reduce crime and disorder, in cooperation with the **police** and other local agencies (introduced by the **Crime and Disorder Act 1998**).

crime prevention any of a wide variety of interventions aimed at making the commission of crimes less likely, ranging from educational initiatives to the use of closed circuit TV cameras in public areas. The term covers both the precautions taken by individuals and businesses to protect themselves and their property from crime, and the steps taken by **local authorities**, the **police** and other agencies (including **crime and disorder partnerships**) to prevent crime. Individuals and businesses can choose to fit burglar alarms, bolts and bars to property or to employ private security companies; the **police** can decide to give priority to potential cases of repeat victimization or to Neighbourhood Watch and other inter-agency activities.

The 'situational' approach to crime prevention involves 'target-hardening': making the prospective targets of crime, such as homes, less inviting to potential offenders through measures such as the visible introduction of closed-circuit TV cameras, placing security staff in car parks or improving street lighting. At an earlier stage, prevention also includes approaches to architecture and planning aimed at 'designing out crime', for example by ensuring that public areas of housing estates are in view by local householders, the so-called 'eyes on the street'. Crime prevention may also rely on the use of social networks, including neighbourhood watch schemes, **community reparation** projects, measures to support people who are repeatedly the **victims** of crime, and other **Victim Support** projects. Other efforts at 'social crime prevention' include educational programmes with schoolchildren and others, providing activities for young people, publicity programmes and a range of interagency **community** safety initiatives.

A distinction is often made between primary, secondary and tertiary crime prevention. Primary prevention concentrates on the general public or the environment and tends to involve educational and situational work. It attempts to prevent crime by raising awareness and by improving security of homes and business premises. Secondary prevention pays attention to people seen as being at risk of offending or becoming **victim**s, and includes many of the social approaches to crime prevention described above. Tertiary prevention involves working with people who are already identified as **victim**s or offenders to prevent repeat crimes, and is the business of agencies such as **probation**, **Victim Support** and the rest of the voluntary sector as well as the **police** and local authority agencies such as housing departments.

Crawford, A. (1998) *Crime prevention and Community Safety: politics, policies and practices.* London: Longman.

criminal court a court dealing with the prosecution of people accused of committing crimes. Criminal courts deal with behaviour considered harmful to society as a whole, as opposed to civil courts, which deal with legal disputes between one private interest (whether an individual or an organization) and another. The main criminal courts in England and Wales are the **magistrates' courts** and the **Crown Courts**. Magistrates' courts deal with the great majority – over 95 per cent – of criminal cases. They hear the facts of a case, make decisions about guilt or innocence and give **sentence**s. They have the **power** to impose any **sentence** up to the legal maximum for the offence, except that the maximum **prison sentence** they can impose is currently six months for one offence or a total of twelve months for more than one offence. If **magistrate**s consider that an offence requires a greater punishment than they have powers to impose, they commit the defendant to the **Crown Court** for trial by a judge and jury, or for sentencing. Summary offences, such as minor criminal damage can be dealt with only in magistrates' courts, whereas indictable offences (such as murder and rape) can be dealt with only by the Crown Court. Many offences, however, (including theft and burglary) are triable either way. When the defendant pleads not guilty, either the **magistrate**s or defendant can insist on the trial taking place at the **Crown Court**, but the case may be tried in the magistrates' court if both the defendant and magistrates agree. If the defendant indicates a plea of guilty, the trial and conviction will take place at the magistrates' court, but the magistrates may still commit the case to the Crown Court for sentence. The Crown Court hears appeals from magistrates' courts (against conviction, sentence, or both); some appeals on pure points of law may go to the Queen's Bench Division of the **High Court**. Appeals from the **Crown Court** go to the Court of Appeal (Criminal Division), and may ultimately reach the **Supreme Court**. Young offenders under the age of 18 are normally tried in the **youth court**.

Criminal Defence Service (CDS)   the service that replaced the previous system of criminal legal aid, providing defence services for those accused of a criminal offence. Established by the Access to Justice Act 1999, it is run by the **Legal Services Commission**. It provides free legal **advice** to suspects detained and questioned in **police** stations, advice and assistance before trial, and legal representation at trial. It mostly operates by contracting with private practice law firms to provide **Criminal Defence Service**s in a locality. In some places the CDS also employs its own salaried 'public defenders'.

Criminal Justice Act 2003   the Act which provides the legal framework for sentencing in the **criminal courts** in England and Wales (see **sentence**). The Act sets out the purposes of sentencing (for adults) as punishment, crime reduction (via deterrence and reform), the protection of the public, and reparation. Courts are instructed to treat previous convictions as an aggravating factor increasing the seriousness of an offence. But courts should not pass **custodial sentences** unless the current offences are so serious that neither a **fine** alone nor a **community sentence** can be justified for the offence. **Custodial sentence**s should normally be for the shortest term commensurate with the seriousness of the offence. **Community sentence**s must only be passed if warranted by the seriousness of the offence. However, specially **extended sentences** continue to be available for the protection of the public from violent or sexual offenders, and the Act also introduced the indeterminate sentence of **imprisonment for public protection**.

The **Sentencing Guidelines Council** was set up and charged with the responsibility (formerly borne by the Court of Appeal) to issue **sentencing guidelines** for the courts. The Act introduced **community orders**, **suspended sentence orders** and statutory **conditional cautions**, and made provision for the introduction of **custody plus sentence**s. A **mandatory sentence** of a minimum five years' **imprisonment** was introduced for unlawful possession of firearms. The **power** previously held by the Home Secretary to veto the **parole** of mandatory life sentence prisoners was abolished, and statutory guidelines were set for their **tariff** periods.

The Act also introduced 'street **bail**', and made amendments to the law on **police** powers of arrest, stop and search, **detention** and questioning, and transferred the responsibility for deciding whether suspects should be charged with offences from the police to the **Crown Prosecution Service**. Changes were made to rules of evidence to make it easier to use evidence of defendants' past criminal records at their trials, and to the rules on eligibility for jury service. Provision was made for certain Crown Court trials to be held without a jury in complicated fraud cases or where 'jury tampering' is feared (see also **life imprisonment**).

Criminal Justice and Immigration Act 2008   an Act of Parliament that made a number of important reforms to criminal justice and **youth justice**. It sets out the purposes of sentencing in relation to young offenders. The principal aim of the youth justice system remains the prevention of offending and re-offending by young people (as laid down by the **Crime and Disorder Act 1998**), but sentencing courts must also have regards to the welfare of the offender, the punishment of offenders, reform and rehabilitation, the protection of the public, and the making of reparation by offenders. The Act introduced the **youth rehabilitation order**, the **youth conditional caution** and the **youth default order**, and extended the circumstances in which a court may make a **referral order** in respect of a young offender. Changes were made to the rules providing for **sentences of imprisonment for public protection** and **extended sentences** and to the recall to **prison** of inmates who have been granted **early release**. The Act also introduced the **violent offender order** and extended the scope of the **Rehabilitation of Offenders Act 1974** to **cautions**.

Criminal Records Bureau   an executive agency of the **Home Office** that keeps records on all criminal convictions in the UK including records held by the **Department of Health** and the **Department for Children, Schools and Families** where concerns about individuals might have been registered which have not necessarily led to a conviction.

The key objective for the CRB is 'safer recruitment' of staff to agencies working with children, young people and vulnerable adults. Only agencies registered with the CRB can submit a request for a 'disclosure' and such agencies must comply with the CRB's Code of Practice. People who want to work with children, young people and vulnerable adults must reveal all past convictions. In these circumstances the exemptions described in the **Rehabilitation of Offenders Act 1974** do not apply. (See also **databases**.)

crisis intervention   a **social work** approach to episodes that users find extremely difficult or impossible to handle and to understand how services might be organized to help people through such events. A crisis can also be an emergency but often it is not although it may feel that way for a **service user**.

Crises are precipitated by hazardous events, which may be a single catastrophe or a series of mishaps. They may be brought about by something external to the person or by something that appears to be rooted in him or her (although on further investigation an external cause may be revealed, such as an earlier trauma or crisis). The same hazardous event may bring about a crisis for some people but not for others – although some events (for example, the unexpected death of a loved one) bring about a state of crisis in most individuals. The hazardous event is likely to disturb the person's 'balance' and arouse feelings of extreme vulnerability. Most people attempt to deal with such difficulties by employing their usual coping mechanisms. If these coping mechanisms do not help, the person may employ rarely used emergency methods as a measure of desperation. If the problem persists and cannot be alleviated or avoided, the person is likely to enter a period of acute discomfort. This period is thought to be the state of *active crisis*. The interval between the onset of a crisis and its resolution will vary, but the active state of crisis is unlikely to last more than four to six weeks.

As individuals experience a crisis, and during the early stages of conflict resolution, they may be more amenable to help. They may even embrace help that they had earlier rejected. Minimal focused effort at this time, because of emotional accessibility, may bring about a substantial change. As the person recovers, new 'ego sets' and adaptive styles may be learned that may enable the person to cope with future crises. Complete, rather than partial, recovery seems to be dependent upon a 'correct' understanding of the event. Thus, a woman who has been in a violent relationship needs to understand that she was not responsible for the event and that she has been a **victim** of a man's abuse of **power**. Services dealing with crises have to be able to give the time to help people through these events. Intensive support is required, and services need to be organized so that an appropriate response is possible. Rape crisis centres and women's refuges, for example, are in some measure organized in the expectation of crises, but other services clearly are not; for example, children's services are thought to be relatively good at 'rescue' but poor at helping children to heal.

Payne, M. (2005) *Modern Social work Theory*, 3rd edition. London: Macmillan.

critical practice a generic term for a set of practices that draw upon critical theory to promote greater social justice through methods that are inherently transformational. In **social work** it may be viewed as an emancipatory approach that locates individual experience within wider social structures and seeks to challenge oppression through progressive welfare policies and practice.

Critical practice may be situated within a historical context as part of a 'radical tradition' that emerged during the 1970s and reflected a number of trends. First, it was informed by a Marxist critique of traditional welfare that resulted in the publication of various critical texts. Here it was suggested that the care function of **social work** could also be seen as part of the state's control of the working class and the reproduction of relationships that ultimately serve the interests of capital. Second, this critique gave rise to the 'critical social policy' movement in universities and the development of a more theoretical and political approach to the study of the **welfare state**. The third trend concerns the growth of new social movements for change both in Britain as well as other European counties. Such movements placed concerns, for example, about the emancipation of women, **institutional racism**, **discrimination** in **mental health**, disability rights as well as a host of local **community** campaigns on the mainstream political agenda.

The new social movements were very much an urban phenomenon that arose in response to what was seen as the 'crisis of the inner city' and the problems of disinvestment and decline in the old industrial areas. At the local level many small **community** groups were set up to tackle specific issues or areas of unmet community need. Social workers began to embrace community action alongside individual **casework** and this was reflected in the growth of an extensive **community work** literature. Community work and community based **social work**, along with area based initiatives like the national Community Development Projects, became part of the state's response to the challenge of managing 'problematic communities'. Social work became involved in finding new ways to tackle what had been dubbed 'urban deprivation' by the **Home Office**.

Critical practice very much developed out of this broader context, and can therefore be seen as part of a long tradition of promoting radical change at the local level. In particular, working with local people and community groups, to find solutions to the problems of urban **poverty** and conflict during periods of rapid social and economic change.

Although many social work writers adopt a 'critical' perspective, there have been relatively few studies explicitly about critical practice published in the UK. The majority of contemporary writing concerning critical practice has come from Australia and Canada – see suggestions for further reading. Critical practice is informed by a number of theoretical traditions and this makes it a rather slippery concept that is not easy to define. It follows that there are numerous versions of **critical practice** drawing on one or more of the following traditions: Marxism, **feminism**, **postmodernism**, realism, a strengths perspective and constructive approaches, reflecting a very wide field. All draw upon critical theory to develop practices that are progressive and inherently transformational.

Three have been chosen as brief illustrative examples:

i) Critical Marxist feminist practice. **Feminism** has helped to refine classical Marxist theory and its economic base/superstructure model to explain conflict between different social groups, in particular, stressing the need to understand domestic labour and women's caring responsibilities through the concept of **patriarchy** as the basis of oppression within the family. This helped to produce a new perspective committed to greater social justice in society but based upon multiple starting points involving gender, race and other divisions alongside class.

Critical practice in this tradition would be women centred and designed to work with women to raise consciousness, transform oppressive relationships and replace them with more supportive structures. Although it is problematic to over-simplify the category of 'woman' in practice, this approach challenges mainstream services to consider the impact of gender, class and other divisions in work with both men and women.

ii) Critical postmodernist practice. Postmodernists believe that reality is not something fixed and handed down to people but can be shaped by language and different meanings through contemporary speech, relationships and writing. Reality is therefore not just concerned with the external world but reflects our internal ways of thinking. And it is the latter that offers scope for the practitioner to work with **service user**s in new ways – for example, beginning with their own experience and formulating new ways forward that will lead to change.

The belief that 'knowledge is **power**' and constructed by people in local interactions is seen as an important resource in this model of critical practice. If we begin with practitioner/**service user** interactions, the practitioner through critical reflection is able to unpack the dominant language used to explain their problems and the assumptions that sustain them and substitute more enabling language ('can do' rather than 'can't do') as the basis of solutions that empower the **service user**.

iii) Critical realist practice. Critical realism draws upon critical theory and adopts a view of reality that maintains that events in the world exist independent of our knowledge of them. This 'external reality' provides the context for practice and can be approximated in research albeit imperfectly. The central task is to explain the human condition and individual actions in a way that takes into account the influence of social structure. Critical realism seeks to do this by being sensitive to subjective experience but views this within the context of wider structures, conditions and policy that are shaped by the external world. It shares with postmodernism the view that knowledge is socially constructed and, as such, partial, provisional, and encoded with cultural values, but takes a more objective view of reality. Thus, critical realism is quite an ambitious and complex approach that draws upon critical theory and seeks to offer causal explanations for social problems and identify the precise mechanisms that produce **outcomes**.

The practice that follows from this approach attempts to link the wider structural context of problems with outcomes through the conduit of human experience. Participatory methods are preferred drawing upon a variety of knowledge, practice wisdom and theory, set in its appropriate policy and community context. This enables strategies of prevention alongside protection to be deployed, particularly important in high risk areas of childcare and mental health. By integrating methods that are task-centred, grounded in ecological systems theory and community based, hybrid models of critical practice may be produced.

Criticisms of critical practice Various criticisms of critical practice can be made. Firstly, the theoretical foundation is built upon something of a 'shotgun marriage' between different philosophical positions associated with postmodernism, neo-Marxism and feminism. Forming alliances in this way is contested because these perspectives view reality in different ways and make contrasting assumptions about knowledge, thus producing a potentially explosive and incompatible mix. This makes critical practice relatively unstable without some clear safeguards built in, particularly in adopting a coherent view of reality. Secondly, while critical practice aims to be theoretically sophisticated this can lead to a high level of abstraction that appears to be far removed from the world of practice. It must therefore offer the practitioner useable knowledge and concern itself with issues of effectiveness. Thirdly, the different perspectives are likely to view **power** and social change in different ways and these tensions will need to be reconciled.

There are clearly many theoretical obstacles and ideological conflicts that need to be overcome before critical practice can be used effectively. However, if the tensions between the different traditions underpinning critical practice can be reconciled, then this approach has much to offer in terms of emancipation and **empowerment**. Critical practice is therefore much more than a trendy theoretical concept, and aims to achieve concrete improvements in **service** users' lives as well as contributing to greater social justice.

Fook, J. (2002) *Social Work – critical theory and practice*. London: Sage.

Stepney, P. (2006) Mission impossible? Critical practice in social work. *British Journal of Social work*, 36(8): 1289–307.

Crown Court the **criminal court** which deals with trials for the most serious offences (see also **criminal courts**). Where the defendant pleads not guilty, the case is heard by a judge and jury of twelve lay people, with the jury delivering the verdict on the question of guilt and the judge deciding the **sentence**. In guilty plea cases there is no jury and the judge decides on **sentence**. Depending on the seriousness of an offence, the Crown Court is presided over by a **High Court** judge (for the most serious), a circuit judge or a part-time recorder, all of whom are experienced barristers or solicitors. The Crown Court acts as an **appeal** court against both conviction and **sentence** in the **magistrates' court**.

Crown Prosecution Service (CPS)   the national service in England and Wales with responsibility for deciding whether a case should be brought to court and for conducting the prosecution in court. The CPS is headed by the Director of Public Prosecutions and organized in 42 local areas, each headed by a chief Crown Prosecutor. The decision to prosecute taken by the CPS is based on the evidence gathered by the **police** but is independent of them. The decision whether to proceed with a prosecution is governed by the Code for Crown Prosecutors which provides two fundamental tests: (a) the evidential test (on the evidence, is a conviction more likely than not; and (b) the public interest test (is prosecution in the public interest)? Following the **Criminal Justice Act 2003** the CPS has assumed the responsibility (formerly borne by the **police**) of deciding whether suspected offenders should be charged with offences. The CPS also makes recommendations to courts as to whether defendants should be **remanded** on **bail** or in **custody**.

curfew order   an order requiring a person or group of people to remain at home during specified hours. If applied to individuals, curfews are usually enforced by **electronic monitoring**. In Britain the courts were first given **power** to impose curfews in the form of 'night restriction requirements' attached to **supervision orders** for young offenders, introduced by the Criminal Justice Act 1982 (though without any provision for **electronic monitoring**). In 1989 a pilot experiment was attempted (with limited success) whereby courts in certain areas attached curfew requirements to **remands** on **bail**, monitored electronically. The Criminal Justice Act 1991 introduced the curfew order (with electronic monitoring) as a court **sentence**. Curfews of between 2 and 12 hours per day can now be imposed as requirements of **community orders** or **youth rehabilitation orders**. Numerically, however, by far the most extensive application of curfews on individuals is in the form of **home detention curfew**, whereby inmates serving sentences of **imprisonment** may be granted a period of **early release** with a curfew of at least 9 (typically 12) hours per day.

Curfews (not electronically monitored) may also be imposed on young people generally in particular localities. The **Crime and Disorder Act 1998** enabled **local authorities** to ban all children under 10 years of age (later raised to 16) from being in streets and other public places at night unless accompanied by a responsible adult. Individual young people aged up to 17 can also be made subject to curfews under the Powers of **Criminal Court**s (Sentencing) Act 2000. These can last up to 6 months, for up to 12 hours per day, and may be combined with electronic monitoring, which requires the young person to wear an electronic 'tag'. Where the young person is under 16, courts are required to obtain information about the family circumstances and the likely impact of such an order upon the family, usually by means of a **pre-sentence report**.

custodial sentence a **sentence** which involves the imposition of **custody** on the offender, including **imprisonment, detention and training order, detention in a young offender institution**. Courts are required by the **Criminal Justice Act 2003** to pass custodial **sentence**s only if the current offences are so serious that neither a **fine** alone nor a **community sentence** can be justified for the offence. Custodial sentences should normally be for the shortest term commensurate with the seriousness of the offence.

custody confinement in a **prison** or similar institution, whether following a **custodial sentence** or on **remand**. The term also includes being held by the **police** following arrest and/or charge. Custody for adults takes the form of prison (see also **imprisonment**), while young offenders are held in a range of secure institutions (see **secure estate**).

custody plus a **sentence** intended to replace **prison sentences** of up to 12 months, consisting of between 2 and 13 weeks in **prison** plus a compulsory period of at least 26 weeks on **licence** in the **community** (total maximum 51 weeks) combined with requirements similar to those which may form part of a **community order**. The **Criminal Justice Act 2003** made provision for the introduction of custody plus, but to date the provision has not been implemented.

cycle of change a model of behavioural change that identifies five stages of a potential 'change cycle'. Each stage of the cycle identifies methods of intervention that have been found to be useful with problems that have hitherto been found to be intractable. The model has been demonstrably useful with substance abuse and alcohol problems, smoking and other health related issues, but the 'method' has potential uses with a wide range of problems including, for example, offending behaviour and women who fail to leave abusive partners after trying to do so, perhaps several times over.

The five stages that constitute this model are precontemplation, contemplation, action, maintenance and, possibly, lapse or even relapse.

In the first stage of precontemplation the **service user** may not accept that they have a problem and may be 'in denial'. At this stage they are not persuaded that there is a need to change or that change may be beneficial for their **wellbeing**. In the contemplative stage the **service user** may still be ambivalent about whether they want to change their behaviour, but it is likely that they are discomforted about some of the negative aspects of their current circumstances. When action is embraced the **service user** prepares for change and then begins to implement change in a more or less systematic way with some enthusiasm. At the maintenance stage some substantial measure of the new behaviour has become integrated into the service user's way of life. Change can become permanent at this stage. In these circumstances the service user may leave the cycle and not return if they can continue the 'new way of life' without lapsing. However, some either lapse for a short time before entering the cycle again or relapse entirely embracing the earlier behaviour(s). Both lapse and relapse are regarded as integral to the cycle of change and as likely for many service users. Neither, however, should be regarded as ultimate failure; both may simply be an acknowledgement that change in relation to some chronic problems is very hard to achieve and that several attempts may be necessary before maintenance is finally achieved.

Social workers try to support service users in different ways according to the stage they think the service user is engaged with or 'is at'. At the precontemplation stage social workers will be concerned to build rapport with a service user and may begin to explore the 'problematic behaviours' in a *non-judgmental way*. At the contemplation stage a more active exploration of the positive and negative aspects of the behaviour might be undertaken. Social workers might need to be convinced that a service user is really engaged with trying to understand the nature of their problem. So, before a service user is accepted onto an alcoholics' recovery programme, for example, they may be asked to keep a diary of current drinking habits together with the service user's observations of how drinking behaviour affects social functioning. Failure to collect this kind of information may constitute evidence of the service user's lack of motivation to change at this point. Once the service user has moved into the action phase, services tend to offer support through **group work** activities or through tailored individual counselling or both. The action phase may also begin with a detoxification programme which can be undertaken in a medical residential facility if shock at withdrawal from a drug is thought possible or at the **service user**'s home if this is thought to be feasible. Easy access to **advice** and support is thought to be crucial for service users particularly in the early stages of the action phase. Helplines are often used to provide such support.

Prochaska and DiClemente argue that the cycle seems to work better with behaviours that are related to immediate and tangible stress such as work related problems or say excessive caring responsibilities; and harder with behaviours that have their origins in very negative thought patterns, enduring relationship and family conflicts or in a very unhappy and abusive **childhood**. Very deep-rooted problems may require intensive and specialist psychotherapeutic interventions in addition to the support that might be offered by social workers.

Prochaska, J. and DiClemente, C. (1984) *The Trans-theoretical Approach: crossing traditional boundaries of therapy.* Homewood, Illinois: Dow-Jones Irwin.

cycle of deprivation an explanation for the persistence of **poverty** that focuses on how attitudes, **values** and behaviours are passed on from one generation to the next, mainly through the family but also through communities.

The notion of the cycle of deprivation achieved considerable political prominence at the hands of Keith Joseph, Minister for Social Services, in 1972. It is closely linked to the theories of the culture of poverty, developed in the 1960s by, among others, the North American anthropologist Oscar Lewis, the concept of the **underclass** and some current ideas about **social exclusion**. Governments in Britain and the United States, particularly in the 1960s and 1970s, were influenced by ideas that have roots in the concept of a cycle of deprivation. Attempts to tackle urban poverty, especially in inner-city areas, have often focused upon early education (for example, Educational Priority Areas, pre-school provision and the US Head Start programme and most recently in Britain with the ambitious **Sure Start** programme) in an attempt to improve the life chances of young children from poor homes. Critics of these schemes have argued that wider forces, such as social class, **racism** and gender stratification (and indeed capitalism in general), cannot be so easily overcome.

Oscar Lewis's notion of a culture of poverty conceptualized the existence of poor people in many societies with the suggestion that people living in long-term poverty develop particular ways of coping with life, passing that way of life on to future generations. The term is closely allied to the ideas of a cycle of deprivation, **underclass** and **social exclusion**. Lewis believed that his researches in both developing and advanced capitalist societies revealed a complex culture of interlocking behaviours, beliefs and attitudes that characterize poor people. He found that poor people had a strong present time orientation, valued the cult of machismo, developed essentially matriarchal family structures and had a sense of fatalism. He argued that there might be some minor variations in how these cultural traits were presented in any society but all these traits, he claimed, appeared to be widespread features of the lives of poor people.

Additionally, the inability of the poor to become involved in institutions such as trade unions, political parties and 'normal' economic activity was thought to add to their marginality and to confirm their membership of an **underclass**. Lewis has been criticized because there is a sense in which he seems to suggest that the poor are responsible for their own poverty. If culture is a set of responses for coping with immediate circumstances, the critical issue is how much those attitudes and values rooted in the experience of poverty may prevent a person or **community** from responding to improved circumstances or initiatives to develop their communities. Lewis has it that the culture of poverty will inhibit anti-**poverty** strategies, unless those strategies explicitly address the attitudes, **values** and behaviours of the poor. Critics of Lewis have argued that if life chances are significantly improved for poor people, they will quickly recognize and respond to the new and more positive environment.

Many professionals working in social welfare have been dismayed at what they perceive as the inability of the poor to respond to help offered. Others take the view that social welfare workers (including social workers), in the main, have little to offer poor people in relation to an improvement in life chances. On the contrary, most social welfare workers, they argue, implicitly endorse the *status quo* and in that respect become allied with the forces of conservatism. Community development programmes, designed to improve the lot of poor communities, have been criticized because they do not acknowledge the importance of structural inequality, or attempt to confront it in any meaningful way and therefore must be regarded as superficial in both their objectives and achievements. Although the idea of the culture of poverty is perceived as flawed by its critics, its influence is still acknowledged as substantial. Many social workers probably see at least some individuals, families and communities in terms that imply a view of poverty consistent with that of Oscar Lewis's notion of a culture of poverty. Radical theorists however argue that confronting the culture of poverty needs to attract more substantial resources and that those resources need to be available for the long haul and not just a year or two. Only then can structural inequality be 'taken on' in any meaningful way. In this context the phrase 'inter-generational poverty' has been widely accepted as a better way of describing how and why poverty persists within a family.

Pierson, J. (2010) *Tackling Social exclusion*, 2nd edition. Abingdon: Routledge.

D d

dangerousness the potential to cause physical or psychological harm to others and in **social work** generally used in relation to **sex offender**s, perpetrators of family violence and some psychiatric patients.

The term now has wide application but was first used regularly in the courts in relation to the offender sections of the **Mental Health Act 1983**, referring to some people who are convicted of an offence and who are also mentally disordered (see **mentally disordered offenders**). If the court considers, on psychiatric evidence, that a person is 'dangerous', he or she will be sent to a special hospital offering secure psychiatric provision. He or she will also be placed on a restriction order under the Act and detained until considered by psychiatrists to be no longer dangerous. Psychiatrists are often called on by the courts to give testimony on the degree of dangerousness of a particular offender.

The concept is used also in relation to perpetrators of family violence who may be abusing children or vulnerable relations. 'Dangerous families' are those in which the pattern of interaction between partners, the degree of violence and conflict or the presence of an unstable and aggressive individual exposes the children of that family to physical harm. Social workers try to gauge the potential for causing physical or psychological harm in the behaviour of both individuals and families (see **risk assessment**). They do this in a number of situations, such as with an older person who may have been assaulted or a child who may have been sexually abused. **Social work** has attempted to gauge the 'dangerousness' of an abuser more accurately by developing 'indicators' such as psychological portraits of **child abuser**s and of partners who collude in the abusive acts.

The **Criminal Justice Act 2003** also draws on the concept of dangerousness. That Act created new custodial sentencing options for courts where the person is convicted of one of a range of sexual or violent offences *and* the court considers the offender to be 'dangerous', that is there would be a significant risk of serious harm to the public through further specified offences if a **custodial sentence** were not imposed. The concept of dangerousness has many critics. One argument is that it is used in law and medicine as both have come to play an intertwined role in a penal system that increasingly makes judgements on the criminal rather than the crime. Standard psychiatric diagnoses in particular lack reliability and the results of research in predicting dangerousness raises serious questions about the capacity of psychiatrists to predict the behaviour of specific individuals. In relation to working with children critics have also pointed out that focusing on dangerousness reflects a drift from working toward broad **outcomes** of child **wellbeing** to a narrower focus on risk. Under the dominance of dangerousness the **social work** role becomes more protective by swiftly distinguishing and removing children from the truly dangerous families as opposed to those that are not so dangerous, with which children are, presumably, safe. In working with people defined as 'dangerous' by the courts or other professionals, practitioners need to be aware of the public **stereotype**s of dangerousness – how these are based on images of wild animals and of badness fixed in the person's character. These can lead to perceptions of the person's character being wildly exaggerated, which results in the worker feeling extremely anxious. This in turn makes the building of a relationship or the carrying out of **social work** tasks such as **assessment** highly fraught. Finally some have now included the behaviour of social workers themselves as being capable of dangerousness. Dangerous practice includes taking unacceptable risks, bowing to pressures from aggressive or violent **service user**s or their carers or of claiming to practise in an ethnically sensitive way and in fact ignoring child or adult protection issues.

McCallum, D. (2001) *Personality and Dangerousness: genealogies of antisocial personality disorder.* Cambridge: Cambridge University Press.

databases stores of information concerning particular individuals usually, but not necessarily, kept on computerized systems.

Social workers have increasingly to use various databases in their practice and, in addition, be familiar with other databases that might either affect them personally or the circumstances of **service user**s. The most important databases in this context appear to be the **Criminal Records Bureau**, the two databases held by the **Independent Safeguarding Authority** regarding people considered unsuitable for working with children and vulnerable adults, the **NHS** database containing medical records, Contactpoint (a national database of all children including biographical and contact information and their involvement with particular public services), the **common assessment framework for children**, ONSET (the **Home Office**'s database about children thought likely to offend in the future), the National Pupil Database (containing a wide range of material on school performance, attendance, behaviour and family circumstances), the National DNA Database and finally the proposed new National Identity Register.

Civil rights agencies such as Liberty have highlighted a number of related concerns about the protection of privacy, the retention of information that has been found to be inaccurate or no longer relevant, the security of data and whether it is actually 'fit for purpose'. In recent years there have been well-publicized 'leaks' of sensitive data with officials misplacing IT software, data being sent electronically without being encrypted and evidence of people having access to databases who should not have. A well-researched report, Database State, published in 2009, has also argued that although all of these IT systems have a purpose and rationale that have a measure of public and political support, many of them are probably illegal under human rights and data protection law. In this respect, it is argued, the UK is out of line with many other advanced societies that tend to keep sensitive material in local databases apart from exceptional circumstances. Further the report claims that 'the benefits of data sharing are often either illusory or overstated and that such sharing has the potential, because of insecurity, to harm the vulnerable and increase **discrimination** and stigmatization'.

It should be the responsibility of social workers to familiarize themselves with every database that they use and to satisfy themselves as to its legality. In addition, social workers need to satisfy themselves that **service user**s' interests are being upheld and that they will not be made additionally vulnerable. Key issues for **service user**s (where they might expect support from social workers) include the need to be informed if information about them is held on databases, of their rights in relation to particular databases and of how to access personal material about themselves especially where they wish to contest information recorded there. See also **Safeguarding Vulnerable Groups Act 2006, Data Protection Act 1998**.

Anderson, R., Brown, I., Dowty, T., Inglesant, P., Heath, W. and Sasse, A. (2009) *Database State*. London: Joseph Rowntree Reform Trust.

Data Protection Act 1998 legislation that regulates the way information is collected, stored, used, and shared by data users and others, including social services and welfare agencies. It implements provisions in EC Directive 95/46 on the protection of individuals with regard to the processing of personal data. The Act is particularly concerned with personal data. 'Sensitive personal data', which includes information as to a person's physical or **mental health** or condition, sexual life, the commission or alleged commission of any offence, or proceedings for alleged offences, is particularly relevant to **social work** practitioners: such data is subject to special protection measures.

The Act requires all organizations handling personal information to comply with requirements regarding privacy and disclosure. It also gives individuals the right to know what information is held about them. It provides a framework to ensure that personal information is handled properly. Broadly, any individual or organization processing personal information must comply with eight principles which require that personal information is:

1. fairly and lawfully processed; in particular, personal data may not be processed unless at least one of the stipulated conditions in the Act has been satisfied; and in the case of sensitive personal data at least one of the additional conditions imposed by Schedule 3 to the Act must have been satisfied;

2. only obtained for one or more specified, lawful purposes; it cannot be further processed, having been obtained, in any manner that is incompatible with that purpose, or purposes;

3. 'adequate, relevant and not excessive' in relation to the purpose for which it is processed;

4. accurate and, where necessary, kept up to date;

5. not kept for longer than is necessary for the designated purpose or those purposes;

6. processed in accordance with the rights of data subjects under the legislation;

7. protected against unauthorized or unlawful processing, and against accidental **loss**, destruction, or damage;

8. not be transferred to a country or territory outside the European Economic Area unless that country or territory ensures an adequate level of protection for the rights and freedoms of data subjects in relation to the processing of personal data.

Accessing personal information. Individuals have the right to find out what personal information is held on computer systems and in most kinds of paper records. This can be done by making a subject access request. Subject to some important exceptions, a person is entitled to be informed by data controllers whether personal data of which that individual is the 'data subject' are being processed. If so, she or he is entitled to be given a description of the data; the purposes for which they are being or are to be processed; and the recipients or classes of recipients to whom they are or may be disclosed. There are limitations on the scope of the duty to supply information, for example where a data controller cannot comply with the request without disclosing information relating to another individual who can be identified from that information, he is not obliged to comply with the request (unless the other individual has consented to the disclosure of the information to the person making the request, or it is reasonable to comply with the request without the consent of that other person). Applicants can be assisted by the Information Commissioner's Office, for example through informal and formal complaints processes. If necessary, enforcement action can be taken. The Information Commissioner provides guidance on compliance, 'good practice notes', and codes of practice.

Particular Acts may also provide for access to information, and government departments may operate their own arrangements enabling people to access information held about them. In the areas of health and **social care**, for example, the **Department of Health** operates an independent internal complaint process. If applicants are dissatisfied with the outcome of their request for information they can seek to resolve the issue by initiating the complaints process, and complaining about the 'initial response' to their request. This will trigger 'a full reconsideration of the handling of the case', as well as a 'final decision'. If the complaint is unsuccessful, the applicant will be informed of his or her right to complain to the Information Commissioner.

Special provisions operate in relation to health, education and **social work**. In particular, section 30 of the 1998 Act enables the Secretary of State, by order, to exempt from the subject information provisions (or modify those provisions) in relation to personal data consisting of information as to the physical or **mental health** or condition of the data subject. Among other things, she may make exemptions or modify provisions relating to people who are or have been school pupils; information processed by government departments, **local authorities**, or voluntary organizations designated by or under the order, and 'processed in the course of, or for the purposes of, carrying out social work in relation to the data subject or other individuals'.

Sharing information is the subject of important 'guidance' in key areas of social work. For example, guidance has been developed for workers in the **youth justice** system to try to secure improved **outcomes** for children and young people. This has necessitated even greater care to be taken, particularly if information needed for effective decision-making and **assessment** is held by other agencies. Access to accurate and up-to-date information is essential, and this may necessitate sharing information appropriately to help to reduce the risk of crime and harm to children and others. Among other things, guidance deals with statutory and non-statutory sources of law on information-sharing and **confidentiality**, including the common law duty of confidentiality (where there is a confidentiality relationship, perhaps based on a spousal or other familial link that may operate to require a recipient of information to retain it without passing it on to a third party unless the person to whom the duty is owed has given consent to pass it on, or there is an overriding public interest that authorizes disclosure. Exceptionally, and assisted by relevant 'guidance', disclosure may help to prevent the person who gave the information, or someone else, suffering harm.

day care/services a variety of caring facilities for people in need who are still living predominantly in their own homes.

Day services have been devised for virtually all client groups where people are regarded as at risk or have conditions or problems that would benefit from **contact** with others. Previously known as 'day care', there has been a focus on monitoring, rehabilitation, giving carers a break and providing social contact for people who otherwise might be socially isolated. Day services can be found in statutory, voluntary and private agencies. Most often, activities still take place in specific premises known as 'day centres', although some day services are run alongside residential provision such as residential homes for **older people** and hospices. Activities taking place in day services tend to reflect the differing objectives of these services and the **service user** group for which the service is provided. Some day services are specialized, for example those focusing on the development of **independent living** skills (and even modest projects where people are employed in what were previously called adult training centres) for people with **learning disability**. Some day centres, previously called adult training centres, offer small scale projects where learning-disabled people are actually employed in simple assembly projects or craft activities where a modest wage might be earned. Other day centres may attempt to meet the needs of all service user groups. Day services may also be provided for people with enduring **mental health problems**, people with terminal conditions, **older people**, disabled children and adults, and pre-school children. 'Day care' has been an important component of **community care** provision. However, recent policy, particularly in respect of learning disability, has referred to 'day services' rather than 'care' or adult training centres. The modernization of day services has resulted in fewer services being delivered exclusively on a segregated site, and in **service user**s being encouraged to use mainstream facilities with the support of day services staff.

deaf-blind being both deaf and blind; this refers both to people who were born with one or more sensory **impairment** and to those who become deaf and/or blind through illness, injury or ageing.

In practice, the term 'deaf-blind' is used interchangeably with 'dual sensory impairment'. Recognition of a person as deaf-blind does not require clinical diagnosis of total blindness and total deafness. There may a degree of residual vision and/or hearing. The **Department of Health** stresses that ability to function can vary and that people whose 'combined sight and hearing impairment cause(s) difficulties with **communication**, access to information and **mobility**' can be regarded as deaf-blind. Deaf-blind people communicate in a range of ways, depending on preference and any abilities developed before the onset of acquired dual impairment. Some may use methods adopted by blind or deaf people, while others may use methods based on touch such as the Deaf-blind Manual Alphabet.

In 2001, the Department of Health estimated the prevalence of deaf-blindness to be at least 40 people per 100,000 population, but those **local authorities** that have made a determined effort to identify deaf-blind people have found prevalence rates of over three times that figure. Although there are deaf-blind people of all ages, the charity Sense estimates that about 90 per cent are aged over 75 and have acquired rather than congenital impairments. The causes of deaf-blindness among children have changed since the 1950s, when rubella was the most common cause. Vaccination has greatly reduced the number of children affected in this way. Now, the majority of children who are congenitally deaf-blind also have other serious impairments.

There is no form of registration particular to deaf-blindness, and, until 2001, no formal system for **recording** the identity and numbers of deaf-blind people. Deaf-blind children and adults are often not identified or offered appropriate services by **local authorities**. Many are not recognized as deaf-blind, as staff awareness of deaf-blindness can be 'masked' by other impairments that are regarded as the primary reasons for service provision. In particular, deaf-blindness is often overlooked in **older people**, possibly due to assumptions that sensory **impairment** is something to be expected in later life. The impact of this lack of access to appropriate services on people's lives and health has been documented by recent research. Due to the barriers deaf-blind people experience in relation to communication, substantial support is needed in order to maintain autonomy and achieve an acceptable level of **participation** on the **community**. The Department of Health has acknowledged that because of the organizational division between adults and children's services, and the development of separate teams for **service user** groups within adult services, older people, people with **learning disability** and children are less likely to be referred to specialists in sensory services. However, mainstream services or those for either deaf or blind people may not be suitable.

In 2001 the Department of Health issued statutory guidance requiring local authorities to 'identify, make contact with and keep a record of deaf-blind people in their catchment area'. The guidance aimed to increase the involvement of specialist staff in assessments under the Children Act and community care legislation, and to provide more widespread access to trained one-to-one support workers when needed. Research carried out in 2007 by the **charity** Sense indicated variability in the way that local authorities have been implementing the guidance, and that in some cases services had actually deteriorated since 2006, when the guidance expired. The statutory guidance was reissued in 2009, and requires local authorities to identify deaf-blind people in their areas, to ensure assessments are carried out by specialist workers, provide appropriate services (including skilled one-to-one support where necessary), provide information in a suitable format, and ensure that a senior manager is given responsibility for deaf-blind services. The Department of Health has indicated that this time the guidance will not have a cancellation date.

deaf/Deaf people   *deaf* – the audiological condition of not hearing; *Deaf people* – those who identify themselves as part of a linguistic and cultural minority group. (The lower- and upper-case d/D is used in the USA and Britain to make this distinction.)

A construction of deafness from the perspective of Deaf people, based on their experiences in a predominantly 'hearing' society, is in the early stages of articulation. This perspective describes a group of people who share a common language, that is, sign language (see **British Sign Language**), and whose culture is historically created and transmitted across generations. Being Deaf usually means the person has a hearing **loss**, but the degree of **loss** is not in itself a criterion for being Deaf. There is also the common notion of deafness as a sensory **impairment**, that is, lack of hearing. This view of deafness as a physical deficit has dominated most professional discourses (such as medical, audiological, educational and welfare services) and lay discourses (such as film and fiction). Deafness is seen as a deviation from the so-called 'normal healthy state', and emphasis is placed on **normalization** and cure. In psychology, deafness has been seen as a defining characteristic of a Deaf person. The two main models of deafness are therefore the clinical / pathological model, which focuses predominantly on audiological factors, and the cultural model, which emphasizes social factors.

Social work with Deaf people has its origins in the missions or welfare societies that were established for social and religious purposes throughout Britain during the 19th century. In common with many social welfare services, the missions were church-based organizations concerned with the religious and moral affairs of Deaf people. These organizations were developed initially by people who had some **contact** with Deaf people but were rarely Deaf themselves. Their motivation was compassion, charitable concern and a response to Deaf people's desire to meet together. As the societies developed and became more complex, they became the centre for social, educational and vocational activity for Deaf people. A person, usually male, was appointed to carry the responsibility of organizing activities and fund-raising. This person was the missioner, the predecessor of the social worker with Deaf people. The work of the missioners included visiting and advising, job-finding and interpreting, while at the same time managing and organizing the society. They concentrated on adult Deaf people who were users of sign language. In the 1920s in-service training was offered to people working in the societies, a large part of which was the development of sign language and interpreting skills. Missioners were involved in the daily life of Deaf people, available day and night for preaching or interpreting at church services, and interpreting at job interviews and doctors' appointments. They had the opportunity to develop sign-language skills and to understand Deaf culture in a way that is perhaps unavailable to some present-day social workers with Deaf people. Some Deaf people view the time of the missioner positively, as they had ready access to sources of help, while others see it as a time of oppression when the missioners' involvement in so many aspects of Deaf people's lives created dependency on the mission.

The services of the missions constitute almost the only welfare service provision for adult Deaf people for over a century. The first statutory funding became available in 1933, and services became mandatory in 1960 following the Younghusband Report in 1959. From this time, **local authorities** took a more direct interest in the welfare of Deaf people by funding either their own services or those of a voluntary agency.

The majority of social workers with Deaf people are employed by local authorities offering direct services, and a minority of workers are located in voluntary organizations that provide services on behalf of their local authority. Despite reports highlighting the need for skilled workers, social workers with Deaf people are less likely than their generic colleagues to have a social work qualification. Even more rarely do they have the dual qualification of basic social work and a post-qualifying certificate in the specialism. Only a small percentage of social workers have the requisite signing skills to practise, as recommended by the Social Services Inspectorate report *Say It Again* (1988). In some local authorities there are no services at all, with posts vacant or filled by unqualified people. About 20 per cent of social workers with Deaf people are deaf themselves. It has been argued that section 11 funding (Local Government Act 1966) could be used to ensure that posts are designed for Deaf people themselves to work with their own **community** group. Yet this would require a shift in thinking on the part of the policymakers towards the view of Deaf people as a cultural minority group rather than as disabled (that is, dependent). Similarly, the numbers of Black social workers with Deaf people and Black Deaf social workers are small. The city of Bradford has been referred to as an example of emerging good practice – it employs an **Asian** social worker to work with Asian Deaf families. Overall, however, there has been a decline in the provision of specialist social workers employed to work with Deaf people, as there has been a move towards setting up separate interpreting services and employing technical officers to deal with environmental equipment.

Social services departments provide services to all 'hearing-impaired' people, which includes people who are audiologically deaf but do not identify with Deaf culture. Greater emphasis may be placed on their actual hearing **loss**, adjustment to it or management of it when referral is made to social services. Some local authorities and their agents' services for Deaf people are provided by social workers with Deaf people who have particular information and knowledge about deafness, but others are not. This results in a distinction between service providers who are employed to work bilingually and trans-culturally with people from a minority group – that is, Deaf people – and mainstream social workers who, with information and appropriate **communication** skills, work with people whose hearing is 'impaired', that is, deaf people. However, both Deaf and deaf people do share experiences of oppression and **discrimination** in a society that seeks to 'normalize' those who are seen as 'deficient' (see also **disability**, **impairment**).

Social workers with Deaf people have inherited the role of the missioners, and whether they should or should not interpret is probably the single biggest issue of debate in services to Deaf people. That interpreters are required is not in question, but responsibility for the funding and provision of such services is. Where social workers with Deaf people work in isolation, are 'hearing' people and have sign language skills, they have often been expected, by the employing body and by Deaf **service user**s in that area, to carry the interpreting role. Some have done this willingly and have not accepted the argument that a social work role is, in the main, in conflict with that of an interpreter. For example, interpreters follow a code of practice that includes not offering personal opinions or advice and keeping all matters confidential, which would be inappropriate for a social worker to adhere to. It has been argued that combining the social work and interpreting roles actually oppresses Deaf people by denying their rights of 'self-determination, independence, choice and equality'. Some local authorities, responding to opinion from both service user groups and some service providers, recognized the need for separate interpreting services and are acting accordingly. The provision of equipment for daily living has been another task that social workers with Deaf people have traditionally undertaken. It is an important service in terms of quality of life for service users, but because of the high demand, it is also very time consuming. In many areas, this is now being undertaken by technical officers as part of the overall service offered to Deaf people.

So far reference has predominantly been made to Deaf people – those who, regardless of their degree or age of onset of hearing loss, identify with Deaf culture and use British Sign Language. Such people are frequently referred to in social services departments as 'profoundly, pre-lingually deaf' or 'deaf without speech'. These categorizations are misleading and often inaccurate, but they reflect the model of deafness predominating in service provision, namely the medical model of deafness as a deficit rather than the recognition of Deaf people as a minority group. As service users, Deaf people may present the same problems as other **service user**s, including childcare issues, debt or **housing problems**, and mental ill-health, which are not directly related to their 'hearing **loss**' but will be influenced by the fact that they are from a minority group in a society that does not widely recognize sign language and de**values** the experience of Deaf people.

Although Deaf people share experiences around 'being Deaf', the Deaf 'community' also reflects the wide variety of human beliefs, lifestyles and attitudes. Deaf people are therefore of all ages and ethnic origins, male, female, gay/lesbian, bisexual, heterosexual and mentally or physically disabled. Prejudice is evident in the Deaf community as in any other, and some Deaf people are marginalized and have different experiences of using social services. For example, from a study of the experiences of both Deaf/deaf people from ethnic-minority groups, it was concluded that Black Deaf people are isolated and generally receive poor services. Other reports suggest the same is also true for deaf-blind people (see also deaf-blind).

Deaf people are not often born into Deaf culture but rather they acquire it, as the majority of Deaf people have hearing parents and families. As such, it is difficult to describe a deaf child as culturally Deaf before he or she has developed a self-identity as a Deaf person by mixing with other Deaf people, using sign language, etc. Given the general lack of awareness about Deaf issues, parents sometimes find it difficult to take on board the idea that their child will become a Deaf adult. Also, the place of sign language and the role of Deaf people in the education of deaf children are part of an ongoing controversial debate that again highlights the different ways of understanding deafness. These issues have influenced the provision of social work services to deaf children and their families.

Ladd, P. (2003) *Understanding Deaf Culture: in Search of Deafhood.* Clevedon: Multilingual Matters.

death and dying the permanent end of life in a person and the last stages of a life. Given the inevitability of death, individuals who know that they are dying and social workers involved with them and their families may try to work towards bringing about a 'good death'. What constitutes a good death is of course a matter for debate. Many people seem to be preoccupied not just with death itself but also about the process of dying. A life ending without a lot of pain is one clear objective; thus **palliative care**, sometimes in a **hospice** setting, has become a key feature of direct work with dying people with a clear focus upon the management of pain and the enhancement of a feeling of **wellbeing** as circumstances allow. Other aspects of a satisfactory death might include trying to deal with problems that are of significance to the dying person such as unresolved problems in close relationships or dealing with issues related to economic matters for dependants.

It is known that some people when they have an incurable disease where there is great pain, or their dependence on others is likely to be substantial, consider **euthanasia** or they issue other instructions to caring and medical staff such as 'do not resuscitate' or a living will that makes clear that doctors should not continue with their efforts if there is little chance of recovery. They take the view that they have a right to die when and in a manner of their choosing. Some others oppose this view, claiming that life and its cessation is a matter for God. In this context there may be a counselling role for social workers to ensure that people are making informed decisions free from any external coercion.

Attitudes to **suicide** too are similarly wide ranging because it can seem to embrace extreme social solidarity as with **suicide** bombers or a way out of an unbearably difficult and painful life; although most faiths seem to discourage it if not explicitly disapprove of it. The **social work** task here is likely to be about supporting the people who are close to the person who has ended their own lives or helping those whose attempts to end their lives has failed.

Kubler Ross has been an influential thinker in relation to her analysis of how people respond when they learn that they have a terminal illness. The five stages that she identified seem to involve an initial denial (there must be some kind of mistake or maybe the tests were not conclusive); second, a stage of being very angry or a feeling that this '**sentence**' is wholly unjust (why do I have to die? I have always tried to lead a healthy life); a third stage might include some bargaining or negotiating, although implying some kind of acceptance (if I can only see another Christmas or survive long enough to see my first grandchild); fourth, a depressive stage of withdrawal, of having reclusive inclinations; and finally a kind of acceptance that might entail preparation for death or dealing with important issues having accepted the inevitable. Although Kubler Ross later acknowledged that not everyone proceeds through the five stages of coming to terms with imminent death, she claimed that many people do or that they experience at least some of these stages although not necessarily in the order specified. Later she claimed that these stages might also be useful in understanding personal responses to **loss** in a more general sense – **loss** of a loved one or of, perhaps, a social status attached to some occupation or member of a **community** or the refugee in a strange land grieving for their homeland and lost relatives.

Social work with the dying is a significant specialism within interdisciplinary **palliative care** teams that might operate in hospitals, hospices or in outreach services where people opt to stay in their own homes. See also **bereavement and grief**, **euthanasia**, **loss**, **palliative care**.

Earle, S., Komaromy, C. and Bartholomew, C. (eds) (2009) *Death and Dying: a reader*. London: Sage.

Kubler Ross, E. (2008) *On Death and Dying*. London: Routledge.

debt advice (money advice) **advice** for people with financial difficulties, typically including advice on how to maximize income, how to manage debt and how to budget, as well as the money adviser acting as the person's advocate with creditors and the courts.

Maximizing income (see also **income maximization**) can include helping people to ensure that they have the best tax arrangements for their circumstances, that they are claiming all the state benefits to which they are entitled, that claims are backdated where feasible and that their wages or salaries are as high as possible (that employers are paying the statutory minimum wage for example).

In addition, some advisers try to raise lump sums to alleviate immediate problems or pressing debts, sometimes from statutory sources, for example a claim for a **community care** grant – see **welfare rights (8)** – from the Benefits Agency and sometimes from charitable or other sources.

Maximizing income will often include 'better-off' calculations so that people can make considered judgements about whether work will pay enough or whether they will maintain a better standard of living by relying on welfare benefits.

Debt in itself does not constitute a problem as long as debtors can manage their contractual obligations to repay a creditor through agreed arrangements. It is default debt that is the problem, that is, a situation of not being able to honour contractual obligations. The management of default debt is a complex process that, first, entails working out detailed income and expenditure accounts in order to determine what sums, if any, can be used to deal with debts. In this context, it is usual to distinguish between priority and non-priority debt (priority debts are those that could ultimately entail **imprisonment**, repossession of property or disconnection), although the consumers may have their own views on which are important. There are some young men, for example, who might value a car above a home.

The next stage involves negotiating arrangements with creditors that are practicable for the debtor and are seen as sensible and fair by the creditors. In some cases it may be possible to challenge the legitimacy of a debt (for example, is it really owed by the person or is it their ex-partner's debt?) or to get a debt apportioned between people held to be jointly responsible for it.

In other cases, non-priority debts may be written off by a creditor if the debtor has no long-term prospect of realistically dealing with them. Other strategies include trying to make informal arrangements with creditors to deal with default debt in the short or long term, having periods when payments might be suspended, restructuring debts or payment periods or more formal arrangements through the courts of administration orders, individual voluntary arrangements or even bankruptcy. Administration Orders (see also **Debt Relief Orders**) can be useful devices for people with multiple non-priority debts (see relevant sections for more details).

Budgeting entails giving **advice** about the relative costs of fuel and how fuel might be used more efficiently, information on cheaper sources of food or on the nutritional value of cheaper foods, **advice** on cheaper sources of credit or help in reflecting on the economic costs of lifestyles. Frequently, budgeting includes advising consumers on how expenditure might be managed, where, for example, some bills are to be met weekly, some monthly and others at less frequent intervals. For those people who find it difficult to budget and who have a track record of having essential services disconnected or eviction from their home threatened, other tactics such as having fuels and rent paid direct by the Benefits Agency might be usefully considered.

To be an effective debt adviser involves the ability to unravel complex financial matters, often with individuals who are themselves confused, anxious and embarrassed by their situation. The middle classes have long used solicitors and banks to advise them on financial matters, but the past 20 years have witnessed the growth of **advice** agencies prepared to help poor people with money difficulties.

The **Citizens Advice Bureaux** (now called Citizens Advice) are pre-eminent among them, but in some areas neighbourhood offices of **local authorities** as well as independent **advice** centres have developed money advice services. During 2008/9 Citizens Advice offered free, independent, impartial advice to over 1.9 million people. Debt remains the largest category of enquiry in terms of volume of problems with advice being given to 575,000 clients on 1.9 million debt problems. In 1980, 22 per cent of those in the lowest income group used credit; by 2000 this figure had risen to well over 70 per cent. Figures from the Council of Mortgage Lenders show that during 2008 there were 40,000 repossessions (1 in 290 of all mortgages) and that by the end of 2008 almost 219,000 mortgages were more than 3 months in arrears, a significant rise from the 127,000 in the same position at the end of 2007.

A rigorous analysis of debt and default debt has yet to be undertaken in Britain, but it is known that many people who develop problems do so as a result of unforeseen difficulties, such as unemployment, short-time working, **divorce** and separation, bereavement, sickness and the failure of businesses. Although there are examples of consumers whose behaviour could be construed as reckless, the vast majority seem to be those who cannot, rather than will not, pay. Indebtedness is mostly rooted in **poverty**, but the apparently foolhardy behaviour of some debtors still needs to be understood and **advice** offered. Wider social forces, such as the availability of credit, high and variable rates of interest and the general pressures to be a consumer, are critical in this context.

Contemporary research into the access to credit for very poor people has consistently found that they are obliged to use moneylenders, 'loan sharks' and other credit agencies that charge extremely high rates of interest despite the regulatory constraints of the Consumer Credit Act 1974. Often social security claimants or residents living in particular areas will be denied access to normal sources of credit such as banks and finance houses. The **credit union** movement, which aims to give poor people access to relatively cheap loans based upon savings societies, is well developed in some areas but not at all in others. The Social Fund (see **welfare rights 8**), administered by the **Department for Work and Pensions**, is another source of cheap loans, but the quota system with cash limits means that access cannot be guaranteed.

Most social workers now accept the connection between money problems and personal and social functioning. Stress caused by **poverty** is clearly acknowledged. Few social workers, however, develop expertise in this area of work, preferring to refer individuals to agencies like Citizens Advice (which in many areas cannot cope with the volume of work). Yet consumers value practical help of this kind very highly. Some social services offices have their own **money advice** and welfare rights specialists, but these are uncommon. The part that social work has to play in anti-poverty strategies is as yet unclear and poorly developed.

Wolfe, M. (2008) *Debt Advice Handbook*, 8th edition. London: Child Poverty Action Group.

decentralization the transfer of staff from social services headquarters to local and **community** level offices. Decentralization has become an increasingly important approach to the delivery of social services by **local authorities**. The aim is to establish a closer link between officials and the local community they serve. The main services affected by decentralization are those of housing and social services, although some authorities are experimenting with a wider range of services. The introduction of decentralization has been associated mainly with Liberal Democrat local authorities and Labour authorities, particularly those of the Left. It has been noted that decentralization is principally of three kinds: departmental decentralization, in which departments are reorganized into neighbourhood or community-level teams; corporate decentralization, where a range of services are decentralized into what are often termed 'mini-town halls', with the aim of providing almost the full range of services at community level within easy reach of local people; and political decentralization, where local-level committees of elected representatives are also devolved to advise the neighbourhood offices. With the latter approach, the aim is to provide a political reform that encourages local groups to become more involved and to increase levels of **participation**; emphasis is often placed on those groups who are most often excluded from the traditional **networks** of representation, including the disabled, ethnic-minority groups and women.

While decentralization approaches have sometimes proved very successful, they have also resulted in opposition. In particular, corporate and political decentralization has proved to be expensive, and in periods of financial constraint there has been some retrenchment. Costs have been high because of a number of factors – first, there is a need for training as junior officers are given greater responsibility; second, there is some capital cost in setting up neighbourhood offices; third, the relative success in the area of housing has led to an increase in demand from the public for services. However, departmental decentralization in the provision of social services has been maintained, as the development of **community care** has often been seen as more effective within a decentralized structure. Also, many senior managers have seen the devolution of some day-to-day management responsibilities as a way of freeing themselves to concentrate on more strategic planning of services. In addition, the **Audit Commission** is promoting decentralization as a way of challenging entrenched **power** structures within local authority **social services departments**. The Audit Commission has argued that these vested interests militate against the interests of **service user**s; in particular, the Commission sees the need for budgets to be devolved so that decisions on the level of service provided for an individual can be made as close to the client as possible.

declaratory relief a term used to describe legal proceedings to determine what is in the best interests of a person if there is disagreement relating to care provision.

Based upon the evidence that is provided a judge will decide what is in the best interests of the person. For example, this can occur when a person with a proposed care plan or their carer do not agree with a planned **social work** intervention. In these circumstances, the recipients or carer would be the defendants and the court must make the ultimate decision whilst taking into consideration all available information. This process originates from situations where people in receipt of medical support needed to continue with treatment but were not necessarily able to give informed consent. This is based upon the common law doctrine of necessity; and might apply to, for example, emergency medical treatment.

deferred sentence a decision by a court to postpone passing **sentence** for up to 6 months, during which time the offender undertakes to comply with requirements about his or her conduct imposed by the court. Requirements could for example be to attend a training programme or perform **reparation**. If the offender re-offends during the period of the deferment or fails to comply with a requirement, the court can re-**sentence** for the original offence plus any fresh offence. Deferment can be used where the decision is a borderline one between either **custody** and a **community sentence**, or between a community sentence and a **fine** or **discharge**. If the period of deferment is successfully completed, the more lenient sentence should be the outcome.

dementia a progressive and irreversible decline in intellectual abilities, usually of gradual onset, affecting all areas of the brain.

The disorder is associated with old age but affects those in younger age groups as well. At age 75, the proportion of all people of that age who are affected is approximately 10 per cent. The prevalence doubles with every five years of increasing age so that it can be calculated that by age 85, as many as 40 per cent of this age group has dementia, whereas at age 65 the risk is only at 2.5 per cent. Dementia can also appear in middle-aged people, when it results in more rapid deterioration.

Indications of dementia are **impairment** in short- and long-term memory and in judgement, inability to learn new information, to remember past personal information or facts of common knowledge, to perform routine or basic tasks, or to make and carry out plans. In addition, there may be significant changes of **personality** and major disorientation in time and place. There are differences in the degree of symptoms, however. Those with mild dementia have some impairment of social activities, although the individual retains adequate control over tasks associated with daily living. Sufferers of moderate dementia require some **supervision** of daily tasks, while the activity of those with severe dementia is so impaired as to require constant **supervision** or institutional care.

Definitions of dementia have become much more precise over the past twenty years in terms of the clinical features by which it should be identified. Other causes of impairment, such as general medical illness or drug toxicity must be excluded. There are also distinctions made between different sub-types of dementia. **Alzheimer's disease** is the principal, but not the only, cause of dementia, accounting for some 55 per cent of all cases. Other causes include minor strokes, degenerative disorders such as Parkinson's disease, alcohol toxicity, head injuries, infections of the central nervous system and transmittable diseases such as AIDS and Creutzfeldt-Jakob disease. Whatever the cause, the condition results in emotional, motor and behavioural problems, which often require interdisciplinary care from both health and social services, including the services of consultant geriatricians, community psychiatric nurses, social workers and domiciliary carers.

Assessment of need under the **National Health Service and Community Care Act 1990** sought to promote interdisciplinary work and to involve **service user**s and their carers to the fullest extent possible. Care of people with dementia should take account of the clinical features presented, the **personality** prior to outset and any subsequent changes, accompanying medical conditions and the psychosocial pressures on the person and carers. Dementia may be accompanied by anxiety, sleeplessness, agitation, paranoia, **depression** and apathy. While medication may relieve some symptoms, careful **assessment** should identify whether any of these relate to a monotonous environment. Sufficient levels of stimulation in the person's immediate environment have proved to be a critical factor in maintaining optimal mental functioning.

Department for Children, Schools and Families (DCSF) the government department responsible for children's services, including both education and **social care**, and primarily delivered through **local authorities** and schools. It was created in 2007 when the Department for Education and Skills was divided into the DCSF and the Department for Innovation, Universities and Skills. Its oversight is vast – responsible for schools, pre-schools, **Ofsted**, the **Every Child Matters** agenda, and **children's centres**.

Department for Work and Pensions (DWP) the central government department responsible for the regulation of welfare benefits, pensions and employment services. The creation of the DWP in 2001 was a clear signal in the development of **New Labour** policies towards welfare benefits and issues concerning rights and responsibilities. Increasingly, there has been much debate about the role of the benefit system and the levels of dependency of people on the state. This originally was associated with the new right and authors such as the American, Charles Murray. They argued that the **welfare state** had undermined the independence of increasing numbers of people who had become more and more reliant on the benefit system. This **underclass** was increasingly separated from the rest of society and gave rise to the concept of **social exclusion**. **New Labour** identified **social exclusion** as being a key issue it wished to tackle as well as the problems associated with an increasing level of expenditure on social security, which had become the largest area of public spending in the UK, as in many other European **welfare state**s.

The creation of the DWP aimed to directly link employment services and the benefit system with the aim of ensuring that the receipt of benefits is tied into pressures to accept employment, with the removal of benefits from those who do not accept work offered. The first of these initiatives was targeted at single parents, with the idea that there was a significant section of the population who would benefit from access to employment. The relative success of this policy in the government's view led to the restructuring of the department to promote further the link between benefits and work.

The DWP incorporates a number of service areas including the Pensions, Disability and Carers Service and Jobcentre Plus. The Pension Services, Disabilities and Carers Service looks after benefit issues for the retired and those who are planning retirement as well as those receiving Disability Living Allowance, Attendance Allowance, Carers' Allowance and Vaccine Damage Payments.

Department of Health (DH) the main central government department responsible for personal social services for adults (but not children) and policies affecting **social work**.

The Department of Health was created in 1986 with the dismantling of the Department of Health and Social Security. Its responsibilities include the **National Health Service (NHS) community care** policy, implementation of major parts of the children Act, the operation of the social services inspectorate and health promotion. As with all other central government departments, the DH is headed by a Secretary of State, who sits in the cabinet as a senior minister. This cabinet minister is accountable to Parliament for the policy of the DH and sits on the government's front bench. Legally and constitutionally subordinate to the Secretary of State is a group of ministers responsible for aspects of the department, served by a group of senior civil servants who provide **advice** on health and social services policy and manage the department's business. Within the department, there is a National Health Service Management Executive and a National Health Service Policy Board. These are responsible for NHS organization and policy matters and report directly to the Secretary of State through the **NHS** chief executive.

In respect of **social work** activities, the Secretary of State for Health has been given important powers under the **National Health Service and Community Care Act** and the **Children Act**. The first requires all local authority **social services department**s to develop **community care plan**s, which have to be submitted for approval to the Secretary of State. The second has given the Secretary of State **power** to have DH officials enter and inspect all premises where children are kept under the Act and the children in these premises. The department also communicates policy guidance to local authority social services through a series of circulars and ministers' letters. These follow up on points of detail to clarify aspects of government legislation but do not necessarily have the same force as Acts of Parliament. They are influential, however, and allow the government to work towards national standards in the application of legislation. The use of other agencies including the **Care Quality Commission** also helps to communicate policy guidance to providers as well as furnishing the department with information on the response from providers to legislation.

Ministers respond to questions on policy on the floor of the House of Commons as well as through a spokesperson in the House of Lords. Both ministers and civil servants respond to parliamentary questioning in front of parliamentary select committees. The DH also works closely with other departments on the development of aspects of policy, notably with the **Department for Work and Pensions** on issues relating to benefit systems. At the same time, the department is often in competition with other departments for resources from the Treasury to try to pay for new and continuing policies.

Department of Health, Social Services and Public Safety, Northern Ireland the department responsible for health, social services and social security within the province of Northern Ireland. This department coordinates all health and personal social services work and has been responsible to the Northern Ireland Executive since the reinstatement of devolved government as part of the Northern Ireland peace process. The health and social care responsibilities of the department are integrated within a Health and Social Care Board. The board is responsible for these services through five commissioning groups which commission services from five health and social care trusts, plus a sixth trust for ambulance services. The board is also responsible for resource management and the performance management regime. There are also five professional groups led by chief officers, including the Chief Social Services Officer who is the lead executive officer for social care within Northern Ireland. The other professional groups are for dental services, nursing and midwifery, medical and allied services and pharmaceutical services.

depression   feelings of hopelessness, sadness, tearfulness and intense anxiety.

These feelings may in some situations be regarded as an understandable response to a situation – for example a recent family bereavement. But where they are more prolonged, or more extreme than would seem appropriate within the person's culture, these feelings may be understood as **mental health problems**, traditionally diagnosed as **depression** (see **mental health problems**).

Depression is the most commonly diagnosed mental health problem, and surveys have suggested that between 10 and 15 per cent of the population may be experiencing the symptoms linked to it. It is a condition or experience which is quite widespread, and it is especially important for social workers to be aware of it because they work with groups who are exposed to even higher rates. Significantly, for example, groups who experience social inequalities such as **poverty** and **discrimination**, including Black and minority ethnic groups, women and **older people**, experience **depression** at perhaps twice the rates of more valued groups. Thus it could be affecting a woman **service user** in **poverty** experiencing postnatal depression; an older person who has recently faced the onset of a serious health condition, and may be socially isolated; or a member of a minority ethnic **community** who is unemployed.

A person suffering from depression can feel often overwhelming feelings of sadness, lack of energy and motivation, low self-esteem and hopelessness, or more extreme feelings such as total despair, complete worthlessness, and intense guilt. Tasks require extra effort, thinking becomes difficult, and the person can be affected by persistent fears or thoughts of **suicide**. Disturbed sleep patterns, poor appetite, slowed speech and movement, gastric problems and bodily pain are all physical experiences linked to **depression**. These difficulties together will have a major impact upon the person's functioning, with implications for all aspects of her or his life – for example work, close relationships, friendships, and day-to-day coping. Suicide is strongly linked to depression, and risk to the person and others cannot be ruled out – e.g. a parent with depression may find it very difficult to cope for long periods at a time with a young child's needs. Traditionally depression has been classified as *endogenous*, potentially biological in origin, and more serious when it seems to have no connection to stressful circumstances, or *reactive*, milder and more short-lived when it can be viewed as an understandable response to such circumstances. People with more serious depression may also experience the symptoms usually associated with **psychoses**. Recent years have brought challenges from several perspectives to the medical model as the definitive explanation of mental health problems, and depression has been no exception to this. Links between experiences of **abuse** and poor care in **childhood**, long-term difficulties such as poverty and unemployment, and life events such as bereavement have been found to be influential, as with all mental health problems. But the experiences linked to depression, even if it is easy to see a link to a recent life event, are very disabling and incur much suffering, and therefore require a response.

Workers may respond when someone has already received a diagnosis, in which case they will be coordinating their interventions with other professionals such as medical doctors, nurses and psychologists. But equally, awareness of depression and its consequences may alert the worker to the possibility that someone not receiving services for these concerns may benefit from a response to them – and that response may be essential if crisis is to be avoided. This is a sensitive issue, given concerns about the traditional **stigma** conferred by receiving help related to mental health problems. But current responses involve integrated health and **social care** working, with considerable importance placed upon non-medical understandings and approaches, and supports to live an ordinary life. Social workers have statutory duties to provide **social care** help to people with **mental health** concerns, and can contribute much to their greater **wellbeing** and control over their lives.

Pritchard, C. (2006) *Mental Health Social Work: evidence-based practice*. London: Routledge.

Deprivation of Liberty Safeguards measures introduced in April 2009 for people who lack capacity to decide about their care or treatment and who are deprived of their liberty to protect them from harm but who are not covered by the **Mental Health Act 1983** safeguards (Department of Health 2005).

These safeguards may apply to people in hospital or people living in residential or nursing care registered under the **Care Standards Act 2000** in such circumstances as preventing someone from being able to leave, using cot sides, using restraint or administering medication. These safeguards apply to anyone over 18 years who has a **mental disorder** or disturbance of the mind, for example, **dementia** or profound **learning disability**. The safeguards link directly to Article 5 of the European Court of Human Rights, Right to Liberty. An independent **assessment** is carried out to ensure that decisions are made in the best interests of the person in order to protect them from harm. The best interest **assessment** will be carried out by a relevantly and appropriately trained professional and also a **mental health** assessor who must meet prescribed post-qualifying criteria. Neither party must be directly involved with the applicant, be compromised by line management loyalties or directly in support of the person being assessed.

The safeguards can also be used as an interim measure in order to provide life-sustaining treatment before a decision is made by the courts. Otherwise they must be approved by either the Court of Protection, or procedures where authorization is given by the higher authority where the care is being delivered for example a **primary care trust** or local authority. The assessment may also involve insight from family, friends, carers or **independent mental capacity advocates**.

The safeguards have a direct link to the case of R *v* Bournewood Community and Mental Health NHS Trust, ex p L [1998] 3 All ER 289. In this a 48-year-old man with autism was an informal patient in a hospital having been admitted following disruptive behaviour at a day centre. This admission was based upon common law principles of necessity. His adult **foster care**rs wished him to return to them and challenged the decision of health care staff to keep the man as an informal patient. The European Convention on Human Rights upheld that deprivation of liberty had been unlawful. This showed a shortfall in current process now referred to as the 'Bournewood Gap', whereby people who were voluntarily admitted to hospital would be prevented from leaving if they attempted to do so. It was considered that best interests decisions made under common law were inadequate and resulted in a consultation process in 2005 which influenced the deprivation of liberty safeguarding process.

Department of Health (2005) *The Mental Health Act Deprivation of Liberty Safeguards in England*. London: DH.

designated person/teacher a term widely used in schools to identify the person responsible for **safeguarding** issues (the person may not always be a teacher). It may also refer to the person responsible for children who are **looked after** (often the same person, especially in primary schools).

detention the deprivation of liberty, which can occur in a number of contexts. Persons suspected of criminal offences may be detained by the

police following arrest for a limited period under the provisions of the **Police and Criminal Evidence Act 1984** (see also **appropriate adult**). The term may also refer to **detention** under the **Mental Health Act 1983**, and is used in relation to **custodial sentences** (see **detention and training order, detention in a young offender institution**).

detention and training order (DTO) a custodial sentence for young offenders aged 12 to 17 introduced by the **Crime and Disorder Act 1998**, half of which is served in **custody** and half in the **community** under the **supervision** of a **youth offending team**. The minimum overall term is 4 months and the maximum 24 months. The custodial half of a DTO is served in a **young offender institution, secure training centre** or **secure children's home** (see **secure estate**). A DTO can be passed only if the court is satisfied either that the offence is so serious that only a **custodial sentence** can be justified or, where the offence is a violent or sexual one, the **sentence** is defined necessary to protect the public from serious harm. Those under 15 cannot receive a DTO unless they are **persistent offenders**. Longer **sentences** of **detention** for young offenders are possible for certain 'grave crimes' under 'section 53' under the **Crime and Disorder Act 1998**.

detention in a young offender institution a custodial sentence for offenders aged 18 to 20, equivalent to **imprisonment** for adults aged 21 and over. The **sentence** is served in a **young offender institution** (YOI), which also houses offenders aged 15 to 17 serving **detention and training orders**.

The **sentence** was first created by the Criminal Justice Act 1988. The Criminal Justice and Court Services Act 2000 contained provision for abolishing this **sentence** and amalgamating it with the adult **imprisonment sentence**, which would have the effect of separating custodial institutions for children under 18 from those for all adults of 18 and over, but would seem likely to end the current separation of young adult (18 to 20) inmates from older **prison**ers. This has not yet been implemented.

detention (schools) keeping a child at school beyond the usual hours. **Detention** is widely used, mainly in secondary schools, as part of a behaviour policy, usually in response to fairly minor incidents of poor behaviour or lateness.

School staff can lawfully detain a child provided they have given 24 hours notice to their parent, so it cannot be imposed on the same day (except during the lunch break). A parent does not have to consent but may make representations about whether the **detention** is appropriate on that particular day, for example, because of transport issues or a pre-existing commitment. Children who do not cooperate with the detention may find themselves subject to a short **exclusion from school** as an alternative.

deviance a sociological term referring to behaviour perceived to deviate from socially constructed and accepted norms and role expectations. It may also be described as social 'rule-breaking' or a **breach** of social order.

Deviant behaviour need not be criminal (for example, mentally ill people are often classified as deviant), but explanations or theories of crime are frequently regarded as specific examples of more general theories of deviance. Deviance tends to be studied in two ways: as an objective reality or as a subjective experience. Those who view deviance as an objective phenomenon argue that there is widespread consensus on norms and **values** in society and that this basic agreement makes it relatively easy to identify deviants. Standard negative sanctions can then be imposed, and this act of punishment or control reaffirms for the group that it is bound by a set of common values and norms. Those who view deviance as a subjective experience are concerned with its social definition. They are concerned to examine how particular people are identified and set apart and what the consequences are both for such people (in terms of developing a deviant identity) and for those who impose the label of deviance. (See also **labelling** and **theories of crime and deviance**.)

diagnostic testing one of the two stages of tests under the **Mental Capacity Act 2005** which informs an **assessment** to establish whether a person has capacity to make a decision.

A test for capacity is decision and time specific; the more complex the decision the greater the level of capacity required. For example, a person may be able to make an informed decision as to whether or not they would like a drink, but they may not be able to understand the complexity of making a decision about moving to residential care or taking medication to treat a life-threatening condition. A diagnostic test would therefore be carried out to establish clarity on issues such as general intellectual ability, memory, ability to concentrate or sustain attention, making reasonable judgements and being able to comprehend information offered or indeed to express their views and wishes as a result of a given situation. Sensitivity to and awareness of the wider cultural and social influences are essential when working alongside vulnerable people who are, by the very nature of their circumstances, in a position of powerlessness.

How we support and present information can impact upon the **outcomes** of those decision-making processes. Social workers must therefore be willing to explore and constantly evaluate their **communication** skills and be willing to offer innovative and creative approaches to problem solving. In her work on **safeguarding adults**, Martin (2007) helps practitioners to engage with the notion that our environment, the space in which we exist at any given time can have adverse effects upon how we perceive ourselves and our surroundings. Social workers should be mindful of how, for example, an **interview** with a person on a bustling hospital ward or a residential care home lounge with the television blaring, or a social services duty room, or a person's home with other distractions may impact upon the information divulged or the expressed wishes of a person under pressure to prove that they are well enough to return home or adamant that they do not wish to do so. It is fundamental also to remember that essential or unwise decision-making does not necessarily indicate capacity deficit, nor indeed does a person's **communication** techniques if this does not fit in with established or expected norms. Sometimes the social worker's willingness to work outside of the boundaries of their own comfort zones can have an empowering influence upon **assessment outcomes**.

When establishing capacity the **Mental Capacity Act 2005** requires that a person must have an **impairment** of or disturbance in the functioning of their mind or brain. This must be established by a qualified medical practitioner. This disturbance must render the person then unable to make a particular decision and both elements must be applied and shown to apply. See also **safeguarding adults**.

Martin, J. (2007) *Safeguarding Adults*. Lyme Regis: Russell House Publishing.

direct payments local authorities transferring funding directly to **service user**s who could then purchase their own services.

Prior to the groundbreaking Community Care (Direct Payments) Act 1996, **local authorities** were not permitted to provide cash in lieu of **community care** services. Therefore the Act was of crucial importance for **service users** who had campaigned for the right to have more control over the services provided for them. Direct payments can make an important contribution to promoting autonomy, flexibility and choice, to the benefit of people who use care services. Under the 1996 Act, a local authority could provide cash payments to service users where, following **assessment** under section 47 of the **National Health Service and Community Care Act 1990**, it had determined that services should be provided to meet assessed need. The cash must then be used by the service user to arrange his or her own care.

Whilst the original provision related to disabled people aged between 18 and 65, this was extended in 2000 to people over 65. The **Carers and Disabled Children Act 2000** further extended the facility for direct payments to carers, including 16–17-year-olds, for services to meet their own assessed needs as carers, and to 16–17-year-old disabled children for services to meet their own needs.

There were certain exclusions, notably for people subject to compulsory orders under the **Mental Health Act 1983**, people on probation with requirements for psychiatric treatment, and people who cannot manage the payments even with assistance. Certain services could not be purchased: residential care exceeding 4 weeks in any one year; services provided by the local authority; help from close relatives or other residents of the household; health care; housing.

As indicated above, since 1996 there has been further legislation and regulation which have made direct payments available to a wider group of service users. The 1996 Community Care (Direct payments) Act was repealed by the 2001 Health and Social Care Act, which is now the key legislation with respect to **direct payments**. However, there have continued to be changes in regulation and guidance since 2001. As originally conceived, **local authorities** had discretion about whether to operate such a scheme, but from 2003 direct payment schemes became mandatory and some of the rules governing exclusions were relaxed. Local authorities now have a duty to offer direct payments as long as the service user consents.

disability social oppression on the basis of physical or mental **impairment**. Disability is increasingly recognized as those disadvantages, restrictions and exclusions that arise as a result of the failure of society to take into account the requirements of people with impairments when determining social and environmental arrangements. The notion that disability is socially constructed is relatively recent, and it is still commonly assumed to be an individual attribute. Exclusion from the mainstream of social life and reliance on segregating forms of welfare were considered inevitable consequences of the need for assistance with 'normal' activities of daily living. It was not until disabled people themselves identified that there was nothing inevitable about such exclusion that dominant assumptions were challenged. An important tool in this struggle has been the redefinition of disability as a form of social oppression and exclusion, and the development of a **social model of disability**.

Disabled activists have challenged definitions of disability based on impairment. Such definitions have had a long-standing influence on policy, practice and research, and imply that the inability of many disabled people to gain paid work, engage fully in social life and maintain autonomy results directly from their impairments. The distinction between disability and impairment has been crucial to the arguments of disabled activists, who have pointed out that many of the restrictions disabled people experience are imposed by disablist attitudes and practices based on dominant notions of normality. The **social model of disability**, as developed by disabled activists, identifies that social and physical environments have been constructed so as to systematically exclude disabled people. It is argued, therefore, that disability is not a medical or individual matter but a social construction. In practice, the barriers faced by disabled people include individual prejudice, inaccessible transport and public buildings, segregated education and employment, and welfare regulations and practices that restrict autonomy.

There was a long struggle on the part of disabled activists to achieve full civil rights for disabled people. The legislation that was eventually passed fell far short of guaranteeing access to full **participation** in society, but the **Disability Discrimination Act 1995** did provide for the first time a degree of protection against **discrimination** in employment and access to goods and services. The definition of disability in the Act, however, is based on the inability to carry out 'normal' activities.

Social care legislation defines disability in terms of individual impairment. The definition first used in the **National Assistance Act 1948** is still used with minimal adaptation in both adults and children's legislation, and refers to 'the blind and partially sighted, the deaf and hard of hearing, the dumb, persons who suffer from any **mental disorder**, and other persons who are substantially or permanently handicapped by illness, injury or congenital deformity'. Entitlement to services is grounded in this Act, and also in the **Children Act 1989**, the **Chronically Sick and Disable Persons Act 1970**, the **Disabled Persons (Services, Consultations and Representation) Act 1986**, the **National Health Service and Community Care Act 1990**, and the Health and Social Care Act 2001 (in relation to direct payments). Despite the medical and individualized definition adopted in legislation, guidance issued to social workers suggests that practice should be based on the **social model of disability**. The focus of this should be on the rights of **service user**s, with a consequent emphasis on inclusion, choice and autonomy. Commentators on **disability** policy have identified that these principles may be inconsistent with a system in which 'need' is based on a professional assessment and purchasing decisions made without any service user involvement.

Despite the fact that professional education now emphasizes the way that needs-led assessment and care planning can be undertaken in more empowering ways, research evidence suggests that some disabled people have not gained access to assessment and that, for others, care packages have been restricting rather than enabling. When working within a care management system, social workers need to develop skills in negotiating care packages that reflect the needs and aspirations of disabled people, in working with other agencies to deliver these, and in fully involving service users in the whole process of care management.

However, current policy is to increase autonomy and choice for disabled service users through **personalization** and self-directed support. Direct payments are considered to be a crucial tool in achieving this. Since 1997, disabled adults have been eligible for payments which enable them to purchase services of their own choice. This is reported to increase the flexibility of care packages and the degree of autonomy experienced by disabled recipients. Services for disabled children are provided by children and families teams, and disabled children are regarded as '**children in need**' under the **Children Act 1989**. Services should be provided to minimize the effect of disability and facilitate 'normal' life. The Act emphasizes that disabled children are 'children first'. In meeting the needs that arise from disability, social workers should ensure that needs as a child are given priority. As a result of this philosophy, far fewer disabled children now live in permanent residential care and the emphasis is on family support. The transfer of support services for disabled children and their families to children and families teams, however, meant that in some local authorities these services had to compete for staff time with safeguarding and were regarded as low priority. There are now more specialist teams working with disabled children, and the increased emphasis given to family support in the recent **framework for assessment of children in need** is likely to benefit this group.

Oliver, M. and Sapey, P. (2006) *Social Work with Disabled People*, 3rd edition. Houndmills: Palgrave Macmillan.

Disability Discrimination Act (DDA) 1995 legislation that aims to combat **discrimination** against disabled people in the fields of employment, education, trade organizations and qualifications bodies, the provision of goods and services and the buying or renting of land or property.

Since the passing of the Disability Discrimination Act in 1995, several important changes have been made to its provisions and operation. Some of these have been as a result of the recommendations of the Disability Rights Task Force, a body set up by the Labour government on its election in 1997, and others have resulted from European Directives and subsequent UK legislation. Originally the DDA included very limited coverage of education, but this has now been amended by the passing of the Special Educational Needs and Disability Act 2001. The DDA's provisions in respect of education are now similar to those covering other areas. Another major change since the passing of the DDA was the establishment of the Disability Rights Commission (DRC) to oversee the operation of the Act. Originally there was no independent organization responsible for advice, conciliation and enforcement, which marked out the DDA as noticeably weaker than corresponding legislation of 'race' and sex.

Individuals who consider that they have been discriminated against can complain to an employment tribunal, a county court or a **special educational needs** tribunal, depending on which section of the Act applies. Research into the operation of the DDA during its first 19 months of operation found that almost 2,500 employment cases were brought, which was substantially higher than the equivalent period for other anti-discrimination legislation. However, only 22 per cent of cases were actually heard at a tribunal. Others were either settled in other ways or withdrawn. Of the cases heard at tribunal, the applicant was successful in only 16 per cent. Recruitment cases were less likely to succeed than dismissal cases. It was found that applicants who were legally represented were more likely to win their cases and also that people with sensory **impairment**s were more successful than those with physical or **mobility impairment**s. Levels of **compensation** ordered by tribunals were significantly lower than those awarded under the Sex Discrimination and Race Relations Acts. Since the DRC commenced work in 2000, applicants have had better access to advice, support and legal representation. The Disability Rights Commission (DRC), and now its successor organization the Commission for Equality and Human Rights, also has a wider enforcement role and can carry out investigations, issue non-discrimination notices and apply for **injunction**s in cases of failure to comply.

The DDA still differs considerably from other anti**discrimination** legislation, as it covers **discrimination** against *disabled people* rather than discrimination on the *grounds* of disability. It is not enough to show that discrimination took place for reasons associated with disability; the individual discriminated against must meet the Act's definition of disability. Disability is defined as 'a physical or mental impairment which has a substantial and long-term adverse effect on his [*sic*] ability to carry out normal day to day activities'. 'Long-term' refers to conditions lasting at least a year and 'substantial' to effects that are more than minor or trivial. 'Mental impairment' refers to both **learning disability** and **mental disorder**s. As a result of the amendments brought in by the Disability **Discrimination** Act 2005, it is no longer essential that the mental disorder is 'clinically well recognised'.

The DDA definition of disability covers a wide range of long-term medical conditions and mental impairments as well as the mobility and sensory impairments more commonly associated with the term 'disability'. It also covers progressive conditions in which the effects might initially be minor. From 2005, people with HIV, cancer and multiple sclerosis are covered by the DDA from the point of diagnosis. The effect of medication or equipment that helps a disabled person to overcome the effects of an impairment is ignored in determining whether the person can be considered as disabled under the Act with the exception of wearing glasses which correct sight problems. However, people who are registered as blind or partially sighted with a local authority will automatically be considered disabled. The definition is based on functional deficit in individuals rather than the disadvantages that people may experience as a result of prejudice and discrimination. The only exception to this is its inclusion of people with facial disfigurements.

The Act identifies several types of discrimination. Direct discrimination involves treating a disabled person less favourably than someone else who has similar circumstances and abilities for a reason relating to the person's disability. Often, direct discrimination results from inaccurate assumptions about what a person with the particular impairment will be able to do. Failure to make 'reasonable adjustments' is also a type of discrimination under the Act. Discrimination against a job applicant, therefore, might not only result from employers' decisions to deliberately exclude disabled people but also from failure to ensure that selection procedures are adjusted to take account of applicants' impairments. Once a disabled person is employed, failure to make 'reasonable adjustments' to enable her or him to do the job would also be regarded as discrimination. In service provision, discrimination involves refusing to provide a service, providing it on worse terms or providing a lower standard of service. There is guidance for employers and service providers on the type of adjustments that might be regarded as 'reasonable' and, conversely, those that might be 'unreasonable'. The Act makes it clear that direct discrimination and failure to make adjustments that are 'reasonable' can never be justified. Victimization of someone who has taken action against an employer or service provider under the DDA is also regarded as a type of discrimination. This provision can provide protection to people who have supported a disabled person in taking such action. The fourth type of discrimination identified under the Act is disability-related discrimination. This involves discrimination for a reason that is related to a person's disability and that results in less favourable treatment than the way in which others. To whom the reason does not apply, are treated. The Act also prohibits the **harassment** of a disabled person.

In only very limited circumstances can employers and service providers claim that less favourable treatment was 'justified'. There can be no justification for direct discrimination, failure to make reasonable adjustments or victimization. The only type of discrimination which can ever be justified is disability-related discrimination, but there are several provisos in relation to this. First, if reasonable adjustments would have made a difference the treatment cannot be justified. Also, the reason for the treatment must have been material (that is, relevant to the particular circumstances) and substantial (or must carry real weight).

The provisions of the DDA were phased in gradually, with the employment rights coming into force first in 1999, followed later by access to goods and services and education. Service providers have been required to make necessary changes to buildings in order to facilitate access for disabled people since October 2004.

The scope of the DDA was widened further as a result of the 2005 Disability Discrimination Act, bringing private clubs within its remit, requiring private landlords to make reasonable adjustments, and introducing the Disability Equality Duty. This is a requirement that all public bodies promote equality of opportunity for disabled people. This intends to address the limitations of the existing system, in which legal challenges could only involve individual cases rather than the impact of policies, practices and prejudices on disabled people as a group. It has been argued that this is more consistent with the **social model of disability**. Public bodies are required to produce a Disability Equality Scheme, and to involve disabled people in planning their policies.

In 2007, the duties of the Disability Rights Commission were taken over by a single equality body, the Commission for Equality and Human Rights. The Disability Discrimination Act is soon to be replaced by the Equality Bill 2009, which will cover all dimensions of inequality and discrimination.

Disabled Persons (Services, Consultation and Representation) Act 1986 an Act of Parliament that provides a right to **assessment** of individual needs if requested by a disabled person or his or her carer.

This Act was intended to achieve improvements to the position of disabled people in relation to three areas. First, it gave the right to **assessment** of individual needs: section 4 of the Act provides for assessment of need on request by any disabled person or his or her carer. This was intended to plug the loophole left by the rather weaker section 2 of the **Chronically Sick and Disabled Act 1970**, which stopped short of conferring an assessment duty. In providing for assessment on request, it confers the strongest kind of mandate for assessment, that of an absolute duty. Even so, it remained necessary for disabled people to know of their right to request an assessment in order to activate the duty. This loophole was eventually closed by section 47 of **National Health Service and Community Care Act 1990**, which requires a local authority, if undertaking a **community care assessment** of someone who then appears to be disabled, to inform the individual of his or her rights under the 1986

Act and to undertake a concurrent **assessment** under section 4 of the **Disabled Persons (Services, Consultation and Representation) Act 1986**.

This is important, first, because this section 4 assessment is specifically for services under section 2 of the Chronically Sick And Disabled Act 1970, which the local authority is bound to provide once it has identified that the individual has needs and that it is necessary to meet these needs. Second, it provided for coordination of services for young people at the point of transition to adults' services: sections 5 and 6 require **local authorities** to identify and assess disabled school-leavers and to ensure smooth transition to adult service provision.

Under the Act local education authorities must also notify social services of all potential school-leavers who have **statements** of **special educational needs**. Social services must then determine whether these children are disabled (within the meaning of the definitions within section 17 of the **Children Act 1989** and section 29 of the **National Assistance Act 1948**). For those who are disabled, social services must ensure that appropriate **assessment** of their potential needs as adults is undertaken. Third, the Act requires the publication of information about services, and section 10 requires consultation with organizations of disabled people in relation to appointments to public bodies.

Sections 1 to 3 of the Act, providing for **advocacy** and representation, have never been implemented. Section 8 of the Disabled Persons (Services, Consultation and Representation) Act contains provision for carers. This is not as extensive as in the later **Carer's Recognition and Services Act 1995**, in that it stops short of a full carer's assessment, but it nevertheless requires a carer's ability and willingness to care to be taken into account when deciding on service provision for the disabled person. The duty arises whether or not the carer has requested such consideration.

discretionary leave gives an asylum seeker limited leave to remain even if they do not qualify for refugee status or **humanitarian protection**. A person is likely to qualify if they have serious health problems: they are given leave for shorter periods and do not qualify for family reunion.

discrimination see **ageism, anti-discriminatory practice, anti-oppressive practice, disability, Equalities and Human Rights Commission, equal opportunities policies, Equal Pay Act 1970, gender, homosexuality/homophobia, positive action, racism, sexism, sexuality**

dispersal order an order which **police** officers can be empowered to make against groups of two or more young people under the age of 16 in designated areas requiring them to disperse and (if after 9 p.m.) return home. These powers, introduced by the **Anti-social Behaviour**

Act 2003 are available when a **local authority** has designated an area in response to an application by a **police** superintendent who is satisfied that people in the area have been affected by **anti-social behaviour** on the part of groups in the locality.

diversion   a variety of ways of dealing with offenders without using the courts and, in general, keeping them out of the criminal justice system.

Diversion from prosecution enables the criminal justice system to avoid unnecessarily **labelling** people as offenders when they have committed only minor or one-off offences. The evidence is that most offenders who are diverted do not go on to re-offend whereas formal prosecution can reinforce a sense of **deviance** and is also costly and time-consuming. Diversion takes a variety of forms in the different countries of the UK. In England and Wales, reprimands and **final warnings** are used with young people as well as referral orders for first offences. With adults, the **caution** allows the **police** to divert minor offenders and those with mitigating circumstances such as certain types of **disability**. In Northern Ireland, the **caution** is used extensively with young offenders (including restorative **caution**ing) and with adults as an alternative to prosecution. In Scotland the **police** and prosecutors have the discretion to issue **warning**s as an alternative to prosecution. In addition to these various means of processing offenders without recourse to **criminal court**s, it is also possible to refer offenders to various agencies for assistance rather than criminalizing them. The **police** have discretion in certain circumstances to take 'no further action', and this is often used, for example, to deal with offences committed by people suffering from **mental illness** or severe stress. Rather than simply letting the matter go, there would normally be an expectation that the person concerned seek assistance from psychiatric services, housing or **social work** agencies.

divorce   the legal ending or dissolution of a **marriage**, often preceded by a period of separation that may or may not be legally ratified.

Successive UK governments, faith-based organizations and social welfare agencies have registered concerns over the high rates of **divorce** and separation experienced by **couple**s and families especially where there are dependent children. According to Social Trends 2009 'divorces granted in the UK peaked in 1993 at slightly more than 180,000. In 2007 the number of divorces granted in the UK was close to 144,000'. Around 50 per cent of **couple**s divorcing in 2007 had at least one child aged 16 or younger. Of these about 20 per cent were under the age of 5 and 63 per cent were under the age of 11. It is still the case that approximately one **marriage** in three will fail leading to a divorce with second marriages even more hazardous with almost twice that proportion leading to divorce.

There is much less social **stigma** attached to divorce and separation and, in broad terms, the variety of family formations in the UK is substantial. Single parents and reconstituted or blended families are recognized by many as part of a wide variety of different contemporary family forms. This is not to say that there is no opposition to these developments. Many faith groups especially remain strongly opposed to divorce. The concern about rising divorce rates in the UK led to the Family Law Act 1996, which introduced the concept of 'no fault' in divorce proceedings but also introduced the possibility of a more reflective requirement to the divorce process in the hope of 'saving' at least some marriages. It was hoped that family **mediation** would lead to some **couple**s staying together and others, still intent on divorce, separating on better terms especially in relation to continued co-parenting. The Act has still not yet been fully implemented.

The impact of divorce upon adults can be traumatic and can involve considerable adjustments, although these changes will vary depending upon various factors such as the length of a marriage; whether there are children; and the emotional, economic and social investment of each partner in the relationship. There are also likely to be significantly different individual experiences of the adults including feelings of betrayal and abandonment or conversely considerable relief if the relationship was abusive. Although some partners may recognize that a marriage is not working at the same time, most break up because one partner is unhappy or dissatisfied first; in a sense their suffering may precede the other partner's unhappiness which is likely to be felt most keenly later. Bohannan and Bernard (1970) in their book *Divorce and After* have usefully identified six different dimensions to divorce:

- the emotional divorce – expressing stress in the relationship and beginning to think that a marriage might be floundering, leading to a decision to separate temporarily or permanently, leading to . . .;
- the psychic divorce – an individual begins to withdraw emotionally from an ex-partner, although emotional involvement is rarely dissolved completely. People who have lived together for some time are unlikely to be emotionally indifferent to each other;
- the economic divorce – the division of the couple's property and resources including financial arrangements concerning maintenance for an ex-spouse or dependent children;
- the co-parental divorce – adjustments about how parenting is to be continued and issues of **custody** and access;
- the community divorce – changes in social relationships as a result of divorce involving friends, relatives including ex-in-laws and the wider community (schools and public services, for example);

- the legal divorce – the formal process of terminating a marriage which may include ratifying formal arrangements.

The **outcomes** for children after their parents have separated/divorced can be negative or they can result in children/young people who are content with the arrangements and more or less unaffected by the experience. The key variables affecting outcomes appear to be: the age of any children and their level of understanding; the explanations offered to children if any; the quality of the conjugal relationship before separation; the quality of the relationships between children and their two parents before separation; how resilient individual children are.

After separation these factors continue to be influential but, in addition, new variables are likely to come into play especially for the resident parent such as a possible move to new accommodation, a new **community**, reduced income, a parent becoming a full-time carer where previously they worked, potential **loss** of social and family supports and new schools and peers for children. A major issue is whether children have to become parts of 're-ordered' families where perhaps one of their parents establishes a new relationship with another person who may have children too, either resident or as visitors. And finally a key issue in relation to **outcomes** is that of whether parents cooperate in relation to their offspring or whether there is distrust and conflict and the degree to which children are exposed to these problems. These is a lot of evidence that **contact** between a non-resident parent and children can be problematic and many men in particular lose contact with their children within a few years. Organizations campaigning for 'fathers' rights' argue that legal and welfare systems discriminate against men and devalue a father's contribution to the welfare of his children. By contrast, some women's groups argue that there is substantial evidence to demonstrate that fathers can be indifferent to the needs of their children and ex-partners, as evidenced by the significant lack of success of the **Child Support Agency**.

The role of professionals in this field can be important, especially from the child's perspective. The **Children and Family Advisory and Support Services for England and Wales (CAFCASS)** has a key role to play to ensure that the 'voice of the child' is heard, when arrangements post-divorce are being determined. Family mediators are sometimes helpful in facilitating discussion between disputing and separating adults/parents to negotiate their own agreements, which subsequently can be legally ratified, although **mediation** has not been the obvious success that was at one stage hoped for. Social workers in community teams dealing with children and families have routinely to deal with parents in conflict and children experiencing stress as a result of such conflict and/or problems of adjustment to new circumstances in new communities, schools and re-ordered families. Interventions in these circumstances are always justified by reference to the paramount interests of any children.

Butler, I., Scanlon, L., Robinson, M., Douglas, G. and Murch, M. (2003) *Divorcing Children*. London: Jessica Kingsley.

Wallerstein, J., Lewis, J. and Blakeslee, S. (2002) *The Unexpected Legacy of Divorce: a 25 year landmark study*. London: Fusion Press.

doli incapax (from a Latin legal phrase meaning 'incapable of evil') the rule that a child aged under 14 was not legally capable of committing a crime unless it could be proved that he or she fully understood the difference between right and wrong. This rule was abolished by the **Crime and Disorder Act 1998**. Prior to this the prosecution of a child under 14 for a criminal offence had to establish to the satisfaction of the court that the child understood that difference – in other words the burden of proof rested with the prosecution. Now it no longer does but rather lies with the defence to establish that the particular child did not understand right and wrong.

domestic violence a term that usually refers to the physical, sexual and **emotional abuse** of women by their male partners or ex-partners. Such abuse on the part of the man can include social isolation, intimidating, bullying and belittling behaviours as well as economic deprivation.

The term and its definition are controversial. One view argues that the term 'domestic' implies a cosiness that detracts from the seriousness of the violence and prefer the term 'partner abuse'. Terms such as 'marital violence', 'spouse abuse' and 'battered wives' imply that the **couple** must be married when many are not. It has also been pointed out that the terms 'battered wives' and 'battered women' divert attention from the key issue, which is one of violent behaviour by current male partners or ex-partners. Others have used the term 'family violence', which appears to group many different kinds of relationship violence, including **child abuse, elder abuse** and sibling abuse. Violence can clearly occur between any two or more members of families or cohabiting people. It can also refer to violence between couples who are lesbian or gay and to relationships where the abuser is a woman and the **victim** a man. Relatively recent research has established that date violence also characterizes a significant proportion of relationships even in the early stages.

Attitude studies have indicated that a high proportion of boys and young men feel it is reasonable to 'physically chastise' their girl friends. However, convention seems to have established that the term 'domestic violence' is restricted to those who are, or have been, in a close, sexual, cohabiting relationship where the abuser is a man and the abused a woman. The term includes violence in cohabiting relationships that have only recently been established, relationships that have lasted many decades as well as relationships that have been terminated and where the couple no longer cohabit. In this respect violence in the relationships of elders who have been together for a long time should properly be characterized as domestic violence rather than elder abuse. Similarly, domestic violence is not confined to the home but may occur in many locations, including public places. Given the complexities of all these issues, it is clear that the term is by no means watertight and that it lacks clarity at the 'edges'.

Attempts to understand domestic violence have been wide-ranging. At first commentators emphasized pathological aspects of men's behaviour, arguing that domestic violence is perpetrated by damaged individuals or whose personalities are warped. Pathologies of this kind were thought initially to be rare. Such explanations have been undermined by compelling evidence that domestic violence is widespread, found in many societies and among all ethnic groups and social classes. In the same vein, others have suggested that there are continuities between the attitudes and **values** of non-violent men with violent men.

Biology has been thought of as offering another plausible explanation. Men, it has been argued, are predisposed biologically to be aggressive. In this context high levels of testosterone in men have been held responsible for their violent behaviour. Critics of this theory have pointed out that any 'natural' drive does not compel a man to be violent. Any predisposition to behave in a particular way can be diverted, modified or even denied. There are, after all, many people who have sexual instincts but do not choose to express them. To further undermine this theoretical perspective, others have pointed to studies that have found no discernible differences in the levels of testosterone in violent men compared to non-violent men.

Other theorists have focused on accounts given by many women that appear to associate violent events with alcohol. Many men, it is alleged, are violent only when under the influence of alcohol, as if the man could somehow be 'other than himself'. This theory has been criticized on the grounds that although some men are violent in a generalized way after taking alcohol, most men 'under the influence' are able to confine their violence to their partners or ex-partners or possibly other family members lacking **power**.

Social stress is another alleged cause of domestic violence. Theorists who favour this kind of explanation have tried to link structural inequality with an increased propensity for men to be violent. Thus, unemployment, **poverty**, poor housing and, in general, few life chances are thought to be instrumental in creating social stress, which is more likely to be expressed in violence to women. Others have argued that the evidence is equivocal. First, middle-class women are to be found in refuges although, in absolute terms, in lower numbers. Second, more middle-class women, because of their comparative wealth, are likely to have more options when trying to leave an abusive relationship. Third, analyses of accounts of violent relationships by survivors and by their children have revealed that domestic violence is widespread in all social strata.

Some have perceived domestic violence as a problem caused by family dysfunction. These theorists perceive families as social systems that have structure, reciprocal relationships, boundaries and that seek to maintain some kind of equilibrium. Any family's equilibrium can be affected if the structure, reciprocal relationships or boundaries are disturbed. Violence in this context is regarded as evidence of something fundamentally wrong with any of these features of the system. Thus, if the established roles and responsibilities that brought about equilibrium are challenged or changed, then families can develop negative relationships. Critics of this approach point out that families are not systems where **power** is distributed evenly between members. Usually it is the man who is the dominant actor, and it is the abuse of **power** on the part of the man that explains the unhappiness within families rather than a 'neutral' system that has somehow become unbalanced.

Feminists have provided persuasive critiques of the perspectives outlined above. They believe that the issue of domestic violence is best understood by analysing the patriarchal relationships that seem to characterize most societies. Domestic violence, they argue, is part of a generalized oppression of women. Men occupy most of the significant positions of **power** in economic, religious, political and social institutions. This dominant position is maintained through men's control of ideas or, more broadly, of **ideology**, reinforced by violence or its threat. Women are in effect covertly persuaded to adopt attitudes and **values** that are instrumental in their own oppression. Thus, pornography, the perception of women as sexual objects, child bearers and carers, and as having primarily domestic roles with few claims on resources (both within society and within families) are all indicative of a pattern of inequality and a consistently subservient position for women. Feminists acknowledge that there are stresses within society, within communities and families, and that these stresses can be severe for individual men and women too. In this sense women are not being idealized. The key question for feminists is 'why do men feel that it is reasonable to use violence?' For them, the answer is that a patriarchal culture legitimates unequal power and the use of force to maintain such inequality. Records of the **police**, health and social welfare agencies, organizations dealing with **victims**/survivors and the British Crime Survey have consistently found that domestic violence is the most common form of interpersonal violence. Although estimates from these diverse sources vary, it is now

generally accepted that domestic violence is a very significant
social problem.

The **Crime and Disorder Act 1998** now requires **local authorities**
to establish a **community safety plan**, which among other duties calls
for estimates of the incidence of the problem to be established within
communities. The **Supporting People** initiative is also supposed to
estimate numbers of vulnerable people, including victims of domestic
violence, in any locality in order to be able to plan specialist supported
accommodation suitable for their needs including refuges. Various
estimates have also been made of the costs to the public purse of the
problem. These estimates have included the costs incurred in intervening
with victims, children and perpetrators by helping and justice agencies,
such as the **police**, social services, **probation service**s, health services,
Women's Aid, voluntary advice and counselling services, housing
agencies and the Benefits Agency. Domestic violence often leads to the
separation of partners, childcare support issues, re-housing, including
relocation to other areas, **loss** of jobs, landlords having to find new
tenants (and possible loss of rent), individuals becoming reliant upon
benefits, and many other social costs. It may be that the recognition of
the costs of domestic violence both to individuals and to statutory and
voluntary services has led to a renewed interest in how best to coordinate
the services currently delivered by many agencies.

There is compelling evidence that domestic violence is connected to
child abuse. First, children living in households where a woman is being
abused can be directly abused emotionally. Second, abusers of women
are often intentional abusers of children. Current **social work** practice
is much more explicit about the need to intervene in families where
there are children and domestic violence is also present. The **common
assessment framework** includes **assessment** criteria that focus upon
domestic violence with an implicit expectation that the effects of the
abuse are determined in relation to any children as well as the mother's
parenting capacity and, very explicitly, their ability to protect their
children. There is also evidence that domestic abuse is a common
ingredient in the backgrounds of women with **mental health problems**.
Similarly, it is now known that **older people** and people with disabilities
are especially vulnerable to domestic violence. Despite this evidence,
surveys of **social services department**s' policies and practices across the
country have revealed very patchy provision and a lack of clarity about
what abused women can expect by way of support and resources. There
are similar findings in relation to the **police**, the **probation service**, legal
practices, housing and refuge services, counselling and victim/survivor
support services. Some have argued that the problem of domestic violence

is so important and so widespread that a major government initiative is warranted that should prescribe which agencies must have responsibility for the problem and how such agencies should work together in multi-agency **partnerships**.

To date, **Women's Aid** has probably been the lead agency, but many have argued that in matters of personal safety and of the human rights of both women and children, statutory agencies should be the key players. Multi-agency working is clearly very important and in this context local **domestic violence forums** can be crucial in orchestrating coherent and accessible services enabling a victim to secure the **advice** and support needed often in very difficult and sometimes dangerous circumstances.

The scale of the problem of domestic violence has been estimated in several ways using broad studies like the British Crime Survey and **Home Office** data, as well as samples of particular populations such as a particular ward in a city, studies of student groups, psychiatric in-patients and **service users** presenting themselves to particular helping agencies. Although estimates vary, an emerging consensus suggests that one in four women are abused in the course of their lifetimes and of these most will at some point have needed medical attention. In any year, it is thought that more than 10 per cent of women will have been severely physically abused and two women are likely to die each week at the hands of partners or ex-partners. Violence in same-sex relationships seems to be on a similar scale and the gay **community** often experience particular difficulties because justice and helping agencies are not as responsive to their needs and may well be actively discriminatory. Disabled people also experience very similar problems in accessing support from social welfare and justice agencies; and in some instances, with people with significant learning disabilities, will face potential **communication** difficulties too. Newly arrived women, whose immigration status may still be insecure, are also extremely vulnerable. Some of these women have felt compelled to stay in an abusive relationship when their partners have threatened them with a return to their country of origin. The social work tasks in relation to domestic violence have many dimensions. Assessing the needs of potentially vulnerable children and adults is core, including securing the immediate and future safety of a woman and any children, enabling a woman to make considered decisions about her future, and helping both women and children to recover from the trauma of abuse and violence. In this context there are many practical and legal problems that may have to be considered, including the safeguarding of children, issues of income and shelter, and long-term protection from a man who may be intent on further violence. A key issue is that of helping women decide whether they can be safe in their home, assuming that they have a right of residence, or whether they need to leave. Even when a woman has a right to reside in the home, her view of her likely safety even with **injunctions** and responsive local **police**, must guide choices. Women's Aid have advised all women to devise a 'safety plan' that will address the particular configuration of problems that she faces. Many have argued that broad strategy should be targeted at ensuring that a woman and her children should be able to stay in their home. It is argued that too many resources are devoted to 'getting her and the children away'. The avoidance of disruption for already stressed women and children is clearly important, but that has to be balanced against a realistic risk assessment of whether they can be kept safe.

Hester, M., Pearson, C., Harwin, L. and Abrahams, H. (2006) *Making an Impact: children and domestic violence.* London: Jessica Kingsley.

Harne, L. and Radford, J. (2008) *Tackling Domestic violence: theories, policies & practice.* Maidenhead: McGraw-Hill.

Domestic Violence, Crime and Victims Act, 2004 an important piece of legislation that strengthens protective measures for people, mostly women, experiencing **domestic violence**.

Section 1 of this Act has sought to address the problem of breaches of **non-molestation** and **occupation orders** that were not being enforced effectively. From July 2007 a breach of a non-molestation order became a criminal offence, carrying a prison sentence of up to five years. This new power replaced the attachment of the 'power of arrest' to such an order that was the previous arrangement. In addition the Act allows same-sex couples and cohabiting couples to apply for non-molestation orders.

The most contentious new clause in the Act was that of encouraging the police to prosecute regardless of the woman's (victim's) wishes. This is a measure that has been in force in Canada for many years and has been widely regarded as having changed the social environment so that domestic violence is now so clearly unacceptable to the Canadian public. Women's Aid in the UK has suggested that there are both advantages and disadvantages to the new measures. The advantages include taking the decision away from women who may no longer be coerced by partners or ex-partners to withdraw a complaint. The sanctions too are now much tougher and, finally, women become witnesses rather than complainants. The disadvantages are that decisions are now taken out of women's hands, and that Black women in particular will fear very negative repercussions for their partners at the hands of the police especially in 'criminalising' them. Other technical objections include the lack of a criminal sanction when an occupation/exclusion order is breached. Such breaches are dealt with in civil courts so that a breach of an occupation/exclusion order and a non molestation order will require a woman to deal with both a criminal and a civil court, a source of additional stress during already difficult times. Many commentators have suggested that this is confirmation of a need for further simplification in the services, both justice and welfare, in relation to the multi-faceted problem of domestic violence.

domestic violence forum a group of agencies, comprising a mix of statutory and voluntary sector organizations, that have an interest in some aspect of the problem of **domestic violence**, who come together to try to work in a coordinated and considered way to support **victim**s and their children.

There are around 150 domestic violence forums in England and Wales. The composition of forums varies widely across the country although the Crown Prosecution, **police**, probation and social services are usually the statutory members together with **Women's Aid** as the most likely voluntary agency representative. Other agencies often involved include local authority housing departments and social landlords, health authorities, education departments, the Benefits Agency, youth services and other voluntary sector agencies such as **Victim Support**, Rape Crisis and various children's agencies such as NSPCC, Barnardos, Action for Children, Save the Children, and the Children's Society. A minority of forums have a small number of paid staff who are given the task of coordinating services, acting as a signposting agency for women actively seeking **advice** and support and ensuring good **communication**s between key agencies. Most forums however are 'virtual' entities meeting monthly, less frequently or occasionally.

It is apparent that attendance at forum meetings is also variable with some forums attended by senior officers able to commit resources to the forum while others will have front-line workers with little **power** beyond their own commitment. Yet domestic violence forums have considerable potential if statutory services in particular committed significant resources to them. Some have argued that the problem of domestic violence is at least as important as juvenile offending and that there is a compelling case to be made for establishing something like **youth offending teams** where key staff work together in a **team** wholly devoted to supporting women and children living with violence. Such dedicated resources in a 'one-stop' shop have the potential for the effective coordination of services as well as delivering coherent policy and relieving considerable stress in traumatic times.

drug and alcohol policy For many decades there has been public concern regarding the misuse of drugs and alcohol in non-medical contexts.

Historically, problematic use of drugs and alcohol misuse became recognized both as a medical disease, and as a criminal justice issue in the early 20th century, due to the harmful consequences of misuse for the

individual user and wider society. Modern policy continues to focus on
these dual concerns, taking its mandate from the enormous social and
economic costs of misuse – estimated at £20 billion a year for alcohol
misuse – relating to crime; disease and consequent use of health and **social
care** services; **loss** of productivity, and harm to families and communities.
A particular concern of current drugs policy is with the lifetime damage to
children's health and social functioning when parents misuse drugs.

In response to these concerns, criminal justice legislation prohibits the
use and supply of a range of drugs, and subjects alcohol use to a range of
restrictions and penalties. In parallel to these provisions, recognition of
misuse as a health matter means that the **NHS** and Adult Social Services
have legal powers and duties to provide assessment, treatment and services
to address related health and **social care** needs.

Drug and alcohol misuse takes place at different levels of severity,
linked in policy to different levels of response. These include *dependent
use*, diagnosed as a disease in the World Health Organization (2000)
International Classification of Diseases. Alcohol misuse is classified as
moderate dependency and *harmful and hazardous use*, while drugs
misuse is more generally classified as *problematic*. There are an estimated
350,000 problematic drug misusers in England and Wales, responsible
for 99 per cent of the social and economic costs of drugs misuse; about
7.1 million people who drink hazardously and harmfully, and over
1 million people dependent on alcohol. People with these levels of
problematic use often experience a range of other concerns including
unemployment, **poverty**, and physical and **mental health problems**,
and research has highlighted strong relationships between **childhood**
experiences of **abuse** and neglect, and **domestic violence** – for example in
Keene and Alison's (2001) study, one fifth of drug users misused drugs as
'self-medication' in relation to traumatic experiences of abuse.

Current drugs and alcohol policy are set out in the *Alcohol Harm
Reduction Strategy for England* (Department of Health 2004) and
The 10-year Drug Strategy (Home Office 2008). Both have the major
objective of harm reduction. This is to be achieved in relation to drugs
misuse through strategies concerned with the supply of drugs; access to
treatment, for drugs offenders; interventions with families where there are
drugs misusing parents; and strengthening of measures in treatment and
aftercare to promote recovery and social integration. **Personalization**
approaches including the use of **individual budgets** are also important.
Alcohol policy is similarly concerned with effective treatment, together
with criminal justice measures, better identification of alcohol problems,
and **community** education.

These policies are translated into practice by Models of Care for Drugs

Misuse Update, and Alcohol Misuse (National Treatment Agency 2006). Models of Care involve tiered multi-agency systems for **assessment** and response, and incorporate access to treatment through the criminal justice system – the Drugs Act 2005 for example, involves referral for assessment at arrest, and the courts can make treatment and testing orders on conviction.

Assessment and responses within these frameworks are carried out by both 'generic' agencies including adult social services, and by specialist drug and alcohol teams based within **primary care trust**s. Provisions for offenders are structured within drugs interventions programmes, and delivered by Criminal Justice Integrated Teams. Adult social services have had a key responsibility for drug and alcohol misuse under the **National Health Service and Community Care Act 1990**, and workers are brought into an even closer convergence with current policy through the concerns of drugs policy with substance misusing parents, and a new concern about misuse amongst other adult **service user**s such as learning disabled people and **older people**.

The multi-agency tiers within Models of Care include:

Tier 1 – Drug and alcohol-related information and advice, screening, referral to more specialized services, and brief interventions. 'Generic' services including social services assess and respond in this tier.

Tier 2 – Specialist provision of assessment, treatment and harm-reduction interventions, and assessment and referral for care-planned treatment for those presenting harmful and hazardous levels of misuse.

Tier 3 – Community-based, specialist and structured care-planned treatment involving coordinated, comprehensive multi-agency assessment and service provision for those with moderate to severe dependency levels. Many people with these dependency levels have complex needs with co-existing multiple concerns such as disability, mental health problems, poverty, domestic violence and housing problems. Integrated care pathways operate to coordinate the different services needed by these service users.

Tier 4 – Specialist in-patient treatment, residential rehabilitation, and care planning and coordination to promote 'continuity of care and aftercare'.

Social work is involved at most of these levels. At Tier 1 care managers in social services departments would conduct a screening for fair access to care eligibility assessment under the provisions of S47 National Health Service and Community Care Act, but they would also relate their assessment to drug and alcohol misuse. To do this, workers need a broad understanding of how drugs and alcohol misuse can impact on people's health, functioning, roles, family and wider environment, and to be able to identify different types of misuse and degrees of harm as a basis for referral. Generic services may also provide brief interventions for people at lower levels of misuse.

In Tiers 3 and 4 social workers will also be involved in comprehensive assessment and care planning, and a major concern of both frameworks is with supporting successful engagement with treatment, rehabilitation, recovery and re-integration with society. Social workers' powers under S46 of the National Health Service and Community Care Act enable them to fund residential rehabilitation. Importantly also they can provide community care services and supports related to housing, finances, transport, and access to occupation, education and employment – essential supports to service users in undertaking their 'drug treatment journeys'. Access to these services can not only meet practical needs, but social, psychological and emotional needs, all highly significant in relation to the complex needs, traumatic memories and adverse social circumstances faced by so many with these levels of misuse. These holistic supports to community re-integration also address one of the 'critical success factors' for improved treatment **outcomes**, and social supports generally have been found to be important with complex needs.

Home Office (2008) *Drugs: protecting families and communities*. London: Home Office.

National Treatment Agency for Substance misuse (2006) *Care planning Practice Guide*. London: NTA.

Keene, J. and Alison, L. (2001) Drug misusing parents: key points for health professionals. *Archives of Disease in Childhood*, 85: 296–9.

drug rehabilitation requirement a requirement which may be included in a **community order** or **suspended sentence order**, obliging the offender to submit to treatment for drug dependency and to mandatory drug testing. Such a requirement can only be included in an order if the offender expresses willingness to comply with the requirement.

drug treatment and testing order (DTTO) a court order requiring an offender who misuses drugs to submit to treatment for drug dependency and to mandatory drug testing and other conditions. DTTOs were introduced by the **Crime and Disorder Act 1998**. Although the order no longer exists as such, similar requirements can now be incorporated into a **community order** or a **youth rehabilitation order** (see also **drug rehabilitation requirement, drug treatment requirement, drug testing requirement**).

drug treatment requirement, drug testing requirement requirements which may be included in a **youth rehabilitation order**, with similar effect to an adult **drug rehabilitation requirement**.

E e

early release the release of a **prisoner** or other person **sentenced** to **custody** before the end of the **sentence**, whether automatically or by a discretionary process. Early release arrangements include **parole, home detention curfew** and **end of custody licence** (all discretionary). Automatic **early release** occurs at the halfway point of most **custodial sentences**. Release is on **licence**, and may be subject to conditions (for example regarding residence or **supervision**) imposed by the **Justice Secretary**. Following early release and up until the end of the **sentence**, the offender is at risk of being returned to **custody** if the **licence** conditions are **breached**, or if a further offence is committed or anticipated.

early years the term now used to denote children under 5 and the services provided for them.

A wealth of research has reported how important the years 0–5 are in terms of the child's development and accomplishments and for adult **wellbeing. Attachment**, environmental circumstances and parenting styles – authoritative, rather than authoritarian or permissive – all heavily impact on later educational attainments and sense of wellbeing. Neither 'nurture' nor 'nature' are influential in their own right but can only be defined in relationship to the other. There is an inter-relationship between environment and a child's natural endowments; hereditary strengths and vulnerabilities establish pathways that evolve together with stresses or buffers in the family, the neighbourhood and the school. That is why early experiences of **abuse**, neglect, **poverty**, and family violence are of such concern.

In the first two years of life the child passes through a number of thresholds that mark moving from individually mediated learning to wider socially based learning. For example, paying attention as part of a group, participating in social routines, responding with feeling to reciprocally developing relationships, engaging in independent, purposeful and sustained activities and use of language to establish joint meanings are all indicators of this development. Recent studies have revealed several pointers for practice. First, children from 0–4 need a variety of learning experiences that are active, relevant and enjoyable throughout that entire period. Second, education and care should be integrated in a well-planned, stimulating and healthy environment. Third, an appropriate curriculum should encourage active learning and 'purposeful **play**', and fourth, a **partnership** between parents and educators is essential to make that curriculum work.

Investment in early years programmes are highly cost effective. A stream of research has demonstrated that they discourage the development of criminal careers thus saving later significant expenditures on custodial regimes for those who would, but for the programme, have embarked on criminal or anti-social careers. Research has also established the benefits to parents in warmer, more nurturing relationships and reduction in stress with tangible cost benefits to families – for example in increased parental working hours. As a result of such findings government has taken several key initiatives to strengthen early years services. **Sure Start** local programmes encouraged new mothers to breastfeed their infants and underscored the importance of close and stimulating interaction with their child from infancy. A nationwide network of **children's centres** have provided care and education services and a provision of a foundation curriculum for children under 5 at **children's centres** and nursery schools demonstrate the extent of government investment in children's learning and development before the age of 5.

Sylva, K. *et al.* (2004) *The Effective Provision of Pre-School Education (EEPE) Project: findings from pre-school to end of key stage 1.* London: Department for Education and Skills.

early years foundation stage the statutory framework that all schools and registered **early years** providers have to use underpinning all care and education provision for all children from birth to 5 years of age. These include: reception and nursery classes in maintained and independent schools, day **nurseries**, childminders, playgroups, after school and breakfast clubs, holiday **play** schemes and **Sure Start children's centres**.

The framework identifies six areas of learning and six stages of development for children from birth to 60 months. There is an emphasis on learning through play and the importance of child-initiated play – rather than a diet of adult directed activity – is key. The foundation is designed to support the five **Every Child Matters outcomes**: staying safe; being healthy; enjoying and achieving; making a positive contribution; and achieving economic **wellbeing**. Children's achievements are monitored, assessed and recorded through the

Foundation Stage Profile, which has 13 **assessment** scales, each with nine progression points. The results of this record keeping are shared with parents.

EC Directive 79/7 concerned with the implementation of the principle of equal treatment for men and women in matters of social security. The directive applies to the working population, including self-employed people and workers whose employment is interrupted by illness, accidents at work and occupational diseases or involuntary unemployment and those seeking employment – and to retired or invalided workers and self-employed people. It does not, however, apply to schemes concerning family benefits other than those that provide for increases in benefits relating to risks that are within the scope of the directive (for example increases linked to unemployment). Nor does it extend to survivors' benefits. The UK courts have used the legislation to strike down legislation that directly or indirectly discriminates against groups like fathers, particularly if access to benefits is restricted on gender grounds and this does not serve any legitimate policy objective, and cannot be 'justified'. In *Hockenjos v Secretary of State for Social Security* (2004), for example, the Court of Appeal held that it was unjustifiable **discrimination** to withhold Jobseekers Allowance additions from a father who had a shared residence order, and therefore shared care responsibilities, on the basis that the mother received Child Benefit and was therefore treated as responsible for the children's care. The court ordered that the additions be paid to the father following his successful appeal. Although *Hockenjos* is less important than it used to be, especially since the Child Tax Credit replaced such additions, it remains an important precedent in relation to other benefits and support schemes that have discriminatory features, or which are operated in ways that are discriminatory.

ecological approach a perspective in **social work** that emphasizes the adaptive and reciprocal relationship between people and their environment.

The perspective sees a person's social environment as a set of concentric circles through which it is possible to picture how institutions, social attitudes and family dynamics promote or curtail the opportunities and **wellbeing** of individuals. Individuals develop within the *micro-system* of home and family, the *meso-system* of school, neighbourhood, and other local institutions such as churches, clubs and associations, and the *exo-system* through which more distant but powerful institutions and practices bear on the individual's life. For a child such institutions may be the parent's workplace (and their level of pay and working conditions), the conduct of local agencies such as youth clubs or something as everyday as the local public transport system. For a young adult it may be how information regarding job opportunities or skills training is transmitted. For a person with **disability** it may be the attitudes of local employers or the supported employment opportunities or more skills training. Finally, there is the *macro-system* – a large field embracing the cultural, political, economic, legal and religious context of society. It includes social attitudes and **values** that, although not always perceived in daily life, have a huge impact on individual lives. For example, our dominant images and opinions on gender, **older people**, HIV, crime and punishment emerge often from the macro-system.

The ecological approach lies behind the **assessment framework for children in need**. It helps social workers to highlight a range of factors that might otherwise have been overlooked in understanding the problems and needs of a person, family or local **community**. These include the importance of income and concrete resources, like childcare and employment opportunities, and better coordinated services around health, education and housing. It also shows the changes that can be achieved only by **community** building where the capacities of local people and neighbourhood organizations are developed. The ecological approach has features in common with **systems approaches** in its invitation to examine any and all parts of the **service user**'s social environment. But some critics argue that this tends to overplay societal consensus and as a result in practice social workers have tended to neglect the economic and neighbourhood environments within which families function.

Payne, M. (2005) *Modern Social Work Theory*, 3rd edition. London: Macmillan.

ecomap a diagrammatic representation of a network of people that have some kind of relationship with a focal person. The network, which can also be thought of as a 'mini-social system', might include family members, friends, neighbours and important others who have or have had some significance for the focal person. Some **social work** practitioners will also include non-human things that are important to the focal person such as a pet or some valued object such as a bicycle or a personal computer.

The convention is to use a number of small circles to represent the key players in the focal person's social system or network. The focal person is usually put into the centre of the page and the significant others are named and distributed around them. A line is then drawn between the focal person and the others; but the line will vary according to the nature of the relationship between the focal person and any individual. An unbroken line represents a close or strong relationship; a line with dashes represents a weak relationship; and, finally, a dotted line represents a stressful relationship. Of course it is also possible to draw lines directly between significant others to illustrate the quality of the relationship say of a child's parents, or of the relationship between a parent and a grandparent. In essence an **ecomap** is a device that can be used to explore the social environment of anyone.

Although ecomaps are used with a wide range of client groups they are routinely used in direct work with children to uncover stresses and conflicts in a child's family and social network. The process of compiling an ecomap with a child can be revealing if undertaken carefully and patiently. Some social workers use them when working on **life story books** especially for **looked after children** or adopted children and sometimes with young offenders. Ecomaps are also used to help social workers, in **partnership** with **service user**s, identify who might be invited to a **family group conference**, to mobilize whole families and significant others to try to solve their own problems. Ecomaps can be very helpful in uncovering problems that are not immediately visible and thus can be helpful in suggesting the nature of further enquiries and potential **social work** interventions. The use of ecomaps may be consistent with work undertaken especially with **systems approaches** and **ecological approaches** in mind. See *Assessing Children in Need and their Families: practice guidance*. Department of Health, 2000.

Education Act 1996 the current framework for most educational provision, which replaced the previous core Education Act 1944. The Act consolidated all earlier legislation on the education of children. Under it, the local authority has a duty to make provision and parents have a legal obligation to secure their child's education either by regular attendance at a school or 'otherwise'. If the local authority is satisfied that the child is not receiving a suitable education, it may take legal action against the parent (see **prosecution**) or, for children not registered at a school, may serve a **School Attendance Order** on the parents. Failure to comply with such an order by admitting the child to a school is an offence. The Act also defines arrangements for **special educational needs** where a child has **learning difficulties**. Many school organizational issues, for example, the introduction of Academies (effectively state-funded private schools outside the management of the local authority) have been dealt with in subsequent legislation.

Education Act 2002 the legislation that defines the duty of a school, through its governors or proprietors and in both the public and private sectors, to ensure that procedures are in place to 'safeguard and promote' the welfare of children. This is the basis of a requirement that all schools have an effective **safeguarding** policy and that they operate a process of **safer recruitment**, as well as systems for combating **bullying**.

Education Act 2006 requires parents to ensure the education of their child, either by regular attendance at school or 'otherwise'. **Unauthorized absence** i.e. absences for which the school has not given permission, constitute an offence, (s.444) though the number that may be required to justify **prosecution** will vary according to circumstances, especially the parents' attitude. Most **local authorities** have a process of initial **warning**s, meetings to try and resolve the problems and placing parents under formal notice or **caution** that any further absences may result in prosecution. **Penalty notices** may be issued as an alternative, especially for a first offence. The most common outcome is a **fine**. Subsequent prosecutions for the more serious offence under section 444 can result in higher **fine**s or, in very exceptional circumstances, **imprisonment** of up to 3 months.

There has always been a lively debate over the effectiveness of prosecution. The National Foundation for Educational Research published two reports in 2004 that concluded that prosecution was effective in about two-fifths of cases, in that the children concerned subsequently improved their attendance (NFER 2004). But many local authority officers and parents also reported that the proceedings often made little difference, or that the threat of court action was actually more use than actually going ahead with it, especially in response to situations that had already become entrenched. Further research by Ming Zhang in a lecture at Cambridge University in 2007 (unpublished) came to similar conclusions. Nothing always 'works' in all situations. There is a general signal from the government that 'good' authorities and schools are frequent users of the courts, though some would argue that having to prosecute a parent is a sign of failure that is always best avoided if possible.

There is no obvious evidence that those authorities or schools that make most use of prosecution also have the best attendance figures; that would in any case be an unfair measure. Neither are prosecutions best evaluated by how high the **fine**s are – some of which will not actually be paid or will be reduced later on appeal. Prosecution is time-consuming for the individual officer and little evidence is currently available that can demonstrate the facts one way or the other, but it is important to reinforce the right messages by taking action when appropriate. But **education welfare officer**s also know that many families do not necessarily respond to court action. If there are major family problems, action under the **common assessment framework** is likely to be preferable, but this requires the cooperation of the parent (and the child or young person). Severe cases of non-attendance may actually be evidence of neglect that should be addressed under **safeguarding** procedures and, in extreme cases, might even result in **care proceedings** alongside other issues of **significant harm** (see also **emotional abuse and neglect**).

Whitney, B. (2004) *A Guide to School Attendance*. London: David Fulton/Routledge Falmer.

Department of Health (2000) *Assessing Children in need and their Families: practice guidance*. London: DH.

National Foundation for Educational Research (2004) *School Attendance and the Prosecution of Parents: effects and effectiveness*. London: NFER.

education requirement   a requirement which may be included in a **youth rehabilitation order**, obliging the offender to comply with arrangements for his or her education made by the offender's parent or guardian and approved by the local education authority.

education social work   see **education welfare service**

education supervision order (ESO)   provision under the **Children Act 1989** (section 36) whereby a local authority education officer may apply to the **family proceedings court** to have a child who is not being 'properly educated' placed under the local authority's **supervision**, initially for one year. The order may be extended for up to 3 years.

As with all Children Act orders, an ESO must be considered to be better for the child than making no order. In practice, these powers have been used to only a very limited extent, largely because **local authorities** lack the necessary resources to ensure effective involvement at such an intensive level but partly because making an order, in itself, will often not resolve the problems of a child who is not attending school. An ESO places a parent under a duty to follow the 'directions' of the supervisor, usually an officer of the **education welfare service**. This is likely to be helpful only where parents are failing to act responsibly or where a child has complex needs, including **special educational needs** that the parent cannot meet unaided.

An ESO is unlikely to be helpful in addressing the needs of a young person who is entirely disaffected with education or beyond the control of his or her parents. **Local authorities** have a duty to assess whether other services and orders may be needed in the event of the child failing to follow reasonable directions. An ESO may be a useful alternative to a **School Attendance Order** where a child on **elective home education** is defined not to be being properly educated by their parents, but where it may still not be appropriate for them to attend a school.

education welfare service/officers   a local authority service that supports the education of vulnerable and marginalized pupils and promotes and enforces attendance at school or other forms of compulsory education.

Increasingly officers are also involved in strategic support to schools in raising attendance and meeting targets, especially those to reduce **persistent absence**.

Education welfare is one of the oldest forms of public welfare provision for children, dating back at least to the Education Act 1870 and the extension of compulsory education through local school boards. Whether such work is '**social work**' is a matter of some debate, not always resolved by the title chosen by the local authority for its particular service. The Ralphs Report of 1973 highlighted the nature of the tasks as being substantially the same as other forms of **social work**, but governments have generally taken the view that their role should be more 'educational' and less 'social work' in focus. There is no national professional career standard or qualification though increasing numbers of education welfare officers (EWO) are obtaining an NVQ level 4 qualification as part of the children's workforce and most are graduates. **Social work** qualification is not a requirement in most current services, although some **local authorities** still seek to appoint qualified staff as EWOs and may have other roles for non-qualified staff.

Attendance officers were historically responsible for identifying children in their area who were not registered at any school or receiving education in some other way and establishing whether they should be enrolled. Much of this work involved seeking to assist children who could not attend school because of **poverty**, supervising children at work and protecting children found to be at risk of harm. These duties still form the core of such officers' responsibilities, including **children missing education**. The traditional perception of the role of attendance officers as based only on legal enforcement does not do justice to what were quite sophisticated attempts to approach the work from a 'welfare' perspective. Although the failure of parents to ensure that their children are 'properly educated' has always been an offence (currently with a maximum **fine** of £1,000 for a first offence and up to £2,500 or brief **imprisonment** subsequently), contemporary commentators noted as early as the beginning of the 20th century that these officials were acting as the 'children's friend and the parents' adviser' rather than relying too much on their **power** to prosecute. With the provision of financial assistance for meals at school from 1902, as well as the administration of charitable funds for clothing and footwear, the welfare of children at school formed a much wider agenda than simply forcing children to attend.

With the Children Act 1948 much of this wider responsibility passed to the children's committees and then to social services departments. The **power** to have children placed into the care of the local authority for not attending school disappeared with the **Children Act 1989**. Education welfare has tended to be seen as of lower status than other forms of local authority social work provision, though EWOs may still have a key role in local **safeguarding** procedures and work under the **common assessment framework**. The major focus has continued to be school attendance, although EWOs may also be involved in monitoring the **employment of children**, and assisting children with special educational needs or reducing **exclusion from school**. With a continuing debate about the future of **local authorities**, their declining role in the day-to-day management of schools and the growing emphasis on delegating resources to schools, EWOs still face an uncertain future, as they have for several years. Some EWOs feel that recent changes have tended to undermine their traditional role of being independent advocates for children and have made them more accountable to head teachers than they would prefer.

In many situations it will now be a teaching or non-teaching member of the school staff who should be the first point of **contact** when a child has a problem at school rather than the EWO. Many schools are appointing their own staff, such as attendance officers or home/school liaison workers. These have taken over much of the low-level work previously done by EWOs who will be likely to concentrate more on statutory work, data analysis, specialist **advice** and assistance in policy development as much as **casework**. All schools will normally have a named EWO, increasingly as a member of a **multi-agency** team, usually working with the school under a service level agreement that defines the role and the time available in which to do it.

Whitney, B. (2008) *A Guide to School Attendance*. London: David Fulton/Routledge Falmer.

educational inclusion a term used by the Office for Standards in Education (**Ofsted**) to describe educational processes, structures and policies that promote more effective **outcomes** for children who are currently marginalized from learning or facing **exclusion from school**.

Many of these children will be **children in need** as defined by the **Children Act 1989** or 'vulnerable' children and will therefore be receiving services from a variety of agencies. Guidance from **Ofsted** for school inspectors talks of the importance of local authority and school staff 'identifying those at risk of missing out and taking positive steps to promote their involvement'. Many **local authorities** will be promoting the interests of such children through their education welfare service or other staff appointed to promote **social inclusion** and through school improvement advisors working with schools at policy level. Schools will also be developing their own responses, such as the appointment of staff to follow up children who are absent or in-school learning support units.

This whole approach often has to be held in tension with other educational priorities that tend to encourage selection and separation rather than maximizing the achievement of the whole population. Promoting educational inclusion is a key task of all schools but is often tempered in practice by national and local political decisions about the organization and management of schools and the significance of performance tables.

There has been a strong political commitment to promoting inclusion in recent years. For example, 'By 2020 the government would like all schools to be models of social inclusion, enabling all pupils to participate fully in school life while instilling a long-lasting respect for human rights, freedoms, cultures and creative expression' (National College for School Leadership website). This clearly links to the **Every Child Matters** agenda in seeking to promote educational opportunity for children from disadvantaged groups traditionally disaffected with mainstream education. **Outcomes** for this group have consistently been poor. Teachers have been encouraged to use ways of teaching that differentiate between the various needs of their pupils, while maintaining a universal entitlement to a national curriculum. This is difficult and challenging in practice but case studies from many schools testify to its possibility.

However, critics of inclusion would argue that many pupils are not able to cope in a mainstream environment and that specialist provision, either in separate classes, units or even special schools, is more likely to address their needs. This is especially the case where the source of the child's difficulties is social and behavioural as much as cognitive or intellectual. Part of this argument will also be that the learning of other pupils may be seriously disrupted by the inclusion of those who either do not really want to be there or who simply do not understand what is going on around them.

Similar arguments also apply to the approach to educating certain ethnic minority groups. While the principle of inclusion in schools clearly contributes to a more inclusive society beyond the school gate, it is argued by some that some groups will inevitably dominate and that the needs of less articulate or culturally inhibited students will be overlooked. Teachers need to be adept at recognizing different learning styles, cultural norms and attitudes to authority. This may be easier if the range of learners is more restricted but such an approach may also do little to promote their engagement with the wider **community,** or promote wider recognition of their particular contribution to society as a whole. This is a major debate in education which has many practical implications for what school children may go to and what they may be offered when they are there. See also **inclusion** and **social inclusion.**

For an overview see: Black-Hawkins, K., Florian, L. and Rouse, M. (2007) *Achievement and Inclusion in Schools.* London: Routledge.

educational maintenance allowance see **welfare rights 4**

educational psychologist a psychologist with additional training in all matters concerned with addressing learning difficulties or social and emotional problems that impact upon learning.

Educational psychologists are usually employed by local education authorities. They have responsibility for conducting statutory assessments of **special educational needs**, determining what educational provision is appropriate and for giving **advice** as to how a child's needs might best be met. Educational psychologists also devise packages to assist learning, to support parents and school staff, and to facilitate behaviour change. If provision within a school under **school action and school action plus** is not meeting the child's needs, they may be asked to assess the child with a view to more specialized provision, either in a mainstream or special school. (See also **statement of special educational needs**.) Working directly with children, educational psychologists may observe, **interview** and assess; and recommend strategies to children, teachers and parents to enhance children's learning. They may also work indirectly with other professionals seeking to understand a child's behaviour and apparent difficulties.

elder abuse see **adult abuse**

elective home education the right of a parent, arising currently from the **Education Act 1996** section 7 (but with a much longer history), to educate their child 'otherwise' than at school if they wish. Ensuring that all children are 'properly educated' is a universal requirement on parents, but requiring their attendance at a school to receive the education offered there is not, unless the child is a 'registered pupil'.

Nobody knows how many home educated children there are as there has traditionally been no requirement on parents to register their provision with the local authority. (This may change following an Inquiry in 2009 and possible new legislation.) About 25,000 children under 16 are known to be home educated but the number could be as high as 80–100,000. There has been concern that some may in fact be working illegally, subject to neglect of their educational needs or at risk of other forms of abuse. There have been examples of children subject to serious case reviews where the fact that the child was not expected to attend school, and therefore was not noticed to be missing or injured, has proved to be at least a contributory factor in the parents' ability to keep professionals from finding out what was happening behind closed doors.

However, many parents deliver their own forms of education effectively and are staunch defenders of their right to do so. The organization

Education Otherwise, for example, provides web-based and other resources to support parents and promotes the right to teach their own children without what they see as excessive local authority intervention and **supervision**. Parents do not have to deliver the national curriculum, arrange tests or examinations or even spend any time in formal lessons. The education does not have to look like what would happen in a school but it does have to give the child opportunity to develop the skills they may need for adult life. However, this can be interpreted in a very narrow sense, especially by some adherents to particular religious faiths, rather than opening up the child's experience to possibilities and insights beyond those shared by their immediate family. Parents are required to produce evidence of the child's learning, and the local authority can serve a **School Attendance Order** or seek an **education supervision order** if they are not satisfied with the provision. However, given the current vague requirements about what a 'suitable' education must contain, this can often be very difficult to prove in practice.

electronic monitoring   the practice of electronically 'tagging' offenders to check their compliance with **curfews** and other restrictions ordered by courts (notably **exclusion requirements**). Electronic monitoring began in North America in the 1980s. The equipment involved consists of a transmitter about the size of a wristwatch, which is attached to the offender's wrist or ankle in such a way that it cannot be removed without this being detected. Equipment is also installed at the offender's home, requiring a telephone line, and this sends signals to a computer at the offices of the private company that runs the monitoring arrangements.

   Electronic monitoring is normally used merely to enforce a home curfew imposed for a number of hours in the day. (See **curfew**.) More advanced systems are also capable of 'tracking' an offender using satellite technology to establish their exact whereabouts at any time, and thus can be used to monitor compliance with **exclusion requirements**. Many of the early technical problems associated with electronic monitoring have been surmounted or reduced, but the technology is still far from perfect. There are also concerns that curfews and monitoring may have the effect, not of reducing the **prison** population by providing an acceptable alternative to **custody**, but of net widening by being applied to offenders who might otherwise have been subjected to less intrusive or more helpful measures.

   Shute, S. (2004) *Satellite Tracking of Offenders: a study of the pilots in England and Wales*, Research Summary 4. London: Ministry of Justice.

emergency protection order (EPO)   an order under section 44 of the **Children Act 1989** allowing a local authority social worker (or an officer of the National Society for the Prevention of Cruelty to Children) to remove a child from his or her parents or other adults, or to retain the child in a safe place, such as a hospital, if the worker has reasonable cause to believe that the child is suffering or is likely to suffer **significant harm**. The order may also be applied for if the social worker is unreasonably denied access to a child who is likely to suffer **significant harm**, the so-called 'frustrated access' condition.

An EPO is usually obtained by the practitioner's application before a **magistrate** without other parties to the case, such as the child's parents, present (see *ex parte*). The application must outline the circumstances in detail, including why the child is likely to suffer **significant harm**. If the social worker thinks that entry to the home where the child is living will be refused, he or she can ask the court for a warrant to enter the premises and for a **police** officer to assist in this.

The order lasts for 8 days, with a possible 7-day extension in exceptional circumstances. A consequence of the order is that the local authority shares **parental responsibility** with the child's parents while the order is in force but should exercise it only as it is reasonably required to safeguard or promote the welfare of the child. During this time the local authority must decide on the course of action it is to take, such as returning the child home or preventing the child from going home by asking the court for a **care order**. While the order is in force the local authority has a continuing duty to keep the case under review. If at any time while the order is in force the authority thinks it is safe to return the child home, it must do so. On the other hand should the local authority do this whilst the EPO remains in force it may again remove the child without any further judicial intervention if it appears that a further change of circumstances make this necessary.

Every person with parental responsibility should receive a copy of the application for an EPO at least one day prior to the hearing *unless* the hearing is to be *ex parte*, that is without parents or other parties to the case being present. However, under rules governing the EPO, if the hearing for the order is *ex parte* the application as well as the order itself is only required to be served on the parents within 48 hours *after* it has been made, thus delaying in practice any application to **discharge**. There is no **appeal** against the making of an EPO or its extension. Parents, the child or anyone with whom the child was living before the order was made may apply for a discharge of the order after 72 hours only if the original order were made *ex parte*.

As long as the order is in force, parents and their representatives enjoy reasonable **contact** with the child, unless the court has made a specific direction to the contrary (see **contact direction**). One of the main objectives of the **Children Act 1989** is to ensure that **local authorities** remove children only when this is necessary in order to protect life and limb. **Department of Health** guidance says that authorities should try to secure the child's safety through measures other than the EPO, if at all possible, such as providing family support services. The Act succeeded in this objective in the **early years** after implementation in 1991 when the number of emergency protection orders taken by authorities had fallen significantly compared with emergency removals of children under previous childcare law. But particular cases more recently have triggered greater pre-emptive use of emergency protection orders – particularly **Victoria Climbié** and '**Baby Peter**'.

In general cases of **emotional abuse** and non-specific allegations of **sexual abuse** where there is no evidence of immediate risk will rarely warrant an EPO. Underscoring the draconian nature of the EPO Justice Mumby in *X Council v B (EPO) [2005]* wrote that an EPO is a 'terrible and drastic remedy' requiring 'exceptional justification and extraordinarily compelling reasons'. Each local authority and the court, he said, in granting an EPO should approach every application with an 'anxious awareness of the extreme gravity of the relief being sought' and a scrupulous regard for the European Convention of Human Rights. Notice of application should normally be provided to parents; an *ex parte* application will normally 'be appropriate only if the case is genuinely one of emergency or other great urgency . . . or if there are compelling reasons to believe that the child's welfare will be compromised if the parents are alerted in advance . . . (See also **child assessment order**.)

Department of Health (1991) *Guidance to the Children Act. Vol. 1: Court Orders*. London: HMSO.

emotional abuse and neglect terms used rather loosely by many writers to describe negative psychological effects on people resulting from the damaging behaviour of others.

'Neglect' is a term suggesting systematic or major inattention by a parent, close member of a family or carer. Emotional abuse has been considered by some to be an active process and neglect an act of omission, but this distinction is hard to sustain and is probably not useful. Emotional abuse and neglect clearly overlap. Emotional abuse can be a result of physical or **sexual abuse**, or it can be a consequence of other behaviours rooted in sustained unpleasant and unhappy transactions between two or more people. In **social work** most recent attention on this issue has focused on children, although emotional abuse can relate to adult relationships within whole families or specifically to vulnerable elders, adults with disabilities and to marital and partner relationships.

Some writers prefer the term 'psychological abuse' because they regard emotional reactions as properly the province of psychology. Others differentiate between matters pertaining to the mind as against issues of feelings or emotions. Clinical psychologists would regard the distinction as unsustainable, arguing that feelings and emotions are the concern of psychology and provide crucial evidence of personal adjustment or maladjustment. The distinction, in their view, possibly originates in a confusion about means and ends. Physical, sexual or emotional abuse can all, singly or in combinations, lead to psychological maladjustment. Different forms of abuse (means) may result in psychological problems (ends).

Whatever term is used, there is some consensus about the kind of behaviour that can be described as emotionally abusing. Intimidating behaviour, deprivation of a carer or loved one, loneliness and isolation, withholding approval or a consistent negative response, constant refusal to recognize someone's needs or worth and the encouragement of negative or **anti-social behaviour** can all be usefully cited. Physical and sexual abuse can be emotionally damaging too. To have been physically or sexually assaulted, and perhaps to live in fear of it happening again, is almost certainly to experience at least some of the circumstances described above. The severity of the abuse depends on a number of factors, including its duration, the age and maturity of the abused, and the degree of **power** exercised by the abuser.

In relation to children, it is comparatively rare for courts to issue an **emergency protection order** on the basis of emotional abuse alone. Even with children who are clearly very unhappy and are displaying major indicators of psychological disturbance, and even with non-specific allegation of sexual abuse, courts have encouraged social service departments to pursue an application for an **interim care order** rather than an EPO, with justices then prepared to transfer the application up to a County Court or **High Court**. Yet establishing proof of allegations of emotional abuse and meeting the **threshold criteria** for an order is difficult in part due to the varying levels of resilience of the children involved. A range of programmes, some school-based, focusing on the 'emotional intelligence' of the child and family aim at adjusting relationships within families to tackle the emotional difficulties that families construct for themselves. Social workers appear to be more confident about dealing with neglect. For children to develop normally, they require regular stimulation for them to become emotionally, intellectually, physically and socially mature. Neglect can lead to ill-health because of a failure to provide a child with appropriately nutritious food or an unwillingness or inability to keep them reasonably clean. Significant under-stimulation of children in their first years has similar effects, leading to poor development of intellectual capacity; if there is lack of interaction with other children or adults, then social abilities and skills will be stunted too. One of the major objectives of **children's centres** and **early years** programmes in general is to help educate parents on how important diet, stimulation and **play**, and interaction with parents and others are to the capacities of the child.

Emotional abuse and neglect exist in relation to adults with some parallels to that of children, particularly in relation to adults who are dependent on carers or family members for care and social interaction. Adult safeguarding teams have to make judgements that balance risk, the degree of neglect and physical abuse and the closeness of the relationship to the caregiver(s). Deprivation of food, speaking harshly over a period of time, taking advantage of cognitive confusion, continuous criticism, denying **contact**s with others are some of the forms of emotional abuse and neglect that occur. A similar balance of factors is applicable in cases of **domestic violence** where a male (or less likely, female) is stalking or otherwise harassing an estranged partner.

O'Hagan, K. (2006) *Identifying Emotional and Psychological Abuse: A Guide for Childcare Professionals.* Maidenhead: Open University Press.

emotional, social and behavioural difficulties (ESBD) a defined category of **special educational needs** (SEN) that result in a child's learning being significantly impaired.

Clearly not all instances of unacceptable or unwelcome behaviour on the part of a child should be treated as evidence of difficulty. For some children their learning and social and emotional development may be adversely affected by persistent patterns of inappropriate behaviours. Such behaviours could include: being withdrawn or isolated, disruptive or disturbing, hyperactive with poor concentration; being violent or self-harming; having long-term **mental health problems** or eating disorders. Schools will be expected to try and meet and manage the needs or these children through consistent application of published behaviour policies. Generally teachers and school staff will be trained to adopt a supportive and positive attitude rather than being punitive towards children. Where 'in-house' management is judged to be insufficient, schools – in **partnership** with parents – should take action in line with the **Special Educational Needs Code of Practice**.

employment of children the part-time employment of children still of **compulsory school age**. The employment of children is subject to regulation and **inspection** by the local authority in accordance with national legislation and local bylaws.

The primary legislation governing the employment of children, the **Children and Young Persons Act 1933**, is badly in need of reform. Although new bylaws were introduced in 1998, many elements of the primary legislation remained unchanged. These regulations cover only employment in any commercial undertaking carried on for profit, whether or not the child is paid; i.e. working in a business. Consequently, jobs such as babysitting or washing neighbours' cars are exempt, but newspaper delivery, shop work, waitressing and so on must all be licensed individually or the employer (not the child or their parent) is committing an offence.

No child can be employed at all under the age of 13 (14 in some **local authorities**), before 7.00 a.m. or after 7.00 p.m. on any day, or for more than 2 hours on a Sunday. A child may not be employed for more than 12 hours in any week (including the weekend) in which he or she is also required to attend school. There are various other limits on the number of hours for which a child may be employed and a wide list of prohibited employments. Thirteen-year-olds can only do jobs on a 'specified list'.

There are widespread **breach**es of the law involving both the work that children do and the hours in which they do it. Research shows that most children work at some point before they leave school and that most work is unlicensed and therefore illegal. Prosecution of employers is rare, partly because of the antiquated nature of the regulations, which do not command widespread public support, but partly because the issue is not seen as a priority in government thinking and there are no targets to achieve improvements. Some local authorities are more vigilant and proactive than others, and there is some concern at the level of injury and exposure to risks by children in the workplace which is largely tolerated. Different regulations govern work experience as part of approved **alternative educational provision**, and there are also rules relating to the protection of children who take part in professional entertainments, film, TV, theatre etc. and sports.

It is interesting to consider why this area of children's lives has remained subject to so little reform and new regulation for almost 80 years, in marked contrast to so many other areas. The rules are essentially the same as they were when the school-leaving age was 14, when shops were all closed on Sundays and long before the creation of many of the currently available opportunities. School term dates still essentially reflect the need for children to be available to help with harvesting! Indeed rules have sometimes been set aside entirely (for example in wartime) and there was widespread protest when it was proposed that the hundreds of thousands of children who look after horses in commercial stables should be defined as 'employed'. It may be true that much of what children do is acceptable, though it could be also argued that delivering newspapers alone at 7.00 in the morning on a February school day is hardly consistent with contemporary notions of what is in a child's best interests, and there is also ample evidence that some work is exploitative and inappropriate. But it appears to be true that children who work part-time tend to be better motivated than their peers and most still achieve well at school. It seems that the benefits gained in achieving positive **outcomes** outweigh the risks.

Lavallette, M. *et al.* (1999) *A Thing of the Past? – child labour in Britain in the 19th and 20th centuries.* Liverpool: Liverpool University Press.

empowerment any process whereby those lacking, comparatively, in **power** become or are helped to become more powerful. The acquisition of power is thought appropriate to them as citizens, consumers or **service user**s. There are both personal and political dimensions to the concept.

Empowerment implies a kind of 'power deficit' theory, very much in the same territory as the **social exclusion** paradigm. Empowerment can refer to, for example, **self-help**, to **community** action, to an involvement in a political process but also to any transactions between a service user and a social worker or helping professional. In relation to the latter 'micro' definition, empowerment means that service users can become more powerful as a result of engaging with helping professionals in particular ways in attempts to solve their problem(s). Empowerment can be regarded as liberational in intent. In relation to service users it is concerned with several inter-related issues. First, many service users do not understand their own needs or problems or they have an incomplete understanding of them or, indeed, they have attributed their problem incorrectly to a particular cause. Further, some may have an understanding of their needs or problems but find it difficult to articulate them. Finally, many do not know how to solve their own problems or, if they do know how, lack the confidence to initiate action.

These kinds of problems of disempowerment may have their roots in low levels of education, including illiteracy, in problems of confidence or self-esteem, in difficulties of **communication**, such as English being a second language or in being profoundly deaf and without access to an interpreter or someone conversant with British Sign Language, in having lived a marginalized life in which decisions or even opinions were not required.

Practical approaches to empowerment can include detailed explanations of problems and of possible solutions to those problems; helping people to make informed decisions about the 'way forward'; helping them to write their own letter; rehearsing what might be said in a forthcoming interview, telephone call, review or case conference; helping them to access an appropriate form of **advocacy**; or sharing any of these tasks with the service user so that they might feel more confident to 'go it alone' in the future. Empowerment can rarely be achieved in one step; it is often incremental especially for those wholly unused to representing themselves or their own feelings and needs and especially if they have previously experienced consistent oppression.

Professionals in helping and caring occupations believe that it is possible to empower service users by working with them in open, transparent and non-oppressive ways. In this context, minimizing the 'social distance' between professional and service user is thought to be crucial, as is working to the service user's agenda, facilitating understanding, supporting or sharing problem-solving activities, being prepared to review problems and tasks, building social skills and, in general, trying to increase the service user's abilities to deal with his or her own problems. In sum, this view of empowerment embraces the idea that people can acquire more power and, crucially, be able to use it effectively in meeting their needs and problem solving.

Other writers have perceived **self-help** activities as having great potential for empowering service users. This view of empowerment emphasizes the importance of not involving professionals and of learning from experience with others who have or have had the same problems. Empowerment is thought more likely to come about because the learning experience will be more profound, service users will be able to act more freely in exploring the utility of problem-solving activities and, if resources are delegated to service users (as with **direct payments**), they will be able to have control over which services are purchased. This view of empowerment rests upon a view that service users are, in a sense, experts in their own problems or needs, or at least that their experience of their problems or needs is valuable in deciding how best to develop services. **Radical social work** has taken the view that the key issue in empowerment is to explicitly connect 'people with problems' with the political process.

Regardless of whether the impetus to connect the personal to the political is driven by professional **advice** or **self-help**, the crucial issue is to uncover the political nature of health and social welfare services and of the political structures within which they operate. In this context the point is not that service users should be 'consulted' but that they should be a core and necessary part of the political process. Empowerment is thus a concept that invites analyses of professional service user relationships, of how power unavoidably colours that relationship, of how that relationship might be reconfigured to make it more equal (and by so doing, empower both service user and professional) and of how power imbalances characterize the relationship between service users/citizens and social institutions, including political institutions and agencies concerned with health and social welfare. In sum, empowerment admits of the possibility of change in both key personal relationships and in the relationship between people and social and political structures. (See also **advocacy**.)

end of custody licence a form of **early release** introduced in June 2007 in response to rising numbers of **prison**ers. **Prison** governors were authorized to make wider use of existing rules to release on **licence prison**ers serving **sentences** of 4 years or less (who have not been released under **home detention curfew**) up to 18 days before their normal release date. Although announced as a temporary measure, the scheme is still operating.

Equality and Human Rights Commission (EHRC) a statutory body which was established under the Equality Act 2006. The EHRC enforces equality legislation around seven key areas or 'protected' grounds: age, **disability**, gender, race, religion or belief, sexual orientation or transgender status. They are also able to provide guidance around equality issues, promote good practice, and influence policy.

The EHRC replaces the previous equalities organizations (the Equal Opportunities Commission, the Commission for Racial Equality and the Disability Rights Commission) and operates in order 'to reduce inequality, eliminate **discrimination**, strengthen good relations between people, and promote and protect human rights'.

The Scottish Commission for Human Rights was established by the Scottish Human Rights Act in 2006 accountable to the Scottish Parliament. The Memorandum of Understanding between the EHRC and the SCHR indicates that both bodies hope to work collaboratively where there are areas of common interest and, so far as is possible, to 'arrive at common policy decisions'. In Northern Ireland the Equality Commission has been established to address the same seven 'protected' groups as the UK EHRC and, in addition, has absorbed the roles, responsibilities and powers of the former Fair Employment Commission which sought to eliminate discrimination in Northern Ireland in relation to the employment of Catholics and Protestants.

The move towards a unified equalities commission signals a shift in thinking about equal opportunities and diversity and emphasizes the intersecting nature of inequalities, for example, in relation to gender and race inequalities. Whilst many have welcomed this realization and shift away from what Bagilhole (2009) describes as a 'mono focus' approach, it remains the case that there is a continued need for adequate recognition of the complex nature of contemporary discrimination and disadvantage as experienced by certain groups.

Bagilhole, B. (2009) *Understanding Equal Opportunities and*

Diversity: the social differentiations and intersections of inequality. Bristol: Policy Press.

equal opportunities policy a **statement** of intended practice adopted by an organization to confront **discrimination** in relation to both the employment of staff and the delivery of services.

Equal opportunities policies are usually prefaced by a guiding **statement** of principle. Such **statements** usually indicate which groups are recognized by the organization as experiencing **discrimination** within the wider society. Thus **gender**, 'race', marital status, **disability** and religious commitments are invariably found in such statements. Age, ex-offenders, social class or social status and sexual orientation or preference are mentioned less often, especially the latter. In the case of public bodies and agencies there is less discretion given in the way policies are formulated, and statements are implemented, especially given the statutory duties imposed on them by anti-discrimination legislation like the Equality Act 2009.

In relation to employment practices, some social welfare employers operate procedures that are more rigorous than they once were. Thus, job descriptions, person specifications, **interview** schedules and formal decision-making procedures have been adopted as good practice by many organizations. The willingness of organizations to adopt additional procedures to address revealed **discrimination** within their organization is much more limited. Monitoring of applications, the effectiveness of targeted advertising, appointments, promotions and uptake of training opportunities are indicators of organizations' willingness to identify problems and to take **positive action** to address them.

All organizations ought to be able to present annual reports in which they can specify progress made in relation to agreed policy targets. For example, a report should be able to indicate how many employees with disabilities are currently part of the workforce, what efforts have been made over the past year to increase the numbers of disabled workers (if, indeed, this had been an acknowledged problem in the previous year), an evaluation of those efforts and finally an action plan for the forthcoming year. The organization's plan should include all groups experiencing discrimination.

With reference to issues of service delivery, social welfare organizations' performance has been very uneven. A full and comprehensive **equal opportunities policy** should contain an analysis of **anti-discriminatory** measures needed with all user groups. Thus with **older people**, as a user group, the needs of black, poor and disabled elders should all be separately identified, as should those who have a religious affiliation or are gay or lesbian. Where little is known about a particular group's needs, plans should be devised to collect critical information. Also, action plans need to be drawn up to address particular policy objectives. An example will serve to illustrate this sequence. It may be noted, as a result of monitoring processes, that no Black elders use social service day-care facilities, and it is not known why this is so. A plan to consult Black **community** organizations is devised. Offers are made to arrange visits to day-care centres for individuals, families and community groups. Critical information leaflets are translated into the appropriate languages, and efforts are made to highlight the services with other key social welfare personnel such as doctors and other support health workers.

Such a process shows the link between reviews of policies, monitoring and planning. Sometimes, however, it is possible to have policies in place, but an organization may make little progress in relation to anti-discriminatory practice. Researchers have sought to understand this problem by looking at the organization's culture or climate. Where people are actually involved and committed to policies they are more likely to work in practice. In this respect, it is likely that a commitment to equal opportunities in relation to service delivery will enhance an organization's commitment to equal opportunities in employment practices. An organization that actually employs disabled people, has women in senior positions and has Black people at all levels is more likely to deliver services that promote equal opportunities.

Equal Pay Act 1970 an Act of Parliament that seeks to deal with **discrimination** against women specifically in relation to pay. Under the Act, women are defined to have an 'equality clause' in their contract. This has a number of legal effects, the main one being that where the woman is employed on like work with a man in the same employment if any term of the woman's contract is (or becomes) less favourable to her than a term of a similar kind in the contract under which that man is employed, that term is to be treated as modified so as not to be less favourable. However, this and the other 'equality clauses' in the scheme can be, in practice, difficult to rely on. There are a number of potentially difficult obstacles to overcome. For example, an equality clause does not operate in relation to a variation between the woman's contract and the man's contract if the employer can show that the variation is 'genuinely due to a material factor which is not the difference of sex'. Furthermore, a woman is only to be regarded as employed on like work with men if, but only if, her work and theirs is of 'the same or a broadly similar nature, and the differences (if any) between the things she does and the things they do are not of practical importance in relation to terms and conditions of employment'.

Subsequent legislation has included the provision of equal pay for work of equal value. Employers have over a very long period of time sought to exploit women by giving them lower pay and inferior conditions of work to men. Justifications – or, more accurately, rationalizations – for this behaviour have included the excuses that women work only for pin money, that they are temporary employees only and that men are breadwinners. Since many women work on a part-time basis, other dubious practices have limited the payment of bonuses to full-time workers only. Some employers have women do virtually the same job as men in most respects but have used the minor differences between men's and women's jobs to justify major differences in pay. Under the legislation women can ask for job evaluation exercises to determine the value of their jobs in terms of some agreed criteria about responsibility and skill. Although not without their difficulties, such exercises have helped women in some important cases.

Despite the legislation, women still earn significantly less than men in comparable jobs across the whole occupational spectrum. This has prompted further attempts at reform to the equality legislation, most recently in the Equality Act 2009. Among other things, the legislation imposes duties on public-sector bodies in regard to socio-economic inequalities, and introduces the concept of 'protected characteristics', which include sex and marital status. It also caters for the possibility that a person is suffering the effects of discrimination if she has more than one protected characteristic, for example sex, age, and pregnancy and maternity.

ethical codes bodies of guiding principles or value **statement**s for professional organizations to set the standard for good practice in relation to service delivery, relationships with clients, or **service user**s, and professional relationships including relationships with other occupations and the 'world at large'. Codes should also be seen as binding on research, evaluation and any consultative processes.

The **British Association of Social Workers** has produced a code of ethics that has become influential within the profession, regardless of whether practitioners are members of the association or not. The code has been drawn up to be consistent with the Ethics of **Social work**: Principles and Standards devised for the International Federation of Social workers in 1994. The British **statement** has been revised several times, most recently in 2002. The United Nations Universal Declaration of Human Rights 1948 has also been influential in the drafting of the British code. The British version has much in common with that produced by the Australian Association of Social workers and emphasizes the importance of five basic values, namely, 'human dignity and worth', 'social justice', 'service to humanity', 'integrity' and, finally, 'competence'.

Each of these guiding principles is discussed further in the material supporting the code with some acknowledgements, here and there, about potential problems of using them in practice. For example, the **statement** on 'human dignity and worth' has it that all human beings have intrinsic value and that everyone has a right to '**wellbeing**, self-fulfilment and to as much control over their own lives as is consistent with the rights of others'. The commitment to 'social justice' brings with it some strong **statement**s about a 'fair and equitable distribution of resources', 'fair access to public services', 'equal treatment and protection under the law' and 'advocating strategies for overcoming structural disadvantage'. The latter is interesting given that there is evidence to suggest that social workers on the whole are not involved in explicit political activity either through political parties or pressure groups, and that the gains made by social workers on behalf of **service user**s tend to be essentially modest.

In regard to the principle of 'service to humanity', the commitment to contribute 'to the creation of a fairer society' is repeated along with the view that the fundamental goals of **social work** are to, first, 'meet personal and social needs' and, second, to enable people to meet their potential. The commitment to integrity is every bit as demanding. The code states that 'integrity comprises honesty, reliability, openness and impartiality' and that it has a primary place in underpinning **social work** practice. Finally, social workers need to be competent, and this umbrella **statement** brings with it a need to continue personal development, use **supervision** appropriately, take proper steps to deal with personal ill-health and stress among many other exhortations to work to a high standard.

The Code of Practice devised by the **General Social Care Council** covers similar territory. The six statements of principle are that social workers should:

- safeguard and promote the interests of service users and carers;
- strive to maintain the trust of service users and carers;
- promote the independence of service users and carers and protect them as far as possible from danger or harm;
- respect the rights of service users while seeking to ensure their behaviour does not harm themselves or other people;
- uphold public trust and confidence in social care services;
- be accountable for the quality of their work and take responsibility for maintaining and improving their knowledge and skills.

There are strong sections in both codes on dealing with conflicts of interest, promoting service users' interests and self-determination and the ability of service users to reach informed decisions and that action will not be taken, unless required by law, without the 'informed consent' of service users or unless 'their behaviour does not harm the interests of others'. Similarly, in relation to cultural awareness, social workers should 'acknowledge the significance of culture in their practice', 'obtain a working knowledge and understanding of service users' ethnic and cultural affiliations and identities' and, ideally, 'communicate in a language and by means which they understand, using a qualified interpreter where appropriate'. However, these codes do not really address the issue of potential conflicts between ethnically sensitive services and human rights or, indeed, whether cultural relativism needs to be measured against any 'universalistic framework'.

Both codes are in many respects impressive statements of good practice underpinned by key principles that most people would feel able to support. The codes place a duty on individual practitioners (and, it is hoped, their employing organizations) to work in ways that safeguard the interests of vulnerable people, support competent service delivery and seek a substantial redistribution of society's resources in order to combat structural oppression. These are laudable objectives and very hard to implement in a comprehensive and whole hearted way especially in relation to combating structural inequality.

ethnically sensitive practice **social work** practice based on a recognition of the cultural traditions of a particular group of people, including family patterns, lifestyles, language and culture.

The problem for **social work** practice is that services may often be undertaken with scant knowledge or understanding of minority client groups, as the Association of Black Social workers and Allied Professions has argued with regard to Black and other ethnic-minority communities. Some commentators hold that the provision of an ethnically sensitive service is not simply a matter of adjusting social work practice to take into account cultural differences, with the **service user**s being the passive beneficiaries, but should instead be a two-way process, with Black families actively involved in and contributing to the social work service offered. The notions of 'ethnicity by consent' and 'compulsory ethnicity' have been used to distinguish between individuals' differing abilities to reject or adopt a specific ethnic identity.

Compulsory ethnicity refers to the institutionalization of ethnic identification as a basis for the assertion of collective claims concerning the distribution of scarce resources. Additionally, many clients have interpreted the cultural pluralist approach of **social services department**s as an attempt to impose a form of compulsory ethnicity, with efforts to provide a more 'ethnically sensitive service' serving as a further instrument of oppression rather than redressing the balance of past injustices. The provision of an ethnically sensitive service should be seen not as 'extra' or 'special' but as a basic service user entitlement. While the importance of such ethnically and linguistically sensitive practice has to be recognized, however, it should not be allowed to overshadow forms of anti-racist practice. That is, while ethnically sensitive practice recognizes the importance of cultural difference, anti-racist practice goes a step further in recognizing the significance of assumed cultural (or 'racial') superiority.

Cultural relativism however can pose difficulties when any customs, beliefs or **values** of any ethnic group appear to conflict either with UK law or with some international code such as the UN Declaration of Human Rights 1948 or the UN Convention on the Rights of the Child 1989. Examples of recent debates about the 'legitimacy' of cultural differences in the UK have focused upon the role of the physical chastisement of children, arranged but not 'forced' **marriage**s, Sharia law, **female genital mutilation**, gender roles and expectations, public holidays and religious festivals, notions of family honour in relation to **domestic violence** and **divorce**, faith based schools, segregated communities and the use of social welfare services. Most of these issues continue to have committed exponents 'both' for and 'against' core beliefs, although some might represent very small minorities.

Unpicking differences in a 'reasonable' way to try to promote understanding and avoid oppression can be challenging. A very general useful way forward however might be to look at the two UN codes as a comparator with the belief, value or behaviour in question as a neutral starting point to have open ended debate. At a child protection conference in Europe in the 1980s a Turkish delegate asked the question of some UK delegates: 'How can you speak of **child abuse** when you make your children sleep alone?' This interesting question offers a gentle challenge to Eurocentric assumptions. (See also **anti-racism, anti-sexism, anti-oppressive practice, anti-discriminatory practice**.)

ethnocentrism an **ideology** that produces a strong orientation towards the norms, values, history and beliefs of a particular ethnic group, so that the interests of that group are always or frequently placed above the interests of other ethnic groups in the attitudes of both individuals and institutions of ethnocentric societies.

Ethnocentrism exists in any society where the dominant ethnic group seeks to persuade others that there is only one ethnic group, which has a monopoly of ideal and desirable attributes, or is more 'civilized' than others. This is based on the assumption that it is both possible and desirable to define that which is 'ideally human' or more worthy of belonging to humanity than other ethnic groups. Ethnocentrism assumes that the culture, **values** and moral standards of the dominant group are necessary to the **wellbeing** of people in other ethnic groups. Ethnocentrism discourages efforts to maintain or promote the history, language, religion or customs of ethnic groups outside the dominant culture if they go beyond the limits of that which the dominant group has defined as acceptable or appropriate.

The influence of **eurocentricism** is culturally pervasive. It shapes opinion. The 'values' of British society are essentially based on Christian ethics and Western European philosophy. Eurocentricism features in the way history is written and the perspective from which it is taught. It is part of the socialization of children, the production and transmission of images and language. It is an omnipresent feature of human **communication** and relationships. Ethnocentrism must therefore be continually challenged and questioned simply in order to recognize the extent of its influence on society and on the thought processes of individuals.

Eurocentrism a form of **ethnocentrism** that involves understanding and interpreting the world exclusively, or nearly so, through the experiences and perspectives of (white) Europeans.

A Eurocentric perspective, which by implication places Europe at the centre of the world, may be detected in such apparently 'objective' activities as the presentation and interpretation of historical events and definitions of 'correct' methods of child-rearing and organizing family life. Eurocentric textbooks, teaching methods and underlying philosophies reinforce negative perceptions of many non-European peoples and fail to inform about the diversity and strength of the many cultures, languages, ethnic communities and religions that enrich and make positive contributions to human society. One compelling example of Eurocentric beliefs about the slave trade had it that progressive thinkers in the UK and other countries were responsible for its abolition. Other historians interested in the resistance of the oppressed would argue that slavery in many locations was abolished principally because the plantation owners could not cope with slave uprisings and, in effect, a developing guerrilla war.

euthanasia (voluntary) the act of killing someone painlessly, where that person has capacity and has chosen to die. This is most likely to happen to help someone who has an incurable disease or an irreversible condition where intense pain is likely or where they are so incapacitated that their quality of life is seriously compromised and they are wholly reliant on others. The term has its origins in the classical Greek idea of an easy or good death.

Euthanasia has in the past been regarded very negatively partly because of the behaviour of the Nazi regime in Germany where 'involuntary' euthanasia was practised especially with severely disabled people. These practices were really driven by eugenics; in this context, the notion then was that inferior 'races' and people had to be eliminated so that superior, Aryan, 'races' might flourish without any possibility of 'contamination'.

However, euthanasia driven by the more humane idea of ending a life because of suffering has had a long history. Many societies have debated the issue for centuries and there are currently several societies where euthanasia is currently legal in some circumstances; for example, Holland and Switzerland. The context for debate has changed first because of the development of life prolonging drugs and 'life support' technology. In addition, there has been a tangible shift in Western societies which has changed the doctor–patient relationship so that the patient is now perceived as having more control over key decisions affecting his/her life. However the complex ethical and legal arguments are unaltered with strong and competing feelings about **impairment**s and disabilities, about how much pain anyone should be expected or allowed to experience and whether a human being has the right to deliberately end their life. A brief summary of the key issues follows.

Advocates for euthanasia and assisted **suicide** argue that a person has a fundamental right to shape their own lives including when and how such a life might be given up. A secondary argument is that unbearable suffering should not be tolerated. Those who oppose euthanasia argue that 'human life is sacred' and that nobody can be entirely sure about the quality of any person's life in the future. Further, the limited use of euthanasia will inevitably lead to a weakening of law so that it becomes increasingly common and will possibly lead to people dying who really do not want to die. The notion that chronically sick people with no hope of recovery can be a burden to society and to their families economically, socially and emotionally is used as an argument both for and against euthanasia; with one side counting the cost to everyone other than the dying person as the key issue(s) with the other side arguing that an emphasis upon economic issues will motivate survivors who stand to gain from the death of a relative, thus devaluing the life of the dying person.

In recent decades there has been an increasing use of 'living wills' drawn up by people to provide instructions to both family and medical staff should they become unable to make decisions for themselves. If a living will is explicit about a person's wish to die or not to be given life prolonging treatments if there is no reasonable prospect of recovery, it is hard for family members or medical staff to ignore such instructions.

Current debate is focused upon the role of relatives or friends who might be involved in helping a person who wishes to die. In early 2010 the **Crown Prosecution Service** (CPS) issued the document *Policy for Prosecutors in Respect of Cases of Encouraging or Assisting Suicide*. Whereas the earlier consultation document gave significance to the **victim**'s condition or illness from which there was no possibility of recovery, the new policy stresses, more than any other factor, the importance of the helper's motivation. The key factors are:

- that the victim had a clear, settled and informed wish to die;
- that the victim had indicated very clearly to the helper that they wanted to die;
- that the request for help to die had come from the victim on their own initiative;
- that the helper was motivated solely by compassion; that the helper was a family member or friend who had had a long-term relationship with the victim;
- that the actions of the helper were only of minor (and reluctant) assistance or influence and that the victim needed such assistance to kill themselves;
- that the helper had tried to dissuade the victim from killing themselves and had considered other treatment and care options seriously;
- that the victim had previously tried to commit suicide and was likely to do so again;
- that the helper had assisted the **police** fully in their investigations.

Stearman, K. (2009) *Euthanasia: ethical debates.* London: Hodder.

Every Child Matters (ECM) the broad cluster of policies for developing the **wellbeing** of children through health, education and social services.

The government published a green paper on children's policy in 2003 entitled *Every Child Matters* based on many of the recommendations of the Laming enquiry into the death of **Victoria Climbié**. From the outset it was recognized that this particular Green Paper was announcing a fundamental recasting of children's services and, although put out for consultation, was going to be enacted swiftly. The very title itself became the banner under which services for children were unified particularly in regard to promoting **wellbeing**, child and family **assessment** and the development of local children's plans. Following the consultation period the government published *Every Child Matters: The next steps* and *Every Child Matters: Change for children* which, along with the Children Act 2004 established the ECM framework.

That framework is geared around **outcomes** – universal elements of child wellbeing which all children should enjoy. There are five outcomes that practitioners from all services dealing with children – hospitals, schools, police, youth work or social services – must promote in relation to the children they work with. These are: i.) being healthy: having good physical and **mental health** and living a healthy lifestyle; ii.) staying safe: being protected from harm and neglect; iii.) enjoying and achieving: getting the most out of life and developing the skills for adulthood;

iv.) making a positive contribution: being involved with the **community** and society and not engaging in anti-social or offending behaviour; v.) achieving economic wellbeing: *not* being prevented by economic disadvantage from achieving their full potential.

ECM requires all services dealing with children – youth service, schools, health and social services to promote these five **outcomes**. To do this each local authority area should have an integrated strategy based on a joint assessment of local needs involving children, young people and parents. This strategy forms the basis of the three year **Children and Young People Plan** showing how local services integrated in **children's trusts** will respond to identified need needs and promote the five outcomes above. Joint Area Reviews regularly appraise progress on the plans and inspect local children's services.

For social workers the biggest impact of the ECM approach has come in the integration of frontline delivery. Services built around the needs of children and young people in relation to the five outcomes are to be accessible and personalized and not based on conventional service boundaries. All staff should have a common core of knowledge and understanding about children's needs and deploy collaborative approaches across the services such as co-location in **extended schools** or **children's centres**. The **common assessment framework** offers a unified start point for appraising a child's needs for all practitioners working with children.

evidence-based practice (EBP) an approach to decision-making, policy-making and intervention based upon a judicious, systematic and thoughtful consideration of the best available evidence to achieve the most effective **outcomes**. There are two broad versions of EBP, one has its origins in medicine where the evidence is informed by scientific methods of inquiry, such as random controlled trials, while the other offers a pluralist model that draws upon a more diverse range of research methodologies. The latter version is the one most likely to be found in **social work**.

EBP is an approach that has made a considerable impact in all public services during the past decade. Its expansion in an 'age of uncertainty' may be seen against a backdrop of increasing concern with managing risk, criticisms of professional performance, perceived weaknesses in public services, and the growth in new forms of public management. The tragic death of **Victoria Climbié** in 2000 highlighted many of these concerns and the need for practice to be informed by better quality evidence. Best practice, it is argued, comes from a rational and objective **assessment** of the evidence and this leads to the **adoption** of the most appropriate course of action. Hence, EBP is inextricably linked to the search for greater effectiveness and efficiency to achieve the best possible outcomes.

The concept of EBP originated from the natural sciences, in particular medicine through the Cochrane Collaboration, and in terms of evidence-based medicine adopts a neo-positivist approach to knowledge building. This infers that knowledge is derived from a process of scientific measurement and observation, through experimental methods such as clinical trials, and this contributes to general laws that underpin an objective reality. These laws are seen to be independent of sectional interests, politically neutral, and developed on the basis of social facts as absolute truths.

In the medical version of EBP proponents propose a hierarchy of research methodologies that favour randomized controlled trials and systematic reviews of the evidence, as these are seen as the gold standard in research. In **social work** a pluralist model of EBP has evolved that draws upon a more diverse range of methodologies, including qualitative methods even though these may still be considered too subjective and lacking in the scientific rigour of the natural sciences. The influence of EBP in social work has increased since the 1990s and led to a preference for practice methods that emphasize short-term intervention that can be evaluated, such as **cognitive behavioural therapy** and task centred practice.

EBP can be criticized on a number of grounds. Firstly, while few practitioners would dissent from the need to become more evidence-based and research minded, the question of what constitutes the most credible evidence and best research methodology remains contested. This has quickly led to arguments between 'champions and critics' and one of the problems with narrow versions of EBP is that their factual scientific approach presents a rational world view that may constrain the choice of the most suitable methods of intervention. This is one of the reasons why evidence always requires careful interpretation and practitioners become confused when faced with a range of research findings that leaves them uncertain about which to follow.

Secondly, the complexity of reasoning and difficulty in interpreting the evidence are not always given sufficient recognition. Further, rational decision-making may be more problematic than proponents of EBP acknowledge and likely to be influenced by prevailing social norms and political realities. This could reinforce a 'top down' model where knowledge is handed down to the practitioner to use in predetermined ways that fit in with prevailing systems of working to meet centrally determined targets and the governments modernizing agenda.

Thirdly, while practitioners accept the need for greater efficiency, public accountability and transparency, an overemphasis on evidential processing if taken to its logical conclusion could lead to the 'McDonaldization of social work'. There is a genuine fear that in such a climate the moral-political dilemmas faced by social workers in their everyday practice could become submerged within the technical-rational task of processing evidence. The end result may be a limited and functional 'what works' or 'what works now' approach that encourages rather mechanistic forms of practice. In this sense, narrow versions of EBP might offer false certainties by encouraging an instrumental, de-contextualized, and competence-based approach that supports managerial priorities.

However, a more balanced and positive view can be maintained by recognizing that no one theoretical orientation towards practice can be said to have become dominant, and this diversity is still seen as one of **social work**'s enduring strengths. The growth of EBP has been facilitated in part by the way it has been able to laminate itself onto the foundation of other theoretical approaches, creating in the process more research informed models of practice. This has undoubtedly been one of the most positive legacies of the EBP revolution. There are thus many different versions of EBP, and as a generic concept it has been generally endorsed by social workers. The more pluralist model of EBP in the hands of the skilled practitioner, set in its appropriate policy context, has undoubtedly contributed to the development of a more effective and research minded practice.

Newman, T., Moseley, A., Tierney, S. and Ellis, A. (2005) *Evidence-based Social Work: a guide for the perplexed.* Lyme Regis: Russell House Publishing.

exceptional leave to remain leave to remain in the UK for a limited period, usually between one and 4 years.

Until 2007 asylum seekers who were refused refugee status could be given 'exceptional leave to remain' if it would be unsafe for them to return to their home country but their application for asylum is not based on a 'convention reason' (see **asylum seekers and refugees**). People given exceptional leave to remain could work, claim benefits and access social housing like any member of the indigenous population. They could not, however, bring dependants over to join them. Before their leave to remain expires they can apply for **indefinite leave to remain**. 'Exceptional leave to remain' has now been replaced by '**humanitarian protection**'.

exclusion from school the correct term for what is usually called 'suspension' or 'expulsion'. A child is officially prevented from attending school, usually following unacceptable behaviour.

There are only two types of exclusion from school: *fixed term* (which can amount to no more than 45 days in total in the same school year) and *permanent*. Head teachers cannot exclude children indefinitely or remove them from the admission register without formal procedures. Unless an incident is extremely serious, schools are expected to have already tried every possible attempt to meet a child's needs in other ways before permanent exclusion becomes appropriate. Detailed procedures, which are statutory, can be found in guidance from the **Department for Children, Schools and Families** (2008) *Improving Behaviour and Attendance: guidance on exclusion from schools and pupil referral unit*. London: DH.

In recent years local education authorities have had targets to meet for the reduction of permanent exclusions, but these have now been reached and no further targets have been set. Full-time **alternative educational provision** must be provided from the sixth day of any period of exclusion. Until then, parents must keep the child at home under their **supervision** and may be committing an offence if they do not do so. Parents have the right to make representations about exclusions over 5 days to the discipline committee of the school's governing body, which has the **power** to reinstate. In the case of a permanent exclusion only, they may then **appeal** to an independent panel, whose decision is binding. There are usually financial incentives for schools not to exclude permanently. Except in the case of children who have been permanently excluded more than once, permanent exclusion will normally result in transfer to another school, but provision may be through alternatives such as vocational/home tuition or a **pupil referral unit**.

Whitney, B. (2007) *Social Inclusion in Schools*. London: NASEN/David Fulton.

exclusion requirement a requirement which may be included in a **community order, youth rehabilitation order** or **suspended sentence order**, prohibiting the offender from entering specified places or areas for a period of up to two years. It can be enforced by **electronic monitoring**.

ex parte hearing the legal phrase for a court hearing that is held without all the parties to the case being present, *ex parte* literally meaning 'without the parties'.

Social workers are most likely to come across *ex parte* hearings when applying for an **emergency protection order** in relation to childcare issues or an **injunction** in relation to the problem of **domestic violence**. With the first example, these can be heard *ex parte*, without the parents or the child present, and usually involve a single **magistrate**, the magistrate's clerk and the social worker on the case. The aim of such a hearing is speed, since time may be short to protect the child concerned. *Ex parte* hearings can be organized quickly and sometimes occur in a magistrate's own home if out of hours. In cases of **domestic violence**, the term is used where one party, usually the woman, seeks an injunction to prevent something happening. The injunction will be in force without the defendant being present and until such time as a full hearing can be arranged.

expulsion see **exclusion from school**

extended schools provision outside school hours and in school holidays that offers activities for children, and often for their parents as well. Most schools will offer something but some are 'full service' extended schools that have a comprehensive range of activities on offer and may also be the base for other services normally outside education. In 2010 the government expects that all schools will provide services that meet the needs of their communities. Schools, colleges and **local authorities** are expected to work together to identify **community** interests and then meet those interests at a minimum financial cost to extended **service user**s.

These services might be of benefit to children – by providing breakfast clubs, after-school and homework clubs, for example. The premises might provide childcare places from 8 a.m. to 6 p.m. which could benefit children and parents. For adults there might be evening classes, or fitness and parenting classes. It is argued that there are also gains for the schools in that their place in the community is cemented and it can raise the self-confidence and self-esteem of both parents and pupils.

extended sentence a sentence of imprisonment for violent and sexual offenders introduced in its current form by the **Criminal Justice Act 2003**. It entails an especially long period of mandatory **supervision** in the **community** following release from **custody** if the sentencing court deems this necessary for the protection of the public from serious harm. Significant changes to the rules for such **sentence**s were made by the **Criminal Justice and Immigration Act 2008**. They may now only be passed if the offence is a particularly serious one, or if the normal term of **imprisonment** for the offence would be at least 4 years; courts no longer have to initially presume that an offender is dangerous if s/he has a previous conviction for a violent or sexual offence; and extended sentence prisoners are now automatically released on licence halfway through their prison sentence instead of their release being at the discretion of the **Parole Board**.

fabricated or induced illness a psychological condition formerly known as 'Munchausen by Proxy', in which the person feels compelled to engage in frequent **contact** with medical authorities such as hospitals and doctors. This can be done 'by proxy' – by using another person, almost always a child, as the person who requires persistent medical attention. Concern arises when there is a poor response to prescribed treatments for the presumed ailment, new symptoms are reported when older ones are resolved and are not observed independently of the carer reporting them. Any instance of fabricated or induced illness will have three elements: the fabrication – or induction – of an illness, the mental state of the fabricator, and the effects on the child's development. The latter can include the suffering and emotional difficulties for the child, the effects of continuous medical intervention such as tests or drugs, loss of school time. In extreme instances children have suffered physical damage and disfigurement as the person harms the child in order to provide the reason for contacting the hospital or doctor. On such occasions protective action may have to be taken by the local authority.

failure to thrive the term applied to children who are not receiving adequate nutrition to achieve normal growth.

One common form of measuring whether a child is failing to thrive is through a **centile chart**, which plots the child's weight, head size and height against national averages for the child's age. If a child falls below the third centile in one or more of these for a period of time, this is an indication of failure to thrive. Certain factors in a child's background are associated with, but not the cause of, failure to thrive. These are **poverty**, which may severely restrict the child's diet, social isolation of a parent and the child's having severe behavioural problems. Failure to thrive is rarely the product of deliberate parental neglect. Support for the parents is usually given in the form of guidance on diet from health visitors and doctors. In extreme cases, brief periods of hospitalization or accommodation help the child to gain weight and size. Significantly **centile chart**s have been reconfigured to take account of norms for breastfed babies who tend to grow at different rates from bottle-fed babies. Once a common phrase in **social work** parlance and even grounds for taking a child into care before the implementation of the **Children Act 1989** it is now less often invoked in any empirical or scientific sense.

Fair Access to Care Services (FACS) guidance provided to **local authorities** for setting their eligibility criteria for adult **social care** services with the aim of ensuring fairer and more consistent approaches to the **allocation** of scarce resources nationally.

Eligibility is graded into four bands, critical, substantial, moderate and low. These categories of assessed need pertain to levels of risk and vulnerability. For example, a critical need would be established if life would be threatened should the service not be provided. This may occur if a person is unable to light a fire safely, turn off a gas appliance or access essential provisions such as food and drink or maintain personal cleanliness and toiletry needs. A substantial risk would suggest that **abuse** or neglect had occurred and that this would be exacerbated without intervention. Moderate needs might link to a change in family circumstances; for example, carer issues linked to tasks such as shopping or collection of prescriptions, whilst low criteria would indicate that the person has lost the ability to carry out one or two domestic routines which do not pose a serious risk to their **wellbeing**. **Social work** practitioners often feel that resources are scarce and that an essential element to **assessment** is in taking preventative measures in order to engage with the longer-term needs of vulnerable people whilst retaining a focus upon the retention of autonomy and independence. The philosophy of well-intentioned policy however is often not borne out in practice due to a lack of resources. Many local authorities are only able to offer services where there is a critical or substantial need, often signposting people to alternative sources of support elsewhere if **service user**s can only meet the lower bands of eligibility.

family assistance order an order under section 16 of the **Children Act 1989** available in matrimonial disputes involving children and where the court may be considering a section 8 order that allows the court to appoint a **probation officer** or local authority social worker to advise, assist and befriend any person named in the order.

The aim of the family assistance order is to provide short-term help in 'exceptional circumstances' to resolve conflict between parents or to help overcome problems associated with their separation or **divorce**. The work is often undertaken with the parents rather than with the child, although the court's main concern in making the order is the child's welfare. The order lasts for 6 months and may be made only with the consent of every person named in the order (other than the child). Social workers have found it difficult to use the order effectively. Judges are uncertain about what the order actually means and what constitutes 'exceptional circumstances', while **local authorities** have no specifically designated resources for practitioners to carry out the work. Nevertheless, it has some potential as a consensual platform for offering guidance and help to a family experiencing separation or **divorce**.

family centre see **children's centre**

family group conference a family-led planning meeting, sometimes involving significant others, to try to address concerns and problems in relation to a child or young person. Most family group conferences have focused upon issues concerned with **children in need**, **safeguarding** or juvenile offending.

The Family Rights Group has usefully identified the stages usually adhered to in a family group conference (hereafter FGC). The initial stage is a referral made often by a social worker, health visitor, **youth offending team** worker, teacher and sometimes by a family themselves. Although there may be an element of compulsion in some **social work** processes concerning children, the process of referral for a FGC is a wholly voluntary process which the family may choose or refuse. The second stage involves the appointment of a coordinator who will make **contact** with the family and any children involved and will help them to decide who to invite to the meeting. In the event of disagreements about who should attend a FGC, the coordinator will try to help to resolve any conflict. Children who have any measure of understanding will also be consulted. Preliminary information about how a FGC is conducted may also be presented at this stage in addition to decisions about where and when the meeting is to take place. The conference is the third stage of the process comprising three separate parts. The first part is regarded as **information giving** where the coordinator will brief the family about any relevant legal matters and any resources that may be available to the family. The next part of stage three offers the family 'private time' to discuss the issues and problems and to devise plans for how they might be addressed. The final part of stage three involves the family presenting their plans to the coordinator and any other professionals that may be involved. It is important to stress that no professionals are involved in the family 'private time'. The professionals then have to decide whether the plan is acceptable to the social welfare services and, if it is, then the plan is implemented. There may or may not be a need for legal ratification of the plan. If the professionals feel that the plan is unlikely to be effective or they have objections on grounds of risk, then the matter may have to be referred to the relevant court.

In New Zealand, where the concept originated in Maori communities, the family group conference has replaced the child protection case conference, thus marking a significant reallocation of **power** between professionals and family members. Although the concept is viewed with some suspicion by social work professionals in Britain because it accords the family considerable new powers and status to make decisions, it is gaining adherents as a way to develop protection plans that are both effective and tend to include arrangements for keeping the child within the extended family. New Zealand research has indicated that families often devise plans that are innovative and workable that might not have occurred to social welfare agencies. The same evidence also suggests that children and young people are more likely to stay with their families given family solutions to family problems. There has also been some limited experimentation with the use of family group conferences with other client groups and problems; for example, work with adult offenders and families where there is **domestic violence** and other vulnerable children and adults. Much of this work has yet to be rigorously evaluated.

family proceedings a group of court proceedings involving disputes about children. Family proceedings are defined under the **Children Act 1989** as including most proceedings that originate in that Act, such as those for care orders, **supervision order**s and section 8 orders. They also include proceedings under other laws, such as **divorce** proceedings, **adoption** proceedings and **injunction**, and non-molestation proceedings between married or unmarried **couple**s. By designating this range of proceedings in this way, the Act allows courts greater flexibility in dealing with cases before it. (See also **family proceedings court**.)

family proceedings court created under the **Children Act 1989**, this court deals with non-criminal matters relating to children, such as care proceedings, **adoption**, child protection, and residence and **contact** following **divorce** (see also **criminal court**). It is staffed by lay **magistrate**s who have undertaken additional training to fulfil this specialist role.

family therapy a range of techniques and strategies for helping families to resolve relationship problems, attain goals and function more harmoniously.

There are many variants of family therapy. Most of them work on the central premise that relationships between family members can become rigid, so that behaviour between members tends to repeat compulsively a familiar destructive pattern. This pattern may involve blaming or scapegoating a particular member of the family or coercive behaviours such as shouting, physical abuse, isolation and withdrawal. Such patterns provide a kind of 'solution' – the family survives but in a way that prevents further development and often at immense cost to the individuals. The central insight of family therapy is drawn from the **systems approach**, namely that relations between family members are circular – how each member behaves affects the way everyone else behaves, and so on. An oft-cited example is where a parent continually criticizes an adolescent, who withdraws from family life but who then elicits more criticism, only to withdraw even more. The therapist or social worker begins with the assumption that no one is to blame. The therapist's role is to provide an outside view of the way the family interacts as a whole and to try to minimize the 'blame games' that inevitably occur in a family deeply at odds with itself. Maintaining a position of neutrality, the therapist explores with the whole family how to achieve a different overall pattern and how to view behaviours more positively. By doing so, the therapist may enable the family to change attitudes, viewpoints and behaviour.

female genital mutilation (FGM) may include removal of the clitoris, cutting the labia and stitching to reduce the vaginal orifice (infibulation). It is practised in many African countries but to varying degrees. In the UK the largest practising communities are from Somalia, Sudan and Eritrea. FGM is recognized by the UN as a human rights violation and is illegal in the UK under the Female Genital Mutilation Act 2003. Under this Act procuring FGM in the UK or abroad can be punished by up to 14 years in **prison**. FGM has extensive adverse health consequences including short-term complications from bleeding or infection and long-term problems including menstrual difficulties, urinary infection and pain. Pregnancy and childbirth present particular problems which may be exacerbated by late access to antenatal care. FGM is commonly performed on girls in their early teens and presents as a child protection issue so that some **local authorities** have proactively sought the parents of young girls to educate and persuade them to reject the practice.

femininity a term that describes the way gender roles of women are socially constructed. Notions of femininity are therefore experienced differently in different groups within society. Concepts of *appropriate* femininity vary according to social differences of age, class and ethnicity etc. For example, in relation to differences of ethnicity and race in differentiating norms of femininity, Black feminists have suggested that the cultural construction of femininity among African-Caribbean women differs immensely from the forms of femininity surrounding white women. Rather than adopting a eurocentric understanding of gender roles based on the distinction between male and female abilities with regard to the labour market, the Black women in some studies had adopted a model of femininity based less upon such distinctions and more upon notions of equality. Indeed, such concepts of **masculinity** and femininity are essentially culturally defined and refer specifically to the way people believe that they and others *should* behave in terms of their biological sex.

Placing emphasis on the word 'should' here highlights that **values** are integral to these concepts, thereby producing ideas that are necessarily subjective. Gender roles, therefore, can be said to represent ideological frameworks that exist both to tell us how to behave appropriately in terms of our biological sex and, most importantly, represent a form of social control since they lay down guidelines for people to follow. While this is the common understanding of gender roles, post-structural theorists have increasingly challenged this dichotomous understanding of **masculinity** and femininity. For example, Judith Butler has argued that we act out our gender roles through a 'gender performance'. The ultimate question is what form that gender performance will take. Essentially, the argument is that by adopting different performances, we might work to disrupt existing gender norms. (See also **gender, masculinity, postmodernism, queer theory.**)

Butler, J. (1999) *Gender Trouble: feminism and the sub-version of identity.* London: Routledge.

feminism a theoretical perspective, social movement and **ideology** that has at its core a recognition of gender equality, especially in relation to women's subordination to men.

Feminism, especially in the context of political struggle, has a long history. Most accounts of feminism, however, have focused on Western conceptions despite the fact that women in former colonial states played an active part in challenging both their gender subordination and colonial rule. In the West, feminism as a social movement and **ideology** is commonly divided into two distinct periods. The first 'wave' is usually located towards the late 19th century and early 20th century, from the writings of Mary Wollstonecraft through the Suffragette movement to the enfranchisement of women. The second 'wave' emerged during the latter half of the 1960s alongside the emergence of the New Left. While feminism is separated in this way, it may be more useful to think of feminist thought in terms of a continuum that has arisen and developed alongside other social movements, including anti-slavery campaigns and the fight for Black civil rights. Feminist theory has informed practice, from fighting for civil rights to votes for women and the development of women's refuges and rape crisis centres.

While it is useful to talk of a 'universal' feminism, it is nevertheless vital to recognize that this is in itself an umbrella term used to group together different strands of feminism. These include:

Socialist-Marxist feminism: this prioritizes social class as the prime factor in determining the place of women within capitalist societies. Consequently, this approach relies heavily on the work of Marx and Engels and argues that gender inequality is a product of capitalism and class oppression. It is critical of the essentialism inherent within radical feminism and also challenges the ahistorical approach to **patriarchy**.

Liberal feminism: the suffragette movement of the early 1900s was founded on the concept of basic equality and justice and rose from the abolition of slavery and equal rights through to the civil rights movements in the USA. Liberal feminists view the route to equality through the mechanism of the state, i.e. legislation to prohibit **discrimination** on the grounds of gender. In this respect, liberal feminists can be seen to have achieved some progress, most evident in the 1975 Sex Discrimination Act, which outlaws direct and indirect discrimination in employment on the grounds of gender, and the **Equal Pay Act 1970**, which stipulates that women and men must receive equal pay for equal work. Numerous studies have challenged the effectiveness of this legislation, however, pointing to the continuing inequalities between women and men in the labour market, and between different groups of women.

Radical feminism: characterized by the belief that patriarchy is the universal cause of women's oppression. As a result, radical feminists focus on **power** and the unequal power between men and women. Radical feminists' central argument has at its core the notion that all women are subordinated by male oppression (patriarchy), which is exercised through institutions such as **marriage** and the family. For example, radical feminism particularly focuses on accounts of violence against women in the home to greatly inform the wider women's refuge movement in both the USA and the UK. An important offshoot of the radical feminist movement, lesbian/separatist feminists, provided a useful critique of the notion of compulsory and/or institutionalized heterosexuality.

Black feminism: developed during the 1980s in response to the universalized discourse of feminism as a whole, Black (and 'third world') feminists challenged white/Western feminism for ignoring issues of race/ethnicity in women's experiences of oppression and for focusing largely on the lives of white Western women in their accounts, thereby denying and excluding the voices and experiences of Black women.

While these strands of feminism are central to the concept of feminism, this list is not exhaustive. Additional elements include academic feminism, cultural feminism, psychoanalytic feminism and political lesbianism.

There has been recent debate around whether feminism (and therefore a feminist 'movement') is still relevant in 21st-century Britain. However, there is widespread evidence of continued inequalities between men and women for example in relation to pay, alongside new and emergent gendered practices and relations (e.g. the increasingly sexualized images of **femininity** in certain male magazines and forms of popular culture, from lap dancing clubs to music videos). **Feminist social work** emphasizes the importance of a gendered analysis and approach, emphasizing the continued inequalities between women and men whilst also celebrating womanhood in all its diversity.

Donimelli, L. (2002) *Feminist Social Work Theory and Practice.* London: Palgrave.

Mirza, H.S. (ed.) (1999) *Black British Feminism: a reader.* London: Routledge.

feminist social work a diversity of **social work** approaches that have as their common element recognition of women's oppression and the aim of overcoming its effects.

Feminism regards all aspects of social relations as being shaped by the great inequality of **power** held by men over women in all aspects of life: in the family, in the professions, in politics, in work and employing organizations, in purchasing power and in **community** institutions. Feminist **social work** begins with this fundamental perspective and develops a practice that attempts to address this inequality. When women social workers are working with women as **service user**s, it adopts strategies of **empowerment**. This often places it at odds with the traditional role of **social work**, which seeks to control difficult or poorly adapting individuals or to regulate families in difficulty. A significant part of feminist social work takes place in the small local organizations that have developed as responses to male violence, including **domestic violence**: rape crisis centres, women's refuges and incest survivors' groups among others. Feminist social work places heavy emphasis on the role that the oppression of women plays in creating the very problems that social work deals with. One notable example is in the field of child **sexual abuse**, where much of the conventional analysis from both inside and outside social work assigned the 'cause' to distorted family relationships and implicitly blamed poor mothering. Conventional analysis ignored the fact that by far the greater number of abusers were men and that this rested on the extreme differences of power held by men and others in the family. This analysis applied to much of social work with children, where the content of case records, court reports and case conferences blamed women as individually poor mothers rather than focusing on **poverty** and lack of material resources. Feminist social workers have also looked more closely at the behaviour of the male abuser, have called attention to the secrecy that male abusers demand and have called for protective solutions that remove the abuser, rather than the child, from the family (see **injunction**).

One of the major concerns of feminist social work is the inequality based on gender within social services organizations themselves, particularly in the management structures of those organizations, which are dominated by men although women form some 80 per cent of employees overall. How to structure management jobs so that they are more appealing to women, as well as allowing more flexible working arrangements, including part-time and job share, are objectives that feminists have at least succeeded in having social services organizations discuss, if not put into practice. It is argued that greater representation of women in social work agencies will likely lead to a more effective 'woman-centred' practice.

final warning a semi-official term for a **warning**. Final warnings and **reprimands** were introduced by the **Crime and Disorder Act 1998** to replace **cautions** for offenders under the age of 18. They are alternatives to court proceedings for an offence which is admitted by the young person. A final **warning** may be used where a young person has previously received a reprimand for a minor first offence, or it may be given for a more serious first offence. These decisions are at the discretion of the **police**. Final **warning**s and reprimands may be cited in court in the same way as previous convictions. After receiving a final warning, the young person is referred to a **youth offending team** so that a **rehabilitation** programme (commonly known as a 'change programme') aimed at preventing further offending can be drawn up. Such plans may include **reparation** to the **victim** of the offence and other elements of **restorative justice**. (See also **youth conditional caution**.)

fine a **sentence** which requires the offender to pay a sum of money to the state. It is by far the commonest penalty, being imposed for around 70 per cent of summary offences and 20 per cent of indictable offences (see **criminal courts**). A **magistrates' court** cannot normally impose a fine of more than £5,000, and Acts of Parliament fix maximum fines for many offences. The amount of the fine should reflect both the seriousness of the offence and the means of the offender. It may be paid by instalments at the discretion of the court; normally this should mean that the fine will be paid off within 12 months. Non-payment of fines can lead to sanctions which include **imprisonment**, but courts should not imprison for default unless they have assessed the offender's means, considered other methods of enforcement (which include ordering deductions from earnings and benefits) and concluded that the default is due to the offender's wilful refusal or culpable neglect. In the late 1990s a concerted effort succeeded in significantly reducing the number of fine defaulters sent to **prison**. See also **fixed penalty notice**.

fixed penalty notice a financial penalty (current maximum £80) which can be imposed by **police** officers and other specified officials for a widening variety of minor offences. Fixed penalty notices were first introduced by the Criminal Justice and Police Act 2001 and extended nationally in 2004. They can be used for a number of minor offences, notably relating to **anti-social behaviour** in public, but now also including shoplifting up to value of £200. They do not amount to a criminal conviction, and unlike **cautions**, they cannot be later cited as part of a person's criminal record. Those who are issued with a fixed penalty notice can choose to pay the penalty, or if they contest their guilt they may be prosecuted in the **magistrates' court** in the traditional manner (running the obvious risk of incurring a greater penalty and receiving a criminal conviction if found guilty). Fixed penalties are also referred to as 'spot fines' or **penalty notices for disorder**. (See also **Respect Agenda**.)

forced marriage protection order a court order made under the Family law Act 1996 for the purposes of protecting a person from being forced into a **marriage**. Orders can also be made to protect a person who has already been forced into a marriage. Judges, when deciding whether (and how) to exercise their powers, must have regard to all the circumstances of the particular case including the need to secure the health, safety and **wellbeing** of the person to be protected. They must also have regard to the person's wishes and feelings, as appropriate in the light of the person's age and understanding. The scheme was introduced by the Forced Marriage (Civil Protection) Act 2007, and protection extends to cases where 'force' in the form of coercion by threats or other psychological means is used, as well as physical violence.

foster care the placement of a child with a family or lone carer who is able to offer the child full-time day-to-**day care** in place of the child's natural parent(s). It is sometimes referred to as substitute family care.

There are many possible fostering arrangements and, with the exception of private fostering, they are regulated by the **Children Act 1989**, the National Standards for foster care and the Fostering Regulations 2002. A child may be placed in foster care by a parent, by anyone with **parental responsibility** for the child or by the local authority where the child is normally resident. Foster care usually refers to a placement with local authority foster carers or with foster carers from recognized fostering agencies (again with the exception of private fostering), who are recruited and trained by **local authorities** or the recognized agencies; recruitment is a long process involving **assessment** and approval or rejection of applications. Financial maintenance of the child is through a fostering allowance paid by the local authority to foster carers at a locally set scale of payment. Alternatively, the local authority may pay a fee to a fostering agency that in turn makes monthly payments to its own foster carers while a child is in placement. Foster care is the preferred way of providing care and nurture for children who need to be **looked after** by a local authority because it provides family-based as opposed to institutionally based care. Foster care has enabled local authorities to develop flexible patterns of care for the children they look after.

There are different kinds of local authority foster placements, as follows:

Short-term placements: the child is placed with foster carers who take care of them on a short-term basis until long-term plans are made for the child. The range of goals for a short-term placement can include 'shared' or relief fostering, holiday fostering, emergency protection, assessment of needs, a bridge to a long-term placement and pre-adoptive fostering. There is no universally agreed duration for short-term placements, which can last from days to months, depending on the child's situation. Research indicates that short-term foster placements become long-term placements with variable success. It is generally agreed that it is poor practice to let a short-term placement drift into a *de facto* long-term placement with no agreed long-term plan.

Bridging or link placements: these are used when a child's long-term placement has broken down or the short-term **foster care**rs cannot continue to look after the child and a long-term placement has yet to be found. Some children are placed in bridging placements after a period in residential care. The task then is to help the child to readjust to family life. The duration of the bridging placement varies according to the child's situation and the speed at which suitable long-term carers are identified for the child.

Long-term placements: the child is placed with foster carers on a planned long-term basis; this is sometimes referred to as a permanent foster placement. The intention is that the child will live with his or her foster family until ready to live independently. It is an alternative to **adoption** for some children, taking into account factors such as the child's age, any special needs, the level of ongoing contact with family of origin and the child's wishes. Studies indicate that long-term fostering is less successful than adoption. It is recognized in current childcare practice that children need a sense of permanence and a sense of identity if their developmental needs are to be met. This is more difficult to achieve in long-term foster placements because the **foster care**rs do not acquire **parental responsibility** for the child, and a sense of insecurity may result from the involvement of the social worker in supervising the placement and in the way reviews and medicals are carried out.

Respite or shared care: this arrangement involves the day-to-day care of the child being shared between the family of origin and foster carers. This kind of placement may be offered if the child has special needs or if the quality of the care available at home can be enhanced. It enables the child and the family to have regular breaks from each other and provides the child with additional caring relationships outside the family. It is good practice to ensure that the same respite foster carers look after the child on each occasion and that respite care is offered on a planned, predictable basis rather than only in response to a crisis. Specialist placements are designed to meet the needs of a child with specified special needs in accordance with a scheme set up by a local authority or voluntary agency to provide a family-based alternative to residential care. Each scheme recruits foster carers to look after children who are defined hard to place by reasons of their age, **disability** or behaviour. Foster carers involved in these schemes receive special training and are often referred to as 'professional **foster care**rs'. They are paid enhanced fostering allowances in recognition of the skills they offer and the additional costs incurred in caring for children with such special needs.

Fostering with a view to adoption: a child may be placed with foster carers who are recruited as prospective adopters. This enables the placement to be tried before a decision is taken to make an **adoption order**. It is possible for short-term or long-term **foster care**rs to apply to adopt their foster child. In these instances, the foster carers have to be reassessed as prospective adopters by an **adoption agency** (usually the child's local authority).

Foster placements with relatives: a child who is unable to live with his or her birth parent may be placed with an extended family member. A relative can become a local authority-approved **foster care**r for a particular child. The local authority has the same legal obligations in respect of a child fostered by a relative as to any child in a local authority foster placement. This includes the payment of a fostering allowance. Research suggests that long-term placements with relatives are among the most successful for children. Relatives can care for a child without the need for them to become approved **foster care**rs. The local authority has the discretion to provide financial support under section 17 of the Children Act or through payment of a residence order allowance if the relative acquires a residence order under the Act.

Special Guardianship Orders operate in a similar way; financial support may be available without social services placement **supervision** guidance under the Children Act, together with a more recent code of practice issued by the **Department of Health** in 1999, and National Minimum Fostering Standards (Fostering Services Regulations) 2002 now govern the placing of children with foster carers by the local authority. The foster carers (except private foster carers) have to be approved by the authority. This process usually involves lengthy discussions as to what the responsibilities of fostering are and why they want to become foster carers. Authorities now also have to make rigorous checks when recruiting to ensure that **paedophiles** do not gain approval. From 2001 assessments have included **police** checks on all people over age 10 in the foster household. Additionally, adults will have to account for all their time in education and for all their addresses and will be probed on their views on safeguarding, diversity, discipline and sexual attitudes. In addition, prospective foster carers will be asked about their social history, their current *lifestyle* and the issues around the **outcomes** of **Every Child Matters**. Foster carers are expected to meet the full range of day-to-day needs of the child placed with them, such as supporting the child's progress through school or undertaking all health and developmental checks. The National Standards now require that foster children receive encouragement to develop their talents and interests, that they participate in decisions related to their care or their future and are provided with **advocacy** and support where necessary to exercise these rights. The children, their birth families and foster carers should have a copy of the care plan within 2 weeks of the placement beginning, with a **written agreement** based on the plan also provided. Any placement will be subject to '**looked after** child' placement and care planning review, placement **supervision**, foster carer review and **Ofsted inspection**.

Matching the child with an appropriate family is also an important **social work** task. The **written agreement** should contain, according to National Standards, specific references to the elements of matching taken into consideration for the child concerned. There is strong evidence to show that a child's identity is best preserved when the foster carers share the same ethnic and cultural origins as the child. As a result, many authorities have policies stipulating same-'**race**' placements wherever possible and actively engage in recruiting foster carers to reflect the diversity of the community they serve. The National Standards also now require, for transracial placements, that the foster family be given additional training, support and information. They also stipulate that children be equipped to deal with all forms of **discrimination** and that Black and minority ethnic children are helped to develop specific skills to deal with **racism**. Children with disability should be helped to maximize their potential, including any necessary equipment or adaptations to the foster homes.

Recruiting foster carers and finding appropriate placements for the children who need them is a perennial problem. The reasons for this are well known: the needs of the children requiring foster care have increased and are more diverse and perhaps more difficult for families to respond to. At the same time, changes in women's working patterns and families' expectations about their lifestyles have reduced the number of prospective carers coming forward. Local authorities themselves have not always nurtured and supported foster carers nor given sufficient thought to remuneration packages. As a result, carers have moved increasingly to independent fostering agencies. To tackle these difficulties, local authorities have been encouraged by the **Department of Health** to examine closely how their services measure up to other competing independent agencies – whether in unit costs, timescales for approving carers, the responsiveness in matching children with carers, which includes race, language and religion and, in general, measures of positive outcomes for 'looked after children'. They have also been urged to provide fees and allowances that recognize the time and skills demanded of carers and offer support 24 hours a day throughout the year.

fostering requirement a requirement which may be included in a **youth rehabilitation order** directing that for a specified period the offender must reside with a **local authority foster** parent.

foyers supported accommodation for vulnerable young people designed to help them negotiate the transition to a secure and independent adulthood. The support services attached to **foyers**, or services with close links to them, include counselling, health services concerned with both mental and physical health, education, training and preparation for employment. Foyers claim to be 'holistic' in regard to the services they provide for young people.

The concept of foyers was introduced in the early 1990s since which the Foyer Federation has grown rapidly and now operates in over 130 locations. In 2008 foyers worked with over 10,000 young people. Foyers are found predominantly in urban areas but there are also some rural projects too. Some foyers have been purpose-built, others have adapted older buildings. Facilities can vary substantially with some having high quality leisure facilities including gyms, cafes and IT centres; others are more basic. All foyers however have single rooms for each individual. Residence is wholly conditional on engagement with training or employment preparation schemes. Involvement with other services will be optional unless behaviour is challenging and/or anti-social in which case there is an expectation that appropriate services will be accessed to address identified problems. Young people using foyer services to date have tended to have a background in care and/or to have had spells in young offenders' institutions, be young parents or be vulnerable in some other respect, often with a **mental health** problem. Foyers are one element of the **Supporting People** initiative designed to identify and help vulnerable people of all ages and with all vulnerabilities.

framework for assessment of children in need the systematic approach to assessing vulnerable children, issued by central government.

The framework covers a wide range of factors that should be taken into account in any **assessment** into three domains and maps them out on the three sides of a triangle. One side has the child's developmental needs, which includes the child's health, education, emotional and behavioural development, family and social relationships, self-care skills and identity. On the second side is the parents' capacity to provide basic care, ensure safety, emotional warmth, stimulation, guidance and boundaries. On the third side are family and environmental factors, which include **community** resources, the family's social integration, the family's employment and income, housing and family functioning. This third dimension has been described as the 'missing side of the triangle' in **social work** assessments indicating by inclination and training social workers do not always give full consideration to environmental and neighbourhood based factors including income and resources available to families locally.

The framework explicitly adopts an ecological perspective that focuses on the interaction between the characteristics of the particular family of the child, the wider neighbourhood institutions and the social and cultural influences of the area. As a consequence, the impact of specific social factors, including housing and economic disadvantage, is given relatively greater prominence than in child assessment approaches of the past. The framework also explicitly addresses the assessment of Black and disabled children and provides ways that it expects social workers to use in assessing each of the three main domains in relation to Black or disabled families with **children in need**. This multiplicity of factors is explained in considerable depth in official guidance issued alongside the framework.

The framework distinguishes between an initial assessment and a core assessment. An initial assessment should address the dimensions of the framework but is brief and should be completed at the most within seven working days of the **social services department** receiving the referral. Its objective is to determine whether the child is in need, what services may be provided and by whom, and whether a more detailed core assessment is needed. An initial assessment may include interviews with the child and family, if appropriate, as well as contacts with other agencies that might be involved in the child's life for the purposes of gathering information. A record of the decision of any further action, or, indeed, no action, must be made and communicated in writing to the family and the agencies involved.

A core assessment is lengthier and in greater depth. It considers the most important elements of need in the child's life and looks more closely at the parents' capacity to respond to these needs as well as the context of the wider family and **community** in which the child lives. A core assessment is led by practitioners from the social services department but will draw on the work of specialists from other fields who may undertake assessments of their own. Planning the assessment is crucial to its outcome. Matters such as who will undertake the assessment, what resources are needed to do so, which family members will be included, what methods for collecting information will be used, how the assessment will be analysed must be thought through in advance. At its conclusion, the core assessment should provide an understanding of the child's needs and circumstances and underpin the further provision of services and the expected objectives of the work. The assessment should be completed within, at most, 35 working days.

The process of assessment – how and in what manner relationships are developed, especially with the family – is as important as the information sought. The framework lays great stress on explaining the assessment process to family members in both oral and written **communication**. It particularly calls for communication and direct work with children, especially if there are child safety issues to be addressed. It stipulates that any assessment must include seeing the child, however young and under whatever circumstances. Practitioners must also develop a relationship with children – enabling them to express their thoughts, concerns and opinions. Talking to children, the framework makes clear, requires time, skill and careful preparation and takes culture, language and other communication needs into account. The framework also draws on research that shows that parents seek clear explanations even in the most trying circumstances and want to be treated with openness, honesty, respect and dignity at all times. It is one of the positive elements of the framework that it provides examples for practitioners to emulate, for example in explaining the assessment process to family members. The objective of an assessment is to produce an improvement in the **wellbeing** of the child. The final stage, then, is the analysis of the child's needs, a decision about what intervention is required and devising a plan that details who is to take what action, with a timetable and a process for review. Along with the framework, to help practitioners with such an analysis the Department of Health has issued a number of scales and questionnaires that correspond to the kinds of information the assessment will have gathered.

The introduction of the **common assessment framework** and the **outcomes** formulated in **Every Child Matters** have expanded the scope of child assessment but not replaced the factors for assessment in the framework.

Department of Health (2000) *Assessing Children in Need and their Families: practice guidance*. London: Stationery Office.

functional testing one of the two stages of tests under the **Mental Capacity Act 2005** which informs an **assessment** to establish whether a person has capacity to make a decision.

Under the Mental Capacity Act 2005 a person is defined unable to make a decision if she or he is unable to understand the information relevant to the decision, retain that information, use or weigh that information up as part of the process of making that decision, or communicate his decision (whether by talking, using sign language or any other means). The focus is on the functional ability to understand, retain, explore risks and communicate insight into the decision-making arena. It is important to retain a sense of perspective when working alongside vulnerable people who may be experiencing changes in their cognition and understanding and to remain mindful that there are many influences which can impact severely upon how a person may be perceived or assessed. Having a sensitivity to and an awareness of these possible influences such as environmental restrictions, **physical disability**, relationships of **power**, visual or hearing difficulties, cultural norms, our own perceptions of self and difference is a vital part of professional and effective practice.

gender the social and psychological characteristics attributed to men and women.

Social scientists maintain that whereas sex is determined by biology or anatomy, gender is determined by social processes that can vary significantly between social groups and historically within societies. Socialization is regarded as the key process by which gender characteristics are conveyed to individuals, a process that is influenced by social class, membership of ethnic groups and other factors. There is still a substantial debate concerning the issue of whether there are any biological bases to behaviour that are rooted in biological differences between the sexes. For example, does a woman as child-bearer have a biological predisposition also to nurture that is different from that of a man? Most social scientists now believe that such behaviour is a matter of social expectation, pointing to major differences between societies with regard to parenting. Increasingly, however, the understanding of gender has become more subtle and complex. Theorists have pointed to the need to see gender as constructed through and in relation to other differences such as race, ethnicity and class.

The issue of 'gender' is fundamental to all social analysis not just in isolation but rather as integral to all other aspects of identity. This has wide implications for **social care** practitioners who need to recognize how gender intersects with other aspects of identity such as ethnicity, age, and sexuality. At other situations however practitioners should recognize that whilst gender might not at first appear to be important, for example in cases of **homelessness, mental health** and **substance misuse** where the primary concern may be meeting those immediate needs, practitioners must also be aware of how issues of gender both impact and differentiate such experiences. This points towards the need for practice and service provision which is gender-specific and gender-aware to best meet the needs of **service user**s, both male and female. (See also **femininity, masculinity, postmodernism, queer theory**.)

Spelman, E. (1990) *Inessential Woman*. London: The Woman's Press.

General Social Care Council an agency of the **Department of Health**, established by the General Care Standards Act 2000, to regulate the **social care** workforce and register social care and social workers (hereafter social care workers) including students on social work qualifying programmes.

The purpose of the Council is to ensure that the social care workforce is of an appropriate standard, and it has done this by setting codes of conduct and practice (see **ethical codes**) as well as regulating and supporting training. In addition, it has established a register of social care workers, a new degree in social work to replace the former diploma in social work and a regulatory framework for both social care professionals and their employers. A further important role for the GSCC is that of parliamentary work; providing government and cross-party Select and Joint Committees with briefings and evidence. The Council has also established a 'Conduct Group' which examines complaints and instances of alleged professional misconduct. Investigations into reported concerns about an individual worker, a social work agency or an institution of higher education offering qualifying courses are dealt with by the Conduct Group under new rules that came into force in 2008.

The General Care Standards Act 2000 gave notice that the title of 'social worker' would be protected by law from 2005. It is possible for **service user**s, carers and employers to check with the Council's register to confirm the credentials of people claiming to be social workers. The process of registering includes checks on qualifications, health and character. Registered social workers are encouraged to undertake post-qualifying training to develop and update their knowledge and skills. Renewal of registration with the Council every 3 years is now a requirement. The GSCC intends to add other workers from the **social care** sector to its register in due course. (See also **ethical codes, profession, whistleblowing**.)

genogram a diagrammatic device used principally by social workers, family therapists and mediators to depict a family tree. The tree may include step and cohabiting relationships. Social workers often use genograms in conjunction with **ecomap**s and other **assessment** tools to try to understand individuals, families and their problems, biographies and social contexts.

grief can be perceived as a way of coping with **loss**, although it is important to stress that 'recovery' may be affected by a wide variety of factors including the support available to a person, their own adaptive powers, their self-esteem and their new social and economic circumstances. Emotions experienced can include feelings of helplessness and hopelessness, **anxiety** and stress, anger and a profound feeling of unhappiness. Behaviours might include self-imposed social isolation, lethargy and a **loss** of motivation, panic or even hyperactivity. In sum there is no 'normal' or right way to handle **loss**. And there may be social expectations about dealing with grief. In many societies widowhood, for example, carries some clear expectations about how long a Black dress should be worn; the extent to which the widow might participate in social activities; or the period before which any notion of establishing a new relationship can be considered to be 'respectable'.

The **social work** tasks in supporting **service user**s who have experienced **loss** are wide ranging. The general themes underpinning such support could usefully include helping **service user**s to explore the nature of their **loss** and their associated feelings; encouraging the service user to continue to value positive and constructive things from their past; to help them recognize negative thoughts and behaviours that need to be dealt with so as to preserve a positive sense of self; to help them accept loss; and finally to help them 'move on' in as constructive a way as is possible given their new circumstances. These general themes run through a wide range of social work 'set-pieces' such as helping an older person after a long **marriage** to adjust to the death of a spouse; to help a child or young person adjust to a new life in care; to support a **service user** adjust to a serious brain injury following a road traffic accident; to help someone awarded refugee status to begin to adjust to a new life in another country; and dealing with a miscarriage or a stillborn child. With some losses there may be some ambiguity about the chances to 'restore' that which has been lost. For example, a child might wish his/her parents to get back together again. Another person might harbour hopes that their **marriage** might be 'saved'. Although the agenda has to be set by the **service user**, the social work task might be to help the service user to be realistic and to take account of the evidence; which might point to such aspirations being questionable.

In relation to practical tasks there is no necessary agenda but common problems that have to be dealt with might be funeral arrangements, a review of income and benefits, housing, a need for specialist counselling, support for difficult decisions about a range of needs including perhaps the need to consider residential or domiciliary care, help with caring tasks and dealing with reconfigured family relationships. (See also **maternal deprivation, death and dying, bereavement and grief**.)

group home a very broad term to indicate a type of service provision utilizing ordinary houses and other domestic settings to provide a home for small numbers of **service user**s. Commonly the term is used for homes for groups of about four people, but it has also been employed to describe accommodation for considerably larger groups. This pattern of service provision is often used for people with **learning disability** and people with **mental health problems**. Staffing levels vary according to the need of **service user**s and may range from no permanent staff at all to staff being on duty at all times. 'Floating support' is increasingly the preferred way of staffing a number of group homes so that a **team** of support workers might routinely visit homes with the possibility of providing more intensive support when needed in 'office hours' and skeletal support in the evenings/nights and weekends.

group work a method of working with personal and social problems where there are three or more people, towards some common end or purpose. Group work can involve self-help with all group members nominally having the same 'status' or they can have leaders or facilitators who might be social workers.

Social work has traditionally been perceived as having four major methods of intervention namely individual casework, work with families, group work and **community work**. It is probably the case that **casework** and family work are now more dominant and that community work and group work interventions are less commonly utilized. Nevertheless group work continues to be a highly effective intervention in some circumstances although the rationale for its use needs to be very clear because it is sometimes clearly inappropriate and unlikely to deal effectively with a **service user**'s problem and, exceptionally, may actually damage individuals. It is also the case that group work may not be a sufficient intervention by itself and that it needs to be supplemented by individual work such as casework or counselling; such individual work may be as a prelude to group work to help 'prepare' an individual for group activities or as a supplement to group work to help an individual cope with the particular stresses of a group.

Group work is used in a wide variety of settings – for example, regular meetings of children, young people and adults in various residential settings where the focus might be upon issues concerned with communal living. Support groups have also developed very rapidly in recent decades for people occupying a variety of roles such as carers (including young carers), **foster carer**s or relatives of people with a particular problem such as alcoholism or gambling. Other kinds of group work might entail therapeutic objectives such as 'recovery' from, for example, a **mental health** problem, a traumatic period in an abusive relationship, reminiscence for an elder with problems of memory or a bereavement. Another form of group work might have social skills and confidence as the objectives; such as in work with bullied children, young lone or teenaged parents or learning disabled **service users**. Yet other campaigning groups might be focused upon problems within a **community** such as **anti-social behaviour** of teenagers, the presence of sex workers, drug dealing or various kinds of urban neglect and decay.

The popular wisdom with group work is that it brings together people with the same problem and that this will inevitably bring some comfort because they have thought that they were the only person with 'that kind of problem' and it is intrinsically good to know that there are others in the same predicament. In addition, there is the probability that they will acquire some insight into a problem because others will inevitably have different and potentially useful experiences of a problem and how to cope with it. Such empowering opportunities are undoubtedly to be found in many groups, but some **service users** find it difficult to cope with groups because of personal reticence and/or they find it very hard to share personal experiences especially if they were belittling or abusive events. From another perspective, it is possible that young offenders meeting in groups will simply learn additional bad habits from others and that they will collude with each other in 'resisting' a rehabilitation and reparation programme. So, the appropriateness of the group as an intervention needs to be carefully thought through.

There are many specific group work skills that social workers should try to develop. A key issue to be satisfied is that of legitimization; of how the group was formed, who decided that a group was an appropriate mechanism to deal with an identified issue or problem and who determined the group's objectives and curriculum. Although social workers may have a role in suggesting a group as a way of addressing a problem, groups have essentially to be a response to expressed individual **service users**' needs and wishes; and that consultations with them have to be painstaking if they are to pass that test. If group objectives and curricula are set in this way a useful and additional important problem to address is that of evaluation; in effect to be able to answer the question 'has the group been successful in its objectives?' The issue of realistic objectives is best thought about as part of planning any group. Evaluations can use hard data that might be about, for example, the incidence of bullying, or the ability to do something that previously could not be contemplated or ways of supporting another that were found to be stressful and now are not. Hard data can be supplemented by 'soft' data; that is, data about how people feel or their sense of **wellbeing** or their confidence.

Preston-Shoot, M. (2006) *Effective Group Work*. London: Palgrave Macmillan.

Gypsy and traveller communities a diverse range of different nomadic ethnic and social groups, including English Romany Gypsies, Welsh Gypsies, Scottish Gypsy/Travellers, Irish Travellers, New (Age) Travellers and Occupational Travellers (Travelling Showpeople and Circus Travellers). Like all ethnic labels and social categories, the terms 'gypsy' and 'traveller' are highly contested. Two of the main groups that are recognized as ethnic groups under British Race Relations legislation are Irish Travellers and Roma or Romany Gypsy groups. Both are distinct ethnic groups, with differing practices, traditions and histories. They have also had differing patterns of migration to the UK. Roma Gypsy groups are believed to have originated from Northern India and have for centuries lived a nomadic way of life across Europe. Historical sources have documented their presence in England since the 15th century. The Irish Traveller communities' movement to England has been more recent, occurring through two major phases in the 19th century (influenced by the Irish potato famine and expansion of British railways) and the 20th century (due to Irish housing policy and post-war labour shortage in England).

Over time, members of both communities have settled and inter-married within sedentary communities. What both groups do share are long histories of **racism**, marginalization and even persecution. Many commentators have commented on the 'normalization' and relative acceptability of **racism** towards Gypsy and traveller communities within contemporary Europe when compared with **racism** towards other ethnic groups. Many live in **poverty**, suffer high levels of unemployment and face difficulties in accessing adequate health care and educational provision, with high levels of infant mortality, lower life expectancy, poor school attendance and high levels of illiteracy.

Historically, planning policy has discriminated against those who lead a nomadic lifestyle and there continues to be a lack of available and suitable sites, with an estimated 20 per cent of the Traveller community not having a legal place to hold their caravans (House of Commons 2004 Report *Housing, Planning, Local Government and the Regions Committee, Gypsy and Traveller Sites*). The Caravan Sites Act 1968 made it a statutory duty for **local authorities** to provide caravan sites for Gypsy and traveller communities. This was then removed with the Criminal Justice and Public Order Act 1994, which gave both the **police** and local authorities powers to evict Gypsies and Travellers from unauthorized encampments. However, under section 225 of the Housing Act 2004, local housing authorities have responsibilities to make an assessment of the accommodation needs of Traveller and Gypsy communities and develop a strategy to meet their needs. There are increasing calls for this responsibility to be a statutory duty for local authorities.

Cemlyn, S., Greenfield, M., Burnett, S. *et al.* (2009) *Inequalities Experienced by Gypsy and Travellers Communities*: Review, Research Report 12. London: Equality and Human Rights Commission.

H h

harassment by a landlord (or landlord's agent) is defined as 'acts likely to interfere with the peace and comfort of a residential occupier or members of his household' or 'persistently withdrawing or withholding services reasonably required for the occupation of the premises as a residence' (Protection from Eviction Act 1977). See also **illegal eviction**.

hate crime a crime motivated by hatred, prejudice or negative attitudes on the grounds of race, religion, **disability**, gender or sexuality. The term 'hate crime' is American and has no legal status in the UK. However, a number of **racially aggravated offences** were introduced by the **Crime and Disorder Act 1998**, attracting more severe **sentences** than the non-aggravated offences. More generally, under the **Criminal Justice Act 2003**, any offence motivated by hostility based on the **victim**'s race, religion, sexual orientation or **disability** must be treated by a sentencing court as an aggravating factor making the offence more serious.

health inequalities differences in life expectancy (mortality) and illness (morbidity) that are persistent and appear to be related to socio-economic and structural features of society, including social class, gender and ethnicity.

Death rates have been falling in the UK over the past century, and life expectancy has increased for all social groups. There are differences in death rates, however, and in the incidence of illness between social classes, and these differences are increasing. Social class in this context is denoted by occupation. Thus class I includes professional occupations, such as those of accountants, doctors or architects. Class II comprises managerial, technical and intermediate occupations, such as those of teachers, nurses, computer programmers. Class III includes both manual and non-manual skilled occupations, such as those of carpenters, plumbers or bank clerks. Class IV comprises occupations such as those of farm workers, machine tool operators or caretakers, and, finally, class V comprises unskilled occupations such as those of labourers, cleaners or factory packers. A series of government reports that have appeared over the past 25 years (notably the Black Report, 1980, and the Acheson Report, 1998) have found that health inequalities have been remarkably persistent and that in some respects such differences are widening. For example, as the Acheson Report states, 'in the late 1970s death rates were 53 per cent higher among men in classes IV and V compared with those in classes I and II. In the late 1980s they were 68 per cent higher. Among women, the differential increased from 50 per cent to 55 per cent.' In relation to morbidity (the incidence of diseases), there are similar differences. For example, there is an increased incidence of depressive illness and **anxiety** disorders, lung cancer, coronary heart disease, stroke and respiratory disease from social class I to social class V, and these significant differences have also widened over the past 20 years.

Explanations for the higher incidence of death rates and poor health among social classes VI and V in particular are to be found in a constellation of factors – low incomes, unemployment, low educational achievement and poor housing. Poor dietary habits, in part influenced by low incomes, less usage of health services and increased smoking in particular, were also cited as contributory factors in the maintenance of health inequalities. As a result, many of the recommendations of both the Black and Acheson Reports focused on anti-**poverty** strategies, increased employment opportunities and improved housing as well as restructured health services to involve more people, especially **older people** and mothers with children in order to increase usage of health services, including preventive services.

The **social work** task in relation to health inequalities, often discharged in conjunction with health service professionals, is multi-faceted. Work in relation to income maintenance, such as an involvement in benefit take-up work, work to encourage the provision of public services without charge or at low cost, encouraging a healthy diet for **service user**s, support for teenage parents and their children, child protection activities, work with people with significant and enduring **mental health problems**, support for vulnerable **older people**, activities associated with improving housing, including work to secure more appropriate housing to meet individual need, and many other areas of work impact upon health. There have also been some useful local initiatives recently emphasizing the importance of good physical health for those recovering from **mental health problems** or trying to live with them on a long-term basis. Successive governments have encouraged cooperation between health and social work/care professionals through new structures. Initially **primary care trust**s, Health Action Zones (until 2004) and **Sure Start** were given the task of establishing a 'seamless' service that acknowledges the complexities and inter-relationships between social and economic factors and health **outcomes**. The most recent initiative, 2007, is focusing upon the 'Spearhead Group' of **local authorities**, comprising the bottom fifth nationally of areas where at least three of five key indicators of mortality or morbidity have a high incidence, namely male life expectancy at birth; female life expectancy at birth; cancer mortality rates in the under 75s; cardiovascular disease mortality rate in the under 75s; and the government's own index of multiple deprivation. The Spearhead group includes many urban areas with a high incidence of ethnic minority communities.

Bywaters, P., McLeod, E. and Napier, L. (eds) (2009) *Social work and Global Health inequalities: practice and policy developments*. Bristol: Policy Press.

High Court the court which hears the most important civil legal disputes in England and Wales, superior to the **magistrates' court** and county court. The High Court is composed of three different divisions, known as the Queen's Bench, Chancery and Family Divisions. The largest is the Queen's Bench Division, which deals with civil disputes including personal injury claims, commercial disputes and administrative issues, for example the **judicial review** of government and **local authority** decisions. The business of the Chancery Division includes matters of taxation, wills and trusts. The Family Division is concerned with disputes about **divorce**, children and family property (see **family proceedings**). Appeals from **magistrates' court**s about civil family matters are heard in the Family Division. The Divisional Court of the Queen's Bench Division also has some criminal jurisdiction, hearing appeals on some points of law from magistrates' courts and **Crown Courts**. (See also **criminal court**.)

HIV/Aids HIV (abbreviation for human immunodeficiency virus) is the virus that may lead to Aids (acronym for acquired immuno-deficiency syndrome). HIV damages the body's defence (immune) system, making it more vulnerable to the effects of opportunistic infections.

The HIV virus is spread by an interchange of bodily fluids, which must pass from an infected person into the body of an uninfected person. The behaviour most likely to affect this interchange is penetrative sexual intercourse and the sharing of needles and other drug-using equipment. The transmission of the HIV virus through blood transfusions from infected people is now much less likely because of improved screening of donated blood. The virus may also be passed from an infected mother to her unborn child or to the child at the time of birth. The HIV antibody test shows whether or not the body has developed antibodies to the virus. If it has, this means that the body at some time has been infected by HIV, but it may take up to three or more months for the antibodies to develop after the virus has been contracted, so ideally two tests with 'safe' behaviour in between are necessary. **Social work** has important roles to play in responding to both, whether through counselling, **advocacy, social action** or policy development. **Social work** with people living with HIV and Aids has changed considerably in the last few years. Significant advances in medical treatment of the virus have been made using highly active anti-retroviral treatment that slows the impact of HIV and has extended life expectancy dramatically.

This progress has added only further complexity to the social work task however. In addition to needing broad counselling skills around momentous life events – relationships with sexual partners, **dying, death and bereavement** – social workers now work with Aids survivors who need support in planning for their futures, becoming informed about intricate drug regimes and in returning to work or job training. In promoting **empowerment**, the social worker helps people to normalize HIV and to hold open different possibilities for their future, whether developing aspects of their social and sexual lives or learning to take an active role in their own medical management. The social **stigma** surrounding a person with HIV or Aids, fuelled by fear, ignorance and **discrimination**, is still immense and requires challenging by practitioners and survivors. At the core of oppressive public attitudes are physical intimidation and violent displays of **homophobia. Prison**ers and drug-related offenders are particularly vulnerable to contracting HIV/Aids. The Prison Service has consistently refused to issue condoms to prisoners, except on home leave, or to countenance needle exchange schemes despite the prevalence of homosexual practices and drug taking in **prison**s. Practitioners should also bear in mind evidence suggesting that families from minority ethnic communities and low income groups are less likely to seek early treatment. A culturally sensitive approach to **assessment** and intervention using key health providers from within specific communities is an important element of the interdisciplinary work required.

Miller, R. (n.d.) *Social Work and HIV/Aids*. London: BASW.

home detention curfew a type of **early release** from **prison** which includes a **curfew** enforced by **electronic monitoring**. The system was first introduced by the **Crime and Disorder Act 1998**. Currently it allows **prison**ers serving **sentences** of 3 months or over to be considered for release up to 135 days before the normal automatic release at the halfway point of the sentence. Those serving **extended sentences** for violent or sexual crimes are excluded from the scheme, and other **sex offenders** are only exceptionally to be released. Release is on **licence**, and the conditions include a home curfew for at least 9 hours per day, enforced by electronic monitoring. The decision as to whether a prisoner is released is a discretionary one, with the discretion resting formally with the **Justice Secretary** but in practice normally with the prison governor. The governor's decision is taken on the basis of a risk assessment carried out by prison and **probation** staff. Around 2,500 prisoners are on home detention curfew at any one time. See also **early release, end of custody licence**.

homelessness the condition of being without a home or shelter or of living in circumstances wholly inappropriate to personal and social needs.

Definitions of homelessness, and consequently estimations of the extent of homelessness, have varied widely in Britain. Official registers are unreliable because many people do not bother to report themselves in need of housing. Statistics usually reflect only those people who are accepted as homeless by housing departments of **local authorities**. However, there have been a number of initiatives that have tried to estimate the size of particular groups of homeless people, such as rough sleepers or young people. Many people who are not in priority categories do not report themselves as homeless because they believe that local authorities cannot help them. Others despair of lengthy waiting lists, often accepting poor-quality accommodation in the private sector. Official statistics therefore grossly underestimate the extent of the problem. Some analysts would add to the homeless list all those who are in inappropriate accommodation, that is, people living in **hostel**s, temporary accommodation or in overcrowded or insanitary conditions. In addition, there are many thousands of people living in abusive relationships who warrant alternative, safe accommodation. If all these groups are admitted as homeless, then the problem is clearly substantial.

The Housing Act 1996 imposes duties on local **housing authorities** to provide social housing for those who are eligible, homeless, in priority need, and not **intentionally homeless**. The Homelessness Act 2002 requires local authorities to publish a strategy for the prevention of homelessness in their area. There is a code of guidance to which local authorities must have regard and which attempts to interpret the law. *Eligible* in this context means not subject to immigration control; but exceptions are refugees and people with settled status or **exceptional leave to remain**.

Homelessness is more than just rooflessness; it includes people who have no accommodation anywhere they are legally entitled to occupy, or who cannot reasonably remain in their home, for example, due to a risk of violence, overcrowding, or the level of disrepair. It includes those who are threatened with **homelessness** within 28 days, and those in emergency accommodation.

Priority need includes: people with dependent children; someone who is pregnant; someone who is vulnerable because of old age, mental or **physical disability**, or other special reason; people who are homeless as a result of an emergency such as flood, fire, or other disaster; 16- and 17-year-olds (unless the responsibility of social services); care leavers aged 18 to 21; people who are vulnerable through having been in the armed forces or **prison**, or who have been in the care of the local authority; people who are vulnerable because they have left accommodation due to violence or threats of violence. The issue of vulnerability has been extensively debated in the courts, and the code of guidance reflects the current definition: someone should be considered vulnerable if, when homeless, 'they are less able to fend for themselves so that injury or detriment will result'. Supporting medical evidence can help someone argue that they are vulnerable. Those in priority need should be given temporary accommodation while investigations continue.

Being *intentionally homeless* means having deliberately done, or failed to do, something that leads to loss of accommodation which it was reasonable to continue to occupy. Acts or omissions carried out in ignorance or good faith should not be considered intentional (see Code of Guidance for examples).

The local authority to which the application has been made has the duty to provide accommodation, although they may refer an applicant to another authority if there is a stronger connection with that authority (unless there is the risk of violence in that authority). *Local connection* means: living in an area for 6 out of the last 12 months, or 3 out of the last 5 years *or* having a close family member who has lived in the area for 5 years *or* employment in the area (but not casual work) *or* 'special reasons', for example, where someone grew up.

The 'full homelessness duty' is owed to those who pass the first four tests. This may be an offer of local authority housing, an assured tenancy with a registered social landlord, or a 'qualifying' offer of an assured shorthold tenancy in the private sector (which an applicant does not have to accept). Accommodation should be suitable for the applicant and their family. Those not owed the full duty should be given **advice** and assistance to enable them to find suitable accommodation.

There is increasing recognition of the association between homelessness and some social problems. For example, the educational attainment for children of homeless families often suffers. This is because there are often delays in finding places in schools and because children find it difficult to adjust to new schools even if a school can be found to accept them. For families who make many moves, these problems become very difficult indeed. Both mental and physical health can be seriously affected as a result of poor or insanitary accommodation and because of difficulties in accessing health services. However it is possible for homelessness to be both a cause and consequence of poor **mental health**. For example, failure to recognize the support needs of people with enduring **mental health problems** can lead to them leaving accommodation or being asked to leave. Other chronic problems include difficulties in claiming benefits and in securing employment. Feelings of powerlessness among homeless people are common, especially where people have been housed temporarily away from their communities of origin and their support **networks** in often poor-quality accommodation. In this context, oppressed groups such as single parents (mostly women), ethnic minorities, care leavers and ex-forces personnel figure prominently. See also **vagrancy**, **night shelters**, **rough sleepers**, **foyers and housing problems**.

Department for Communities and Local Government (2006) *Homelessness Code of Guidance for Local Authorities.* London: HMSO.

Fitzpatrick, S., Quilgars, D. and Pleace, N. (eds) (2009) *Homelessness in the UK.* London: Chartered Institute of Housing.

Home Office the government department responsible for the **police**, crime, **anti-social behaviour**, drugs policy, anti-terrorism and immigration, headed by the Home Secretary. Until recently it was the central government department responsible for most criminal justice policy in England and Wales and oversaw **prisons**, the **probation service** and sentencing policy. However in 2007 the work of the courts, **probation service** and **prison**s was separated into the new **Ministry of Justice**. The Home Office now concentrates on the work of the police and the security service with its involvement centred on counter-terrorism, drugs and anti-social behaviour.

homophobia an intensely negative feeling about homosexuals and **homosexuality** which, sufficiently strong, may lead to **discrimination**, **harassment** and physical intimidation.

Homophobia may be an irrational fear and possibly a deep-seated hatred of homosexuals and of what is perceived as their lifestyles. It is thought to be widespread in society, although for most people the feeling is relatively dormant, brought occasionally to life by anti-homosexual jokes. It is rare for people to be involved in active anti-homosexual politics or campaigns, although there have been incidents of **hate crime**s on gay men sometimes resulting in deaths, perpetrated by individuals known to have homophobic attitudes. Some have hypothesized that homophobia may itself be evidence of repressed or latent homosexuality.

homosexuality a socially constructed term used to define same-sex desire, particularly among males.

Although same-sex desire between men has been found historically within all societies, the term gained usage within the 19th century. The death penalty for 'buggery' was not abolished until 1861 in England and Wales. Yet this did not herald liberalization of the law but rather represented the tightening of its grip, and in 1885 the Criminal Law Amendment Act effectively made male homosexuality itself 'illegal'. The Vagrancy Act 1898 also criminalized homosexual soliciting and extended the meaning of homosexuality beyond buggery. Homosexuality between women (lesbianism) has had a much lower profile and has not had to face the same degree of condemnation from the average citizen or governments.

From this time and well into the 20th century, homosexuality was seen as a pathological disease that could be cured. It was not until 1973 that the American Psychiatric Association removed homosexuality from its list of '**mental disorder**s'. The alleged pathological nature of homosexuality was actively challenged by the Gay movement from the 1960s onwards, and the term 'homosexuality' itself began to change into a more positive affirmation of sexual desire. Under the Sexual Offences Act 1967, homosexual acts were decriminalized as long as both parties are consenting and, later, both have reached the age of 16 (as amended by the Sexual Offences (Amendment) Act 2000).

Homosexual acts are defined in law as 'buggery' or 'gross indecency'. The 1967 Act is used largely to prosecute gay men accused of 'cruising' in a public place, whether or not there is anyone else present. Such legislation relating specifically to gay men further enforced the idea that homosexuality is wrong; confirmed by the thinking that inspired section 28 of the Local Government Act 1988 in its prescription that no local authority shall either 'promote homosexuality' or 'the acceptability of homosexuality as a pretended family relationship'. This legislation was repealed in Scotland in 2000 and in the rest of the UK in 2003, although there was continued support for section 28 from various faith based groups including the Roman Catholic Church, the Church of England, the Muslim Council and various Christian evangelical groups. There are specific implications for **social care** practitioners, especially with regard to fostering and **adoption**. The Guidance and Regulations to the **Children Act 1989** states: 'It would be wrong arbitrarily to exclude any particular groups of people from consideration.'

This principle was reinforced in 1997 in a landmark decision when a judge concluded that the law 'permits an adoption application to be made by a single applicant, whether she or he . . . lives alone, or cohabits in a heterosexual, homosexual or even a sexual relationship . . .' While there has been a significant shift in both attitudes towards and images of homosexuality in society, in part because of the efforts of the lesbian and gay movement, in many respects it has been unsuccessful in achieving legislative social change, and **discrimination** on the basis of homosexuality remains, especially within the workplace. In 2004 the Civil **Partnership**s Act was passed (implemented in December 2005) providing some legal recognition of same-sex **couples**. The 2009 edition of Social Trends reported that in the month of December 2005 2,000 civil **partnership**s were registered; for the complete years of 2006 and 2007 the figures were 16,000 and 8,700 respectively. See also **queer theory**, **sexuality**.

hospice see **palliative care**

hospital orders orders, available under sections 37 and 38 of the **Mental Health Act 1983**, allowing **Crown Court** to detain a **prison**er for up to 6 months in a psychiatric facility. The orders are renewable.

Two doctors have to be convinced that a prisoner or defendant is suffering from a serious **mental health** problem and that they need treatment or need to be detained if treatment is thought not to be possible. Where such people constitute a **risk** to the public a restriction order under section 41 of the Act may also be imposed. Hospital orders may also be applied to someone serving a **prison sentence** at the direction of the Home Secretary again with a recommendation from two doctors.

hostel a residential unit that offers a measure of support, **supervision** and, sometimes, protection.

Hostel facilities are often a halfway house between a long-stay institution and 'normal' **community** living, or they may be designed to help vulnerable people to live more independently and thus at some later stage effect a move into community living. They may offer both **supervision** and support to ex-offenders without family support, especially after a long **prison sentence**. Such facilities are often appropriate to those on **parole** and where a conviction has included an offence against the person. Hostel accommodation, together with a **probation order**, is also increasingly offered to **sex offender**s as an alternative to **imprisonment** as part of a rigorous regime of 're-education'. Supervision and support are also pertinent to people with **mental health problems**, either as a temporary measure to reintroduce them into the community or, conceivably, to prevent admission to hospital, or as a long-term placement for those who cannot manage alone. Other vulnerable groups, including **older people** (see also **sheltered accommodation**), people with learning disabilities (see also **group home**), children leaving care, alcoholics 'drying out' and homeless people or families (as a prelude to finding more settled and secure accommodation), have all benefited from hostel accommodation of varying kinds. Hostels differ in terms of **social work** support, which is provided intensively on the premises in some cases and more distantly in others, with workers visiting from time to time offering 'floating support'. (See also **bail hostel**.)

housing association a non-profit organization involved in the building and maintenance of housing. **Housing association**s are organized in a variety of ways reflected in their status, which can range from that of a friendly society through to charitable companies under the Charities Act. Under the changing legislation of the 1980s, housing associations have expanded to become an increasingly important part of public or social housing provision. As a result of this expansion, they are responsible for approximately a third of all newly built housing. This has been largely because of the way central government has aimed to reduce the role of the local **housing authorities** in providing and managing public-sector housing. This change has also allowed central government to have greater direct control over the housing programme, bypassing **local authorities**. In 1964 the government established the Housing Corporation as an agency for financing housing associations. Through the Housing Corporation the government can channel funds through a system of deficit loans that allow housing associations to engage in building new housing without being dependent on raising finance through more commercial channels such as the banks.

As housing associations have increased their role in providing new housing, so have they also established themselves as a major provider of supported accommodation for people emerging out of long-stay hospitals (including people with enduring **mental health problems** and people with learning disabilities) in addition to recovering alcoholics, drug users, elders and women fleeing violent relationships. **Social services department**s have worked with housing associations in the development of new forms of sheltered and supported accommodation, often maintaining allocation rights in return for contracts with housing associations. This has enabled social services departments and health authorities to develop new initiatives, particularly in areas where the district housing authority is a limited supplier or in response to the government's emphasis on non-statutory provision. Housing associations are likely to play a major role in the government's **Supporting People** initiative.

Malpass, P. and Rowlands, R. (2009) *Housing, Markets and Policy*. London: Routledge.

housing authorities the housing departments of local district councils and unitary authorities, primarily responsible for the management of council housing stock.

Housing authorities are involved in the provision of public-sector housing, as both builders and managers. Within the metropolitan areas they are part of the metropolitan district council alongside **social services department**s. Similar arrangements are now in existence in other unitary authorities established when local government was last restructured in 1997. This has allowed for some close working relationships to develop, and in some authorities, including Tower Hamlets in London and St Helens in Merseyside, there has been a move towards the integration of these services as a response to the demands of **community care**. However, local authority housing provision has come under severe strain since 1979, when the Conservative government introduced a range of financial and statutory controls on housing finance. Most important was the introduction of the statutory right to buy in the Housing Act 1980, which resulted in approximately two million sales of council dwellings by 2005. The financial benefit to **local authorities** from the sale of council dwellings was restricted because of capital controls on the use of receipts from sales. These and other controls led to a fall in capital spending on housing by local government and housing associations becoming a more significant provider of public housing.

The Conservative government introduced its controls on housing finance with the stated objective of reducing the role of the state in providing public housing. The aim was to increase the role of the Housing Corporation and housing associations in public housing and to provide more incentives for the private sector both in owner-occupation and in rented accommodation. Additionally, the government introduced measures to ensure that local authority housing was provided at a price closer to its market value. Local authorities' housing revenue accounts can no longer be subsidized from other sources, so management, repair and maintenance costs must come out of the rents charged. This has inevitably resulted in an increase in rents in recent years and consequently a major increase in housing benefit payments – see welfare rights 6 – as tenants find rents outstripping their ability to pay. Critics have argued that the introduction of the right to buy, together with controls on capital spending, resulted in a reduction in the housing stock available to local authorities for housing the poor. This gave rise to an increase in the number of cases of homelessness and the use of temporary accommodation to try to resolve the problem.

With all these financial pressures, some local housing authorities concentrated more on providing sheltered accommodation. The approach adopted involved the use of wardens and introduced an element of care into the service. Some of the largest housing authorities including Bristol and Stoke-on-Trent have argued consistently against the view that housing authorities should concentrate on the 'bricks and mortar' aspects of housing management and instead emphasized their welfare role in caring for tenants. It is increasingly common for local authorities to transfer all or part of their housing stock to Registered Social Landlords (large scale voluntary transfer), thus further increasing the role of housing associations as providers of public housing, and social services frequently see these as partners in providing accommodation for clients rather than the district housing authorities. The election of a Labour government in 1997 did not significantly reverse these trends in housing developments, and the emphasis remains on a mix of providers of public-sector and low-cost housing.

Morgan, J. (2007) *Aspects of Housing Law.* London: Routledge-Cavendish.

housing benefit see **welfare rights 6**

housing problems a wide range of problems, involving social workers and support workers, concerning access to housing, the relationship between housing and personal needs, security of tenure, housing and **community** context and **homelessness**. A distinction is often drawn between a shelter and a home. The functions of a shelter are to provide protection from the elements and some measure of personal security whereas a home, additionally, includes notions of privacy and seclusion for individuals and families to express themselves in a manner that meets their personal needs and reflects the standards of the society in which they live. A home is thus a basic requirement without which people cannot adequately function in relation to their principal social roles (for example, work, raising a family or being in a married or cohabiting relationship and living in a community). Although the **Human Rights Act 1998** has been invoked in the courts on the issue of interference with a person's home, there is no universal right to a home in Britain. The state recognizes a need to house 'vulnerable' people, but housing agencies are inconsistent in the help offered to such groups (see **homelessness**). In addition, numbers of households are increasing, while the supply of new housing has fallen.

Access to housing or appropriate housing, both for people in general and for those with particular needs, continues to be a major problem that engages social workers. Research has identified young people (and especially care leavers), ex-prisoners, people with enduring **mental health problems**, drug abusers, **older people**, lone parents, ethnic minorities, people in violent relationships and disabled people as experiencing persistent problems of accessing suitable housing. This was acknowledged by the addition of some of these groups of people in the priority need categories in 2002. Mental health problems are now perceived as both a cause and effect of **homelessness**. This cause and effect is heightened if a person is drug or alcohol-dependent. Given that some mental health problems are episodic in nature, requiring varying levels of support, suitable accommodation may be hard to access. The best-planned provision includes a range of services, with spare capacity, to meet often short-term needs. These services allow people to move between packages of care, support and accommodation as their problems improve or deteriorate. The work of **assertive outreach teams** and **active rehabilitation teams** can help to both prevent the need for moves or to make them short term. In both scenarios there is the potential for significantly increased stability for **service user**s.

The issue of how independent or dependent a lifestyle can be sustained is also especially important to both **older people** and to disabled people. Britain has an ageing population, and although there is no necessary association between age and **disability**, some older people do acquire both physical and mental disabilities. Younger people can be physically or learning-disabled from birth or through illness or traumatic events such as accidents. Planners have devised a number of supported housing options for both groups, with varying levels of social support ranging from people living in their own homes (with visiting or domiciliary support) to clustered accommodation through **group home**s and **sheltered accommodation** to residential and nursing homes.

The social and caring support needed can also be conceived of as being on a continuum from a few hours a week to 24-hour cover, depending upon a person's needs. A different issue arises for women wishing to leave a violent partner. Women have to decide whether, with appropriate measures in place, they can seek to oust the partner or whether they need to get away to some place of refuge. Many women have felt it necessary to leave, but increasingly justice and community agencies have tried to put together a package of legal and protective measures designed to enable women and their children to feel safe in their own homes. Better that women and children can maintain important aspects of their daily lives, such as schooling, work and social supports, than to have to start all over again in another area.

Other housing problems concerning social workers and support workers involve issues that could be broadly labelled as 'neighbour relations'. This clutch of problems includes some very testing issues such as racial **harassment**, **anti-social behaviour** and the problem of housing known sex-offenders. Work on these problems requires the careful balancing of rights and risks. Black and ethnic minority groups clearly need to be able to live without fear from racists in any community, and social workers and housing workers need to act decisively in the event of racist behaviour. With sex-offenders living in the community, the issues are those of wishing to rehabilitate people but also ensuring that women or children are not put at risk. Similar issues arise in relation to people exhibiting behaviour labelled as anti-social. Social workers are required to ensure that there are good reasons why anyone should be evicted and that suitable alternative accommodation is found for those so regarded. Social landlords have a range of powers to tackle anti-social behaviour.

The threat of eviction can arise for additional reasons, such as rent or mortgage arrears, from the behaviour of unreasonable landlords (especially where landlords will not make essential repairs or there are indefensible rent increases) or because of an alleged failure on the part of tenants to maintain property. Such difficulties often result from personal and relationship problems, such as redundancy, **divorce** and separation or financial mismanagement. Social workers can help through **debt advice (money advice)** and negotiations with mortgagors or landlords and by sometimes helping **service user**s to maximize their incomes. Social landlords are required to comply with the Pre-Action Protocol for rent arrears, which obliges them to attempt to resolve the problem before taking court action.

The past decade has witnessed a reconfiguration of **social work** services focused on housing issues. Increasingly, social workers and social support workers are being employed by housing agencies concerned with vulnerable groups rather than being located in **social work** agencies and acting as advocates for service users in their dealings with housing agencies. This movement is epitomized by the **Supporting People** initiative, which was implemented in 2003. The movement is also evidence of a new thinking about complex social problems, namely, that specialist workers can most effectively work together if they work in dedicated teams within the same organization.

Housing inequalities reflect broader structural social and economic features of society. These inequalities concern not only the quality of accommodation, but also community infrastructures and, often, other 'life chance' issues such as health, education and employment. Housing is therefore an important locus for social work and community work activity and it must be seen as an important dimension of urban and rural regeneration strategies.

Morgan, J. (2007) *Aspects of Housing Law*. London: Routledge.

Human Rights Act 1998 a law that sets out the rights of the citizen, incorporating the provisions of the European Convention on Human Rights into UK law. Under this Act, all public authorities – including, for example, health authorities and trusts, **social services department**s and their employees – are under a legal duty to respect the rights recognized in the European Convention on Human Rights. These include rights to life, liberty, security, respect for private and family life, freedom of thought and expression and the right not to be subject to inhuman or degrading treatment. British courts are bound where possible to interpret UK law so that it is compatible with the Convention. If the court decides that UK law is clearly incompatible with the Convention it must make a formal declaration to this effect; the government then has special powers to swiftly introduce legislation to remove the incompatibility. However, the courts have no **power** themselves to overturn UK laws which infringe Convention rights.

These changes represent an enormous shift in the legal culture of the UK, although they are based on a limited and conditional view of **citizenship**. They potentially extend rights to the whole population that were previously available only to those with the resources or backing to take test cases to the European courts. The rights protected include the right to life, the right to liberty unless this is lawfully taken away and then to a fair trial, the right to respect for private and family life, freedom of thought, conscience, religion, expression, assembly and association, the right to education and the right to marry and set up a family.

humanitarian protection gives an asylum seeker the right to remain in the UK even though they do not satisfy the UN Convention. They are given the right to remain for up to 5 years because their life is threatened for some other reason. They are able to work, claim benefits, apply for social housing and family reunion.

I i

ideology an organized system of ideas and beliefs concerning the political, social and cultural views of an individual or group.

For most, ideas about political and social structures tend to be unformed or not fully thought through. Few people have a developed system of ideas that are logically integrated within a system and, as such, tend to react to changing issues in an *ad hoc* and pragmatic way. Ideologies, on the other hand, are more formally established sets of ideas and beliefs that can be seen as a guide to action. Political ideologies are for the most part the classic example of sets of formulated ideas concerning behaviour, organization, responsibility and action. These often have a well-established history behind them, having been developed during the period associated with the development of popular democracy in the 18th and 19th centuries. Ideologies associated with the main political parties, including socialism, conservatism and liberalism, all emerged in the 19th century and are clearly associated with the way in which society, the economy and the political system should operate. They are also linked closely with the development of the **welfare state** and debates around its future.

Liberalism and socialism were bodies of thought that identified to varying degrees a role for the state in providing support for the most disadvantaged within society, with socialism seeing the collective good of society being of greater concern than individual need. Conservatism has largely been pragmatic in its response to these developments and, until recently, has not reversed the trend towards more collectivist approaches to welfare. Within conservatism, however, there is a strong trend that believes that the role of the state should be minimal as it leads to dependency and the undermining of individual freedoms. These conflicting ideologies have been powerful forces in the development of welfare services and play a key role in debates over the future of welfare. For example, the relationship between the level of state provision and the role of the private sector in areas such as pensions, residential homes or health care insurance is a key debate where the ideologies of the main political parties ensure that such issues are always of high political importance.

Some would also argue that while most people have not formulated clearly their political and social beliefs, they still respond to issues from an ideological position. Evidence for this is that people who tend to support one issue, such as equality of treatment for women, will tend to support other related issues, such as **disability** rights. Indeed, pragmatism itself may be seen as an ideological position.

Leach, R. (2009) *Political Ideology in Britain*. Houndmills: Palgrave Macmillan.

illegal eviction under the Protection from Eviction Act 1977, it is an offence if any person 'unlawfully deprives the residential occupier . . . of his occupation of the premises or any part thereof, or attempts to do so . . .'. Tenancy relations officers are part of a local authority's housing team. Their main role is to make sure that tenants in private rented accommodation do not experience **harassment** or are not illegally evicted by their landlord. Local **housing authorities** are specifically authorized under the Act to prosecute offences of **harassment** and illegal eviction.

Immigration and Asylum Act 1999 an Act that introduced new arrangements for providing accommodation and support for asylum seekers. Under it asylum seekers are not eligible for social housing or welfare benefits but set up separate arrangements from April 2000 under which they were accommodated and supported by an agency of the **Home Office** – now the UK Border Agency. The agency makes arrangements by contracting with private providers and **local authorities** for accommodation and providing cash for daily living needs.

impairment a physical, sensory or psychological characteristic or aspect of functioning that falls outside norms established in medical practice. The distinction between impairment and **disability** is vital to the critique that disabled activists have developed of approaches to disability based on the limitations of individuals. Impairment has been defined by disability activists as 'lacking part or all of a limb, or having defective limb, organism or mechanism of the body', whereas disability is regarded as the social restrictions and exclusions imposed on people with impairments. These result from the way that the requirements of people with impairments are disregarded in social and environmental arrangements. Impairment can be caused by differences at birth or by illnesses and accidents. However, it is more common in later life.

There are many types of impairment, and the above definition from within the disability movement does not mention mental distress or **intellectual impairment**, more usually referred to as **learning disability**. Recent discussion within the disability movement has focused on whether there should be more emphasis on impairment and the restrictions and discomfort this imposes on some disabled people. In particular, it has been argued that the movement could be more inclusive by acknowledging difficulties arising from illness and impairment. The counter-argument to this has been the danger of focusing on impairment rather than on the external barriers that can be tackled by political action. Academic critics have pointed out, however, that impairment is itself socially constructed on the basis of dominant conceptions of normality and that this should also be subject to analysis.

Thomas, C. (1999) *Female Forms: experiencing and understanding disability.* Buckingham: Open University Press.

imprisonment   the **custodial sentence** whereby a court orders that an adult offender (aged 21 or over) be confined in a **prison** for a specified period. The **sentence** can be passed by any **criminal court** as long as statute law specifies that the offence is imprisonable, but imprisonment is only supposed to be used as a last resort. Courts are required by the **Criminal Justice Act 2003** to pass sentences of imprisonment only if the current offences are so serious that neither a **fine** alone nor a community **sentence** can be justified for the offence. Before a **sentence** of imprisonment is passed, a **pre-sentence report** must normally be obtained, and the court is required to give its reasons for passing the **sentence**. The maximum length of a sentence of imprisonment is laid down by Act of Parliament (as is, occasionally, a minimum or mandatory term: see **mandatory sentences**) but under the 2003 Act the sentence should normally be for the shortest term commensurate with the seriousness of the offence. **Magistrates' courts** are currently limited to a maximum of 6 months imprisonment for a single offence. Sentencing courts must also have regard to **sentencing guidelines**. The length of time that the offender spends in **prison** will not be the same as his or her stated **sentence** because, under the arrangements for **early release**, a proportion of the sentence will be served in **prison** and the remainder on **licence** in the community, sometimes under **supervision**. See also **custody, prison, early release**.

imprisonment for public protection (IPP)   a **sentence** introduced by the **Criminal Justice Act 2003** and imposed on adult offenders who have committed a serious violent or sexual offence and are considered dangerous, but who do not qualify for a **life imprisonment sentence**, either because the maximum penalty for the offence is less than life, or because the court does not consider that the seriousness of the current offence justifies a life **sentence**. The effect of IPP is however almost entirely identical to a life sentence (see **life imprisonment**).

When first introduced, IPP was mandatory for offenders aged 18 or over who had committed one of the specified offences where the court believed that the offender posed a significant risk to the public. The use of the sentence by the courts far exceeded expectations, threatening to add thousands to the **prison** population on a long-term basis. Following a review by the Chief Inspector of Prisons the government responded by introducing measures in the **Criminal Justice and Immigration Act 2008** which made the sentence discretionary instead of mandatory, and forbade the passing of an IPP sentence unless the court thinks that a **tariff** period of at least 2 years is appropriate. An equivalent sentence of 'detention for public protection' exists for offenders aged under 18.

inclusion (education) an approach to the education of children that requires **nurseries**, schools and colleges to plan to meet the diverse needs of all pupils.

The term has specific implications for meeting the needs of children with **special educational needs**, and most children with SEN are taught for most of the time in mainstream schools with their peers rather than in special schools or units. More generally the notion of educational inclusion includes the recognition that schools have a part to play in tackling **discrimination** in their communities. The Education and Inspections Act 2006 introduced a duty on schools to promote **community cohesion**. Schools should, for example, recognize the range of cultural, religious, ethnic and social class experiences locally and work to foster cooperation and a sense of **community** and belonging.

income maximization see **money advice**

incontinence an inability to control bladder or bowels in socially acceptable ways. Incontinence comprises enuresis which is defined as involuntary wetting during the day or at night by non-disabled children aged 5 years and over; and encopresis which is defined as the passing of stools into clothing or in other inappropriate places by a child who has reached an age at which this is no longer socially acceptable.

Incontinence may result from a wide range of physical, emotional and environmental causes and is a common phenomenon that may be temporary or permanent. Its incidence may be under-estimated because people affected by it are reluctant to seek help because of **stigma**. Many health authorities now employ incontinence advisers; nurses specializing in this area of work who may supply relevant equipment.

Enuresis has been more specifically defined as the 'involuntary discharge of urine by day or night or by both, in a child aged 5 years or older, in the absence of congenital or acquired defects of the nervous system or urinary tract'. Night-time 'bedwetting' is the more common form, and it is found more frequently among boys. A number of factors are involved, such as delayed physical maturation, stressful life events or infections in the urinary tract. Enuresis may be a source of unhappiness for children and in their relationship with their parents. It can bring with it a **loss** of confidence and affect social life, such as overnight stays. There are also practical problems to consider – increased washing and cleaning and the financial costs of these. A child's individual needs should guide treatment: these can be established only by a detailed assessment, including a medical examination. The child should be encouraged to actively participate in any programme aiming to tackle it. Treatment is frequently behavioural, including star charts, bladder training and using an alarm system to wake the child before wetting at night.

There are several different definitions of encopresis. US definitions are broader and tend to cover all possible causes of 'soiling', while in the UK definitions have been restricted to those cases in which the causes are psychological and where the child has physical sensation and control. This is further complicated by the fact that children may experience emotional distress and other psychological reactions as a *result* of encopresis, whatever its cause. The age at which 'soiling' can be regarded as encopresis is not clear. Some definitions place this as low as four but also emphasize that 'soiling' should be regular and of at least one month's duration in order to be regarded as encopresis. In practice, parents may seek help when the child reaches school age if the encopresis is causing embarrassment to the child and adverse reactions from staff and other children. Specialist treatment may be available from paediatricians or Child Guidance Clinics and usually includes behavioural approaches and support for parents. In some cases treatment is effective only temporarily. However, some children with encopresis improve without professional intervention.

Both forms of incontinence can also be found in **older people** and with some young people and adults of all ages. Loss of control of both bladder and bowel is a feature of later life for some elders for which treatments may be limited. Issues concerning the personal care of elders can be a major stress for carers in domestic settings and for care staff in both **day care** and residential settings.

indefinite leave to remain the right of a person to remain in the UK without time limit or conditions. Indefinite leave to remain gives a person the right to work, claim benefits and access social housing and other services. It is normally granted after a period of limited leave to remain. If they have not already made 'family reunion' a person with indefinite leave to remain can bring over members of his or her family for settlement under the normal immigration rules.

independent living a concept developed by disabled people involving the achievement of control over their own lives and the ability to live in settings of their own choosing.

The term 'independent' is often used by professionals in connection with the ability of a disabled person to carry out everyday tasks without assistance from anyone else. Disabled people themselves, however, have emphasized the link between independence and personal autonomy. In order to pursue personal ambitions and aspirations in the same way as non-disabled people, disabled people need to maintain control over their own living arrangements and personal assistance. For most people, this involves moving out of institutional settings and obtaining independent accommodation.

Centres for independent living are run by disabled people and offer information and support to those who are seeking more independence. An important factor in the development of independent living has been the opportunity for disabled people to be the employers of their own **personal assistants** rather than the clients of care organizations. The wider availability of **direct payments** for **community care** services is beginning to make these arrangements more common. Before it was permitted to provide payments for community care services directly to **service users**, **social services department**s sometimes made arrangements for **direct payments** schemes to be run by centres for independent living, which can still provide support to disabled people in carrying out their duties as employers.

Morris, J. (1993) *Independent Lives: community care and disabled people*. London: Macmillan.

independent mental capacity advocates (IMCA) representatives for those who have been assessed as lacking capacity and who have no one to advocate on their behalf.

An Independent Mental Capacity Advocacy service is commissioned from the **advocacy** sector and considered a safeguard for people. There is a legal duty to refer eligible people to this service when a key decision about, for example, medical treatment or where a person should live is to be made. Under the **Mental Capacity Act 2005** this would apply to people who are in receipt of private or public social and health care support and in cases where allegations of **abuse** or mistreatment have occurred. The first annual report from the **Department of Health** 2007/08 showed that 5,175 people received support from this service in its first year, 3,047 of those people were supported in decision-making regarding accommodation moves, 191 in reviews of care, 671 in decisions related to receipt of medical treatment and 675 people relating to adult protection issues (Department of Health 2008).

The role of the IMCA is to explore with the person what their needs and wishes are using the preferred means of **communication** of the person whose life will be directly affected by the decisions in question. If all creative options of communication have been explored and more information is still needed, family and friends and historic records may be consulted in support of the process with full consideration being made to the maintenance of privacy and dignity in line with human rights principles. The IMCA will also examine the **assessment** process thus ensuring that this has been carried out equitably and exhaustively and that all possible avenues of referral and support have been explored. A large proportion (1,165) of those people supported to make decisions relating to moving accommodation directly affected people who were hospital in-patients. It is therefore important to consider, in line with current delayed **discharge** processes, how this may impact upon timely, considered assessment of people who may have extreme difficulty in communicating their needs and wishes.

Independent Safeguarding Authority (ISA) the principal organization charged with ensuring that unsuitable people are kept from working with children and vulnerable adults. It works in **partnership** with the **Criminal Records Bureau** and other partners in order to assess every person who wants to work or **volunteer** with vulnerable people. All would-be staff and volunteers need to apply to register with the ISA and will be vetted by it, drawing on relevant criminal convictions, **police** intelligence and other sources. Only applicants who are judged not to pose a risk to vulnerable people can be ISA registered and employers or voluntary organizations who work with vulnerable people will only be allowed to recruit those who are ISA registered. It is estimated that some ten million individuals will require registration – including those working in children's services, youth organizations, **prison**s and the **National Health Service**.

independent visitors a **volunteer mentor** to befriend, advise and support children and young people in the care system. Many damaged and vulnerable children and young people living in residential units or with fosters parents often find it difficult to sustain trusting relationships with adults. Independent visitors are vetted and trained volunteers who hope to provide a positive influence on children and young people by meeting with them regularly to undertake activities which both parties enjoy. The aspiration is to provide life affirming experiences and opportunities to share anxieties that will hopefully result in greater confidence and enhanced self-esteem for children and young people.

individual behaviour plans school based plans for responding to problematic behaviour from particular pupils. The plan specifies the kinds of **challenging behaviour** the pupil engages in along with the time, frequency and context in which that behaviour occurs. It also specifies the behaviours that are to be encouraged. Carrying out the plan relies on the teaching **team** to provide appropriate role models and age-appropriate rewards, and to apply agreed consequences when the pupil fails to comply or achieve the changes in behaviour sought.

individual budget funding allocated to an individual on the basis of need which can be spent as directed by the **service user** in order to achieve agreed **outcomes**.

Individual budgets, personal budgets and **direct payments** are tools for achieving self-directed support and greater control for **service user**s. The **social care** concordat *Putting People First*, published in 2007, argued that almost all **social care** users should have access to a personal budget. This could either be taken as a direct payment or as a notional budget. The latter could be useful for people who do not wish to take on the responsibility of managing the money directly or of acting as an employer of **personal assistant**s. Personal budgets allow service users to design a package of services to meet their own needs. This may draw on non-traditional sources of support including the use of mainstream leisure services, **community** groups and family and friends. Some **local authorities** have introduced resource **allocation** systems to guide **assessment** and determine the size of the personal budget.

The idea of individual budgets was then taken up in the Green Paper *Independence, Wellbeing and Choice* in the same year, and later in the White Paper *Our Health, Our Care, Our Say*. The **social care** concordat *Putting People First (2007)* also strongly supported individual budgets as a means to achieving the **personalization** of adult social care, and local authorities were expected to make progress in transferring service users to personal budgets or direct payments. Individual budgets have now been piloted in 13 local authority areas and the results of the evaluation published in 2008 are encouraging. The 'IBSEN' study and other relevant research evidence indicates that many **service user**s experience improved quality of life and a greater degree of choice and control. However, there has been considerable variation between **service user** groups, with **older people** generally expressing less satisfaction. The evidence suggests that investment in support and brokerage will be necessary. In particular, people are likely to need assistance with managing money and accounts, accessing services and meeting their responsibilities as employers. Staff training will be needed in order to increase the confidence of front-line **social care** staff and to address the issues that may arise in respect of safeguarding **service user**s and managing risk.

While personal budgets are associated with **social care** services, 'individual budgets' is the term usually associated with budgets drawing on a number of different funding streams. Research has shown that there can be challenges involved in aligning funding streams available under varying legislation. However, the **Department for Work and Pensions** has taken up the idea in the 2008 Green Paper *No One Written Off: reforming welfare to reward responsibility*, referring to 'a new right to control for disabled people'. This would involve identifying a combined budget which includes the money spent on support by several different government departments including Access to Work funding from the Department of Work and Pensions and social care funding. Working to agreed outcomes, service users would have a degree of control over the way their budget was spent. The White Paper which followed later in 2008 promised to legislate to ensure the 'right to control' and to carry out further pilots before deciding on the exact nature of the scheme. Individual budgets and the 'right to control' are now included in the Welfare Reform Act 2009.

Social Care Institute for Excellence (SCIE) (2009) Research Briefing 20: *The Implementation of Individual Budget Schemes in Adult Social Care*. London: SCIE.

Glendinning, C. *et al.* (2008) *Evaluation of the Individual Budgets Pilot Programme: final report*, the 'IBSEN' study. Social Policy Research Unit, York: University of York.

individual education plan (IEP)   an outline of the strategies and provision being employed to ensure that an individual child with **special educational needs** (SEN) receives educational opportunity appropriate to their needs. The plan is normally drawn up by the school's special educational needs coordinator (SENCO). It should include information and targets, the nature of the provision being made available, success and exit criteria, and arrangements for review. All children with identified SEN should have such an individual plan.

individual racism   a form of personal prejudice which relates to a person's racial or ethnic origins, which can result in unfair, discriminatory, and sometimes violent treatment (see **racism**). The core of individual **racism** consists of people acting as though ideas about '**race**' are valid criteria for differentiating among human beings, yet there is wide support for the view that there is no adequate biological basis for believing in 'race' as a legitimate, scientifically proven term. Racism is not, however, simply individual prejudice but rather a reflection of discriminatory structures and institutional practices. The net effect of this is that **racism** is built into social structures and dominant social institutions. (See **anti-discriminatory practice**, **institutional racism**, **racism**, **anti-racism**.)

Thompson, N. (2004) *Anti-discriminatory Practice*. London: Macmillan.

individual support order   an order which a court attaches to an **anti-social behaviour order** made on a young person under 18 if the court is satisfied that this would be desirable in the interests of preventing further **anti-social behaviour**. The order requires the defendant to comply for up to 6 months with requirements specified in the order and with directions given by a **responsible officer** from a **youth offending team**.

information   in social work, knowledge that may be acquired or transmitted about services and about legal and **social work** processes.

There is increasing recognition of the importance of good information about a wide range of services and transactions in social welfare organizations. The Children Act, for example, requires that **social services departments** publicize their services to **children in need**, and often the relevant information includes details about voluntary provision where the voluntary sector works closely with the statutory services. The **National Health Service and Community Care Act** has a requirement that **community care plans** are published for public consumption and consultation.

Organizations need an information strategy to inform potential users of all services. The strategy should include an analysis of the most likely points of contact with particular client groups and an appreciation of the forms of **communication** most suitable to their needs. For example, a leaflet for children might have to be written in a different way from one designed for young people or adults. Similarly, deaf and blind people have very particular needs. **Social work** processes and users' and parents' rights could also usefully be described in written or another appropriate form. When, for example, an **emergency protection order** is served, parents need to be able to understand what has happened or, if invited to a case conference, they need to know what might happen. Similarly, **service user**s or their representatives will benefit from information about sources of help, if they are in dispute with social welfare agencies, or about how to make a complaint. Some agencies have made considerable progress in the development of information services, although others have not. (See also **recording, information giving**.)

information exchange   the process by which public authorities, welfare agencies, and other bodies exchange and cross-match data, for example to facilitate **assessment** and decision-making processes. Data exchange is also widely used to combat welfare fraud, and facilitate investigations and prosecutions. Particular Acts and regulations provide for such processes. For example, under the Social Security Administration Act 1992 and the Social Security Fraud Act 2001 government departments and

local authorities obtain and hold information about benefits claimants and others; and may require banks, public utilities, credit agencies, and other organizations to share data with them. If necessary, agencies may require organizations to enter into agreements to provide electronic access to information they hold; and the agencies may then, in turn, share and cross-match data for certain specified purposes. Local authority officers are supposed to 'have regard to' codes of practice on information-gathering and sharing arrangements. The legislation includes provisions aimed at safeguarding such data, and preventing its abuse; create offences in cases where there has been abuse, for example by local authority employees. Authorized officers are also subject to any **Data Protection Act 1998** provisions that have not been displaced by other legislation; and action is taken from time to time against officers who abuse their powers, for example by making unauthorized data checks on clients and claimants.

information giving the lowest level of **participation** in which practitioners and service managers inform users and local people about specific services or projects in their area.

Giving information to people is fundamental and a necessary requirement for any service that aspires to have user **participation**. Clearly, users or local residents need to know specific details of a project or service that is going to affect them in all but the most select instances. If, however, practitioners provide *only* information and seek no opinion or feedback in return, it amounts to a take-it-or-leave-it approach that may produce even more aggressive feedback. Information giving is appropriate if practitioners have no room for manoeuvre with regard to the services they are providing and must follow one course of action or if it is the start of a wider consultation process with the opportunity to participate later.

In providing information to user groups it is important to be familiar with the target audience: what do they already know and what might they expect? Practitioners should make sure that the audience understands the ideas being advanced and the language in which they are expressed. Be clear from the start about the need for providing information alone rather than consultation. The principal means for channelling information to users include leaflets, newsletters, posters and other printed material; presentations at meetings; briefing the media with press releases and conferences; advertising, exhibitions and video.

Chanan, G. (1999) *Local Community Involvement: a handbook for good practice*. London: Community Development Foundation.

injunction a 'civil court order', available under Part IV of the Family Law Act 1996, that requires someone to do or not to do something. In the context of **domestic violence**, an injunction is designed to keep someone safe and to restrict or restrain the behaviour of a partner or ex-partner and to make any further violence less likely. **Non-molestation order**s and **occupation order**s are the two particular injunctions that are widely used in this context.

The non-molestation order prohibits a partner/ex-partner from pestering, intimidating, harassing or assaulting a woman and her children. This order may also prohibit particular behaviour such as telephoning or texting a woman or visiting a particular street or part of a town. The order also includes prohibitions about getting, for example, a friend of the man to do the telephoning or behaving in a threatening way on his behalf. An **occupation order** (also known as an ouster order) is designed to exclude a partner/ex-partner from a particular property, even if he is still living in the dwelling. It is possible to secure an injunction without the perpetrator being present. This is called an injunction 'without notification' (formerly called an 'ex parte' injunction). Injunctions 'without notification' are served by civil courts in circumstances where the court believes that violence may be prevented before a full hearing can be held with the perpetrator present to 'put his side of things'. Injunctions 'without notification' do not become active until the papers are served, that is given, directly to the perpetrator and there may be problems in locating the man. Courts can exceptionally send injunctions in the post.

Applications for injunctions are made in civil courts which are closed; that is, no members of the public or the press are present and the woman can ask that her private address be kept secret. In the full hearing with the perpetrator present a woman can ask for protection from court officers should she feel immediately unsafe. Injunctions about **domestic violence** have a 'power of arrest' attached to them, since the Domestic violence and Victims Act 2004 was implemented in 2005. Copies of all injunctions are given to the **police** who would be expected to arrest any man who disobeys the terms of any order. The perpetrator would then be presented to the court (the woman would also have to be in attendance) where it is possible that he would be **fine**d or given a **prison sentence** of up to 5 years.

A key issue for women subject to violence is whether they are prepared to report a man who breaks the terms of an **injunction**. A woman may feel ambivalent about an ex-partner going to **prison** or the father of her children having a criminal record and she may be persuaded that he will change. However, it needs to be recognized that many men do not accept injunctions and that many will do serious harm to their partners or ex-partners. These risks have to be accurately assessed for any woman's safety plan to be both realistic and practicable.

inspection a process of external examination that is intended to establish whether a service is managed and provided in conformity with expected standards.

Three bodies now have inspection functions for work in the **social care** and **social work** field; these are the **Care Quality Commission** (CQC), the **Audit Commission** and **OFSTED**. Nationally the Care Quality Commission is the chief regulatory body in social work in England. The CQC together with the Audit Commission undertake a programme of reviews of **social services department**s. These major inspections raise issues about the quality of local social services. Areas of good practice are highlighted as well as areas that need to be improved or developed. In between these 5-yearly joint reviews, there are usually separate inspections by the CQC alone of adult care services, while OFSTED undertakes inspection of children's services, bringing together education and social care issues.

In Wales a similar role is undertaken by the Care Standards Inspectorate for Wales, in Scotland the Scottish Commission for the Regulation of Social Care and in Northern Ireland the Regulation and Quality Improvement Authority.

institutional racism the processes that lead to **discrimination** against members of particular racial or ethnic groups. It has long been understood that not only individuals but also institutions can systematically discriminate against members of oppressed and excluded groups. This need not be intentional nor even as a matter of deliberate policy: an institutional practice may simply not take account of ethnic or racial differences sufficiently to prevent discrimination occurring in practice. Thus, it may be institutionally racist to fail to provide appropriate support to someone present when a murder is committed because he is a potential suspect. This is what happened in the case of Duwayne Brooks, who was a co-**victim** with Stephen Lawrence, a traumatized witness of a racist attack, but was not treated as such. **Police** procedures gave priority to trying to obtain evidence and prevent it from being 'contaminated' at the expense of providing support and information to Mr Brooks. For this and other failures of the investigation, the Stephen Lawrence Inquiry Report found the Metropolitan Police guilty of institutional **racism**, incompetence and poor leadership. While there may have been no explicit racist intent on the part of individual officers, the cumulative effect was the same as if they had all been deliberately racist. The report also made it clear that part of the problem was ignorance, prejudice and stereotyping, demonstrating that the line between institutional and intentional racism is a fine one in practice. The indignant police reaction to the report tended to concentrate on the allegation of institutional racism rather than on the evidence provided of ignorance, prejudice and stereotyping.

Institutional racism can be tackled only at a systemic level: removing individual 'bad apples' from the staff of the institution makes no real impact upon it. As such, the failure of criminal justice and social services to provide appropriate professional services to Black people has to be addressed at a policy level. The **Macpherson Report** made recommendations in respect of the treatment of **victim**s and witnesses of crime, and also on **police** training, the ways in which racist incidents should be defined and recorded, and the enforcement of the law on racial **harassment** and violence.

During the mid-1990s, **social work** training was attacked for its emphasis upon **anti-discriminatory practice**, but this is now becoming a more orthodox approach to professional training. Institutional **racism** can partly be addressed through staff training, but changes may also be required to **complaints procedure**s, **recording** processes, the collection of statistics, the evaluation of services, and prosecution or administrative action against racist offenders. Public-sector institutions such as the probation and social services and **youth offending team**s, as well as the **police**, have enormous powers that can be used responsibly against perpetrators of racial harassment and violence.

Knight, C. and Chouhan, K. (2001) Supporting victims of racist abuse and violence, in B. Williams (ed.) *Reparation and Victim-Focused Social Work*. London: Jessica Kingsley.

Integrated Children's System (ICS) the overarching framework to support practitioners and managers in all aspects of their work with **children in need**.

The system aims to bring together the range of processes that are used in local authority **contact** with a child, including assessment, planning, intervention and review. It builds on the assessment framework and the **looked after children** (LAC) system. The ICS provides the basis for electronic **recording** of children's records and interventions practitioners have with children and their families. The system has not been embraced uncritically and there is a growing concern suggesting that the system is not working, does not make efficient use of **social work** time, and limits the amount of time social workers have for direct **contact** with children and their families.

intellectual impairment a level of intellectual functioning that is more limited than that of the majority of the population and with norms established in medicine and psychology. People with intellectual impairment may experience barriers as the social environment has been constructed without their requirements in mind. 'Intellectual impairment' is often used interchangeably with **learning disability**, but, strictly speaking, it has a more limited meaning that is confined to the attributes of individuals. Learning disability, however, indicates the barriers that may arise as a result of the interaction between individual ability and the social environment. The term 'intellectual impairment' does not appear in legislation. Education legislation refers to **learning difficulty** (severe or moderate) and **social care** legislation to learning disability or **mental handicap**. The **Disability Discrimination Act 1995** refers to mental impairment in its list of disabilities. However, mental impairment includes both learning disability and any recognized **mental disorder**.

intensive supervision and surveillance programme (ISSP) community programmes for serious and persistent young offenders which may be attached to **supervision** under **community orders, youth rehabilitation orders, early release licences** or **bail** conditions. First introduced in 2001, they were originally intended to be reserved for use on **persistent offenders** who have been charged or warned at least four times within a 12-month period, and who have previously been subject to a **custodial sentence** or community order. The criteria were later extended to include offenders who were less persistent but who had committed more serious offences, or who had a history of repeat offending while on bail. ISSPs involve intensive monitoring of the young offender's movements and whereabouts by means including **electronic monitoring** and telephone monitoring using voice verification technology. They also include highly structured individually tailored packages of measures that are intended to address the young person's offending behaviour (for example, training and education programmes lasting up to 5 hours per day) and may include elements of **reparation**.

intentionally homeless describes people identified by a local authority as having made themselves homeless by virtue of unacceptable behaviour or by giving up accommodation that might reasonably have been kept.

If a local authority has decided that an applicant for public housing is intentionally homeless, it is not required to offer that person permanent housing, although in some circumstances (if the person is in priority need) temporary accommodation may be offered. The usual criteria applied by councils in such decisions include substantial rent arrears, anti-social conduct including criminal activity and the misuse of property.

They may also decide that a person is intentionally homeless if they believe that the person has left the property without sufficient cause, as in the case of a woman who is not experiencing **domestic violence**. There are often major differences between **housing authorities** in their interpretations of the criteria and in their willingness to use the appropriate legislation. The social worker's and housing **advice** worker's task is often to challenge a local authority's decision and the alleged evidence upon which such a decision has been made. Since evidence from a tenant's past behaviour, often over many years, may be cited, the task of helping such tenants can be complex.

The Homelessness Code of Guidance contains useful examples of when **homelessness** should not be considered intentional (see **homelessness**).

interim order an order made under the **Children Act 1989** for a limited duration. A court may make interim orders in respect of care, supervision, residence or **contact**. When hearing an application for any of these orders, it may decide to adjourn the proceedings. To make an interim care or **supervision order**, the court must be satisfied that there are reasonable grounds for believing that the child in question is suffering or likely to suffer **significant harm**. This is a less stringent test than for a full care or supervision order, which requires the court to be satisfied that the child is actually suffering or likely to suffer significant harm. The making of an interim order should not prejudice a final hearing on the full order, as the situation may have changed considerably following a further period of **assessment** and **social work** intervention. Interim orders when first made may last up to 8 weeks (but can be shorter) allowing the local authority to complete its investigation; the court however may extend the order by periods of 4 weeks unless the original order was under 4 weeks duration in which case it can be extended by 8 weeks. Should the authority decide *not* to apply for a full care or **supervision order** the court must be informed of the authority's reasons, including outlining any services or other actions it may have taken with the family in the interim period.

The whole aim of interim orders is to provide further flexibility to the court in settling the **outcomes** of care or supervision proceedings. They provide a short-term legal intervention into a family's life if the situation warrants it. Where there is need for an assessment of a child and his or her parents arising from suspicions of **abuse** the court may attach conditions to the interim order to enable such an assessment. An 'exclusion requirement' can also be attached to an interim care order if there is reasonable cause to believe that if by excluding a particular individual from the dwelling house in which the child lives the child will cease to suffer or be likely to suffer significant harm and that another person in the household is both willing and able to give the child a standard of care expected of a parent and consents to the exclusion requirement.

In general a court is not being asked to make a final conclusion on whether a full care order is required; the interim order in effect establishes a holding position after weighing all the relevant risks pending the final hearing which should be scheduled at the earliest appropriate date including considering transferring the case to an adjacent **family proceedings court**. When an interim order leads to a substantial change in the child's position swift resolution of the full order becomes all the more urgent.

The powers given the local authority are the same as under a full order but they are of limited duration. The court determines how long the order is to last and may give directions to the local authority to carry out a medical or psychiatric examination or other assessment with the child's, but not parents' consent. In the main, interim orders are used to follow a period of emergency protection for a child, particularly if the authority has not yet completed inquiries. If the authority thinks that direct **supervision** of the child and parents is required for a short time but that it does not need to obtain **parental responsibility**, then an interim **supervision order** is sufficient. If the authority concludes that it must remove the child and acquire parental responsibility for a limited period of time, then it will ask for an interim care order. Interim orders are commonly used during the course of care proceedings, which average between 6 and 12 months from initial application to final hearing.

Department of Health (1991) *The Children Act 1989 Guidance and Regulations Vol. 1 Court Order*. London: HMSO.

intermediate care a policy to ensure smooth coordination between health and **social care**, in particular for **older people**, to promote **wellbeing** and reduce or shorten stays in hospital.

Intermediate care forms part of policy promoting health, independence, and peoples' capacity to participate in society to the full, maximize control over their lives and manage risks. Achievement of these aims by prevention rather than by a crisis response has become a major policy focus. Strategies, service frameworks and practice guidance have therefore been developed to maximize the prevention of long-term disabling health conditions, deterioration in health, increased dependency, **social exclusion** and risk.

Intermediate care became formalized in policy in the **NHS** Plan (2000), and enshrined in the health and **social care** standards set out in the **National Service Framework for Older People** (2001). It was intended to apply mainly to potentially frail **older people**, and research has shown that the majority of people using the service are older. It aimed to create 'integrated teams to promote faster recovery from illness, prevent unnecessary hospital admissions, support timely discharge, and maximize **independent living**'. As such, it is concerned with the forms of prevention which forestall crisis involving hospital admission; provide early intervention preventing deterioration and potential admission to residential care, and offer rehabilitation and re-ablement following hospital discharge.

In order to achieve these aims of prevention, intermediate care involves a range of services, mainly offered by integrated health and social care providers. These involve: rapid response services providing rapid **assessment** and access to short-term support at home; hospital at home, offering intensive support to avoid acute admission to hospital or facilitate earlier discharge; residential or day rehabilitation on a short-term basis avoiding admission to hospital or following hospital discharge, which usually takes place in a care home; supported discharge, offering a short-term period of support at home.

Important features of these interventions include their time-limited nature; a person centred ethos; systematic health and **social care** assessment and care planning; shared health and **social care** assessments, records and protocols; and exemption from charges for **social care** services (including use of a residential or day **social care** service for rehabilitation).

Research has shown a fair degree of success in preventing admission to long-term care following hospital discharge, with one study showing nearly two-thirds of people able to return home after residential rehabilitation, and **service user** satisfaction with the improvements in their ability and confidence. However, in tandem with the **Community Care (Delayed Discharges) Act 2003**, which promotes rapid discharge, there has been a focus on the post-discharge aspect of intermediate care, and there have been concerns that this has been at the expense of services preventing deterioration, crisis and hospital admission. There have also been concerns about the very limited time-frame for the service, especially given the value of longer-term interventions with psychological and social wellbeing. A further concern has been with the limited access for people with **mental health problems** and cognitive difficulties to the service.

intermittent custody a sentence of part-time **imprisonment**, introduced by the **Criminal Justice Act 2003**, whereby offenders could spend part of the week in **custody** and part in the **community**. It was hoped that such a **sentence** could be useful in allowing some offenders to serve a **prison sentence** while staying in employment or maintaining their caring roles. Critics however feared that it would have the effect of net widening, imprisoning many who would otherwise have been given a **community sentence**. The scheme was introduced in two **prison**s in 2004 on a pilot basis, but proved a wasteful use of **prison** resources with almost all spaces in the intermittent custody units empty during the week. In 2006 the scheme was terminated.

internal market arrangements for different units inside large public service organizations to buy and sell services from each other.

Throughout the 1980s the Conservative government reorganized many public services so that parts of, for example, the **National Health**

Service took on the sole function of buying services from other parts of the same organization. The intention was to set up market-like transactions inside the organization itself, whereby separate units buy and sell the service in question on behalf of clients or other members of the public. The aim of the reform was to compel the public services, such as **local authorities** and the health service, to behave as if they had to deal with market conditions. This, it was argued, would encourage them to be more responsive to the public and to provide services with greater efficiency, which are the chief characteristics of any market. These large public service organizations were in particular need of such reforms, since they had previously provided their service under monopoly conditions and grown complacent and bureaucratic as a result.

In one form or other, internal markets have been introduced into education, with the introduction of local management of schools, into local authority services, such as refuse collection, by means of compulsory competitive tendering, and into the health service by establishing **NHS** hospital trusts and fund-holding general practitioners. Purchaser/provider units within community care services are a form of internal market arrangement that has affected social services agencies considerably. In each case, the aim of the policy was to achieve greater efficiency and responsiveness of the service by introducing a sense of competition and the discipline of cost control.

The proponents of internal markets hoped that they would provide a third way between forcing public service organizations into open, external markets and the old style of central control and monopoly provision. While the **New Labour** government formally abolished the internal market the legacy is seen as one where markets and competition are favoured by proponents of greater efficiency within the public sector. As a result, competition is still a key part of the agenda for political parties of all persuasions.

interview and interviewing a formal and purposeful discussion or exchange between a social worker and a **service user**, carer or significant other to explore issues and problems as part of an **assessment**.

Social work interviews are usually conducted face to face or by means of a telephone or, exceptionally, video link. For any interview it is more likely that it will be productive if the setting is comfortable, quiet, safe and free from interruptions. If these conditions can be achieved the service user is more likely to be at ease. This can be brought about in social work offices, the service user's own home or sometimes in 'neutral' territory, although there will be circumstances that make this difficult to arrange or achieve. Telephone interviews can involve additional difficulties. The lack of visual information about a service user may make it difficult to fully comprehend how they are feeling. If an assessment involves looking at documents to try to understand problems, telephone interviews then rely heavily upon the service user's literacy and their ability to summarize key information that may be found in letters or other written **communication**s. In addition, in some circumstances it may be wholly inappropriate to contact service users by telephone if their safety is a potential issue; for example, where **domestic violence** may be an issue.

Some interviews might involve investigations of issues such as alleged **abuse** or whether a service user is a danger to themselves or others. These 'difficult' interviews can sometimes generate hostility and aggression and they are all the more difficult to conduct in the service user's home with the television on, a threatening relation or partner present and a large dog growling in the corner. Even in these difficult circumstances clarity about who you are, your role and the nature of your enquiries will help. Where the service user is presenting a problem to you the same courtesies apply together with a clear **statement** about what you can and cannot do. It will always also be necessary to inform service users of the circumstances in which **confidentiality** will have to be **breach**ed. Interviews can be highly structured affairs when, for example, a service user is being assessed to determine whether they are eligible for a particular service or benefit. In other circumstances the service user may be consulting a social worker to try to access help with a problem that they may understand in whole, in part or not at all. In these circumstances interviews need to be exploratory to begin to give shape to some ill-defined symptoms or difficulties. Closed questions are thought to be most useful to secure accurate information about dates of birth, addresses, occupations, schools and other key information about service users' relationships to significant others (**genograms** are useful in this context) and open questions where it is crucial that social workers listen closely to begin the complex task of understanding problems, stresses, behaviours, relationship difficulties, needs and wants. Where social workers are required to investigate allegations of, for example, child or **adult abuse** or where a service user's **mental health** is a concern then interviews are likely to be driven by particular agendas associated with key assessment vehicles such as the **Framework for the Assessment of Children in Need** or the checklists used for assessing mental capacity. Other problems may require the same rigour in interviewing service users but the agendas may be more of a reflection of service users' concerns and not the social workers'.

A key issue is that of conducting interviews at a pace that is comfortable for the service user. This may mean allowing for silences to permit the service user to collect their thoughts. The aspiration is to help the service user be relaxed but focused. It makes sense to try to start 'where the service user is at'. This means trying to see things through the service user's eyes; in essence to be as sympathetic and empathetic as possible. To make sure that the issues and problems that are explored are being clearly defined and understood, a key listening skill is to be able to summarize what the service user has said at intervals to confirm understandings. In this context it is important to use simple language and to avoid technical jargon. It is also helpful to avoid being distant by hiding behind a desk. To be too close might make some service users uncomfortable, to be too distant may be experienced as a remote professionalism by the service user and make them feel tense. Social workers however will need to be aware of the need for safe retreat should an interview prove difficult with a service user known or thought likely to be aggressive or violent.

It is worth remembering that many issues may be embarrassing for service users so that it is important to present a non-judgmental face that actively avoids any hint of disapproval. For example, it is well known that a service user with serious multiple debt may reveal just a part of their difficulties as a way of 'testing the water'. If they receive an encouraging response, it is more likely that they will tell the whole story, and in this instance it is crucial to know about all the debts because it is more likely that the adviser will prepare a plan to deal with creditors that is realistic and practicable. Cultural and gender issues often need attention either because the topic to be discussed is sensitive such as **sexual abuse** or because women from some cultures are not used to talking to male social workers. Asking a service user if they would prefer to talk with a social worker of a particular gender or from a particular ethnic background should be routine in any social work agency.

There are some circumstances too where interviews can only be conducted with a service user if they are supported by either an interpreter or **advocate/mentor**. An interpreter is engaged where a service user's English language skills are likely to impede communication. An advocate or mentor may also be involved in an interview where a service user needs assistance to represent their wishes and to help them articulate their problems. There are now useful codes of practice available for both interpreters and advocates/mentors to advise on professional practice. These codes spell out the need for interpreters to confine themselves to interpreting and to avoid adding their own perspectives on problems; and for advocates/mentors the issue is also to do justice to the service user's wishes or to help them represent their own 'case' and no more. Both interpreters and advocates/mentors have to guarantee confidentiality. For some service users it may also be crucial that interpreters and advocates/mentors are of the same gender. A useful benchmark by which to judge the success of any interview is the extent to which a service user has felt **empowered** to reveal everything they wanted to.

Allen, G. and Langford, D. (2007) *Effective Interviewing in Social Work and Social Care: a practice guide.* Houndmills: Palgrave Macmillan.

intoxicating substance requirement a requirement which may be included in a **youth rehabilitation order** requiring that the offender must submit to treatment to reduce or eliminate the offender's misuse of intoxicating substances. It is similar to the **alcohol treatment requirement** for adults, but is not restricted to alcohol.

J j

joined-up action the concept of a more integrated approach to the planning and delivery of services across government. British government has traditionally been characterized by 'departmentalism', whereby each government department pursues its area of activity with only limited reference to the work of other departments. Ministers are seen as defenders of their departmental interests, and this has led to problems in coordinating policies across government. Similar problems exist at other levels of government and service delivery, with the area of health and **social care** being seen as particularly problematic. The needs of a range of user groups, such as **older people** and people with disabilities, cross the boundary between the **NHS** and social services. This organizational separation is complicated by the existence of different models of need, often identified as the social model versus the medical (or individual) model in which social workers and health care workers view the cause of problems faced by individuals with needs differently. This complex range of barriers to effective care has been identified by government as in need of resolution, and joined-up action is one proposed solution. The approach is centred on the idea that different government departments and levels of government should work together. The aim is to provide coordinated action to tackle the needs of communities and individuals where those needs cut across organizational barriers. The identification of lead agencies, such as **primary care trust**s, is seen as a way in which such problems of coordination can be overcome. These are long-standing problems, however, and the concept of joined-up action faces significant barriers to successful implementation (see **partnership**).

judicial review a process whereby the legality of decisions by government (whether national or local) can be challenged in the **High Court**. The grounds for review include: (1) that the public body has exceeded its legal powers (*ultra vires*), for example by not following mandatory procedures or failing to comply with the **Human Rights Act 1998**; (2) that there has been a **breach** of 'natural justice', for example because a party with a legitimate interest in the decision has not been consulted or allowed to have their say, or there has been the appearance of bias; or (3) that the decision is manifestly unreasonable.

just deserts the theory of punishment which holds that offenders should be penalized in proportion to the seriousness of their offences. The 'justice model' argues that the offender's welfare or public policy considerations, such as deterring or preventing future offences, should be irrelevant to individual sentencing decisions: offenders should simply receive the **sentences** they deserve for having committed the current offence.

von Hirsch, A. (1993) *Censure and Sanctions*. Oxford: Clarendon Press.

Justice Secretary the shorthand phrase for the government minister who oversees the **Ministry of Justice**. The full title is Lord Chancellor and Secretary of State for Justice. This ministerial post, one of the major offices of state, replaced the ancient office of Lord Chancellor in 2007 when the new Ministry of Justice was created. The Justice Secretary is responsible at Cabinet level for the running of the ministry which deals with criminal, civil and family justice as well as with civil and human rights and issues arising from the British constitution.

juvenile justice see **youth justice**

K k

key worker a named worker responsible for coordinating service arrangements for a person using residential or day-care services and who usually forms an important relationship with that person.

Originally the **key worker** was a named worker to whom a child in residential care could turn to discuss his or her plans and problems. Now the role includes acting as a focal point for the coordination and **communication** about a particular **social work** case and assumes greater responsibilities as a result. The **key worker**, particularly in child protection cases, completes core assessments, convenes and chairs core group meetings and coordinates the contribution of family members and other agencies in putting the plan for the child into action. Additionally he or she oversees contact with other agencies, ensures that records are promptly completed and that a child requiring safeguarding is seen regularly.

L *l*

labelling (and labelling theory) the process whereby people holding
positions of **power** or influence sometimes attribute generalized negative
characteristics to particular categories of individuals, tending to produce
or amplify the characteristics attributed.

Influential groups who may label include the **police**, judges, the
communication media and social workers. As the outcome of such a
labelling process, the individuals or categories of people labelled (for
example, as 'drug addicts' or 'the mentally ill') tend to live up to the
negative label, thus tending to confirm, reinforce or amplify the behaviour
that led to the initial label. In these circumstances, it may become
difficult for a person to counteract or ever escape the implications of the
application of a label (see **stigma**). The people or categories of people so
labelled may acquire what sociologists refer to as a 'deviant identity'.
Deviance has been famously described as not a quality of the act that a
person commits but rather a consequence of the application by other
people of rules and sanctions.

At one level, the insight of sociologists with regard to labelling
may appear relatively trite, seeming to assert little more than such
commonplace or folk conceptions as 'Give a dog a bad name and it will
tend to live up to its reputation.' Guided by the theoretical approach in
sociology known as 'symbolic interactionism', however, labelling theory
directs systematic attention to several features of human social behaviour:
the way behaviour is highly influenced by the social expectations that
others have of one; that, far from always successfully explaining deviant
behaviour, some forms of 'scientific' (or positivistic) social science (such as
would-be genetic explanations of criminal behaviour) can operate as part
of the labelling process; the widespread operation of 'labels' and labelling
in modern societies, in which both individuals and agencies often operate
on the basis of stereotypical conceptions of particular categories or groups
of people (see **stereotype**); that individuals can become caught up in an

escalating process initiated by labelling that leads to an increasing exclusion from conventional social intercourse or even incarceration; that institutional labellers, including social workers, and labelling state agencies, such as **social work**, possess considerable **power** to attach labels that can radically influence the lives of others. Labelling theory can be seen as part of a distinctive 'social-interactionist' approach to social problems. Criticisms can be directed at labelling theory: for example, that it sometimes overstates the effects of labelling while ignoring the intrinsic features of some deviant behaviour. Nevertheless, an awareness of labelling theory and the widespread operation of labelling processes is useful to social workers, first because many clients of **social work** can be seen as adversely affected by the application of social labels, and second because social workers must be aware of how they themselves operate as labellers. A concern to offset the more negative effects of **labelling** processes can be seen as central to the orientation of much modern social welfare practice, with its aim of limiting discriminatory practices both within **social work** and in wider society. (See also **underclass**, **culture of poverty**.)

Becker, H.S. (1963) *Outsiders: studies in the sociology of deviance.* Glencoe, Illinois: Free Press.

Lasting Power of Attorney (LPA) a document which is arranged whilst a person still has capacity to make the decision to give authority to someone else to act on their behalf should they lose capacity in the future.

Unlike the previous Enduring Powers of Attorney, Lasting **Power** gives the appointed person (the attorney) ability to inform key decisions relating to care, services and medical treatment as well as other issues relating to property and estate, bank accounts and financial management and benefits of the person they are acting on behalf of (the donor). This agreement must be registered with the **Public Guardian** for which there is a charge. In situations where there is suspicion of abuses of **power** the Court of Protection can revoke the Lasting Power. If someone loses capacity without having made previous arrangements this becomes a matter for the Public Guardian and Court of Protection (Johns 2007). It is important to choose someone who is felt to be trustworthy and capable of making fundamental and possibly life-changing decisions on another person's behalf. Anyone over 18 years can become an attorney and there can be more than one person identified. This provision can offer a deal of reassurance to people in the knowledge that if they were to lose capacity their affairs and care needs will be overseen by a person of their own choosing. Within practice this can often help to clarify and resolve issues of dispute or uncertainty.

Johns, R. (2007) Who decides now? Protecting and empowering vulnerable adults who lose the capacity to make decisions for themselves. *British Journal of Social Work*, 37(3): 557–64.

learned helplessness the inability of a person to act in situations in which he or she has learned previously that he or she will have no control over the outcome.

The origins of the idea of learned helplessness are in animal behaviour experiments where animals learned that they could not avoid a negative experience or punishment and thus developed a kind of passivity as a coping mechanism. Learned helplessness has three components: an environment in which some important outcome is beyond a person's control; the already learned response of giving up; and the person's expectation that no voluntary action of his or her own can control the outcome. Learned helplessness has been implicated as a contributory factor to **depression**, since one aspect of depression is the giving up of attempts to control one's own life. It has also been associated with problems associated with **domestic violence** and in particular women's frequent return to a partner who has been violent to them and/or their failure to leave after sustained abuse. Feminists have been critical of this hypothesis arguing that abused women are 'survivors' rather than **victims** and that they often make choices that they perceive as the least harmful to themselves and/or their children given the often inadequate response from social welfare and justice agencies to known and documented abuse.

Seligman, M.E.P. (1992) *Helplessness, Development, Depression and Death*, 2nd edition. New York: W.H. Freeman.

learning difficulty a term indicating **intellectual impairment**; this is still used in education, but has now been replaced by **learning disability** as the term approved by government for use in **social care**.

The term 'learning difficulty' replaced **mental handicap** as a way of referring to people with intellectual impairments. Criticism of 'learning difficulty' focused on the fact that there can be many reasons for difficulty with learning, not all of which result from **intellectual impairment**. The term is still used in education, however, as part of current definitions of **special educational needs**. In education, a child is defined to have a learning difficulty if she or he has significantly greater difficulty in learning than the majority of children of the same age; or has a **disability** which prevents her or him from using standard educational facilities. Therefore a child who is disabled (as defined by either the **Children Act 1989** or the **Disability Discrimination Act**) may not have a learning difficulty or special educational need, but may meet both definitions. Learning difficulty can refer to generalized intellectual impairment or may be more specific, as in the case of dyslexia. It can also refer to children without intellectual impairments who have difficulty accessing standard educational resources as a result of a physical or sensory impairment. Therefore not all children with learning difficulties will also have a learning disability, which is the preferred term in social care.

However, many self-advocates prefer the label 'learning difficulty'. As a result, the term is still used in some publications to which they have contributed. There have also been arguments from some social scientists that the term 'difficulty' better promotes a focus on the interaction between the individual and the social environment and that it is in fact more consistent with the **social model of disability** than the term 'learning disability'.

Goodey, C. (1999) Learning disabilities, in S. Hood, B. Mayall and S. Oliver (eds) *Critical Issues in Social Research: power and prejudice.* Buckingham: Open University Press.

learning disability a level of intellectual functioning that is more limited than that of most people in the general population.

The government now urges professionals to give priority to capacity for **communication** and independent social functioning over the level of a person's IQ in determining the need for learning disability services. The White Paper on learning disability, **Valuing People**, published in 2001, defines learning disability as 'a significantly reduced ability to understand new or complex information, to learn new skills (impaired intelligence), with a reduced ability to cope independently (impaired social functioning), which started before adulthood, with a lasting effect on development'. Traditionally, **social care** services have focused on people with an IQ of below 70 for the allocation of learning disability services. The White Paper suggests that level of social functioning should be a more important criterion.

It is estimated that 210,000 people in England have severe learning disability, including 65,000 children. About 1.2 million people have mild/moderate learning disability; this amounts to about 25 out of every 1,000 people in the general population. Severe learning disability is fairly uniformly distributed around geographical areas and social groups, but there is a link between **poverty** and mild to moderate learning disability.

Relatively few people with learning disability now live in large institutions. Most are either with their own families or in small residential homes and supported housing projects. Although this appears to be more inclusive, in reality most have limited access to mainstream social life. Many adults with learning disability are users of **day services**, being poorly represented in the labour force. Access to education and leisure is also limited. The exclusion of people with learning disability was associated with the segregation of groups perceived as non-productive in the late 19th century. The introduction of mass education also made the intellectual limitation of some children more visible than it had formerly been. Systems of medical classification were developed for these children, and these became **stigma**tizing labels that diverted attention from any potential for learning. The Mental Deficiency Act 1913 reinforced these trends and created an entirely separate set of services based on institutional care. The environment in the large hospitals was very poor and was associated with institutionalization. In some cases, there was proven **abuse** of patients.

The move towards deinstitutionalization for people with learning disability has been influenced by a number of factors, but the philosophies that have had the greatest impact on professionals are those of **normalization** and **social role valorization** (SRV). These have emphasized that people with learning disability should be able to live in the **community** and enjoy the roles and styles of living that are valued in society generally. A criticism of these approaches is that they fail to challenge the attitudes and practices of other people towards people with learning disability, as they accept uncritically that **service user**s should adopt prevailing norms of behaviour in order to be accepted. There have also been challenges to **normalization** on the basis that it does nothing to expand the range of social acceptability or to ensure that services meet needs in terms of gender, ethnicity and sexual orientation. **Normalization** has been introduced by service providers rather than struggled for by **service user**s. However, the principles of community presence, community participation, choice competence and respect, which are associated with normalization, have influenced the more progressive service settings to support people in making choices, gaining skills and taking part in community life. This often involves using mainstream education and leisure facilities rather than spending all the time in a segregated day centre.

Rather than providing a standard service for groups of people with learning disability, there is now individual planning. The system of individual programme planning (IPP) involves regular reviews of progress towards goals and involves the service user and any professionals involved with her or him. In practice, however, this has had a strong emphasis on assessing individual competence, and many people with learning disability have found it difficult to put across their views and aspirations sufficiently assertively.

Person centred planning is intended to increase the contribution of service users and has been promoted in the White Paper *Valuing People* (2001). In order to achieve this, people with learning disability will require support in preparing for meetings, and also access to **advocacy**

and **self-advocacy** in the assessment and planning processes. Citizen advocacy offers the opportunity to have an independent person to speak on behalf of those who cannot do this for themselves. Self-advocacy simply means a person speaking up on his or her own behalf. This can be on an individual basis, but the development of self-advocacy groups to take up common issues has been a strong feature in learning disability services.

Current policy stresses the principles of: rights, independence, choice and inclusion. The government has identified a range of problems with the existing system, including: the poor coordination of children's services and transition planning; lack of involvement, choice and control for service users; the neglect of health, housing and employment needs of people with learning disability; lack of attention to the needs of ethnic minorities; and poor interagency coordination. In order to tackle these, it is planned to increase access to advocacy, **direct payments**, and person centred planning, to set up local learning disability partnerships with service user representation to plan and coordinate local services, to modernize day services, and to increase the support available to particular groups: people from minority ethnic groups, children with severe disabilities and adults living with informal carers aged over 70.

There is evidence that people with learning disabilities are still abused in institutional settings and that they can be victimized in the community. An investigation by the Parliamentary Select Committee for Human Rights heard evidence about abuse in two hospital settings, violent crime against people with learning disabilities, and a number of breaches of human rights. Recent research has also highlighted concern about treatment in the criminal justice system, where learning disability is not always identified. It is suggested that people with learning disabilities and learning difficulties are over-represented in the prison system, but it is only recently that attempts have been made to investigate this.

Williams, P. (2006) *Social work with People with Learning Difficulties.* Exeter: Learning Matters.

learning theory a cluster of theoretical explanations that seek to explain how experience at a particular point in development affects subsequent behavioural and mental activities.

Learning theory embodies such perspectives as behaviourism, cognitive views of conditioning, observational and ecological explanations. (See also **behaviour modification**.)

Legal Services Commission (LSC) a public body set up by the Access to Justice Act 1999, which replaced the previous legal aid system. The LSC runs both the **community legal service** on the civil side, and the **criminal defence service**.

licence conditional freedom at the end of a **custodial sentence** as part of **early release**. Licences may contain conditions regarding residence or **supervision**. During the period of the licence, the offender remains liable to be recalled to **custody**.

life course the process of personal change, from infancy through to old age and death, brought about as a result of the interaction between personal and social events.

Growing interest in exploring and defining the concept of life course in recent years has been from two broad perspectives: first, the biological, which emphasizes stages in psychosocial development, the common process underlying the human life course (in this usage often referred to as the *life cycle*); second, the experiential, which emphasizes the importance of unique experience and significant life events, that is, the contrasts between lives rather than their similarities. While the biological model provides a framework, each individual life course is unique; individuals have the **power** to make choices, and each constructs his or her own biography within broad biological and social constraints. Acknowledging the importance of both age and experiences when considering an individual's current concerns, a model has been proposed that describes the adult developmental process, not tied to age stages or to typical life experiences but distinguishing concerns. It describes the establishment of self-identity, the establishment of relationships, the extension of **community** interests, the maintenance of position, disengagement and the recognition of increasing dependency. While this may be seen as a life course process, individuals may pass in and out of these areas of major concern, become stuck in one, cope well or badly, and experience crises and development as a result of the interactions within them. Social workers and educators particularly may find this and other models of the life course useful in interpreting reactions to crises at transition points, problems of adjustment, and failures of **communication** between family members, and in assisting individuals to gain insight, use their experiences developmentally and improve their social relationships.

life imprisonment a **sentence of imprisonment** that is potentially lifelong. This is the **mandatory sentence** for the crime of murder, and the maximum sentence for a number of other serious crimes including rape and robbery. When a life **sentence** is passed, the judge must specify a **tariff** period. This is the minimum period which must be spent in **prison** before the offender becomes eligible for **early release**. When the tariff period has expired, the offender may apply to the **Parole Board**, which will only order release if it is satisfied that there is no longer an unacceptable risk of serious re-offending. Partly because of the mandatory life **sentence** for murder, partly because of the wide definition of murder in English law, and partly due to the large number of offences for which life is available as a maximum **sentence**, there are more inmates serving life sentences in England and Wales than in all the rest of the European Union combined.

life story book a scrapbook or folder put together for children and young people that provides an account of a child or young person's life to date.

More recently life story books have been used with elders, especially when difficulties with memory have become a feature of their lives. Life story books can comprise **genogram**s, photographs, drawings, stories, letters, reports and any other memorabilia that provide information about the life of a child, a young person or an older person. There are some similarities between a **case history** and a life story book although they have quite different purposes.

Life story work has its origins in direct work with children and young people who have entered the care system or have been adopted, many of whom experience multiple moves as well as troubled backgrounds in their families of origin. The life book can help the child to begin to grapple with trauma, and to make sense of their own lives, to help with identity problems, to help with resolving possible separation and **loss** issues and to unravel fantasy, misunderstandings and facts. Life story work must be undertaken at a pace suitable for the individual child taking into account their age, understanding and emotional readiness to begin the exploration of their backgrounds. It is usually best to allow the child to decide which parts of their life to explore and record first, especially if the professional worker undertaking the life story work is in the process of establishing a relaxed working relationship with them. Although it is likely that the social worker with strategic responsibility for a child in the care system will undertake the life story work, it is possible for the role to be taken on by a family support worker, a **foster care**r or a residential childcare worker provided they have recourse to professional advice.

Life story books are usually prepared or at least planned before a child moves to a permanent placement, although for very damaged and troubled children such work may not be possible until they begin to feel safe and settled in their new setting. It is important to add to the book as later events of importance to the child take place. In this sense the book becomes, in effect, living history and it is possible that later happy events will trigger memories that are more painful, but are now easier to deal with because of a happier outcome in relation to similar events. It is also clear that life story books successfully completed will help carers understand what has happened to a child and to recognize their needs. The overarching objective however for the child is to help them feel more worthwhile, valued and secure; and, by implication, enable them to establish new attachments and feel able to deal with life's later difficulties.

With elders life story work can be an important strand in helping people to retain their identities when poor memory and the early symptoms of **dementia** are present. **Reminiscence therapy** can usefully include **group work** supplemented by individual work that might include life story work.

Shah, S. and Argent, H. (2006) *Life Story Work: what it is and what it means.* London: BAAF.

listening skills abilities associated with hearing and understanding what a **service user** is communicating in a comprehensive way in any **social work** transaction.

Listening is a key social work skill enabling practitioners to accurately hear and understand the feelings, attitudes and problems of service users with sympathy and empathy. To listen well requires concentration, an encouraging manner and patience, especially when the service user is upset and/or experiencing stress. Accurate listening will enable social workers to ask the 'right question at the right time'. A key dimension of good listening skills involves summarizing understandings at intervals to both corroborate what has been said and as a way of encouraging the service user to continue to if they have more to say and to reveal. It is also more likely that service user's concerns will be heard faithfully if social workers work at an appropriate pace, use accessible language and act in a warm but professionally purposeful way. (See also **interviewing**.)

local authorities the democratically elected bodies responsible for providing public services at a local level. The present local government system was established by the Local Government Act 1972, implemented in 1974 and later reformed in 1997. This created a two-tier system of shire and metropolitan county councils as the upper tier, with district (including London borough) councils as the lower tier. Each tier of government had a council composed of elected local people who are part-time councillors, increasingly members of one of the main political parties. Serving the councils are full-time officials, including general administrators and professionals such as social workers and housing officers. Services are divided between the two levels, with services defined to require a larger geographical and demographic component to work effectively being at county level. The districts provide services that cater for more local needs. For example, large departments providing education and social services are the responsibility of the shire counties, while housing, refuse collection and street lighting are provided by the districts. The metropolitan counties operated slightly differently, as their districts had very large populations and were therefore defined to be able to provide some of those services provided by the counties in the rural shire counties themselves, including education. However, in 1985 these metropolitan counties, including the Greater London Council, were abolished as the result of a mixture of administrative reasoning and political conflict. All their responsibilities were devolved down to the district authorities, so that in areas such as Greater Manchester, South Yorkshire and the West Midlands a single-tier system of district authorities is in operation. The problems associated with two-tier authorities continued to exist into the 1990s and a commission was established to resolve them throughout the non-metropolitan areas. While the Conservative government of the time favoured single-tier authorities the issues of local identity proved to be more complex. As a result, when the commission finished its tour of the **local authorities**, their recommendations were varied and complex with some authorities emerging as single-tier systems while others retained their two-tier format. Often the restructured authorities emerged as a compromise solution combining both approaches, with single-tier cities surrounded by two-tier counties.

Clarke, J.J. (2008) *Local Government of the United Kingdom*. Charleston, SC: Bibliobazaar.

local safeguarding children boards the key statutory mechanism for coordinating relevant organizations in safeguarding and promoting the welfare of children in a given area. Members of the boards include **local authorities**, **police** and health bodies. They were created by the **Children Act 2004** replacing area child protection committees from April 2006. Their remit includes oversight of the protection of particular children and young people, work with **children in need** and **preventive work** with all children and young people in the area. However, guidance makes clear that the first responsibility is to ensure that effective and responsive child protection work takes place and if there is a conflict between resourcing that work and other preventive responsibilities the former takes priority.

Department for Children, Schools and Families (2001) *Working Together to Safeguard Children*. London: DCSF.

lone parent family a family with one parent on his or her own raising dependent children.

Lone parent families arise for different reasons but often share similar difficulties. They include single mothers who have never married and mothers who have either separated, **divorce**d or been widowed. Lone fathers form a small but evident percentage of all lone parent families – approximately 9 per cent. Whatever the source of lone parenthood, over the past 20 years the number of lone parent families has increased significantly. Altogether, over 3 million children are currently being raised by a lone parent, and lone parent families now constitute some 24 per cent of all families with dependent children. However, the incidence of lone parent families does vary significantly within different ethnic groups. The current figures are (*Social Trends*, 2009; Office of National Statistics) 23 per cent for white families; 39 per cent for mixed race families; 48 per cent for Black and Black British families; and 13 per cent for **Asian** families. Lone parents usually face financial hardship, having to rely primarily on welfare benefits and only to a lesser extent on earnings because employment compatible with looking after children is difficult to obtain and often poorly paid. Research indicates that lone fathers are usually better off financially because they are more likely to be in full-time employment as well as receiving higher wages than women for comparable work. Maintenance is not a major source of economic support for many lone parents, on average accounting for no more than 7 per cent of their income, despite successive governments' **child support** initiatives to encourage fathers to acknowledge responsibility for their children.

The circumstances of lone parent families have caused unease across the political spectrum. Commentators from the far right are concerned that lone parenthood is a matter of individual moral failure that undermines the integrity of the family as an institution linked to the growth of an amoral **underclass**. Liberal and social democratic analysts point to the fact that because a high proportion of lone parents are reliant on state benefits, a great many children are raised in families on unacceptably low incomes. Recent **New Labour** governments have fallen somewhere in between, with policies that encourage lone parents, including mothers raising young children, to find work through the New Deal for Lone Parents.

Lone parent families have repeatedly been shown to be worse off materially than the poorest categories of two parent families. A large percentage of all children in **poverty** live in a lone parent household. For the parent coming off benefit and going into work there can be gains in income, improved **networks** and wider social contacts. But such gains vary greatly from individual to individual and depend on their earning capacity. Researchers have established that to secure these gains, investing in 'human capital' – that is, qualifications, job-related training and accumulated work experience – is crucial to lone mothers' obtaining higher wages. Interestingly, employment rates among lone parents from various ethnic groups do vary significantly with Black/Black British/ Afro-Caribbean lone parents being the most economically active. Other barriers to work for all lone parents from all ethnic groups may also arise, such as cultural or social **values** that restrict the search for potential jobs, or lack of suitable kinds of work at local level, the prejudice of employers or the costs of transport or childcare. Given the association between poverty and lone parenthood and the stresses of parenting alone, it is not surprising that lone parent families figure prominently on social workers' caseloads.

long-term conditions   a recent term for chronic diseases. They are a major social concern today, forming the subject of international World Health Organization, and UK policy initiatives. Statistically, they tend to constitute the main health concerns or causes of morbidity in modern societies: in the UK 17 million people experience at least one of these conditions, and almost half of these individuals have multiple conditions. As many as 72 per cent of people over the age of 40 have at least one long-term condition. Although these conditions are found amongst higher proportions of **older people** than younger people, large numbers of younger people experience them.

Long-term conditions are often controlled by medication which can reduce the effects of the symptoms and slow deterioration in the condition. In many cases, this means the individual can live an ordinary life. Very importantly for **social work**, however, some of these conditions, despite the fact they are controlled by medication, result in **disability**. Disability refers to the ways in which the symptoms, and the physical and sometimes the cognitive and emotional effects of the disease impact upon the individual's capacities for daily living and social functioning: as a consequence the person may experience difficulties in self-care and daily living tasks; in carrying out social roles such as work or parenting; and in activities of social **participation**. These effects and difficulties altogether can have many further implications for individuals, increasing their exposure to **risk** and **abuse**. All of these issues and concerns come within the remit of social workers in adult **social care** services, and form the focus of wider health and **social care** frameworks for assessment, care planning and intervention.

The **social model of disability** raises awareness that difficulties in daily living and social functioning should not be attributed to the individual, but to the limited provision of social arrangements by which individuals experiencing **impairment**s can access the means of ordinary life such as housing, work, leisure and safety in relation to risk and abuse. Use of these wider understandings supports work with the **service user** which maximizes rights and effective and person centred supports, thus enabling the service user to maximize control over his or her life. However, practice with long-term conditions crucially involves the worker also in awareness of and responses to people's experiences of specific symptoms and other physical and intrapersonal consequences of the condition, and their effects. People in poverty are more at risk of developing these conditions through the impact of poverty both directly upon health, and upon lifestyle factors which also influence health (see **health inequalities**). Through these processes, individuals in poverty may additionally be more likely to develop multiple conditions. In turn, people developing long-term conditions can enter poverty through unemployment. In combination, these concerns increase the risk of people with long-term conditions developing **depression** and cognitive **impairment** and, often, both. And poverty and **disability** resulting from long-term conditions is likely to lead to **social exclusion** involving social isolation and few opportunities for social participation. **Substance misuse** is a further possible consequence of this combination of difficulties, affecting substantial numbers of **older people** (see **alcohol abuse**). In the UK, responses are shaped by a number of inter-related policies with important implications for **social work** practice. First is the vision of government for transforming **social care**. Central in this is a planned shift in adult social care generally, from intervention with health crisis and dependency to prevention and the promotion of **wellbeing** and independence. For those who have existing long-term limiting conditions, the aim is to prevent further crisis and deterioration and promote peoples' control over their lives and the care they receive. These aims are to be achieved in wider health and social care policy by promoting healthy lifestyles and social participation, linked statistically to improved health, re-ablement or rehabilitation (see **intermediate care**) and **personalized social care** including self-assessment (see **assessment**) and self-directed care including **direct payments** and **individual budgets**. The standards and principles for integrated health and **social care** working in relation to **long-term conditions** are set out in the National Service Framework for Supporting People with Long-term Conditions (DH 2005).

Supported self-care is particularly emphasized amongst these principles through its connections with overall health and adult social care aims for optimal prevention and control over one's life and the care received. Further policy frameworks relevant to working with long-term conditions include recent **mental health** strategies including the refocused care programme approach, and the government's vision for mental health services – New Horizons in Mental Health Care – and the **Mental Capacity Act 2005**. Both these sets of provisions relate to the greater risk of experiencing **mental health problems** and cognitive difficulties amongst people with long-term conditions. The higher rates of mental health problems experienced by people with these conditions are particularly noted in New Horizons: Models of Care for Alcohol Misuse (see **alcohol misuse**), and again highlight the risk of **substance misuse** amongst people with chronic diseases. Social work practice in these contexts can maximize benefits to service users through a fully comprehensive assessment in collaboration with health colleagues, and by care planning which is responsive to the range of health, personal distress, social functioning and social adversity issues impacting upon the service user. Of particular significance in assessment are mental health, substance misuse and mental capacity issues on the one hand, and the barriers created by social conditions on the other. Care planning is especially important to help prevent crises and deterioration in health, support self-care and rehabilitation with the use of **evidence-based** health and **social care**. For example the ability to provide transport has been found to facilitate social participation and access to social support, important in preventing depression.

looked after the phrase used in law to describe a child being cared for by the local authority. Under the **Children Act 1989** a child is looked after by the local authority if either the child has been provided with **accommodation** at the request of the parents or the child is in the care of the authority. The whole point of the concept is to underscore that the responsibilities of the local authority are the same for any child, regardless of whether the child has been voluntarily accommodated or is the subject of a **care order** or **emergency protection order**. The primary duty of the authority is to safeguard and promote the welfare of children they are looking after, including taking decisions in their long-term interests. In planning the placement of children it is looking after, the authority must consult all those concerned with the children as well as the children themselves before placement decisions are reached. The Act also requires that the authority place children as near to their homes as practicable. The authority is responsible for drawing up a plan for the future of every child being looked after, including how long the placement will last, when that child will be reunited with his or her family and the amount of **contact** between child and family while on placement. Investigations into the quality of life of children while they are being looked after as well as the conduct of the local authority itself as a corporate parent indicate a high level of variability in promoting the child's **wellbeing**. Whether in educational attainment, in job finding or in their life following care, children or young people who have been looked after by the local authority have often been at a large disadvantage to their peers. For example, a substantial proportion of the homeless and of the **prison** population have had care experiences in their past. Much effort has gone into improving the situation. The **assessment** and action records from the **Department of Health** provide age-related checklists for continuing assessment of the child's or young person's progress while being looked after. The **Children (Leaving Care) Act 2000** has also specified the tasks a local authority must undertake as it prepares a looked after young person for independence. It also stipulates that **local authorities** continue to support in various material ways a young person up to the age of 25 if necessary.

looked after children in education (LACE) a **team** of professionals, either stand-alone or integrated with others within a local authority, with specific responsibility for promoting improved educational **outcomes** for children who are **looked after**. The **outcomes** for such children have traditionally been significantly below those of their peers but there has been a sustained effort at improvement in recent years. Given that many of these children and young people will have had disrupted educational experiences before coming in to care, and that many will have **special educational needs**, this deficit is not entirely surprising. But a LACE **team** will work directly with schools, carers and children and young people themselves to try and overcome barriers to their **participation** and achievement. Each looked after child should have a **personal education plan**. It is likely that attendance at school or at **alternative educational provision** will be closely monitored in this context as the local authority will have specific targets as part of its duty as a corporate parent. Some **local authorities** are also experimenting with 'virtual schools' that may even have a 'virtual head teacher' to support the learning of looked after children, both those who are still attending school and those who may not be doing so at present. This is an attempt to provide continuity in the face of the many likely changes of school that a looked after child may have and to ensure their participation in examinations and standard assessments wherever possible.

loss a profound feeling of disadvantage or deprivation resulting from losing someone or something. Loss can be associated with a **bereavement**, a separation from someone where there was an **attachment** or a significant or radical change in circumstances such as redundancy, retirement or needing to claim asylum from a war-torn country. Sometimes **loss**es can be multiple and integrally related where, for example, a serious illness might lead to a **loss** of a job, the need to adapt to a new *lifestyle* because of a chronic condition and a consequent loss of status. A key issue for social workers is that of determining the significance of any **loss** to a particular **service user**. A death of a partner or a parent for example might be a profound loss or it could be liberating if the relationship that has been severed was oppressive or abusive for the service user. All social and interpersonal changes, as a result of loss, are likely to bring problems of adjustment. Any really significant change, such as a movement from a rural area to a city, being given refugee status in another country or leaving a long-stay psychiatric hospital or **prison** might unsettle a person's sense of self, their feeling of personal security, their 'world view' and their social status. In relation to the problem of adjusting to loss, much will depend upon a number of factors including the person's own robustness, their support systems and the nature of their new social circumstances. It is entirely possible for the loss to also be an opportunity for positive change as new ideas may have now, post-loss, to be considered. In addition the person's own adaptive capabilities can influence how a loss is managed. As with all crises, some will experience the loss as quite disabling and others will deal with it comparatively equably.

low pay income that barely permits individuals and families to meet the basic requirements of life.

Conventionally, low pay covers the poorest sections of the working population, although these sections will vary according to the economic climate of a country and prevailing government economic policies. Low pay correlates closely with **poverty**. Low-paid jobs are frequently associated with a lack of security, training and retraining opportunities and fringe benefits (including holiday entitlement and pension rights). Women, disabled people and people from ethnic minority backgrounds are significantly over-represented in the poorly paid occupations. Jobs such as bar work, cleaning, portering, shelf-filling in retail stores, labouring, agricultural working, waiting in restaurants, cleaning, car park and petrol station attending, care working and similar posts have been poorly paid for many decades in Britain. The National Minimum Wage was introduced by the Labour government in April 1999. From October 2009 the minimum wage has been set at £5.80 per hour for those over 22, £4.83 per hour for those aged 18–21 and for 16–17-year-olds (excluding apprentices) £3.57 per hour. It is now illegal for employers to pay less than the minimum wage, regardless of whether workers are part-time, casual, temporary, agency or home workers, although a small minority of employers continue to do so. Other unscrupulous employers may deduct unreasonable amounts from minimum wages for meals, protective clothing and, where relevant, tied accommodation. Seasonal immigrant workers are particularly vulnerable to this kind of exploitation. The task of social workers and other **advice** workers is to ensure that people in work are claiming all the benefits (for example, housing and council tax benefits) and tax credits (Working Tax Credits and Child Tax Credits) to which they are entitled and to press for greater fringe benefits for all workers.

low-vision aids equipment to assist people with **visual impairment** to maximize useful sight. Although medical treatment may not be available for some eye conditions, much can be done to make the most of existing vision. Low-vision aids include relatively 'low-tech' solutions such as magnifiers, improved lighting, large-print books and more effective colour contrasts. There are now also text enlargement and other specialist programmes for computers. Low-vision aids are available commercially but can often be provided by **social services department**s, voluntary organizations and hospital eye clinics.

M m

Macpherson Report effectively the *Stephen Lawrence Inquiry Report* chaired by Sir William Macpherson and published in 1999, which examined the investigation of the murder of Stephen Lawrence in London in 1993 and the responses of official agencies, including the **police**, who were condemned within the report for their **institutional racism**. The failure to provide appropriate support to Duwayne Brooks, who was with Stephen Lawrence when he died, was part of the Inquiry Report's argument for this finding. Instead of treating him as a traumatized witness of a racist attack, Brooks was treated as a suspect. Police procedures gave priority to trying to obtain evidence and prevent it from being 'contaminated', at the expense of providing support and information to the Lawrence family and Mr Brooks. While there may have been no explicit racist intent on the part of individual officers, the cumulative effect was the same as if they had all been deliberately racist. The report also made it clear that part of the problem was ignorance and stereotyping, demonstrating that the line between institutional and intentional **racism** is a fine one in practice.

The indignant police reaction to the report tended to concentrate upon the allegation of institutional racism rather than on the evidence provided of ignorance, prejudice and stereotyping. What the report said was that institutional racism results in a failure to provide an appropriate professional service to the public because of prejudice, ignorance, thoughtlessness and stereotyping. This clearly applies equally to all other public services, including those in criminal justice. Since the publication of the report, almost all of whose recommendations were accepted by the government, policies within the courts, the police, and the prison and **probation service**s have changed substantially in order to introduce ethnic monitoring of staff grievances and of those receiving services, and to increase the representativeness of the workforce of these agencies. All public authorities have been given a legal duty to promote racial equality under the **Race Relations (Amendment) Act 2000**.

A report by HM Inspectorate of Probation has applied the Stephen Lawrence Inquiry Report findings directly to probation policy and practice, reintroducing quality measures for **pre-sentence report**s and encouraging specific new provisions for Black offenders and racially motivated offenders. Local services are encouraged to develop new **partnership**s with Black **community** organizations, and a programme of staff training is under way. Much of this has been done before, however, and it remains to be seen whether the probation service can maintain its commitment to these measures. Earlier this year, the **Home Office** reported that the majority of Macpherson's recommendations have been either fully or partly implemented. Whilst the use of the term 'institutional **racism**' by Macpherson has been viewed as controversial by some, it is apparent that this **labelling** has undoubtedly led to a targeted emphasis on challenging racism within the police and on establishing better relations with Black and minority ethnic communities. However, there remain significant ongoing issues for the **police**, for example relating to stop and search; figures for which still indicate that Black men are significantly more likely to be stopped and searched than either white or **Asian** men and similarly relating to the career opportunities for **police** officers from Black and minority ethnic communities.

Home Affairs Committee (2009) *The Macpherson Report – ten years on*. London: House of Commons.

magistrate   a lay person who sits as a judge in the **magistrates' court**. Magistrates, also known as Justices of the Peace, undergo basic and ongoing training but are not legally qualified. Magistrates are meant to be representative of the local **community**, and recruitment has become a more open process in recent years; nevertheless they are still predominantly white, middle-aged and middle-class. 'Stipendiary' magistrates (professional and legally qualified judges who also sit in magistrates' courts) are now known as district judges.

magistrates' court   the **criminal court** which deals with the great majority – over 95 per cent – of criminal cases. (See **criminal court**.) Lay **magistrates** sit in these courts in panels, usually of three, known as benches, with legal advisers (formerly known as justices' clerks). District judges (legally qualified professionals) sit on their own. The court makes decisions about **bail**, hears the facts of cases, pronounces verdicts about guilt or innocence and passes **sentence**. The court has the **power** to impose any **sentence** up to the statutory maximum for the offence, except that the maximum **prison** sentence it can impose is currently 6 months for one offence or a total of 12 months for more than one offence, and it cannot normally impose a **fine** of more than £5,000. There is a specialized version of the magistrates' court for young people under 18 years of age, known as the **youth court**. The magistrates' court also has an important civil jurisdiction in family matters (see **family proceedings court**).

Makaton a system of signs and symbols used to assist **communication** for people with **learning disability** who cannot use conventional speech. Makaton originated in the 1970s in connection with a research project into communication methods for deaf adults with learning disability. Makaton signing is described as an aid to communication rather than a language, as it does not have grammar of the same complexity as **British Sign Language** (BSL). However, the vocabulary is based on BSL Makaton symbols, which is designed to be easy to draw by hand and aims to represent meaning in pictorial form.

mandatory sentence a **sentence** which it is compulsory for a **criminal court** to impose on the offender. The only fully mandatory sentence in England and Wales is the **life imprisonment sentence** for murder. A number of other sentences are mandatory (or require a mandatory minimum) for certain offences but with allowable exceptions. For example, disqualification from driving is a 'semi-mandatory' sentence for the offence of driving with excess alcohol, but need not be imposed if the court finds that exceptional circumstances exist in the particular case. Mandatory sentences include the **'three strikes and you're out'** measures which originated in the USA and were imported into England and Wales by the Crime (Sentences) Act 1997. This Act and its successors require a minimum sentence of 7 years' imprisonment for an adult offender convicted of a Class A drug trafficking offence for the third time and a minimum 3 years for an offender convicted of a third offence of domestic burglary unless the court considers this to be 'unjust in all the circumstances'. The **Criminal Justice Act 2003** additionally introduced a minimum **sentence** of 5 years' imprisonment for unlawful possession of firearms unless the court finds that there are 'exceptional circumstances'.

manic depression see **bipolar disorder**

marital and relationship problems problems arising between two people who are living in a committed relationship. This kind of work includes both heterosexual and homosexual relationships.

Marital and relationship problems are subjective difficulties that either or both partners may choose to define as problems. Sometimes **couples** will ask a counsellor to explore their problems with them and in these circumstances it may be that a counsellor will suggest some 'reframing' of their problems so that, in these limited circumstances, problems then might be 'defined' or interpreted by someone else. But in the early stages of couple counselling it is essential that partners are encouraged to describe their experiences, feelings and hopes as fully as possible, in their own language and at their own pace.

Key issues in relationship counselling are communication difficulties between couples as their lives change, often imperceptibly, as a result of, for example, stressful jobs, new caring responsibilities in relation to children and/or dependent adults, illness or the development of chronic conditions. Other well-known stress factors include: a woman returning to work after a period of child-rearing; redundancy; working away from home; and retirement. Couples can lose the habit of 'tending' their own relationship, taking old habits for granted even when the evidence suggests that one partner is becoming dissatisfied. A pattern of poor communication can become both cause and effect of a deteriorating sexual relationship too, and in these circumstances partners may seek to express their sexual needs in other ways that begin to further undermine the relationship.

The primary agency dealing with these kinds of relationship difficulties in the UK is Relate (formerly the **Marriage** Guidance Council), although their efforts are often about helping partners to separate on the best possible terms, especially for their children, as well as helping couples to resolve problems so that a relationship becomes viable and as fulfilling as possible. Although Relate hope to work with both partners useful work might still be undertaken with just one person to help them begin to acquire coping skills and ideas for both renewal of a relationship or its ending. Where couples attend together it is possible to work with one or two counsellors and it is also possible that counsellors will recommend both joint and separate sessions and possibly referral on to other kinds of specialist help such as a sex therapist or a family mediator. For those with dependent children who decide that separation and later **divorce** is the only acceptable solution a referral to the **Children and Families Court Advisory and Support Service** (CAFCASS) will be necessary. Relationship counselling services for ethnic minority couples are still hard to find and there are also special difficulties attaching to working with couples where there has been **domestic violence**. For the latter it may be necessary to have undertaken a risk assessment before counselling is considered safe. Counselling involving people who have been violent can only begin when there is a demonstrable commitment from the person who has been violent to change. (See also **mediation, divorce**.)

market a means through which products and services may be bought and sold. Markets bring buyers and sellers together in a particular place (for example a farmers' market) or through other mediums such as linked computers (the Stock Market). Often the word 'market' or 'marketplace' is used to denote the aggregated transactions for a given product within the country as a whole, such as the housing market. Markets are one, but not the only, mechanism for allocating goods and services in conditions where resources and personal incomes are limited but demand tends to be unlimited.

Two factors, supply and demand, are central to the functioning of a market. As consumers we have wants for goods and services but a limited income with which to obtain them. We have to make decisions as to which goods and services we should buy. Demand for a particular product arises from the extent to which consumers are willing to pay for it (if at all). In general, market theory holds that the higher the price for a product, the lower the consumer demand for that product will be. Supply is the quantity of goods or services available from its producers and, in general, depends on costs such as materials and labour; the lower the costs for producing the product in relation to the price obtained for it, the greater the supply of that particular item. To put it another way, the higher the price at which the product can be sold, the more resources producers will put into its production. Economists talk of the theory of the 'perfect' market. In reality, markets are frequently distorted by various pressures and are not necessarily stable. Supply of a particular product can remain in the hands of a few producers or even one. The latter case is called a monopoly, which can often result in the consumer paying an unjustifiably high price. Or the reverse can be true: too many producers produce an excess, or glut, so that quantities of goods remain unsold regardless of price; then producers suffer, since they often do not recoup their costs. The use of a market to allocate goods and services assumes that consumers are placed in the best position to make the decision as to whether a particular good or service is worth paying for at a particular price, that is, the consumer is best placed to decide on the value of the goods or services. This finds expression in the notion that 'the consumer is sovereign' or 'the customer knows best'. In practice, there are important questions concerning the quality and accuracy of the information that consumers hold, and whether their decisions are affected by such external influences as advertising.

From roughly 1990, and specifically with the passage of the **National Health Service and Community Care Act**, successive governments tried to introduce market-like mechanisms into health and **social care**. Advocates of market principles noted the lack of choice in the provision of services because their supply is dominated, in effect, by public monopolies – the **local authorities** and the **National Health Service**. They concluded that this fosters a co-dependency: people do not try to provide for themselves but also are forced to accept a limited range of service options. Providing organizations have no incentives to offer a greater range of service for people to choose from. They viewed the introduction of the market mechanism into **social care** services as the only way to increase both choice, by encouraging other suppliers to come forward, and efficiency, by containing rising costs. Government continued to expand the role of market mechanisms in determining **allocation** of both health and **social care** services. It began by separating the *purchasers* of services, those who assess needs and buy the services to meet those needs for a particular individual, and *providers*, those who organize and sell the services required. These two distinct roles became widespread within local government and the health service, and are undertaken by different personnel in an attempt to change the culture and the way of thinking. One consequence was that local authorities have greatly reduced or abandoned their direct provision of services – such as housing or residential care for **older people** – and have relied on commissioners to purchase those services from suppliers from the private or voluntary sector. Further market pressures were exerted as government opened a greater range of services to competition among private, public and voluntary organizations. This could be seen in the number of organizations that entered the youth training field, provided **day care** for under-5s and employment services for those on benefits. **Service users** themselves, particularly those with **disability** or **older people**, were given the option of purchasing their own services under **direct payment** schemes from the mid-1990s on and greater numbers are doing so within a personalized service framework (see **personalization**).

Evidence is mixed as to whether the introduction of markets and market-like mechanisms in the provision of services has achieved their stated objectives of increased choice and more efficient use of resources. Translating social need into a purchaser–provider framework has been more difficult than at first thought. Competition between suppliers is essential to a fully functioning market and while one can see, for example, a market in care and education for the under-5s, parents have no real way of assessing the quality of that care available in their area. Research on private organizations delivering youth training schemes has also indicated limited quality in those programmes.

Furthermore 'choice' is difficult for a would-be consumer to exercise in **social care** since it involves pulling triggers in systems that, though familiar to the practitioners, are unknown territory for users. Users are prepared to enter into choosing services and, moreover, prepared to spend their money in pursuit of those choices, but not where they are uncertain about what they are getting. Numerous obstacles remain, especially for older citizens, in understanding the care system. Primarily these have to do with conflicts in **values** and culture of the systems they become enmeshed in. A basic feature of public-sector care is that health care is generally free at point of use while **social care** levies a charge. While this is clear to practitioners it is not always so to users. The care management role of **social work** remains shadowy, even confusing, and providing information on its own is not sufficient to overcome this. In any case user difficulties with the system are not to do with practicalities of care so much as with the emotional difficulties that follow in the wake of a crisis which triggers the need for a service in the first place. Experience within the **National Health Service** suggests that, because of the obvious need to preserve continuity of service provision, purchasing bodies increasingly adopt a **partnership** model – involving long-term contracts for a wide range of services – as opposed to a competition model, although this blunts somewhat the objective of free and open competition.

marriage a socially acknowledged relationship or union between two adults. In the UK a legally ratified **marriage** must be between a male and female over the ages of 16.

Marriage in traditional or pre-industrial societies appears to serve kin interests and to be regulated by kin relationships. Marriage within capitalist or industrial societies is more likely to be a matter of choice between the two adults concerned, although choice seems to operate within a comparatively narrow range; that is, most people marry others of roughly comparable social status. In Britain individual choice seems to predominate, although there are situations where more traditional forms of marriage still occur, for example among some Muslim and Sikh groups or in some parts of rural localities such as Wales, Ireland and Scotland. Sociologists have noted at least two kinds of models for marriage in developed countries. One is marriage based on *functional equality*, where both spouses work, maintain separate bank accounts, pay separate taxes and equally divide household and care giving tasks. The other is the *domestic partnership model*, which emphasizes the partners making more personal choices and rewards partners for making mutually considerate decisions on how best to use their time, resulting in varying patterns of paid and **unpaid work** to emerge in relation to different family needs.

Arranged marriages play an important role within specific ethnic communities. In arranged marriages, the families of both spouses take a lead role in arranging the marriage but the choice of whether to accept the arrangement remains with the individuals. The emphasis on mutual respect and sustained lifelong support for partners and family members is often balanced by Western observers with the dominance of male authority in the relationship and within the family as a whole. There is a distinction between an arranged marriage and a *forced marriage*, in which one party does not consent to the marriage and an element of duress and criminal offence is involved, including threatening behaviour, harassment, assault and kidnap. It should be noted that not all **victim**s of forced marriages are women, with husbands forming some 15 per cent of unwilling partners.

In general, the majority of people continue to believe in the importance of marriage although many will also spend periods with a partner in a cohabiting relationship often as a prelude to marriage. The average age at which men get married for the first time is now around 31 years of age, up from 21 years in 1970 and 29 years old in 1996. The corresponding figures for women are aged 27 in 1996 and currently very nearly 30 years of age. There have been delays before married **couple**s have children. Increasing **divorce** rates have also further clouded the image that people hold of what marriage actually means. **Cohabitation** before marriage is also increasing.

Powerful social and economic changes have clearly weakened the once close link between marriage and parenthood. Compared with 30 years ago, it is easier for women to raise children without men and for men to escape the responsibilities of fatherhood. More women go to work so their financial need for marriage may be supposed to be less than it was. One widespread view among social theorists suggests that marriage restricts self-development and individual freedom at a time when society places a strong emphasis on precisely these same values. In addition there is the thesis that marriage can now be 'unreasonably long' given significantly increased longevity, implying that it is very difficult to sustain a lively and interesting relationship with one person over the course of very long life. Others argue that divorce is too easily accessed and, consistent with this notion, that marriage is too easily entered into. The proponents of these arguments would have greater social seriousness attached to marriage and that careful preparation is needed before people might be permitted to marry. Others have argued that pre-nuptial agreements or a clear contractual approach to marriage will also help would-be partners be more conscious of the consequences of failure, especially if the needs and costs of children are acknowledged in the contracts. (See also **domestic violence**, **marital problems** and **mediation**, and Civil Partnership Act 2004.)

masculinity notions of 'what it means to be a man' viewed as a social construct and how these ideas impact upon **social work** practice. Traditional traits of masculinity include strength, physical ability, autonomy and **power**, and ideas of hegemonic masculinity ensure the reproduction and reinforcement of **patriarchy** within society. The term is subject to academic debate and discussion, and more recently it has been argued that it may be more useful to talk of masculinities in the plural rather than a single all-encompassing notion of masculinity. This allows for a consideration towards notions of 'difference', most specifically in relation to ethnicity, sexuality and class. In terms of practice, this can be understood as a need for recognizing the complexities of human experience as differentiated by masculinity and its relationship with other aspects of identity such as ethnicity. An example of the importance of this would be in the case of an **Asian** lone male parent who would need to negotiate his masculine role both in relation to the interpersonal setting, the cultural context and that of the wider social structure.

The relatively new focus upon 'men' and 'masculinity' can be said to have arisen partly in response to (or indeed as a backlash from) the 'second wave' of **feminism**, yet also as a result of changes in employment patterns and the make-up of the family. These developments have increasingly led to a problematization of 'man' within contemporary society, especially in response to the underachievement of boys in education and their over-representation within school exclusion rates. Current debates focus on how best to respond to this 'problem', be it via structural changes in the delivery of education or more interpersonal responses evident in schemes such as **mentor**ing, which aim to provide a suitable role model for young men on their transition to adulthood. There have been a number of explicitly 'masculinized' social policy measures (Featherstone *et al.* 2007), for example, in relation to fathering through targeted schemes such as **Sure Start**.

Featherstone, B., Rivett, M. and Scourfield, J. (2007) *Working with Men in Health and Social Care*. London: Sage.

Maslow's hierarchy of needs see **needs**

maternal deprivation a theory that has sought to demonstrate a connection between an unsatisfactory relationship between a child and its mother and difficulties for that child in later life.

Deprivation here may be understood either as the **loss** of a mother entirely or as her absence for lengthy (if temporary) periods, or as a mother who acts distantly or indifferently towards the child. The originator of the theory, John Bowlby, conducted research that appeared to show that maternal deprivation can lead to juvenile delinquency and to behavioural disorders in later life. Bowlby's work has been read to imply that even short and temporary separations can have profound and lasting effects upon the child's later ability to function as a mature adult. The debate on maternal deprivation seems to reappear vigorously from time to time. Some, for example, have argued that a pre-school child attending a nursery or with a childminder should be seen as experiencing **maternal**

deprivation. More recent considered criticism of Bowlby's ideas has it that there are many important ingredients in a (separated) relationship between a child and its mother, including the age of the child, the quality of the relationship before separation occurred, the length of separation, the quality of substitute care and the quality of maternal care after child and mother are reunited. Where a period of separation is relatively brief, where the child understands what is happening and why, and where a warm and loving relationship exists both before and after separation, it is unlikely that any harm will come to the child. A more negative experience on any of these criteria might increase the chances of later difficulties for the child.

Feminists have argued that the theory is oppressive to mothers and is essentially 'woman blaming'. They argue that in times of war or periods of economic expansion, men are content to encourage women into paid employment; in periods of recession, however, women are reminded of their domestic responsibilities and especially the duties of motherhood. Government thinking in the early part of the 21st century, in its encouragement of women to work to combat **social exclusion** and **poverty**, is clearly convinced that adequate childcare arrangements do not lead to damaged children. The theory can be perceived as trying to control women directly and indirectly, the latter by avoiding the question of what the role of the father should be in relation to child-rearing and what consequences for the child may result from paternal deprivation. Recent government initiatives encouraging 'flexible employment options' may permit fathers to become more involved in active parenting.

mediation a voluntary process by which people in dispute negotiate an agreement or partial agreement with the aid of a mediator or, less commonly, co-mediators.

The Family Law Act 1996 explicitly encouraged **mediation** as a non-adversarial approach to solving problems. The Act hoped to encourage people to be responsible parents even if their relationship had irretrievably broken down. Mediation as a form of **alternative dispute resolution** is used with family problems but has also been successfully used with other kinds of disagreements such as neighbour disputes and employment problems. Any agreements secured through mediation are often subsequently sanctioned by a solicitor. It is argued that negotiated agreements arrived at through mediation are more likely to provide acceptable and workable solutions to problems than those 'imposed' by the courts as a result of litigation. Mediation is 'legally privileged' so that any matter discussed in mediated sessions cannot be cited in a family court, unless the matter involves someone having been hurt or in danger of being hurt or parents have benefited from the proceeds of crime. In these circumstances mediators can stop proceedings and report matters to the **police**. Mediation services can be provided free of charge by voluntary sector agencies, but more often fees are payable although agencies will take account of parents' resources.

Family courts may also offer 'in-house' mediation although their services usually involve just one or two meetings as a supplement to litigation. Family problems that can be addressed through mediation include all arrangements concerning children, financial matters, the family's home, any practical issues associated with a possible separation or **divorce** and possibly issues concerned with **communication**s between the parties. Mediation can begin at any point whether people have already separated or divorced and are living apart or where the **couple** are still cohabiting. Usually mediators meet with the disputing parties separately to brief them about what they should expect from the mediation process and the ground rules that apply to meetings to encourage reasonable behaviour in the negotiations. Mediation typically takes one to six meetings. Where there is considerable hurt and anger between the parties some mediators will try to secure partial agreements between people to re-establish some measure of trust. This may mean that additional meetings will be delayed to determine whether new arrangements are actually working and, if they are working, then further meetings may then help the parties negotiate solutions to hitherto difficult and intractable problems. Some mediators are prepared to include children in some sessions to determine their views of key issues, and to have parents hear their children's views. This is consistent with contemporary commitments to 'hear the voice of the child'. However, mediators will be mindful of the age and maturity of children as well as the likely behaviour of parents and the effects of such behaviour on children. So, sessions with children could be undertaken without parents but with mediators reporting children's feelings to parents in subsequent meetings.

Mediation is often not successful because parties in conflict cannot establish any measure of mutual trust by which to negotiate in a meaningful way. Special attention has to be given to any relationship where there has been **domestic violence**. In this context mediation may not be possible or the risks may be too high to proceed. Some have argued that the gender of mediators can be key and that if co-mediation is the preferred model, then to have a man and a woman working together in an even handed manner can be helpful. It was hoped that mediation would become an essential and widely used method for resolving problems between separating and divorcing couples. However, currently the majority of couples actively reject mediation seeming to prefer litigation. Indeed some sceptics have argued that mediation is only successful with 'reasonable' people who would probably have worked things out without professional help. One possible explanation for the widespread preference for litigation is that relationships often become untenable for the two parties at different stages; so that one person is likely to become unhappy before their partner and may decide that the relationship cannot be retrieved. In effect partners 'do their suffering' at different times and when it comes to **mediation** one partner may be in recovery mode whereas the other is still experiencing stress and rejection.

men (social work with men) **social work** practice where ideas of **masculinity**, held by practitioners, **service users**, families, communities and society, impact upon helping objectives and processes.

Whereas sex is thought of as a biological entity, gender has been held by social scientists to be socially and culturally constructed and subject to historical change. Feminists have for several decades encouraged critical analyses of the idea of gender and, in particular, of the treatment of women in society. These analyses have been driven by both empirical research and by significant theorizing. Inevitably, the behaviour of men has come under scrutiny by feminists and others. In this context a variety of key issues concerning the behaviour of men as social workers and as service users, and in social work transactions, have preoccupied researchers and practitioners. These issues include violence, including **domestic violence**, equal opportunities and **anti-oppressive practice**, parenting (including **child abuse** and neglect) and offending behaviour (see **parent education and training**).

One important issue, especially in relation to **social work** with children and their families, has been the relative invisibility of men unless they have been suspected of abusing their children or their partners as with domestic violence. Where families include both a woman and a man, social work records habitually contain much more information about the woman than the man. This appears to be a reflection of social workers' predisposition to think of women as having primary responsibility for the care of children, a tendency that may lead, as some feminists claim, to 'woman blaming' when things go wrong. Some have argued, however, that social workers prefer to engage with mothers rather than fathers, even where fathers are involved with the childcare. Mothers are construed as more compliant or reasonable as service users or clients whereas men are regarded as being more difficult, aggressive or even violent. Another contributory factor may be the heavily gendered nature of childcare and parenting services, which are staffed almost exclusively by women. Thus there may be disincentives for fathers or male carers to participate in services for a parent and a child, as with **Sure Start** centres. Yet the objective, perhaps, should be to involve more men in both childcare and in caring services if the responsibilities of parenting are to be acknowledged by both men and women.

Those working with perpetrators of domestic violence have increasingly found it useful to deconstruct men's accounts of their abusive behaviour. This work has highlighted the tendency of men to rationalize, to minimize their personal responsibility for injuries, and to redefine violence in a narrow way to exclude a variety of controlling and abusive behaviours that are not physical violence. Rationalization includes blaming the woman for 'not having the dinner ready' or 'not controlling the kids' or 'looking at another man' or regarding the incident as essentially an accident, as in 'I did not intend to hit her that hard' or 'I did push her, but I did not realize she was next to the glass door'. Locating the problem in stress is also common, including financial pressures or unemployment. Blocking, confining, intimidating or bullying behaviours or socially isolating a woman or denying her economic resources are all excluded from some men's idea of violence, although such behaviours are underpinned by violence or its threat. The task of social workers has been to reveal the interconnected nature of these behaviours, to demonstrate that they are essentially about the misuse of **power**. The key objective is to bring men to the point that they will understand their behaviour, accept responsibility for it and, by so doing, control and develop other more appropriate strategies for dealing with personal relationships.

Similar objectives underpin other kinds of work with boys, youths and men in relation to such problem areas as teenage pregnancies, adult and youth offending, and residential care. One part of the strategy to reduce teenage pregnancies is to encourage what educationalists call 'personal and social education', whereby young people take responsibility for their sexual behaviour. Such programmes include contraceptive advice, **advice** about personal and sexual relationships, and issues of **parental responsibility**. Although evidence suggests that teenage fathers are unpromising sources of support, services for teenage mothers rarely seek the involvement of the father, regarding them as essentially irresponsible and likely sources of additional problems. Some of this work takes place in residential childcare settings because young people in care, both males and females, are more likely than other young people to become teenage parents. Work with both young and adult offenders includes topics and issues that concern offenders' ideas of masculinity.

Victim reparation schemes, **community service** and offence behaviour analysis all have elements that emphasize personal responsibility for actions, developing awareness of the repercussions of offending behaviour for victims, understanding the personal and peer pressures that may lead to offences and the development of strategies for dealing with opportunities and temptations to offend. A number of commentators have explored the issue of whether the gender of workers affects the response of male **service user**s or clients. At times some have argued that it is the responsibility of male workers 'to deal' with the men and the boys. Yet there is compelling evidence to suggest that women are quite able to deal with offenders of all ages, including **sex offender**s, violent men and parenting issues, and that there are very positive reasons for not offering 'segregated' services. Problems can sometimes occur when male and female workers co-work and male clients attempt collusion with male workers, or where male workers presume the role of leader. Consciousness of these issues, together with planned strategies for dealing with them, are necessary and may be instrumental in helping males to accept a more responsible notion of masculinity.

Featherstone, B., Rivett, M. and Scourfield, J. (2007) *Working with Men in Health and Social Care*. London: Sage.

Mental Capacity Act 2005 legislation concerned with issues of competence and decision-making. The Act has three main sections; section 1 is concerned with the person who lacks capacity, Lasting Powers and the role of the courts; section 2 is devoted to the role of the Court of Protection and the **Public Guardian**; and section 3 with miscellaneous issues and general areas of application. There are five key principles with a focus upon the pursuit of human rights freedoms and best interest practices, including the rights to make eccentric or unwise decisions, to be supported to make your own decisions wherever possible, to have an assumption of capacity unless otherwise proven and to have the least restrictive intervention. This legislation will apply to all those who are working in a professional capacity including social workers, lawyers, doctors, dentists, health workers, anyone involved in research that would include the **interviewing** of vulnerable people, people who have **Lasting Power of Attorney**, the Court of Protection deputies and **independent mental capacity advocates**. An **assessment** will be triggered if there are concerns for a person's ability to make an informed choice regarding a specific issue and initially to ascertain whether the decision can be postponed until capacity is restored or whether there are sufficient grounds to pursue an assessment in view of enduring criteria being met. There may be changes in behaviour, circumstances or concerns of carers, health care workers or others. The best interests of the person to which the assessment refers should be at the heart of all decision-making and must ensure that the person concerned is fully consulted about their cultural needs and wishes, their personal interests and choices are considered, conflicts are explored and evaluated, family and carers are consulted and assumptions avoided.

A person must be assumed to have capacity unless it is established that he or she lacks capacity. A person is not to be treated as unable to make a decision unless all practicable steps to help him to do so have been taken without success. A person is not to be treated as unable to make a decision merely because he makes an unwise decision. An act done or decision made under this Act for or on behalf of a person who lacks capacity must be done, or made, in his best interests. Before the act is done, or the decision is made, regard must be had to whether the purpose for which it is needed can be as effectively achieved in a way that is less restrictive of the person's rights and freedom of action. (See also **Deprivation of Liberty Safeguards, diagnostic testing, functional testing, independent mental capacity advocates** and **Public Guardian**.)

mental disorder an important term, providing a gateway to compulsory **detention** and treatment under the **Mental Health Act 2007**, and to service entitlements in the adults social services context, under **disability** legislation. Mental disorder has traditionally been understood to relate to **mental health problems** – thought to originate in the person's 'mind' or mental functioning. Under the **Mental Health Act 1983**, mental disorder was taken to include '**mental illness**, arrested or incomplete development of mind, psychopathic disorder and any other disorder or **disability** of mind', and longer-term compulsory **detention** or guardianship was conditional upon diagnosed mental illness along with the other categories if certain conditions were met. There were certain exclusions from the use of compulsory powers – those connected with behaviour such as **drug and alcohol dependency**, and sexual **deviance**. However, under the Mental Health Act 2007 which amended the Mental Health Act 1983, someone assessed as having 'any disorder or disability of mind' fulfils one of the criteria for any compulsory interventions, and sexual deviancy is not excluded. This has been viewed as a very broad definition which could have the advantage of ensuring an adequate response to a wide range of distress. Critics have identified the potential for it to be applied very widely, to conditions which may not be categorized as mental health problems. For example, under the **Mental Capacity Act 2005**, someone is defined as lacking mental capacity if they are unable to make a decision for themselves in a particular matter because of 'an impairment of, or a disturbance in the functioning of the mind and brain'. The latter phrase can refer in this legislation to **mental illness**, but importantly, it can also refer to a physical disease, or perhaps other more temporary experiences, which impact on the functioning of the mind and brain.

Mental disorder is also an important term within **social work** practice. Under the **National Assistance Act 1948** someone who suffers from 'mental disorder of any description' (section 29) is entitled to **assessment** and **community care** service provision for disabled people under section 46 and section 47 of the **NHS and Community Care Act 1990**. These provisions can be used in social services **assessment** and care management, and under the care programme approach (CPA). Importantly, if someone with mental health problems is not eligible for services under the CPA, they may still potentially be eligible for social services provision.

Further, people have rights under the **Disability Discrimination Acts 1995** and **2005**, if they have a 'mental impairment which has a substantial and long-term adverse effect' on their 'ability to carry out normal day to day requirements'. This provides social workers with many powers and duties in relation to people defined as having a mental disorder. Both as Approved Mental Health Professionals under the Mental Health Act 2007, and in the full range of **social work** practice, workers therefore need, in order to maximize the **service user**'s rights, to use their powers with a sound and critical appreciation of relevant legislation and of the range of mental health and related issues.

Barber, P. (2009) *Mental Health Law in England and Wales: a guide for professionals.* Exeter: Learning Matters.

mental handicap a term referring to **intellectual impairment**; it has now been replaced by the term **learning disability**. The term 'mental handicap' is regarded as offensive by many self-advocates and tends to be associated with long-stay hospitals and segregated services of **mental health** professionals who can act in the Approved Mental Health Professional role. Potentially this could reduce their opportunities to perform in and thus to contribute their specifically **social work values** and knowledge-base to this role. However, they have much to offer in this role and to the work in many other areas of the legislation, with their traditions of **assessment** and knowledge of services which respond to the person's mental health concerns in the context of his or her rights and experiences of **discrimination**, **social exclusion** and inequalities. Indeed, with both the increased rights and increased controls provided for within this legislation, there are a range of significant opportunities for social workers to use their distinctive values, understandings, and practice knowledge to promote the person's rights and enable him or her to access the supports she or he requires to be able to maximize his or her own control over his or her life.

Archambeault, J. (2009) *Social Work and Mental Health.* Exeter: Learning Matters.

mental health the World Health Organization has defined health in general, including mental health, as 'a complete state of physical, mental and social **wellbeing**, not merely the absence of illness'. This definition incorporates two different perspectives on mental health which have had major significance in recent years.

The first of these perspectives – mental health as the 'absence of illness' – is linked with traditional Western **psychiatry** and the professions associated with it, including **social work**. From this viewpoint, mental health or the absence of **mental illness** is viewed as the norm, with mental illness representing a significant departure from that norm, hence regarded as 'abnormal'.

The second perspective – defining mental health as 'mental wellbeing' – has resonance in many societies, and has been influential in Western societies prior to, but also alongside psychiatry. Historically, for example, it was associated with the 'moral treatment' movement in the late 18th century in the UK, and again with 'anti-psychiatry' in the 20th century.

From this viewpoint, most departures from a state of personal and social wellbeing may be understood as being within the range of 'normal' human functioning, rather than indicative of the presence of abnormality and illness. Thomas Szasz, a proponent of anti-psychiatry, regarded these difficulties as 'problems of living', and it was the individual's triumph over them, his or her personal growth, which allowed him or her to attain the full state of mental health or mental wellbeing. In contrast, radical approaches to mental health, expressed for example by Laing in the same period, saw this state as the consequence of making changes in society, overcoming the **power** inequalities that inhibited people in fulfilling their potential.

These understandings have great significance within the **recovery** approaches influential in recent international and national **mental health policy**, and in wider social model and service-user led perspectives in mental health. Both World Health Organization (2002, 2008) and UK (DH 2009) policy regard medical considerations as only one of a number of influences, social, environmental and personal, on mental health. They thus place emphasis upon living an ordinary and fulfilling life with or without symptoms, envisaging personal growth and social **participation** as the main route to prevention of more serious mental health problems, or to recovery. As a consequence, services are expected to give a significant place to psychosocial interventions and more 'ordinary' forms of help in the wider **community** – and indeed the document 'Capabilities for inclusive practice' (Care Services Improvement Partnership 2007) requires workers to prioritize ordinary community facilities where possible over health and **social care** services. Alongside this approach, however, psychiatric and medical approaches to mental health remain pivotal to the services – primary care, hospitals, and community mental health teams – in which workers would engage with service users with mental health problems.

The implications of these different understandings of mental health for practice must include recognizing the importance of sensitivity to the service user. If mental health is defined as positive wellbeing, what counts as wellbeing will always be informed by the values of the particular society, culture or social group. Thus attention to what service users perceive as wellbeing is crucial in communicating respect, and providing meaningful and effective support.

Second, social workers are particularly well placed through their legal powers to provide social care services, and through their professional 'person in situation' skills and knowledge-base, to provide the supports needed to promote social participation and personal growth, as indicated in a study concerned with promoting wellbeing amongst **older people**.

Third, is that although social inclusion and personal growth are important to many service users, the barriers arising from mental distress and experiences of symptoms on the one hand, and social inequalities and **discrimination** on the other, should not be underestimated. This is illustrated in one study concerned with access to employment, where service users experienced both symptoms and discrimination in the workplace as barriers to entering and sustaining employment. Thus assessment and supports need to be holistic, responding to the range of personal, social and health difficulties faced.

Department of Health (2009) *New Horizons: a shared vision for mental health and wellbeing.* London: DH.

Mental Health Act 1983 legislation that governs the **assessment** and treatment of people with **mental disorder**, including the conditions under which a person can be compulsorily detained in a psychiatric hospital.

The Act sets out four specific categories of mental disorder. Three of the four – mental impairment, severe mental impairment and psychopathic disorder – all share similar characteristics: incomplete development of the mind, which may include significant impairment of intelligence and social functioning and is associated with abnormally aggressive behaviour or socially irresponsible conduct. The fourth and most important category, **mental illness**, is left undefined in the Act. Consultative documents issued by government at the time the Act was passed, however, defined mental illness as having the following characteristics:

- persistent interruption of intellectual functioning as indicated by a failure of memory, orientation, comprehension and learning capacity;

- persistent alteration of mood to such a degree that it gives rise to the patient making a delusional appraisal of his or her situation;
- the presence of delusions or other persecutory or grandiose beliefs;
- thinking so disordered as to prevent the person from making a reasonable appraisal of his or her situation.

Section 2 of the Act provides for a person to be admitted to hospital for psychiatric assessment for up to 28 days if he or she is suffering from a mental disorder (that is, one of the categories above) to the extent that **detention** is justified and that the person ought to be detained in the interests of his or her own health or safety or that of others. Compulsory admission for assessment can take place only on the recommendation of two registered medical practitioners. After the 28 days have elapsed, the person must either remain in hospital as an 'informal' – voluntary – patient or be detained for treatment under section 3. An order for the person's **discharge** may be made at any time during the 28 days. The person may seek his or her own **discharge** by making an application to a mental health tribunal within 14 days of admission. A person may be detained under section 3 of the Act for treatment on the grounds that he or she is suffering from mental illness, severe mental **impairment** or psychopathic disorder to the degree that it is appropriate for him or her to receive medical treatment *and* it is necessary for the health or safety of the person or others that he or she receives treatment that would not otherwise be received without detention. Again, the application for compulsory treatment requires the written recommendation of two medical practitioners.

The Act also allows for compulsory admission for **assessment** for 72 hours in cases of emergency. An emergency application may be made by a person's nearest relative or by an approved social worker and the written recommendation of a medical officer who is familiar with the person in question. The application cannot be renewed at the end of the 72-hour period. The Act also allows for the appointment of a guardian for people over the age of 16 who are suffering from mental disorder to a degree justifying the appointment. The guardian is usually a local authority social services officer, who can require the person to live at a specified place, to receive specified medical treatment and to permit access by a medical practitioner or approved social worker. The value of guardianship has been the subject of considerable debate, since it contains no powers of enforcement and must rely on the cooperation of the person.

Mental Health Act 2007 amendment to the **Mental Health Act 1983**; it also replaces provisions under the Mental Health Patients in the Community Act 1995, and provides important new **Deprivation of Liberty Safeguards** in relation to people lacking capacity under the

Mental Capacity Act 2005 who may be deprived of their liberty. The Act seeks to rebalance **empowerment** in the light of the **Human Rights Act 1998**, and protection as a response to public concerns about the risks people with **mental health** concerns may present in the **community**. These latter concerns arose in the 1990s and more recently as a result of a small number of high profile homicide and **suicide** cases pertaining to people with serious **mental health problems** receiving **community care**.

The aspiration for empowerment comes from understandings about mental health problems which emphasize the influence of the person's social environment and their coping capacity upon mental health. These understandings have been influential at different times in history, and have been prioritized in **mental health policy** over the past decade in efforts to modernize services. After the Second World War, the asylums came under the **National Health Service**, treating mental health concerns as illness, just as physical illness, and the Mental Health Acts of 1959 and 1983 reflected these understandings by making compulsory admissions as short-term as possible, treating compulsory admissions as the exception to informal admissions, and passing powers of decision-making about admission from the courts to doctors.

The Code of Practice for the Mental Health Act 2007 is broadly the same as that underpinning the Mental Health Act 1983. They include the purpose of the legislation to minimize harm, and maximize safety and **wellbeing**; use of the least restrictive alternative; respect for the individual and for diversity; the maximum **participation** of the person; and the most effective and efficient use of resources.

The Mental Health Act 2007 makes a number of important amendments to the Mental Health Act 1983 across a range of provisions, including definitions, compulsory powers to treat people in the community, 'treatability', consent to treatment, professional roles, **advocacy**, rights of minors, and **Deprivation of Liberty Safeguards** for people lacking mental capacity under the **Mental Capacity Act 2005**.

The following amendments are of particular importance for social workers.

*Grounds for compulsory **detention** and treatment* – these have in the 1959 and 1983 Acts included the presence of a diagnosed mental health problem together with a risk to the health and safety of the person or others. Under case-law related to Article 5(i) in the European Convention for Human Rights, incorporated into the UK Human Rights Act 1998, compulsory detention can only take place if it is proportional to nature and degree of the person's mental health problems, and the extent of harm which could arise as a result of these problems. These considerations are incorporated into the grounds for compulsory detention and treatment in the Mental Health Act 2007.

Definition of mental disorder – the definition of mental disorder forming one of the criteria for compulsion in the Mental Health Act 1983 has been amended. Under the 1983 Act, a general definition of mental disorder formed the basis for admission for assessment (section 2 Part 2 Mental Health Act 1983), but people could only be detained for compulsory treatment under Section 3 Part 2 of the Act on the basis of more specific diagnoses together with a requirement of 'treatability' in respect of **personality disorder** and mental impairment (see Mental Health Act 1983). The 'treatability' consideration has meant people with the latter diagnoses have been excluded from these provisions when, as is often the case, they are defined 'untreatable'. To avoid these and other exclusions, both in the person's own interests and in the interests of public protection, the Mental Health Act 2007 therefore sets out only one generic definition of mental disorder in section 1 (2) – 'any disorder or disability of the mind'. Special provisions are retained for people with learning disabilities, who can only be compulsorily detained under the Act if these disabilities are associated with 'abnormally aggressive' or 'seriously irresponsible' conduct.

Treatability – section 3 Part 2 of the Mental Health Act 2007 provides for compulsory treatment for renewable periods, initially for up to 6 months. The 'treatability' condition in the 1983 Act required the treatment to be of benefit to the person. The 2007 Act instead has an 'appropriate treatment' test, taking into account both clinical and social considerations in assessing the 'appropriateness' of hospitalization and available treatments.

Approved Mental health Professionals (AMHP) – The approved social worker is replaced by the Approved Mental Health Professional. This role can be carried out by a range of non-medical mental health professionals, including for example, psychologists and mental health nurses besides social workers. In this role, the professional is required in relation to assessments for compulsory admission to hospital and to Guardianship, to conduct an independent assessment as a basis for deciding – as did the approved social worker under the 1983 Act – whether or not to apply for compulsory powers. The Nearest Relative, however, still retains potential powers in connection with these decisions from the 1983 Act. The AMHP is required to take into account in the assessment, the impact of social factors, the views of the nearest relative, and the relative merits of admission compared with community alternatives. These professionals require specialist training before they can perform this role: arrangements for approval are set out in the Mental Health (Approval of

Persons to be Approved Mental Health Professionals) (England) Regulations 2008.

Responsible Clinician and Approved Clinician – Significant amendments are made to the 1983 Act concerning who can make decisions about the person's treatment. These changes are in accord with the emphasis of modernizing **mental health policy** upon the role played by non-medical factors in mental health. For the first time, clinical decision-making is not vested in the psychiatrist and does not require a medical training. The Responsible Clinician has overall responsibility for the person's treatment, and the Approved Clinician is likely to have the lead role in the multi-disciplinary **team** treating the person. Both are required to have specialist training and practice competence across the range of mental health concerns. Importantly, social workers like other mental health professionals can assume these roles. The Approved Clinician has the **power** to detain patients for up to 72 hours in a holding order (section 5), and this would be a new responsibility for social workers and for some of the other professionals who can perform this role.

Consent to treatment – Under Part 4 of the Act, some treatments for a detained patient can be given without consent or a second opinion – and cannot be subject to **advance directives** under the Mental Capacity Act 2005. However, importantly, it is possible for patients to withhold consent to certain treatments if they are assessed as having capacity to make that decision under the Mental Capacity Act 2005. This has been upheld in case-law.

Community Treatment Orders – New powers are inserted under 17A of the 1983 Act to allow for Supervised Community Treatment. Subsections are inserted into section 64 of the 1983 Act regarding the conditions under which such treatments may be given to people who lack capacity. People liable for these Orders have been detained under section 3 Part 2 of the Act or a Hospital Order or Transfer Directions under Part 3, the criminal sections of the Act. The person has to be assessed as presenting a risk to his or her own safety or that of others, together with the presence of mental disorder. The Responsible Clinician decides on the use of this **power**, but the **written agreement** of the Approved Mental Health Professional is also required. The Order can continue for up to 6 months and can be renewed.

Mental Health Review Tribunals (MHRT) – Under section 65 of the Act, the MHRT can decide, as under the 1983 Act, whether the person should continue to be formally detained. Under the 2007 Act, they also have the power to decide if the person should remain on a Community Treatment Order. The social worker can support the person in relation to his or her **appeal** in a number of important ways, including providing **advice** about free specialist legal services, acting as an expert witness, and providing a social circumstances report. Independent Mental Health Advocates – under section 130 of the Act, any person subject to compulsory powers, with the exceptions of sections 5(2) and 5(4) (holding powers), and sections 135 and 136 (powers pertaining to assessment under the Act in the community) is entitled to have an IMCA, and to be made aware of this entitlement. Importantly, IMCAs can assist the person both when detained in hospital and on a Community Treatment Order.

Section 117 Aftercare – This was a duty based upon the local social services authority and the **primary care trust**s under the 1983 Act, and continues as such under the 2007 Act. Importantly this allows for social workers to assess and provide for the full range of **community care** services under section 26 of the **NHS and Community Care Act 1990**, free of charge. This takes place in collaboration with health staff under the 're-focused' Care Programme Approach 2008.

Overall, the 2007 Act provides some additional rights, such as the right to independent advocacy and the right to withhold consent to some forms of treatment if she or he has the capacity to make that decision. However, the introduction of Community Treatment Orders has not been welcomed. These are viewed from some **service user** perspectives as overly coercive, and questions have been raised by academics about the potential of the Orders to breach human rights. There are also questions about their effectiveness – evidence from other countries has not been able to show a connection to positive **outcomes**. However, one study shows that people subject to the orders experienced satisfaction because they were able to access easily a range of services they needed, but at the same time, found the controls upon them a source of considerable unease. Social workers as Approved Mental Health Professionals under the 2007 Act retain their former powers as Approved Social workers, but form only one of a range of mental health professionals who can act in the AMHP role. Potentially this could reduce their opportunities to perform in and thus to contribute their specifically **social work values** and knowledge-base to this role. However, they have much to offer in this role and to the work in many other areas of the legislation, with their traditions of assessment and knowledge of services which respond to the person's mental health concerns in the context of his or her rights and experiences of **discrimination, social exclusion** and inequalities. Indeed, with both the increased rights and increased controls provided for within this legislation, there are a range of significant opportunities for social workers to use their distinctive values, understandings, and practice knowledge to promote the person's rights and enable him or her to access the supports she or he requires to be able to maximize his or her own control over his or her life.

Archambeault, J. (2009) *Social Work and Mental Health*. Exeter: Learning Matters.

mental health policy ideas, assumptions, ideologies, services and institutions underpinning government policy in relation to people with **mental health problems**. At the birth of the **welfare state** under the **NHS** Act 1946, asylums became hospitals, and mental health problems were understood as illness, just like physical illness but located in the mind. In relation to these understandings, the humane response became prominent, and under the **welfare state**, legislation gave people with **mental health problems access to a wide range of health** and **social care** services. Importantly for **social work**, people with 'any problems of mind' were included in the definition of a disabled person under the **National Assistance Act 1948**, and subsequent disabled persons' legislation, thus making them eligible for social services for disabled people. Through this period, compulsory **detention** continued to take place, but **service user**s had far more rights in the process; they were detained for shorter, time-limited periods, and voluntary treatment comparable with treatment for any other illness was the norm.

From 1990 the **NHS and Community Care Act** brought a more extensive programme of deinstitutionalization and emphasized **values** of **community** treatment and care, **independent living** and quality of life. This involved social workers – now care managers – in social services, in coordinating health and social care services to provide a package to support the person in ordinary living. However, risk became a renewed social concern following from some high profile homicides by people with mental health problems in the community, and responses to this included the risk emphasis of the integrated Care Programme Approach, together with new legal controls in the community. **Modernization policy** has extended these concerns further, developing a powerful new approach and making very significant changes to mental health services. The impetus for this was outlined in an early White Paper *Saving Lives* 1999. It pointed to the human, societal and financial costs of mental health problems, manifesting at high rates in modern societies including the UK. Effective and efficient services were therefore required, The National Service Framework in Mental Health 1999 for the first time set standards for health and social care service provision, intended to maximize effective practice and positive health and social care outcomes for **service user**s.

These standards and subsequent policy documents such as the Care Programme Approach guidance 1999, *Making it Happen*: Mental Health

Promotion 2001, The Journey to Recovery 2002, and Mental Health and
Social Inclusion 2004, were concerned to go beyond ordinary life and
community care, and to promote social inclusion; access to mainstream
roles – notably employment – and facilities rather than segregation in
services; capacity building and self-management of symptoms, as major
approaches to mental health improvement. This involved new concerns
with the importance of social factors such as inequalities and **social
exclusion** in the onset and persistence of mental health problems;
recovery on the basis that many of the determinants of mental health
problems were social and psychosocial and thus could be intervened with;
with prevention of mental health problems and relapse; and with service
user empowerment and self-management. In relation to risk, still a major
concern of the CPA, **risk-taking** was viewed as important in promoting
the **service user**'s **empowerment**. However, for those who could not
manage risk or engage with services, intensive multi-agency support was
offered, as for example with **crisis intervention** and **assertive outreach**,
and the Government embarked on reform of the Mental Health Act
1983. One major rationale for this was to align the legislation with the
Human Rights Act of 1998, but there was an equal concern to extend
controls in relation to people thought to pose the greatest risk, including
those with **personality disorder** and those with severe problems who
would not engage with services in the community. The conclusion of the
reform process with the Mental Health Act 2007, has legislated for
greater controls in the community in respect of the latter group.

mental health problems difficulties linked, in societies historically
influenced by Western European culture, with the 'mind'.

From the time of Descartes in the European Enlightenment of the
18th century, a clear distinction was made between 'mind' and body,
and 'mind' was defined as the workings of a person's 'consciousness',
including perception, thought and judgement, emotions and behaviour.
Thus, in these societies, mental health problems are located in a person's
thinking, feelings and experience and actions, in turn impacting upon her
or his psychological and social functioning. Many cultures have a similar
concern with this area of personal and social functioning but may not
make such a strong distinction between 'body' and 'mind': instead,
people may experience mental health problems holistically – as expressed
in descriptions such as 'my heart is squeezed'. In Western cultures
too, however, physical illness, discomfort and pain often accompany
these problems.

Range of mental health problems. Internationally, about 16 per cent
of the population at any one time may be experiencing mental health
problems. Proportions are higher in poor and socially excluded areas.

Women, Black and minority ethnic groups, disabled people, and **older people**, more likely to be exposed to **poverty**, also experience these problems at higher rates. Traditionally, Western **psychiatry** has divided mental health problems into the following categories:

- Stress and **post-traumatic stress** – the latter has been linked for example, to survivors of natural disaster, combat and torture, but more recently it has been recognized that **victim**s of violence or **abuse** can also experience this condition;
- **neuroses**, including the 'common mental health problems' of **anxiety** and **depression**, together with eating disorders, obsessional compulsive disorder, **phobias**, and psychosomatic illness – people with anxiety and depression make up the greater proportions of those experiencing mental health problems at any one time;
- **psychoses**, regarded as serious mental health problems, including manic **depression** or **bipolar disorder**, schizophrenia, **personality disorder** (including psychopathy), and organic diseases of the brain, such as the **dementias**. Traditionally these conditions have been understood as different diseases of the mind, on the model of physical disease and diagnosis. However, there has been debate over some time, reflecting the different ways of understanding **mental health**, regarding how far **neuroses** in particular should be regarded as illness rather than simply as reactions, or over-reactions to stress. Use of the term 'mental health problems' as distinct from **'mental illness'** has thus become customary when referring to all these different conditions.

From a disease perspective, the person is thought to experience different sets of biologically generated psychiatric disease symptoms affecting thoughts, feelings, experience, judgement and behaviour. Indeed people with mental health problems do face what are often very distressing and disabling inner experiences which can affect their behaviour and responses. However, the relevance of a range of diagnoses to these experiences has been subject to question from different perspectives. One reason for this is that research has indicated there can be more differences between the symptoms experienced by people with the same diagnosis, than between people with that diagnosis and no diagnosis at all, thus suggesting that the diagnoses do not reflect disease entities after the model of physical illness diagnoses.

But more influential is the development of social and **recovery models** of mental health, recognizing the powerful role of social and personal factors in the emergence of, resilience to and recovery from mental health problems. These considerations have given strength to powerful concerns concordant with both modernization policy and social work values of **empowerment** – concerns that notions of mental illness deny the individual's capacity for self-determination. Social work additionally has traditionally been sympathetic to the anti-psychiatry argument that psychiatric diagnoses give a scientific label to what is only a social judgement of abnormality. Some mental health survivor perspectives view psychotic symptoms such as auditory hallucinations such as hearing voices, not as an illness at all, but as understandable human reactions to extreme experiences and points, for example, to the high percentage of people with psychoses as having suffered childhood physical or sexual abuse (see **post-traumatic stress disorder**). Psychology is a further influential perspective challenging the use of diverse diagnoses with mental health problems, suggesting that the experience of symptoms may be contributed to substantially by learned behaviour. Even within psychiatry, the 'critical psychiatry' perspective, questions the above traditional diagnostic understandings.

From these perspectives, notions of illness and symptoms are not ruled out, but tend to be viewed as only one amongst a range of factors to intervene with. This trend is also reflected in the definition of **mental disorder** in the Mental Health Act 2007. At the same time, medical models and the use of the above diagnostic systems retain considerable influence in mental health services.

What are mental health problems? At the advent of psychiatry late in the 19th century, mental health problems were understood as mental illness, viewed solely as the result of genetic abnormality in mental functioning. Psychodynamic theory in the earlier part of the 20th century was influential in the understanding and treatment of neuroses. A major development later in the 20th century particularly in relation to psychoses, however, was the 'stress-vulnerability' model, still important today. These understandings acknowledge a genetic component in mental health problems, but suggest these – often biochemical – disorders in mental functioning will only emerge if they are triggered by developmental and social stressors which the individual lacks the capacity to cope with. Relapse in these conditions has also been understood in this model as a consequence of stress 'triggering' the re-emergence of symptoms. Social psychiatry, a development in the wider discipline of psychiatry in the later part of the 20th century aligned itself with these understandings, producing a wealth of research and approaches to service provision, especially with psychoses. These understandings and approaches came to be viewed as the 'bio-psycho-social' model, leading to the promotion of a multi-disciplinary response to mental health problems. Social work was and is regarded as one of the key participants in the multi-professional mental health team.

With **community care** and modernization policy since the 1990s, policy-led and critical and **service user**-led social models of mental health have had increased influence. These models emphasize theories and research which link social factors such as social **discrimination** and abuse, **poverty**, social isolation, unemployment, and social stress, to mental health problems – and we can see some of these connections in the statistics referred to above, indicating higher rates of mental health problems amongst poorer, socially devalued and socially excluded groups. Policy models further highlight the important role of social **wellbeing** – e.g. social **participation**, social support, a sense of control – in the development of resilience in relation to these problems (see **mental health policy**). These models have given support to already existing opposition to medical models of mental health. Critical and service user-led social models further challenge the power of the medical profession in relation to people with mental health problems, pointing to a need instead for changes to power inequalities in society and more development of non-medical forms of intervention. All of these models, although most do not deny a medical component at least in more serious mental health problems, view these concerns generally as largely understandable reactions to social discrimination and inequalities, on a continuum of normal human functioning.

Consequences of mental health problems Just as in the stress vulnerability model mental health problems are viewed as having biological, psychological and social components, so the impact of mental health problems can be seen to have consequences for biological, psychological and social functioning, and importantly, for distress in these areas of experience. Experiences traditionally viewed as symptoms – e.g. hearing voices, depressed mood – can often be very distressing and debilitating. They can have consequences for physical suffering and discomfort – for example anxiety can lead to digestive problems – and can lead, at least indirectly, to physical illness through, for example sustained high levels of stress or a poor diet. They can profoundly affect functioning through their impact on perception, judgement, emotions, motivation, concentration, comprehension. These experiences can have major implications for roles such as work or parenting. They can also have a far-reaching impact on relationships, both close and more distant – e.g. lack of concentration, mis-perceptions of the other person, or emotional responses inappropriate to the situation would make it difficult to maintain or initiate friendships or colleague relationships at work. In turn these difficulties can result in unemployment, loss of children into care and social isolation, further leading to **poverty** and **social exclusion**. There is a significantly raised risk of **suicide** amongst people with mental health problems, perhaps related to the above range of substantial difficulties experienced. Other risks can also result from these experiences – e.g. a risk of accidents through poor concentration.

Social model understandings of these difficulties – corresponding in some ways to the **social model of disability** with disabled people (although some social model perspectives in mental health do not align themselves with that model) emphasize that it is the discriminatory societal reaction to the different experiences and responses of people with mental health problems, which creates unemployment, social isolation and social exclusion: thus statistics in recent years indicate that as many as 82 per cent of people with mental health problems were unemployed. The medical model and the power of professionals in mental health services are further regarded as contributing much to their disempowerment.

Social work has powers and duties to provide community care services in response to the **social care** aspects of these problems (see **NHS and Community Care Act 1990**). This is because people with 'any' **mental disorder** are included in the definition of a disabled person under the **National Assistance Act 1948**, rendering them eligible for **assessment** and for services for assessed need under the **Disabled Persons Act 1986**, and the **NHS and Community Care Act 1990**.

All of the above difficulties are substantial, and often they can be as serious for people with what are regarded as minor or 'common' mental health problems, as for people with **psychoses**. This is not always appreciated, as indicated in case-law examples where people with diagnoses of **depression** have been unlawfully defined by social services as ineligible for **community care** services.

Responses to mental health problems. People with mental health problems are responded to mainly in primary care, but those with more serious mental health problems are referred to the mental health services, comprising community mental health teams and in-patient psychiatric beds. They can be subject to compulsory detention and other provisions under the Mental Health Act 2007. Promotion of mental **wellbeing** in wider society is a further very important policy development.

Social work may be involved in both primary care and in mental health service settings, through its duties under the Disabled Persons and Community Care legislation as indicated above. Workers are further involved in the mental health services through **participation** with health agencies in the **care programme approach**, informed by the principles of the **recovery model**.

In both settings, medical, psychological and social work services are of significance, and under the **Health Act 1999** community mental health teams are structured in accord with arrangements for integrated health and **social care** services. Medication and psychological interventions emphasizing cognitive behavioural approaches are important interventions in primary care and mental health services, intended in accord with the stress vulnerability model to enable people to cope better with stressors as a means of preventing relapse and diminishing symptoms. Family interventions are also a focus. Access to employment and to ordinary community supports and facilities is of major importance in both settings, viewed in mental health policy on the basis of social model understandings, as a means of promoting recovery and social inclusion. It is of particular significance to social work that social factors have been found to have strong links with mental health problems. On this basis, it has been argued that social work could do more not only to address the social difficulties experienced by people with mental health problems, but also to contribute to the prevention of relapse and promotion of recovery by working to provide appropriate supports to accessing the mainstream, and to reduce social stress, discrimination and its impact.

More mental health awareness amongst social workers could also result in enormous benefits to service users. Because service users are predominantly in poverty, rates of mental health problems are high. There is a dilemma where the person has not been identified as experiencing mental health problems – referral carries a risk of **stigma** due to the meanings attached to a mental health 'label', but equally, the absence of an appropriate mental health response can seriously disadvantage the service user, and could lead to crisis, such as **suicide**, for example, or loss of children into care. Awareness of all of these issues in assessment, involving **service user**s in formulating appropriate responses, and advocating with or on behalf of the service user in relation to other mental health professionals and service providers, could thus potentially prevent crises and make all the difference to service user outcomes and experiences.

Golightley, M. (2008) *Social Work and Mental Health*, 3rd edition. Exeter: Learning Matters.

mental health treatment requirement a requirement which may be included in a **community order, youth rehabilitation order** or **suspended sentence order**, directing the offender to undergo treatment by or under the direction of a medical practitioner or psychologist with a view to the improvement of the offender's mental condition. Treatment as an in-patient or as an out-patient may be specified. Such requirements can only be included in an order if the offender expresses willingness to comply with the requirement.

mental illness traditionally understood as 'disease' of the mind and of reasoning faculties that distorts a person's thinking, perception of reality and problem-solving capacity.

These understandings have been modelled by **psychiatry** after the notion of physical disease. They are believed to involve a biological disorder in the functioning of the 'mind' which results in symptoms affecting thought, perception, feelings, and judgement with wide-ranging implications for personal and social functioning and behaviour. They have traditionally been divided into different diseases, broadly grouped into **psychoses** and **neuroses** (see **mental health problems**). However, important challenges to medical model understandings of these difficulties have been made from several influential perspectives.

Although both physical and mental illness have been viewed thus as having a physical reality in biological dysfunction, mental illness has also been viewed traditionally in society and sometimes in the services as failing to equate with the 'real' concerns around pain, discomfort or poor functioning associated with physical disease; rather symptoms of mental illness have been regarded as simply distortions produced by the mind. Indeed, part of the **stigma** attached to people with mental health problems stems from this – it is thought they cannot be taken seriously; that their difficulties are not 'real'. In countering these stigmatizing views, social models of **mental health** have focused away from these debates to identify real experiences of mental distress, as a largely cognitive and emotional reaction to social **discrimination**, inequalities and stress. Indeed, **service users** experience these and other forms of distress, but in addition there is research evidence to suggest that most symptoms associated with mental health problems are associated with biochemical disorders which involve suffering and can affect both physical and mental functioning. **Service users** have described experiences corresponding to these findings. It is important therefore to take these findings pointing to suffering and substantial effects upon functioning fully into account when working with people with mental health problems.

What are the causes of mental illness? There have been different explanations of mental health problems over the past century and before. The medical model and concepts of mental illness have formed only one of these explanations, but became the dominant approach particularly when asylums for people with mental health problems became incorporated with hospitals for physical illness into the **National Health Service** in 1946. Medical models of mental illness have changed over time, with genetic biomedical models influential from the late 18th century onwards, eventually giving way to 'stress-vulnerability' understandings later in the 20th century. The 'stress-vulnerability' model is based on an accumulation of research evidence that the emergence and persistence of the symptoms of mental illness is linked to various forms of social stress, including **poverty** and unemployment, and life events such as bereavement, job loss, traumatic experiences such as childhood **sexual abuse**, and critical family attitudes known as 'high expressed emotion'. In the model, these stressors are thought to 'trigger' mental health-related biochemical disorders in people with a genetic predisposition to mental illness – although research has also found that a range of social stressors and trauma have distinct biochemical effects which can lead to both physical and mental health problems.

Although these understandings were first applied to **psychoses**, research relating to neuroses suggests they can similarly be applied to these conditions. Research in the 1970s showed, for example, that in a sample of 500 women in an inner London suburb some 33 per cent experienced some degree of **depression**, against a background of bad housing and unhappy **marriage**s/relationships. Those with depression were more likely to have three or more children aged under 14 living at home; lack of an intimate or confiding relationship; **loss** of mother in **childhood**; and a lack of employment outside the home.

What is involved in mental illness? In general, symptoms of mental illness are understood to involve experiences and responses which represent a departure from what others in the individual's culture would consider understandable. Symptoms of neuroses such as depression and anxiety have been understood as extremes of ordinary feelings seemingly out of proportion to the situation – e.g. pessimism, anxiety, sadness – alongside physical symptoms such as poor appetite, fatigue and palpitations. Psychotic symptoms on the other hand, involve experiences viewed as outside ordinary experiences. These are defined as hallucinations, delusions and thought disorder, involving sensations, beliefs and cognitions which appear to diverge from how others in the person's culture understand reality. Severe depression, and post-traumatic stress also may be associated with some of these symptoms. Importantly these symptoms will have further consequences for the person's experience, emotions and functioning, also often viewed as symptoms – e.g. someone may withdraw from social **participation**, or shout apparently at nobody, if severely troubled by hearing voices.

Responses to mental illness. The symptoms of mental illness have been responded to since the 1950s primarily by medication from within a medical model of mental health problems. However, Community Care and Modernisation policies have emphasized the importance of an integrated health and **social care** response rather than a medical approach alone, with psychology playing a significant part in helping people to manage their symptoms and the stressors that may exacerbate them.

These policies have also sought to respond to concerns about risk, associated in the public consciousness with the symptoms of mental illness. Because these symptoms are thought to undermine peoples' capacity to problem solve, control the environment around them, and their own reactions, fears of risk, danger and incompetence associated with people with mental illness are great, and policy has responded by extending compulsory powers over people in the **community** (see **Mental Health Act 2007**).

However, these fears result from historical beliefs about mental illness as taking over completely from the person's agency and integrity, and are thus exaggerated: in contrast for example, to public fears of violence, and homicide, research has shown that risk is only very minimally larger proportionately than amongst the population as a whole, and the numbers involved are very small. At the same time, there are occasions when risks more generally can be substantial and the person may lack the capacity to manage them or use the supports available at that point. It is in these situations that workers may have to consider the use of compulsory interventions under the Mental Health Act 2007. But in most practice situations, recovery models and social model approaches to risk aim to work with peoples' strengths, aspirations, and the different medical, psychological and social barriers to an ordinary life, to support the person in meeting needs and managing risk. And against the background of the discrimination experienced by people with diagnoses of mental illness, it should be no surprise that the worker's commitment to the person is of enormous value to **service user**s, and makes a real difference both to **wellbeing** and to the person feeling able to engage with the services. These **values** should also lead the worker to help address discrimination towards the **service user**, whether in use of compulsory provisions, in the community, or from service providers.

Thus although many of the exaggerated and discriminatory beliefs and responses linked to the symptoms of mental illness have been rightly challenged, there is evidence that these experiences can have serious implications for suffering, functioning, and sometimes risk. The significance of social factors in the emergence and persistence of these experiences, and the importance of the person centred relationship to **service user**s, suggests **social work** powers, knowledge-base and **values** can make a major contribution to integrated mental health practice.

Golightley, M. (2008) *Social Work and Mental Health*, 3rd edition. Exeter: Learning Matters.

mentally disordered offender person who commits a crime and is additionally diagnosed as suffering from a **mental disorder** (which may or may not be linked to the offending). Such persons may be removed from the criminal justice system by various measures of **diversion** to more appropriate treatment services. Comparatively rare are court findings of 'not guilty by reason of insanity' and 'unfit to plead' which can result in a **hospital order** or **supervision order**. Following conviction, a **criminal court** can make a hospital order, guardianship order, or **community order** with a **mental health treatment requirement**. Imprisoned offenders can also be transferred from **prison** to **detention** in hospital. Diversion schemes seek to identify **mentally disordered offender**s at an earlier stage, so that they can receive attention from **mental health** treatment services as an alternative to prosecution. Despite all these diversionary possibilities, an enormous number of people with **mental health problems** continue to find themselves in **prison**, where the quality of psychiatric services has been found to fall well below standards in the **National Health Service**. Detailed surveys have consistently shown that fewer than 10 per cent of **prison**ers showed no evidence of **mental disorder**, and seven out of ten showed signs of two disorders or more. The commonest diagnoses were for **personality disorder**, with high rates also for **drug and alcohol dependency**, and much smaller rates for **psychoses**. An influential official reports Bradley (2009) have sought to reduce these numbers by encouraging diversion and suggesting reforms to facilitate it.

Department of Health (2009) *The Bradley Report: Lord Bradley's review of people with mental health problems or learning disabilities in the criminal justice system*. London: DH.

mentor a person with experience of a particular situation or problem offers **advice** or support to others in a similar position. Mentor means 'a trusted counsellor or guide'. Mentoring is a consciously developed relationship that mixes an informal educative role with personal support and encouragement, together with the roles of change agent and advocate. Broadly any mentoring project aims to develop a one-to-one voluntary relationship, with a more experienced person coaching, guiding and transferring their skills and outlook to a less experienced person. Mentoring provides a young person with both a role model – that is, a successful example to follow in terms of a career path, personal conduct or in studying – and a source of instruction and guidance.

The act of mentoring involves several roles – as good listener, critical friend, counsellor, network and coach. Perhaps one of its key assets for socially excluded young people is to provide a bridge to areas of life that have been habitually closed off. This may include useful prospective employment **contact**s, access to social **networks** and resources outside the neighbourhood, and guidance on how to make those contacts effective. Mentors are potentially a key element in what is called 'bridging social capital', assets stored in social relationships that are outside the young person's immediate neighbourhood, family and friends.

While the term is often used informally (for example, 'she was my mentor' meaning someone who helps a new member of staff settle into an organization) what is asked of mentors for young people is substantially more. There are three key features of a mentoring relationship:

- It is a voluntary arrangement as required by the person being mentored and can be ended by either party at any time;
- Mentors are equipped with the necessary interpersonal skills to manage and monitor the relationship;
- Both those mentored and mentors understand the boundaries and purpose of the relationship.

Mentor schemes can assist in work with young offenders or those at risk of offending, poor school achievers, homeless young people and care leavers to name a few. In setting up a mentoring scheme you need to think about who the scheme is for: is it intended for pupils with a substantial record of unexplained absences, for those aged 16 plus who are looking for work, for care leavers in a particular area or for those **caution**ed by the **police**? The group may be large or small, focused or general – but from the beginning thinking about who the scheme is for is closely linked to the purpose and the aims of the scheme. Be sure to collect data on how many young people are likely to be interested. Establish aims and objectives: the project needs to think through what its prime purpose is, what it is trying to accomplish, and what kind of achievement it wants to be known for. Its objectives are the more specific steps outlined to achieve those aims. Careful thinking around gender is needed: will the scheme be for girls or young women only, for example? What will be the gender balance in the likely supply of mentors? Careful thinking around ethnicity is needed: are shared cultural or religious norms between those being mentored and likely **volunteer** mentors important? Overlap: make an audit of existing voluntary and statutory services to ensure that what you want to achieve is not already being done in your area. Decide where the project will be placed within that map of current services. Recruiting mentors calls for accurate judgement of people. Potential mentors should feel comfortable in front of others, have the capacity to speak about their feelings and be open about themselves and their experiences. They need to believe that individuals can cope with difficulties when supported and not to feel threatened when challenged by others. Above all they should be able to imagine themselves in others' shoes and perceive the mentor's role as enabling and not controlling. (See also **modelling**.)

Minicom   a brand name for a type of text phone used by deaf people; it is often used as a generic term for text phones. Text phones enable deaf people to communicate with other text phone users by typing messages. They have a keyboard and a screen, which allows received messages to be displayed. It is possible for text phone users to communicate with people who use standard telephones through the Typetalk service, operated by British Telecom and the Royal National Institute for the Deaf. Messages are channelled through an operator who can receive and transmit both speech and text.

minimum intervention the theory (based on **labelling theory**) that formal responses to crime involving prosecution and punishment and other intensive interventions can increase the likelihood of re-offending, as it can lead to counter-productive labelling and **stigma**tization and reinforce 'deviant identities'. Consequently the best approach is one based on **diversion** from prosecution and **custody** and minimizing other interventions. In the field of **youth justice** this has been summed up as 'leaving the kids alone' as far as possible to allow them to 'grow out of crime' (as most young offenders do). The opposing school of thought (see **zero tolerance**) favours early intervention on the grounds that misconduct ought to be 'nipped in the bud' by teaching pro-social behaviour at the earliest opportunity.

minimum sentence see **mandatory sentence**

Ministry of Justice ministry created in May 2007, replacing the Department for Constitutional Affairs and assuming responsibility for the **National Offender Management Service**, criminal justice policy and **youth justice** (formerly the responsibility of the **Home Office**). Also responsible for courts, civil law and legal aid but also the more contentious and potentially controversial issues of human rights, democracy and the nature of the constitution.

Misuse of Drugs Act 1971 the major piece of legislation in Britain concerning the use and misuse of drugs. The Act lists drugs which are controlled, and divides them into Classes A, B and C, a classification which is intended to reflect their relative harmfulness. Those in Class A – for example heroin, cocaine, ecstasy and some hallucinogenic drugs – carry the most severe penalties. It is illegal to possess, supply, produce or allow premises to be used for the use of these drugs. The Act also gives **police** officers the **power** to stop and search people in public places if they have reasonable suspicion that they are in possession of controlled drugs. In 2004 the government reclassified cannabis from Class C to Class B, a decision it subsequently reversed in 2009.

mixed economy of care the provision of services from a variety of sources, including the statutory agencies and the private and voluntary sectors. Many policy analysts, both inside and outside the Conservative

Party, believe that the provision of welfare services purely by the state sector reduces choice for individual users, undermines efficiency through monopoly and benefits welfare professionals and local bureaucrats rather than those in need. An important core belief of Conservative **ideology** is that choice equals freedom and that by opening up the provision of care to a greater variety of providers more choice will be available to users of services, who will therefore experience greater freedom. The Conservatives also argued that through the existence of what is largely a state monopoly there is inevitably more chance of inefficiency and waste. Some analysts see the state as being too insulated from the 'discipline of the market' because it does not suffer the threat of bankruptcy that the private sector experiences, which in their view acts as a spur to efficiency. Thus, they argue that there is a need to open up the state sector to competition from the non-state sector and to introduce an **internal market** through identifying purchaser/provider roles within **social services departments**. In addition, the private sector has complained that the criteria that **local authorities** use to register private residential accommodation are more rigorous than those used for their own in-house provision. Consequently, the Conservative government increased competition through encouragement of the mixed economy made up of both the private and voluntary sectors.

The development of the mixed economy of care should not be identified solely as a cost-saving exercise. The belief that the private and voluntary sector can provide care at a lower cost played an important part in the policy. Privatization and competitive tendering were seen as ways of reducing public expenditure and the **power** of public-sector trade unions. The fiscal crisis of the state, emerging out of welfare commitments and the changing demographic structure, put pressure on governments to seek ways of reducing the role of statutory provision. Local authority social services departments, however, still retain a core regulatory role and involvement through the purchase of services. The **NHS and Community Care Act** placed local authorities at the centre as enabling bodies that purchased services from the private and voluntary sector in competition with their own in-house providers. The contractual relationship created between the state and the non-state sector was aimed at ensuring that users were provided for and that the level and quality of provision would be guaranteed and open to scrutiny.

While the Labour government since 1997 has argued and legislated against the maintenance of competitive tendering as a compulsory element in public-sector provision, competition still provides a place for the private and voluntary sectors. Its commitment to the mixed economy of care can be identified through the role of best value and now the

Comprehensive Area Assessment and the questions asked of local government providers through that process.

mobility the ability of people to get around indoors and to get to places they want to go. The term can be used in connection with individual capacity for movement or with the skills and facilities that are needed in order to negotiate the physical environment. Mobility **impairment**s are bodily characteristics that restrict the capacity of individuals to move around without personal assistance or aids. People with **visual impairment**, however, also experience difficulties in getting around, and rehabilitation programmes emphasize the skills needed to avoid hazards in the physical environment. Mobility goes beyond individual abilities and skills, and involves access to transport and the places to which people want to go. For example, many disabled people have limited choice of employment or leisure because they are restricted by the limited transport or assistance available. Much public transport has been inaccessible for disabled people, although there has been some improvement since accessibility regulations were introduce for trains in 1998 and for new buses in 2000. Amendments to the **Disability Discrimination Act** ensure that transport providers must make 'reasonable adjustments' for disabled people using the service.

modelling essentially, learning by example, and originally a therapeutic technique in **behaviour modification**. The term is now widely used to refer to any situation when a person or group follows the pattern, behaviour or general example of another person or group. In behaviour programmes the person being treated watches another person coping appropriately with an anxiety-provoking stimulus, including anything from a social event to spiders. He or she thus learns the inappropriateness of his or her own reactions and more effective ways of responding. Many studies have confirmed that modelling is a speedy and effective treatment method. See **mentor**.

modernization policy concerned with promoting effective, **evidence-based** health and **social care**. To this end the **Social Care Institute of Excellence** was set up, providing a wide range of research and especially research into practice resources for practitioners.

money advice see **debt advice**

Moon a system of reading and writing for blind people that is based on tactile symbols.

   Moon is simpler to learn and use than Braille, but the materials are considerably more bulky. It cannot be produced by hand, and the available literature is small. There is a relatively small number of Moon users, and they tend to be **older people**.

motivational interviewing a set of counselling techniques used in many situations where service users express ambiguity in the wish to change some problematic aspect of their lives. The techniques have been found to be especially useful in work with people with addictive behaviours involving alcohol and drug/substance abuse.

Motivational interviewing has been characterised as a particular style of counselling in its concern to establish a constructive atmosphere or conversation in which to discuss possible changes to problematic behaviour. Five different conditions have been identified to make it more likely that service users will both perceive a problem clearly and to want to engage in attempts to change behaviour. These are:

- expressing empathy – in essence to convey an understanding and an acceptance of how difficult life is for the service user;
- avoiding arguments – challenging the service users reasons and/or justifications for their negative behaviour is construed as counterproductive and likely to lead to increased resistance to change. The task is to get the service user to identify what needs to change;
- supporting self-efficacy – this is a key aspect of the counselling process in its attempts to accept that previous attempts at change have failed, but that further attempts at change will not inevitably fail. This could entail recognising more precisely what needs to change, identifying when help is needed when the going gets tough and accepting such help;
- rolling with resistance – the core issue here is to not to challenge behaviour but to sensitively challenge the thinking that supports it. Offering a service user an alternative explanation or understanding can be helpful in deconstructing unhelpful behaviour;
- developing discrepancy – identifying opportunities to highlight the differences between where a service user 'is at' and where they 'want to be' as a mechanism for revealing goals that are not imposed by the therapist but may offer a starting point for a genuinely self-motivated change.

Many perceive these core elements of motivational interviewing as a restatement of a committed and competent social work underpinned by the GSCC Code of Practice combined with the application of principles of person centred counselling. Such skills are indeed an important part of the armoury of effective social work practice. (See also **Cycle of change; strengths perspective** and **solution focused therapy**.)

Rollnick, S & Allison, J, Motivational Interviewing in *The Essential Handbook of Treatment and Prevention of Alcohol Problems*, edited by N. Heather & T. Stockwell (2004), Chichester, Wiley and Sons

multi-agency public protection arrangements (MAPPA) the process whereby the **police, probation** and **prison** services work in teams with other agencies to manage the risks posed by violent and **sex offenders** living in the **community**. Since 2001 local **police** and probation authorities have been required to set up such joint arrangements to ensure that serious offenders are the subject of appropriate **risk assessment** and **supervision**. MAPPA promotes the sharing of information about offenders between all the agencies.

Offenders are managed at one of three levels. Level One offenders (the majority) are assessed as presenting a low or medium risk of serious harm to others and receive normal management by appropriate agencies. Level Two offenders are assessed as high or very high risk, and have their risk management plans being regularly discussed by regular meetings of multi-agency public protection panels (MAPPPs). Level Three offenders (around 3 per cent of the total) pose the highest risk of causing serious harm: their management involves senior officers and the use of special resources, such as **police** surveillance or specialized accommodation.

multi-disciplinary work work undertaken jointly by workers and professionals from different disciplines or occupations.

In **social work** and in general social welfare provision, there is increasingly an expectation that services will be delivered collaboratively by several agencies or that a particular problem can be addressed only if professionals work together in the same organization or **team** with perhaps a devolved budget. An example of the first approach is **community care** services involving collaboration between social services and health services in relation to vulnerable **older people** or those with chronic **mental health problems** where social workers, health workers and sometimes housing workers may need to work together, but still have their bases in their own original professional agencies. An example of the second is a **child and adolescent mental health team** or **assertive outreach teams**, where social workers may be found in the same **team** as a psychologist, counsellor, community psychiatric nurse and psychiatrist from the same work base. Other examples include **youth offending teams** where a social worker will work closely with a **probation officer**, a **police** officer, representatives from education and health services and sometimes additional professionals. There are difficulties associated with multi-disciplinary work. Sometimes professionals can disagree about the causes of and solutions to problems. They may have different objectives for their work (or their parent organization may have) because of differing professional paradigms. Consider, for example, the differences between the medical model and the **social model of disability**. There can also be relational problems because, for example, of differences in status, **power** and language. Multi-disciplinary work requires effective decision-making and a clear **allocation** of roles and responsibilities. Successive governments since the early 2000s have made it clear that organizations that need to work together to do so in order to bring down the 'Berlin Wall' that has characterized relationships between some agencies especially health and social services. There is increasing evidence that co-training of different professionals where possible helps to emphasize a more collaborative approach to multi-disciplinary working; as does working in the same work base.

Munchausen's syndrome by proxy see fabricated illness

N n

National Assistance Act 1948 a legal cornerstone of the **welfare state** giving **local authorities** the duty to provide residential accommodation for vulnerable adults who need it.

This Act, introduced as part of the welfare state after the Second World War, provides the statutory mandate for the provision of residential accommodation by local authorities to those in need. Under section 21, local authorities have a duty to provide accommodation for people over 18 who 'by reason of age, illness, **disability** or any other circumstances are in need of care and attention which is not otherwise available to them'. The duty is owed to anyone ordinarily resident in the authority's area or who is not so resident but is in urgent need. Much accommodation so provided is found in residential and nursing homes, or special housing, but ordinary housing may be provided if this will meet a need that would otherwise have to be met by other **community care** services. Charging for the care and shelter provided in such accommodation has proved a highly contentious point. Charges must be levied (section 44) for the care provided in such accommodation and local authorities must follow regulations in relation to charges made (Community Care (Residential Accommodation) Act 1998). In the late 1990s, however, a Royal Commission on long-term care for **older people** concluded that personal care should be provided without charge to individuals. Both Scotland and Wales have signalled the intention to follow this recommendation, but in England only nursing care is to be made available free of charge to recipients.

Section 29 of the National Assistance Act gives local authorities both duties and powers to make arrangements for promoting the welfare of disabled people. The duties relate to social work services, **advice** and support, social rehabilitation or adjustment to disability, registers, occupational, social, cultural and recreational facilities, workshops and **hostel**s. The powers relate to holiday homes, travel, assistance in finding accommodation, warden costs, warden services, and information. Section 29 provides a definition of disability that, despite its dated terminology, remains one of the determinants of eligibility for services for disabled people: 'persons aged 18 and over, who are blind, deaf or dumb, or who suffer from **mental disorder** of any description, and other persons who are substantially and permanently handicapped by illness, injury or congenital deformity or such other disabilities as may be prescribed'.

Both section 21 and section 29 are in Part III of the Act, which falls within the definition of **community care** services developed in section 46 of the **National Health Service and Community Care Act 1990**. Eligibility for Part III accommodation is thus determined through **assessment** of needs undertaken under section 47 of that later Act.

National Association of Probation Officers (NAPO)   the professional association and trade union representing **probation officers** and other professional staff in the **Probation Service** in England, Northern Ireland and Wales.

National Association of Social Workers in Education (NASWE)   the professional association for **education welfare officers** and social workers in education settings. NASWE represents its members' interests to the **Department for Children, Schools and Families** and the interests of its primary client group under the slogan 'For every child a chance'. It also promotes professional standards, training and staff development.

National Asylum Support Service (NASS)   the agency that was responsible for establishing the system for providing accommodation and support to asylum seekers under the **Immigration and Asylum Act 1999**. The service is now provided by the UK Border Agency.

National Health Service (NHS)   the organization for the provision of state-funded health care. Established in 1948, the **NHS** aims to provide health care for the entire population on the basis of need. The original intention of the NHS was the provision of health care without reference to a person's ability to pay, based on the belief that expenditure would decrease as the population became healthier as a result of the benefits of the services provided. However, a number of significant problems emerged out of the original structure of the **NHS**. First, the service was centred on existing hospital provision, and there was therefore an uneven geographical distribution of resources. Second, demand for services proved to be greater than anticipated and expanded as new technologies emerged. This resulted in pressures on costs that led to the intention of providing free health care being undermined and the introduction of prescription charges shortly after the creation of the service. Third, with the concentration on hospital services, other areas of provision were overshadowed by developments in surgical and other interventionist procedures. The so-called 'Cinderella' services included care for people with learning disabilities, **mental health** services and provision for **older people**. The NHS became subject to an increasingly frequent series of reorganizations in order to tackle its problems, including the development of health authorities to replace hospital boards and a move to change the balance in resource distribution through the establishment of the Regional Allocation Working Party, which channelled resources towards under-funded areas. More recently, concerns with cost containment led to a major review of the service, resulting in the publication of a government policy statement, Working for Patients, in 1989. The most significant changes introduced by this review included the following reforms: the introduction of an **internal** market in which general practitioners and district health authorities purchased health services from hospitals, creating a purchaser/provider split within the NHS; the establishment of trusts in which hospitals and other services, including ambulance services and mental health hospitals, are managed independently of the health authorities; the introduction for some general practices of budgets that they had to manage themselves and from which they could purchase hospital services, screening services and sometimes the services of social workers and other carers. These changes were criticized for potentially creating a two-tier system of health care in which resources were directed towards those hospital services with trust status and general practices that are budget- or fund holders. Partly because of these changes, the **New Labour** government abolished the internal market and introduced further major reforms.

In 1997 the White Paper *The New **NHS**: Modern, dependable* was published, which replaced purchasing of services by the concept of commissioning. All general practices were to be joined together in primary care groups whose role is to establish local health care needs and ensure that these are met through the commissioning of services from hospital trusts and other service providers. The primary care groups will have representatives from social services and community nurses to ensure that issues around community-based care are taken into account as well as acute services. In 2001 a new reform paper, *Shifting the Balance of Power*, reinforced this development by establishing all primary care groups as trusts by April 2002, thus giving them greater control over their resources and provision. As part of this process, all district health authorities were abolished and larger strategic health authorities were created with a broader role, leaving the **primary care trust**s to concentrate on needs and provision.

The NHS has continued to be both the recipient of significant increases in expenditure and the target for reform and reorganization. As such it maintains its position as one of the most significant areas of political debate in the UK while being well loved by a major part of the population.

Ham, C. (2009) *Health Policy in Britain*, 6th edition. London: Palgrave.

National Health Service and Community Care Act 1990 a watershed Act of Parliament that established the main mechanisms for providing **community care** services for adults with health and **social care** needs.

The legal provision for community care has developed in a piecemeal fashion over many years, with different pieces of legislation reflecting the different policy principles of their time. It has also been a constantly changing picture because of the impact of case-law – judicial interpretation in the Court of Appeal and House of Lords. From 2000 too, the implementation of the **Human Rights Act 1998** has had major ramifications for this interpretation. At the time of writing there are proposals for the reform of this legislation, not only to iron out the inconsistencies in the principles implemented by the different pieces of legislation, but also to bring it into line with the concerns of developments in **modernization policy** to promote **personalization**, prevention of crisis and dependency – the 'inverted triangle of care'.

The Act provides a single gateway for access to a range of services provided under other, in many cases older, legislation. It is an Act of Parliament that was primarily concerned with the restructuring of the **National Health Service**, establishing arrangements between health authorities, general practices and **NHS** trusts, which have subsequently been modified by later reforms. One part of the Act, however, gave to local authority **social services department**s significant new duties, with very important implications for **social work**. The Act arose from the then government's philosophy that tax and hence welfare cuts were necessary, and that a purchaser–provider split, together with a **mixed economy of care** was a more efficient means of delivering cost-effective services to adults with health and **social care** needs, than were previous arrangements. Under previous arrangements, social workers assessed and intervened with need, drawing upon services provided by local authority social services departments. Henceforward, however, social services departments were to become 'enabling' authorities. This involved social workers, renamed 'care managers' implementing an **assessment** and care management process. This first involved establishing need through assessment. Then they would put together 'packages of care' to meet the needs, rather than intervening themselves. These would come from services commissioned by the local authority social services department from a range of providers, with a particular emphasis upon independent sector – private firms and voluntary organizations – agencies. In addition to bringing cost advantages, this was intended to promote **service user**s' choice and greater flexibility in the arrangements to meet their needs. It also meant, significantly, that staff employed by these organizations would not have professional qualifications – and indeed, well into the first decade of the 21st century, as many as 75 per cent of these staff lacked any care-related qualifications.

The emphasis on care in the **community** arose in response to a growing discontent with institutional care and a concern to promote more autonomous, independent lifestyles for people with health and **social care** needs. The guidance accompanying the Act (Department of Health 1990) thus required **social services department**s first, to promote the development of services to enable people to live in their own homes wherever feasible; second, to make practical support for informal **carers** a high priority; third, to make individualized assessment of need and good **care management** the cornerstone of high-quality care; fourth, to promote the development of a flourishing independent sector alongside good-quality public services; fifth, to clarify the responsibilities of social services, so making it easier to hold them to account for their performance; and sixth, to secure better value for taxpayers' money. Modernization policy under Labour governments from 1997 onwards restated these objectives as being to support people not only to live independently, but to access social inclusion; to take active responsibility for their health and their lives through self-care and more **participation** in the community; and to have more control of the care they receive through **direct payments**, and subsequently **individual budget**s. Person centred and individually tailored assessment and care planning was viewed as essential in promoting these principles and implemented in Guidance such as the single assessment process. Policy for informal carers also came to encompass social inclusion besides support in the caring role.

The key to community care service provision is assessment of need. The local authority's assessment duties are contained in section 47 of the National Health Service and Community Care Act 1990. Section 47(1) states: '. . . where it appears to a local authority that any person for whom they may provide or arrange for the provision of community care services may be in need of any such services, the authority: (a) shall carry out an assessment of his needs for those services; and (b) having regard to the results of that assessment, shall decide whether his need calls for the provision by them of any such services.' The duty implies three decisions: Is the person someone to whom provision might be made? What are the person's assessed needs? Is it necessary to meet those needs? Case-law has established that anyone to whom the local authority has the legal **power** to make provision must be assessed, even if services are not available.

If the person being assessed is disabled (within the definition of disability in section 29 of the **National Assistance Act 1948**) then under section 47 there are additional duties on the local authority to undertake an assessment under section 4 of the **Disabled Persons (Services, Consultation and Representation) Act 1986**. This is an important provision for disabled people, making the section 47(1) assessment a duty. Research has shown, however, that disabled **older people** may not be responded to as such, thus denying them their right to an assessment. Section 47 also requires notification to health and **housing authorities** by social services if a person being assessed appears to have needs that could be met by these agencies.

Guidance on assessment issued by the Department of Health when the Act was implemented further states that assessment should actively involve **service user**s and take their views into account; be needs-led, consider risk factors and a range of health and **social care** needs; establish priorities and objectives for intervention; achieve, maintain or restore social independence, normal living and quality of life at home where possible; and be informed by **values** of dignity, fulfilment and choice. Essentially these principles have not changed in Guidance issued under subsequent governments. Once an assessment has been undertaken, professional decision-making establishes which assessed needs meet the local authority's eligibility criteria for service provision. Eligibility criteria formed a further major new requirement of social services departments under the Act, with the aim of targeting services only upon the most needy. Under section 47 of the Act, the local authority is empowered to use eligibility criteria to define the needs it is going to meet, and in Guidance at the time of the Act and previously, it was allowed to take resources into account by these and other means. The Labour government in 2002 established **Fair Access to Care Services**, a national framework for setting eligibility criteria, and determining eligibility in the individual case. Once eligibility for provision has been established, it was expected in the original Guidance that **service user**s should have choice about what particular services will meet their needs, although the ultimate decision on this rested with the local authority. However, the Community Care (Direct Payments) Act 1996 allowed the local authority to offer service users **direct payments** to purchase their own care, and this started what has become under modernization policy and personalization, the main legal and policy expectation for the design of care packages.

The services available to someone assessed as eligible for provision are those that fall within the definition of 'community care services' under section 46 of the **National Health Service and Community Care Act 1990**. These are social care services provided mainly under pre-1990 legislation, although certain pieces of this legislation have been re-drafted since 1990. Broadly, the services that can be provided under this legislation are intended to meet needs related to health finance, education, employment, leisure, accommodation, abilities, transport, personal care and social support. These services, as indicated above, are provided largely by the independent sector. They are regulated by the **Care Standards Act 2000** and by the **Safeguarding Vulnerable Groups Act 2006** – although research conducted into the kinds of services purchased by service users with direct payments and individual budgets suggests they may often fall outside the scope of these regulatory instruments.

The legislation includes: *Part 3, National Assistance Act 1948* includes duties to provide residential accommodation and community services to disabled people; *section 2 of the Chronically Sick and Disabled Persons Act 1970* includes duties to provide a wider range of community services to disabled people; *section 45 of the Health Services and Public Health Act 1968* provides for the **power** (but not the duty) to make arrangements for promoting the welfare of older people; *section 21 and schedule 8 of the National Health Service Act 1977, subsequently section 254 and schedule 20 of the National Health Service Act 2006* include duties and powers to provide for the prevention of illness, the care of people who are ill, and aftercare of people who have been ill, together with home help and laundry services to expectant or nursing mothers, and people who are old, disabled or ill; *section 117 of the Mental Health Act 1983, subsequently the Mental Health Act 2007,* provides for the duty to provide aftercare services for people **discharge**d from compulsory **detention** in psychiatric hospital under certain sections of that Act.

While **local authorities** may not charge for assessment and care management, under section 17 of the Health and Social Services and Social Security Adjudications Act 1983, they may, if they choose, charge for the services they arrange or provide. It is up to local authorities to decide what to charge, but charges must be reasonable and services must not be withdrawn because of inability to pay. Charges can be waived or reduced to what it is reasonable to expect an individual to pay. There are, however, important exceptions to charging. Statutory aftercare services provided under section 117 of the Mental Health Act 2007, and **intermediate care** provisions are exempt.

In the context of resource constraints, the use of eligibility criteria and the purchase of care largely from the independent sector which unlike the local authority relies on income from purchases to stay afloat, many needs have gone unassessed and unmet, and service quality and availability has been in question. As a consequence, case-law judgments have proliferated surrounding the correct balance to be struck by local authorities between taking account of resources and meeting needs. Summary judgments require local authorities to take their resources into account, but not at the cost of neglecting their legal duties around assessing and responding to need. This allows, for example, for a full range of needs, including psychological and emotional needs besides physical needs to be assessed and properly responded to.

Mandelstam, M. (2008) *Community Care Practice and the Law*, 4th edition. London: Jessica Kingsley.

National Offender Management Service (NOMS) an organization set up in 2004 combining the **prison** and **probation service**s. This restructuring, based on the recommendations of the 2003 Carter Report on the management of offenders, was intended to introduce a more integrated approach to offender management. The organization has a regional structure, with a Director of Offender Management responsible for each English region and Wales. It is envisaged that NOMS will in future commission services from both the probation service and the private and voluntary sectors. In 2008, following an internal review NOMS was itself restructured, bringing the **prison** and probation services under a single headquarters.

National Probation Service the unified national structure for the **probation service** created in 2001, replacing the previous system of local accountability. The National Probation Service is now part of the **National Offender Management Service**. Subsequently the Offender Management Act 2007 abolished local **probation board**s and transferred from them to the **Justice Secretary** the duty to make arrangements to provide **probation service**s. The Justice Secretary may in future commission 'probation services' from providers in the public, private and voluntary sectors.

National Service Framework for Older People developed by government to improve services for **older people** and eliminate the **discrimination** against **older people** in health and **social care** services.

To promote improving quality and to tackle existing variations in care, the National Service Framework sets national standards for the care of older people, defines service models, proposes strategies for implementation and sets performance measures against which to assess progress. The framework is directly linked to other policy developments such as maintaining independence by the development of **intermediate care**. It also reaffirms the push for more integrated approaches by health, social care and housing in their responses to service development and the need for greater support for informal carers.

There are eight standards:

1. no age discrimination – only criteria are clinical or assessed needs;
2. intermediate care – reduce avoidable admission to hospital or institutional care through effective rehabilitation and recovery;
3. person-centred care – treat older people as individuals with respect and dignity, involve them in decisions about care and develop a single assessment and integrated care;
4. general hospital care – shorter waiting times in accident and emergency, involvement in discharge planning, better trained staff and care;
5. stroke – action to prevent strokes, access to specialist units, coordinated rehabilitation and support for carers;
6. falls – improved prevention through greater access to health promotion services, specialist assessment and coordinated action to reduce risk, coordinated rehabilitation;
7. **mental health** – improvements in early diagnosis and treatment of **depression** and **dementia**, best cost-effective drug treatments;
8. active healthy life – promotion of health and **wellbeing** of older people, including smoking cessation and flu immunization, wider initiatives such as exercise, healthy eating, keeping warm.

It is worth noting that the standards set by the National Service Framework are primarily focused on the physical independence of older people. While quality of life in older age is affected by physical health, the importance of social inclusion and maintaining socially valued roles does not feature; although for some older people they may be physically able to be maintained at home this may not address their psychological needs.

National Standards for the Management of Offenders detailed criteria for the **supervision** of adult offenders issued by the **National Offender Management Service** in 2007. These replaced the National Standards for the Supervision of Offenders in the Community formerly issued by the **Home Office**. The purposes of national standards are to provide a clear framework of expectations and requirements for **supervision**, to facilitate professional judgement within a framework of accountability, to encourage the development of good practice and to ensure that service delivery is fair and consistent. National standards specify the frequency and promptness with which offenders must be supervised, the expected contents of **pre-sentence reports**, and the planning of supervision, record-keeping and enforcement. The 2007 standards provide a framework for offender management based on **allocation** of offenders to one of four 'tiers' based on a **risk assessment** and an appraisal of the need for offender's **rehabilitation**.

The development of national standards reflects a desire by central government to ensure accountability, consistency and rigour in the work of the **probation service**. Critics argue that they have stifled initiative and creativity in work with offenders and eroded the professional autonomy of field workers.

National Standards for Youth Justice Services detailed criteria for the **supervision** of young offenders by the **probation service** and **youth offending teams** (see also the **National Standards for the Management of Offenders**). They are issued by the **Justice Secretary**, advised by the **Youth Justice Board**. The standards were revised in 2009 to coincide with the introduction of the **Youth Rehabilitation Order**.

National Vocational Qualification (LDSS) the qualification increasingly being obtained by **education welfare officers** at Level 4 for those working in Learning, Development and Support Services. The same generic qualification, with a different specialist pathway is also studied by **Connexions** staff, learning **mentors** and **parenting education and training** workers.

A National Voice the **advocacy** organization for children and young people **looked after** by the local authority. It was established in 1998 with initial funding by the Department for Education and Skills and is managed by looked after children and young people themselves. Since 2006 A National Voice has been a freestanding independent company the aim of which is to ensure that looked after children's and young people's own voices challenge negative perceptions of young people in care. Some of the important functions of the organization are to help young people set up in-care groups and raise awareness about the needs and experiences of looked after children and young people.

needs the necessary requirements for maintaining life at a certain standard. To have a need means requiring something in order to live a life to some agreed standard. This standard may be little more than subsistence living, such as that provided by the 19th-century workhouse for its inmates. Or the standard may be higher and relate to a person's **wellbeing** or fulfilment in life. Maslow suggests that needs could usefully be ordered into a hierarchical continuum beginning with very basic, but essential, needs for food, shelter and safety to 'higher order' psychological needs of belonging, approval, love and finally 'self-actualization'. If these needs are indeed distinctive, the issue for some social thinkers is whether these needs, in part or in whole, indicate some universal functional prerequisites for all societies regardless of their complexity.

Debates over the concept of need always centre on the question of what this standard should be and who should define it. Often the standards for determining need are set by a mixture of influences, such as social consensus, Acts of Parliament, activist groups and professionals in the field. As a result, what constitutes need changes over time. A good example is provided by campaigns against **domestic violence** and the need for physical safety and for safe places, such as a **women's refuge** where women and children can safely stay for a period. Such a need was scarcely recognized a generation ago, although it is now widely accepted. Needs, or what a person requires, are often distinguished in theory from 'wants', or what a person prefers or desires. In practice, however, defining what a person needs as opposed to what he or she wants is fraught with difficulty. For example, a homeless person can be said to need shelter, but shelter can mean many things: a temporary bed in a **hostel**, a room in **bed and breakfast** accommodation, a permanently rented room, a rented flat or an owner-occupied house. What are the real needs of a homeless person and who decides? In the attempt to resolve some of the conflicts over the definition of needs, a classification has been developed by Jonathon Bradshaw consisting of: normative needs, that is, needs as defined by a norm or standard set by professionals; felt needs, which individuals declare as their needs (the same as 'wants'); expressed needs, that is, felt needs turned into a demand through some action; and comparative needs, which are defined by the fact that others, living in the same conditions, have been recognized as having a similar need and requiring a service.

The creation of the **welfare state** in the middle decades of the 20th century focused the discussion of needs around the kinds of services that were available, such as housing needs, income assistance, and long-term incapacitating illness or **disability**. When social workers define need they usually do so on the basis of the definitions used by their agency and from formal guidance issued by government, such as the **Department for Children, Schools and Families** or the **Department of Health**. While most people meet their needs through their own efforts, through family or friends or through arrangements they make themselves, social workers and **social care** professionals often work with **service user**s who, for a variety of reasons, have many basic needs that they have not been able to meet themselves. Workers decide what these needs are through **assessment**. In doing so they often have to consider a broad range of needs, such as physical care, the provision of shelter and food, cultural and religious sustenance, emotional and psychological needs arising from isolation or violent personal relationships, and social contacts. Very often people in the same household have different needs that have to be met in different ways. Because needs are so much a matter of interpretation, it is essential that service users should participate in the process of deciding what their needs are, and that their wishes and preferences be taken into account. Welfare professionals have in the past often interpreted a person's needs in terms of the services that they could offer. Thus a frail older person might have been assessed as 'needing' a place in a day-care centre or in a residential home, rather than the worker looking at what specific care needs he or she had and then deciding how these might best be met. The only way to overcome this is to consult closely with users, to include their wishes and preferences and to think how they might be most suitably met.

Social workers are continually involved in assessing needs of the people they work with. When working with children and families social workers focus on the care and developmental needs of children in order to ascertain whether a child's development is broadly in line with a general norm of health and welfare. The needs of a child or family are assessed according to the **framework for assessment of children in need** by a social worker and others before the family can receive services to help them look after that child. Typically these needs may include such factors as any lack of skills on the part of the child's parents, as well as any educational or health needs the child might have. When working with adults, practitioners concentrate on those needs that will allow an older or disabled person to live as independently as possible. The **Department of Health** has outlined six broad areas of adult need that should be assessed: personal and **social care**; health care; accommodation; finance; education, employment and leisure; transport, **mobility** and access.

Needs can be met only if resources are there to enable this to be done. Because resources are so limited, social services professionals have often used a system of prioritizing needs and of developing criteria for eligibility. This invariably places greatest importance on the need to protect the health and physical safety of the client and less importance on those needs that would improve the person's wellbeing but are not essential to physical survival. At the same time, there are opportunities to widen the definitions of need. Groups of users are urging this across a number of services, including those for children and families, disabled people and people with **mental health problems**. Such groups can be involved in setting local policies on need, since **community care** reforms in particular envisage a growth of new services from the independent sector. (See also **assessment**, **common assessment framework**, **needs-led assessment**, **single assessment process**, **special educational needs**.)

needs-led assessment an **assessment** that defines an individual's real **needs** and not just his or her needs in terms of services that the local authority has to offer. Before the passage of the **National Health Service and Community Care Act 1990** need, it was argued, was defined in terms of the services the **local authorities** had to offer. Thus a person with a **learning disability** was declared as 'needing' a place in a training centre, regardless of whether the centre helped such people overcome their **disability**. The individual's need was defined in terms of the service available ('Mr X needs a place in a day centre') rather than in terms that specified the needs of the individual ('Mr X lacks the skills to make basic purchases at his local shop and needs to acquire those skills'). The tendency to define need in terms of available services was heavily criticized as a way of protecting the interests of local authority staff. On this basis, the beds of residential units were filled, as were places at day centres, thus apparently demonstrating users' 'need' for such establishments.

Those arguing in favour of the reforms under the Act claimed it introduced the concept of needs-led assessment, that is a person's real needs would determine the service response and not be governed by the routine and limited services provided by the local authority or health service. One of the basic reforms aimed to make the assessment function independent of providing a service so that an independent judgement of need could be reached, taking into account the person's own view, instead of his or her needs being expressed simply in terms of existing service interests. For example, a frail, older person who is socially isolated may have a need for regular social **contact** that could be met by arranging regular outings with family or friends rather than by offering a place in a day centre. It is debatable however as to whether these reforms actually allowed practitioners to undertake authentic needs-led assessments that noted needs specific to the individual and a budget to allow them to respond to those needs by whatever means necessary. A number of barriers thwarted this desirable objective. First, it became clear from research throughout the 1990s and beyond that budgets remained tightly controlled at senior levels within **social services department**s and failed to devolve to practitioner level so that a social worker's discretion as to how a need should be met was highly constrained. Second, preoccupation with risk, whether in relation to children or **older people**, meant that safeguarding services which essentially focus on relatively small groups of users (compared for example to the large pool of users who have everyday needs for social interaction, leisure pursuits, maintaining ties with family) received larger shares of budgets at the expense of informal, community-based groups which could have met these kinds of needs. In current practice the notion of **personalization** is attempting to restore something of what was intended in the earlier reforms – a framework for responding to need in ways that allows the user to define and direct how their needs will be met.

neighbourhood a geographic zone or area that is continuous and small enough for residents to have some familiarity with one another, with local landmarks, institutions and organizations such as schools or shops. A neighbourhood is smaller in size than other common spatial areas such as a district, **community** or city. It may be based on recognized common boundaries, whether physical, such as roads, or cultural, such as ethnic make-up, or by social **networks** and local associations, income levels or housing tenure. Usually a person's home is the central reference point for determining a neighbourhood for that person. However, neighbourhoods can be defined in other ways, for example on the basis of a single economic function or dominant business activity. Often neighbourhoods do not have precise borders but are informal judgements about where one small area begins and another ends. Accumulating evidence shows that the area where a person lives profoundly affects their life chances and opportunities, referred to often as 'neighbourhood effects'. The differences among neighbourhoods, in terms of institutional resources, patterns of social organization and social networks, levels of community safety, quality of physical environment and levels of trust, either support or undermine how people are able to overcome difficulties and develop resilience. The concept of 'neighbourhood effects' refers to the powerful environmental impact that living in a particular area has on the health, **wellbeing** and **life course** of individuals who live in that area.

William Wilson's classic study *The Truly Disadvantaged* first outlined the structural dimensions of those neighbourhoods where a high concentration of low-income people live, the ghettos of Chicago, and how this geographic isolation of the poor, from services, jobs, education and labour markets shaped the behaviour of all the residents living there. Wilson discovered that the structure of forces in these neighbourhoods – such as the **discrimination** by employers towards residents, the total lack of investment, the lack of jobs and job opportunities, the poor levels of services in health and education, the social isolation and lack of transport, the 'redlining' by mortgage companies (the informal practice of estate agents which stops mortgage lending in specific low income areas) – narrowed individual choices and undermined residents' lives at every turn regardless of individual character and behaviour. Such deprivation, Wilson noted, especially impacts on unskilled young men who encounter so many barriers to the labour market that they adapt to a different, often criminal lifestyle. In such neighbourhoods the middle class withdraws, social and economic isolation increases to constrain significantly the life chances of children and families who reside there. The concept of neighbourhood, like **community**, has only recently re-emerged as a focus of **social work** concern. The idea that **social work** should focus on a single small area fell from favour from the late 1980s, partly because of the pressure to focus on individual risk and protection and partly because of increasing specialization around groups of users rather than geographical areas. There was also distrust within the profession of the very notion of 'neighbourhood' and 'community', which were seen as potentially repressive entities intolerant of difference or behaviour outside certain norms.

Pierson, J. (2008) *Going Local: working in communities and neighbourhoods.* London: Routledge.

neighbourhood forum a semi-formal organization bringing together the representatives of local organizations, users and residents to express their opinions on services and projects. Neighbourhood forums in particular have become prominent as one way of consulting local people and to hear neighbourhood opinion. They have a semi-formal role in current regeneration initiatives and in some best-value reviews, where they are usually organized around particular subjects of local concern – young people, **community** safety, job development. Neighbourhood based initiatives often rely extensively on the work of forums to bring plans together and to monitor progress. On the basis of the trust developed in that process, the forums' roles are formalized; they received their own devolved budgets for implementation of their sector of the plan while remaining accountable to the **partnership** board.

neighbourhood management team a multi-disciplinary **team** that organizes and coordinates services in a given locality or neighbourhood.

Restructuring services around a neighbourhood agenda has become an important element in the strategy of public services in tackling **social exclusion**. The concept of 'neighbourhood management' best embraces what these new developments are trying to achieve. Neighbourhood management brings together several threads in the fight against **social exclusion**:

- local government **decentralization** – physical, administrative and political;
- interagency working and joint planning;
- drawing mainstream service budgets into activity that counteracts disadvantage.

The **Social Exclusion Unit** laid out the key elements of neighbourhood management in its *National Strategy for Neighbourhood Renewal* in 2000. These include:

- a neighbourhood board involving residents, the local authority, other public agencies, and the voluntary and private sectors to plan and steer a programme of local regeneration;
- a multi-agency **team** to deliver the plan to address joblessness, community safety, poor housing and poor health, with an emphasis on building human and social capital as a way of overcoming these problems;
- provision of accessible services that are integrated with continuously improving **outcomes** for local people;

- services that place an emphasis in their practice on prevention, drawing on evidence of 'what works';
- building capacity by preparing residents to participate in strategy development and local control to the maximum that they are able;
- 'bending' mainstream programmes of the principal services so that they routinely target resources in areas of greatest need and in ways that have maximum impact.

The development of neighbourhood management teams inevitably means a changed relationship between frontline practitioners and management. Neighbourhood teams require devolved budgets (with which social services already has some valuable experience, as does education) to the front line, with the teams then held accountable for achieving holistic outcomes that actually show up in the improvement of quality of life and the promotion of inclusion in the locality. This can then lead to pooled budgets in which service agencies and local authority departments look at the combined resources at their disposal and then, after discussion and the creation of jointly agreed action plans, proceed to commission the services required. To be effective, such neighbourhood teams will often deploy local 'one-stop shops' from which people can find advice for navigating the various service systems, advocates who will speak and work for their objectives as well as access to services themselves – whether family support, **social care** or housing. They also typically will need high levels of **participation** by local residents and users in determining service strategies and yearly action plans. (See also **neighbourhood forum**.)

Taylor, M. (2000) *Top Down Meets Bottom Up: neighbourhood management*. York: Joseph Rowntree Foundation.

neighbourhood renewal rebuilding both the physical and social fabric of a **neighbourhood**. Neighbourhoods where there are high concentrations of people living below the **poverty** line have a range of social problems that impinge on every person who lives there, whether individually poor or not. Such neighbourhoods are generally found in the decaying owner-occupied or privately rented terraced housing of older cities and the peripheral housing estates that ring many of Britain's urban areas. Social theorists use the phrase neighbourhood effects to describe this impact that a neighbourhood has on the lives of residents. For instance, decaying or abandoned homes and buildings have a severely negative effect on the morale of residents, providing a major incentive to move elsewhere. Highly disadvantaged neighbourhoods also frequently lack organized activities and **community** facilities. As a result, residents do not see themselves as being in control and what they want is to have influence over regular services rather than special projects. Neighbourhoods do matter to residents, however, and it is wrong to characterize disadvantaged areas as lacking social cohesion and interaction that survive in difficult places. What cuts a disadvantaged neighbourhood off from the economic, social and political activity of the city or region within which it is located? The nature of the housing and physical layout has much to do with it. Social housing has become a residual service, that is, an under-resourced basic service for those individuals and families who could not find housing in other parts of the housing system (in the main through home ownership). As a result, certain low-income groups are channelled towards specific areas within a local authority area. The consequence is a rise in the number of people in **poverty** and households where no one is working. There may also be a rise in vandalism, making housing hard to let, with tenants wanting to stay for as short a time as possible. Shops close, and amenities such as playgroups for children disappear. The social fabric of the estate – the way people relate to each other and the strength of local organizations such as residents' associations and clubs – is also weakened.

Pierson, J. (2008) *Going Local: working in communities and neighbourhoods.* London: Routledge.

networking the process of linking together individuals, groups and/or communities with common interests in order to spread information, knowledge, resource sharing, and mutual support. It assumes that there networking increases the capacity for problem solving, to meet organizational or individual challenges and to promote a common aim.

networks the web of social relationships through which people are connected. Networks exist in relation to individuals and families as well as entire neighbourhoods. They also exist for specific groups of people, for example gays or lesbians, or around the workplace or shared interests or predicaments. When working well, networks transmit certain forms of trust and commitment. Network **poverty**, on the other hand, is centrally a deficit in the means of securing trust and is strongly associated with a culture of fatalism in which people have little trust either in the reliability of systems or of other persons.

Social networks vary considerably in their impact on specific individuals and families. Networks are not confined simply to 'close personal relationships'. They may provide support or undermine, be plentiful or virtually non-existent, close and intense or far-flung and distant. The quality and purpose and functioning of networks varies dramatically whether in the numbers of people involved, the degree of interconnectedness and frequency of contact, the quality and duration of the relationships and the degree to which they are supportive or undermining.

There are various ways of describing and measuring the characteristics of networks. One helpful distinction is to think of networks for 'getting by' and those for 'getting ahead'. They are very different and perform very different functions.

Networks for getting by are the close supportive networks embedded in everyday relationships of friends, neighbourhood and family. When we think of the social supports offered by extended families and friends or by close-knit communities – these are networks for getting by. They can supply gaps in childcare, look after a person when he or she is ill, provide small loans and cash to make ends meet and participate in family celebrations or rites of passage. Social workers have an interest in how networks for getting by are viewed by the people with whom they are working. They may be seen as affirmative, nurturing or accepting or as antagonistic and inaccessible. At their very worst they can be sources of heavy responsibility, aggression and scapegoating. Understanding how natural networks function help us to better understand the distinctive characteristics of socially excluded and isolated individuals and families.

Networks for getting ahead provide crucial information for individuals and families on jobs, education, training and on a range of options for advancing one's interests. In many ways they are the opposite of networks for getting by but can achieve so much more. They are more occasional and episodic in nature and are more tenuous than a close personal relationship. They may be based on 'someone who knows someone' about a job possibility or on the links obtained through a skills agency half a city away which a person visits only occasionally. But such networks can be very powerful when finding a job or a place on a training programme.

A number of structural factors dramatically affect the kinds and quality of networks that a person has, such as income, educational background, age, gender, **disability**, ethnic origin and employment. As a person moves through old age they tend to have smaller, less reliable networks, while people with higher incomes, in employment and with higher education tend to have richer social networks.

Networks can be crucial to families in their struggle to care for children or older dependent adults. Taking stock of these networks jointly with family members should be part of a routine assessment, and an important part of **social work** practice should be to facilitate the growth of networks. Network mapping, capitalizing on existing strengths within networks for getting by, creating new **networks** around existing points of service, such as **children's centres** and schools, or using **mentor**s and **volunteers** are all approaches that social workers should be developing.

They are particularly important when working with individuals that employment gatekeepers view stereotypically as ill-equipped for the jobs market, such as young males – Black and white – or disabled and **older people**. Using an **ecomap** or **social network map** helps in this work. The map collects information on the composition of the family's network and also the extent to which the networks are supportive or undermining or conflicted. By simply putting initials or first names of people into the various segments network members are recorded in any of these seven areas: household or people lived with; family/relatives; friends; people from work or school; people from clubs, organizations or religious groups; neighbours; agencies and other formal service providers. Once the strengths and weaknesses of a family's network is clear, practitioners can use the map to ask further questions regarding the nature of the network relationships. These cover the types of supports available, for example, whether they provide information or emotional support, how critical a member of the network might be and the closeness or intensity of the relationship, or other features such as frequency of **contact** and length of relationship. Although any one map is constructed from the point of view of a single family, through use practitioners will become more familiar with the different characteristics of families' networks. These include the size, perceived availability of different types of support through the network, the degree of criticism that networks contain and the extent of reciprocity.

Pierson, J. (2009) *Tackling Social Exclusion*, 2nd edition. London: Routledge.

neuroses traditionally understood as a group of **mental disorder**s, including **depression**, **anxiety**, **phobia**s, hysteria, psychosomatic disorders, eating disorders like anorexia nervosa, obsessional compulsive disorders, post-traumatic stress syndrome and adjustment reactions (see **mental health problems**). There have, however, been important challenges in recent years to the use of these categories in relation to mental health problems, and there have been shifts generally, in the way mental health problems and their symptoms are understood and responded to in **mental health policy** and services. People do, however, undergo experiences which correspond to the symptoms traditionally linked to neuroses. Although they are often regarded as less serious than those linked to **psychoses** – for example, Schizophrenia – this cannot be assumed: very often their consequences for the person's life, coping and risk to self and others can be just as serious. Workers respond to neuroses as they do to other mental health problems: in this they have important statutory roles, and have much to contribute to **service users' wellbeing** and greater control over their lives.

New Labour the term given to the new policy orientation that the Labour Party adopted from the mid-1990s on to underscore the changes that took place in the organization of the Party and on traditional issues such as public ownership and taxation. The Labour Party found itself out of office for 18 years after the Conservatives gained **power** in 1979. A series of general election defeats and significant internal battles had led some to believe that the party had become unelectable. Battles between the left and the right of the party in the 1980s resulted in an internal split (giving birth to the Social Democratic Party), a serious conflict over the election of the Deputy Leader and efforts to exclude the far left. The leadership of Neil Kinnock, the late John Smith and then Tony Blair saw a series of victories for the centre-right of the party in their efforts to regain power. One of the most important events was the decision in the 1990s by the leadership to remove Clause 4 of the party's constitution, which committed the party to the public ownership of the means of production and tied the party in the public's mind to nationalization of key parts of the economy. However, the apparent success of the Conservative government's policy of privatization, in particular the sale of council houses to their occupants, led many at senior levels in the party to believe that Clause 4 was a key obstacle to re-election. The combination of these events led the party to reposition itself towards the political centre, although for some in the party this was in reality a shift to the right and the acceptance of key elements of the Conservative agenda, notably an increased role for the private sector in the delivery of services, a closer relationship with employers and the business **community**, and a low-tax economy. These policies were seen by senior members of the party as important in their election success in 1997 and their continuation in power.

For social services and the continuation of the **welfare state**, the acceptance of the core features of this agenda, including an increased role for the private sector and a low-tax regime, presents a significant challenge to more traditional Labour views about the role of the state in the provision of welfare services. Increased resources are part of the New Labour policy for health and **social care** but only in exchange for a modernization of these services, making increased use of performance measurement and a more managerial approach. For traditional Labour supporters and many workers within the public sector, the maintenance of aspects of Thatcherite policies is seen as highly problematic and creates tensions within the Labour movement as a whole, including relations with public service workers' trades unions. With the change in Prime Minister from Blair to Gordon Brown some saw a return to aspects of an older Labour tradition. However, the impact of the Credit Crunch and the resulting economic downturn has for many seen the possibility of such a change of direction put on hold while the consequences for the public sector economy are worked through.

Giddens, A. (2007) *Over to you Mr Brown*. Cambridge: Polity Press.

new youth justice the system of **youth justice** introduced by the **New Labour** government after 1997 by means of Acts such as the **Crime and Disorder Act 1998** and the **Youth Justice and Criminal Evidence Act 1999** and other reforms. The system involved new court orders and measures such as **reprimands, final warnings** and **referral orders** along with new institutional arrangements including **youth offending teams, youth offender panels** and the **Youth Justice Board**. Its underlying principles included the prioritization of preventing offending by young people, a wish to see young offenders held more responsible for their behaviour, an emphasis on early intervention (see **zero tolerance**), and a secondary and subordinate emphasis on **reparation** and **restorative justice**.

Goldson, B. (ed.) (2000) *The New Youth Justice*. Lyme Regis: Russell House.

night shelter temporary accommodation for homeless, usually, single people. Such **hostel** accommodation is invariably very basic, often organized in dormitories and, as the name implies, unavailable for shelter in daylight hours; people are usually asked to leave the premises by 9.00 a.m. Meals and bathing facilities are often available too, and some night shelters have second-hand clothing stores. Night shelters are mostly offered by the voluntary sector, with religious organizations like the Salvation Army playing a prominent role. Staffing is often dependent upon the efforts of **volunteers**. A limited number of night shelters have connections with longer-term housing projects that seek to help provide more stability in relation to accommodation for the rootless. A particular voluntary organization, Night Stop, has developed over the past decade or more where private households, with a spare bedroom or two, will offer emergency accommodation to young homeless people for a few nights. Informal night shelters are also often offered by faith based institutions, especially for destitute **asylum seekers** who have exhausted the appeals processes but have not yet been 'removed' from the UK. (See also **vagrancy**.)

non-molestation order one of a number of remedies in the Family Law Act 1996 available to **victims** of **domestic violence**. A non-molestation order prohibits a respondent from molesting another person who is associated with the respondent, or a child. An order can be made, with or without a specific application being made. Typically, orders are made in the course of **family proceedings**, including proceedings in which the court has made an **emergency protection order** under the **Children Act 1989** section 44 which includes an **exclusion requirement** (as defined in section 44A(3) of that Act). In some cases a court is obliged to consider making a non-molestation order, for example if it is considering whether to make an **occupation order**. A non-molestation order may be expressed so as to refer to molestation in general, to particular acts of molestation, or to both; and it may be made for a specified period or until a further order is in place. **Breach** of an order is now a criminal offence, and a person guilty of the offence is liable on conviction on indictment to **imprisonment** for up to 5 years; or on summary conviction for a term not exceeding 12 months or a fine or both.

no recourse to public funds (NRPF) not eligible to claim welfare benefits or social housing. Typically the disentitlement is a reflection of the person's immigration status. For example, a sponsored wife brought from abroad is unable to claim benefits for 2 years so that if the **marriage** breaks down within that period when she already has a baby she will need to seek support under the **Children Act 1989**. Similarly failed single asylum seekers may be supported under the **National Assistance Act 1948** if they have care **needs**.

normalization a service philosophy that emphasizes access to lifestyles that are valued by society as a whole for people with **learning disability**. Normalization is based on the assumption that integration with non-disabled people and the **adoption** of societal norms of behaviour are likely to lead to greater acceptance and respect for people with learning disability. It arose from the recognition that the regimes in which people with learning disability lived made it impossible for them to live ordinary lives and therefore added to their **stigma**tization. The concept was originated by Wolfensberger in Scandinavia and further developed in North America. Wolfensberger later referred to '**social role valorization**' (SRV), by which he meant 'the creation, support and defence of valued social roles for people who are at risk of devaluation'. Challenges to normalization have come from both the **social model of disability** and from minorities using learning disability services. Both sets of challenges have identified the emphasis on social conformity as problematic. For example, women with learning disability may be expected to adopt behaviour based on dominant gender **stereotype**s, and Black and minority ethnic people may find themselves subject to white norms.

Advocates of the social model of disability argue that the social barriers experienced by people with learning disability should be tackled directly and that social acceptance should not be conditional on 'normal' behaviour or roles. Such critics point out that **normalization** is not a means for promoting respect for diversity. The methods used by Wolfensberger to assess services are known as **'pass'** and **'passing'**. They focus on how far services enhance the social image and personal competence of users. In this context, the promotion of age-appropriate behaviour is seen as important. Despite these reservations, normalization and SRV have been associated with a greater recognition of dignity and choice in service provision and integration into mainstream services and leisure activities for people with learning disability. It has been pointed out that normalization is managed by service providers and does not arise out of **service user** activism. It has been associated, however, with greater access to **advocacy** and more participative forms of **assessment** and planning.

No Secrets guidance on developing and implementing multi-agency policies and procedures to protect vulnerable adults from **abuse** (Department of Health 2000). Abuse is defined generally as a violation of an individual's human and civil rights by any other person or persons, and can take many forms: physical, sexual, psychological, financial or material, neglect and **discrimination**. It is recognized that the abuser could be a member of staff within an existing service, another professional, a **volunteer** helper, another **service user**, a relative or spouse, a 'friend', carer, neighbour or others intent on targeting vulnerable people for means of exploitation. The policy examines the roles and responsibilities of agencies in **adult abuse** investigations, such as health, housing, and **police**, with the local authority taking the lead role. If there are concerns that a criminal offence has been committed the **police** should be informed and plans for the protection of the vulnerable adult put in place. The level of vulnerability of the person, the nature and extent of the abuse, the length of time the abuse has been occurring, the impact on the individual and the risk of repeated or increasingly serious acts are all factors to be taken into account. **Confidentiality** should be preserved within a clear line of **communication** and discussion of factors and detail amongst designated and appropriately identified people.

Any intervention must be seen to be in the best interests of the individual and in the best interests of the public when considering prosecution. One of the challenges here may be if the alleged perpetrator is also perceived as a vulnerable adult, therefore meeting criteria under the **National Health Service and Community Care Act 1990** or indeed if the alleged perpetrator is the main carer for the vulnerable adult who would otherwise be unable to care for themselves independently. These real issues can create ethical dilemmas in practice. This document has now been built upon with *Safeguarding Adults: a national consultation on the No Secrets guidance* launched in 2008.

Department of Health (2008) *Safeguarding Adults: a consultation on the review of the No Secrets guidance.* London: HMSO.

not in education training or employment (NEET) collective term for young people between 16 and 19 who have finished school and have not, for various reasons, gone on to college or university or found employment or a place on a job training programme. Central government has long focused on this group, variously estimated at roughly 5 per cent of 16-year-olds but as high as 15 per cent of 17-year-olds, as vulnerable to **social exclusion** in later life. In its reform of education and training that followed from the White Paper *Education and Skills 14–19* in 2005 it set out plans to extend the period of compulsory training and education for all young people. The '**participation** age' – that is being in full-time education or training – is to be raised to 17 in 2013 and 18 in 2015. It is recognized that the traditional academic route for post-16 education is not what all young people want and so a number of routes or pathways have been established with the intention of providing appropriate choices that guarantee quality. The reforms should result in flexible options including study that could lead to higher education, study that directly supports vocational training and apprenticeships in the workplace. (See also **Connections**.)

nurseries facilities providing supervised **early years** care and education for children from soon after birth until they start school (usually around the age of 5). The government guarantees some free nursery hours for all 3- and 4-year-olds. From 2010 that will be 15 a week delivered flexibly over a minimum of 3 days.

Most nurseries are provided by private companies or through the **Sure Start children's centres**. In planning, delivering and assessing care and education, **nurseries** are bound by the requirements of the **early years foundation stage**. Mostly relatively young women have staffed the **early years** sector – in part because the pay is low and hours are often long. Rates of pay are commonly in line with the national minimum wage. This has meant that standards of care and provision have been variable – as young, inexperienced workforces have struggled to meet the requirements of owners, parents and policymakers. All nurseries are subject to the **Ofsted inspection** regime and reports are published. Nurseries have to comply with adult:child ratios that depend on the ages of the children but in any space there should be at least one nursery nurse for every eight children.

Government has recognized that the early years workforce needs to be better trained and rewarded. There is a target that by 2015 all nurseries employ at least one member of staff educated to graduate level and qualified with Early Years Practitioner Status (EYPS). This status typically requires 9–12 months further training for graduates. Otherwise most nursery staff will have qualifications at NVQ levels 2 or 3. The children's centres model for nurseries – which is endorsed in the **Childcare Act 2006** – requires that nurseries work in a more collaborative, holistic fashion. This will put additional pressures on nursery staff to work alongside social workers, health visitors and other welfare professionals.

O o

occupational therapy a rehabilitative profession concerned to help people recover from illness or to adapt to or cope with a **disability**.

The key objectives are optimal personal functioning and thus **independent living**. Occupational therapy is one of the three rehabilitative professions recognized by the **National Health Service** (with physiotherapy and speech therapy). It is equally represented in physical medicine and psychiatry. Occupational therapy services are also provided by **social services departments**. Occupational therapy has a practical emphasis and is concerned with the problems and activities of daily living. In hospital settings with the focus on physical problems, occupational therapy typically includes retraining for daily living skills (for example, washing and dressing), the prescription of therapeutic activities (for example, artwork, woodwork, group discussion) and provision of orthotics (for example, splints) and prostheses (for example, walking sticks and wheelchairs). In psychiatry, occupational therapy is concerned with the provision of therapeutic activities, skills training for a return to the **community** and possibly some aspects of psychotherapy. Patients within the **community** receive occupational therapy from **social services departments**. A wide range of aids and adaptations to buildings to enhance daily living and the quality of life are the major concerns for this work. Close collaboration with social workers within adult teams is necessary for the effective **assessment** of **needs**.

occupation order one of a number of orders available to assist **victims** of **domestic violence**, including partners and children. An occupation order can regulate who is to live in the family home. It may also restrict abusers from entering an area near the home. Applicants must normally have a legal right to be in the home, for example as a joint tenant; or the applicant must be the spouse or domestic partner of the owner or tenant. The order may be subject to conditions, for example that the applicant takes responsibility for the rent of the property.

offending behaviour programme a training programme for offenders
(typically based on **cognitive behavioural** principles) which seeks to
challenge and alter the offenders' attitude towards offending and thereby
alter their activities and patterns of behaviour which lead to the
commission of offences. Such programmes are offered both in **custody**
and in **community** settings; in the latter case offenders may be obliged
to attend by a **programme requirement** in a **community sentence**.
Programmes may focus on general offending, violence (including anger
management training), **sex offending, substance misuse** or **domestic
violence**.

**Ofsted (Office for Standards in Education, Children's Services and
Skills)** the body that inspects schools, other children's services and **local
authorities** and publishes reports on its findings aimed at improving
standards. **Inspection**s may also be carried out through partner providers.
Ofsted has also taken over the duties of the previous inspection regime for
social care, including **safeguarding** and **children's homes**.

older people the term now widely used in practice, in preference to
'elderly' or 'old people', to refer to those who may have age-related **needs**.
The phrase 'older people' is commonplace in **social work, social care**
and health care for the good reason that it is less **stigma**tizing than the
alternatives. It is difficult to say precisely at what age a person becomes
'older' but that is the point behind using the phrase: it is a relative
designation that allows for flexibility of application and a great range of
capacities and competences. As a result it is more inclusive and does not
stigmatize the way the phrases 'old people' or 'the elderly' do. While one
could say that in general the term applies to people of state pensionable
age (for men at 65, women at 60 but rising to 65 in the future) it usually
refers to people older than that. As a rough rule of thumb, from the age
of 70 onwards individuals may well be regarded as 'older' in certain
dimensions of their life – as a parent or driver for example – without being
considered so in other areas, such as consumer of health care, jazz
musician, religious leader or judge. The different aspects of identity and
functioning only differentially become 'older' as the person's **life course**
progresses.

  The **wellbeing** of older people hinges on elements of life that most
citizens of any age want: to participate, to be interdependent and be
able to engage in reciprocal social relationships. Survey research has
repeatedly shown that older people want to be seen as full citizens of their
communities and not just as consumers of health services. They want to be
able to create their own options and to be in full control of their lives.
Dignity is highly valued and preserving it should be defined as an outcome
in its own right. Easily eroded, it is hard to shore up after it has been

diminished. Dignity is constitutive of identity, autonomy and control. But this is jeopardized by a lack of **community** focus and the absence of structured choice within that community – diminished by being patronized, excluded from decision-making and being treated as an object. The Green Paper on adult services, *Independence, Wellbeing and Choice* (Department of Health 2005), promotes specific **outcomes** for older people: independence through choice and personal control, equal opportunity for work, **participation** in society without facing discriminatory hurdles, intentional or unintentional, improving health and quality of life, enabling people to make a positive contribution and have choice and control, ensuring freedom from **discrimination** or **harassment**, economic wellbeing and maintaining personal dignity.

Social networks can offer concrete forms of support, whether emotional ties or material aid such as **contact**, visits, errands or phone calls on behalf of an older person. Such networks are, however, subject to a range of variables – size, density, composition (in terms of roles, gender, age, material resources) and geographical spread of members. The capacity of networks relies on the strength and continuity of these personal ties – but also on the ideas and views that those in the network have about how much support should be offered and how much accepted, and the **values** and **personality** of the person at the centre.

For practitioners aiming to strengthen parts of a network it is important to configure what effect each element of the network will have on **outcomes** such as dignity, independence and participation. To achieve this, elements of networks such as brokering roles, network reach, boundary spanners and peripheral players need to be clearly identified along with the specific kind of social sustenance they provide. Identifying the extent and capacities of support and care networks can only be done with a thorough knowledge of local resources, connections between community groups and the role of informal carers. The most effective way is to establish specifically who is part of the network and who thinks of themselves as part of the network and then ask what the capacity of these network members is to undertake the care tasks.

The White Paper on health, *Our Health, Our Care, Our Say* (DH 2006), has emphasized the necessity of moving social services and health services to a preventive orientation and working for improvement in adults' wellbeing. It envisages new roles for social workers as navigators and brokers for local authority adult services, while relying on the voluntary and community sector not only to provide services but also to be advocates for individuals and innovative practice. Such an orientation requires considerable changes. The trend in services for older people is to offer fewer services at higher cost. Disabled people discover this when crossing the age line – turning 65 – and suddenly find they are classified as 'older people' by **social services department**s with an accompanying lower level of service than they had previously received. While home care plays a critical role in preserving independence – every unit increase of home care the likelihood of remaining at home rises by as much as 8 per cent – pressures on the home care services has led to a bureaucratic, impersonal style of delivery that is risk averse and leaves little time for staff to focus on anything other than personal care.

Effective **day care** services, home care and chiropody can all be said to support wellbeing, but independence requires more than that. Fear of crime, poor transport and inaccessible buildings also undermine independence and choice. Prevention in the context of older people's services means taking action in the present to prevent the need for intensive or intrusive interventions in the future. In contrast to children's services, what is being 'prevented' is not the loss of developmental capacities early in the child's **life course** but a forestalling of the intrusiveness, loss of dignity and stripping of autonomy which accompany institutional intervention such as enforced hospitalization and entry into residential care with the consequent loss of network and onrush of social isolation. Preventive practice means tackling **social exclusion** and the **stigma** of **ageism** in order 'to build community capacity and to support communities of interest, as well as geographical communities to look after and manage their own affairs'. By itself **social care** cannot address this scale of task but has to work with other sectors of the local authority, all departments of which should be consulting **community care** user groups.

Choice in services is often difficult for older people to exercise since it involves pulling triggers in systems which, though familiar to the practitioners, are quite unknown territory for users. Users are quite prepared to enter into choosing services and, moreover, prepared to spend their money in pursuit of those choices, but not where they are uncertain about what they are getting. Numerous obstacles remain to older citizens understanding the care system, primarily to do with **values** and culture of the systems they become enmeshed in. A basic feature of public-sector care is that health care is generally free at point of use while **social care** levies a charge. While this is clear to practitioners it is not always so to users. The care management role remains shadowy, even confusing, and providing information on its own is not sufficient to overcome this.

In any case user difficulties with the system are not to do with practicalities of care so much as with the emotional difficulties that follow in the wake of the disturbances to their known and scripted routines. To remedy the situation, advocates have proposed walk-in community centres offering **mental health advice** and access to specialist services, more psychological treatment and wider user choice. The aim is to change the system previously geared to risk management and acute illness into one that meets the **needs** of people with long-term or more common **mental health problems**. Within such an arrangement 'access workers' would provide entry to the system rather than GPs. The centres would act as a base for health, social care and voluntary sectors, and provide information and support focusing on physical and **mental health** and wellbeing. (See also **elder abuse, No Secrets, outcomes.**)

ombudsman a government official who investigates complaints of maladministration made by members of the public against statutory authorities, including, for example, complaints about delays in dealing with claims for a benefit or a service. The system is based on a Scandinavian model.

The ombudsman does not investigate any matter where there is a right of appeal. If the ombudsman finds that there has been maladministration, he or she will recommend action by the authority, including an apology and possibly compensation. The Parliamentary and Health Service Ombudsman investigates complaints against the various executive agencies of the **Department for Work and Pensions** and HM Revenue and Customs. The Local Government Ombudsman investigates complaints against **local authorities**; these complaints should first of all be made directly to the authority, but, if still dissatisfied, the complainant can then approach the ombudsman. The Housing Ombudsman Service is for complaints about registered housing providers, which include **housing association**s and social landlords other than local authorities. All the ombudsman services have their own websites.

organization theory attempts to understand how organizations work with respect to their internal structures and processes, both formal and informal, and their external relations.

In relation to social welfare agencies, policymakers have been concerned to answer several related questions. First, how can services be organized and delivered most effectively? Second, what structures will be most supportive of workers in what are widely recognized as stressful occupations? Third, how are social welfare agencies to relate to **service users**? Fourth, how are social welfare organizations to relate to each other? **Social services department**s have experimented a lot in the past few decades to try to develop more effective models of service delivery. Three kinds of models have emerged. Departments using 'functional' arrangements are organized into sections based on setting – typically fieldwork, residential and day-care services. Other functional sections might comprise research, **inspection**, staff development, and so on. Departments increasingly structure services around 'client groups', with the integration of all residential, fieldwork and day-care services for each client group in one section of the organization. Finally, some have a 'geographical model', dividing up the organization into smaller units that then usually employ either the functional or client group models. In practice, hybrids of various kinds are often devised. Research seems to indicate that client/service user group models work best because all resources for a case are contained within one section of the organization. Such a model, however, is not without its difficulties: how are services to be organized, for example, when two client groups are involved in one case such as some childcare problems because of concerns about a parent's **mental health**?

Most social welfare workers have a clear preference for flat hierarchies; that is, they appear to want few levels or tiers within the organization. Such arrangements give them access to decision-makers and make plain where the responsibilities for decisions actually lie. Similarly, they want direct access to support staff without having to go through intermediaries. For example, a worker with a case of child **sexual abuse** will wish to consult with the department's adviser without complex referral systems to that adviser. 'Chains of command' vary a lot within welfare and justice agencies. Some agencies operate almost as collectives or with one manager only (often in the voluntary sector); others may have as many as seven or eight tiers (typically some social services departments) with many with fewer tiers as with probation departments.

Service users will wish to have reasonable access to services. Agencies should pay attention to the siting of offices in relation to populations and to public transport routes. Many social services departments have devised outposts for isolated communities, and in large densely populated areas neighbourhood offices may offer the first point of contact with several local government departments. Policies to promote access frequently include the provision of transport by the social welfare agency. With the efficient coordination of services as the objective, it is clearly advantageous for welfare and justice agencies to have the same area boundaries. With some functions this has proved possible, but with others both boundaries and forms of accountability vary significantly. Some organizations are accountable to local government, others increasingly to central government or to **quango**s. Where these organizations also have different boundaries, coordinating mechanisms are required. Not surprisingly, the service user, required to deal with two or more agencies, can be confused. (See **multi-disciplinary work**.)

outcomes identified universal aspects of **wellbeing** that collectively services are aiming to achieve for the people they work with. More and more government has attempted to frame its policy objectives in terms of outcomes, that is those aspects of wellbeing that are defined to be what we all want for ourselves. While the concept of outcomes can be critically analysed it does mark a shift away from the idea that providing outputs from a service is *per se* of a benefit to those who receive the service. For example just because a frail older person has two days a week attendance at a day centre (an output) does not automatically mean that their sense of wellbeing, of social engagement, of cleanliness and self-respect are improved. The latter are outcomes and provide the test of whether the day centre is achieving what the **service user** wants. The five outcomes for children promoted in **Every Child Matters** – being healthy, staying safe, enjoying and achieving, making a positive contribution and achieving economic wellbeing – constitute a kind of definition of wellbeing for all children against which services now measure their effectiveness. Regardless of the service, whether school, **youth justice**, health and sexual health promotion they all are to aim to see that children enjoy good physical health, are safe from abuse and exploitation and show better behavioural and cognitive development than they would have otherwise enjoyed had they or their families not received those services. Outcomes now also shape work with young people. In addition to the five outcomes for children there are others expressly set out for young people in the Green Paper *Youth Matters*: improve a sense of security, self-efficacy and the capacity to plan their future; secure the assets, or 'human capital', they need to reach adulthood, particularly requisite levels of education; achieve a sense of wellbeing and the capacity to form relationships and ultimately households and/or families. In pursuing these outcomes, social work should focus on providing support for the key transitions facing young people such as **independent living,** finding a place in the world of post-16 education and/or training. This includes helping them to secure a decent income that enables them to make a real choice as to whether to find work or pursue education, and if the former to decide what work they are best suited for. The Green Paper on adult services, *Independence, Wellbeing and Choice* (DH 2005), promoted similar outcomes: independence through choice and personal control, equal opportunity for work, **participation** in society without facing discriminatory hurdles, intentional or unintentional, improving health and quality of life, enabling people to make a positive contribution and have choice and control, ensuring freedom from **discrimination** or **harassment**, economic wellbeing and maintaining personal dignity.

overpayments – criminal liability in addition to civil liability for overpayments, a person who has received overpayments may be liable, in some circumstances, to criminal prosecution. In particular, under the Social Security Administration Act 1992 a person who has made dishonest representations in order to get benefits or tax credits, or who dishonestly fails to give prompt notification of a change of circumstances affecting entitlement (for example by failing to report that he is in remunerative work, or living together with a partner who is in remunerative work or who has access to capital in excess of capital limits) may be prosecuted. In some cases a **caution** or penalty may be given instead of the matter proceeding to court.

P p

paedophile a **sex offender** who commits sexual crimes against children under the age of 16. Such crimes can involve a high degree of coercion, secrecy and cruelty, and can cause lasting psychological and physical harm. Offences range widely and include meeting a child following 'grooming', sexual assault, sexual activity with a child, and rape.

Public and professional interest in paedophiles has expanded enormously in recent years. This has been prompted by several factors, including high-profile murders of young children by known paedophiles, the arrival of the internet, which provides a means for paedophiles both to **contact** one another and children themselves, and the exploitation of children by paedophiles who had found employment in children's homes and schools. The paedophile has been described as the 'folk devil' of today, serving as a convenient focus for public hatred. In the 1990s and 2000s, some newspapers waged vigorous campaigns to 'name and shame' paedophiles, in some cases 'outing' individuals by publishing names and photographs, arguably encouraging vigilantism.

Within the UK **police**, a Child Exploitation and Online Protection (CEOP) Centre has been established to tackle paedophile crime. Official interest has focused not only on paedophiliac assaults themselves, but also on the commercial sexual exploitation of children, which includes the prostitution of children and young people, the production of child pornography and its distribution via the internet, and specialized operations such as Operation Ore have targeted the consumers of internet child pornography. Like other **sex offenders**, paedophiles can be made subject to **sexual offences prevention orders** and placed on the **Sex offenders Register**.

A long-running controversy surrounds the question of whether local communities should have the right to know whether a convicted paedophile is living locally. In the USA, laws collectively known as 'Megan's Law' establish such a right, and in the UK campaigners including Sara Payne (mother of Sarah Payne, abducted and murdered by a known paedophile in 2000) have urged the enactment of a similar 'Sarah's Law'. Proponents of such a law contend that parents have the right to know and thereby to safeguard their children from danger; opponents claim that such information will be of no practical value to parents and that providing it will encourage vigilante actions, hamper the rehabilitation of offenders and lead to greater numbers 'going underground', avoiding any monitoring or surveillance and devoid of support. In 2008 the government introduced very limited pilot projects giving parents the right to ask the **police** whether or not a named person who has **contact** with their children is a known sex offender.

Paedophiliac orientation is not an illness which can be cured but part of the **personality**. Available evidence suggests that paedophiles do not respond positively to traditional therapeutic interventions, such as individual psychotherapy. **Sex offender treatment programmes**, based on **cognitive behavioural** principles, are thought to offer more promise.

Howitt, D. (1995) *Paedophiles and Sex Offences Against Children.* Chichester: John Wiley.

palliative care defined by the National Institute for Health and Clinical Excellence (NICE) as the active holistic care of people with advanced progressive illnesses. The aim of palliative care is the best quality of life for seriously ill people and their families and or **carers**. Palliative care is best understood as a very specialist part of supportive care. NICE describes supportive care as helping patients and their families cope with the illness and treatment of the condition, 'from pre-diagnosis, through the process of diagnosis and treatment, to cure, continuing illness or death and into **bereavement**. It helps the patient to maximize the benefits of treatment and to live as well as possible with the effects of the disease'.

Supportive care is supposed to include helping the patient to help themselves and involving them in all stages of diagnosis and treatment. The provision of clear information to help patients make informed decisions is seen as key. Other aspects of supportive care include symptom control including the use of complementary therapies, rehabilitative interventions where possible, the use of social and spiritual supports and finally end of life and post-death support for family and carers. Whereas supportive care admits of the possibility of recovery, palliative care does not. Palliative care includes many aspects of supportive care but, according to NICE, it places special emphasis upon 'affirming life and to regard dying as a "normal" process; to provide relief from pain and other distressing symptoms; to provide integrated psychological and spiritual supports; to offer other supports to help patients live as actively as possible until death; and finally to offer help to families and carers so that they can cope with the patient's illness and death as well as possible'.

Palliative care is provided by specialist teams comprising health and **social care** professionals with, sometimes, the addition of personnel representing various faith groups. These will include doctors, nursing staff, social workers, counsellors and sometimes physiotherapists and **occupational therapists**. Palliative care teams work in hospitals (sometimes in specialist units), hospices and often in the **community** supporting patients in their own homes. It is also often possible for patients to spend time in several locations depending upon issues concerned with managing the condition, providing intensive therapies, giving respite for both patients and families or carers. Although hospices are often used to support patients in the very last weeks of life, many patients use hospices for much shorter periods and sometimes as day patients usually returning to their homes. The modern hospice movement began in the UK with the work of Cicely Saunders. She established a hospice in south London in the 1960s, but the hospice movement has grown rapidly in the UK and there are estimated to be well over 200 units for adults and about 40 dedicated to children. Saunders' work still had care of terminally ill people at the hands of medical and health staff at its core but its focus shifted in very important ways from the illness to the person experiencing the illness. This led to her involving other professionals including religious personnel together with counsellors, social workers and others to attend to other matters of importance to the dying person. Most hospices are located in communities although some can be found within the grounds of hospitals or even as specialist wards within hospitals.

Although some hospices are wholly funded by the **National Health Service** the majority have to raise most of their funds from charitable sources. Services to patients however are entirely free. Hospice services include a number of beds for the use of patients who are close to death, others that will be for short-term use as respite services as well as 'day-care' units where patients can access specialist services such as counselling or physiotherapy or simply to take part in various social and leisure activities with other patients. Many hospices also have their professional staff working with patients sometimes in the hospice and sometimes in their own homes. Patterns of attendance of patients vary; some patients might use a hospice for just a few days and others for many years.

Children's hospices now routinely deal with children and young people with conditions such as motor neurone disease, cystic fibrosis and muscular dystrophy which usually lead to shortened lives, but may take several decades before death occurs. For these young persons a normal day might entail attendance at school before going to a hospice for a few hours for various therapies or just some fun.

Some have argued that hospices are part of attempts to manage death in ways which marginalize and exclude the dying and in some more general sense 'sanitize' death itself. The hospice movement however argue that they are acknowledging the inevitability of death in an open and honest way, that hospices are not closed institutions and that they seek to work with terminally ill people and their families and carers in a holistic manner and that crucially they address the expressed **needs** of patients. The evidence suggests that many terminally ill people do value the range of services and the holistic intentions of hospices and others prefer the seclusion of home and family as they approach death. With a society that is rapidly ageing it has to be acknowledged that many dying people will have no close family to support them and that hospices can make a real difference to end of life experiences. (See also **death and dying, loss, bereavement and grief**.)

Connor, S. (2009) *Hospice and Palliative Care*. London: Routledge.

parental responsibility as defined in the **Children Act 1989** spans the rights, duties, powers, responsibilities and authority that in law parents have in relation to their children.

The term is used in sections 2, 3 and 4 of the Act to emphasize that parents have inescapable responsibilities when bringing up children and so should not view the relationship with their children as based solely on the concept of parental rights. Parental responsibility is automatically conferred on both parents of a child as long as those parents were married at the time of the child's birth. If the parents are not married at the time of the birth, both parents acquire responsibility as long as they have jointly registered the child's birth. If this has not happened, only the mother has automatic parental responsibility; the father does not and can acquire responsibility only through a court order or by agreement with the mother.

A parent who has parental responsibility for a child cannot lose it except through **adoption**. It can be shared, however, delegated by a parent or acquired by others who are not the child's parents. For example, foster parents who have **looked after** a child for a period of time can acquire parental responsibility through a **residence order**, and the local authority itself acquires parental responsibility when it holds a **care order** on a child. In both instances the parents do not lose parental responsibility but have to share it with the foster parents or local authority.

Knowing who does or does not have parental responsibility for a particular child is extremely important for social workers and other care professionals working with families. Although the **Children Act 1989** does not define what the specific responsibilities are, people with parental responsibility have an important role in decision-making concerning a child who is being looked after by a local authority. They also have certain rights to maintain contact with a child unless there are compelling reasons why they should not do so.

parent education and training services that help parents and prospective parents understand key aspects of parenting in order that they might become more effective carers of children. These services seek to help parents to understand the emotional, intellectual, physical and social **needs** of children as well as their own needs. Such services seek to enhance the relationship between parents (or their surrogates) and the children for whom they have responsibility. The over-arching objective is to assist parents to help their children to achieve a mature and independent adulthood. In the past decade there have been persistent calls for the creation of a range of accessible services to assist parents with parenting. This loose movement has been driven by a number of concerns.

First, many commentators have pointed out that, in the past, most adults have assumed the role of parent without any formal education or training to help them prepare for parenthood or to assist them when they encounter difficulties. Second, it is acknowledged that parenting is a complex process, especially in stressful circumstances or where children have particular kinds of problems or needs. Most parents appear to benefit from opportunities to discuss their problems and to learn from the experiences of others. Third, many have argued that statutory childcare services have been preoccupied with child protection at the expense of family support services. Family support services, it is held, are perceived as less **stigma**tizing than having social workers intervene in the lives of families. As a result, such services are thought capable of playing an important preventive role so that more complex and entrenched parenting and childcare problems are less likely to develop.

It is useful to distinguish between 'support for parenting' and 'support for parents'. The first refers to services that have the parent–child relationship as its focus. Such services can be generalized in nature or be concerned with problems of varying seriousness. Hardiker's typology of services is useful in this context. She distinguishes between primary, secondary, tertiary and post-crisis services. Primary services are concerned to convey basic skills in parenting, as with the health visiting service or a parenting education programme offered by the local adult education college. Such first-line services are open-access in character, designed to inform parents and would-be parents about some of the common problems and some of the solutions to successful parenting. Secondary services are designed to assist parents with some identified problem that the parent is keen to resolve, say a young lone parent is consulting a doctor because her child is very wakeful at nights and she is exhausted. Tertiary services are those designed to deal with serious problems, such as parenting in a household where there is **domestic violence** and **emotional abuse** of the child or in another household where the parents of a multiply disabled child cannot cope. Post-crisis services refer to work with parents following some critical event, such as an admission of a parent to a psychiatric hospital, a child being taken into care or a woman and child retreating to a women's refuge.

Hardiker argues that parents should have reasonable access to such support services and that statutory and voluntary agencies should work together to provide them within a coherent and planned framework that takes account of local needs. Services to 'support parents' are those that have a direct bearing upon parents as individuals but which may fundamentally affect parents' abilities to parent. Such services focus upon an adequate income, affordable and quality childcare services, family friendly employment practices, good housing, effective health and education services and reasonable **play** provision for children. The need for these kinds of services is located in a view that emphasizes the importance of the social and economic context to parenting. This view also underlines the need for governments to foster both kinds of services, for to emphasize parents' responsibilities for their children without providing them with the resources to do the job adequately might be regarded as oppressive.

There are many kinds of parenting problems. Some are located in special needs that children might have, such as autism, some in a parent's behaviour, condition or social context, such as a health problem or being imprisoned. Recent reports from the Social Services Inspectorate, based upon **inspection**s of a wide range of **social services department**s, have identified particular clusters of problems that have been recognized as being especially complicated. The same reports have found that **social work** services, both statutory and voluntary, dealing with these problems are often inadequate or poorly coordinated. The reports have highlighted **domestic violence, mental health problems** in parents, drug-abusing parents, parents with learning disabilities, teenage parents, parenting after **divorce** or separation (including step-parenting) and children with multiple disabilities as key areas warranting better services both to help parenting and to support parents. At least some of these difficulties in service provision arise out of the separation of children's services from adult services in social services departments. There is now a widespread consensus that coordinated services to support parenting are needed. These services should take a holistic view of parents' needs, should include fathers and men yet to be fathers, should offer a range of services to deal with broad-based parent education as well as services to offer support to parents in times of stress and crisis, should be non-stigmatized and should try to promote the idea that to want to seek **advice** about parenting is normal rather than exceptional. All these principles are to be fostered by the new government **Sure Start** programmes and the National Family and Parenting Institute.

parenting contract a **written agreement** between a school and a parent aimed at improving a child's behaviour or attendance. These contracts are voluntary but further sanctions such as **exclusion from school** or **prosecution** of the parent under the **Education Act 1996** could follow if the situation does not improve. Some parenting contracts may also involve officers of the local authority where there are wider issues to be considered.

parenting order a court order (introduced by the **Crime and Disorder Act 1998**) requiring parents and guardians to participate in activities aimed at preventing their child from committing crime or disorder. Such activities include counselling and guidance (once a week for up to 3 months) designed to improve their parenting skills. Additional requirements such as school attendance or the child being home by a certain time can be added for the total length of the order (a maximum of 12 months). Orders are enforced by **youth offending teams**, and parents who fail to comply with an order can be **fined**. A parenting order can be made if the child is convicted of an offence or is made the subject of an **anti-social behaviour order**, a **child safety order** or a **sexual offences prevention order**, or if the parent has failed to secure the child's regular attendance at school. Clause 9 requires that, where a child under 16 has been convicted of an offence and the court is satisfied that a parenting order would help prevent a reoccurrence of the offending behaviour, the court shall make a parenting order. It also: requires that the court shall take into account information about the family circumstances and shall explain the effect and consequences of the order to the parent in ordinary language before making the order; allows the court to **discharge** or vary the order in certain circumstances; and provides for a **fine** not exceeding level 3 on the standard scale (currently £1,000) for a parent failing to comply with an order. Clause 10 provides for an **appeal** against parenting orders.

parent partnership service a service that must be provided either by a local authority at 'arms-length' or independently and that offers advice, support and information to the parents of children with **special educational needs** (SEN). Provision will also include procedures for resolving disagreements between schools, **local authorities** and parents about the provision that is being made available for individual children as an alternative to using the more formal process of the SEN tribunal.

parole **early release** from **prison** granted at the discretion of the **Parole** Board, a body whose members include judges, psychiatrists, **probation officers** and criminologists. Under the **Criminal Justice Act 2003**, the Parole Board now only decides on the release of **prison**ers serving **sentences of life imprisonment** and **imprisonment for public protection**, although it still also deals with the cases of long-tem prisoners sentenced under previous legislation. The Parole Board is independent of the government, but is bound by directions issued by the **Justice Secretary**; these state that the Board must primarily focus on the risk of future offending. In existence since 1967, the **Parole** Board's procedures were originally highly secretive, and its decisions could be overruled by the Home Secretary. Over the years, and especially as a result of test cases under the European Convention on Human Rights (see **Human Rights Act 1998**), its procedures have been progressively 'judicialized' and brought more in line with normal standards of 'natural justice', while the powers of the Secretary of State (now the **Justice Secretary**) to veto its release decisions have been removed.

participation 'taking part in'. In **social work** practice this is understood to mean the process of involving **service user**s and carers in the decisions that affect their lives and achieving change.

Defining exactly what is meant by the term 'participation' is problematic, since terminology such as 'participation', '**partnership**', 'involvement', and '**Working Together**' can invariably be used interchangeably in relation to the involvement of service users in decision-making and have become integrated into social policy and service provision. Principally, however, *participation* describes an activity where people using services are involved in influencing and changing their lives where previously they had little control or influence.

The level and nature of participation may vary from 'taking part in' or 'being present at' to knowing that one's actions and views are being taken into account and might be acted on. These are significant differences indicating what occurs and the associated levels of activity (or passivity). Service users may participate as individuals in decisions concerning their lives (agreeing personal care plans; attending decision-making meetings); as individuals in wider events (focus groups or consultation events), through membership of an organization – where service users have formed an identity (a **self-help** group or user-led organization), or as a representative of a wider grouping (a network for carers or local **community** group). Participation may be a single event or ongoing. For example questionnaires and feedback forms, focus groups and group interviews, or consultation events provide an opportunity for a number of people to contribute their views. On the other hand people who live in residential care may have regular group meetings, service users may choose to join subcommittees and working groups, be part of a newsletter group or be regularly involved in specific activities such as recruiting and training staff.

Discourses of participation acknowledge the complex power relations present in a given situation. Participatory practice is therefore a dialogic process professionals listen to and respect the views of service users or carers and are open and honest in their **communication**s. The relationship then is neither a hierarchical one between professionals and service users nor is it an approach where the professionals relinquish their **power** completely. Rather, it is one where professionals are reflective and reflexive in their relations with service users and carers with the notion of participation linked to the institutional contexts of practice. (See also **Arnstein's ladder, neighbourhood management teams**.)

McPhail, M. (ed.) (2007) *Service User and Carer Involvement: beyond good intentions*. Edinburgh: Dunedin Academic Press.

partnership a working relationship that involves a number of different organizations in formal or semi-formal arrangements in which goals are agreed upon, some resources are pooled and common strategy planned. A partner may be defined as 'one who has a share or part with others', implying that there is an overall goal or framework of which individual partners are aware although each partner may be responsible for implementing a different part of that strategy. Successive governments have invoked the concept of partnership when proposing ways that services and different professions should join together in tackling specific problems. Over the last two decades government has strongly encouraged a partnership approach to service provision: **youth offending team**s, **children's centres**, resettling **older people** at home after a stay in hospital, employment and training for socially excluded individuals, **community** safety and crime and disorder. Virtually all aspects of **social work** and **social care** now include an element of partnership working – in joint **assessment** of **needs**, in providing social care at home, in work with young people.

Partners that are frequently linked together in providing services are: **local authorities**, which are often the dominant or leading players in local partnerships and have developed experience in partnerships for delivering services; public service agencies, such as the **police**, the health service, local schools, and **social services department**s; voluntary sector agencies, whether large and well known or small locally based organizations representing specific groups in the **community** or providing specific services, for example an **Asian** women's refuge; local community organizations, such as tenants' or residents' associations, which bring local knowledge and experience to bear on the needs of specific local constituencies and neighbourhoods; the private sector, which can embrace a range of employers, job trainers, consultants and other experts.

Partnerships have become central to resolving social problems because of their sheer complexity. Tackling **social exclusion**, securing the full development of the child under 5, addressing **anti-social behaviour** and youth crime, providing for the needs of older people all have many strands to them – beyond the capacity of any one service organization to address on their own. Historically the major public services have had a particular culture interested first and foremost in their own set of responsibilities and concerns. It proved difficult for them to step outside this perspective and view social problems as rooted in many different causes. Linking services within a partnership structure facilitates a collaborative, holistic approach to complex problems. Partnerships are also needed to improve coordination. Users may have several different services circling around them each claiming a need for information particular to them and each wanting to collect and assess their own information.

Effective partnerships are often built on the following:

- developing standards of success that relate to creating awareness and supportive local attitudes (although relatively intangible) rather than tangible units of service;
- choosing a base for organizing efforts – a neighbourhood, demographic group or cluster of professions;
- balancing this organizing with service delivery demands and not letting the latter drown out the former;
- sharing leadership and roles of influence as the collaborative constituency building evolves;
- bridging class, racial and ethnic divides.

Communication, cooperation and coordination are crucial to success. Different tasks can be allocated among individuals with the various skills to contribute. Sometimes collaboration means recognizing differences and finding ways to accommodate those differences. Each partnership should undertake a self-study of preferred styles – reflecting on their own styles and those that they feel most comfortable with.

Forming partnerships does not in itself guarantee smooth collaborative working or achieving stated objectives. At times they may be worse than no partnership at all. For example they may exist only on paper simply to provide a smokescreen for capturing resources. Or the individual organizations in a partnership may have vastly different levels of influence allowing dominant agencies to smother the interests of smaller, often community-based organizations. Centrally imposed conditions for bidding for partnership funding carry their own drawbacks. These often stipulate a short time-frame for submitting applications giving considerable advantage to those major agencies with a specialized workforce and the capacity to do the hours of necessary planning and report writing. Local organizations, users and residents usually have no such resource to fall back on so for them to enter into a partnership on equal terms is difficult.

Douglas, A. (2007) *Partnership Working*. London: Routledge.

pass and **passing** methods of determining a service's quality by measuring how far that service meets criteria associated with **normalization**. The techniques of pass and passing are proposed by their authors as suitable for assessing services for people from any devalued group, but are most commonly employed with regard to people with **learning disability**. They focus on how far services enhance two main areas affecting **service users**: their social image and their personal competence. Pass and passing are similar, but passing includes only measures of normalization, while pass includes additional criteria associated with service quality. Workshops are utilized to train people in these assessment techniques.

Wolfensberger, W. and Thomas, S. (1983) *Passing Program Analysis of Service Systems' Implementation of Normalization Goals*. Ontario: Canadian National Institute of Mental Retardation.

pastoral support programme (PSP) a programme of support designed by a school, in consultation with parents and others, to assist a child at risk of **exclusion from school** and to promote improvement in his or her behaviour in order to prevent the need for more serious sanctions. Some schools may use an **individual behaviour plan** or other mechanism instead for the same purpose. Other professionals should be consulted, with parental permission, and involved in the programme where they are working with the family. Such a package of support should normally have been attempted by the school before permanent exclusion becomes appropriate, unless the child has committed a very serious **breach** of the school's discipline policy, usually involving violence or supplying drugs. Where complex problems exist, it may be more appropriate for the school to make use of the **common assessment framework** rather than acting in isolation.

patriarchy any form of social system whereby men achieve and maintain dominance over women and younger men in relation to social, familial, economic, political and cultural institutions.

Sociologists, especially feminists, have emphasized the negative aspects of patriarchy perceiving it as likely to keep women in subordinate positions in many societies and in all aspects of life. Further they argue that patriarchy prevents women from exercising full equality of opportunity and that as a result women's life chances are seriously curtailed. Younger men too are seen to be controlled by patriarchal systems although such control is seen as less pervasive because as men age they assume **power** that is denied to most women.

Although violence or its threat is regarded as underpinning patriarchy, it is reinforced through multiple systems, especially the control of media and **ideology**. In relation to **social work** there are many examples of patriarchy 'in action'. Some have pointed to the workforce in health and social work organizations being predominantly female and yet senior managers being mostly male. Others point to the attention that women attract in **social work** 'surveillance' and that women blaming is rife in relation to lone-parenthood, to lone parents who work (neglectful mothers) and lone parents who do not (welfare dependent). Yet other problems include **domestic violence** and the widespread **abuse** of women including deaths and the consistent inadequate responses of welfare and justice services in relation to issues such as rape. The lack of representation too of women in positions of power in politics, religious institutions, trade unions, law and the economy is seen as definitive, as is women's relatively low income especially in work considered to be 'women's work' even though it is often both demanding and crucial to society.

peer group a group of people with the same social standing or status.

Although peer groups are thought to be especially influential among young people, the term has general application to other age groups. Peers may be a specific group (such as colleagues in a **social work** organization) or a wider group (such as the **social work** profession in general). Both groups can act as reference points for individuals, enabling them to make judgments about how they are faring in some particular respect. Judgement by peers is regarded as a crucial part of being a professional, in relation both to education and training and to disciplinary matters.

By far the greatest attention has been paid to adolescent peer groups and the effect they have on the behaviour of young people. While such an effect is often the source of worry for professionals, parents and the public at large, it is by no means clear that peer pressure always has a clear negative impact on adolescent behaviour. Voluminous research on the subject suggests that many young people do go through an experimental phase, partly in response to peer pressure and expectations, which may entail risky or anti-social activities. But there is also well-documented recognition that such responses increase towards mid adolescence and then diminish as a sense of individual identity and the importance of social roles and achievement in the context of class and gendered expectations becomes dominant. Most young people become less dependent on the affirmation of peers rather than small friendship groups. However, in very deprived communities **peer group**s in the shape of gangs can be more persistent in terms of their longevity and be more anti-social too in response to socially excluded lives.

penalty notice for disorder (PND) see fixed penalty notice

penalty notices (for unauthorized absence from school) provision under the **Anti-social Behaviour Act 2003** which enables a local authority, usually through the **education welfare service**, to issue parents with a penalty **fine** in response to **unauthorized absence** from school. This process is an alternative to court action but still results in a conviction for the offence. The **fine** is currently £50 per parent and per child if paid within 28 days and £100 if paid within 42 days. If the parent chooses not to pay then **prosecution** under the **Education Act 1996** must follow. A penalty notice must be paid in full, not by instalments, and there is some evidence that some parents choose to go to court and argue their case there. This may result in a larger fine but with a negotiated arrangement available about paying it over a longer period. Some **local authorities** have targeted their use of penalty notices on particular schools, or on parents who have taken their children on holiday in term-time without the school's permission. Others use them as part of their overall **casework** response to unauthorized absence. A local protocol must set out the arrangements. See also **prosecution**.

persistent absence individual pupil absence from school at a rate of 20 per cent or more, i.e. less than 80 per cent attendance over the school year. This is the key focus for **local authorities** (National Indicator 87) to reduce the number of pupils in secondary schools under 80 per cent attendance to no more than 5 per cent of pupils in any school by 2011. While there is no formal target for primary schools, local authorities will be working towards the national average of around 2.5 per cent of pupils. This priority will largely determine the workload of the **education welfare service** rather than absence at a less significant level. This measure relates to the overall percentage, both **authorized absence** and **unauthorized absence** totalled together. Pupils at risk of falling below this level of attendance (the equivalent of missing one day a week or one whole half term in a year) should be identified by schools and plans put in place to promote improvements. There has been a significant shift away from focusing only on unauthorized absence in recent years. While only unauthorized absences can constitute an offence by the parent, evidence suggests that if a school authorizes absence too readily, this may adversely affect overall attendance, even if unauthorized absence is low. Schools have been encouraged to be more robust in challenging explanations for absence that may not be appropriate. Consequently there has been a rise in the level of unauthorized absence, sometimes presented by the media as a rise in **truancy**, but there has also been a rise in total attendance in recent years. The concern now is much more about those pupils who miss a substantial amount of their education, whatever the reason for their absence. The annual performance tables for schools no longer publish the level of unauthorized absence but the total. This has enabled many schools to be more pro-active, especially where absences might previously have been authorized without question.

persistent offenders offenders who commit crimes repeatedly (also known as 'recidivists'). Persistent offenders, even those whose crimes are relatively minor, are likely to receive disproportionately severe **sentences** as a result of accumulating a lengthy list of previous criminal convictions. A very high proportion of people in **prison** are recidivists, and this contributes greatly to prison overcrowding. Persistent offenders have been a particular focus for attention by the **New Labour** government, who have always insisted that persistence should indeed be a ground for more severe treatment, even for those individual offences that are relatively trivial. This approach is defended by claims (disputed by some) that 100,000 offenders are responsible for half of all crimes. The **Criminal Justice Act 2003** provided that a poor previous offending record should be regarded as a factor aggravating the seriousness of the current offence and hence leading to more severe **sentences**, while schemes targeted upon persistent offenders include **intensive supervision and surveillance programmes** for young offenders and Prolific and Priority Offender Schemes for adults.

Garside, R. (2004) *Crime, Persistent Offenders and the Justice Gap.* London: Crime and Society Foundation.

personal assistant an employee who carries out specified tasks under the direction of a disabled person. This may be in order to facilitate **independent living** or to enable the employer to participate fully in the workplace. Disabled people have argued that in order to gain autonomy and social **participation** they need to have control over their support and the way it is provided. Until recently it was assumed that they needed the services of 'carers'. The concept of personal assistance, however, better describes a relationship in which the disabled person is in charge. In the workplace, help with funding for personal assistants may be obtained from the **Department for Work and Pensions. Social services departments** may provide **direct payments** for **community care** services, and these may be used by disabled people to pay personal assistants. Sometimes personal assistants are employed by an organization managed by disabled people, such as a Centre for Independent Living, on behalf of the **service user**. These organizations, however, also provide support to disabled people so that they can themselves fulfil the responsibilities of being employers. Disabled people have reported that they are more able to maintain autonomy and the lifestyle of their choice when they have a personal assistant in comparison with conventional care arrangements. It is also easier to change a personal assistant if the arrangement has not worked well.

Priestley, M. (1999) *Disability Politics and Community Care*. London: Jessica Kingsley.

personal education plan (PEP)   a plan outlining educational provision for a child of **compulsory school age** who is **looked after** and which deals with any necessary changes in the light of events, such as **exclusion from school** or change of carer. All children of school age in the care system should have a PEP. Standard proformas are usually available in each local authority area. The responsibility for initiating the plan lies with the appropriate social worker, in close collaboration with the child or young person's school, where a particular member of staff should have a designated role in supporting all the looked after children. The PEP should be reviewed six-monthly in conjunction with the young person's care plan.

person centred planning   a planning style mainly associated with **learning disability** services. This focuses on improving the quality of a person's life in a way that is grounded in her or his own perceptions and goals rather than those of professionals or others.

While traditional styles of planning in learning disability services tend to start with professional assessments of ability and what needs to be done to increase 'independence', person centred planning begins with who the person is and what her or his aspirations are. This is by no means straightforward, as many people with learning disability have become used to deferring to the goals of others and some do not use traditional means of **communication**. An important starting point in any attempt to make planning person centred, therefore, is to assist people to share and communicate their preferences and hopes for the future. Person centred planning is, therefore, grounded in self-determination and **self-advocacy**. It often involves bringing together those people who are important in the life of the person with learning disability, or who have the **power** to bring about the changes that are necessary if the identified goals are to be met.

There are several styles of person centred planning, the best known being Path, Personal Futures Planning, Maps and Essential Lifestyle Planning. Sanderson and colleagues (see below) describe these as different lenses for looking at a person's life. The White Paper *Valuing People* (2001) endorses person centred planning as the way forward in learning disability services. Guidance issued by the **Department of Health** stresses, however, that it is not just a new way of doing individual programme planning or care management and assessment. For example, care management and **assessment** may be triggered by person centred planning where this has revealed a need for services. The Department of Health stresses that person centred planning involves continual listening and learning about a person's aspirations and working towards these with the support of family and friends. It also stresses the importance of good facilitators, many of whom are currently found in service-providing agencies, including **advocacy** organizations. It is not to be seen as an end in itself, however, and current government statements suggest that the quality and outcome of person centred plans are more important than generating large numbers of plans as a 'paper exercise'.

The government has prioritized certain groups for early access to person centred planning. It hopes this will be available for everyone still living in long-stay hospitals and for young people moving from children's to adults' services by 2003. It is envisaged that people using large day centres, living in the family home with carers, aged over 70, and people living on National Health Service campuses will be able to use person centred planning by 2004.

Official guidance distinguishes between person centred planning and person centred *approaches*, which refer to service planning and commissioning that are carried out in collaboration with **service users** and which reflect their views and aspirations. **Valuing People** should be implemented at local level by groups that include people with learning disability and use person centred approaches.

Thompson, J., Kilbane, J. and Sanderson, H. (2006) *Person Centred Planning for Professionals*. Buckingham: Open University Press.

personality those aspects of an individual's character that remain relatively permanent across different situations.

There is a debate over the degree of permanence and how to describe an individual's personality. At one extreme, some theorists have argued that an individual differs so much between situations – for example, with friends, family or at work – that there is no element that is constant. The ways of describing personality range from classifying people according to type, such as an authoritarian personality, or according to a set of traits, such as neurotic and extrovert, to the ideographic approach that one should not try to classify people but treat them as individuals. A further debate concerns whether the structure of personality has unconscious elements. Psychoanalysts such as Freud and Jung have suggested that some parts of personality are unconscious. Numerous methods have been employed to assess personality, ranging from clinical interviews to paper-and-pencil tests, and the method adopted reflects the theoretical position of the designer.

Psychometricians such as Cattell and Eysenck utilize questionnaires containing explicit questions about a person's behaviour. These questions have been selected partly to reflect the specific structures that the designer of the questionnaire believes to constitute personality and partly through a statistical technique called factor analysis, which helps to identify the most useful questions to address such structures. An alternative approach, employing a projective test, is to give people ambiguous pictures that they are asked to interpret. The reasoning behind this approach is that a person will project aspects of himself or herself, some of which may be unconscious, through the interpretations that are given. Examples of such tests are Rorshach's inkblot test and McClelland's 'thematic apperception' test. Two questions that anyone wishing to employ a test should ask are: how valid is the test, and how reliable is it? A valid test is one that measures what it was designed to measure, and this is usually checked against criteria such as the clinical judgement of a psychiatrist. A reliable test is one that produces the same **assessment** of an individual from one occasion to another. The validity and reliability of a personality test are usually reported in the manual that accompanies it.

personality disorder   traditionally viewed by **psychiatry** as one of a range of **mental disorder**s, or **mental health problems**, manifested in a wide-ranging and persistent pattern of maladaptive behaviour.

Some of these difficulties can be seen in a quote from the Diagnostic and Statistical Manual 2000, which defines people with personality disorder as: 'impulsive people who make recurrent **suicide** threats or attempts, are affectively unstable and often show intense inappropriate anger. They feel empty and bored and frantically try to avoid abandonment' (NIMHE 2003). Additionally, a small group of people said to have 'severe anti-social personality disorder', traditionally categorized as 'psychopathy' have been a major concern at the start of the 21st century because of their presumed **dangerousness**. **Drug and alcohol problems** also can be a frequent set of difficulties for people with personality disorder diagnoses.

Problems linked to personality disorder have been traditionally viewed as more a matter of **personality** or behaviour than of **mental illness**. At the same time, however, the very extent of the **deviance** these difficulties represent from social expectations has contributed historically to their classification as a mental disorder. A key consideration here, noted by Herschel Prins, an important writer on personality disorder, is that people with these difficulties may not only act in ways that can be difficult for other people to cope with, but equally do not act in their own interests.

There are, however, major consequences of the understandings that the difficulties associated with this diagnosis may not perhaps derive from 'illness'. The responses people with personality disorder receive from the services may often be rejecting, treating the person as 'undeserving'. Another significant consequence has been that people with these difficulties may be excluded from services, defined as 'not treatable' – a response that led to the proposals contained in the Mental Health Act reform.

Policy has, however, sought to improve the service frameworks and access to treatment for this group of **service users** (NIMHE 2003). Of significance in these developments has been a recognition that **childhood** experiences of **abuse** are frequently found in the backgrounds of people with personality disorders, and some have argued that the difficulties associated with this diagnosis may relate to **post-traumatic stress disorder** for this reason. In relation to this it has been recognized that **service users** with these difficulties benefit from the experience of a 'secure attachment' when therapists engage with them in a person centred relationship, and that in contrast, abandonment by services is likely to exacerbate the difficulties.

Services focus, as do other **mental health** services, on an integrated health and **social care** response. Within this context, social workers have statutory duties towards people with **mental health problems**, and there is much they can offer to people with personality disorder. This is in terms of helping to address the range of **social care** difficulties and **discrimination** – in society and the services – experienced by this service user group; providing appropriate supports in tandem with psychiatric psychological; and sometimes criminal justice services, and engaging with the individual in the person centred relationship, together with an anti-discriminatory awareness of the kinds of circumstances that may lie behind often very challenging behaviour.

National Institute for Mental Health in England (2003) *Personality Disorder: no longer a diagnosis of exclusion*. London: NIMHE.

personalization the strategic reorientation for health and adult **social care** based on the twin principles of early intervention and user choice and control over the service they receive.

The broad transformation of **social care** services for adults was outlined in the White Paper *Our Health, Our Care, Our Say* published by the **Department of Health** in 2006, which declared that both health and social care should meet people's aspirations for independence and greater control over their lives. To achieve this more resources were to be directed toward health promotion and preventing crises in the lives of those needing care. More flexible commissioning, innovation and bringing services closer to individuals were all part of the projected development.

Personalization has been defined as enabling 'individuals to make real choices and take control, with appropriate support whatever their level of need. Everyone with support if necessary will be able to design services around their own needs, within a clear financial allocation' (DH 2008).

Personalization involves the following elements:

An outcomes approach. **Outcomes** are those elements of **wellbeing** that we all share irrespective of illness or **disability**. Under personalization there are specific **outcomes** that all people should enjoy irrespective of illness or disability. These are: i) to live independently; ii) to stay healthy and recover quickly from illness; iii) to exercise maximum control over their own life; iv) to sustain a family unit so that children do not have to take on an inappropriate caring role; v) to participate as active and equal citizens in their locality; vi) to retain maximum dignity and respect. **Assessment** should enable the person to explore the outcomes they seek together with the strengths, resources and preferences he or she has in relation to attaining these outcomes. Services are then provided to enable people to realize the same life satisfactions and capabilities as everyone else with the understanding that the individual is best placed to know what they need and how those needs can best be met.

Self-directed support. A range of services have been incrementally introduced and now – should – provide users with the tools for directing their own support systems. These include **direct payments, individual budgets** which involve a more flexible use of different funding streams and allow the person to receive cash or services within his or her resource allocation. Other services include planning assistance. Workforce changes to support personalization involve a focus on advocacy and brokerage, enabling individuals to design their own care packages in ways that will best meet their needs and achieve sought outcomes. Emphasis is also placed upon enabling people to access appropriate assistance in relation to managing their own care budgets.

There are many implications for social workers' roles in personalization. Good practice involves drawing upon only the best in traditional person centred and social model practice in assessment; real **service user** involvement, and professional skills in areas such as brokerage where the person is enabled in designing a care package tailored to his or her individual requirements. It should also be kept in mind that here are those who argue that 'personalization' is simply a means through which public services transfer responsibility for care away from themselves and on to individuals who, the policy notwithstanding, have few significant resources at their disposal.

Department of Health (2008) *Transforming Adult Social Care.*
London: DH.

phobia an intense fear of a particular situation, organism or object – for
example spiders; supermarkets.

Most people may have a phobia of some kind, but when these are
such as to cause severe and persistent distress, and to have significant
implications for the person's behaviour and functioning, the difficulties
may be diagnosed as a **mental health problem**. As such, the person
would receive treatment and a **social work** response within the general
provisions of **mental health** services and of social work services under
the **NHS and Community Care Act 1990**. (See **mental health
services** and **mental health policy**.)

physical disability the restrictions associated with a physical rather than an
intellectual impairment. It is argued that all disabled people experience
restriction as a result of social oppression and that to describe a **disability**
as 'physical' is to suggest that the restriction arises from **impairment**. The
distinction between physical disability and **learning disability**, however,
is often made in practice, and the nature of the restrictions experienced
by these groups may vary. Sometimes sensory **impairment**s are included
within the overall category of physical disability. Some **deaf** people,
however, regard themselves as a linguistic and cultural minority and
would reject the labels of impairment and disability.

play a complex set of processes undertaken by both adults and children
that involve exploration and learning in many contexts and situations.
Play may be unstructured or 'free-form', as with a child playing without
adult intervention in an unfamiliar situation, or highly structured, as
with a well-known game with agreed rules.

Play serves many purposes, including the development of motor or
physical skills, the development of the intellect and the development of
the person both emotionally and socially. Social workers and other social
welfare workers are mostly concerned with the issue of play with respect to
children and young people (although play may have a therapeutic role
with mentally ill people, with reminiscence therapy with **older people** and
with other client groups too). Here play is regarded as a key process in
socialization; without it, children will be developmentally inhibited. The
ability to play is thus perceived as a significant indicator of a child's health
in its broadest sense. If a child is seen as in need of help, programmes of
play can be devised to promote particular skills that are seen to be lacking
or poorly developed. **Nurseries**, nursery schools and specialist units for
play therapy are facilities where help may be available for children with
such needs. Play is also a very useful tool for social workers and therapists
working with abused children; it can provide a medium for revealing and

understanding what has happened to a child and for therapeutic work with children who have been damaged by their experiences. The value of play for young children is recognized in government policies and legislation. The **early years foundation stage** assumes that children learn best while playing. The **Every Child Matters** framework assumes that play opportunities are important for the physical, social and emotional health of children and young people. (See also **toy libraries**, **under-fives provision**.)

Else, P. (2009) *The Value of Play*. London: Continuum Press.

police the main civil (as opposed to military) state body empowered to enforce the law and maintain order. The police investigate alleged criminal acts and gather evidence which may be used in the prosecution of accused persons. In England and Wales the police service (or 'police force' as it was previously more commonly known) is comprised of 43 regional forces plus a number of specialized agencies such as the British Transport Police. Each force is headed by a chief constable (known as the Metropolitan Police Commissioner in the case of the Metropolitan Police). Scotland has eight police forces and Northern Ireland the single Police Service of Northern Ireland.

Police officers are granted a wide range of legal powers by laws such as the **Police and Criminal Evidence Act 1984** (in England and Wales), which empower them to arrest, stop, search, detain and question suspects and other citizens. It is the police who charge suspects with offences, administer **cautions** and grant **police bail**, although since the **Criminal Justice Act 2003** it is usually the **Crown Prosecution Service** which decides whether a suspect should be charged.

The police are increasingly involved in a wide variety of **crime prevention** work, including being central participants in **crime and disorder partnerships** along with **local authorities** and other local agencies. Police officers also participate in **youth offending teams**.

A substantial amount of **social work** is undertaken jointly with the police or in close liaison with them, notably in the area of child protection. Social workers often play the role of **appropriate adult** when the police **interview** juveniles and other vulnerable persons suspected of offences.

Police and Criminal Evidence Act 1984 an Act codifying **police** powers in relation to suspected offenders and thus defining more sharply than before the rights of citizens in relation to the police. The Act sets out clearly the powers and obligations of the police in relation to stopping and searching, entering premises, arrest, **detention** at a police station and interviewing. It also sets out the machinery for investigating complaints against the **police**, lays down rules for the admission of certain types of evidence in criminal trials and has introduced in statutory form the concept of **community** involvement in policing.

For social workers and **probation officer**s, the most important aspect of the Act is probably that relating to the role of the **appropriate adult**, and this is covered in the codes of practice issued by the Home Secretary. Social workers and (less frequently) **probation officer**s may act as appropriate adults in relation to either juveniles or mentally disordered people who are arrested and interviewed by the police. In the absence of parents or close relatives, they are required to be present throughout the proceedings, not just to observe but also to offer advice, help **communication** and make representations where appropriate. The Act's procedures, for example in relation to the conduct of interviews (whether under **caution** or otherwise) have been adapted and extended for use by other agencies – for example fraud investigators working for the Department of Work and Pensions when they **interview** in suspected **overpayments** and welfare fraud cases (in the Fraud Investigators' Guidelines); or UK Border Agency officers investigating **breach**es of immigration control.

Police and Justice Act 2006 a wide-ranging act that amends earlier statutes and introduces further provision concerning **police bail** and conditional **cautioning, anti-social behaviour** (particularly in relation to **parenting contract**s) and the **inspection** of **prison**s.

police protection provision under section 46 of the **Children Act 1989** whereby a **police** officer may remove a child to suitable accommodation or ensure that he or she remains in a safe place, such as a hospital, if the officer has reasonable cause to believe that the child might otherwise suffer **significant harm**. A child may remain under police protection for a maximum of 72 hours. During that time the child's parents and others should have reasonable **contact** with the child if it is in the child's best interests. Neither the police constable taking the action nor the 'designated officer' for the constabulary acquire **parental responsibility** for the child. Having taken a child into police protection, the designated officer must notify the child's parents and the local authority, ensure that the child knows what is happening and take steps to find out what the child's wishes and feelings are. If it is appropriate to seek an **emergency protection order** the police officer may do so on behalf of the local authority, even without the authority's knowledge. More usually the police will notify the local authority, which in turn will apply for the order from the court. If an emergency protection order (EPO) is already in place it takes priority unless the police have compelling reasons to conclude that it is not reasonably practical to exercise that order. Once a child is in police protection the local authority makes such enquiries as necessary in order to decide whether they should take any action to safeguard or promote the child's welfare.

Poor Law a system for dealing with **poverty** and unemployment laid down in 1598 during the reign of Elizabeth I. With various amendments, notably the Poor Law Amendment Act 1834, the Poor Law remained the law of England until the introduction of the **welfare state** and the passage of the **National Assistance Act** in 1948 which finally removed the Poor Law from the statute books.

The introduction of the Elizabethan Poor Law Act in 1601 arose from genuine concern to help the poor and from concern to control the numbers of unemployed people roaming the country in search of work. Under the system, parishes were empowered to raise local taxes to support sick, old, disabled and unemployed people. In general, the law recognized that **poverty** was a misfortune and not always within the control of the individual. Those in need could apply to their parishes of origin for assistance, but the effect was to severely curtail the migration of those looking for work. The **Poor Law** Amendment Act of 1834 substantially altered the older Elizabethan system based on recognized reciprocal duties between local society and the indigent.

Following the rapid industrialization of Britain, the requirements of a market economy were articulated by political economists such as David Ricardo and reformers such as Edwin Chadwick, who saw the old Poor Law as a fetter on economic activity. They wanted to ensure that the system of poor relief allowed workers greater **mobility** to move to industrial urban areas and at the same time to ensure that poor relief was run as efficiently as possible. The Poor Law (Amendment) Act of 1834 (or the 'New Poor Law' as it was dubbed) introduced the 'workhouse test' to establish whether an individual was genuinely in poverty or not. Only those faced with near starvation would choose to enter the workhouse where conditions were Spartan at best. A basic diet, separation of men and women and highly repetitive work, such as stone breaking, were often central to workhouse regimes, although there were many examples of humanely run establishments that sought to flout the spirit of the 1834 Act. The underlying philosophy of the **Poor Law** (Amendment) Act was that of deterrence: able-bodied people had to be discouraged from seeking poor relief rather than entering the labour market. A guiding principle of the 1834 Act was that of 'less eligibility' (meaning less satisfactory or rewarding): that is, poor relief should be set at a level *below* that of the lowest paid labourer. Only those who could not work and were threatened with starvation would choose to receive relief of their poverty from the public purse. The cornerstone of deterrence under the Act was the workhouse: to receive any kind of benefit meant entering the workhouse and submitting to what was frequently a semi-punitive, certainly institutional regime, one which ensured that even for **older people** and other groups of people at the **absolute poverty** line were set to tedious, hard and repetitive labour in order to receive a basic subsistence diet.

Throughout the 19th century, the pace of industrialization, the ever larger numbers out of work during depressions and the continued predicaments of the old and frail placed great pressure on the system and led to a general rise in 'outdoor relief', which to some extent diluted the workhouse system. The 'deserving poor' – the sick, old, disabled and genuinely unemployed – could apply for outdoor relief, that is, payments or goods and/or parish work outside the poorhouse. Other efforts to move beyond the structures and attitudes of the Poor Law gathered pace in the early 20th century but only slowly. Providing school meals (in 1906), old age pensions (1908) and family allowance for children (1945) were all hotly contested for decades prior to their enactment largely on the ground that they would undermine people's need to work.

Social work as a profession came into being in the late 1860s to determine exactly who was deserving and undeserving in terms of charitable relief. It can be fairly said that this basic **assessment** category was widely used by early **social work** such as that practised by the Charity Organization Society and remained a touchstone of professional attitudes well into the 20th century. Behind that practice was the refusal to acknowledge that in most instances **poverty** was not the result of personal failure or moral irresponsibility. It is also important to remember that the **Poor Law** system operated within a framework of **charity** and amid widespread **anxiety** among professional, governmental and influential charitable circles that people would inevitably try to avoid the labour market if they were given even the smallest incentive to do so. The notion of rights did not take root until later in the 20th century and came to fruition with the introduction of the **welfare state** in the late 1940s.

Jones, K. (2000) *The Making of Social Policy in Britain: from the Poor Law to New Labour*. London: Athlone.

positive action measures permitted by the Race Relations Act 1976 and the Sex Discrimination Act 1975 to help members of ethnic minorities and women achieve more equality (in comparison with white people and men respectively) in relation to seeking employment or promotion.

British law does not permit discrimination at the point of selection for employment or promotion. Positive action measures mostly concern training opportunities targeted at women and members of ethnic minorities. Such training might include special attempts to equip and encourage women to apply for jobs in areas of employment hitherto dominated by men, such as in engineering. Similarly, it might be demonstrated that Black people are a substantial proportion of the population within a particular area but are practically invisible as local authority employees. Training in these circumstances might be to familiarize Black people with an area of work or occupation relatively unknown to them and to help them acquire the specific skills necessary to secure a job. Other measures might include networking, that is, telling particular **community** groups that an organization really does want to recruit more people from ethnic minorities. The use of particular newspapers and advertisements in various languages would send strong signals to particular communities about the seriousness of an organization's equal opportunities' policies. It is also possible to appoint a Black person or a woman to a post (in competition with a white person or a man respectively) if he or she is considered to be equally competent to do a job and women or Black people are under-represented at that level within the organization. A limited number of posts can also be 'reserved' for Black people and for women where the job could be said to offer a personal service that only somebody of that ethnicity or gender could reasonably be expected to provide. Thus a woman and only a woman should be considered for a job in a rape crisis centre, and only a Black person for a job as Afro-Caribbean **advice** worker. Some employers have also made attempts to recruit older workers, although such initiatives are not required by law despite recent legislation giving people the right to claim discrimination on grounds of age.

postmodernism   a theory that holds that our understanding of social reality is limited, partial and personal, depending on individual or group perspective. 'Modernism' is generally thought to originate in the scientific revolutions in Europe in the 17th century and confirmed in the rational and technical cultures that developed in Europe and North America from that point on. Modernism is characterized by notions of economic progress, the **power** of reason and rational thought, and hierarchical **poverty** social and commercial organizations. Gender hierarchies in particular associated reason and rationality with men, and emotion and irrationality with women. Equally, modernism produced comprehensive 'world views' – whether a belief in continuous (economic) progress through the operations of the market or the conviction that a socialist revolution, led by the industrial working class, was inevitable. Postmodernism rejects such notions as well as the idea that there is a single reality or social truth that only awaits discovery. Thus it heralded the dismissal of 'grand narratives' such as Marxism and psychoanalysis. For the social sciences it encourages a turn away from methodologies that aim to establish social truths. Rather, postmodern theorists have emphasized the need to look at the complex, interwoven patterns within society with a diversity of viewpoints and experiences. The relevance of postmodernism for **social work** is that it encourages the exploration and expression of multiple voices and perspectives. Under its influence, social work theory has placed greater emphasis on the importance of 'narrative' and the personal 'stories' of users. Postmodernism also favours making explicit underlying assumptions and perspectives and emphasizes the value of emotion and personal experience.

Postmodernism at first seemed to place great emphasis on aspects of an individual's social identity – such as **'race'**, gender or disability – as virtually determining that person's view of society. By the late 1980s and 1990s, however, it played a significant part in challenging these simplistic notions of social identity by encouraging a more fluid understanding of identity and subjective experiences.

Gorman, J. (1993) Postmodernism and the conduct of inquiry in social work. *Affilia*, 8(3).

post-traumatic stress disorder a person's reactions following an 'extraordinary' or 'catastrophic' experience that shatters his or her sense of invulnerability to harm.

Stress itself describes the state of discomfort arising in a person's emotions and mental and physical state when struggling to cope against overwhelming odds. The experiences leading to post-traumatic syndrome, in order to shatter the person's sense of invulnerability to harm, would involve a major betrayal of trust. This may mean the betrayal of trust in a particular human being (the experience of child **sexual abuse** has been identified in the literature as an outstanding example of this in society); or the betrayal of trust in the government or an official agency, such as the **police**, if such an agency attacks the person's basic human rights through, for example, torture or **imprisonment** without trial; or the betrayal of trust in society through serious crime against the person, such as rape, assault, mugging or housebreaking, especially while the person is present. Devalued groups in society – Black people, women, **older people**, disabled people, and gay and lesbian people – are particularly likely to be the **victim**s of crime and abuse from the general population and may be treated unjustly by professionals and officials, so members of these groups are more likely than others to experience post-traumatic stress syndrome.

The feature shared by all the above experiences is that trust in a parent, in official agencies and in other people in society may be very fundamental and taken for granted as a reality to depend upon. Children trust their parents to protect them from harm in every area of life, as they have little **power** to do this for themselves. Members of society expect the government and official agencies, such as the **police**, to be active in protecting, or at least not compromising, their basic human rights, and people have a measure of trust in others also not to infringe the latter. It may be that a person has never been able to trust parents, official agencies or other people, but even so, being the **victim** of harm from any of these sources may still shatter the person's sense of safety and security to the degree that he or she has no other source of safety to which to retreat. It is the very fundamental nature of these sources of security that makes harm from any of them such a devastating experience, one from which it is said by some writers to be very difficult to recover. Professional **abuse** from a doctor, therapist or social worker – whether it involves sexual or other forms of malpractice – may also fall into this category, if the harm is significant, because of the expectation, from professional ethics, that the professional will protect the client's interests first. Other forms of trauma betraying trust would include personal disasters, such as a house fire or involvement in a serious accident, and major disasters that again destroy or shatter the person's taken-for-granted experience of safety in his or her home or car or in a public place such as a football stadium.

All the above experiences, which are likely to lead to post-traumatic stress syndrome, are familiar to social workers, including the experiences of torture and other human rights' violations by refugees coming from abroad. Practitioners are particularly likely, however, to encounter clients who have experienced **childhood sexual abuse** (and perhaps other forms of **child abuse**) and crime, while the dangers of professional abuse also need to be borne in mind. It is therefore important to understand the effects that these experiences can have and helpful forms of intervention.

Writers on post-traumatic stress syndrome have identified two different stages of this condition: post-traumatic stress reactions, which refer to the person's immediate or short-term responses to the trauma, and post-traumatic stress disorder, referring to the longer-term responses. Post-traumatic stress *reactions* can include hysteria, involving perhaps loss of memory and even consciousness, restlessness, impaired concentration and coordination, impulsiveness, weeping, confusion and perhaps psychotic experiences such as hallucinations or delusions (see **psychoses**). Soldiers experiencing 'shell shock' in the First World War exhibited these symptoms. The fact that psychotic symptoms are sometimes experienced may lead the worker to conclude that the person is mentally ill, or may have led to a referral for **assessment** under the **Mental Health Act 1983**. Workers should be aware that such symptoms may arise from other causes and assess the person's circumstances fully. Post-traumatic stress disorder is a continuation of these symptoms into the longer term, along with chronic disturbance of sleep, anxiety,

depression and impulsiveness. Lack of concentration and coordination, impulsiveness and perhaps even impaired vision or hearing may lead to accidents. In addition, there is a risk that hallucinations, 'flashbacks' of the experience, impulsiveness and depression may result in **suicide** attempts.

In the very long term, adult survivors of **childhood sexual abuse** are highly likely to suffer the **mental health problems** of depression, self-harm, **anxiety** and low self-esteem. **Substance misuse** is also highly likely. People suffering other severe traumas may well experience similar long-term difficulties. It is important to be aware, however, that the original trauma, especially if it occurred in **childhood**, may be repressed from memory, but change and crises in the person's current life may trigger the memories, and this may result in all the original post-traumatic stress reactions. **Crisis intervention** alone is not sufficient to relieve the distress of the post-traumatic stress syndrome, either after the original trauma or if memories of it are triggered in later life. Long-term help is always needed, and this may often be most effective in a long-term group. This is especially so for survivors of childhood **sexual abuse**, where the one-to-one client–worker relationship may so painfully remind the person through transference of the abuse situation that distress, distrust and dissociation act against any benefits the therapy might provide. The main benefit that **group work** can bring is to help the person, through exploration of what has happened, to develop greater self-esteem. One of the major long-term effects of trauma, and especially of violence or abuse to the person, is a feeling of guilt and unworthiness, as if the person himself or herself had wanted such treatment.

When working, either in a group or performing other **social work** duties with the person, reliability and consistency are essential if the person's trust is not to be betrayed again. Nevertheless, the person may very early perceive the worker as untrustworthy, through transference, and this needs to be understood by the worker, not taken personally, and perhaps acknowledged and worked with in whatever depth is appropriate within the particular client–worker relationship. A further consideration in work with people experiencing post-traumatic stress syndrome is the likelihood that the psychiatric services, or at least the general practitioner, will be involved, and thus the worker needs to liaise with these services constructively (see **mental health, multi-disciplinary work**).

poverty a condition in which people are inhibited from **participation** in society because of a serious lack of material and social resources. Poverty is defined in two ways: absolute and relative poverty. Absolute poverty refers to conditions that will not sustain physical life. It is defined by a fixed standard below which individuals and families experience complete destitution in which they cannot meet even minimum **needs** for food and shelter. The United Nations Development Programme (UNDP) uses such a standard for measuring poverty in the developing world: this is fixed at an income of roughly 1 (US) dollar a day. Below that families face severe deprivation of basic human needs, including food, safe drinking water and shelter, resulting in malnutrition and dangerous levels of ill-health. Absolute standards have the virtue of allowing us to calculate poverty across different countries. At the time of writing, UNICEF estimates that around one quarter of all under-5s in the developing world are underweight. Relative poverty refers to the lack of resources to obtain the types of diet, participate in the activities and have the living conditions and amenities that are customary or at least widely encouraged and approved in the society to which a person belongs. Poverty cannot therefore be understood only as a subsistence threshold but can be defined more accurately in relation to the society of which it is a part.

The basic standards of living, which most people enjoy, are implicitly defined within each society. These standards have not only to do with income but also consumer purchases, levels of health and **wellbeing**, and access to goods and services. Those investigating relative poverty look at the ways that individual and family life is affected by the experience of deprivation. The notion of relative poverty focuses on the degree to which people are prevented from sharing the living standards, opportunities and norms of **wellbeing** that society as a whole has created for itself.

The concept of relative poverty implies that as society and its norms and institutions become more sophisticated so does what an individual or family requires. Information and **communication** technology (ICT) presents a good example. Thirty years ago computer operations were specialized functions performed on huge, room-sized machines by small numbers of highly trained operators. In a relatively short time, skills in ICT have moved from the margin of economic activity to its core. Add its research and educative functions and its social **networking** value through email and it becomes a central tool that impacts on individuals. Families with no access to, or knowledge about, ICT have another dimension in which they are poor – now referred to as 'information **poverty**'.

Studies have also analysed the distribution of resources within families where there is an adequate income to reveal that the woman's share is disproportionately small. Members of minority ethnic groups, similarly, are more likely than other people to be unemployed or to be in low-paid work.

Since 1998, the Joseph Rowntree Foundation has been providing an annual report on poverty and **social exclusion** in the UK, analysing data from various official statistics and indicators. At the time of writing, data suggests that more than 13 million people are living in poverty in the UK, which roughly equates to around one fifth of the population. With the current economic recession, this figure is likely to rise. Since 2005, the incomes of the poorest have fallen and those of the rich have risen. Particularly vulnerable groups include lone parents, the unemployed, the disabled or long-term sick, and minority groups, especially Pakistani and Bangladeshi. Other groups vulnerable to poverty include adults living in one-person households, those who left school at 16 or under, and those living in local authority and **housing association** tenancies.

In general, those on the right of the political spectrum, and particularly those supporting the notion of an '**underclass**', believe that poor people are responsible for their own poverty through lack of work discipline and unstable family relationships. Selective coverage of poverty in some of the press compounds this with a set of negative images of poor people as lazy and welfare-dependent. The belief that the poor are responsible for their own difficulties is persistent. In the public domain, the idea of the **cycle of deprivation** and, among sociologists, the theory of culture of poverty seek to explain the persistence of poverty by reference to ideas and behaviours transmitted from one generation to another. Critics of these views point to the major changes that have occurred when governments have pursued policies that seek to redistribute wealth – the clear implication being that poverty is a structural feature of society and not a question of individual behaviour.

Poor people form the largest group of consumers of social services. Poverty is a major source of stress, and although it cannot be regarded as a simple causal factor (because many who live in poverty manage to escape major personal and family difficulties), it has strong associations with **mental health problems**, with crime, with family problems including **child abuse** and with ill-health. Yet, while **social work** has worked with predominantly poor people since its inception in the second half of the 19th century, it has also tended to 'pathologize' poor people, that is, to view users' **poverty** as the result of the poor person's perverse choices, for example, spending too much on alcohol and tobacco (or drugs) and being apathetic towards work and family responsibilities. As a result, the dominant **casework** tradition in social work tried to secure good personal habits, such as thrift, sobriety and hard work, through developing the personal relationship with the social worker. Today the role of social workers in trying to alleviate the poverty of consumers of social work services is full of ambiguity. Many still do not see such work as part of their brief, preferring to perceive it as the responsibility of other agencies. Often such social workers align themselves with therapy, or at least regard helping with relationships as their major focus. Others may limit their assistance to, for example, help with second-hand clothing or a grant for a holiday.

Few social workers have poverty 'centre stage' or indeed are required or permitted to develop an effective **anti-poverty strategy**. Such an approach might entail income-maximization programmes, **money advice**, housing improvement programmes and programmes to facilitate the involvement of poor people in employment (for example, adult education services, nursery provision, and work and food cooperatives). Many such ventures would require at least a **community** focus and methods rooted in the approaches of **community work** and action. (See also **child poverty, social exclusion, poverty trap, health inequality**.)

Ridge, T. and Wright, S. (eds) (2008) *Understanding Inequality, Poverty and Wealth: policies and prospects*. Bristol: Policy Press.

poverty trap the situation of people when the gains they make from increased income, typically earnings from employment, are exceeded by losses through increased payments of tax and national insurance and reductions in means-tested benefits. In practice, the phrase 'poverty trap' is used to describe any situation in which it is difficult for a person to make significant improvements in disposable income by working or increasing earnings. Since 1997, New Labour has focused explicit attention on 'making work pay' with an emphasis on paid work as the best route out of **poverty** and **social exclusion**. In an attempt to increase the numbers of people engaged in paid employment, whilst also seeking to challenge the 'poverty trap', those engaged in employment have become able to receive additional support in the form of tax credits (e.g. Working Families Tax Credit and now Child Tax Credit).

Ridge, T. and Wright, S. (eds) (2008) *Understanding Inequality, Poverty and Wealth: policies and prospects*. Bristol: Policy Press.

power the ability to command obedience or exert control over people by using force, persuasion, example or incentives. Individuals, organizations, bureaucracies and even large social formations such as a specific social class or gender all utilize it to gain various objectives.

The most common way is to think of power in terms of domination and resistance, of using it to compel people to do certain things. In this sense power is 'power over' others – the thing that allows one person, organization or nation to compel, pressure, influence, cajole, or coerce other people, groups, organizations, social classes or nations into doing something. This is *instrumental power*, something held over others and used to obtain leverage. Power *relations* in this sense are often unequal: those that are dominant pursue their interests and have the power to see that they are realized over those who have less power. Moreover, the structures of a whole society may be so laden with power and the power relations within that society so unequal that the dominant groups rarely have to exercise it in obvious ways since the inequality of power and the coercion is hidden in widely accepted ideas, in the media, in religious faiths and, in family relationships.

The very fact of inequality in this kind of power may breed resistance as rising social movements, subordinate social classes or political underdogs seek to develop their own countervailing forms of power in order to even up the balance between 'us' and 'them'. This is a familiar story in history – rebellion, protest, riots and revolution at its most spectacular – but also in other ways such as resistance to rape and **domestic violence** or moves to defend animal rights. Equally an extreme imbalance of power may create a feeling that 'nothing can be done' about a particular injustice resulting in a sense of fatalism and powerlessness.

Some sociologists note that power generally arises from different sources: *physical sanctions* such as punishment or other forms of direct coercion, *material power* based on the control of resources such as wages and services, *symbolic power* based on conferring or withholding generally desired rewards such as esteem, status or respect, and *ideological power* which shapes the way people think. Others focus on the power to make and implement decisions, the power to prevent certain issues even being discussed – whether in a meeting or in the media or the political process.

Some of the sources are:

Sources of formal power	*Sources of informal power*
authority vested in positions and titles	ability to cope with uncertainty
control of scarce resources	interpersonal alliances and networks
control of structure, rules and regulations	systemic **power** arising from social class, ethnicity, race, gender
control of decision-making processes	control of symbolism and management of meaning
control of knowledge and information or expertise	control of beliefs and custom
control of work boundaries	charisma and confidence
control of technology	ability to communicate

There is, however, another way of looking at power, one that lends itself more to **social work**'s purposes and methods. This can be identified as *relational power* or 'associational power', which is exercised with others. This is expressed as the 'power to' rather than 'power over' when people come together to talk and to act. This kind of power provides the capacity to accomplish things that comes from people getting together, discussing, deliberating and reaching agreement on what should be done and how to do it. To nurture this kind of power requires the ability to build relationships and to be able to discuss matters freely in the public domain. It is achieved through recognition of the positive contributions and capabilities of others and nurturing these in others. When social work has talked about **empowerment** it has in general been thinking of **power** in the first sense – the 'power over' others and how to rebalance that in favour of relatively powerless **service user**s. Yet the second meaning of power affords greater opportunity for social work to directly apply its skills and knowledge in building local **partnership**s. In developing relational power, listening to personal narratives and developing trust and mutual regard are key steps – as they are in the way social work develops relationships and uses self. Often social workers undertake just this but do so in particular ways outlined by the dominant **casework** paradigm.

The same skills can be used for different, wider ends – empowering people, and building collaborative capacity. People want recognition (which is often what the overworked term 'respect' is about) of who they are, what their life story is and what their hopes and fears are. They want to be able to carry forward a meaningful story of their life and to have it validated by others. Social workers have many relationship building, narrative-forming and **listening skills** to encourage and develop this aspiration. (See also **empowerment**.)

Lukes, S. (2004) *Power: a Radical View*. London: Palgrave Macmillan.

pre-sentence report (PSR)   a report compiled by a **probation officer** or member of a **youth offending team** that provides courts with information to assist the decision on **sentence**. The content of PSRs is laid down in the **National Standards for the Management of Offenders**. They normally include information about the offender's background, circumstances and attitudes, the offence (especially its seriousness), and the effects upon the **victim**. It concludes by proposing possible appropriate **sentence**s.

Sentencers are normally required by the **Criminal Justice Act 2003** to consider a PSR before imposing either a **custodial sentence** or **community order**. However, for adult offenders, sentencers may dispense with a PSR 'if, in the circumstances of the case, the court is of the opinion that it is unnecessary to obtain a pre-**sentence** report'. If the offender is under 18, a new PSR is required unless the court considers a previous PSR made in respect of the same young person. It has been found that around 15 per cent of adult offenders are given custodial sentences without the benefit of a PSR, but **community sentence**s are rarely imposed in the absence of such a report. In some cases a shortened form of PSR, known as a 'specific sentence report', can be used by courts when considering the offender's suitability for a particular sentence the court has in mind without going into much background detail. PSRs were known as 'social inquiry reports' before 1992. The change of name reflected a shift in emphasis in sentencing from the welfare needs of the offender to the seriousness of the offending. Since then proposals for sentences in PSRs have become significantly more severe, with explicit proposals for **custody** doubling from 2–3 per cent to 5–6 per cent between 1990 and 2000.

preventive work/prevention any work that seeks to stop a potential problem emerging or an existing problem becoming more acute, whether for individuals, families or whole neighbourhoods. Preventive practice aims to direct resources and intervention towards addressing early signs of social difficulties or social problems before they accelerate and intensify into emergencies that require vastly greater resources in terms of time, energy and money.

The notion of 'preventive work' is not wholly satisfactory, first, because it raises the question of *what* exactly is being prevented and, second, because it suggests that it is a kind of optional extra as if **social work** is not really social work until it is reacting to harm or imminent catastrophe. The phrase takes on greater clarity when defined by its opposites such as 'reactive work' or '**crisis intervention**'. Preventive work in health offers a clear example: between 1997 and 2002 there was a decline of 23 per cent in deaths from heart disease; some of this was a result of improved acute surgical intervention – angioplasty, transplants, bypass procedures; but a good percentage was achieved also because of improved life choices, better diet, taking exercise or giving up smoking. In other words heart disease was reduced through a double-pronged approach combining both acute intervention *and* prevention.

Social care and social work services have comparable arenas for preventive work. For example, in order to forestall **social exclusion** and its impact on **youth justice** and **anti-social behaviour** arising from low educational achievement social workers should be promoting stimulating environments for child development. Providing and promoting activities for young people in order to prevent or diminish anti-social behaviour in a particular locality is another example. Strengthening caring **networks** in a locality to reduce rates of **older people** going into hospital is a third. Yet the commitment to prevention has been taken on very slowly. Social work and social care have found it difficult to move beyond programmed responses to individual casualties of a winner/loser society, almost inviting the perception that it is a residual service, the ultimate safety net.

Child protection services perhaps provides the best example of how the heavy emphasis on risk swallows up resources for **preventive work**.

Despite the well-known association between specific environmental stressors and **child abuse**, child protection systems are only triggered when circumstances of imminent danger to the child are reported or after harm has been done. While a formidable research effort has described in detail how social workers working with children and families could use resources more effectively if they got out from under the shadow of reactive protective work, the required shift in social work thinking and resource **allocation** proved difficult to bring about. Significant instances of abuse, such as the death of **Baby P** reported widely in the media make this a difficult, even courageous undertaking. A similar perspective applies to work with older adults or those with **disability** where protection and preventive work compete for resources and practitioners' time. Gerald Smale and colleagues (see below) use the phrase 'development work' to distinguish the kinds of **preventive work** they have in mind from 'curative'.

Smale, G., Tuson, G. and Statham, D. (2000) *Social Work and Social Problems*. Basingstoke: Macmillan.

primary care trust (PCT) the lead organizations ensuring the delivery of primary care health services in the **National Health Service**. Their role is to take the lead in ensuring that community-based services are delivered based on needs **assessment** of their relevant population. For the purpose of fulfilling this role, the PTCs are composed mainly of general practitioners (GPs), but in addition have representation from community nurses and social services as well as lay members. As part of this, a key relationship is with social services with the aim of fulfilling the aims of the government's modernization agenda and joined up health and **social care** services.

Ham, C. (2009) *Health Policy in Britain*, 6th edition. London: Palgrave.

principles of sentencing a collective term for the explanations and justifications given for imposing punishment or treatment on people who break the law.

It is usually argued that there are two broad philosophies of punishment, known as retributivism and utilitarianism. Retributivism maintains that the punishment of wrongdoing is a moral right and duty, an end in itself: it is simply right to mete out to offenders the suffering or deprivation of liberty they deserve through having committed the crime. It follows from this theory that, firstly, it is essential to establish that the person to be punished is indeed guilty of the offence, and secondly that the severity of the punishment is proportionate to the seriousness of the crime (also known as the principle of '**just deserts**'). Utilitarianism seeks to bring about 'the greatest happiness of the greatest number', and maintains that the suffering involved in punishment is itself an evil that can be justified only if it brings about a greater good, namely the reduction of wrongdoing. This reduction in crime may be achieved by deterrence (making potential offenders afraid to break the law for fear of punishment), by incapacitation (making it impossible for criminals to re-offend, for example by confining them in **custody**), or by bringing about the reform or **rehabilitation** of the offender. Punishment in this view is a means to an end, not an end in itself. The main criticism of utilitarianism is that it takes insufficient account of the relationship between punishment and the seriousness of the crime, while the main criticism of retributivism is that it takes insufficient account of the consequences of punishment. Various attempts have been made to combine and reconcile the two approaches, including 'limiting retributivism', the theory that punishments may be inflicted for utilitarian purposes, but restrained by the notion of just deserts.

Retributivism and utilitarianism are not the only possible justifications for punishment. Denunciation is the theory that punishment can be justified as an expression of society's emphatic condemnation of the offence. Some believe that the principle of **reparation** provides a basis for a system of **restorative justice** radically different from existing arrangements. The 'communicative theory' of punishment seeks to conceptualize punishment as an attempt at moral dialogue with offenders. Attempts have also been made to construct theories based on the principle of human rights which can synthesize the concerns of a number of these different approaches.

The term 'principles of sentencing' is also used in a different sense, to refer to various overarching considerations that **criminal courts** should adhere to when passing sentence. These include the principle of proportionality (that sentences should in general be proportionate to the seriousness of the offence), and the principle that custodial sentences should only be passed as a last resort.

Cavadino, M. and Dignan, J. (2007) *The Penal System: an introduction*, 4th edition. London: Sage Publications, Chapter 2.

prison a secure institution providing **custody** for adult offenders (currently those over 21) serving **sentences** of **imprisonment**, and also for defendants on **remand** in **custody**. The term is also used more loosely to include custodial institutions for young offenders (**young offender institutions** and **secure training centres**). There are currently 140 **prison**s in England and Wales (including 20 YOIs). Most of these are run by the Prison Service (now part of the **National Offender Management Service**), but some are privately run (see below). Prisons are categorized according to their function and the level of security. Adult men's prisons are divided into local prisons (which house prisoners on remand and immediately after **sentence**), closed training prisons, open prisons (for low-risk offenders) and high-security prisons (formerly known as 'dispersal' prisons). There are 14 women's prisons in England (none in Wales).

The prison population of England and Wales has reached record numbers in recent years, and has been consistently among the highest in Western Europe in proportion to total population. One of the major criticisms of prisons has for many years been the levels of overcrowding, especially in the local prisons, many of which were built in Victorian times, and associated poor conditions of confinement. Governments have responded with massive prison-building programmes and the introduction of privately run prisons, but inmate numbers continue to rise, and many observers argue that providing increased numbers of places will inevitably lead courts to make use of them.

The Prison Service is constantly faced with serious problems that have often been characterized as 'crises'. They may be summarized as problems of security (preventing escapes), of conditions (squalid accommodation and the **poverty** of regimes, with inadequate work, education and time out of cells), of authority (relating to poor industrial relations and low staff morale), of control (maintaining discipline among prisoners and preventing riots), and of legitimacy (maintaining a belief that the system of **imprisonment** is just).

A significant recent development in UK prisons has been the policy of privatization, whereby private firms have been paid from public funds to design, build and run prisons. The arguments in favour of privatizing prisons are both ideological (that it is appropriate to a free market economy) and pragmatic (the need to build more prisons quickly and to maintain them economically, to hold management more accountable and to make staff working practices more flexible). The arguments against privatization are similarly ideological (that punishment should remain a direct responsibility of the state) and pragmatic (that privatization does not in actuality represent good value for money, that private security staff are not sufficiently competent to contain, care for and treat prisoners, and that private prisons create vested interests in maintaining a high prison population).

The work of the **Probation Service** within prisons was initially concerned with routine welfare matters, but **probation officers** have become increasingly involved in **offending behaviour programmes**. Probation staff contribute to **sentence** planning and **risk assessment** and prepare reports on prisoners' progress towards **early release**. Probation officers from prisoners' home areas also maintain **contact**, prepare reports and supervise some offenders on **licence** when they are released early. This is known as 'through care' or resettlement.

Despite all attempts to care for and rehabilitate prisoners, prison is widely viewed as ineffective in controlling crime, 'an expensive way of making bad people worse' in the words of a government White Paper of 1990. Three-quarters of young offenders and two-thirds of adults sentenced to custody are convicted of another offence within two years of their release. A high proportion of prisoners have **mental disorders** (see **mentally disordered offenders**), and large numbers also have a history of drug misuse. Conditions in overcrowded prisons are not conducive to **rehabilitation**, and rates of **suicide** and self-harm are high. Nevertheless, prison retains enduring support from those who assert or assume (with little supporting evidence) that it effectively serves to control crime by deterrence and incapacitation (see **principles of sentencing**).

Cavadino, M. and Dignan, J. (2007) *The Penal System: an introduction*, 4th edition. London: Sage, Chapters 1, 6 and 7.

probation board local body formerly responsible for employing probation staff and overseeing the work of the local **probation service**. Probation boards were abolished by the Offender Management Act 2007, and are being replaced by **probation trusts**.

probation centre premises run by the **probation service**, to provide **group work** and other activities which offenders may be obliged to attend under **activity requirements** or **programme requirements** in **community orders**.

probation hostel see **bail hostel**

Probation Inspectorate a national monitoring body responsible for inspecting and enforcing standards in the **probation service**. The inspectorate conducts thematic **inspections** of particular aspects of probation work and periodic reviews of the overall performance of local services as well as analysing statistical returns.

probation officer a qualified officer of the **probation service**. See also **probation service officer**.

probation order the name given prior to 2001 to a court order requiring an offender to be subject to the **supervision** of a **probation officer**. In 2001 the name of the order was changed to **community rehabilitation order**, and the **Criminal Justice Act 2003** replaced it with the **community order** containing a **supervision requirement**.

probation service the statutory agency responsible for providing reports to **criminal courts**, supervising offenders on community-based programmes and working with them in a **prison** welfare role. It also has responsibilities in the area of **crime prevention** and liaising with **victims**.

Originally probation services were all local entities, but since 2001, the **National Probation Service** has overseen the work of local probation services in England, Northern Ireland and Wales. The National Probation Service is now in turn (since 2004) part of the **National Offender Management Service**. Each local probation service has a chief **probation officer** with assistants and often a deputy.

Probation workers (probation officers and probation service officers) supervise adult offenders (and young offenders aged 16 to 17) given **community sentences** by the **criminal courts**, in particular **community orders** with **supervision, activity, programme requirements** and **unpaid work requirements**, supervise offenders released on **licence**, and work with offenders in **prison** to encourage them to change their attitudes and behaviour in such a way as to avoid reoffending. They also provide an information service to **victims** of crime where the offender has been sentenced to **imprisonment**. Probation officers may be seconded to work in other agencies, including **youth offending teams** and **multi-agency public protection** panels. One of the major roles of **probation officers** is to prepare **pre-sentence reports** for the courts. Probation staff work is governed by the **National Standards for the Management of Offenders**.

Until the 1990s, the probation service was generally perceived as a **social work** agency, and probation officers trained alongside social workers. More recently, a specialist diploma in probation studies has replaced the social work qualification, and many observers feel that the service as a whole has moved away from its **social work** roots. There is now a greater emphasis on 'offender management': managing the risks posed by offenders as opposed to working for their welfare.

Ward, D., Scott, J. and Lacey, M. (2002) *Probation: working for justice*, 2nd edition. Oxford: Oxford University Press.

probation service assistant former name for **probation service officer**.

probation service officer (PSO) a member of **probation service** staff without a formal qualification as a **probation officer**, working either to support a field **team** or to provide a specialized service. Unlike **probation officers, PSOs supervise only low risk offenders.** Their duties can include providing **pre-sentence reports**, overseeing **unpaid work**, delivering **offending behaviour programmes** and providing support to **victims** of crime and their families.

probation trust a local public-sector body (introduced by the Offender Management Act 2007) from whom the **Justice Secretary** may commission **probation services**. It is envisaged that probation trusts will compete for such commissions with alternative private and voluntary sector providers.

'problem family' a term widely used in the post-Second World War period in British **social work** agencies to describe families thought to have persistent problems over time that either were impervious to help or required constant support.

The concept of the 'problem family' was closely associated with the idea of a **cycle of deprivation** in the 1960s and 1970s which broadly held that problems such as child neglect, criminal behaviour, or periods of **homelessness** were transmitted from one generation to another through the process of socialization within the family and close **peer group**s. Although the actual term is no longer used by social welfare professionals, certain **risk factors** are used by agencies and in government policy-making to identify 'multi-problem' families or 'families at risk' (both of which are still used) who generate a persistent need for a range of services. Many of these risk factors outlined in recent government policy – lone parent, a parent with a criminal record, homelessness for example – closely parallel those of the problem family. In truth since the beginnings of social work in the **charity** organizations of the last quarter of the 19th century the family beset by many problems and disadvantages has been the regular target of intervention. Often discussion of such families have been tied to theories of the **underclass**, of parents who fail their basic responsibilities to their children and avoid entering the labour market. While the discussion today is more muted there is still within the discourse of **social exclusion** the strand of opinion that such families through their own actions and refusal to accept services have in one way or another excluded themselves from the mainstream.

Social Exclusion Task Force (2006) *Think Families*. London: Cabinet Office.

profession a group or body, of some social standing, claiming expertise in an area of work.

Features thought to characterize a profession include lengthy training in relation to some clearly demarcated area of knowledge and skill, the idea of public service or even altruistic practice, impartial service regardless of client or **service user**, competent service regardless of practitioner, and a code of ethics or conduct. The classic concept of the profession, based on the medical and legal professions in the 19th century, included a scale of fees and a commitment to independence, the latter implying that none could possibly judge the individual professional except a peer or colleague.

The process of professionalization seems to involve a sequence of developments. A particular skill or area of knowledge emerges in response to changes in economic and social activity; people gather together to exchange ideas and to develop the new territory; if the 'field' has commercial or social potential, the group will increase in number; the members seek to define and set boundaries on the new activity and by so doing seek to distinguish it from associated activities; decisions are made about who can be a member and later a 'practitioner'; and the final stages involve controlling the qualifying process and the conduct of members. The state will incorporate the training of professionals into the mainstream of higher education if the activity is regarded as sufficiently important, although professional organizations will still have some measure of autonomy.

There is no doubt that **social work** has emerged as an occupation in the way described above. Most commentators, however, question whether social work is or can be a fully fledged profession, preferring to regard it as a 'quasi-' or 'semi-profession'. They point, first, to the roots of social work in voluntary activity and to the continuing debate about how much social work requires genuine expertise and how much of it might be undertaken by communities, in **self-help** activity and by **volunteers**. Second, they point to the lack of agreement among social workers about the knowledge and value base of the occupation, although there is increased convergence about the core social work curriculum as a result of National Occupational Standards prescribed by the **General Social Care Council**. Third, social workers operate within a bureaucratic context. They are part of hierarchies and, far from exercising autonomy, they are clearly accountable to a line manager on a day-to-day basis and use proformas both for the **assessment** of problems and to determine eligibility for services. Additionally, given that many important decisions concerning social work activities are actually made by the courts, the claim that social workers are professionally autonomous is further undermined. Indeed, there have been significant debates in recent years about the extent to which social workers are allowed to make decisions within general guidelines laid down by judges, as against a perception that judges are making many more 'casework' decisions than they did before. Finally social work operates in a political context and is vulnerable to public opinion about the competence of social workers in the light of, for example, child deaths. Recent evidence indicates that many more children are coming into the care system since the death of Baby P. There have been consistent concerns that social workers, their managers and elected representatives are very concerned about how the public view their competence, their diligence and their management of risk, even though social workers are also often accused of being too intrusive in their pursuit of child or adult protection.

Critics of the idea of profession have pointed to the self-interested behaviour of professional bodies. Such bodies may speak the language of public service and of a commitment to high-quality practice for all, but their tactics often restrict entry to the profession, discriminate against women and members of ethnic minorities and seek to maintain, if not improve, high salaries. The social class origins of the established professions are principally from the same social groups. Given these general criticisms of professions, some social workers have questioned the desirability of adopting the idea of the profession as the occupational goal. If the average social worker does accept structural inequality as the major explanation for the social problems that they have to deal with then maybe, they argue, the occupation should aspire to a strong trade unionism. Trade unions too are interested in competent, high-quality services.

professional network the range of **contact**s that practitioners establish with other professionals in their own or other agencies and with local residents in **community** organizations. A professional's own network is a critical tool in achieving certain objectives. **Partnership**s, for example, grow out of **networks** as trust and confidence in the capacity of network links deepen. Networks also generate innovative projects and multi-dimensional thinking. Purposeful, work-oriented networks are different in nature and purpose from users' networks and the techniques for strengthening them also differ. Practitioners should keep in mind that networks are reciprocal. Asking others for information or help in solving a problem means that similar assistance be offered in return at some point in the future. Networks are created and maintained the way most social ties are created. Shared experience and common interests are powerful glue to cement relationships. These may arise from a practitioner's personal life, shared adversity or **discrimination** or from simply having to knuckle under to the same set of organizational tasks. Lengthy chat with the same set of colleagues everyday while pleasant and supportive does not create the kind of network that practitioner's need for developing partnerships or a collaborative multi-agency initiative. Whether a **social care** worker, social worker or social services manager, the practitioner looks across his or her agency, and outside the agency for those productive links that in time may pay off. Networks also thrive on use. Depending on the nature of your relationship, some form of regular contact is probably desirable.

profound and multiple learning disabilities (PMLD) children and adults who find learning and communicating very difficult. Many will also have additional sensory or physical disabilities, complex health needs or **mental health** difficulties. The combination of these needs and/or the lack of the right support may also affect behaviour. Some examples of conditions and syndromes that are more usually associated with PMLD are: Rett syndrome, tuberous sclerosis, Batten's Disease. All children and adults with PMLD will need high levels of support from families, carers and paid supporters. This will include help with all aspects of personal care, such as washing, dressing and eating, as well as ensuring that each individual has access to high-quality and meaningful activity throughout their lives. Those who offer this support will need access to good-quality and appropriate training, especially around particular skills; for example, on particular feeding needs and **communication** approaches. Good support is person centred, flexible and creative to enable the person with PMLD to learn and to achieve their full potential.

programme requirement a requirement which may be included in a **community order, youth rehabilitation order** or **suspended sentence order**, requiring the offender to attend an accredited individual or group programme. Typically this will be an **offending behaviour programme**.

prohibited activity requirement a requirement which may be included in a **community order, youth rehabilitation order** or **suspended sentence order**, forbidding the offender from participating in specified activities on a day or days.

prohibited steps order a court order under section 8 of the **Children Act 1989** that prevents a parent or any other person specified in the order from taking, without the consent of the court, a particular action that could be taken in meeting **parental responsibility**. Examples of possible prohibited steps orders are an order preventing the removal of a child from the United Kingdom, an order preventing a child undergoing certain surgery or an order preventing a change in a child's schooling.

prosecution (for unauthorized absence from school) legal action taken by a local authority, usually through the **education welfare service** to enforce school attendance for a child of **compulsory school age**.

Protection of Vulnerable Adults (POVA) a scheme set out in the **Care Standards Act 2000** and implemented in 2004 to provide a 'workforce ban' for those who have harmed people in their care, an employment safeguard, alongside **Criminal Records Bureau** checks (Department of Health 2004). To try and further protect vulnerable people from abuse, this scheme was introduced to enable a record of people known to have abused or mistreated others to be made available to potential employers; this is referred to as the POVA list, a list of those people held by the Secretary of State. People who have harmed others or placed others at risk either in their personal or work life will not be able to enter into further work with vulnerable people and it is the responsibility of the employing agency to check the status of an applicant. This is now superseded by the vetting and barring scheme (VBS) under the **Safeguarding Vulnerable Groups Act 2006** and POVA referrals shall be made to the **Independent Safeguarding Authority** (ISA). The effect of an ISA decision to place a person on the adults' barred list will be to prevent them from working in those workplaces covered by the POVA Scheme (DH 2009). From October 2009 it will be an offence to employ someone either voluntary or paid who is barred by the ISA.

Department of Health (2004) *Protection of Vulnerable Adults (POVA) Scheme in England and Wales for Care Homes and Domiciliary Care Agencies: a practical guide.* London: HMSO.

PSR see pre-sentence report

psychiatry the medical approach to the understanding and treatment of **mental health problems**.

Psychiatrists are qualified medical practitioners with a specialist postgraduate training in psychiatry. They are specialists and therefore have operated traditionally from the hospital base. Today they continue to practise in psychiatric in-patient units, but predominantly operate in community-based specialist **mental health** services. These are usually in the form of integrated health and **social care** teams, including social workers as **team** members with key roles in relation to their own statutory duties towards mental health **service user**s under the **NHS and Community Care Act 1990** and the **care programme approach** in mental health (see **mental health problems**).

Psychiatrists have further powers as **mental health** specialists, to implement compulsory interventions in respect of people with any form of mental health problem under the **Mental Health Act 2007**.

psychodynamic approach an approach to **social work** that uses some of the main concepts of psychoanalysis.

Social work theory and practice were heavily influenced by psychoanalytic ideas in the 1940s and 1950s. They particularly adopted the concept that children develop through a number of stages and the notion that if this development is incomplete children's behaviour can become 'fixated', remaining stuck at a certain level, or 'regress', returning to that of an earlier stage of development. The psychodynamic approach also viewed the adult **personality** as a product of **childhood** development. Adults suffered **anxiety** when **childhood** relationship conflicts had not been fully resolved. Adults deal with **anxiety** by employing a number of defence mechanisms, such as regression, denial (refusal to accept that something is a problem or causes distress) or projection (an unacceptable feeling such as hatred or anger is attributed to another person).

Social work theorists developed a model using psychodynamic concepts but in a way more applicable to relatively fluid and less intensive relationships between social workers and **service user**s. They saw service users' problems and distress as arising from childhood needs and drives (often as a result of poor relationships with parents) that persisted into adulthood because they had not been adequately dealt with at the time. The service users experience distress arising from poor ego functioning – that is, an ego that has not mastered living in the day-to-day world. Social workers used a number of techniques to help service users. Among these were: *diagnostic understanding*, understanding the precise origins of a service user's distress; *ventilation*, allowing the service user to express feelings; and *corrective relationship*, whereby the relationship with the social worker enabled the service user to compensate for previously unsatisfactory relationships. Above all, by exploring and giving insight into the origins of conflict the practitioner helped the service user to become aware of how to change. The psychodynamic approach was widely criticized in later decades for lacking a way of addressing the social origins of problems. Indeed, a number of psychodynamically oriented theorists did introduce a social dimension into their analysis. Even so, the main legacy of the approach was a deep impact on **social work** terminology, which, in its crudest terms, was used to describe service users in a patronizing way. Behaviour could be described as 'infantile' or refusal to accept a social worker's point of view as 'denial'. There was also the tendency to examine a service user's current difficulties as reflections of deeper problems of unsatisfactory relationships and to overlook the very real dilemmas of current relationships or environmental pressures.

psychopathy see **personality disorder**

psychoses a group of incapacitating **mental health problems** that severely disrupt thinking, speech and behaviour, and coping. Psychoses include **schizophrenia**, **bipolar disorder** and serious forms of **depression**. About 3 per cent of the population may be diagnosed with these conditions.

Psychoses have traditionally been contrasted with **neuroses** as a more serious set of **mental health** concerns. This is because the symptoms associated with psychoses are understood to sever the person's link to the realities of life in whatever way these are viewed by the person's culture. In turn, these are thought to result in serious difficulties affecting every area of the person's life and coping, and sometimes in serious risk for the person themselves or for others. The seriousness of these difficulties is reflected in findings that in modern societies, only about a third of those who have been admitted to hospital fully recover, while many experience severe, persistent difficulties with frequent relapses. However, cross-national research shows that in traditional societies where people with mental health problems may be more socially included, recovery is at much higher rates.

People with psychoses have traditionally been responded to primarily by psychiatry. However, although **psychiatry** is still prominent in mental

health services, many debates and changes have taken place over recent
years in relation to the kinds of understandings and responses thought
appropriate to the issues experienced by mental health service users.
Looking back over time, primarily biomedical genetic models of psychoses
gave way to models which took more account of social factors.
Consequently, the stress vulnerability model has been dominant in mental
health services, in which it is believed that the biochemical processes
linked to psychotic symptoms only emerge in the face of an accumulation
of stressors. More recently, however, social and **recovery models** have
become influential, bringing the assumption that many of the problems
associated with psychoses can be overcome by social **participation**,
access to employment and by developing self-management strategies –
and where difficulties remain, it is thought that people can still lead an
ordinary, fulfilling life. Changes have also taken place in recent times in
thinking about the legislation required for the protection of **service user**s
and the public in respect of mental health risk.

These changes in understandings of psychoses have had an impact on
mental health services. With social and recovery models gaining influence,
there is more recognition that medical interventions are only one of a
range of interventions needed to promote recovery and quality of life.
There is particular recognition that social factors have a very significant
influence upon all mental health problems, and the principle that people
even with the most serious mental health problems should access an
ordinary life. Thus it is recognized that both health and **social care**
professionals including **social work** have their part to play.

Social workers are therefore likely to work with these **service user**s with
more serious mental health problems, in an integrated mental health
team, using the **care programme approach**. Social workers have statutory
duties towards mental health service users under the **NHS and
Community Care Act 1990**, and have much to contribute to
their improved **wellbeing** and their greater control over their lives
(see **mental health problems** and **mental illness**).

Archambeault, J. (2009) *Social Work and Mental Health*. Exeter:
Learning Matters.

Public Guardian the role of the Public Guardian is to protect people
who lack capacity from abuse. The Office of the Public Guardian was set
up in October 2007 to facilitate and oversee the registering of Enduring
Power and **Lasting Power of Attorney** arrangements and to supervise
Court of Protection deputies who are appointed to protect vulnerable
people. The Public Guardian, supported by the Office of the Public
Guardian (OPG) helps protect people who lack capacity by: setting up
and managing a register of Lasting Powers of Attorney (LPA); setting up

and managing a register of Enduring Powers of Attorney (EPA); setting up and managing a register of court orders that appoint Deputies; supervising Deputies, working with other relevant organizations (for example, social services, if the person who lacks capacity is receiving **social care**); instructing Court of Protection Visitors to visit people who may lack mental capacity to make particular decisions and those who have formal powers to act on their behalf such as Deputies; receiving reports from Attorneys acting under LPA and from Deputies; and providing reports to the Court of Protection, as requested, and dealing with cases where there are concerns raised about the way in which Attorneys or Deputies are carrying out their duties.

The Public Guardian is also personally responsible for the management and organization of the OPG, including the use of public money and the way it manages its assets. A separate Public Guardian Board scrutinizes the work of the Public Guardian and then reports to the Lord Chancellor. This links directly to the **Mental Capacity Act 2005**, **Lasting Power of Attorney** and Court of Protection.

public inquiry a form of inquisitorial investigation into past events where problems of public concern are evident. These proceedings are frequently utilized to investigate failures in areas of **social care** and are often high-profile events involving significant expenditure of public money. The most important cases in recent years have been those involving investigations into areas of **child abuse** or the death of children while in care or identified as at risk. In these cases social service departments are often identified as having a responsibility for care or protection and as not having adequately executed that responsibility. In the area of care, an example was the inquiry into the operation of care homes in North Wales where significant levels of organized abuse were discovered. The **Victoria Climbié** Inquiry investigated the death of a child while in the care of relatives and revealed failures on the part of social services, the **police** and other key agencies of the state to protect a child evidently at risk of serious abuse. However, calls for a public inquiry are not always met and normal prosecutions through the courts may be seen as an alternative, as in the case of **Baby P** in 2009. These inquiries normally involve a senior member of the judiciary, who takes evidence from a wide range of interested parties, cross-examines the witnesses and then makes significant recommendations on the responsibility of the participants and for improvements in the service. The **advice** emerging from the inquiries are then provided to the Minister, who decides whether to act on the findings.

Corby, B., Doig, A. and Roberts, V. (2001) *Public Inquiries into Abuse of Children in Residential Care*. London: Jessica Kingsley.

Public Interest Disclosure Act 1998 see whistleblowing

pupil referral unit (PRU) provision made by a local authority or a
partnership of schools for children who cannot currently be educated
in a school, usually as a result of **exclusion from school** or more general
behavioural difficulties. (They may actually be called something else:
inclusion unit; support unit; re-integration centre.) **Local authorities**
and schools operate different models of PRU provision, developed to
meet local circumstances and in line with local policies. Models of
provision that may be included in the blanket term 'PRU' include:
provision on a single site; provision on several sites under a single
management structure; a peripatetic Pupil Referral Service (particularly
in rural areas); 'E-learning' provision using ICT and web-based resources;
hospital and home teaching services, or discrete parts of a service
which provide education in a unit or school-type setting; some hospital
provision; provision for young mothers/pregnant schoolgirls; 'umbrella'
provision to register pupils who follow individual programmes elsewhere.
Legally, any centre maintained by a local authority for children who,
because of exclusion or other reasons, are not able to attend a mainstream
or special school is a PRU regardless of whether it is described as such.
They are subject to **inspection** by **Ofsted** on the same basis as schools.
PRUs may provide full or part time education, in **partnership** with a
school or as an alternative to mainstream provision. They may offer
provision directly or can organize packages of educational provision
involving other providers, e.g. further education (FE) colleges,
work-based training and programmes offered by the private
sector (including independent schools), voluntary and **community**
organizations and by other statutory agencies. See also **alternative
educational provision**.

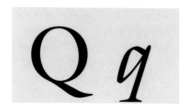

quango a form of government agency used to provide services or carry out other duties determined by government. The term, which is North American in origin, is subject to some dispute as to what it means. Originally an acronym for 'quasi-autonomous non-governmental organization', it referred to voluntary and non-profit organizations that had become dependent on grants and funding from government and were thus seen to be linked into government policy implementation, and questions were asked about their independence. In Britain the term more frequently became associated with agencies established by government departments, among the best known example being the Equalities and Human Rights Commission. For this reason, the term sometimes refers to 'quasi-autonomous national governmental organization'.

queer/queer theory part of the wider development of gay and lesbian studies within academia, queer theory emerged as an attempt to challenge essentialized and fixed definitions of sexuality by adopting a more inclusive and exploratory understanding of sexual location.

Central to the idea of 'queer' is the postmodern notion of identity as fluid and changeable. Queer thinking also allows for the possibility of reinventing identity through gender performance. See also **femininity, masculinity, postmodernism**.

R r

'race' a term used to describe groups considered to be biologically distinct. The biological characteristics thought to typify such groups were believed to be constant or unalterable unless 'races' intermingled. The term has effectively been discredited by physical scientists and social scientists.

Most sociologists are no longer prepared to use the term **'race'** except in inverted commas, thus demonstrating that they do not accept the biological distinctness of ethnic (the preferred term) groups. 'Race' is clearly a socially constructed concept, which both currently and historically has been used to justify exploitative behaviour on the part of powerful groups. (See **racism**.)

Race Relations (Amendment) Act 2000 an Act that strengthened section 71 of the Race Relations Act 1976 by extending the protection against racial **discrimination** by public authorities and placing a new, enforceable positive duty on public authorities. The Act also introduced other important changes. It made chief **police** constables liable for acts of discrimination by officers under their direction or control. It allows complaints of racial discrimination in certain immigration decisions to be heard as part of 'one-stop' immigration appeals. It prohibits discrimination by ministers or government departments in recommending or approving public appointments and in the terms and conditions or termination of such appointments or in conferring honours, including peerages. The Act also introduced new arrangements for appointing members of the House of Lords. It allows complaints of racial discrimination in education to be brought directly before county or sheriff courts without having to be referred first to the Secretary of State for Education. It also limits the circumstances in which 'safeguarding national security' can be used to justify discrimination. In practice, it will mean that **local authorities** will need to ensure that all services are provided fairly and without discrimination, that policies and procedures do not discriminate directly or indirectly and that all their employment practices – recruitment, selection, promotion, access to training, support to staff – are fair. The first priority should centre on ensuring that systems are in place to monitor both the take-up of services by different groups, and the recruitment, selection and development of staff, and to consult with different groups on service provision. The Act also recognized that public bodies, including the **police**, might be responsible for devising and implementing policies and practices that could be 'institutionally racist' in consequence if not in intent.

Racial Equality Council a voluntary organization, previously known as a **community** relations council, constituted to promote good **'race'** relations within a particular area.

Race equality councils are registered charities. Financial support for the councils is usually from **local authorities** and from the **Equalities and Human Rights Commission**, with some funding from special projects sponsored by central government departments such as the **Home Office** and further financial support from local industries and affiliates. Councils have as their principal objectives: first, the implementation of policies designed to promote good **community** relations, together with the elimination of racial **discrimination** in the private, voluntary and public sectors; second, education and information services for the public; third, support and **advice** for ethnic communities; and fourth, support for individuals experiencing discrimination.

racially aggravated offence an offence which is regarded as more serious because it is motivated by **racism**. (See also **hate crime**.) New offences of racially aggravated wounding, assault, criminal damage, **harassment** and public order offences were introduced by the **Crime and Disorder Act 1998**, attracting more severe **sentences** than the non-aggravated offences. More generally, any offence with a racial or religious motivation must be treated by a sentencing court as an aggravating factor making the offence more serious.

racism(s) a complex process which can take many forms and can operate at an individual, cultural, social and institutional level (see **institutional racism**). It can be expressed through ideas, attitudes, actions and structures within society. These often overlap and are difficult to entangle.

Historically, discussions of race and racism have been associated with physical appearance and ideas of **'race'** ('colour **racism'**), but it has always been far more complex, as evident in academic discussions and debate regarding the term 'race' and processes of racism. In the British context, racism is related to histories of Empire, slavery and colonialism. These periods saw a marked construction of racial difference and a racial hierarchy which was used to justify and maintain **power** and control.

Pseudo-scientific notions of race and racial groups combined with other dominant discourses to construct ideas of particular racial types, resulting in some groups (at this time, white Europeans) being constructed as superior to other, so called racial groups. It is now widely agreed however that 'race' is a socially constructed category, rather than having any biological or scientific basis. This means that race and racism is therefore constructed by social, economic and political conditions. As such, racism is not static, and what was considered as not being racist in the past may become seen as racist over time. Similarly, the perpetrators and targets of racism are also likely to change over time and place. It may therefore be more useful to talk of racisms in the plural, as opposed to implying there is one type of racism. Indeed, whilst early attempts to theorize the complexities of racism and its relationship with **social work**/welfare focused on the racial dichotomy of black/white (as was necessary at that time to highlight issues of racism and to give voice to the previously marginalized and pathologized experiences of Black and minority ethnic groups in the UK), it is now evident that this model is inadequate as it fails to capture the complexities inherent in processes of racism and racialization. This is not to suggest that racism is any less real; indeed, racism continues to shape and structure British society and people's everyday lives. This is evident in statistics for racial **harassment**, new forms of cultural **racism** and continued inequalities between racial/ethnic groups in education, employment, etc. Therefore, processes of race and racialization continue to operate as a form of stratification and social division.

Dominelli, L. (2008) *Anti-Racist Social Work*, 3rd edition. Houndmills: Palgrave Macmillan.

radical social work an attempt to achieve a major rethink of social welfare and of social work theory and practice – by emphasizing the degree to which personal problems are shaped by such oppressive forces as class divisions, sex and racial discrimination or by emphasizing the role of the market in social welfare provision.

Britain has witnessed two loose movements regarded as radical in the field of social work over the past two decades or more. The first, springing from an unorganized socialist movement in the 1970s, held that the welfare state offered an important mechanism for sustaining and improving the conditions of poor and vulnerable people. This movement was united in the belief that social problems are socially constructed and in the main to be explained by structural inequality, notably social class. By contrast, earlier methods employed by social workers implied a view of problems as rooted in personal inadequacy or pathology, or perhaps in family dysfunction, rather than in poverty or differential life chances.

Major ingredients of this movement were 'consciousness raising' (explaining to users the structural origins of their problems), user involvement in the decision-making process, and community work and group work as legitimate methods to neutralize the dangers of casework, which tended to lay the blame for problems on individual weaknesses. It also placed greater emphasis on legal rights (including the right to free welfare services) and the creation of progressive political alliances of community and residents' groups, user groups, trade unions, pressure groups and political parties. This movement has been criticized for its omissions in relation to race and gender stratification, in particular, and for its lack of awareness of the problems of other oppressed groups, including people with disabilities, old people and gay men and lesbians.

The second movement, rooted in the new right of the 1980s, sought to be radical in an anti-welfarist stance. The New Right was committed to the **market**, individual enterprise and initiative, and to a view that public spending should be curtailed. The New Right attacked welfare provision because they believed it interferes with the free working of market forces. It perceived families as the principal source of moral responsibility and therefore of welfare, except where the market had encouraged the growth of welfare within a vigorous private sector. Although the notion of a welfare safety net was not entirely eroded, it was somewhat reduced in the 1980's and 1990's.

Acknowledging the growth of managerialism in social work generally, Ferguson and Woodward (2009) have attempted to 'relight the fire' of a radicalism which is closer in spirit to the earlier form of radical social work. They point to the very limited opportunities currently available to social workers to develop a more incisive anti-oppressive practice which may have some limited potential for inspiring some redistribution of life chances. They have identified the following four aspects of a radical practice as:
- retaining a commitment to good practice;
- "guerrilla warfare" and small scale resistance;
- working alongside service users and carers;
- collective activity and political campaigning.'

Stifled by a preoccupation to 'manage risk' at the cost of genuine preventative work and to restrict access to care services except for those in critical **need** that currently characterises statutory social work, the opportunities for a more radical practice currently seem greater in the voluntary sector.

Ferguson, I & Woodward, R (2009) *Radical social work in practice: Making a difference*, Bristol, The Policy Press

recidivism see **persistent offenders**

recording the process by which a social welfare agency maintains an account of its dealings with a **service user**. Such a record may be kept in written files or, increasingly, on computers (see **databases**).

The selection and recording of relevant information about **service users** and their families are core tasks for social welfare agencies and especially for **social work** agencies. Recording may be understood as an expression of accountability for practitioners to their agency, but it is also, crucially, a means by which there can be accountability to the service user and, beyond, to the general public and the profession. Recording can also constitute evidence in a court of law. It is generally agreed that the overriding principle for ethical and effective recording is the service user's best interests. Good practice to the service user requires clear and purposeful recording. Competent recording facilitates an accurate account of what has actually happened and an understanding of why it has happened. This process will enhance an evaluation or a review of progress in the work. It will also help colleagues if they have to take the work on, in the absence of the responsible worker. Additionally, recording is often used by social work agencies to gather critical information about their own activities for research or monitoring purposes.

There are many interesting practice issues and dilemmas in relation to recording. Access to personal files on the part of the service user, a principle established in law with the Access to Personal Files Act 1987, can in many instances be problematic. Should, for example, a family case file be open to scrutiny by all members of that family? It may be agreed as a basic right of civil liberties that service users should see their own records, but workers may need at times to protect other people's privacy and safety and their sources of information. Similarly, the business of writing an account of an individual's or family's problems that is truthful, that faces up to the considerable difficulties that some service users have but does not damage or label people in discouraging ways and may be shared with all the relevant people, is patently very difficult. A related matter, which can assist in this process, is writing the record with the service user; some regard this as a major change in orientation in dealings with service users. To inform people that they may see their record if they wish is a relatively passive commitment to greater access, but to take the record to them, to invite their scrutiny and to record with them is clearly going significantly further. Fashions have changed in relation to the fullness or brevity with which records are kept. In some critical and sensitive work, great detail helps to reveal hidden patterns; in other work areas, a detailed account of daily events is unnecessary. The depth of **recording** and analysis depends upon the objectives of the work. In all circumstances, however, it is important to distinguish facts from opinions, and where an opinion is ventured, the supporting evidence should always be listed to reveal the worker's thinking and analysis. Increasingly recording is driven by proformas devised to support the **common assessment framework** in relation to children or similar devices (see also **confidentiality**).

British Association of Social Workers (1984) *Ethical and Effective Recording*. London: BASW.

recovery policy the personal process of changing attitudes, values, feelings, goals, skills and roles in order to develop positive meanings in the wake of mental ill-health.

The concept of recovery in relation to illness has traditionally been associated with 'cure'. Cure is often understood as involving medical treatment for the illness, resulting in a return to normal functioning and normal life, the illness gone. However, different understandings of recovery, specifically in **mental health**, emerged with the Retreat movement and 'moral treatment' in the late 18th and early 19th centuries in England, and are currently highly influential in **mental health policy** in the USA, New Zealand and the UK. The prominence of these different understandings today, recognized as the recovery model, can be explained by their resonance with the perspectives of **service user** movements in mental health and **disability**, and with **modernization policy** for health and **social care** in the UK which promotes **citizenship**, social inclusion, independence, choice and control instead of **stigma**, segregation and dependency.

Core principles of recovery include both the use of the full range of effective treatments to minimize the symptoms and processes of mental health problems and mental distress, and crucially, what may be called 'social' or 'personal' recovery. The latter recognizes that a full clinical recovery may not be possible – and significantly, is not important – for an anti-discriminatory and social approach to mental health problems, in accord with service user movements and **social model of disability** perspectives, and recognizes these experiences as human difference which should be valued and accommodated in society. On this basis, personal recovery refers to recovery of hope and the ability to live an independent, fulfilling and satisfying life, despite symptoms. This process has also come to be defined by service users rather than by professionals: service users have led in the development of the model, and workers are expected to support individual service users in their own personal journey of recovery. Although the model has developed within the mental health context, it is being applied in other areas including **dementia** and people with severe learning disabilities, and is used with serious offenders with mental health problems.

The **values** embodied in the recovery model are central to mental health policy in the UK. They guide recent policy developments including the 'refocused' care programme approach in mental health, and the comprehensive cross-government vision for mental health, incorporating the promotion of mental health and **wellbeing** in the population, and the range of responses to people with poor mental health. Recovery values have also informed modernization of mental health policy over the longer term, emerging from the standards set in the National Service Framework for mental health in 1999. Importantly, these policy developments are concerned with the mental health issues experienced by the range of people who use **social work** and **social care** services, including for example, older people, learning disabled people, children, and parents, some of whom, through parental mental health problems may come into contact with childcare services.

Recovery is also a major focus of the capabilities for inclusive practice, promoting best practice in accord with **citizenship** values amongst practitioners. The influence of recovery **values** in all these policy areas means that social work practitioners need to be aware of them, and relate their practice to them. Recovery incorporates a set of values that challenge traditional expectations and practice in mental health, and themes providing guidance for practitioners.

Core to these values and themes is a shift from traditional practice concerned with pathology, illness, symptoms and dependence, to a focus on hope, strengths, wellness, fulfilment and control over one's life. The recovery process involves **empowerment**, which emphasizes the development of self-care and self-management of symptoms; individual responsibility; strategies for social inclusion and access to mainstream social roles; finding personal meaning in life which may involve spirituality, and developing a personal identity which does not involve illness – for example, seeing oneself as 'a schizophrenic'. This process often involves individuals in transforming themselves and their lives, rather than returning to their former selves. The process takes place within **assessment** and care management frameworks.

Treatments, services and supports are all important in promoting recovery – as demonstrated, for example, in refocusing the care programme approach – and the person centred, valuing worker–service user relationship is viewed as a major strand of the approach, supporting the person's motivation, hope, aspiration, and acting as companion in his or her individual journey. Crucial to this relationship is the awareness that the service user is the expert on his or her own life, and the role of the professional is that of **mentor**, coach, and supporter, enabling the person to pursue his or her own recovery. The approach has been critiqued from different service user, policy and professional perspectives. Some service users on the one hand are concerned that the approach will result in a loss of services, or pressure to enter employment when they are not ready, while others are concerned that adoption of the approach by mental health services will lead to professional domination of the recovery process. Some professionals have asserted with service users, that the approach should be accompanied by a full recognition of the services needed to support recovery, and others challenge the feasibility of the approach.

There are rights issues associated with the approach, for the definition of a disabled person under the **Disability Discrimination Act 1995** and **2005** requires the person's **impairment** to have a substantial impact on their life and functioning. At the same time, the approach seeks to maximize citizenship rights for people with mental health problems who have historically faced enormous **stigma** and **discrimination**.

Care Services Improvement Partnership, Royal College of Psychiatrists and Social Care Institute for Excellence (2007) *A Common Purpose: recovery in future mental health services.*

referral order an order imposed by a **youth court** on a young offender, consisting of a referral to a **youth offender panel** for up to 12 months. It is an example of a measure aimed at the **diversion** of young offenders out of the criminal justice system. When they were first introduced by the **Youth Justice and Criminal Evidence Act 1999**, courts were required to make referral orders in the cases of all young people appearing before a **youth court** for the first time and pleading guilty (except when the offence merits an absolute **discharge** or is so serious that only a **custodial sentence** can be justified), but these were the only circumstances when the order could be made. Following the **Criminal Justice and Immigration Act 2008**, courts can now make a referral order for a second conviction, provided a referral order was not previously made, and a second referral order can be made in exceptional circumstances.

Newburn, T., Crawford, A., Earle, R. *et al.* (2002) *The Introduction of Referral orders into the Youth Justice System: Final Report*, Home Office Research Study 242. London: Home Office.

reflective practice the ability to stand back and look critically at one's own practice.

In **social work** education there is an increasing emphasis being placed upon reflective practice both during basic training and also as part of a continuing professional development. The main themes include: an awareness of the impact that the individual worker will have upon the **service user** in terms of **race**, **gender**, **age**, **disability** and **class**; an awareness of the importance of **anti-discriminatory** and **anti-oppressive**

practice and how an individual service user has been affected by an oppressive society or **community**; an awareness of the worker's own prejudices and the impact that these will have upon practice issues; the ability to apply relevant knowledge to practice. Reflective practice is a skill in its own right and owes a lot to the seminal work of Schon. The distinction between 'reflection on action' and 'reflection in action' has been found to be useful. The former is essentially reflecting upon and reviewing past actions, events and decisions with a view to learning lessons and being able to 'do it better next time'. Reflection in action is the more immediate ability to review what one is doing when it is being done. This latter skill requires practitioners to be able to 'take time out' and not be pressed into poor decisions through unthinking habitual behaviour or because of, for example, immediate pressures from service users or management.

refuge a place of safety for women and children who have experienced violence from men within the home.

Refuges provide safe accommodation on a temporary basis for women and children made homeless by leaving violent homes. Refuge is also the name of the national organization that provides a network or refuges (as does **Women's Aid** Federation). There are specialist refuges for ethnic minority women, and many refuges provide additional services such as welfare rights advice, aftercare, **group work** with children and telephone help-lines. Most do not admit boys above a certain age and obtain maintenance and other services wherever possible from female workers. This is designed to create a safe environment for women and children who have been assaulted by men. Some refuges cater for particular groups such as African-Caribbean women, South Asian women or disabled women although such resources are as yet underdeveloped.

regeneration the economic and social revitalization of a disadvantaged area or city. Regeneration conventionally has two sides. One is economic, which aims to rebuild the local economy of a particular area through tax incentives, encouraging small business and corporate investment and improving the physical environment, whether through better transport or leisure facilities. The other is social – revitalizing the social fabric or **social capital** of an impoverished area as the key to improved levels of **wellbeing** for local residents. In the main, regeneration of either kind is associated with inner-city areas and low-income social housing estates that have suffered a cycle of disadvantage over a number of years. But regeneration efforts can also be found in rural areas, such as the former coalfields towns and villages where the abrupt **loss** of work following the mass closure of the mines produced similar levels of area-wide disadvantage.

What has become clear from the research is that to have a chance of success regeneration programmes should tackle simultaneously the different dimensions of **poverty** and disadvantage at the same time. Selecting just one element – for example, economic development or physical rehabilitation of old buildings or providing better social services – will not have sufficient impact on the lives of local residents. The problems of disadvantage and **social exclusion** interlock. Unsafe streets, the abandonment of public places to gangs or drug dealers, poor schools, high unemployment, dilapidated housing, high levels of **anti-social behaviour**, the withdrawal of local commerce all reinforce each other. Any attempt at rebuilding such an area must have a broad enough scope and sufficient intensity to deal with a number of these problems at the same time. Concentrating and targeting scarce resources on an entire area rather than individuals has been shown to be effective. **Participation** by local residents has also become a major theme of all regeneration efforts. But this is easier said than done. The complexity of programmes and the demands on residents' time are enormous. Residents' participation brings with it enormous responsibilities that would test the most powerful agencies of central government. Critics say central government has in effect delegated large responsibilities to local people without providing commensurate powers and resources.

Pierson, J. (2008) *Going Local: working in communities and neighbourhoods.* London: Routledge.

registered social landlord (RSL) housing associations and other agencies registered with the Tenants Services Authority.

Most of these new social landlords have arisen as a result of the transfer of local authority housing stock to new organizations. Prior to November 2008, they were regulated by the Housing Corporation; under the Housing and Regeneration Act 2008, the functions of the Housing Corporation were taken over by the Tenant Services Authority.

rehabilitation a process of restoration or recovery from an illness, accident or from some adverse circumstance or event.

The term was used widely in health settings in the latter part of the 20th century but now has much wider application in **social work** practice and in work in the criminal justice system. In health settings, rehabilitation has described attempts by doctors and other health professionals, such as physiotherapists and occupational therapists (see **occupational therapy**) to help people recover physically, emotionally and socially from physical illness, **mental illness** and trauma.

The term also accurately describes both social and health professionals' attempts to assist alcoholics and **substance misuse**rs (see **drug and alcohol policy**). Similarly, since the **Rehabilitation of Offenders Act**

1974 became law, the concept of rehabilitation has been applied to offenders and especially those who have received **custodial sentence**s. In all these cases, if a holistic approach is taken with recovery from illness, accident, addiction or past offending behaviour, it is clear that interventions often need to be multi-disciplinary. Although medical assistance has an important place in many rehabilitation programmes, there is increasing recognition of the importance of social and practical support in relation to personal and social skills, relationships, employment (where appropriate), housing and income. The other key issue regarding rehabilitation is that any planned programme should be realistic, given the problems/conditions of the **service user** and their circumstances. Such programmes should take into account the person's motivation, personal skills and morale in order to enable him or her to feel that objectives and targets can be met.

Rehabilitation of Offenders Act 1974 an Act whose underlying principle is that people with criminal convictions, especially if they are minor, should eventually be able to put the past behind them in the interests of **rehabilitation**. The legislation assists in this process by making some convictions 'spent' after a 'rehabilitation period' if the person concerned does not re-offend during that time. The Act's provisions were extended to **cautions** (including **conditional cautions, reprimands, final warnings** and **youth conditional cautions**) by the **Criminal Justice and Immigration Act 2008**. After a conviction or **caution** legally becomes 'spent', the ex-offender no longer has to declare it (for example, when applying for a job or obtaining insurance) except in certain specified circumstances (as when applying for jobs that involve working with children or other vulnerable people). Rehabilitation periods vary between instantaneous (for a caution other than a conditional caution) and ten years (for a **sentence of imprisonment** of between 6 months and 2 years. Convictions leading to longer periods of imprisonment are not covered by the Act. Rehabilitation periods for young offenders under 18 on conviction are shorter than those for adults.

reintegrative shaming a process of encouraging offenders to feel, express and come to terms with shame about their behaviour in a manner designed to encourage their **rehabilitation** and reintegration into society.

The theory of reintegrative shaming has been developed by the Australian criminologist John Braithwaite and others over the past two decades, but it has been practised in a range of cultures for centuries. Braithwaite argues that offenders should be dealt with in a manner that shames them before other members of their **community**. However, shaming can be of a '**stigma**tizing' nature which will tend to exclude them from being accepted by the community; this (as **labelling theory** suggests) will be counter-productive, making re-offending much more likely. Instead, the shaming should be of a kind which serves to reintegrate offenders, by getting them to accept that they have done wrong while encouraging others to readmit them to society. Reintegrative shaming often involves a formal or ritualized process of discussion between offenders, **victims** and community representatives, aimed at achieving consensus about the harm done and the way forward. This may take place in a public or semi-public setting, and is followed by gestures or ceremonies which demonstrate that the offender's apology or remorse has been accepted and that the offender is therefore welcomed back into the community.

Reintegrative shaming involves mobilizing community **participation** in criminal justice and giving a formal voice to the victims of crime. At the same time, offenders are treated with respect and their views are heard. This is achieved by involving people who are part of the community of care of both the **victim** and the offender in the process of responding to the offence. The theory of reintegrative shaming underlies much of the practice of **restorative justice**. The practice associated with restorative justice are particularly suitable for pursuing reintegrative shaming, while the performance of **reparation** shames the offender symbolically while seeking to set matters right between the offender, the **victim** and the community. Mechanisms for implementing reintegrative shaming include **family group conferences** and **victim–offender mediation**.

Braithwaite, J. (1989) *Crime, Shame and Reintegration*. Cambridge: Cambridge University Press.

remand temporary disposal of a defendant or convicted offender during criminal proceedings, for example pending trial or during adjournments for the preparation of reports (for example **pre-sentence reports**). Remands can either be on **bail** in the **community** (including in a **bail hostel**) or in **custody**. Custodial remands account for 15–20 per cent of the **prison** population. Young offenders are only meant to be remanded to custodial institutions as a last resort, and although large numbers are still sent to custody, there is a range of alternative placements available to **youth offending teams** through the **Youth Justice Board** (see also **secure estate**). (See also **bail**.)

reminiscence therapy the process of recalling the past, a technique of memory-revival usually used with **older people** who have experienced memory loss.

Reminiscence work with **older people** has developed in the past ten years and is an important strategy for aiding them, particularly in **group work** settings such as residential or **day care**. Reminiscence work is a form of oral history-sharing that involves older people with their

peer group and with carers. It is easy to instigate, yet the **outcomes** can be a rewarding and enriching experience. For example, all members of a small group of older people may be asked to bring a small object to the group that has significance for them and then to tell the group the story of that object, such as a brooch or an ornament. This in turn may stimulate memories in other group participants, and a rewarding diversity of conversation topics may be generated that may have immediate relevance to group participants. Reminiscence work thus creates 'communities' of memories that maintain and re-establish a person's place and role within the **community**.

Shared memories renew a sense of rootedness and connectedness to others that helps to anchor the person with memory difficulties in a social setting. Conventional or pre-existing relationships may change for a little while as the older person shares, with his or her carer or peers, times from the past, giving the older person control over conversation topics. It has been shown that reminiscence group participants arrive early for sessions, greet others with enthusiasm and anticipate the events with pleasure – often wearing their best clothes and jewellery for the sessions, indicating that the group has the status of an event in the older person's life. For some people, however, reminiscence is painful, and the unavoidable recall of **loss** that accompanies later life may mean that sessions can be distressing for all concerned. Workers need to be genuine and skilled in supporting older people through sad memories. Involvement in reminiscence groups has been seen to help residents new to group living and to aid their transition from home and their integration into group life. It has been suggested that groups become 'safe places for sharing both joyful and sad recollections', giving participants an enhanced sense of the value and significance of their past lives and enriching their relationships with contemporaries and workers.

reparation   action undertaken by an offender to make amends for the crime. Reparation can take the form of an apology, financial **compensation** paid to the **victim** of the crime, work performed directly for the benefit of the victim, or for victims generally, or **unpaid work** to benefit the general **community**. It can take place on a voluntary basis, or as part of obligations imposed on an offender under a **community order** (for example by way of an **activity requirement**), a **suspended sentence order**, a **conditional caution**, or a **youth conditional caution** or **reparation order**. Reparation is an important component of the theory and practice of **restorative justice**. Reparation was made one of the statutory purposes of **sentences** by the **Criminal Justice Act 2003**. A reparation order is a community sentence requiring a young offender under the age of 18 to perform reparation, either directly to the victim of the crime or to the community in general. The reparation order was introduced by the **Crime and Disorder Act 1998**. It requires a young offender to carry out up to 24 hours of reparative work within three months of the making of the order, supervised by a **responsible officer**, usually a member of a **youth offending team**. Direct reparation to individual victims requires the victim's (but not the offender's) consent. There is a presumption in favour of making reparation orders in cases where the court has power to do so, and courts are required to give reasons when they decide not to make an order.

reprimand an alternative to court proceedings for offences by young people under the age of 18.

Reprimands were introduced by the **Crime and Disorder Act 1998**, and (along with **final warnings**) replaced **cautions** for young offenders in England and Wales. (See also **youth conditional caution**.) A reprimand is given by the **police**, and at their discretion, for a first offence that is relatively minor; a subsequent offence may receive a final warning, or the offender may be prosecuted. Reprimands can only be given if the young person admits the offence, and may be cited in court in the same way as previous convictions.

research social research is the conduct of systematic study in order to describe social behaviour or to test theories about social behaviour. Much of the knowledge on which social workers draw in the context in which they work is the product of social research. This includes both *primary* research, in which researchers have generated new data, and *secondary* research, in which existing data is re-used for new purposes. The latter constitutes an important source of information, with researchers extracting relevant data about the health, living conditions and working lives of the population from government surveys such as the Census, the General Household Survey, the Labour Force Survey and the Family Expenditure Survey.

Research into **social work** itself, however, has until recently been more limited. There has been disagreement between those who claim that social work and its **outcomes** are too complex to measure and others who argue for a more scientific approach to research and evaluation. This focus on evaluation and effectiveness is reflected in the work of the Social Work Research Unit at the University of Stirling among others, and is consistent with present policy, which emphasizes the importance of research in informing professionals about 'what works' in social work and **social care**. The integration of research-based evidence of effectiveness into practice is often referred to as **evidence-based practice** and was originally introduced in the **National Health Service** to identify the most effective clinical practice. In social work and social care, there can be a range of different types of evidence about the effectiveness of practice and the views, feelings, behaviour and circumstances of **service users**. The type of evidence that is collected, and the way that social work researchers design their research studies, will depend on the nature of the research problem and also practical, theoretical and ethical issues. Social workers should be able to understand how existing research findings have been generated, to identify any weaknesses in research and to accurately identify key research findings and their implications for policy and practice. The **Department of Health** has therefore indicated that, in future, research methodology will be a component of qualifying degree courses.

The reasons for undertaking research can differ considerably, and research studies can be of different types. *Exploratory* research is used in order to gain an initial understanding of an issue or setting that has been little researched in the past. It is often used to identify topics that could be included in subsequent studies and can overlap with *descriptive* research, which aims to provide a picture of patterns of behaviour or the characteristics of a group of people. If researchers need to go beyond this, they may conduct an *explanatory* study that seeks to find the reasons or causes for behaviour or differences between groups. The types of explanation may vary from the discovery of the motives and frames of reference of participants to the testing of a hypothesis about associations or causal relationships between two or more variables, as in overtly *scientific* approaches to research. In *evaluative* research, which assesses a particular intervention or practice, one or more of the above approaches can be adopted depending on the type of evidence which is sought. Whatever the purposes of the research, it is always necessary to clearly identify the research problem or question that it attempts to address. This is usually defined in relation to both empirical and theoretical issues. For example, a study about the needs of children might be framed by drawing on a theoretical approach such as **attachment** theory.

Researchers must also choose the settings in which to carry out their research; the choice of particular settings will, of course, have an impact on the results. For example, in research on **homelessness**, the number of young women affected has often been underestimated because of the practice of researching in the street or in **hostel**s rather than in homes where they are staying temporarily. Having framed the research problem and decided on settings, the researcher has to identify an appropriate methodology. Research strategies include *surveys*, in which standardized methods are used to collect data about a sample of respondents and comparisons drawn; *case studies*, in which a variety of methods are used to collect data about a single setting; *comparative case studies*, in which two or more settings are compared; and *longitudinal designs*, which allow for repeated data collection from the same group so as to chart change over time. An example of this is the New Child Development Survey, in which data is collected about children born in one week in 1958 at regular intervals. Longitudinal designs can be useful for investigating the effect of interventions, although they are not as rigorous as *experimental designs* in this respect. Experiments consist of collecting relevant data from two similar groups before one of the groups receives a new service or treatment in which the researcher is interested. The two groups can then be compared after having a different type of service. However, it is often unethical to withhold a potentially effective or supportive service from one group, and it is therefore more common to use *quasi experimental designs* in which naturally occurring groups are compared. For example, services to **older people** may be about to change in one local authority area but not in another, which allows for before and after comparison of the two groups.

Once the strategy has been determined, a data collection method must be selected. Among the methods a researcher might choose are: in-depth interviewing; **interviewing** using questionnaires; participant observation; structured observation; secondary analysis of official statistics or documentary analysis. In-depth interviews can be used to collect the 'narrative' of the person being interviewed (with only a minimal list of topics for guidance), while a highly structured questionnaire can be used for either an interview or a postal survey. Observation methods can range from **participation** (in which the researcher takes part in the activities of the setting) through to structured observation of others using a structured checklist. In the past, many researchers had a clear preference for either *qualitative* research methods, which generate data in the form of words describing the experience and perspectives of participants, or *quantitative* methods, which generate data in the form of numbers, allowing statistical comparisons between groups to be made. Quantitative methods have been traditionally associated with 'top-down' approaches in which the theoretical orientation, design and interpretation of research were determined by the researcher. The perspectives of research participants were more likely to permeate the design of qualitative studies. It is now increasingly recognized, however, that these methods can complement each other so as to provide a fuller understanding of social phenomena, and that both qualitative and quantitative research can reflect the perspectives of participants. Many studies therefore use a combination of qualitative and quantitative methods.

There remains an ongoing debate, however, about whether researchers should 'take sides' when designing research and interpreting their findings, particularly where these might be used to promote the interests of oppressed groups. The advocates of *emancipatory research* have argued that research claiming to be objective has often been based on the erroneous assumptions of powerful groups rather than being truly objective, whereas others argue against the erosion of the scientific standards that they feel protect the credibility of social research. Recent policy has emphasized sharing the control of research with research participants and taking account of their perspectives rather than relying solely on existing academic and professional frameworks to inform the design of research. However, there should still be transparency in the way that research is conducted and findings interpreted, as it is this that distinguishes social research from less systematic forms of investigation. In quantitative research, this is often achieved through standardized procedures that are replicable, whereas detailed 'reflexive accounts' of the research process can be used in qualitative research.

McLaughlin, H. (2006) *Understanding Social Work Research.* London: Sage.

Research Register for Social care as part of the **Social Care Institute for Excellence** the Research Register will record all **social care** research that has received independent review for scientific merit and has received ethical approval through the research governance framework. This will provide a valuable source of research evidence to support practice as well as work to ensure that research in **social care** complies with the ethical rigour which has been a part of healthcare research since the **Department of Health** published the research governance framework in 2001.

residence order a court order under section 8 of the **Children Act 1989** that specifies with whom the child is to live. It is used primarily in matrimonial disputes, replacing the older concept of **custody**. The aim of the residence order is to reduce tension between divorcing parents, because neither party any longer 'wins custody'; the issue is now merely one of the court's deciding where the child or children should live. Whatever the court's decision, both parents retain **parental responsibility** and are expected to continue to take part in decisions regarding the child. It is possible for the court to grant a residence order to each parent, with the child living alternate weeks with each. The residence order can also be used in other **family proceedings** and can be applied for by people who are not parents and who do not hold parental responsibility for the child. For example, a grandparent may apply for a residence order on a grandchild in care proceedings as an alternative to the local authority's application for a care order or **supervision order**. Or he or she may apply for a residence order some time after a care order was made at a previous hearing; if the application is successful, the care order is automatically discharged. As another example of the order's flexibility, **foster care**rs may apply for a residence order on a child who has been living with them for more than 3 years.

Whenever an applicant is granted a residence order, it automatically gives parental responsibility for the child to the person who has applied, if he or she does not have it already. It thus provides a means by which grandparents or other members of the child's extended family, and indeed foster carers, become included in decisions regarding the child. Children may also apply for a residence order on their own behalf and have done so when they want to live with a person other than their parents. There are no specific grounds for the residence order other than the **welfare checklist** in the Children Act and the consideration that making the order should be better for the child than not making it. The local authority cannot apply but can support others such as foster carers to do so.

residence requirement a requirement which may be included in a **community order, youth rehabilitation order** or **suspended sentence order**, requiring the offender to live in a particular place. This can include a **bail hostel. A youth rehabilitation order** can contain a 'local authority residence requirement', ordering that the young person live in accommodation provided by the local authority.

residence tests eligibility for welfare support in its various forms, including benefits, social housing, **community care** services, and health care is increasingly dependent on satisfying residence tests and migration status requirements such as the 'habitual residence' test. In the case of benefits, for example, a family member of a European Economic Area national must usually reside in the UK with that national and maintain her **right to reside** before she can access UK social housing or benefits. Those who do not have the requisite residence status will generally be excluded from benefits, social housing, and community care services. Key restrictions in this regard are in the **Immigration and Asylum Act 1999** (particularly in barring out those subject to immigration control from benefits and services); and in the Nationality, Asylum and Immigration Act 2002 (which provides further barriers to access to community care services). Such services may, nevertheless, be provided if this is necessary to avoid a **breach** of a person's EU Law or Convention rights. For example, withdrawal of support may interfere in 'family life'; or constitute inhuman or degrading treatment under the European Convention of Human Rights article 3, particularly if the person has no other means of support than benefits or social services assistance, as confirmed by the House of Lords in the leading case of *R v Secretary of State for the Home*

Department, ex parte Adam and Others (2004). In that case, the Lords ordered the reinstatement of support for failed asylum claimants who had no other source of assistance when NASS support was withheld.

residential work social work undertaken within units where people live, either permanently or temporarily.

Residential provision has many purposes: an alternative home, therapy, respite care, **custody**, diagnosis and assessment, or some combination of these. From workhouse to orphanage, from asylum to **prison**, residential work to some social end has existed for some considerable time. In general terms, however, residential provision for many **service user** groups has contracted in the past few decades; some has changed in character, and virtually all residential services have been closely examined. The review of residential provision has been motivated partly by its substantial cost and partly by fundamental criticisms of some residential services.

In relation to children, long-stay **children's home**s have reduced in number very significantly. This change has come about principally because children's experiences of long-term residential care have been very negative – in effect, allowing children to drift without effective care plans; and in some instances residential units have not been able to handle very troubled young people who behave in challenging ways. Most **local authorities** seek to place as many children as they can into **foster care** placements. Strategic policy for children's residential services is undeveloped and many residential facilities experience substantial staff turnover in response to unsocial hours, poor pay and sometimes stressful behaviour of 'residents'. Staff within such services are often unqualified and, although often very committed to the children, felt themselves to be undervalued by their employers. Other residential provision for children, such as observation-and-**assessment** centres, has also attracted criticism because of the problem of trying to assess children when they have been removed from their normal environment. If a family cannot cope with a child any more, such arrangements may still be necessary, but they are now regarded as a measure of last resort.

For old people, the growth of local authority residential homes (under Part III of the **National Assistance Act 1948**) has been reversed, partly by the growth of private provision and partly with a renewed commitment to **community care** services. Cuts in public expenditure have also contributed to this change as providers claim that the funding for residential care is increasingly untenable. Some commentators have questioned the need for **social work** services at all in many contemporary residential facilities for old people, arguing that nursing care applies for some and that for the rest long-term but not demanding support is needed from **social care** 'assistants'. For people with long-term

mental health problems and those with learning disabilities who previously might have been long-stay hospital patients, residential provision has been developed in sometimes imaginative ways, although demand continues to outstrip supply. A range of residential services is available in some areas that reflects the ability of people to live more or less independently. **Group home**s are examples of such provision, with **housing association**s particularly active in this area.

Residential provision is increasingly specialized and focused. Examples are **bail hostels** as alternatives to remand in **custody**, units to help prepare children for leaving care, respite care for a range of client groups to give carers a break or a holiday, secure accommodation for children who are a danger to themselves or to others, and residential facilities with a very particular therapeutic focus – for example, programmes for **sex offender**s. Alongside such developments, the status of residential work is increasing as workers are seen to offer very specialized skills. In the light of the number of incidents of **child abuse** in residential homes, the government has also committed itself to a greater proportion of qualified **social work** staff in residential work.

Respect Agenda a prominent theme in the approach to crime and **anti-social behaviour** pursued by the Labour government following the general election of 2005, formally launched by a 'Respect Action Plan' in January 2006. It comprises a range of measures aimed at curbing anti-social behaviour by promoting the lost social ethos of respect and tackling low-level nuisance behaviour employing novel measures including **anti-social behaviour orders** and **fixed penalty notices**. Such measures often lack some of the formal safeguards associated with traditional criminal justice. This aspect of the Respect Agenda embodies something akin to a **zero tolerance** approach to minor crime and low-level disorder. Other aspects of the 2006 Respect Action Plan included measures aimed at improving parenting, intensive schemes aimed at changing the behaviour of 'problem families', improving children's attendance and behaviour at school, providing activities for children and young people, and empowering local communities to deal with anti-social behaviour. Between 2005 and 2008, coordination of the Respect Agenda was the responsibility of a cross-governmental task force headed by Louise Casey, the Co-ordinator for Respect in the **Home Office** (or 'Respect Tsar'). This body was replaced by a youth task force within the Department for Children, Schools and Families in 2008.

Home Office (2006) *Respect Action Plan*. London: Home Office.

respite care and services care for vulnerable people provided either in their own homes or, more usually, in a residential or day-care setting that supplements the care provided by the main carer – usually a family member or friend. Respite care can also be seen as a positive strategy to enhance the quality of life for the cared-for person.

There is now recognition that good practice in respite care provision should ensure a stimulating and enjoyable experience for the **service user** as well as an opportunity for the main carer to have a break. The pattern of care depends upon need and available resources. It may be for a few weeks a year to permit habitual **carers** to, say, take a holiday, or it may be for a few hours a day or a week. Patterns of respite care may increase as a problem increases in severity, as with a dying person. Usually respite care is provided in residential facilities – services include short-term care beds in **hostel**s, hospitals and small homes as well as care provided in the homes of specially recruited and trained families. In addition, respite may be provided in a service user's own home by the employment of support staff for this purpose. Most respite services are hard pressed and are unable to give as much support to carers as they or the carers would wish. Charges are levied for some of these services, and there are local variations in rates. Concerns about the appropriateness, quality and availability of some respite care have been raised, particularly in the case of service users from Black and ethnic minority groups. (See **palliative care**.)

responsible officer the person with the responsibility for administering and enforcing a **community sentence**. Depending on the **sentence**, this could be a **probation officer**, a member of the **youth offending team**, the manager of an **attendance centre** or (in the case of a requirement enforced by **electronic monitoring**) an employee of a private security firm performing the monitoring.

restorative justice a term used to refer to a wide range of informal processes that seek to deal with offences by involving offenders, **victims** and others affected by the offence, emphasizing reconciliation – the restoration of relationships between offenders, victims and the **community** –, **reparation** and the resolving of conflicts by informal discussion, as an alternative to traditional criminal justice.

According to advocates of restorative justice, the traditional criminal justice system has unhelpfully interposed the state between parties in conflict, and over-emphasized the offender at the expense of the **victim**. Restorative approaches do not remove state agencies from the process altogether, but they attempt to ensure that the participants are enabled to reach their own agreed solutions to the conflicts created by crime. Informal structures can in some cases replace the need for decisions by **criminal courts,** or agreements reached informally (for example, about reparation to be performed by the offender) can subsequently be officially endorsed by courts. Restorative justice processes include **family group conferences, victim–offender mediation**, 'sentencing circles' and 'circles of support and accountability' (see below), and **community** conferences which involve representatives of the local community, while favoured **outcomes** of such processes include reparation of various kinds.

Some of these processes and outcomes can find a place within formal criminal justice processes and measures, including **conditional cautions**, community orders and (for young offenders) **final warnings, youth conditional cautions, reparation orders** and **referral orders**. The introduction of **family group conferences** for young offenders in New Zealand (based on traditional Maori customs) in the 1980s and 1990s was successful in producing informally agreed outcomes and in achieving **diversion** of young offenders from courts and **custody**. In many cases, it also reassured victims and changed the attitudes of offenders. The process has subsequently been adapted for use in other countries and with adults. Another influential development was victim–offender mediation, pioneered in Canada in the 1970s. Changes to sentencing practices along restorative lines also originated in North America, where 'circle sentencing' began in the early 1990s. The idea of a supportive circle of concerned individuals, including those who know the offender best, taking part in decisions about how to respond to their offending was subsequently extended with the development of 'circles of support and accountability' which augment the **community supervision** of offenders (often **sex offenders**) on **early release** from **prison** as part of their **licence** conditions. Friends, family members and **volunteers** 'encircle' the offender with support, surveillance and help in the community but report regularly to the official authorities. Projects of this kind have been established in Canada and, more recently, in the UK.

Restorative justice has found favour with the government in recent years, although critics observe that the restorative principle has been distinctly subordinate to a general increase in punitiveness. Nevertheless, elements of restorative justice have been introduced and encouraged in relation to innovations such as **community orders, conditional cautions, reparation orders, youth conditional cautions** and **referral orders**. Many of these relate specifically to young offenders and/or are in effect restricted to use with minor offenders. However, reparation was made one of the statutory purposes of **sentences** by the **Criminal Justice Act 2003**, and in 2003 the government outlined a general strategy to expand the scope of restorative justice, stating that it had an important part to play at all stages of the criminal justice system. (See also **reparation, reintegrative shaming**.)

Dignan, J. (2005) *Understanding Victims and Restorative Justice*. Maidenhead: Open University Press.

reunification   a term used to describe rights and procedures invoked to secure family members' reunion after a period of separation – for example as a result of immigration restrictions. In particular, EC Directive 2003/86 was enacted to protect the family and respect family life enshrined in many instruments of international law.

The Directive aims to implement fundamental rights and principles recognized by article 8 of the European Convention for the Protection of Human Rights and Fundamental Freedoms, and in the Charter of Fundamental Rights of the European Union. It is also used in the context of returning children to their families after they have been **looked after** by a **local authority** for a period of time. The conclusion of much research in the 1980s was that children who were looked after by the local authority away from home for a period of time easily lost touch with their families. The longer the period of separation, the greater the likelihood that the children would remain in the long-term care of the authority. To successfully reunite looked after children means consciously planning for their return from the very beginning of placements. To do this, social workers and foster parents or residential care staff facilitate **contact** such as visits and exchange of letters and gifts. The intention is to keep the parents and family involved in the life of their child and allow them to make as many decisions affecting their child as possible. The concept of reunification therefore has to do both with the planned return as well as with the actual return of the child to members of their family. The family is understood in the extended sense – the child may be returned to relatives such as grandparents or adult siblings, for example.

For many years the word 'rehabilitation' was used to denote this process of returning the child home, but this implied that parents had to overcome certain personal defects and thereby 'earn' their child's return. This approach has now been firmly discarded. 'Reunification' acknowledges a far greater responsibility resting with the local authority social worker, who often has to work intensively with parents in setting up plans, and facilitating home visits, to ensure the child's return home takes place quickly and effectively.

rights claims to treatment, benefit or protection that an individual can make on the basis of a law, code of practice or declaration.

There are several kinds of rights. *Political and civil rights* both protect a citizen of a particular country from the arbitrary use of **power** by state authorities and entitle that person to undertake certain **positive action**s that enable them to exert some influence, however nominal, in the political process and in influencing public opinion. *Social and economic rights* lay claims to publicly provided goods and services; these rights are not dependent on whether an individual is eligible for them or in some way is deserving. *Human rights* claim a universal status and are usually framed in global terms pertaining to all peoples. *Procedural rights* lay claim to giving people a fair hearing before any decision is made regarding a social benefit or service, such as setting a level of an individual's income support, meeting the **special educational needs** of a child with a **learning disability** or taking a child into local authority care. Those political and civil rights that protect a citizen against abuse of state **power** include the right of free speech, the right to vote, the right to trial by jury, the right to personal security and the right not to be discriminated against on the basis of race. Such rights were established in law, often as the consequence of considerable struggle, from the 17th century onwards in Britain. They are not universal, nor can they be assumed to be permanently irreversible, as recent discussions about the right to silence of the accused in criminal trials indicate.

Social and economic rights include the right to medical care, the right to social security, the right to vocational training and the right to housing. The concept of social and economic rights does not enlist the same consensus as political and civil rights. There is fierce argument as to whether they should exist as rights at all. In general, commentators from the political Right think that, because such claims involve a call on resources such as money and the time of those who would deliver the services or benefits, they cannot be considered as rights because the resources needed to provide them may not always be available and the concept of a right as an unconditional, automatic entitlement would be undermined. Others at the political Centre and on the Left argue that the difference between civil rights and social rights is not as great as it seems because they both depend on a sufficient level of resources being available. The right to personal security, for example, requires an effective **police** force, and the right to a fair trial requires court time and the provision of legal aid.

The best instances of global human rights provision are found in United Nations human rights declarations regarding, for example, the right to work, education, social security and health care. Nations may have such rights enshrined in their laws, but most do not. In practice, they are often ignored even by countries that have assented to particular UN conventions. They continue to exert influence, however, by their claim to universality and through the work of many organizations, both governmental and non-governmental, such as the UN Commission on Human Rights and the World Court.

Procedural rights have a broad political consensus behind them. Increasingly, they are seen by the public as the most effective way for individuals to guard against arbitrary decisions by government bureaucracies, including those of the local authority. This trend has important implications for **social work** and **social care**. The right of a person to participate in the process of defining his or her own needs, the right to be told about the worker's role and powers in a specific situation, the right to give explicit consent or to refuse intervention (except where the worker has statutory protective duties), the right of people to receive information in their first language, the right to **written agreement**s as the basis of any service provided are all powerful examples of procedural rights affecting how welfare professionals undertake their work with users.

The incorporation of the European Convention of Human Rights into British law came through the **Human Rights Act 1998**. Historically, the European Convention on Human Rights has its roots in the philosophical tradition of universal rights that stretches back to the Enlightenment of the 18th century and the French Revolution, although formal **adoption** of the Universal Declaration of Human Rights actually came through the United Nations in December 1948. There is continuous and evolving discussion on the place of rights in social policy and social work. Commentators on both Left and Right sometimes argue that an over-emphasis on rights or 'rights talk' leads to 'entitlement thinking', that is that a person or group of people will assume they have a 'right' to a source of income, service or other privilege while ignoring the responsibilities that go with it. The notion of **parental rights** offers an instructive example in which there are those who argue that simply being the parent of a child entitles the adult to a certain level of mastery over that child without acknowledging any explicit responsibilities in providing for the child. (See also the **UN Declaration on the Rights of the Child**, **advocacy**, **self-advocacy** and **empowerment**.)

Ife, J. (2001) *Human Rights and Social Work: toward a rights-based practice*. Cambridge: Cambridge University Press.

right to reside a national of an EU Member State or European Economic Area country and his or her family member or extended family member enjoy the right to 'move and reside freely' in other EU and EEA states. However, residence in itself does not give EEA residents an automatic right of access to host states' benefits, housing, and other social welfare systems. This requires them to also have a 'right to reside', which in the UK now depends on satisfying the requirements of the Immigration (European Economic Area) Regulations 2006. In particular, the EU/EEA national must be a qualified person, for example by having 'worker' status. This can be problematic for some groups, including those who are not working and do not have work-seeker status. For family members who separate and **divorce** it may be difficult to meet the requirements for retaining a right to reside, particularly if the claimant is not self-sufficient and tries to claim benefits or access social housing and social services at a time when they have lost the right to reside.

risk the chance that the health or development of a person may be damaged by certain conditions or actions of others.

Care professionals use the phrase 'at risk' to indicate that a **service user** is exposed to some source of harm and that possibly some protective measures should be taken. These sources of harm to a service user may be external, such as assault by someone else, or arise from the client's own habits, such as not feeding himself or herself. For example, a 'child at risk' is regarded as vulnerable to physical or **sexual abuse** by one or more people or to other sources of harm through parental neglect. What is rarely stated is the probability that the child will suffer some harm. This is the drawback of the phrase; it is used widely but with little agreement over the actual chance that a service user defined at risk will come to some harm. Care professionals also use the word in the sense of 'risk-taking', which means making a conscious decision to put something at stake in order to make possible a worthwhile gain or benefit for the client (see **risk assessment**).

risk assessment assessing the chances of some harm occurring to a **service user** or other person.

Risk assessment means carefully weighing the chances that particular forms of harm might or will happen to a **service user** or be caused by a service user in a given situation. Analysing the degree of risk is necessary, for example, when discharging from hospital a person with a **mental illness** who has previously been violent, when returning a child home from care who has been physically abused by his or her parents, or when leaving an elderly confused person who refuses to turn on the heat in the winter in his or her home. In each instance, the practitioner has to try to gauge the chance of harm occurring against the benefits.

It is often necessary to accept a certain level of risk, because to try to minimize risk has its own costs and can be detrimental to the interests of a service user. Although the risk could be reduced or eliminated in each of the cases above, to do that would require taking action that would be highly restrictive for the person concerned and might itself present different risks to the service user's health or development. The person with **mental illness**, if not released, could become institutionalized, the child placed long-term with foster parents would suffer from loss of family **contact**s, the older person if removed to a home could become severely disoriented. With risk assessment, the care professional must be clear as to the specific benefits and harms that may result from proposed action. Increasingly this is a joint task, discussed with the service user and the service user's family and carers. After both the benefits and harms are itemized, some attempt must be made to judge the probability or likelihood of each occurring. One of the most difficult examples of risk assessment concerns the level of danger to a physically or sexually abused child if left at home. To undertake risk assessment it is important to know precisely what the nature of the **abuse** was, whether or not it was committed by a member of the family and what the likelihood is of it happening again. Both the severity of the abuse and the probability of it happening again are important considerations. Often the **assessment** will be difficult, since it must try to balance the possibility of immediate harm against the long-term harm the child could suffer if removed from home for a lengthy period of time.

Risk assessments are also a key part of the health and safety policies, especially 'lone working policies', for health and **social work** agencies. Should a service user have a history of aggressive or even violent behaviour social workers will need to devise strategies to minimize harm to themselves and others. Working in pairs, involving the **police** where necessary and making decisions about where service users are to be met are all examples of risk assessments in everyday practice.

As resources available to **social work** agencies become more constrained it has been argued that services become wholly focused upon the 'management of risk' and decreasingly on therapeutic interventions and 'healing'. The pressures on social work agencies to manage risk effectively is clear evidence of social work being asked to devise technical solutions to what are essentially political problems.

role theory and role analyses a role amounts to a set of expectations and obligations to behave in a particular way, arising from a recognized social position, function or status. Roles often carry with them specified rights as well as obligations. The theory has its origins in the language of the theatre: that is, people play parts in everyday life in ways that resemble actors' performances. The difference is that social roles are learned so effectively that a person *becomes* the role, such as daughter, son, soldier or doctor. People identify themselves as the role, having learned and internalized the script (expectations) through socialization processes. Thus roles are a key part of a person's social identity. The theory has been summarized in terms of people's self-concepts being based on how they think others see them, and these perceptions in turn being partially based on the roles people occupy.

People can play many roles – for example, roles of parent, worker and neighbour. People may be seen as belonging to *role sets*, that is, all the people associated with the playing of a particular role. Some people have many role sets; others have fewer, perhaps even as few as one (or none in the case of hermits or recluses). Role sets can be quite separate or they can overlap. For example the people that a person relates to at work might be called the 'work set' and the people a person relates to in their **community** might be called the 'community set'. Sometimes there will be other people who are part of both sets such as a neighbour or friend who also works in the same company as our focal person. People can occupy a number of sets and have varying status in each. So the vicar might occupy an influential and perhaps powerful position in the church but a lowly position in the village cricket team. It is more likely that in urban contexts people will occupy many different role sets than in rural locations. And it is also more likely that in rural locations that the same people will be members of various role sets but with different statuses in each. The analyses of roles and role sets in relation to particular individuals can be helpful in understanding issues of social stress and social solidarity or its lack.

Roles can conflict in two ways. First, there can be 'conflict within a role' – for example, a **team** leader might be expected, by members of the team, to protect them from further pressure if they are already working to capacity, but the same **team** leader could be expected by senior management to get workers to work harder if there are many unallocated cases. Such role conflict is referred to as 'intra-role conflict'. The second kind of role conflict refers to conflicts between roles, that is, 'inter-role conflict' – an example might be a person having to work long hours (role of worker) who is very worried about his or her children (role of parent) but feels unable to alter the situation to meet the obligations of both roles. Roles can also usefully be seen as 'ascribed or achieved'. Here sociologists look at the issues of whether roles are given and are unchanged (as in some traditional societies) or might be developed in later life. Some interesting problems, for example, of how first-generation **Asian** children adapt to both traditional expectations of them from their families and those of their peers, can be usefully analysed using role theory. Similarly, some roles might be considered to be tightly defined (specific) and others to be of a more general nature (diffuse). This typology of roles can be helpful in looking at the range of responsibilities that may be built into a role. A shift from a tightly defined role to something more diffuse, or the same process in reverse, can have interesting repercussions for the parties involved with the role-player. Some social workers, for example, feel constrained by the expectations of statutory **social work** where roles are closely defined and in some cases such individuals find that there is more room to experiment in **social work** roles in the voluntary sector.

Role theory has useful applications for social work and allied occupations in its attempts to make general sense of particular social problems or situations (say, women's roles in modern Britain) and in its potential for helping to understand individual problems, say, within social groups and families. **Family therapy** is an area of work that has developed and applied role theory. Family stress can arise when there are changes to roles that members have occupied for some time. A woman who returns to work after a period of being a full-time parent takes on a new role with the potential for experiencing inter-role conflict. A man who is made redundant may feel a **loss** of a key role and may find adjusting to the unemployed role very difficult. These kinds of changes can have a major impact on morale and family functioning and role theory can be helpful in charting such changes as a prelude to offering **advice** and counselling to deal with stressors.

Role theory places a strong emphasis on understanding the individual within the context of social **networks** and organizations. Thus the concept of role is useful in explaining why a person's behaviour changes when he or she changes social position. Hence if a person's social position is known, it should be possible to broadly predict his or her behaviour. The theory maintains that attitudes and beliefs are shaped by the role a person occupies and that a person tends to bring his or her attitudes into line with the expectations of the role. It follows that a change in role should lead to a change in attitudes. Role theory argues that people spend much of their lives participating in organizations and groups where they occupy distinct positions, formally or informally assigned. Role theory suggests that, in general, people conform to behavioural norms and to the expectations of others, and an individual is evaluated by others on his or her level of conformity to norms. However some commentators have criticized role theory for seeming to imply that people are endlessly compliant to the expectations of those around them, and for suggesting that people receive information about role performance during socialization and interaction processes and then willingly set out to meet those expectations. Thus role theory, it is claimed, ignores the impact of individual determinants of behaviour, motivation and **personality**. The extent to which people are allowed to innovate with a role may be related to the pressures for conformity and tradition in a society or social institution. Clearly some people do break moulds but that may only be permissible in a society that tolerates or even values change.

rough sleepers homeless people who literally sleep outside, often on the street itself, frequently now referred to as 'street sleepers'.

Rough sleepers are by definition the most marginalized and vulnerable of the **homeless**, often requiring multiple forms of support in addition to shelter. There have been several successive Rough Sleepers' Initiatives since the 1990s sponsored by both Conservative and Labour governments. The former Labour government's Rough Sleepers'

Initiative has offered block grant payments to agencies dealing with homeless people to explicitly target street sleepers and to offer them accommodation in shelters and to work toward their resettlement. As a result of the Rough Sleepers' Initiative, there are smaller numbers of homeless young people than in the late 1980s and early 1990s, but those who are homeless are more vulnerable. For example, of homeless young people who approach Centrepoint, an organization that offers services to homeless young people in central London, each year: 44 per cent are women (many under 18); 41 per cent are 16 and 17 years of age with no automatic right to benefits; 40 per cent have no income at all; 43 per cent are young Black or mixed 'race'; and 25 per cent have been in local authority care. Most homeless young people who arrive at Centrepoint, 68 per cent, are looking for work or training. Elsewhere some projects provide temporary winter accommodation for rough sleepers with multiple problems such as alcohol and drug abuse. Successive Rough Sleepers' Initiatives have aimed explicitly to make a visible impact on specific areas of London and the larger cities and to provide a gateway to more permanent support services such as **foyers**.

Projects take a holistic view of the needs of residents and as a result adopt a multi-disciplinary approach that recognizes residents as having complex problems as well as multiple skills and interests. Projects also offer health and psychiatric care together with counselling and alcohol recovery services. Residents can also gain from vocational guidance and various creative activities, including computer use. So the principal barriers to finding accommodation include lack of financial assistance, lack of any legal rights to social housing for some, and lack of adequate support services to make stable accommodation sustainable over time. The geographical dimension to this is that homeless young people come disproportionately from highly deprived urban localities.

An analysis of agency responses to a discussion paper, 'Rough Sleeping 10 Years On: from the streets to independent living' (Department for Communities and Local Government, 2008), acknowledged that the numbers of rough sleepers had been reduced but that some 'entrenched' vulnerable groups were still evident and that coordinated action was needed to focus upon both prevention and more targeted interventions in relation to specific groups. These groups include people released from **prison** and psychiatric hospital, economic migrants from countries who have recently joined the EU, sex workers, young people, gay and lesbian people, asylum seekers (especially 'failed' asylum seekers) and ethnic minority people from all of the aforementioned groups. People with complex **mental health** needs including **substance misuse** were of major concern. There was also general concern that those people 'without recourse to public funds' should not have destitution as the only option. Suggestions for a new strategy included:

- the need for **assertive outreach** to offer support both 'on the streets' as well as support to those who could be 'brought inside';
- this support should address individual needs as well as addressing '**anti-social behaviour**';
- to institute the possibility of 'fast track arrangements' by bypassing **hostel**s for those with lower support needs, and to speed up referral and verification processes through the provision of enhanced night and weekend work;
- improved 'protocols' for people leaving hospitals and **prison**s and greater support for the maintenance of accommodation for both prisoners and patients away from home for short periods;
- plans to reduce evictions especially from hostels;
- improved support from **local authorities** for those not considered to be in 'priority need';
- addressing the needs and improved 'preventative services' for those who 'hide their homelessness' including young people, women, ethnic minorities and gays and lesbians;
- the provision of better **advice** to migrants and those without recourse to public funds to access emergency accommodation;
- to research the possibility of establishing inexpensive **hostel** accommodation to economic migrants who have 'low or no support needs'.

runaway children or young people under the age of 16 who have left home or substitute care without the agreement of parents or carers for at least one night (a higher age for young people/adults with learning disabilities if a vulnerability is known).

There are significant problems with definitions of runaway. The term includes young people who have left their normal place of residence 'of their own volition', those who have been forced to leave, those who are fleeing and those who do not think of themselves as runaways but have simply left their normal place of residence without telling anyone or seeking their agreement. Others have found the notion of 'missing' more useful although this term too includes the child who has lost touch with a carer in a busy shopping centre perhaps for just a short time on the one hand to a child or young person who has been abducted and is never found. In addition many carers report the child or young person as missing but many do not especially if the child/young person has been forced to leave.

Various researches have tried to capture the extent of running away and its core characteristics. There seems to be a rough consensus that there are around 100,000 incidences of running away each year involving probably about 40,000 children/young people, indicating that some young people run away on several occasions. There seems to be consistent evidence that there are many more female runaways than male and that most running away occurs from the age of 13 onwards although a little fewer than a quarter of all runaways are thought to be under the age of 11 (Social Exclusion Unit 2002). In addition there appear to be higher rates of running away among those who think of themselves as having learning difficulties and those that think of themselves as lesbian or gay. There is preliminary evidence that some ethnic minority groups are more likely to run away than others although Pakistani, Bangladeshi and Indian young people seem less likely to run away but there is also the possibility that their running is under-reported. It seems that young people living in step-families are the most likely to leave with those from lone parent families more likely to run than those from a home with both birth parents. The highest rates for running away are of young people in the care system, from both **foster care** and residential care. Accounts of reasons for running away include family conflict and mistreatment, **abuse** including **sexual abuse**, bullying (predominantly in school but also in the **community** at large), unhappiness in their care placements and seeking to avoid justice agencies for young offenders. Runaways are also more likely to be offenders, drug users and truants.

There is considerable diversity in the experiences of runaways with some returning home very quickly after a night on their grandparents' couch to others that are away for a very long period of time, perhaps never to return. Many sleep rough, a small minority of young people are hurt in some way (and this may include sexual assault) and a similar proportion survive by stealing or by begging or both. A small proportion of young people, mostly females, are coerced into prostitution.

Devising appropriate resources to support runaways has been a major preoccupation of agencies working in this field. Section 51 of the **Children Act 1989** made it legal for various projects to provide temporary accommodation for runaways; modifying the earlier Child Abduction Act 1984 with its concern about the illegal 'harbouring' of children/young people. However provision of refuges across the UK is uneven. There are a few services that are 'dedicated' to runaways in addition to some modest emergency fostering projects and a small number of specialist units as part of larger supported housing projects. It is hoped that as a result of a new government commitment announced in early 2008 that there will be increased and improved provision of refuges; revised guidance for **local authorities** about services and clearer guidelines in relation to their roles and responsibilities in respect of runaways. In sum, running away needs to be seen as a critical event suggesting some serious underlying problems in the lives of children and young people. Clearly it is crucial to engage with unhappy and disaffected young people to assess and address problems both before they abscond and on their return should helping agencies get 'another chance'.

The Children's Society (2007) *Stepping Up: the future of runaway services*. London: The Children's Society.

Social Exclusion Unit (2002) *Young Runaways*. London: Office of the Deputy Prime Minister.

S s

safeguarding the work of organizations and their personnel in taking all reasonable measures to ensure that the risks of harm to an individual's welfare is prevented. The term lays out a wider remit than earlier policies designed to prevent **child abuse** and encompasses the more diffuse notion of safeguarding welfare of vulnerable individuals, chiefly **older people** and children but includes adults with **disability** and **mental health problems**. Often the term is combined with action designed to promote the welfare of the individual, creating a broad spectrum of professional activity in relation to **assessment** and intervention. It is now regarded as a complex activity and is not the sole responsibility of a small group of professionals but extends to all who work with or who have **contact** with vulnerable people.

Safeguarding children has three main elements as defined by government in **Working Together**: i) protecting children from maltreatment; ii) preventing **impairment** of children's health or development; and iii) ensuring that children grow up in circumstances consistent with the provision of safe and effective care. Protecting children from **significant harm** such as physical abuse, prolonged neglect, psychological damage and **sexual abuse** remains central to the safeguarding task but is only part of it. But whereas the older notion of protecting a child from abuse was often based on ensuring that an identified perpetrator did not have access to a given child safeguarding tasks can be much wider. As outlined in the **Children Act 2004** they include not only protecting children from maltreatment but ensuring that children grow up in safe and effective care and preventing impairment of children's health and development underscoring the wider, proactive role that children's services should embrace if they are to meet their safeguarding duties fully. Protecting children against maltreatment and preventing impairment of health or development is central but insufficient to ensure that children are growing up in circumstances of safe and effective care. In this sense safeguarding is cumulative action contributing to the five **outcomes** stipulated in **Every Child Matters**.

There is greater awareness now of the increased complexity of safeguarding, looking for example at the interaction between neglect and **domestic violence** and its impact on the child. Young people at risk of community based violence, such as knife crime are also part of the safeguarding process. Indeed the definition of harm in section 31 of the **Children Act 1989** has been amended by the **Adoption and Children Act 2002** to include 'impairment suffered from seeing or hearing the ill treatment of another'.

Safeguarding children has shone a light on the recruitment policies of organizations other than social services and **children's home**s, whether voluntary or professional – particularly following the murders of two schoolgirls by a school caretaker in Soham, Cambridgeshire in 2002. In response government has initiated a thoroughgoing vetting system, particularly checking on previous criminal convictions, for all people working with children in either a paid or voluntary capacity. (See also **serious case review, Independent Safeguarding Authority** and **local safeguarding children boards**.)

Safeguarding adults, as with children, rests on multi-agency coordination and developing strong local leadership to ensure effective responses. Since the publication of **No Secrets** in 2000 government has realized that safeguarding entails more than just preventing physical harm. There are complex issues around the degree of risk that is acceptable, and around how much influence the vulnerable adult has regarding decisions about their own safety. User-led assessments of risk in relation to health services, housing, **police** and adult **social care** services are one way of balancing the extent of acceptable risk with the ultimate need to protect life and limb. There is also greater awareness of the institutional basis – care homes, hospital wards – to much of the abuse that particular **older people** suffer. (See also **personalization**.)

safeguarding adults legislation, policy and **social work** practice associated with the identification of actual or potential **abuse** of vulnerable adults so that it might be prevented.

Since the **National Assistance Act 1948** with its concern to provide for people lacking 'due care and attention' there has been some awareness that adult **service user**s could be abused and mistreated. Following media concerns about 'granny bashing', **adult abuse**, at that time seen largely as 'elder abuse', was seen as public concern, but also as an understandable response by family carers to the stress and 'burden' presented by the person being cared for. In this context, under **community care** policy in the 1990s, following the **NHS and Community Care Act 1990**, government guidelines were developed for the first time. These were followed under **modernization policy** by No Secrets (2000) guidance, produced in the light of the then recently passed **Human Rights Act 1998**, and subsequently the Association of Directors of Adult Social Services (ADSS) provided standards for the implementation of this policy. This guidance has been subject to review, and currently, significant revisions are under consideration.

Abuse has been understood in these policies as a violation of an individual's human and civil rights by any other person or persons. The Association of Directors of Social Services in 2000 added the following to this definition 'the misuse of **power** by one person over another' and upholds the **Human Rights Act 1998** vision that all persons 'have the right to live a life free from violence and abuse' (see **adult abuse** for further discussion of the nature, causes and impact of adult abuse, and how they relate to the Human Rights Act 1998). In the original No Secrets guidance, intervention was expected only when the abuse resulted in '**significant harm**', but the ADSS (2005) suggest that all abuse will have a significant impact on **service users'** 'independence, health and **wellbeing**', and therefore always requires a response.

As highlighted by service user movements, the way we understand an issue will have direct consequences for the kinds of policy and practice responses made to it (Barnes and Mercer 2004). In the adult abuse arena, different understandings with their implications for policy, have been passionately debated. There are four influential models which approach the issues in very different ways, including:

- *Child abuse model* – this is a very influential model. The issues are viewed here as analogous to child abuse and neglect, with the *carer stress model* – informal carers are the main perpetrators of adult abuse through the understandable stress they face from caring, the assumption that adult service users, like children, are unable in the ordinary way to protect themselves and they thus should have legal rights to protection in the same way as children.
- *Domestic or transgenerational violence model* – here adult abuse is part of a long-term pattern in the family. The person is seen as a legally autonomous adult consenting to this behaviour.
- *Unique adult abuse model* – this is the model which informs current policy under No Secrets. Here Adult service users are recognized as different from children in that they have legal entitlements to autonomy and **citizenship**, as all adults in the wider population, and it is through these means – e.g. recourse to mainstream legislation; choosing to leave the situation – that often they can protect

themselves. However, due to the impact of health and **social care** concerns, Adult service users may often need support to be able to do this, and on occasions, they may need to be protected and sometimes treated on a compulsory basis (under the **Mental Health Act 2007**), or become subject to substitute decision-making (under the **Mental Capacity Act 2005**) to ensure protection.

From the perspective of the unique **adult abuse** model therefore, policy has not, up to now, considered the possibility of an overarching legal framework analogous to children and families legislation. Instead guidance has been provided, setting out approaches which seek both to empower and to protect, using existing legislation for both. Importantly, government aims for a balance which maximizes **empowerment** but uses compulsory approaches to protection if necessary. This is in agreement with social work values which require workers to 'safeguard and promote the interests of service users and carers' and 'promote the independence of service users and protect them as far as possible from danger or harm' and 'respect the rights of service users while seeking to ensure their behaviour does not harm themselves or others' (General Social Care Council, Code of Practice).

These objectives led to the following policy principles implemented in practice through the ADSS (2005) standards for abuse work. The principles include raising awareness amongst staff and **service user**s of abuse and its impact; prevention of abuse; the right of the service user experiencing abuse to access justice like any other citizen; and maximization of autonomy and capacity to be able to make decisions in his or her best interests, while having access to protection measures if these are justified. A care plan which focuses on **empowerment**, prevention, and importantly also upon healing work, forms a further crucial element of the policy. These principles are implemented through multi-agency **partnership**s, led by social services, which develop their own policies, procedures and training to support the work.

There are many important elements of the work, calling upon practitioners to draw comprehensively, and with ethical commitment to the service user, upon the range of practice knowledge and evidence-based, skills and values. First, workers need an understanding and awareness of the wide-ranging forms of abuse requiring a response in the policy. These include:

- **physical abuse** such as assaults;
- **sexual abuse** such as molestation and rape;
- **psychological abuse** such as threats, humiliation, blaming;
- **financial or material abuse** such as theft, coercion in connection with wills;

- **neglect** and acts of omission such as ignoring medical needs, failure to provide access to appropriate services;
- **discriminatory abuse** such as racist or disablist abuse, committed as a consequence of negative social **stereotype**s of different groups of **service user**s.

The worker is then concerned to prevent abuse where possible. Effective prevention involves the use of **Fair Access to Care** eligibility criteria. This involves identifying whether abuse could happen in the future, and if so, designing a care plan in **partnership** with the service user and other agencies to minimize the likelihood of this happening. Understanding abuse and the conditions which promote it forms vital knowledge-base in this process (see **adult abuse**). Then, if abuse could actually be taking place, the worker would need to assess sensitively, also taking care not to compromise evidence. There is a duty to investigate, and the multi-agency **partnership** would participate in this, then proceeding to a case conference where decisions are made on the action to be taken. The rights and procedures applying to the alleged perpetrator also have to be addressed, involving a range of different responses in accord with whether, for example, s(he) may be another service user, a relative or informal carer, a paid carer or professional.

Decisions about whether the person may need to be protected without his or her consent would involve reference to the **Mental Health Act 2007**, the **Mental Capacity Act 2005** and the **National Assistance Act 1948** section 47. The **Mental Health Act 2007** has further amended these last two pieces of legislation to provide **Deprivation of Liberty Safeguards** allowing for compulsory admission to a hospital or care home if this would be in the best interests of the person, assessed as lacking capacity in relation to that decision. The **Human Rights Act 1998**, and the **empowerment** provisions in the **Mental Capacity Act 2005** require that deprivation of liberty only takes place if stringent conditions are met, including empowerment and proportionality – the response must be proportional to the degree of harm associated with the abuse. Substitute decision-making is also a **power** under the Mental Capacity Act 2005. Information-sharing between professionals and agencies is also a legal requirement where there is serious risk.

Services which can be provided in a care plan – essential regardless of whether interventions are compulsory or consensual – would be those provided for in the pre-1990 **community care** services legislation coming under section 26 of the **NHS and Community Care Act 1990**. These, including for example help with accommodation, adaptations, equipment, personal care, social support, and access to leisure, occupation or education can support service users' independence and control over their lives, thus making them less vulnerable to abuse.

In seeking redress in relation to the abuse, a range of criminal law and public law can be drawn upon – thus for example financial abuse could be addressed by theft legislation, and a **social care** service could be de-registered if the **Care Standards Act 2000** was breached. There are also legal provisions for **vulnerable witness**es, making it easier for service users experiencing abuse to give evidence. And the Public Disclosure Act 1999 protects workers who 'whistleblow' (see **whistleblowing**). Protection is also increased by the Safeguarding Vulnerable Groups Act 2006 with its vetting and barring scheme which operates across care services.

The current review of the policy is taking place in response to difficulties which have emerged in its implementation, and to challenges from influential groups campaigning for a different approach. One of the difficulties relates to the operation of the multi-agency **partnership**s. Although **participation** in these frameworks is mandatory for social work, it is not so for other agencies, and consequently there can be limited commitment from some partners. Partners also lack resources for the work. Research recommends, therefore, legislation to underpin the process, and dedicated staff to support multi-agency partnerships.

Also, of major significance in the review of the policy is the emergence of **personalization** in adult **social care**. The principles of this approach call for service users' greater empowerment, including self-assessment, and support and information enabling people to make their own decisions, and the balance of these aims with protection is under consideration. From some perspectives, however, including those of practitioners working in adult safeguarding, personalization approaches may go too far, leaving service users more vulnerable to abuse: for example use of **Direct payments** and **individual budget**s often involve **service user**s in purchasing their care from individuals or organizations which are not regulated under the **Care Standards Act 2000**, and where providers are not subject to the Safeguarding Vulnerable Groups Act 2006 vetting and barring scheme.

The policy overall therefore does promote principles consonant with social work values, and within it, workers can make a real difference in service users' lives through the provision of social care services, and through making well-informed, best-practice decisions about compulsory interventions. However, the values dilemma concerning how best to balance empowerment and protection in this area, has been woven into the history of adult abuse policy, and shows very little sign today of going away. (See also **Independent Safeguarding Authority**.)

Mandelstam, M. (2009) *Safeguarding Adults and the Law.* London: Jessica Kingsley.

Safeguarding Children and Safer Recruitment in Education DCSF statutory guidance (2007) arising from the **Education Act 2002** section 157/175, which defines procedures for safeguarding in schools, to be read alongside **Working Together** and London Safeguarding Children's Board's procedures. All schools, including those in the independent sector must have a **designated person/teacher** at senior management level to oversee the school's practice and policy. There may also be a designated governor. This includes appropriate arrangements for referring children thought to be at risk of **significant harm**; ensuring that the school participates as required in local **safeguarding** procedures and addressing any issues within the school itself such as **bullying** and **safer recruitment**. The circular also gives guidance to **local authorities** on the duties of education services, now usually integrated with other children's services rather than in a discrete local education authority as before. Schools have always had a pastoral responsibility for their pupils. But the specific duty on schools to promote and safeguard the welfare of children arose largely as a result of the case of Lauren Wright, who was killed by her father and step-mother in 2000. The resulting inquiry found significant shortcomings in her small primary school and a general lack of awareness of safeguarding procedures. Representations from the NSPCC and others led to a new statutory duty being imposed, rather than relying on the previous emphasis on best practice advice. Schools should have a written policy and, from 2009 the school **inspection** framework contains a specific rating of the quality of a school's arrangements. A school found unsatisfactory for safeguarding by **Ofsted** cannot be rated as 'good' overall and would be required to address the shortcomings identified. Many local authorities will provide an audit tool to assist schools in addressing these responsibilities, as well as training and specialist advice.

Whitney, B. (2004) *Protecting Children: a handbook for teachers and school managers.* London: Taylor and Francis/Routledge.

Safeguarding Vulnerable Groups Act 2006 legislation which aims to prevent unsuitable people from working with children or vulnerable adults.

This legislation resulted from the recommendations of the Bichard Report, which was set up after the murder of two children by a school caretaker in Soham in 2002. The Inquiry recommended that a single agency should vet all applicants for jobs which involved working with children and vulnerable adults rather than leaving it to employers to carry out background checks. A new **Independent Safeguarding Authority** has been set up to coordinate a 'vetting and barring' system which will replace the separate lists of barred persons which previously existed. The Independent Safeguarding Authority (ISA) will keep a list of those barred from working with children, and another of those barred from working with vulnerable adults.

The scheme introduced by the Safeguarding Vulnerable Groups Act is far reaching, and it is anticipated that as many as 11 million people may have to apply for registration in the first 5 years of operation. The scheme covers anyone who wishes to work or **volunteer** with children and vulnerable adults in a role that involves 'frequent or intensive contact'. The Safeguarding Vulnerable Groups Act covers a wider range of sectors than was the case under the previous system. For example, staff in **prisons** and the **NHS** are included, and also people employed in a private capacity in the home.

The ISA became responsible for barring decisions in England from January 2009. Registration with the ISA will be mandatory from November 2010. Applications for registration will be handled by the **Criminal Records Bureau**, which will pass on any relevant information to the ISA so that a decision can be taken on whether to grant registration or bar the individual. There will be continuous monitoring of people registered with the ISA, with employers and other regulatory bodies having a responsibility to pass on to the ISA any information they may have about harm or risk of harm to a child or vulnerable adult.

This legislation aims to deliver consistent decision-making and a more streamlined and comprehensive system to prevent unsuitable people from gaining access to children and vulnerable adults. Employers will be able to check an individual's status with the ISA before offering employment, but will also be able to require their own Criminal Records Bureau check where they consider it appropriate.

safer recruitment a child-centred principle backed by a programme of mandatory training using resources provided through the National College for School Leadership, in order to promote best practice in recruiting staff who are safe to work with children. Initially arising as a result of the Bichard Inquiry and implemented first for school leaders and governors, the training has subsequently been expanded to other members of the children's workforce, including the **third sector**. It consists of either on-line or face-to-face training and is assessed to ensure that appropriate learning has taken place. It covers information on how **paedophiles** and other **child abuser**s operate in seeking to gain access to children; good practice during recruitment, selection and **interview** in order to test out candidates' suitability to work with children; and how to create an ongoing culture of vigilance and safe conduct standards within the organization.

Awareness of such issues is an essential element of any provision for children, especially in schools and voluntary groups. Evidence suggests that those who wish to have **contact** with children for inappropriate reasons may deliberately seek opportunity to work with them or be left alone in a position of trust. The **sexual abuse** of children is rarely a spontaneous activity; it is likely to be preceded by a period of grooming in which otherwise legitimate actions are deliberated and calculated to facilitate the child's cooperation. The safer recruitment training provided by the NCSL makes use of the Finkelhor model: the abuser develops a motivation to abuse; the abuser overcomes his or her internal inhibitors; the abuser overcomes external inhibitors – essentially other people who might have prevented the abuse and protected the child; the abuser overcomes any resistance in their **victim**.

Strategies to make it more difficult for potential abusers to access the organization (it can never be hoped that they will always be deterred entirely), should then be written into the recruitment and selection process. These might include, in addition to **Criminal Records Bureau** checks:

- clear safeguarding messages from the outset a job description and person specification that makes the boundaries of the role clear;
- references obtained before interview so that any issues can be addressed with the candidate before the job is offered;
- probing questions at interview into motives, attitudes and behaviours, not just skills and experience;
- observed interaction with children in a supervised setting wherever possible, or the views of children on the candidate's suitability;
- making it clear that there are codes of professional and personal conduct with which any staff member is expected to comply.

Schedule I   a list of serious offences against children found in Schedule 1 of the **Children and Young Persons Act 1933. Local authorities** are notified of those who commit such offences, and they maintain a register of Schedule 1 offenders in their area. Details of any person on the register who moves to another area should be passed on. Information about a person's Schedule I status may be disclosed to third parties, and Schedule 1 status may severely restrict access to employment involving **contact** with children. Schedule 1 offenders may also be subject to **multi-agency public protection arrangements**. Schedule 1 differs from the **Sex Offenders Register** in that: it only covers offences against children; it is not restricted to **sex offenders**; the register is maintained by **local authorities**, not the **police**; and there is no obligation on the offender to register. Offenders remain on the register for life.

Finkelhor, D. (1986) *Child Sexual Abuse: new theory and research.* New York: Macmillan.

schizophrenia is the most prevalent **mental disorder** amongst those traditionally classified as **psychoses**. See also **mental health problems** and **mental illness**.

school action and school action plus the two stages of in-school provision to support children with **special educational needs**, using budgets allocated specifically for the purpose, under the leadership of the school's **special educational needs coordinator (SENCO)**. All children receiving additional educational support in this way should have an **individual education plan (IEP)** that sets out the strategies being used. School action is the provision of additional and appropriate strategies to support a child's learning, over and above normal differentiation of teaching to take account of the child's needs. This may involve the deployment of additional staff, the use of specialist resources or material and focused work in groups. School action plus involves a request for additional support services from professionals outside the school, such as specialist teachers and advisers. The overwhelming majority of children with special educational needs should have their needs met in this way, without the need for statutory **assessment** or the provision of a **statement of special educational needs**.

School Attendance Order (SAO) an order under section 443 of the **Education Act 1996** that requires a parent to register their child at a named school. The local authority then has the **power** to prosecute the parent if they do not comply. SAOs can only be used where children of **compulsory school age** are not registered at any school, i.e. not as a response to **unauthorized absence** or **truancy**. They are for use where a parent has failed to make any educational arrangements for their child. A series of letters has to be sent first, giving the parent the opportunity to indicate that they are educating the child themselves (see **elective home education**) or to express a preference for which school their child should attend. This process often resolves the problem and the parent arranges for the child's admission. Where they fail to take any action, the local authority will indicate which school it thinks is suitable and then issue an Order naming that school. **Prosecution** by summons then follows with a maximum **fine** of £1,000. SAOs do not always resolve the issue however, especially if parents are deliberately seeking to evade their responsibilities or keep changing their address. There may be a problem identifying a suitable school place, especially if the child has a previous history of absence or has not attended any school for some time. Once a parent has been **fined**, the SAO remains in place and, if they still take no action, further prosecution may be necessary. Situations rarely get this far, but there are cases where parents move away during the process to an unknown address and the procedure has to end. This raises questions of **safeguarding** as well as leaving the local authority not knowing whether the child has subsequently become known to education officials elsewhere.

Whitney, B. (2007) *A Guide to School Attendance*. London: David Fulton/Routledge Falmer.

school refusers or school phobics children who have refused to attend school over a prolonged period. Children may refuse to attend school for a variety of behavioural, emotional and psychological reasons, but their **anxiety** is not necessarily focused on the school experience itself. Wider issues of **abuse** or family difficulty might be relevant, and it is not normally helpful to describe this behaviour as **truancy**. Some of these children might only be able to manage small amounts of tuition, either at home or in other settings, or may need careful programmes of reintegration if they are to return to mainstream education. School refusal is not in itself a **special educational need**, although such children often suffer educational disadvantage and are among those most at risk of **social exclusion**. Opinion varies about whether such behaviour should be seen as deviant, in quasi-medical terms or as an entirely normal reaction where the education on offer is not meeting the child's needs.

school transport the statutory duty of **local authorities** to provide transport to and from school for children who live more than two miles from their 'designated school' if a primary school or three miles if a secondary school. From September 2008 free transport became available for all pupils attending their nearest 'suitable' school *provided* that the school was further away than the 'statutory walking distance': two miles for children under 8 and three miles for those 8 and over. If parents choose an alternative school, they are responsible for providing the transport themselves. This is sometimes a contentious issue for children who are **looked after** some distance away from their homes. Unless special arrangements have been made, the local authority will not normally be responsible for transport to the school and back in the child's home area under **education requirement**s. If the social worker or the parents wish the child to continue attending the same school as before rather than transferring to the designated school for the new address, they will usually have to finance the transport some other way. Local authorities must, however, make provision where a child has been permanently excluded from school (see **exclusion from school**) and is required to attend a setting elsewhere that is over the specified distance.

Scottish Executive with the devolution of power to the Scottish Executive health and **community care** have become the responsibility of the government in Scotland accountable to the Scottish Parliament. **Social care** is delivered through the **local authorities** in Scotland and regulated by the Scottish Commission for the Regulation of Care. The Commission also regulates the work of independent providers and carries out **inspection**s of such providers. The importance of devolution to the people of Scotland is exemplified in the area of social care where a decision was made by the Parliament and the Executive to provide social care free to all users. While this has been an expensive decision it was seen as a clear **statement** of intent on the part of the Scottish Executive to make their independence from the UK national government clear. Similarly, the Scottish Executive is making efforts to develop joined-up working by encouraging links between health, housing and social work. Much of the work is governed by the Community Care and Health (Scotland) Act 2002 which legislated for the Scottish governance of social care through the executive.

sculpting   a technique used in experiential work to help individuals depict their thoughts and feelings about their family, their **social work team** or other collections of people.

   The technique entails individuals moving people around so that they assume particular relationships and attitudes and postures in relation to each other. The configurations produced by sculpting are regarded both as revealing an individual's feelings about particular people and as potentially diagnostic about family, **team** or group functioning. Sculpting techniques can be used in such activities as **family therapy**, team-building exercises or **supervision**. They can also be used as part of role plays as a way of expressing meanings of sometimes complex and difficult relationships.

secure children's home   a secure institution for young people (up to the age of 16) run by a **local authority**. See also **secure estate**.

secure estate   (or 'juvenile **secure estate**') the generic term for all secure establishments for young offenders, comprising **secure children's homes**, **secure training centres** and **young offender institutions**. The intended abolition of the **sentence** of **detention in a young offender institution** would have meant that the juvenile secure estate was reserved for offenders under 18, but with the delayed implementation of this reform **young offender institution**s continue to cater for the 18–20 age group as well as 15–17-year-olds. In England and Wales, the level of incarceration of young people is higher than almost anywhere else in Europe, and the re-offending levels of those released are extremely high. The UK has been repeatedly criticized for failing to meet minimum international standards, particularly under the **United Nations Convention on the Rights of the Child**. The **Youth Justice Board**

(YJB) is now responsible for commissioning and purchasing places for all young offenders given **custodial sentences**, and the secure estate is subject to the Board's accreditation and standards. The YJB has tried to improve conditions and increase the emphasis on **rehabilitation** and challenging young people's offending behaviour. However, these plans depended on a reduction in the use of **custody**, and this has not been achieved: the YJB's target of reducing the numbers of under-18s in **custody** by 10 per cent between 2005 and 2008 was not met. The overcrowding crisis and continued political commitment to incarcerating troublesome young people have made the YJB's other ambitions extremely difficult, if not impossible, to put into practice.

secure training centre privately run secure accommodation for young offenders (boys aged 12 to 15 and girls between 12 and 17) who are serving **custodial sentences** (**detention and training orders** or **detention** under **section 53**). See also **secure estate**.

self-advocacy a process through which **service user**s and other devalued citizens speak up on their own behalf to promote their rights and interests. Self-advocacy is particularly associated with **empowerment** and autonomy for people with **learning disability**. Self-advocacy is one of a range of approaches through which rights and interests can be promoted independently of service providers.

It is particularly associated with group processes, but it can also be undertaken by individuals. It shares some of the features of other forms of **advocacy**, in particular its commitment to challenging the oppression of people using welfare services by ensuring that their views are heard in decision-making settings. It has been argued, however, that self-advocacy should be the goal of all other forms of advocacy, as it is ultimately more empowering for oppressed groups to represent their own interests. Authors such as Goodley (see below) argue that citizen advocacy, in which **service user**s' views are represented by citizen **volunteer**s, relies upon the philosophy of **normalization**, which makes it open to challenge from user-led groups.

The individual benefits of self-advocacy include improved skills, self-confidence and self-esteem. However, self-advocacy is not primarily about individual development. It has become part of the social movements through which disadvantaged groups have pressed for equality and citizenship rights, and as such it has influenced wider policy and practice in welfare services. It began as a movement of people with **learning disability** in Sweden and the USA in the late 1960s, and became firmly established in the UK following the setting up of People First in London in 1984. In the **mental health** field, the self-advocacy organization Survivors Speak Out grew out of the campaigning and advocacy activities of Mind at around the same time. Self-advocacy groups and organizations are involved in representing their interests at a variety of levels. The groups that are located within service settings and represent members' views to the management of the service are perhaps the most familiar. Other self-advocacy groups exist under the general umbrella of either a general advocacy organization or an issue-based organization led by either parents or professionals. The facilitation of such groups can be a problem, especially when this is carried out by a professional who is in a position of **power**. Goodley (see below) maintains that the notion of professional expertise is inconsistent with the **social model of disability**. In self-advocacy groups informed by the social model, the members should themselves determine the nature of the assistance they require as well as the membership, agenda and policy of the group. This is easier to achieve in organizations that are financially and organizationally independent, such as People First.

Recent government policies have encouraged greater recognition of the role of self-advocacy. Both the **Children Act 1989** and the **National Health Service and Community Care Act 1990** have stressed that the views of **service user**s should be taken into account in both the individual and collective planning of services. This has led to increased use of advocacy as well as self-advocacy. However, in the field of **learning disability** this process has gone further. Following the White Paper *Valuing People* (2001), the government has endorsed **person centred planning**, which is grounded in the service user's own views and goals and strongly associated with self-advocacy. There is also a requirement to include service users directly on the interagency boards planning local services, which should use person centred approaches. This has led to greater input from self-advocacy groups and also to individual service users advocating for themselves and their peers at multi-disciplinary meetings. This has raised pertinent questions about the nature of the support such self-advocates need and the adjustments that might be needed in the way such planning bodies operate. (See also **advocacy**.)

Goodley, D. (2000) *Self Advocacy in the Lives of People with Learning Difficulties.* Buckingham: Open University Press.

self-help a process by which individuals, groups or organizations work together with the objective of mutual aid or benefit. The focus of such activity could entail a wide range of experiences including personal and **community** problems.

If **empowerment** is the process by which individuals or groups are encouraged to become more powerful, then **self-help** can usefully be seen as a form of empowering. Self-help activity necessarily usually involves avoiding the status of a **service user** of a **social work** service. Other critical defining characteristics include equality of status among members, shared decision-making by individuals within the group or organization, **confidentiality** with regard to the group's or organization's activities and a common focus, interest or problem on the part of members.

Self-help encompasses a very wide range of activities, including self-sufficiency, **community** living, worker **participation** in industry and industrial cooperatives. In relation to social, health and community concerns, the list is very long indeed and includes carers' and relatives' groups, groups focusing upon some form of therapy and groups for people experiencing major problems of **stigma**. Two of the best known of the large 'anonymous' self-help groups are Alcoholics Anonymous and Gamblers Anonymous, but many more have followed this model. Over the past decade there has been a mushrooming of groups concerned with the needs of carers – for example, relatives of people with **Alzheimer's disease** and relatives of schizophrenics.

A major commitment to self-help has developed from the community worker's perspective. Community development and community action have both had substantial ingredients of self-help, principally because such activities have often rested upon a belief that the normal channels for getting things done are not working and that direct action is required by the people most affected by the problem. In some instances such groups have received some support from social service agencies, but in others they have managed their affairs without any external assistance from the helping professions. Some social and community workers believe that an acceptable way of working is to help establish self-help groups and then, at some later stage, to encourage the groups to 'go it alone'. Many community and interest groups have started in this way. Purists, however, would have it that this form of professional 'contamination' is unacceptable and that such intervention prevents a genuine form of self-help emerging. It is argued that, even where professionals withdraw at an early stage and where their contribution has been minimal, they may nevertheless have fundamentally determined how the group conducts its affairs. There is an obvious danger that this will be so when the 'professional' holds the purse strings for the costs of the groups' activities, as with many carers' groups. Some commentators have been concerned that the growth of self-help groups may be a response to cuts in public expenditure. In this respect self-help may be perceived as a part of voluntary activity and perhaps a substitute for what was previously a professional welfare service. Others have argued persuasively that **social work** and other services have encouraged **service users**' dependence on professionals. Seen in this way, self-help may be a healthy antidote to professional power. The key to this debate may be in discussions about what should be guaranteed by the state and how such services are to be delivered.

sentence an order made by a **criminal court** specifying the punishment or other measure to be imposed on a person who has been convicted of an offence. For any given offence, an Act of Parliament lays down a maximum sentence, and occasionally a minimum or **mandatory sentence**, but subject to these parameters and various other statutory rules the sentencing court has discretion to decide on the sentence, including whether it should take the form of **custody**, a **community sentence**, **fine**, **discharge** or some other disposal. In exercising this discretion, however, courts are bound to have regard to official **sentencing guidelines**.

Sentencing Advisory Panel (SAP) an official body which advises the **Sentencing Guidelines Council**. The SAP was created by the **Crime and Disorder Act 1998** to advise the Court of **Appeal** (see **criminal court**) in its role of issuing **sentencing guidelines**. When this role was transferred to the **Sentencing Guidelines Council** by the **Criminal Justice Act 2003** the SAP remained in existence to advise the SGC.

Sentencing Council an official body created by the Coroners and Justice Act 2009, amalgamating the **Sentencing Guidelines Council** and the **Sentencing Advisory Panel**, with the task of issuing **sentencing guidelines** to the **criminal courts**.

sentencing guidelines official standards, less rigid and confining than rules, which guide **criminal courts** in making their decisions about **sentences**. Guidelines were issued to lower courts by the Court of Appeal (see **criminal courts**) in the course of hearing appeals on **sentence** from the **Crown Court** from the 1970s onwards, and from 1989 the Magistrates' Association also issued guidelines for **magistrates' courts**. The **Crime and Disorder Act 1998** created the **Sentencing Advisory Panel** to advise the Court of Appeal in this function. Subsequently the **Criminal Justice Act 2003** transferred the function of producing guidelines to the **Sentencing Guidelines Council** (SGC). The Coroners and Justice Act 2009 will amalgamate the SAP and SGC into a single body, the **Sentencing Council**.

Sentencing Guidelines Council (SGC) an official body chaired by the Lord Chief Justice with the task of issuing **sentencing guidelines** to the **criminal courts**. The SGC was created by the **Criminal Justice Act 2003**. The Coroners and Justice Act 2009 is to amalgamate the SGC and the **Sentencing Advisory Panel** into a single body, the **Sentencing Council**.

service user the widely accepted generic term for those who are in receipt of **social work** or **social care** services. While 'service user' has the

connotation of someone who has made a free choice to draw on a
particular service as a consumer it also refers to those who have no choice
but to be the targets of social work intervention, whether they wanted
such services or not. In much writing about social work the phrase is
shortened simply to 'user'. The term shows how difficult it is to find a
single word or phrase to cover all those who use or are compelled to use
services. 'Client', 'consumer' and 'customer' are possible alternatives but
themselves are only credible in relation to subsets of people approaching
social services. Few would argue that a parent involved in having a child
removed under an **emergency protection order** is a service consumer and
still less a 'customer' of any kind.

sex education all secondary schools must provide sex education within a
moral framework that focuses on personal responsibility and respect for
others. Primary schools may do so if the governors wish. Sex education is
carried out according to curriculum guidance, usually as part of a school's
Personal, Health and Social Education programme for all pupils. Parents
may remove their children if they wish although not from the Science
elements taught elsewhere. In responding to any disclosure of sexual
activity by older children, school staff may not necessarily follow the same
guidelines as those issued for other support workers in school by the
Department of Health. In general, teachers would expect to involve
parents wherever reasonable to do so, though the young person's wishes
should be actively considered. Young people will often seek help at school,
if not from a teacher then from a school nurse who may be more able to
respect their wish for **confidentiality** providing no issues of **abuse** arise.

sexism the negative and unjustified treatment of any person by virtue of
sex or gender. Sexist behaviour is regarded as discriminatory and may take
personal or institutional forms.

Although men may be subject to **discrimination**, it is women who
experience discrimination on a major scale both within the UK and
worldwide. In **social work** there are many examples of sexism in terms
both of employment practices within social welfare organizations and of
services. The majority of employees in social welfare agencies are female
yet management is predominantly male. In social work departments in the
pre-Seebohm period, women occupied a greater proportion of senior
posts. In terms of equality of opportunity and employment practices,
there is little evidence of progress for women. Services are clearly
institutionally sexist on a grand scale.

The failure of social welfare agencies to grasp and deal with the problem
of violence against women can be understood only in terms of male
explanations for such violence continuing to dominate both policies and
practice. Social services for vulnerable people of all kinds who require care

rest very clearly on an almost unquestioned assumption that women will care. In relation to mothers, **social work** practice often seems unable to look beyond the woman as parent to perceive the individual with individual needs. Women often face multiple problems in relation to their caring responsibilities – **poverty**, social isolation, poor housing and second-class **citizenship** – and yet still seem to attract blame for not being able to cope. The problems of Black women are, of course, compounded by their additional experience of **racism**. Disabled women and lesbian women also experience multiple oppression.

Different analyses and perspectives have been developed to attempt to understand the nature and origins of sexism. Some feminists perceive the problem to be rooted in an almost universal **patriarchy**, that is, that women are everywhere oppressed by men. This oppression takes the form of ideologies, policies and the social fabric within which men and women conduct their personal relationships. That men occupy positions of **power** throughout society is unquestionable, and such occupancy is a primary source of oppression. Other feminists locate the problem within an analysis of capitalism and critically in the roles they play as part of the reserve army of labour (to be taken up and put down by the economy as and when needed) and as bearers and carers of the future labour force. Some have sought to embrace both theories to achieve some kind of synthesis. It has been recognized that each theory leads to quite different anti-sexist strategies, although there is some common ground. (See also **discrimination, domestic violence**).

Dominelli, L. and McLeod, D. (1989) *Feminist Social Work.* Basingstoke: Macmillan.

sex offender person convicted of a sexual offence, examples of which include rape, sexual assault, incest and indecent exposure. **Paedophiles** are one type of sex offender. Sex offenders can be the subject of a number of special measures, including the **Sex Offenders Register, sexual offences prevention orders, sex offender treatment programmes, multi-agency public protection arrangements, extended sentences** and **imprisonment for public protection.**

Sex Offenders Register arrangements first introduced by the Sex Offenders Act 1997 which oblige **sex offenders** who have been convicted or **cautioned** for specified offences to notify the **police** of their name and address and to inform them of any changes and of any plans to travel abroad. Offenders must register with the **police** (commonly referred to as 'signing the Sex Offenders Register') within 3 days of being convicted or cautioned, and then annually. The police have powers to photograph and fingerprint offenders when they register. Compulsory registration periods last between 2 years (one year for those under 18) and lifelong, depending on the **sentence** passed for the offence. Failure to register or notify required information is an offence punishable by a maximum 5 years' **imprisonment**. It is officially estimated that 97 per cent of those required to register do so. In 2007/8 there were 31,392 registered sex offenders in England and Wales. The term 'Sex Offenders Register' is a misnomer, as it has never been a separate register but a subcategory of records on the **Police** National Computer system. A new national **database**, the Violent and Sex Offenders Register (ViSOR), was set up in 2005. This contains details of sex offenders required to register with the police, those jailed for more than 12 months for violent offences, and (controversially) unconvicted people thought to be at risk of offending. ViSOR can be accessed by the police, the **Probation Service** and by the **prison service** personnel.

sex offender treatment programme (SOTP) offending behaviour programme for **sex offenders**. Based on **cognitive behavioural** principles, such programmes seek to change offenders' thinking patterns and improve their moral reasoning by reducing the extent to which offenders minimize and justify their offences and promoting empathy with the **victim**; and to teach offenders more effective control of their own impulses, for example by developing plans to manage their own personally relevant risk factors. A national scheme for a comprehensive system of programmes within **prisons** (also known as SOTP) was introduced in 1992 and has been greatly expanded since then.

Friendship, C., Mann, R. and Beech, A. (2003) *The Prison-based Sex Offender Treatment Programme – an evaluation*, Home Office Research Findings 205. London: Home Office.

sexual abuse forcing or enticing a child or young person under the age of consent to take part in sexual activities whether or not the child is aware that it is happening.

Child sexual abuse involves many kinds of behaviour, such as *non-contact sexual activity* (voyeurism, provocative speech, exposure, rubbing the outside of clothing), *actual contact*, including kissing, fondling, masturbation, as well as various forms of sexual penetration. It also includes sexual exploitation such as prostitution and the making of or watching child pornography.

Most child sexual abuse takes place between two people, but it is possible for more than two people to be involved. The perpetrator is usually an adult, but sometimes both perpetrator and **victim** are children. While men make up the largest group of perpetrators women are also involved. The perpetrator may be adolescent and the victim a younger child, sometimes much younger; or conceivably the victim and perpetrator are the same age, but the victim is at an earlier developmental stage.

Sexual abuse of almost any kind is more likely to be committed by a person known to the victim than by a stranger. Early studies suggested that the incidence of child sexual abuse was very low, but more detailed research has since revealed that the problem is on a greater scale. The principal sources of information are statistics collected by various **social work** agencies that reflect upon the agencies' own work and the disclosures of adults about abuse experienced in their own **childhood**s. Studies consistently indicate a high percentage of children being sexually abused with some indicating that at least l0 per cent of young people over the age of 15 had experienced abuse of some form at an earlier stage in their lives.

The dominant explanations for abusive behaviour have changed significantly over the past few decades. Individual pathology (the belief that it is an individual fault in some sense) and family dysfunction (the view that there must be something fundamentally wrong with the way family members relate to each other) were the major explanations until the 1970s. Such ideas still have wide currency in public circles and in some treatment regimes. One particularly persistent theme at this time was implicitly to blame mothers, either for not discharging their sexual obligations to their partners or for not managing to protect their children from abuse (implying that they had colluded with the abuse). Such theories have been rigorously criticized by feminists, who perceive **sexual abuse** in almost any form as an expression of male **power** and patriarchal institutions. Far from accepting the argument that **sexual abuse** is an aberration on the part of a small number of individuals, feminists have it that sexual abuse is an expression of the widespread abuse of **power** by males and that, in some sense, all men are implicated.

Treatment programmes in many places focus on the offence behaviour of perpetrators, to emphasize their responsibility for the behaviour and to help them develop coping mechanisms for dealing with their attraction, for example, to young children. Few treatment programmes claim that perpetrators are cured, but that many can control their problem. Almost all workers involved with sexual offenders believe that such programmes are more effective than **imprisonment**. The **Probation Service** is active in this field.

The major difficulties in working with the problem of child **sexual abuse** are those of secrecy, denial and incredulity. The major impediment to the protection of children who have been sexually abused has been the disbelief of those working in the field, including social workers, health professionals and the **police**. Although more abuse is perhaps being disclosed than ever before, clearly much more could be done preventively to help children disclose earlier or to prevent abuse taking place at all. (See also **safeguarding, paedophilia**.)

sexuality can be understood as generating sexual identity within contemporary society. Sexuality can therefore be seen as an expression of those socially constructed qualities, desires, roles and identity that have to do with sexual behaviour and activities.

Populist notions of sexuality derive largely from the Freudian notion of libido (a biological impulse) and are commonly understood as an essential, natural and impulsive marker of sexual activity, desire and character present in all individuals. More recently, however, sociological and feminist theorists have pointed to the importance of recognizing the social significance of sexuality. A key figure in this area is Michel Foucault, who examined sexuality in relation to discourse, concepts of **power** and the social construction of sexual practices. While Foucault's work is important, however, it has been criticized, especially by feminist sociologists, for underestimating the significance of gender relations and the unequal **power** between women and men (see **gender**, **homosexuality**).

Sexual Offences Act 2003 new provision about sexual offences, their prevention and the protection of children from harm from other sexual acts and for connected purposes (Office of Public Sector Information). This Act contains new provisions relating to non-consensual offences of rape, assault by penetration, and causing a person to engage in sexual activity. The area of familial offences exists to protect those who are vulnerable and who are sexually mistreated by relatives or spouses. The Act also addresses the administering of substances with the intent to assault (date rape), prostitution, child pornography, trafficking and restricted travel for those convicted of sexual offences.

sexual offences prevention order an order prohibiting a convicted or **caution**ed **sex offender** from doing anything specified. They can be made by a **criminal court** when an offender is convicted and **sentenced**; alternatively a chief officer of **police** may apply to a **magistrates' court** for an order to be made. In either case, the court must be satisfied that the order is necessary to protect the public from serious harm. Introduced by the **Sexual Offences Act 2003**, these orders replaced **sex offender** orders (introduced by the **Crime and Disorder Act 1998**) and restraining orders (introduced in 2000).

sexual problems problems and dilemmas faced by social workers, therapists and counsellors in advising clients and service users in the matter of sexual behaviour and sexual identity.

Sexual problems and issues are a major area of work for social welfare workers that is often not acknowledged and for which professional preparation is as yet piecemeal. The issues include contraception, sexual behaviour and health risks, confronting unacceptable sexual activity and counselling around issues of sexual identity. Work relating to contraception includes advising and providing services for prisoners, children in care and people with learning difficulties. Much of this work involves key dilemmas. For example, should contraception be offered to children under the legal age of consent and should contraception be provided in prison establishments when the Home Office's official policy is that sexual activity should not take place there at all? Similarly, what kinds of advice ought people with **learning difficulties** be given about sexual behaviour and is compulsory sterilization ever justified?

The second area of work refers to general advice about sexual behaviour and health-related matters. The focus of such work might be educational and preventive or it might be concerned with the consequences of sexual activity, such as HIV/aids counselling. The third area includes work with sex offenders and with child sexual abuse. Dealing with sex offenders in the community has become a major focus of work in recent years. Similarly, identifying child sexual abuse and helping children, or adult survivors, to work through their difficulties is also an important and growing area of work.

Counselling people on problems of sexual identity and social responses to those problems – for example, with children in care who feel themselves to be gay or lesbian – is a sensitive and difficult process. Similarly, the consequences for people 'coming out' (publicly acknowledging their homosexuality) can be substantial. Social workers may also become involved in official reports on the future care of children when families break up and one parent decides to live with another person of the same sex. In all these areas of work there are major dimensions of anti-discriminatory practice. This is an area of social work where a practitioner's own values are especially important to avoid oppressive practice. (See **gender, femininity, masculinity, homosexuality, sexism.**)

S Myers & J Milner, 2007, Sexual Issues in Social Work, BASW/Policy Press

sheltered accommodation units of dwellings designed for vulnerable people where some measure of help is available from a paid warden who lives on the premises or nearby.

Most sheltered accommodation is purpose-built for **older people** or people with **disability**. People with learning disabilities also live in such units, although the term **'group home'** is sometimes used for this user group. Sheltered accommodation was thought to be potentially a primary service for old people. Research has revealed that although some old people move to sheltered accommodation when they become frail or less able to look after themselves independently, many do so in anticipation of future vulnerability. Wardens also prefer to have a 'mixed' group of older people, that is, some vulnerable and others relatively robust. Such findings have suggested that people in sheltered dwellings may not be significantly different from those living in their own homes in the **community**. Given these findings, some argue that sheltered housing may not be 'the way forward' that it once appeared to be and that a strong case can be made for supporting people in their own homes with **community service**s such as home helps, meals on wheels and peripatetic warden schemes.

significant harm the degree of harm to a child that is necessary to establish in court to obtain protective orders under the **Children Act 1989**.

The intention of the Children Act 1989 is to ensure that a local authority resorts to a care or **supervision order** when there is no other means to protect the child. Only when the child has suffered serious harm does such a measure find favour with the courts. Section 31 of the Children Act 1989 defines two types of harm: ill-treatment, which includes physical, sexual and **emotional abuse**, and the **impairment** of health or development, which includes the effects of neglect and deprivation on the child's physical, intellectual or social development. The definition obviously includes traumatic injury such as might result from deliberate cigarette burns or an assault that causes bone fractures. It also includes types of harm at the hands of adults that are harder to define, such as repeatedly subjecting a child to sources of terror, keeping a child locked up or depriving the child of even minimal amounts of food. The crucial question for practitioners is: what level of harm is 'significant'? Children Act guidance suggests that 'significant' means 'considerable, noteworthy or important'. It also states that the significance of harm suffered by a child can lie either in the seriousness of the harm itself or in the effects of the harm. A physical injury such as a severe beating inflicted by a parent does not have to have longer-term effects on the physical or **mental health** of the child to be significant. Conversely, a physical injury – for example, to a child's genitals inflicted when he or she was being sexually abused – may be more serious in its emotional and long-term consequences.

Whether a particular harm is significant depends on certain factors such as the age of the child and the length of time for which the child has suffered the harm. Overly harsh physical punishment administered to a 6-month-old child leading to severe bruising would be significant, whereas the same amount of force would not necessarily be significant for a 10-year-old. A 3-year-old child wandering streets late at night could be likely to suffer significant harm, whereas a 10-year-old would be less vulnerable and less likely to suffer significant harm. As a form of harm, the

impairment of health or development includes the effects of neglect and deprivation such as a very young child being left on his or her own for great lengths of time, persistent weight **loss** and the failure to grow over a long period of time. In addition, harm in this sense may be measured in relation to the child's overall development, including intellectual or social development. In general, social workers view the harm suffered by a child as increasing in significance if it is repeated and occurs within the context of constant parental anger, indifference or outright rejection. To establish whether the harm is significant to the particular child, the effects of the ill-treatment or neglect must be considered in detail, particularly if the case is to come to court. This is done by describing the extent of injuries inflicted by parents or other members of the family, or the extent of the neglect, such as persistently low levels of nutrition, and how the child's health and development have suffered as a result. If the harm is to the child's health and development, the Children Act requires that its significance be established by contrasting the harms that the child has suffered with a hypothetical similar child, that is, a child of the same weight, age, size and physical attributes or disabilities.

The most difficult of all forms of harm to identify is emotional or psychological abuse. Constantly criticizing the child, always blaming him or her for things, and prolonged episodes of shouting or screaming at the child may or may not do significant harm. Severe rejection of the child, refusal to speak to him or her over a long period of time and long periods of enforced isolation, depending on the age of the child, probably would be significant harm. In terms of an application to court in such cases, much would depend on the behaviour and reactions of the child; if the child showed severe behaviour problems, the harm, though not physical, could be significant. Undoubtedly, the attempt to establish this as significant harm would require a psychologist's expert opinion. (See also **child abuse, threshold criteria**.)

social action an approach to working with people which stresses **empowerment** and **participation**, often used in relation to young people. The social action approach to practice aims to move away from 'deficit' models in which professionals step in at the outset to define the problems and to embark immediately on what they regard as the remedies. The approach spends much time probing why certain problems are being experienced by groups of young people. Williamson, in *Social Action* writes, 'Only through injecting the "why" question did the structural explanations for the predicaments of young people become more apparent to them, thereby sidelining the tendencies towards individualistic explanations and blame.' The approach underscores the collective situation of young people. It seeks to explore what common experiences they share and what stories they have to tell – whether of separated parents, racial **harassment**, leaving care, or experiences of entry into the job market, the usefulness (or otherwise) of specific **networks** and channels of information. There are several phases of the social action process: identification – asking what are the important issues; explanation – asking why are they important; planning – how these issues can be addressed; action – carrying through with the plan of action; reflection and review – whether the process facilitated participation and **empowerment** or fade-out and disillusionment. The objective is to promote confidence and recognition in order to achieve a variety of ends that are transferable across time. The practitioner's role is as listener and gatherer of stories, as adviser, organizer, advocate and **group work**er.

Williamson, H. (1995) *Social Action for Young People*. Lyme Regis: Russell House Publishing.

social and emotional aspects of learning (SEAL) a structured, whole-school framework and resources for teaching social, emotional and behavioural skills to pupils and for supporting teachers. It encourages an approach to all aspects of school life that promotes self-awareness, managing feelings, improving motivation and developing empathy and social skills across the whole school **community**, adults and children.

social care services provided under section 46 of the **NHS and Community Care Act 1990** for adult **service user**s experiencing significant health and **social care** problems.

The services relate to a range of welfare legislation enacted prior to the 1990 Act, making provision for disabled people – including people with **mental health problems** (see **disability**); for promoting the welfare of **older people**; and to provide assistance in relation to illness. They offer assistance to people to support their physical, personal and social independence and quality of life. Social care can be provided to people at home; in supported housing, residential care, and day or resource centres; and since the 1990 Act, **social services departments** have purchased these forms of care from independent sector providers in the **mixed economy of care**. The services are regulated by the **Care Standards Act 2000**. Services are now often organized by **service users** directly with the use of **direct payments** and **individual budgets** in the context of **personalization** policy and social care reform.

Social care is distinguished from health care and informal care (see **carers**). It includes a certain level of physical and personal care, such as help with bathing, dressing, toileting, eating, and coping with **incontinence**. It also includes social support involving assisting people in maintaining **contact** with family and friends, enabling people to develop social skills and skills for **independent living**, such as food preparation, and making social contacts. Help with transport and with accessing social activities for adult **service user**s, such as for example, resource centres for visually impaired people run by voluntary organizations, or engaging in mainstream activities such as employment and leisure are also important **social care** provisions supporting the **modernization policy** aim for social inclusion.

Social Care Institute for Excellence (SCIE) established in 2001, the purpose of the institute is to help identify and disseminate good practice in **social care**. It has been established as an independent **charity** but funded by the **Department of Health**. This is part of the changes resulting from the 2004 Children Act, but can be seen as in line with the earlier National Institute of Health and Clinical Excellence (NICE) which was a central part of the government's aim to improve quality in health care through the development of the evidence base for practice. Its role of identifying and promoting good practice will be seen as central to the future development of **social work** practice.

Social Care Research Ethics Committee this committee is part of the National Research Ethics Service which is linked to the National Patient Safety Agency within the **NHS**. This committee will be the focus for the development of a procedure for ethical scrutiny of **social care** research and is therefore linked to the Social Care Institute for Excellence. This is seen as filling an important gap in the research governance framework for health and social care where the varied and quasi-independent nature of **social services department**s led to a failure to introduce formal ethical approval procedures in line with the requirements of the government White Paper on research governance and the process introduced within the **NHS**. As a central body it will review research into social care issues covering a range of issues where local or university ethical committees are defined not to be wholly appropriate. Examples are social care studies funded by the **Department of Health** or those studies involving people who lack the capacity to give informed consent. Its aim is to work alongside **NHS** and University research ethics committees and to develop a wide definition of what constitutes research for the purposes of ethical review, including many service evaluations.

social education centre a day service for people with **learning disability** that concentrates on the development of skills and abilities in daily living. Social education centres were introduced in many areas to replace **adult training centres**, which were then regarded as outdated. Adult training centres provided workshops in which **service user**s undertook contract industrial work for token payment. It was recognized that this did little to prepare the users for the demands of living a more independent life and that the tasks were repetitive and unrewarding. Social education centres concentrated on the skills and abilities that service users needed in order to work towards a more independent style of life. This could include **communication** skills, the management of money, using public transport and household management. The focus was on what people needed in daily life. For example, food preparation sessions focused on everyday meals and snacks rather than on jam making, which had featured prominently in day centres in the past. Social education centres have declined since policy has emphasized **day services** rather than day *centres*. The expectation is that service users will be assisted to use mainstream leisure and educational facilities and that they will not spend most of the week within a segregated day centre site.

social exclusion a process that deprives individuals and families, groups and neighbourhoods of the resources required to flourish in society.

As a process, social exclusion is primarily a consequence of **poverty** and low income, but other factors such as poor housing, low educational attainment and deprived living environments also underpin it. Through social exclusion people are cut off for a significant period of their lives from institutions and services, social **networks** and developmental opportunities that the great majority of society enjoys. The process of social exclusion revolves around five components:

- **poverty** and low income;
- lack of access to the jobs market;
- thin or non-existent social supports and networks;
- the overall condition of the local area or neighbourhood;
- exclusion from services.

The concept originated in France in the 1970s and was used by the European Union in the 1990s to describe the condition of certain groups on the margins of society who were cut off from regular sources of employment and the income safety nets of the **welfare state** as well as powerful institutions, such as trade unions, that might have given them a voice. When the Labour Party came to **power** in the UK in 1997, it swiftly adopted the concept as its own. From the start, the Labour administration saw how its range of social goals could be presented in terms of reducing **social exclusion**. As a first important step it set up the **Social Exclusion** Unit (SEU) in the Cabinet Office to ensure that all departments coordinated their efforts. In the transition from the European continent to the UK, social exclusion has become an extremely flexible concept. The Labour government's policies for reducing social exclusion have merged with earlier strands of welfare policy in the UK, particularly around ideas of individual need, eligibility criteria and means testing.

When looked at more closely it is possible to find within the term justification for quite different policy approaches to disadvantage. One is the view that only through redistribution of wealth will poverty and inequality be successfully eradicated in Britain. But another strand within discussions about social exclusion points to the need to tackle the moral failings of families and neighbourhoods, who in effect exclude themselves through detaching themselves from widely accepted social goals. On this account, low-income neighbourhoods are poor because they have fallen prey to individuals with a weak moral code which encourages criminal behaviour and lacks a work ethic, not because of any structural inequality in society. Government has drawn on both strands in devising policy but with a primary focus on paid work and entrance into the labour market as a means for overcoming exclusion. Particular groups, such as lone parents, young adults and adults with incapacity, have been strongly encouraged to return to work with reductions of benefit if they do not.

Exclusion also occurs at the level of neighbourhood or **community**. The signposts of exclusion at this level include overcrowded housing, **stigma**tized social housing estates, low levels of voluntary or community activity, a high percentage of residents without bank or building society accounts and high levels of burglaries among others. For neighbourhoods as for families, social exclusion has devastating effects. Certain long-term trends gather pace: the withdrawal of services and commercial and financial outlets, concentration of vulnerable groups, such as lone parents, in housing and a rise in the incidence of social disturbances. Social workers are now far less familiar than they used to be in addressing social problems on a neighbourhood basis, although once it was a distinctive part of **social work** practice in the form of settlement houses or **community work** itself. For social work to tackle **social exclusion** at this level means drawing on some of that earlier tradition and developing new approaches in practice with neighbourhoods.

For the social work practitioner, tackling social exclusion and promoting social inclusion means developing approaches to practice that addresses each of these areas:

- maximize income – social workers should be able to review the benefits families or individuals are receiving and any further support they may be entitled to; they should also be able to explore users' options for entering the labour market and to explore the gains and **loss**es to income that coming off benefits would entail;
- strengthen social **networks** – mapping **networks** exposes patterns of interaction and activity and highlights available supports and areas of weakness which need strengthening;
- increase levels of user **participation** in planning and shaping services,

whether through consultation, joint action, or citizen **power** (see **Arnstein's ladder**);

- neighbourhood based work – includes moves to decentralize and base services within excluded neighbourhoods; it also can entail developing the capacity of the neighbourhood itself to solve its own problems through **community work and community development**. Pierson, J. (2010) *Tackling Social Exclusion*. London: Routledge.

social model of disability an approach to **disability** developed by disabled activists that explains the restrictions and exclusions experienced by disabled people as the result of social-structural, attitudinal and environmental barriers. The social model of disability was developed by disabled people as a result of their own experiences of barriers to autonomy and full **participation** in society. This contrasts with previous definitions of disability, which have either focused on individual bodily deficits or on the extent to which people can carry out key 'normal' activities. In their practical application, the latter often focused on ability to carry out key tasks of self-care unaided. The social model has not only been a new way of defining and explaining disability but also a political tool for the emancipation of disabled people. It challenges the assumption that disabled people are restricted mainly by their own **impairment**. Instead, disability is seen as the restriction arising from society's failure to take into account the requirements of people with impairments. Initially, the social model was promoted in respect of people with physical and sensory impairments. More recently, it has also been applied to the situation of people with **learning disability**. Three types of barriers have been identified. *Social-structural* barriers include those relatively stable social arrangements that marginalize people with impairments. *Attitudinal* barriers refer to prejudice at the level of individuals or societal cultures, while inaccessible buildings and physical surroundings result in *environmental* barriers.

The social model of disability is beginning to have an impact on policy and practice in welfare services. Social workers are now encouraged to promote autonomy and independence and to have regard to the barriers that impede full participation in society. This contrasts with established approaches, which focused on assisting the **service user** to adjust to the limitations of her or his lifestyle. The concept of **independent living** has been developed by disabled people and argues that **community care** policies should promote social inclusion, autonomy and service user control over arrangements for personal assistance. Advocates of the social model argue that the concepts of 'need' and 'care' have reinforced professional control over the lives of disabled people and that policy and practice would be better based on 'rights' and 'personal assistance'.

Political activism grounded in the social model has increased public awareness of both direct and indirect **discrimination** against disabled people.

The **Disability Discrimination Act 1995**, however, is based on an individual model of disability. It utilizes a definition of disability based on individual functional deficits and allows for situations in which discrimination is 'justified'. This falls short of promoting the full civil rights of disabled people. Recent debates within the disability movement have posed the question of whether the social model should be 'renewed'. Disabled feminists such as Jenny Morris and Liz Crow have suggested that there should be more space for the personal experience of both disability and impairment. It is argued that if the restrictions and discomforts imposed by illness and impairment are not acknowledged, the movement cannot become more inclusive. These critics stress, however, the importance of the social model and argue for its renewal rather than its replacement. Other activists and academics, such as Michael Oliver, argue that the movement should concentrate on matters that are susceptible to political solutions and that by acknowledging illness and impairment the movement could be playing into the hands of those who wish to see a return to individual and medical models of disability.

Oliver, O. (2009) *Understanding Disability: from theory to practice*, 2nd edition. Basingstoke: Macmillan.

social network map a graphic representation of the **networks** of a particular individual, family or neighbourhood.

A social network is the web of relationships through which people are connected. It may be supportive or destructive, thick or thin, close and intense or dispersed and distant. They consist of family, friends and neighbours but also workplaces, organizations and institutions within which a person may be embedded. In mapping a network it is useful to think of *nodes*, that is the persons, organizations or teams in the network and *links* as the relationship between them. *Hubs* are those nodes, whether persons or organizations, that have a far greater number of links than the average for the rest of the network participants. Mapping these connections reveal patterns of interaction and activity that otherwise would not be apparent.

An essential element of **social work** is promoting the development of dependable social **networks** that fulfil certain functions for people. The quality, purpose and functioning of networks vary dramatically: in terms of the numbers of people involved, the degree of interconnectedness, frequency of **contact** and the quality and duration of the relationships. Mapping a person's network jointly with the user is a way of revealing what links and connections that person has, what assets are stored in those relationships and where the exclusion, obstacles or even antagonisms which the person faces are located. (See also **ecomap**.)

social pedagogy a way of working directly with children and young people where the practitioner (pedagogue) works with the 'whole' child or young person over a significant period of time in a close relationship that attempts to deal with the child or young person by occupying the same 'life space'.

Originating in various countries in Europe in several formulations, social pedagogy is thought to have significantly improved **outcomes** for children and young people, especially those in the care system. It focuses on the relationship between pedagogue and child that develops when both occupy the same 'life space'. Doing things with the child is central through which the child/young person develops as a social being.

The White Paper *Care Matters: time for change* (2007) included a proposal to pilot a number of projects designed to assess the effectiveness of social pedagogy in nine residential units in England. Experienced pedagogues from Denmark and Germany were asked to act as advisors to help residential childcare workers to develop an understanding of social pedagogic principles so that they might apply them with confidence to their practice with children **looked after** by the local authority.

To help answer this question it is necessary to review the implications of the principles of social pedagogy for social work practice. Often the lives of **looked after** children are characterized by uncertainty and insecure attachments. The care experience, with multiple moves can add to these insecurities. The pilot projects currently underway are focusing upon the residential care worker with presumably an assumption that close supportive and stable relationships can be fostered in this setting. An alternative model is that the pedagogue might 'follow' the looked after child and would perhaps be the constant in his or her life but not necessarily living in the same locality. Either scenario could work but have implications for the organization of the 'pedagogy service', if the pedagogue is to inhabit the same 'life space' and to be ready for the long haul, including the time after the young person or child has left the care system.

The role of pedagogue clearly runs counter in spirit to the constrained expectations currently attached to social work personnel who work closely with looked after children. Emotional closeness combined with a willingness to give a hug or to put an arm around a distressed child are not explicitly prohibited in the current climate, but social workers are potentially open to accusations of inappropriate behaviour especially with older teenagers who may be sexually vulnerable, especially if they act in a sexualized manner; no doubt a result of earlier **abuse** or exploitation.

A pedagogue is expected to take risks to encourage a young person to embrace independent and responsible living. Of course the usual standards, the **General Social Care Council**'s Code of Practice for example, would still regulate professional behaviour but the relationship between the looked after child and the pedagogue would be more open. But such emotional closeness in a relationship implies **attachment** and that should mean that the looked after child should have some say in how to manage the changing relationship between themselves and the pedagogue and even when and how it should be terminated. It is not clear how the German and Danish approaches to social pedagogy handle these difficult issues.

It seems likely that some experimentation is needed to work out the most advantageous configuration of key professionals with clear roles, responsibilities and, crucially, orientations for each. By implication the issue of training for social workers with children and families and pedagogues cannot be addressed unless and until there is a review of workforce in relation to **social work** and social care especially in relation to looked after children. It is worth remembering that social pedagogy in Europe is a praxis that underpins **early years** workers, educators of younger children in particular, **youth justice** workers as well as those working within care systems although each will have their own dedicated curricula too. It may be that the core curriculum for this wide range of professionals in the UK should also be social pedagogy.

Petrie, P., Boddy, J., Cameron, C. *et al.* (2009) *Pedagogy – a holistic, personal approach to work with children and young people, across services,* Briefing Paper, Thomas Coram Research Institute, University of London.

social role valorization (SRV) a service philosophy applied mainly to **learning disability** that emphasizes 'the creation, support and defence of valued social roles for people who are at risk of devaluation'. Social role valorization is a further development of Wolfensberger's philosophy of **normalization**. Normalization focused on the integration of people with **learning disability** and the development of 'normal' competencies so as to promote acceptance by the wider **community**. SRV takes this further by stressing that people with learning disability should have access to roles that are valued in society generally. While both normalization and SRV have been criticized as insufficiently radical, the principles with which they are associated are acknowledged to have improved practice in many settings. These are: community presence, **community participation**, choice, competence and respect.

social services committee the committee of elected representatives in a local authority that is responsible for local social services policy. **Local authorities** responsible for social services are at present the shire county councils, unitary authorities and the metropolitan district councils. They have a statutory requirement to provide personal social services, and a group of nominated elected councillors comprise the social services committee to oversee the work of the **social services department**. The committee is accountable to the whole council for the running of the department and for the development of policy within the limitations imposed by central government legislation. The committee does not technically make decisions on social services but makes recommendations to the full council for approval.

In reality, most committees are looked to for expert decision-making, with most policy recommendations being passed by the full council. In many authorities, before the committees' recommendations reach the full council they are considered by a policy and resources committee, which assesses the policy in the light of overall council priorities and resource constraints. Central government also has an interest in these decisions and now requires the development of a **community care plan** by each authority. The Secretary of State may intervene to overrule the council if advised that the plan is unrealistic or out of line with government policy. Members of the committee are elected representatives, usually with an interest in the area of social services. They are put forward by their respective parties, and committee membership is allocated in line with the relative strength of the different parties on the whole council. This gives the majority party in the council an automatic majority but also gives minority parties a full say. Prior to recent legislation, the majority party could form a committee made up exclusively of its supporters. During meetings, senior full-time officers sit with the chair of the committee to give **advice** on policy and management issues and also on the constraints imposed by central government legislation and finance.

For some areas of specialist activity, committees utilize subcommittees and working parties. These comprise members of the committee and often appoint non-elected experts to give advice, sometimes allowing them to vote on issues within the subcommittee. These seconded individuals, however, do not normally have a vote on the full committee when it meets to discuss any recommendations from the subcommittee. The members of the committee are councillors and, therefore, in general, part-time politicians. They bring to debates about social services and social work issues more general and political priorities, which may lead them into conflict with full-time officers and professional social workers. These different criteria can, however, often bring a new light to bear on an issue and prevent a more narrow professional viewpoint from dominating decision-making. As elected representatives, they also have the important task of trying to balance the needs of individual **service user**s with the wider concerns of the local electorate. Local government is largely about ensuring the public accountability of the actions of full-time public officials and service professionals. Due to changes emerging from the **Children Act 2004** many local authorities have merged children's care and education with a separate Adult Services committee which reflects the structure of their departments.

social services department the organizational structure for the delivery of personal social services in a local authority. Personal social services departments are the primary deliverers of social services. They are the largest employers of social workers and are the main providers of care for the main **service user** groups. Departments are composed of full-time and part-time officials. They are accountable to elected representatives from the local authority who comprise a **social services committee**. The responsibilities of the departments include arranging care, services and support for people with learning disabilities, **mental health problems** and physical disabilities, and for **older people**. They also have primary responsibility for **children in need** and their families together with children who have been thought to be physically or sexually abused. These responsibilities gradually began to divide following the passage of the **National Health Service and Community Care Act 1990** and the **Children Act 1989**, a division that has become complete with the establishment of children's and adult services after the **Children Act 2004**. Departmental and committee structures have followed this separation which can be seen as a response to key changes in central government structures and the impact on new legislation surrounding child protection and education. Organizationally, departments are structured along a number of lines. Until recently, the major organizational arrangement was on the basis of fieldwork and residential work, with some **decentralization** down to local area divisions.

More recently, pressures to create specialist posts have resulted in user-based approaches for the delivery of services to children and adults, or to **older people**, children, health and **disability**. Such organizational arrangements can have important consequences for the provision of services and have the potential to lead to conflict between different sectors of the departments. After education, social services are the largest spenders of local government finance and one of the largest employers. Within departments, social workers are the predominant professional group although within children's services this is shared with educational professionals and as such are often dominant within the management structure, with directors and their deputies either qualified social workers or from an education background. This, however, does not rule out disputes between managers and those social workers who have direct

contact with clients. The central issue is that of resource constraints and their impact on the provision of services. Managers within the departments have a responsibility to ensure that public money is used with probity, and they are increasingly concerned with value for money. For this they are accountable to the **social services committee** and to central government through the district auditor, an employee of the **Audit Commission**. (See also **organization theory**.)

Social Services Yearbook (2009) London: Prentice Hall.

social work the paid professional activity that aims to assist people in overcoming serious difficulties in their lives by providing care, protection or counselling or through social support, **advocacy** and **community** development work.

From the inception of social work in the mid-19th century, there has been controversy over what in essence it seeks to achieve. The argument has been between those who believe social work is an activity that seeks to provide particular groups of people with the tools and resources to change the social structures that disadvantage them and those who believe it should assist individuals to adapt to their circumstances. The first view was promoted by settlement houses, established in low-income urban neighbourhoods from the 1880s on, which combined educative tasks, research into social conditions and mutual support for local people under one roof. The second was represented by the Charity Organisation Society, which systematized the approach called casework, which combined home visiting, record-keeping and a focus on individual conduct as the source of social problems.

This second view of social work dominated its practice from the very beginning. Social work evolved from the work undertaken by various charitable organizations in the second half of the 19th century. From its beginnings, it was based on personal **contact** between a largely **volunteer** force offering practical assistance, **advice** and support, and people such as abandoned or neglected children, **older people** and infirm, destitute families and the homeless who seemed to be casualties of rapid industrialization. Social work thus formed part of a broader pattern of social concern and social reform that arose as the effects of urbanization, **poverty** and deprivation on the lives of the urban poor were better documented. These early **volunteer** social workers were attached to hospitals, courts and **prisons**. Others, perhaps attached to charitable housing projects, visited people in their homes. Their legacy remains in the **casework** methods that they developed, which the profession has used to this day: systematic interviewing, record-keeping and devising rudimentary plans for improvement. They also devised the basic distinction between the 'deserving' and 'undeserving', or the 'helpable' and 'unhelpable' in a later formulation, which had lasting influence within the profession.

By the middle part of the 20th century, social work had added a strong psychological perspective to its work. Under the influence of psychoanalysis, social workers began to pay more attention to early family experiences, unconscious motivation and the roots of inconsistent or irrational behaviour. The practical consequence of this was to emphasize the relationship between social workers and the individuals and families with whom they worked. Through this relationship, users would find compensating experiences and learn strategies for overcoming their difficulties. While social work never completely abandoned its concern with the effects of **poverty**, it came to place great emphasis on the psychological inadequacies of clients. For much of the 20th century it became an instrument for enforcing social norms, albeit by providing practitioners with sufficient discretion to be able to respond to an individual's or family's particular set of circumstances. In the course of the 20th century, a formidable array of legal powers were provided by Parliament to underpin that practice with people who are unwilling or unable to conform to existing social norms or standards. These applied particularly to standards of parenting and caring for children and to the behaviour of those with **mental health problems**.

In the late 1960s and 1970s, social work, more particularly the radical social work movement, began again to focus on social deprivation and how the wider structures of society contributed to, and even caused, the problems of **service users**. Radical **social work** practice was intent on providing expressions of solidarity with the working class – for example, in work with unemployment centres, in joining with groups of users in **community** and neighbourhood action, in welfare rights work and in **advice** centres. When working with individual clients, radical social workers tried to heighten their awareness of the social origins of their difficulties. Each phase in its development left its mark on social work, but each also tended to generate a number of critics both inside and outside the profession.

In effect, social work came to be many different things, with large objectives, to an extent that a single summary of what it entailed became impossible. It aimed to work with 'individuals in their environment', or, from a different angle, with both the psychological and social dimensions (the 'psychosocial') of the human **personality**. Attempts to define social work became increasingly general, such as that of the **British Association of Social Workers** in 1977: 'Social work is the purposeful and ethical application of personal skills in interpersonal relationships directed towards enhancing the personal and social functioning of an individual, family, group or neighbourhood, which necessarily involves using evidence obtained from practice to help create a social environment conducive to the wellbeing of all.'

Partly because social work seemed to claim such a large mandate with very few methods specific to its own profession and partly because of its tradition of paternalistic attitudes toward low-income people, it became vulnerable to attacks throughout the 1980s as political forces mobilized against the very concept of the **welfare state** itself. The public's antipathy was spurred by high-profile instances where social services failed to remove children from parents who eventually killed them. But the media also rounded on social workers for their overzealous and intrusive behaviour when they removed children from their families without due cause, as in Cleveland in 1987. Public perception of social work was further damaged by the widespread evidence of a **paedophile** network throughout the residential childcare system in the 1990s, particularly in Wales and the northwest of England.

As a result, social work seemed to lose its way, with a number of competing visions as to what its principal mission should be. Some argued that the profession had been too ambitious in its claims to effect change both in individuals and within society at large. Social workers should aim to stabilize individuals who have acute needs and to maintain them to the highest degree possible within an environment familiar to them. Others said no, social work must press on with its mission to practice in a manner that diminishes oppression in society at large. In any case, to make it more accountable, social work practice became the subject of detailed reviews, **inspection**, legal statute, government guidelines and national standards throughout the 1990s and early 21st century.

Vocal and assertive groups of users and their advocates also began to spell out more clearly what they expected of a social work service. Some authorities, such as Bill Jordan in his books, argued that what distinguishes social work from other helping professions is its capacity to negotiate. Social workers are part of a bureaucracy that exerts authority over the behaviour of individuals, families and communities, often under government mandate, but unlike other professional service providers they are willing to move beyond the formality of the role and work with people in their own environment as they negotiate solutions to problems. For them, imposed, formal solutions are a last resort. Rather, they pay special attention to the way users and their families and local networks define social problems and individual needs and work within a collaborative framework to address them.

Today social work still contains some of these earlier different threads.

Counselling, an area of work that attracts so many social workers to the
profession in the first place, forms a diminishing but still significant part of
the work even if now carried out more informally and as part of other
support measures. A more clearly administrative set of tasks has taken
the place of intensive face-to-face work with users. For instance, care
management, in which the social worker concentrates on the **assessment**
of need and the purchase of services, has done much to alter the nature of
social work. It is arguably the greatest single source of change in social
work for the past fifty years and has forced practitioners to become
organizational functionaries.

The direction that social work is to take in the future remains uncertain,
with different pathways still before it. The Scottish Executive in its report
of 2006, *Changing Lives: a review of social work in the 21st century*,
outlined a mission that gives greater prominence to **community**
development and counteracting the effects and causes of family poverty.
In England the work of the Social Work Task Force in 2009 has been
more cautious in examining roles and responsibilities but has focused
instead on powerful obstructions to their work: they are tied up in
bureaucracy, suffer relentless attacks from the media, are unprepared for
the work after training, and rely on management systems that do not focus
on quality. Whether a confident, capable and well trained profession
emerges in the next decade depends on how these obstructions are
resolved.

social work practices social work agencies, emulating GP practices,
designed to assume responsibility for 'looked after children' in relation
to all strategic issues concerned with their welfare. Such practices are
currently being piloted across the country in just a few locations. They are
designed to offer continuity in the relationship between the 'looked after
child' and the responsible social worker.

Many enquiries into the poor **outcomes** for children and young people,
especially looked after children and young people, have revealed the high
turnover rate as well as stress/burnout among front-line social workers
working with children and families in the **community**, especially in urban
areas with high levels of deprivation. It has been argued that the creation
of social work practices where social workers would concentrate wholly
upon looked after children with care orders (section 31 of the Children
Act 1989) as well as those voluntarily accommodated (section 20 of the
same Act) would prevent such turnover and make the responsible social
worker a more stable figure in their lives. Such practices could be
independent private businesses, voluntary sector agencies or a social
enterprise. While **local authorities** would retain responsibility for care
proceedings, once children entered care they would be given a lead

professional from a social work practice, who would provide the consistent parental figure and advocate for the child so frequently missing.

High vacancy rates in children's teams across the country (18 per cent in the major conurbations) and high rates of staff turnover rate (15 per cent in London) in 2005 provided the impetus for the setting up of social work practices. They aim to redress the dominance of managerialism over knowledge-based professionalism and re-establish a sense of professional autonomy. There is as yet no empirical evidence that the model of social work practices will solve such problems. The decision has been made to run a few pilot social work practices over the next few years, taking on children after **interim order**s had been granted but before care proceedings have been completed. For accommodated children the point of transfer would be decided by local authorities.

The preferred 'business model' seems to be a base-line fee for each looked after child plus additional 'bonuses' for achieved **outcomes**. So, an entrepreneurial flavour would inform even the voluntary sector or social enterprise versions of the practices, although the working group seemed to prefer the professional **partnership** where the agency was owned by its employees. The practices would of course be subject to considerable regulation; the local authority would be required to monitor the contract (there is a separate proposal for local authorities to maintain a **database** of information about looked after children with a focus on indicators concerned with their welfare); an **Ofsted**-type organization to deal with registration and **inspection**; the current Independent Reviewing Officer would continue to scrutinize individual cases through case reviews; and a new set of National Minimum Standards for social work practices would be developed to kite-mark good practice.

Predictably, opinion about these proposals is very divided. Arguments for the social work practices include greater professional autonomy and a welcome exclusive focus upon looked after children (as against the current situation where social workers will have a mixed bag of responsibilities). Some believe that the financial incentives will improve staff retention figures and encourage loyalty to practice as against a tendency to go for management positions to increase both salary and status. Critics are worried about potential competition for funds between the needs of children and the wish for practitioners to reward themselves. Similar arguments apply to the **allocation** of funds to professional training and development assuming that social work practices will have responsibility for all staff development needs. Others have argued that financial incentives will undermine the altruism that has and should drive social work practitioners. Yet others feel that social work practices will probably enjoy more resources than current practitioners have and that given similar ring fenced resources local authority childcare teams would do much better, especially if their caseloads were protected to reduce stress and encourage more individual attention to looked after children.

Le Grand, J. (2007) *Consistent Care Matters: exploring the potential of social work practices.* London: Department of Health.

solution focused therapy a form of talking therapy, developed by De Shazer in the USA, that focuses very pragmatically upon what can be achieved in the service user-counsellor relationship that will help service users cope with or resolve problems.

De Shazer argued that most people when consulting professional helpers such as social workers or counsellors spend the majority of their contact time describing the problem(s) with little time being given to solutions. Solution focused therapy has it that the priorities should be upon finding solutions with a heavy emphasis upon the present situation and the future. Any focus on or preoccupation with the past is seen, usually, as unhelpful. Typically, the counsellor is only interested in:

- identifying what the service user wishes to achieve or change. Desired changes are always expressed in terms of small scale, realistic and concrete steps.
- the strengths evidenced by service users (these strengths can also include some reference to positive things in the service user's social networks' and the resources at their disposal);
- reviews of events should take note of any successes as a means for identifying the tactics and coping strategies that the service user has found to be useful in practice. In essence, personal **strengths** are to be brought to the fore and developed further where possible.

Solution focused therapy sets great store by using particular kinds of questions to identify goals (goal setting questions); questions to convey a notion of what the future without the revealed problems might look like (the 'miracle' question); questions to try to capture how negatively the service user currently feels and what might be needed to improve, incrementally, their circumstances (the scaling questions); questions about successful coping and problem solving strategies they have employed in the past (coping questions).

Solution focused therapy has much in common with other methods and approaches in social work including **task centred work, motivational interviewing** and the **strengths perspective**, but is nevertheless a useful summary of some pragmatic tactics and strategies that many social workers find useful.

De Shazer, S. *et al* (2007) *More Than Miracles: The State of the Art of Solution–Focused Brief Therapy* Abingdon: Taylor and Francis.

special educational needs (SEN) severe, profound and multiple difficulties, general learning difficulties and specific difficulties (such as dyslexia), speech, hearing and visual disorders, behavioural and emotional difficulties, and needs arising from restricted **mobility**. The majority of needs will be met at school level through **school action plus**. About 20 per cent of children have particular **learning difficulties** to an extent that requires their identification and extra provision under the **Education Act 1996** and the **Special Educational Needs and Disability Act 2001**. The **Special Educational Needs Code of Practice** (2001) provides detailed guidance for schools and early education practitioners. Only those children with the most severe difficulties will require a **statement** of special educational needs.

Under the general principles of **inclusion**, children with SEN should be educated alongside their peers in mainstream schools wherever possible. Any problems about provision should be raised with the local authority's **parent partnership service** or the school's **special educational needs coordinator (SENCO)**. Parents and educationalists are in constant debate about how best to meet the needs of such children. It is only since the Education Act 1981 that there has been an expectation that they attend a school. Prior to that, provision in 'junior training centres' or as part of residential hospitals and other units was presumed, if it was available at all. There are those who argue that such children may get lost within a large mainstream school and that their needs are still better met in smaller specialized settings. Others claim that the education of the majority of children may be adversely affected by the inclusion of children with, for example, emotional and behavioural difficulties. But there is also an argument that it benefits pupils of all kinds to learn together as far as possible.

There have been considerable changes as a result of legislation such as the **Disability Discrimination Act 1995** in order to improve physical access and remove other barriers that may prevent a child with special needs from attending their local school. In practice, most pupils with SEN remain in mainstream schools, if with specialist support, while even those with the most significant difficulties may still spend part of their time in mainstream settings, even if they are actually registered at a special school. Flexibility in meeting the child's needs is perhaps more important than adhering to an ideological principle one way or the other.

Black-Hawkins, K., Florian, L. and Rouse, M. (2007) *Achievement and Inclusion in Schools*. London: Routledge.

Special Educational Needs Code of Practice guidance, published by the then Department for Education and Skills (DfES), providing **advice** to local education authorities, schools, **early years** settings and others on how to carry out their statutory duties in meeting the **special educational**

needs (**SEN**) of children and young people. The current Code of Practice was published in late 2001 and became effective in January 2002. In deciding on how best to meet the child's needs all those involved – in education, health and social services – must 'have regard' to it; the Code of Practice cannot be ignored. The Code is intended to help effective decision-making; it cannot prescribe what should be done in individual cases.

special educational needs coordinator (SENCO) a teacher in every maintained school or **early years** setting who is responsible for all the children identified as having **special educational needs** (SEN). The SENCO should play a key role, in **partnership** with the head teacher and the governing body, in determining the strategic development of SEN policy and provision within the school. The SENCO takes day-to-day responsibility for the operation of the school's SEN policy and provides professional support and **advice** to colleagues, both in school and from other agencies, in order to ensure high-quality teaching and learning for all children with SEN. Other duties may include the maintenance of records and reports, liaising with parents of these children as well as other relevant external agencies and professionals.

specific issue order a court order giving directions for settling a particular question that has arisen between parents or others with **parental responsibility** for the child concerned.

The order is one of four section 8 orders under the **Children Act 1989**. In effect, it gives the court **power** to settle a dispute over some aspect of raising a child, such as medical treatment or education, stipulating what is to happen. **Local authorities** may apply for the order if they obtain leave from the court to do so. They can, for example, obtain an order directing that a child they are accommodating should have a particular medical operation.

sponsored immigrant someone given the right to enter the UK because a citizen or settled resident has undertaken to maintain him or her. A sponsored immigrant is able to work but not entitled to claim means-tested or non-contributory benefits and cannot access social housing. Sponsorship is required for 2 years for a fiancé or spouse and 5 years for other dependent relatives.

squatting living in a dwelling without the permission of the landlord or owner.

Many people regard the problem of **homelessness** as a political problem, because in Britain it is estimated that there are more dwellings than households. These excess dwellings may be a second home for some people, void dwellings of **local authorities** awaiting repairs before being re-let, properties that are empty pending redevelopment or renewal, and properties empty for a variety of other reasons (ex-army camps, for example). In the face of such apparently wasted resources, squatters' movements have appeared from time to time. Homeless families and single people, sometimes desperate for shelter, have taken direct action by occupying such properties. On occasions, they have succeeded in persuading an owner to let them stay in a property for a negotiated period. More often, disputes occur between owners and squatters, sometimes of a violent nature that have sometimes lead to the forcible eviction of squatters. Legally a court order is required to evict squatters, but on occasions owners have hired their own 'informal' bailiffs. Squatters can also be accused of trespass or criminal damage if they have used force to gain entry or have damaged the property in other ways.

Landlords have sometimes agreed to 'short-life tenancies', whereby a habitable property awaiting demolition is rented to a tenant on a temporary basis – although 'temporary' has been known to be as long as 5 years. Some **housing association**s have put a lot of effort into the renovation of short-life housing. The installation of a decent bathroom, basic heating and some new windows can make a basically sound dwelling habitable for a family for a temporary period and may be preferable to **bed and breakfast** accommodation, although clearly this is not a long-term solution to **homelessness**.

statement (of special educational needs) a written outline of the provision being made by a local authority to meet the needs of a child with **special educational needs** (SEN), (aged 2–19), following a process of **statutory assessment**. About 20 per cent of children have identified SEN but only about 2 per cent should have a statement. The vast majority of children with SEN will have their needs met at school level under **school action and school action plus**. Only children with complex or permanent and life-long needs and disabilities, many of which will be identified pre-school, are likely to need a statement unless there is a dramatic change in their circumstances. Children with a statement will not necessarily require education in a special school, although some will for at least part of their education. In accordance with the general principle of **inclusion**, even children with complex needs should be educated alongside their peers in mainstream schools wherever possible.

statutory assessment (of special educational needs) the process by which a local authority establishes whether a child with **special educational needs** requires a **statement** or other provision. Although these assessments are primarily undertaken by an **educational psychologist** at the request of a parent or school, the input of professionals from other agencies is often crucial in order to ensure a full picture of the child's needs. These assessments should not be confused with the assessments of **children in need** under the **common assessment framework** (although they will often involve the same children).

stereotype a set of biased, inflexible assumptions about an individual or group, based on physical appearance or characteristics, or social attributes or roles. These include sex, ethnicity, age, physical capacity, class, marital status, kinship, language, nationality, religion and sexual orientation. **Stereotype**s differ from typifications in that typifications are flexible sets of assumptions based on individual life experiences. Typifications are open to modification through the acquisition and assimilation of additional life experiences; they are useful as building blocks to help people make sense of their social experiences and assist in the formulation of expectations of behaviour. Stereotypes, by contrast, are formulated through dominant political, social and cultural value systems and promoted by various institutions (such as through cultural traditions, religion and the media) controlled directly or indirectly by a dominant social group. They are used to justify privilege or to discriminate against individuals and groups in society in terms of access to resources or employment opportunities. Social workers often work with people who have been unfairly stereotyped, such as lone parents and people with **learning disability**, and they may have to counter the effects of such negative stereotyping by others.

stigma a characteristic or attribute that conflicts with the expected norms or **stereotype**s assigned to an individual or group and is therefore viewed as undesirable. The term 'stigma' originates from the ancient Greek word for a sign branded on a person to signify something bad about him or her, for example that he or she is a traitor. The concept is now used to describe the process whereby people are allocated social identities based on stereotypes. When we first have **contact** with a person, we anticipate what that person is like from information that we have about him or her. Inferences are drawn from the person's visible characteristics, such as sex, ethnicity and physical capacity. As knowledge is acquired about that person, further assumptions are made on the basis of his or her name, accent, religious belief, sexual orientation, class, economic status and other invisible attributes. An attribute becomes a **stigma** when it is spuriously linked with undesirable behaviour or unvalued experiences: for example, an assumption that being a Black man means that the person is a threat to the social order or that being female means that the person is physically weak. It is possible for some attributes to be ascribed as acceptable or desirable for some individuals but not for others; for example, it is socially acceptable for men to grow facial hair, but facial hair is stigmatizing for women. Dominant political, social and cultural **values** play key roles in the operation of stigma, as they help to formulate individual value systems and reinforce the stereotypes of what is desirable for individuals and groups within society. Stigma strikes at the core of individual identity because stigmatized people either believe messages about themselves as inferior or have consciously to reject the process of stigmatization and challenge the stereotype assigned to them. The concept of stigma is useful in understanding the operation of **discrimination** at all levels – from internalized **racism** and **sexism**, and so on, through individual prejudice to direct and indirect institutionalized discrimination. The process of stigmatization is particularly relevant to **social work** because the use of a **social work** service is commonly perceived as a stigmatizing experience for **service users**.

Goffman, E. (1968) *Stigma: notes on the management of spoiled identity*. Harmondsworth: Penguin.

strengths perspective an approach to working with users that focuses on their strengths rather than weaknesses and on their resources not deficits. In this emphasis it closely aligns with building the resilience of users and their families. The strengths perspective is widely associated with the work of Dennis Saleeby who outlined three assumptions behind it: i.) every person has an inherent capacity for change; ii.) this capacity is the basis for a potent form of knowledge that guides personal and social change and social workers recognizing this create the basis for dialogue and effective exchange of knowledge with the user; iii.) when people's capacities are respected and supported they are more likely to act on their strengths.

The perspective fits within that broad spectrum of approaches based on mutual dialogue with, and empowerment of users. It frames users by their positive attributes and avoids standard professional judgments on behaviour such as 'dysfunctional', 'lack of insight' or 'unwilling to change'. Instead of asking what is wrong with an individual or family it asks 'what are the user's aspirations, talents and abilities?' 'What has allowed them to cope so far?' What social, emotional and material resources do they need to support their growth and well-being?' Particularly in relation to children the perspective works with what it regards as an inherent human quality to work toward healthy development and realization of potential. The approach provides structure and guidance, assesses attainable goals, mobilizes resources and promotes self esteem. (See also **motivational interviewing**.)

Saleeby, D. (2008) *The Strengths Perspective in Social Work Practice* 5th edition London: Pearson Education

subsistence level a standard of living thought sufficient to sustain life in a minimal way.

The idea of subsistence level has been used to define a minimum standard for people living in abject poverty in developing countries where life is constantly hazardous but also a minimum standard capable of supporting an individual in health. The workhouse system in 19th-century Britain attempted to define subsistence through the very Spartan and at times harsh conditions it offered those who were so poor that they were forced to enter the workhouse or face slow starvation. In our own time, the United Nations Development Programme defines a global standard for subsistence as one US dollar a day income for each individual. Below that threshold families face severe malnutrition and dangerous levels of ill-health. (See also **Poor Law** and **poverty**.)

substance misuse the non-medical use of substances that when taken into the body can substantially affect psychological and physical functions. Substances commonly misused may include legal and illegal drugs (amphetamines, cocaine, opiates, cannabis, LSD, Ecstasy), alcohol and prescribed drugs such as tranquillizers and barbiturates. Figures for drug and alcohol misuse have increased over recent decades. Alcohol use has increased by 74 per cent since the 1950s, and heroin users registered with the **Home Office** have increased many times in the same period. Also, illegal drugs and alcohol are used by more and more young people and at increasingly young ages. People using illegal drugs are usually (although not exclusively) aged 20–35 and increasingly poor, unemployed, living in disadvantaged areas with poor housing and facilities, and often involved in criminal activity to sustain their habits. Alcohol users who develop problems from its use are often older, male and with families, but those with very severe problems are usually unemployed and socially isolated. Substance misuse by women, Black people and **older people** is more hidden because these groups do not approach helping agencies (fearing **stigma**, **racism** and/or their children being taken into care) and because agencies do not recognize these groups have substance misuse problems or cater for their particular needs. Studies have shown that there may be extensive use in these groups but resulting in different problems and needs compared to those of the white male user; it is important that services take account of these differences.

Drug and alcohol misuse results in a range of serious problems for users themselves, their families and the wider society. In understanding these problems, it is important to realize there are three different types of drug and alcohol misuse – experimental, recreational and dependent use. There is no necessary progression to dependency, but people experience problems with each type of use. Experimental use can lead to intoxication and death – for example, small numbers of young people taking too large a dose of Ecstasy have died – and also to accidents through lack of control of usage because of unfamiliarity. Recreational use means controlled use in situations in which the user knows that harm is minimized. However, the physical and psychological effects of the substance still take their toll. Symptoms of **psychoses** and **neuroses** may arise – short or long term – with LSD and amphetamines; moderate use of alcohol can affect the functioning of most organs in the body, and intoxication with any substance impairs functioning for several days and may lead to accidents. *Dependent use* means that the person finds it very hard to exist without the substance, and if the person is poor, crime or prostitution may be the only way of financing the habit, with criminal charges and **imprisonment** likely consequences. Dependent use of a substance also leads to longer-term mental and physical health problems along with problems of poor housing, **homelessness**, self-neglect and **loss** of relationships.

Social workers have a duty to intervene in all these areas of difficulty if the person is referred. In addition, there is a strong likelihood with alcohol misuse that children may be physically or sexually abused; in large proportions of child protection cases, studies have shown there to be parental alcohol misuse. Neglect of children is also possible with substance misuse of all kinds, and especially when use is dependent. Thus childcare and child protection work should take full account of the issues of **substance misuse** if intervention is to be appropriate. The risk of **HIV/ Aids** is also increased, not only through injecting substances but through the greater vulnerability to infections resulting from malnutrition and self-neglect. **Social work** has a responsibility to respond to the **community care** needs of people with HIV/Aids in collaboration with the health service and other agencies.

There have been attempts to reduce substance misuse on a number of fronts. First, legislation making the possession and sale of illegal drugs criminal offences is intended to reduce the supply of drugs and deter use. Only specially licensed doctors are allowed to prescribe illegal drugs and opiates, and users have to be notified to the **Home Office**. Second, treatment programmes in general have been health-based, with **drug and alcohol dependency** units located in psychiatric hospitals and, more recently, community drug teams and community alcohol teams funded by health authorities. The authority of licensed doctors to prescribe illegal drugs is one aspect of treatment, intended to keep the user away from the risks of the illicit market. Government policy, however, expressed in the various reports of the Advisory Committee for the Misuse of Drugs, recommends that **social work** should play an important role in treatment. This arose through the idea, still influential, that substance misuse was the result of the person's inability to manage his or her life, because of social or psychological pressures, and the social worker was expected to make a major contribution to the work of the medical **team** by helping the person to cope independently. 'Treatment' thus includes rehabilitation. One important rehabilitation route has been residential rehabilitation in residential care homes provided by voluntary agencies. Social services now have the responsibility of funding these (and other) residential care services under the **community care** legislation. The third approach to reducing substance misuse involves **preventive work**. In the 1980s the Advisory Committee for the Misuse of Drugs recommended that prevention be directed both at the risk of the person engaging in substance misuse and at the harm associated with misuse. Social work has been expected to deal with the former through the generic community work of addressing the sources of stress that bring about coping difficulties and subsequent substance misuse. There are opportunities for such work to be funded now by the Home Office drugs prevention team.

A particular focus of harm reduction strategies since 1988 has been to seek to minimize the spread of Aids and HIV resulting from injecting substances. Emphasis has therefore been placed upon providing easy access to clean needles and prescriptions of substitute non-injection drugs. Other targets for harm reduction include the major problems presented by users for themselves and the wider society, through criminal activity to finance drug use, also unemployment, and distress and disruption in family and social relationships. The relative stability involved when a person receives drugs by prescription alleviates some of these problems and brings the user into **contact** with the services, where he or she may quickly receive support and referral if he or she is ready to try to stop using substances. In the case of people misusing drugs or alcohol, social work is involved in harm minimization through the community care legislation, which requires social services to include the needs of drug and alcohol users in their plans. The fourth approach consists in the important role of social work in both prevention and treatment aspects of working with substance misuse. Traditionally, social workers have regarded the problems as more within the province of **psychiatry** than of social work, and they have been deterred from engaging with these issues through negative social **stereotype**s of people misusing different substances. Social workers need to deconstruct stereotypes, develop understanding of the complex problems associated with drug misuse as a prelude to possible intervention approaches, and learn the skills of appropriately recognizing substance misuse patterns. This will help them identify the key components of **assessment** and intervention to determine both risks and needs.

suicide an intentional act of commission or omission on the part of a person that results in the same person's death. A suicidal act of commission might include self-hanging, taking an overdose of drugs, cutting of wrists, or inhaling carbon monoxide fumes; an act of omission would include failing to take a life-maintaining medicine. Statistics about suicides are notoriously unreliable and almost certainly under-represent the actual suicide rate. There are often very difficult decisions to be made by, among others, coroners and doctors about the cause of death, and strong social pressure exists, where there are doubts, to record causes other than suicide. Suicides affect all social classes. Rates are higher for men than for women, and among **older people**, those without children, the **divorce**d and the widowed. Significant loss of social status is a precipitating factor. There are cultural differences, too, with pre-industrial societies usually having much lower suicide rates. Behaviour can vary a lot historically, with times of war, for example, leading to a lower incidence of suicide if group cohesiveness rises. To determine whether an act is genuinely suicidal entails examining the problem of intent. Suicide attempts are sometimes inadvertently discovered, whereas mock-suicidal behaviour often entails careful planning in the expectation that the person will be discovered. All such behaviour must be taken very seriously, including mock attempts, because such acts are inherently risky and mock suicides usually represent profound unhappiness and major personal problems. Suicidal behaviour, if known of, usually brings about intervention from the statutory sector, although voluntary sector agencies such as the Samaritans also have a lot of **contact** with people contemplating suicide. **Social work** effort tends to concentrate upon the social problems that may underpin, for example, an **anxiety** state or **depression**, or upon attempting to alter a person's self-perception.

supervision oversight of one person's activities by another. This can take the form of a worker being monitored by a superior; or user, child or family being under the supervision of a social worker, **probation officer** or member of a **youth offending team**. In **social work supervision** – the overseeing of the work of **social care** staff, social workers and student social workers by either a practice teacher or line manager (usually a **team** manager) or a consultant. The role of supervisor includes three elements: first, to ensure that workers account for their work (the *managing* or *administrative* function); second, the professional development of workers (the *educative* or *teaching* function); and third, the personal support of workers in times of difficulty (the *supportive* or *enabling* function). The form and content of supervision vary according to the needs of the worker, the nature of the work and the abilities of the supervisor.

Qualified practitioners in any of the established professions (law, medicine, and so on) would maintain that supervision is necessary during training; thereafter the need to 'consult' with specialists would be sufficient. This pattern tends not to apply to social work and social care. There is continuing uncertainty about the status of social work as a **profession** and thus of the ability of even experienced and qualified practitioners to work independently. The location of much social work within bureaucratic **local authorities**, together with the stressful nature of the work, may also account for the widespread use of supervision, at least within fieldwork teams, for even the most experienced practitioner. Within day-care and residential settings, supervisory practices vary, with many workers continuing to receive scant support. The predominant form for supervision continues to be the one-to-one relationship of supervisor and supervised. It is possible for experienced practitioners to be supervised by inexperienced managers, and it is common for women workers to be supervised by male **team** managers and Black workers by white supervisors. Such arrangements may pose problems, although attempts to address possible sources of oppression can help. Potentially useful alternative methods and arrangements for supervision continue to be rejected in favour of line management. The former National Institute of Social Work suggested that pair supervision might be suitable for senior **casework**ers; that group supervision may be especially helpful in residential and day-care settings. A major initiative from the Social Care Association has, however, led to some limited experimentation on the part of some employers in supporting workers under stress, including independent counselling services that are **gender-** and **'race'**-sensitive. A more recent trend has added appraisal of staff to the supervisor's/**team** manager's role – either for the purpose of **National Vocational Qualification**s or for in-house staff appraisal systems. This has tended to dilute the supportive role of the line manager as supervisor by adding to it a watchdog function (including possible promotion to higher grades) that does not always sit easily with the support function.

Hawkins, P. and Shohet, R. (2007) *Supervision in the Helping Professions.* Buckingham: Open University Press.

supervision order (1) a court order under section 35 of the **Children Act 1989** that requires a local authority social worker or **probation officer** to act as supervisor to the child or children named in the order.

The court may make a supervision order only when a child has suffered, or is likely to suffer, **significant harm** and that harm is attributable to the standard of parental care (see **threshold criteria**).

Although the grounds for making a supervision order are exactly the same as those for a care order, it is the less intrusive of the two, since the local authority does not acquire **parental responsibility** for the child. In this sense, the court will see it as preferable to a care order, as long as it is assured that the powers under the order are sufficient to protect the child and safeguard his or her welfare. Under a supervision order, the supervisor has a duty to advise, assist and befriend the child; in practice, this often means giving guidance to parents on, for example, matters of discipline. The supervisor may have the child medically or psychiatrically examined only after seeking the court's approval and then only with the child's consent. The supervisor may also direct the child to live at a specified place for a period of up to 90 days and to participate in designated activities. These provisions are aimed at young people in their teens who may be required to attend certain activities or courses of instruction; they would apply particularly to young people who are likely to suffer significant harm through being beyond parental control. The supervisor also has powers to take all reasonable steps to see that the terms of the order are put into effect. Within the terms of the order the court may appoint a 'responsible person' – often a parent or another adult in the family – with that person's consent. The responsible person must take all reasonable steps to ensure that the terms of the order and the directions of the supervisor, such as a curfew, are met. A supervision order lasts for one year but can be extended to a maximum of three years. It can be varied or discarded by application of any of the parties involved, such as the local authority, the child or the parent.

supervision order (2) order which could formerly be made by the **youth court** in criminal proceedings, placing a young offender under the **supervision** of a social worker, **probation officer** or member of a **youth offending team**. Now replaced by the **youth rehabilitation order**.

supervision requirement a requirement which may be included in a **community order**, **youth rehabilitation order** or **suspended sentence order**, requiring the offender to be subject to **supervision** for the duration of the order. The supervisor (or **responsible officer**) is a **probation officer**, or if the offender is under 18 may be a member of the **youth offending team**. Such requirements are the historical successor to the **probation order**, the **community rehabilitation order** and the juvenile **supervision order** made in criminal cases.

Supporting People a government programme to provide housing-related support services to vulnerable people through one funding stream.
    It was implemented in April 2003, and drew together many disparate funding streams into a single 'pot' that is controlled by a commissioning body including **local authorities**, health authorities and the **probation service**. Local authority **Supporting People** teams are responsible (through consultation with partners) for developing a strategy for the development of housing-related support services. By 1 April 2003 service providers had to have made an 'interim contract' with the Supporting People authority in order to ensure continued funding.

The contract reflected the existing service and funding levels. Thereafter, the schemes have been reviewed, having particular regard to the needs and gaps identified in the strategy. Supporting People is a working **partnership** of local government, **service user**s and support agencies.

The aim of Supporting People is to ensure that, on the basis of a common approach across the country, a comprehensive overview of the needs for support by vulnerable adults is conducted in each area. The programme also matches existing services in each area against these needs. Thus the needs and funding for support services for very different groups of users are brought together within a single framework. Among others, it covers **older people** in sheltered housing or those wishing to remain independently in their homes, young homeless people staying in one place for training or counselling, women escaping **domestic violence**, asylum seekers, those with long-term **mental health problems** and adults with learning difficulties to live in a shared house or other supported accommodation.

The Supporting People programme is partly about rationalizing different funding schemes for supported housing, but it also has the potential for creating active **partnership**s between agencies (public, private and voluntary) to provide the necessary range of supported housing for vulnerable groups in localities. This could entail a significant expansion of provision for those groups mentioned above, which was previously patchy or poorly developed across the country. However, the government underestimated the total cost of the scheme, and subsequently reduced the budget, which has led to some uncertainty at the local level. Supporting People also detaches support services from housing. For example, floating support services can be provided to teenage parents moving into council accommodation and in need of support or to a person with mental health problems who wishes to move back to his or her previous home. It also promotes the interlinking of care and support jointly supplied from different agencies, whether health, housing, social services or probation.

This reshaping of services has led to a significant reconfiguring of **social work** in relation to supported accommodation, providing a range of services from 'floating support' to comprehensive 'on-the-premises' support. Each locality has a Supporting People multi-disciplinary team that should include housing health, probation and social services. It works with other partner agencies, particularly from among the supported housing agencies. One of the principal objectives is to ensure a fuller range of support for Black and ethnic users with more specialist providers available who should have a more stable funding stream to draw on as a result. Black and minority ethnic users and providers must be part of the consultation and planning process in each locality and services must be commissioned from providers who can address the specific needs of existing or potential Black and minority users.

Supreme Court the highest court in the United Kingdom, dealing with appeals on important points of civil law from the whole of the UK and criminal law from England, Wales and Northern Ireland. The Supreme Court replaced the Appellate Committee of the House of Lords (also known as 'the Law Lords', or simply 'the House of Lords') in October 2009 as a result of the Constitutional Reform Act 2005. The 'Law Lords' are now known as Justices of the Supreme Court.

Sure Start a UK-wide programme of **children's centres**, primarily located in areas of high or substantial deprivation, designed to improve the life chances of pre-school children. The centres are all supposed to be within 'pram pushing distance' of the communities they serve. Sure Start has been inspired in part by the US Headstart programme.

Launched in 1998 with a few 'trailblazer projects', the Sure Start programme has expanded significantly and in 2009 there were over 3,000 children's centres. This number is expected to rise in 2010 although further expansion, and indeed the future of the programme overall, is dependent upon continued political support.

The main objectives of Sure Start have broadly remained the same over the last decade although there have been some additional objectives added and some re-configuring of others. Both Public Service Agreements and Service Delivery Agreements of Sure Start projects have also been changed from time to time. The main objectives are: to improve the emotional and social development of children through services to help parents bond with their children and services designed to help the early identification of emotional and behavioural difficulties; to improve the health of children through a variety of strategies to promote healthy development both before and after birth; to improve children's ability to learn by the encouragement of stimulating **play**; the promotion of language skills and services designed to identify children with learning difficulties early; to strengthen families and communities; to involve people in their communities and in the devising and delivery of local services so that they reflect local needs.

Individual children's centres tend to have core services including **day care** for children, parenting classes, services for pregnant women, postnatal support and activities to promote the confidence and **wellbeing** of parents as individuals with a view to them being able to secure paid work. There are many other services which the larger children's centres may offer directly with core staff or, with the smaller centres, accessing specialist services from other health and social welfare agencies. Services may include staff working with teenaged pregnancy and parenthood, postnatal **depression**, speech therapy, support staff for children with learning difficulties, clinical psychologists, support services for child-minders, workers designed to encourage the **participation** of ethnic minority families in children's centres' services, workers helping adults acquire skills including, for example, literacy, numeracy and IT skills, **volunteer** support workers, fathers' support groups and others.

The evidence concerning the effectiveness of Sure Start projects appears to be very mixed. Projects have been subject to both local evaluations and national evaluation, mostly undertaken by Birkbeck College, London. The key issue of whether young children who have enjoyed Sure Start services later perform better in primary school seems to suggest that the **outcomes** are either modest (in some localities) or not discernible. Other outcomes such as reducing the incidence of teenaged parenthood, encouraging breastfeeding, involving fathers in active parenting and encouraging parents into paid work are again variable across projects. The proponents of Sure Start children centres argue that it is still too early to make an overall decision as to the worth of the programme. They also believe that it is crucial that ways of communicating the clear benefits of some individual projects need to be devised so that best practice is identified, disseminated and emulated.

suspended sentence order a **sentence** introduced in this form by the **Criminal Justice Act 2003**. It combines a suspended **sentence** of **imprisonment** with one or more requirements of the kind which can be attached to **community orders**. The suspended **sentence** component consists of a **prison** term of between 28 and 51 weeks which for a specified period (from 6 months to 2 years) is held in suspense (not put into effect) unless the offender re-offends or is in **breach** of a requirement of the order.

The use of suspended sentences had previously declined dramatically (from 6 per cent of all sentences for indictable offences in 1991 to 0.7 per cent in 2004) following the Criminal Justice Act 1991 which restricted its use to cases with 'exceptional circumstances', but this new version of the measure has revived its fortunes (to 9 per cent in 2007). The suspended sentence order seems to be now being used to replace some sentences of immediate **imprisonment**, but also some **community orders**. Concerns have been expressed, including by the government and the **Sentencing Advisory Panel**, that this may be causing net widening and increasing the **prison** population because of the number of offenders who **breach** their **community** requirements and are imprisoned as a result.

suspension see **exclusion from school**

systems approach the undertaking of **social work** based on analysis and activation of the human systems around the **service user**.

A system is a set of objects that are interdependent and inter-related so that they function as a single unit. We often refer loosely to systems in contemporary life, such as sound systems or computer systems, to indicate a grouping of components that produce something through the relationships between them that they could not produce on their own. Systems display a number of characteristics. The parts are *reciprocal*, each is related to every other so that a change affecting one will change the whole. Their *structure* endures over a period of time because systems can adapt to changes in the surrounding environment. A system copes with environmental change by receiving inputs such as information from the environment, processing that information and producing an output that enables it to adapt. Systems have a *boundary* that marks off where each system ends and the environment begins. The boundary may be open, allowing the system to interact with its environment, or closed, preventing influences, information or changes in the environment to affect its internal working. Systems strive for *equilibrium*, that is, some balance in their relationship to their environment so that they may survive with their fundamental nature intact. In the 1970s some **social work** educators turned to systems theory as a basis for developing a single **social work** approach, or 'unitary method', that would be applicable to all **social work** settings.

The concept of systems was applied to the way people interacted with one another. It was theorized that people depend on human systems in meeting needs. People were part of informal systems, such as family, friends and colleagues, as well as formal systems, such as clubs and trade unions, and societal systems, such as schools and employing organizations. Problems arose for people when their systems had broken down or were failing to produce sufficient resources to allow the system to continue working as before. The role of the social worker in this approach is to identify the different systems of which the user is a part (the 'client system'), such as family and employing organization, and to analyse how the interaction of the parts of those systems causes problems. The social worker's task is to make the client system function again by modifying the interactions between people and resources within the system. Such thinking had the benefit of requiring the social worker to see the client as a product of wider forces and to move away from the traditional concentration on the individual client. A client's problems might well be generated by relationships within his or her system so that one had to look beyond the individual to make change occur.

As a theory, systems thinking in the form of the unitary method was criticized for its difficult terminology, lack of practical guidance to social workers and tendency to highlight stability and equilibrium while failing to acknowledge radical changes as options. It has, however, continued to influence social workers' understanding of families. Placing a user in relation to the various systems, often simply understood as networks, often diagrammatically, is a commonly used tool to allow both social worker and user to understand the range of supports present and those areas where they may have to be created. The systems approach has also provided a basis for seeing families as self-regulating systems that function according to rules established through a process of trial and error. Social workers and family therapists emphasize the capacity of family systems to adapt and change as their environment changes. Families that are closed systems, that resist change and do not evolve become 'stuck' in patterns that often place the entire blame for this on individual family members. The use of **ecomaps** is another widespread technique drawn originally from systems thinking. A whole school of **family therapy** has developed around the basic insight that family problems are a product of the relationships between all the family members and that change requires changing how all the family members behave in relation to each other rather than pinning blame on a single delinquent member. (See also **ecological approach**.)

Payne, M. (2005) *Modern Social Work Theory*, 3rd edition. London: Macmillan.

systems management   the application of the **systems approach** to the criminal justice system, associated with the use of managerial techniques to pursue goals such as a decrease in the use of **custody**. This was a particular goal of the systems management approach which was especially influential in **youth justice** in the 1980s and 1990s, and which was in turn heavily imbued with the philosophy of **minimum intervention**. Systems management techniques include monitoring, **diversion**, and interagency cooperation.

T t

tagging see **electronic monitoring**

Targeted Mental Health in Schools a government initiative aiming to transform the way that **mental health** support is delivered to children aged 5–13, to improve their mental **wellbeing** and tackle problems more quickly. It brings together work that goes on in schools (e.g. **social and emotional aspects of learning**) and the clinical and therapeutic expertise available through child and adolescent **mental health** and multi-agency locality teams.

tariff (1) a set of punishments of varying severity which are matched to crimes of differing seriousness or to offenders with different criminal records; (2) the minimum period which must be served in **prison** under a **sentence** of **life imprisonment** or **imprisonment for public protection**.

task-centred work a particular approach to **social work** that places strong emphasis on solving problems that the **service user** considers important by completion of a series of small tasks. Task-centred work is one of the very few approaches to **social work** developed by social workers themselves. It originated in the United States in the 1960s as a response to increasing criticism that long-term **casework** was both time-consuming and ineffective for a substantial proportion of **service user**s. The approach is based on three key principles: first, that the social worker and user together tackle problems that the user has defined as the most important; second, that these problems are resolved through a series of small steps or tasks; and third, that the work is short-term, usually completed within three months. Clear and accurate **assessment** of problems is an integral part of task-centred work.

Task-centred work proceeds through a number of stages. The first stage is *problem selection*. This is achieved by the social worker and user listing all the problems facing the user. From the list of problems the user and social worker agree on which are the two or three most important problems to resolve. The selected problems are written down in language that is clear to the user and expressed in as much detail as possible. For example, a problem such as 'Janice is socially isolated' is general and vague; a better way of framing the problem would be 'Janice has no opportunity to meet people during the week because she has to look after her 18-month-old twin daughters. She has no car and finds the bus service too infrequent to be of use.' It has been suggested that practitioners should use the 'five Ws' to help with problem specification: who, what, where, when and why. The social worker's role is to facilitate this process of problem selection but not to impose his or her views as to which is the most important. There is one exception to this rule: the worker may have to insist that, because of a responsibility in law such as protecting a child, a particular problem must be addressed by the user whether or not the user considers it a priority. If the social worker is unable to convince the user that the problem – say, a parent's habit of going out in the evening and leaving a young child unattended – is important to address, it means that no further task-centred work can take place, at least in respect of that particular problem. In practice, overriding the user's priorities in this way rarely happens. It may also be necessary to undertake a task or even pursue a goal which the social worker feels is likely to be achieved or is going to be helpful; but sometimes it is useful to demonstrate that a user's perceptions of a problem or its possible solution is unrealistic.

The second stage is *goal setting*, that is, moving from what is wrong to what is needed. The goal is what the user wants as a way to resolve the selected problem. Goals should be realistic and achievable in a short time. Choosing goals often involves negotiation between worker and user in order to reach agreement on their feasibility or desirability. If the social worker cannot agree that a particular goal is realistic for the user, this observation is also recorded and reasons are given. As with problems, the goals are written down in the user's own words and in as much detail as possible so that everyone can agree when they have been reached. This has the merit of forcing social workers to think as specifically as possible about the user's goals. Social workers have sometimes been vague in goal setting. 'We will work to reduce Janice's social isolation' is too woolly and does not include any way of satisfactorily measuring when the goal has been achieved. 'I want to visit my friends more often' is better but still unclear. 'Janice wants to visit her mother at least once a week and to meet her best friend two evenings a week in her local pub' is better yet. The goal as expressed is less grandiose but is clear and attainable.

The third stage of task-centred work is the *setting of tasks*. Tasks are the small steps that the user, the practitioner or both undertake in order to move towards the defined goal. In some circumstances it may be reasonable for another person to be asked to undertake a task. In essence

together, each with his or her own particular focus. In hospital settings, psychiatrists are likely to be seen as the managers of the 'case'; in the **community**, the social worker is more likely to play the **key worker** role. Teamwork is enhanced by an effective team manager; few teams operate without a line manager. Effectiveness seems to be related to clear and appropriate policies, active staff support and **supervision** systems, and a **workload management** scheme that ensures both worker protection and good-quality service delivery.

teenage pregnancy conception by a young woman or girl generally understood to be under the age of 18 and particularly those between 13 and 15. One of the key elements of government strategy to improve the health of the nation and tackle **social exclusion** is to prevent unwanted pregnancies across all age groups, but especially among teenage women and girls. For some time Britain has had the highest teenage conception rate among Western European states and despite government sponsored programmes that rate remains stubbornly high. The chances of becoming a teenage parent (both mothers and fathers) are greatly enhanced by social and economic disadvantage. A number of risk factors are associated with pregnancies among teenage women. These include **poverty** (girls from social class 5 are much more likely to become pregnant than girls from social class 1), a background in care, **sexual abuse**, low educational attainment, **homelessness** (teenage pregnancy can be both cause and effect of homelessness) and finally crime (teenagers, both females and males, who have been in trouble with the **police** are twice as likely to become parents as those who have had no **contact** with the **police**).

Explanations for high rates of teenage parenthood in the UK are complex, but a number of themes appear consistently in the research. First, teenagers are seen as lacking knowledge about key aspects of contraception, expectations of adult personal relationships and parenting. Second, low expectations seem to characterize teenage parents' aspirations for employment, housing and life in general. Third, parents, the media and many public institutions provide mixed messages – or no messages at all – about sexual, personal and health-related issues. Teenagers are bombarded with sexually explicit messages and, for some, encouraged by **peer group**s to become sexually active. In addition, many parents, some youth services and some schools are poor at providing accurate and sympathetic information much needed by young people.

Two principal objectives currently concern government strategy: first, a reduction in teenage pregnancies and, second, improved life chances for teenagers who become parents (and by implication their children). As an example of the first, **primary care trust**s provide sexual health clinics where teenage boys and girls can go in confidence during school time to receive contraceptive **advice** and, it must be said, free contraceptives. Local education departments are encouraging more robust personal, social and health education programmes through schools and youth services, in particular the delivery of sex and relationship education. As an example of the second objective government has sought to ensure that the proportion of teenage parents in education, training or employment reaches 60 per cent by 2010 to reduce their risk of long-term **social exclusion**. Local education authorities have made greater efforts to ensure that school age mothers at least receive the chance to complete GCSE units. **Local authorities** have also developed **Sure Start** plus which offers support to pregnant teenagers around issues such as childcare, parenting skills and furthering their own education. While the national rate of young teenage pregnancy remains high where there has been a specific push to invest in services accessible to young people and **sex education** has been seriously undertaken by schools with commitment and resources a dramatic reduction in pregnancies has taken place – even within some of the most deprived areas of urban Britain.

The young teenage mother and father themselves fall within the responsibilities that children's services have under the **Every Child Matters** agenda and the **outcomes** that social services and education must deliver for all the young people they work with. In this the key **social work** tasks with this group lie in providing **advice** and counselling to enhance self-esteem, increase life chances (support and encouragement to achieve educationally, be employable and to access secure and good-quality accommodation), to negotiate support from families and useful significant others and to help with parenting where a young person decides to have and keep a child.

third sector defined by the Department for Communities and Local Government as including 'non-governmental organizations that are value driven and which principally reinvest their surpluses to further social, environmental or cultural objectives' (and sometimes called 'civil society'). This includes voluntary and **community** organizations, not for profit organizations, social enterprises, mutuals and cooperatives. In recent years, the government has placed great emphasis on the role played by third sector organizations; both in terms of service delivery but also in terms of bringing about social changes 'on the ground' and providing a voice to marginalized groups. This has resulted in increased economic investment in third sector organizations and an emphasis on the value of collaborative partnerships between statutory services and the third sector. It is estimated that around 40 per cent of personal **social care** is provided by third sector organizations. Whilst many view this positively, some have suggested that this also relates to shifting welfare provision away from the state and into an increasingly privatized sector (Lavalette and Ferguson 2007).

Lavalette, M. and Ferguson, I. (2007) Democratic language and neo-liberal practice: the problem with civil society. *International Social Work*, 50(4): 447–59.

'three strikes and you're out' laws which prescribe **mandatory sentences** (or minimum **sentence**s) for a third offence. Such **sentence**s originated in the USA and were first imported to England and Wales by the Crime (Sentences) Act 1997.

threshold criteria grounds for granting a care order or **supervision order** to a local authority under section 31 of the **Children Act 1989**. The threshold criteria are so called because it is necessary for the court to be satisfied that the threshold is crossed before the court can proceed to consider whether it is in the 'best interests' of the child to make a care or supervision order. In other words showing the threshold criteria are met in relation to a given child does *not* mean that the court will automatically grant the order being sought. The criteria require the authority to establish that a child is suffering, or likely to suffer, significant harm and that this harm is attributable to the standard of care given by the parents or to the fact that the child is beyond the parents' control. A very young child left to wander streets at night, an infant continuously losing weight because of lack of food and a child suffering fractures as a result of parental assault are all examples that meet the criteria. The grounds are referred to as threshold criteria because, even if they are established in court in respect of a particular child, the court, before making a **care order** or **supervision order**, must consider other grounds as well, including the points in the **welfare checklist** and the principle that making the order must actually benefit the child in ways that would not happen if the order were not made. (See **significant harm**.)

There are two stages in establishing the likelihood of **significant harm**. For the first stage the burden of proof rests with the applicant to establish on the balance of probability that the alleged events occurred. The more serious the allegations the more convincing is the evidence needed to tip that balance. For the second the applicant must assess the extent of future risk and convince the court that there is a real possibility of significant harm; it is *not* necessary however to establish that the harm is more likely than not to occur. Landmark judicial decisions have indicated the wide range of facts that are relevant to reaching a decision such as parental attitudes, threats, abnormal behaviour by a child and unsatisfactory parental responses to complaints or allegations. Recent court decisions have made it plain that courts – and by implication **local authorities** –

must be sensitive to the cultural, social and religious circumstances of the particular child and family. Justice Munby in *Re K: A Local Authority v N & Others [2007]* said that courts 'should be slow to find that parents only recently arrived from a foreign country – particularly a country where standards and expectations may be very different from those with which we are familiar – have fallen short of any acceptable standard of parenting if in truth they have done nothing wrong by the standards of their own community'.

toy library a facility for people to borrow toys for their children. Such facilities are often attached to **nurseries**, nursery schools, playgroups or specialist facilities for young children.

The general purpose of toy libraries is to help poor families to have access to toys that a low income would normally not allow and, in the case of some specialist units, the use of toys specifically chosen to help stimulate a child. This may be with reference to a general under-stimulation or to an identified problem or need, including a **disability**.

trans-racial adoption and placement the placing of children of one 'race' (or of mixed parentage) with the families of another 'race', so that, legally, the fostered or adopted children are to be regarded as it they were born to that family.

In practice, trans-racial adoption amounts to the placing of Black children with white families; the converse has rarely, if ever, taken place. Since British society regards all non-white people as effectively black, what follows utilizes that distinction. The practice of trans-racial adoption emerged from a number of developments in the 1970s: first, changes in the **abortion** law; second, increased availability and usage of contraception; and third, major changes in social attitudes towards unmarried mothers and single parenthood. These three related developments had the effect of reducing the supply of 'healthy white babies' for **adoption**.

Significantly, as a result of changing attitudes to **adoption** too, this was a time when the demand for adoptable babies was in fact growing, especially among middle-class **couple**s. A dwindling supply of suitable babies and at the same time a growing demand for them brought to light the situation of many Black babies languishing in care who had previously been regarded as unadoptable (along with children with disabilities and older children). Not only were Black children considered 'hard to place', suitable Black families were thought 'hard to find'. Early attempts to recruit Black adopters were remarkably unsuccessful, leading to the misplaced conclusion that the idea of adoption was 'alien' to certain cultures. From these circumstances, and from the prevailing 'assimilationist' views on race of the period, the practice arose of placing Black children with white families. Until the mid-1960s the majority of adoption agencies operated in accordance with a strict 'matching' policy whereby the 'race' of the child was the focal issue. The concern in many policy documents of adoption societies was that children should be presentable as the biological offspring of the **couple**. In this context, much attention was also given to matching the religious background of the child's family of origin to that of the adopters.

In the 1970s, major and wider struggles took place to determine how **community** relations were to be handled in Britain in the future. Opposing forces on the one hand sought the total assimilation of immigrant groups into the 'host society' and on the other many supported the idea of cultural pluralism. The former position implied that 'race' in a sense did not matter, or at least should not. This broadly assimilationist view underpinned the commitment to trans-racial placement and adoption. The problem of the child's identity was reduced in importance; if assimilationist policies were pursued, we would all be white in the end (so long as strict immigration policies were enforced, at least in relation to New Commonwealth citizens). In the late 1960s a small group of Black social workers provided the first critique of trans-racial adoption. They argued that the 'Black community' might not survive because it was being 'robbed' of its most precious resource, its children. How, they asked, could the 'Black community' feel any measure of pride in itself if advantage (for children taken into care) was being defined as being brought up by white families? Their second concern was the effect of trans-racial adoption on the psychosocial development of Black children. This point raises the issue of whether white adoptive parents can grasp the problems that blacks have to face in a racist society such as Britain. Can white parents of Black children create in them a pride in their blackness, in effect a positive Black identity? Can such parents equip them with the necessary coping and survival skills to help them deal with racism and disadvantage? In the same vein, will such children be able to take on the social and cultural characteristics that will enable them to move freely in the 'Black community'? Finally, the remaining preoccupation of the social workers was to challenge the assumption that blacks would not adopt. They were fundamentally critical of the unsuccessful methods employed to try to attract would-be Black adoptive parents.

Research has been divided on the issue of whether Black children adopted by white couples can meet the standards implied by the critique from the Black perspective. Some research has apparently indicated that many Black children brought up by white adoptive parents are broadly well adjusted, have succeeded reasonably well at school and are able to sustain good peer relationships. Critics of this research have suggested that these children have a 'defensive' form of self-esteem, that their sense of self-worth is unlikely to stand the test of a lifetime of racism in Britain and that these children are white in all respects (including their consciousness) except their skin. The phrase 'Black skins but white masks' has been widely used about these children.

In relation to the search for Black families for the adoption of Black children, new approaches explored by the London borough of Lambeth in 1980 proved encouraging. The recruitment of Black social workers to help identify, train and support Black families who were interested in adoption was only one ingredient in Lambeth's success but an important one. Other factors included combating racist attitudes in other workers, discarding stereotyped notions of the normal family and the ability to use 'Black networks' in imaginative ways. These experiments have now been repeated elsewhere in Britain with at least some success. By the mid-1980s the placement of most Black children for adoption took place 'in race': that is, the children were placed with families of the same ethnic origin. Key difficulties remain. Not a few **social services department**s still do not have rigorous policies in relation to **adoption** and 'race'. There are circumstances where Black or mixed-parentage children have been in long-term placements with white foster parents and where permanence has been sought with Black adopters. The bonds established between white families and their Black foster children can be strong; criteria must be established to determine whether in these circumstances it is in the children's best interests to be moved. Similarly, it cannot be assumed that Black families necessarily have the best attitudes and **values** to adopt a Black child. Recent discussion documents from the **British Association of Social Workers** and the government suggest that a more flexible practice in relation to same race **adoption**s should be pursued by **social work** agencies, but Black social workers and others have been very critical of what they see as an attempt to undermine the progress made in the past decade.

truancy absence from school without permission, best applied to behaviour that is initiated by children and young people rather than by their parents and which may be recorded as an attendance if they abscond from the premises after registration. 'Truancy' is often used as a generic term for all illicit absence from school, especially by politicians, but this is not strictly correct. There are many reasons why a child may not be at school when they should be, only some of which should be seen as **deviance** on their part. Such behaviour is not an offence by the child or young person (only parents can commit an offence by failing to ensure their child attends a school where they are registered), but it is often regarded as meriting some sanction or disciplinary response.

Truancy is often seen as indicative of wider problems with the child or family, including **anti-social behaviour** or **child abuse**, but since the late 1990s has increasingly been seen as at least equally related to what is going on at the school itself such as avoidance of particular lessons or teachers, relationship problems or as a response to **bullying**. The leading writer and researcher on truancy is Reid. His many published works have chronicled the various initiatives over the last twenty years, looking both at the causes of truancy and the role of related professionals such as **education welfare officers**. Reid's approach is to mix theoretical research-based analysis with practical solutions drawn from case studies in individual schools. His writings give frequent examples of what 'works', such as pro-active interventions by school staff, addressing obstacles to attendance such as **learning difficulties** and effective use of **prosecution**. However, he also retains a healthy scepticism about official statistics which suggest that the level of absence is being reduced. It is easy to conceal the true extent of **truancy**, especially that which occurs from the school and after registration. Such children will still appear in the official statistics as 'present'. Reducing absence from school has become a highly political issue which requires schools to be seen to making progress and achieving targets. Whether it also means that there is a genuinely increased level of **participation** by disaffected and marginalized children and their parents is another question that is open to considerable debate. (See also **unauthorized absence**.)

Reid, K. (2002) *Truancy: short and long term solutions*. London: Routledge.

U u

unaccompanied asylum seeking children are supported by **local authorities** under the **Children Act 1989** while waiting for a decision on their application. If they are not given refugee status they will at least be given **discretionary leave** up to their 18th birthday before which they must apply for an extension. Such unaccompanied children are supported under section 20 of the **Children Act 1989** and thus eligible for leaving care support if they are given the right to remain.

unauthorized absence (from school) the correct term for the legal status applicable when children of **compulsory school age** are absent from school without the school's permission, as distinct from **authorized absence** where leave has been granted for an 'unavoidable cause'. Such absences are an offence by the parent under the **Education Act 1996** and are often referred to collectively as **truancy**, which is only one form of illicit absence, generally at the child or young person's initiative. It is not the child but the parents who are legally responsible for attendance and it will often be the parents who initiate or condone the absence, especially with younger children. That clearly cannot be described as truancy. Parents may be subject to a **penalty notice** as an alternative to **prosecution**.

Technically one half-day's absence without permission is an offence but all **local authorities** will have criteria for determining which cases result in enforcement and which are either tolerated or dealt with in other ways. Unauthorized absence will include taking family holidays without permission or keeping children away from school for inappropriate and trivial reasons, such as shopping or birthdays. It is the individual school/ head teacher that decides whether or not to authorize an absence, consequently the levels vary widely. Government guidance, such as 'Keeping Pupil Registers' (2007) seeks to promote a common understanding of the computerized codes allocated to each half-day session, but given that there are over 20 codes to choose from, there is

room for considerable discretion and variation. If the school chooses
to authorize the absence, no offence occurs. The published school
performance tables no longer distinguish between authorized and
unauthorized absence so there is no longer any incentive for schools to
keep the level of unauthorized absence as low as possible. In the past this
led to schools accepting parents' explanations for absence without much
challenge as authorized absences were ignored. Schools are now much
more likely to be more robust, knowing that rises in unauthorized absence
will not necessarily be seen as increasing 'truancy', especially if overall or
persistent absence is reducing as a result.

underclass a term used both to describe and to explain the over-
representation in the criminal justice system of defendants who live on
state benefits and are unemployed, homeless and/or without stable family
relationships.

    The term is used by the far right in its claim that there is a class of people
who are morally and criminally deviant as a result of being raised in
fatherless families with a welfare dependence mentality. Their argument
runs that in adulthood the underclass is unwilling to work for a living
and expects to take from, rather than contribute to, the good of society.
Left-wing critics either refuse to use the term because of its judgmental
connotations or insist that it should be used only in a descriptive and
not an explanatory manner. According to this view, while many poor,
unemployed, homeless people commit crime, this is the result of social
inequality and injustice. There is no evidence to support the idea that such
people have different moral **values** or aspirations from other people.
Given the opportunity, they would also appreciate a home, a job and a
settled family life. (See **anti-discriminatory practice**; **problem family**,
culture of poverty and **cycle of deprivation**.)

under-fives provision day-care facilities for pre-school children, including
day **nurseries**, childminders, **Sure Start** projects, nursery schools or
nursery classes in primary schools, playgroups and other provision
(nannies, au pairs, **nurseries** in family centres). The **Children Act 1989**
places a duty on **local authorities** to 'facilitate' day-care provision for
pre-school-age children. It also requires authorities to review such
provision, including voluntary and private facilities, every 3 years.
Acceptable standards have to be maintained, and to help providers reach
and sustain these standards, authorities can provide training and guidance.
In comparison with many European countries, Britain's under-fives'
provision is poor and unevenly developed from one area to another. There
is a clear lack of strategic thinking at both national and local levels.
Comprehensive policies are needed to address the issues of childcare
needs and equal opportunities, employment and social security rights. In

Britain there is a bewildering variety of complex regulations about how child day-care provision is to be regarded, costed and charged for. There is also great inconsistency in criteria for access to such provision. Urgent requirements are the development of good-quality under-fives' provision on some scale, improvements in the employment conditions for workers (especially pay) and financial help for the costs of childcare for single parents.

Cohen, B. (1988) *Caring for Children*. London: Family Policy Studies Centre.

United Nations Convention on the Rights of the Child an international treaty, agreed in 1989, that applies to everyone under the age of 18. It codifies **children's rights** and requires countries that have signed it (including the UK) to issue periodic reports of the steps they have taken to comply with its provisions.

In addition to the Convention itself, the United Nations has convened a number of international meetings at which detailed rules for its implementation have been agreed. These include the Beijing Rules on the administration of juvenile justice (1985) and the Riyadh Guidelines on the prevention of juvenile delinquency (1990). The European Convention on Human Rights has also provided additional, detailed guidance – and UK criminal law in relation to young offenders has had to be changed on a number of occasions when European courts have ruled that it **breach**ed the country's international obligations. Some of the most important aspects of European law are recognized in the UK in the **Human Rights Act 1998**. Some of the most important provisions of the UN Convention are:

- that families should be provided with the support and protection they need to bring up children in a harmonious environment where their rights are respected and children are not arbitrarily or unnecessarily removed from home;
- that the child's best interests should be paramount where there are questions of child protection; the right to protection from **discrimination**;
- the right to social services such as education and health.

The two sets of rules provide greater detail on matters such as the right to privacy and **confidentiality** in relation to **contact** with juvenile justice, the establishment of an official **age of criminal responsibility**, a separate **youth justice** system, the right to consideration of **diversion** from formal proceedings, the right to representation and to have parents participate in legal proceedings, and the parsimonious use of **custodial sentence**s (under rule 17 of the Beijing Rules).

There has been considerable debate about the extent to which the legal

framework set out in the **Crime and Disorder Act 1998** meets the requirements of the various international treaties and rules. In some respects, the legislation brought the law in England and Wales into compliance with international standards, but in others it created potential conflicts.

unpaid work supervised work for the benefit of the **community** which offenders perform as a requirement of their **sentence**. This may be under an unpaid work requirement in a **community order**, a **youth rehabilitation order** or a **suspended sentence order**. The order specifies the number of hours to be worked, which under an adult **community order** must be between 40 and 300, and must be performed within a period of 12 months. **Unpaid work** was previously known as **community service**, and has now been given the non-statutory name of **Community Payback**.

In 2006 the government announced that unpaid work should be central to **the community sentences**, and that it planned to double the number of hours performed per year from 5 to 10 million. In 2008 a Cabinet Office report (*Engaging Communities in Fighting Crime*) recommended that Community Payback work should be more visible and demanding, and that local communities should be given information about it. Following this it was decreed that offenders performing unpaid work should wear high-visibility orange jackets emblazoned with the words 'Community Payback' from December 2008, and members of the public in some areas have been given the opportunity to vote online to choose which proposed projects should be started first. To date, unpaid work schemes have been the responsibility of the **Probation service**, but the 2008 Cabinet Office report recommended that the government should consider contracting out the running of 'Community Payback' from the **Probation Service**.

Upper Tribunal a court of record with jurisdiction throughout the United Kingdom set up by the Tribunals, Courts and Enforcement Act 2007. Formerly known as the Social Security and Child Support Commissioners, Upper Tribunal judges decide appeals at the second stage of appeals on social security, tax credits and **child support**. The Upper Tribunal hears appeals in London, Cardiff and Edinburgh, and decisions are available on the Upper Tribunal's website. The full title of the court is the Administrative Appeals Chamber of the Upper Tribunal. It hears appeals against decisions of the Social Entitlement Chamber, the Health, Education and Social Care Chamber, and the War Pensions and Armed Forces Compensation Chamber of the First-Tier Tribunal. As well as dealing with appeals in benefits, tax credits, child support and other 'social entitlement' cases, the Upper Tribunal has taken over some of the supervisory and **judicial review** powers of the Administrative Court (see **judicial review**).

User (service user) the term now widely used to refer to people receiving **social work** services. It was first adopted by **advocacy** and support groups, particularly in the fields of **mental health, disability, learning disability** and childcare, to convey their message that those using services did not regard themselves as the traditional powerless, dependent 'client' of social work literature. For a time the two terms 'service user' and 'client' co-existed in social work parlance with the first referring to those who seek services as an autonomous citizen and the second referring to those who, under law, are compelled to receive a service. But that period did not last for long and 'user' is now universally accepted as the generic term for all who are in receipt of social work services, whether they wanted such services or not.

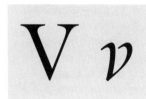

vagrancy the practice of living without permanent accommodation and of having no fixed abode.

The term is often associated with wandering, although vagrants in fact often confine themselves to particular localities. Usually vagrants are single, but families too might be vagrant. Vagrants' lifestyles may vary substantially, involving sleeping rough, using **night shelter**s, taking on temporary work with tied accommodation, and spells, often brief, of living with family or friends. Housing workers, social workers and, to some extent, **probation officer**s have increasingly argued that the 'problem' of vagrancy and **rough sleeping** should be viewed not as personal pathology or inadequacy but as an issue of **homelessness**. Night shelters should therefore be seen as only a first step in trying to secure permanent accommodation for the single and mobile homeless. A recognized additional problem for vagrants is that of securing an income from the Benefits Agency. The process is usually lengthy, with benefit being given on a day-by-day basis. There are strong associations between vagrancy and a background in care and **mental illness**.

value judgement an **assessment** or **statement** based upon one's own ethical code or norms about the worth of a person, group or whole **community**, particularly about their actions or beliefs. Any **social work** system will require a range of value judgements, for it presupposes that there are certain people who need some form of support, punishment, treatment or restraint and that there are others who are in a position to make judgements regarding the kinds of services offered. Inevitably in making judgements about which services to offer to whom and when there will be many disagreements between people about the social and moral significance of certain kinds of behaviour. Much social policy and social work practice rests upon a consensus of belief, that is, value judgements that there are certain kinds of behaviour that require support and other kinds that need to be prevented. Much social work intervention is justified by reference to some value or other – there is simply no avoiding them. The task in education and in policy formation is to reveal one's own assumptions (that is, value judgements), and how they may be linked to social advantage or position or conversely from the personal experience of disadvantage or **loss**. Part of becoming a social worker is to examine one's own value base, to see how it fits (or not) with the professional value base and reach the point where the practitioner is able to defend their own **values** as balanced, reasonable and just.

values   moral standards or principles underpinning the beliefs and behaviour of individuals, families, groups, communities, cultural and ethnic groups, faith based groups, political parties and social institutions including professions. Values are also, in a general sense, a **statement** of what is considered to be good or desirable.

   Social work has had a sustained interest in values from several perspectives. As a profession, now regulated in the UK by the **General Social Care Council,** it has sought to establish a Code of Practice to support the core objectives of social work as well as the behaviour of social workers in practice (see **ethical codes**). Many of these guiding principles are to be found in different formulations in other professional codes for other occupational groups such as doctors or lawyers. The core ideas are to focus on the needs of the recipient of a service (patient, client or **service user**); to do so in a way which promotes their interests as well as others in a close relationship with them and the interests of the wider society; and to be committed to improving practice so that the profession achieves wide public approval and support. These are admirable and widely understood values and principles, although there are sometimes problems associated with the public understanding of how social workers discharge their duties, especially when trying to promote the interests of service users when their behaviour is a concern to carers, neighbours and the wider **community**. Social workers operate in sometimes shifting sands when they are required to protect vulnerable people and yet not be too intrusive in relation to family life and an individual's right to privacy.

   Values also clearly underpin human rights although the implementation of human rights legislation is often contentious for the average citizen. The general principles on which, say, the **Human Rights Act 1998** is founded are widely accepted, but people are then perplexed in its use for groups they find unsympathetic such as those imprisoned for acts of violence, or immigrants whose claims for asylum are hard to demonstrate because of a lack of supporting documentation or travellers camping in a local lay-by. The key aspect of the Act, as with other important international value statements such as the UN Declaration of Human Rights 1948 or the UN Declaration of the Rights of the Child 1959, is that human rights continue to be applied to everyone, although they may have committed an offence (that warrants some 'correction') or they are a marginalized group (and they are reacting negatively to being marginalized) or their legal status is not yet clear.

The value base of social work has also become distinctive because of its avowed commitment to **anti-oppressive** and **anti-discriminatory practice**. This humanitarian commitment of social work to solve problems and enhance life chances means that it has to engage with structures, cultures and individual beliefs and behaviours that oppress and discriminate against people often on grounds of **'race'** and ethnicity, **gender**, **disability**, social class, age, sexual orientation and religious belief. Social workers are concerned to deliver services that are sensitive to the needs of diverse groups to ensure their inclusion; to routinely consult them on their needs; and to ensure equal access to benefits and services based upon assessed **needs**.

Values often influence the way that social workers and service users interpret the world, formulate problems and potential solutions to problems. However all this is contested territory, because many people take opposing or different views of key issues and often, by implication, the social worker's right to intervene. For example, what happens within the home is thought by many to be a private matter that should be of concern only to the people that live there. UK law takes the view that in matters of abuse the right to privacy is subordinate to the right to live free from ill-treatment. Similarly the woman's right to choose whether to go through with a pregnancy or not is contested by those that argue the right of the unborn child to life. Others argue that 'mild' physical chastisement of children is reasonable whereas others regard such behaviour as assault because comparable behaviour between adults would constitute an offence. Social workers share some of these different beliefs and values; it is therefore important that they are conscious of these values and that they are prepared to continue to work with service users, and offer them the support they clearly need, even if the service user makes a decision that differs from the social worker's **advice** or convictions, so long as the resultant behaviour is within the law. A reflective social work practitioner will want to work in **partnership** with service users so far as is possible. Although there will be circumstances when legal authority will result in a social worker compelling a service user to do something, the aspiration is to minimize the occasions on which this is necessary and that, for the most part, it is possible to work with honesty on agreed agendas and goals even where there are differences of opinion and conviction.

Banks, S. (2006) *Ethics and Values in Social Work*, 3rd edition. London: Palgrave Macmillan.

Valuing People a White Paper setting out the government's policy commitments in respect of people with **learning disability**.

Valuing People was published in 2001, and was the first White Paper about learning disabilities for 30 years. It identified a number of major problems which needed to be tackled. These included the poor coordination of services for families with disabled children; poor planning for young people at the point of transition; inefficient support for carers; lack of choice and control for people with learning disabilities; unmet healthcare needs; lack of choice in housing; **day services** which were not tailored to meet the needs and abilities of individuals; limited employment opportunities; lack of suitable provision for minority ethnic communities; lack of **partnership** working between health, **social care**, **service user**s and **carers**.

The White Paper stressed the principles of rights, independence, choice and inclusion. It aimed to deliver better life chances for people with learning disabilities, and set new national objectives concerning the problem areas identified above. In order to tackle problems with existing services and promote the social inclusion of people with learning disabilities, it aimed to increase access to **advocacy**, **direct payments**, and **person-centred planning**; to set up local **learning disability partnership**s with **service user** representation to plan and coordinate local services; to modernize day services; to provide a health facilitator for all people with learning disabilities; to introduce new targets for participation in employment; to complete resettlement from the long-stay hospitals by 2004; to establish a national Task Force including service users to advise on implementation and a national implementation support team; and to increase the support available to particular groups. These are people from minority ethnic groups, children with severe disabilities and adults living with informal carers aged over 70.

In 2009, the government followed this up with *Valuing People Now*, a new 3-year strategy for putting the original vision into practice. This took into account developments since 2001, such as the 2008 report of the Joint Parliamentary Committee on Human Rights, *A Life Like Any Other? Human Rights of Adults with Learning Disabilities*. This had revealed the extent of human rights abuses against people with learning disabilities and influenced the government to take a human rights approach in *Valuing People Now*. Following evidence of breaches of human rights in **NHS** establishments, a decision was taken to transfer the commissioning of **social care** for people with learning disabilities from the **NHS** to **local authorities**. The new strategy also responded to an independent report into access to healthcare for people with learning disabilities which found serious shortcomings in provision, and also to policy initiatives on the '**personalization**' of **social care**, which had gathered pace since the publication of *Valuing People* in 2001. The new strategy also aimed to include those groups whose **needs** appear not to have been addressed so far, in particular people with complex needs; people from minority ethnic groups; people with autistic spectrum disorders and offenders in **custody** and in the **community**. There is also a strong focus on access to employment which was taken forward later in 2009 with the publication of *Valuing Employment Now*.

victim a person injured, harmed or killed as a consequence of crime, accident of illness.

The reactions of victims of crime are unpredictable. Some people put serious offences behind them quickly and without apparent long-term harm. Others, especially if they are vulnerable at the time of a crime, can react strongly even to relatively minor incidents. Common reactions to victimization, apart from experiencing physical harm, include feelings of shock and guilt, a loss of trust in others and in the 'just world' that people normally take for granted, heightened reactions and exaggerated vigilance, fear of being alone in the place where the offence took place or similar settings, anger and humiliation. In extreme cases, the emotional impact can be long-lasting. Where victims show signs of post-traumatic stress syndrome (intrusive thoughts and dreams, emotional turbulence, intense and long-lasting pain, social withdrawal and avoidance of situations that might remind the victim of the offence), they may need specialized professional help.

Until recently, victims of crime were neglected by the criminal justice system. Indeed, their experiences of criminal justice were often so negative that observers referred to 'secondary victimization'. Although practices have changed substantially, the needs of victims and witnesses continue sometimes to be met inadequately. The rise of the 'victims' movement' and of **restorative justice**, coupled with the increasing influence of feminist and anti-racist movements, led to increased attention being paid to victims around the world. In Britain, **Victim Support** has received progressively increased funding from the government to provide direct assistance to individual victims. Other voluntary agencies such as Rape Crisis and **refuge** have also played an important part. In 1990 the government published a Victim's Charter outlining what support and help victims should be entitled to expect, giving the **police**, the **criminal courts**, the **probation service** and the **Crown Prosecution Service** specific responsibilities in relation to victims. The Charter was revised in 1996, and replaced in 2005 by a Code of Practice for Victims of Crime. When asked about their **needs**, victims emphasize information, being treated with respect and sensitivity, **compensation** and support (in roughly that order of priority). It is these needs that have been targeted in these reforms. The Domestic Violence, Crime and Victims Act 2004 provided for the appointment of a Commissioner for Victims and Witnesses. To date this has not happened, although in 2009 Sara Payne, a child protection campaigner and mother of a murder victim (see under **paedophile**), was appointed as a temporary part-time 'victim's champion'.

Victims and their needs and interests loom large in the rhetoric of politicians and pressure groups when discussing criminal justice. The government has repeatedly stated (since the White Paper *Justice For All* in 2002) that it seeks to 'rebalance the criminal justice system in favour of the victim'. Such rhetoric tends to assume that criminal justice is a 'zero sum game' in which the victim can only be benefited by removing or reducing safeguards for defendants and by more punitive measures against convicted offenders, ignoring the substantial research evidence that victims are no more punitive towards offenders than are members of the public generally, that harsh punishment of offenders brings little if any satisfaction to victims, and that developments such as restorative justice can prove more satisfactory to both victims and offenders than traditionally punitive approaches. (See also **victim–offender mediation, victim personal statement**.)

Dignan, J. (2005) *Understanding Victims and Restorative Justice.* Maidenhead: Open University Press.

victim impact statement see **victim personal statement**

victimless crime an offence that has no adverse consequences for the **victim** or has no victims. Some crimes have no clearly identifiable victim, obvious examples being the consumption of illegal drugs or sexual acts between consenting adults in private. Some however argue that there is no such thing as a victimless crime: for example, shoplifting and insurance fraud lead to higher prices, drug misuse may lead people to commit property crimes to fund their drug habits, and speeding offences can lead to serious accidents.

victim–offender mediation negotiations between an offender and the **victim** or victims of the crime, assisted by a neutral third party, that aim to reach a mutually acceptable decision about what the offender should do to put matters right or what punishment is appropriate. Victim–offender mediation was first pioneered by Canadian **probation officer**s in the 1970s and has since been employed in many countries. The approach can be used for offences of a wide range of seriousness, even including murder where surviving relatives of the victim may wish to meet offenders to show what harm has been done and to try to encourage changed attitudes and behaviour. (See also **restorative justice**.)

victim personal statement introduced in 2001, a system whereby **victims** of crime can provide the **criminal court** with a written **statement** explaining the effect that the offence has had on them.

Victim Support an independent **charity** whose **volunteer**s and paid workers offer help to **victims** of crime in the **community** and at court. Victims are mainly referred to Victim Support schemes by the police, but referrals are also received from other agencies and from individual victims themselves. Founded in the 1970s, Victim Support has grown into a national network of schemes covering the whole of the British Isles and receives substantial financial support from the government. In addition to the community-based schemes, Victim Support also runs Witness Support schemes in courts. These began in the **Crown Courts** and have more recently been extended to cover **magistrates' courts**. Although careful to maintain political neutrality and to avoid commenting on sentencing policy, Victim Support has become increasingly influential and is seen as the most representative victims' organization by government. In addition to a small paid staff, the organization employs the services of tens of thousands of **volunteer**s. It began as a 'first aid' agency offering advice and non-judgmental support rather than extended counselling, but some volunteers now receive advanced training to enable them to undertake longer-term work with victims of more serious crime and the survivors of murder. Victim Support schemes usually maintain regular **contact** with local **police**, housing, health, social services, probation and other specialist agencies in order to ensure that volunteers give up-to-date and accurate information and that the victim perspective is taken into account in **crime prevention** and other local strategies.

Victoria Climbié a 9-year-old girl who was abused and murdered by her guardians in London in 2000. She was born in the Ivory Coast and was moved to England when she was 7. Many services had regular **contact** with her and her guardians in London – **police**, social services, the NSPCC, health services – but none intervened sufficiently to prevent her murder. Her circumstances and the comprehensive failure of the major services to intervene caused public outrage and prompted government to launch a major inquiry headed by Lord Laming. Public anger was not helped by the apparent obstruction in presenting evidence to the Inquiry by Haringey social services, the London borough in which Victoria died. The massive restructuring of children's services under **Every Child Matters** and the **Children Act 2004** was the direct consequence of Lord Laming's report.

Violent Offender Order an order introduced by the **Criminal Justice and Immigration Act 2008**, similar to a **sexual offences prevention order**, which can be imposed on an offender who has previously been convicted of one of a number of specified violent offences and **sentence**d to at least 12 months in **prison**. The order is made by a **magistrates' court** on the application of a chief **police** officer, and may contain conditions preventing the offender from going to specified places, attending specified events or having **contact** with specified individuals for between two and five years after they leave **prison**. They are also required to inform the **police** if they change their names or addresses or travel abroad. **Breach** of these requirements is an offence punishable with a **prison sentence** of up to 5 years.

visual impairment eyesight defined as defective in comparison with norms established in medical practice; this includes both lifelong and acquired **impairment**. This is a general term for a wide range of visual disabilities. The wearing of glasses or **contact** lenses is sufficiently common to be regarded as unremarkable and does not automatically signify the difficulties and environmental barriers associated with **disability**. In practice, the term 'visual impairment' usually refers to people whose sight cannot easily be 'corrected' by glasses and who are likely to experience difficulties negotiating a physical environment designed for sighted people. In the UK, there are clinical criteria for **blind and partially sighted registration**.

The World Health Organization also has definitions that distinguish between 'profound blindness' and 'severe low vision'. The former involves the inability to count fingers at a distance of ten feet or less, and the latter at 20 feet or less. Over a million people in the UK are visually impaired, and three-quarters of these are aged over 75. This reflects the causes of visual impairment, which tend to be age-related. The most common causes in Britain are macular degeneration, cataracts, glaucoma and diabetic retinopathy. Over 24,000 children in Britain have visual impairments, however, and over half of these also have additional impairments.

The Royal National Institute for the Blind (RNIB) stresses that visually impaired people are 'just like everyone else' but may need aids or assistance in order to undertake some everyday tasks. Help should be offered, however, rather imposed on people. The types of challenges faced by people with visual impairments include getting out and about (often referred to as '**mobility**'), and coping with everyday tasks in the home and at work, including reading and writing. In connection with these, **social services department**s offer mobility training, low-vision aids and equipment. Some visually impaired people may use Braille, **Moon** or audiotapes in order to read, but many people are also taking advantage of computer technology.

Visually impaired people can work with the right support, but in reality they are disadvantaged in the labour market. This is often because of false assumptions about lack of ability and ignorance of the support and equipment that can be provided. People with serious visual impairments meet the definition of disability used in the **Disability Discrimination Act 1995** and are entitled to have 'reasonable adjustments' made for them in the workplace. Some may be provided with a **personal assistant** to deal with any tasks for which vision is essential. Some **local authorities** directly employ mobility officers and/or specialist social workers for visually impaired people, while others use local voluntary organizations to provide some services on their behalf. Registration as blind or partially sighted is not necessary in order to receive services. It is recognized that the loss of sight can be disorientating and traumatic for many people, and that the prompt provision of **advice** and support is essential. Many **service users** report delays in receiving assistance after diagnosis, however, and **inspections** of services for people with sensory impairments have remarked on the way these services are marginalized within local authorities.

volunteer a person who works for a statutory or voluntary organization without pay. Volunteers sometimes deliver a social welfare service or help in indirect ways so that others may deliver the service.

Such activity is considered altruistic, although for many volunteers volunteering can be a way of securing valuable experience that may lead to paid employment. Volunteers can enact many roles, including those of befriending the vulnerable, offering support in relation to very tangible tasks such as driving or keeping financial accounts, or directly delivering the service, as with **advice** bureaux and **advocacy** schemes. A major contribution made by many volunteers is to the management committees of voluntary organizations. The scale of the contribution varies too – some people helping for a few hours a week and others working almost full-time. Much **social work** and social welfare provision has its roots in voluntary activity. Over the past century in Britain, professional social work services have grown and in the main have been located in the statutory sector. The responsibility to discharge the duties of social welfare provision enshrined in law is mostly placed upon local government or statutory health authorities. The contribution of the voluntary sector to social welfare remains considerable, however. Many voluntary organizations in fact employ only paid professional workers, sometimes to deliver, on the basis of an agency agreement, a service on behalf of a local authority (for example, social work services to deaf people). Others have a mixture of the paid and unpaid, and yet others rely wholly on unpaid volunteers. There is also considerable variation in the extent to which organizations train, support and supervise their volunteers. Some are rigorous in their training programmes (the Citizens' Advice Bureaux, the

Samaritans and the **Probation Service**, for example); others have yet to develop explicit policy on these issues.

The role of the volunteer is a matter of partisan debate, a debate located in the question of what responsibilities properly belong to the state, what to the **community** and what to the individual or family. The period between 1945 and 1975, with some fluctuations, was characterized by the growth of statutory provision. Since that time there has been encouragement for families to look after their own and for voluntary effort to replace statutory provision. There is thus considerable ambiguity in the role of the volunteer, with some seeing it as an indication of **self-help** and of a caring **community**, while others are concerned at the erosion of the minimum standards that should be guaranteed by the state.

vulnerable witness a witness in **criminal court** proceedings (often the **victim**) who is regarded as vulnerable on the grounds of age, the nature of the offence, fear or distress at the prospect of giving evidence or because of **disability**. Once defined as vulnerable, witnesses are entitled to various special measures that affect the way the court case is conducted. These may include video-recorded evidence, evidence given in private or by live video link, reporting restrictions, the removal of court ushers' wigs and gowns, screens to prevent the defendant from seeing the witness, the assistance of an intermediary to help with **communication**, and devices that facilitate **communication**.

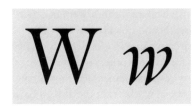

warning the official statutory name for a **final warning**.

welfare checklist the seven points that courts must bear in mind when considering making an order under the **Children Act 1989**. The seven points of the checklist are:

1. the wishes and feelings of the child, taken in the light of their age and understanding;
2. the child's physical, emotional and educational needs;
3. the effect of any change of circumstances on the child;
4. the age, sex and background of the child (which inevitably includes the child's racial, cultural and religious background);
5. the harm that the child has suffered or may suffer;
6. how capable each of the parents is at meeting the child's needs;
7. the range and powers of the court under the Act itself.

The importance of the checklist is immense. It acts as a reminder to the court that it must, above everything else, consider any order it might make in the light of the child's welfare (except the **emergency protection order**, to which the checklist does not apply); and for the first time in child law it itemizes, however broadly, what welfare means. In particular, a court must not make an order under the Act, even if the grounds for that order exist, unless it has also taken into account the effect of making that order on each of those aspects of the child's life contained in the checklist. Although the **welfare checklist** is expressly for the court to consider, social workers and other professionals appearing in court in connection with an application for an order must also bear its contents in mind when presenting their arguments.

welfare rights I an umbrella term that broadly includes trying to maximize the income, in cash or in kind, of **service user**s and their dependants. Such work requires the provision of information to claimants, the education of claimants and, where necessary, the provision of **advocacy** and representation services to assist claimants in securing claims, reviewing and appealing against adverse decisions.

The place of welfare rights work in mainstream **social work** services has long been contentious. Some have argued that social workers should have detailed knowledge of the complex British welfare rights system in order to be able to assist vulnerable people directly and quickly. Such a view emphasizes the importance of material circumstances to social functioning. Others have argued that it is unrealistic for social workers to have these duties, given the, usually, heavy statutory responsibilities that they carry. There is probably now a consensus that social workers should at least have direct access to welfare rights advisers. In addition, social workers should perhaps have at least an outline knowledge of the welfare benefits system in order that they might recognize a possible issue of entitlement, even if others undertake the detailed work to help **service user**s make a claim or challenge an adverse decision (what some have called **signposting**). In some instances, of course, social workers have sole and unavoidable responsibility for determining eligibility criteria for benefits in the form of some **social work** services, such as home helps, meals on wheels, **aids and home adaptations** to be used in users' own homes or charges for residential care services. Statutory sector agencies will only rarely incorporate a welfare rights specialist within social work teams. More often social workers will have formal arrangements with specialist welfare rights advisers located elsewhere within a local authority or with organizations in the voluntary sector, like the Citizens' Advice Bureaux, which will provide **advice** to individual social workers or take referrals from them.

A relatively small number of **local authorities** dispense such services from neighbourhood offices where welfare rights advisers might share advice functions with representatives from **social services department**s. There is great complexity in the British welfare benefits system, including some variations in provision and legal framework in England and Wales in comparison with Scotland and Northern Ireland. The principal benefits are administered by the **Department for Work and Pensions**, HM Revenue and Customs, local authority departments (social services, housing and education departments in particular) and by health services.

Other types of financial support can also be accessed, for example, grants to support disabled people into work from Jobcentre Plus, help with legal costs from the **Legal Services Commission**. There are also areas of welfare rights work where issues impact upon 'private' provision, as in stakeholder pensions, for example (see **welfare rights 8**).

Not surprisingly, welfare benefits' handbooks describing eligibility, rates of benefit, the relationship between benefits, **appeal** mechanisms and many other matters have become voluminous. A key part of the state welfare benefits typology is the distinction, first, between contributory and non-contributory benefits and, second, between means-tested and non-means-tested benefits. *Contributory benefits* are those where entitlement depends upon the claimant having paid (or being treated as having paid) national insurance contributions as well as on other criteria relating to the claimant's personal circumstances – for example, age in the case of *state retirement pension* (**welfare rights 8**), or limited capability for work in the case of *contributory employment and support allowance* (**welfare rights 9**). The other main contributory benefits are contributory *jobseeker's allowance* (**welfare rights 9**) and *bereavement benefits* (**welfare rights 2**).

Non-contributory benefits, on the other hand, are those benefits where entitlement depends only on personal circumstances and not on any means test – such benefits include *child benefit* (**welfare rights 4**) and *disability living allowance, attendance allowance* and *carer's allowance* (**welfare rights 3**). Another category of benefits is *means tested* where eligibility depends on a claimant's other income and capital. People working in the welfare rights field, whether they be specialists or social workers, have a number of key tasks to fulfil. These tasks include trying to maximize income by determining eligibility criteria for benefits and *passported benefits*. For example, if a claimant is found to be eligible for *income support* (**welfare rights 5**), he or she may also be eligible for *housing benefit* and *council tax benefit* (**welfare rights 6**), *free school meals* (**welfare rights 4**) and health benefits. There are issues of *'better-off'* **calculations**, where comparisons can be made about whether a claimant will be better off working rather than being reliant upon benefits. For example, a single parent with a young school-age child would have to compare the value of, say, income support, child benefit, free school meals, free prescriptions and housing benefit with a wage where there may be deductions for income tax, national insurance contributions, a contributory pension, childcare costs (for an after-school club for example) and travel costs as well as the loss of some or all of the housing benefit.

Other major areas of work concern *challenging decisions* or *appeals*, *backdating* of claims, and trying to challenge attempts by welfare agencies to reclaim funds where there is alleged to have been an *overpayment*. Research about the success rates of claims for particular benefits reveals that some benefits are very difficult to secure. For this reason, and because sometimes claimants complete forms inaccurately or fail to provide the required evidence (often because they have found it difficult to understand the claims form), a lot of the work of welfare rights advisers is about challenging decisions. Such challenges can be to a designated decision-maker in the **Department of Work and Pensions** (DWP) or local authority, or appeals to tribunals (a body that hears appeals about social security matters (see **appeal tribunal**).

Although such processes can be time-consuming for workers and anxiety-provoking for claimants, they can be successful. DWP statistics show that, in the first quarter of 2004, 52 per cent of claimants were successful at an oral hearing, compared to 21 per cent whose **appeal** was decided on the papers alone; the success rate is also significantly higher for those appellants who are accompanied by a representative. Since the take-up rate of benefits varies so much (child benefit has the best rate of around 98 per cent, whereas pension credit and council tax benefit are significantly under-claimed), welfare rights workers are increasingly *targeting* (see below) particular groups of potential claimants. For example, campaigns to ensure that people with enduring **mental health problems** are claiming all the benefits to which they are entitled will work through many of the agencies that work directly with the mentally ill. Thus work will be done in psychiatric hospitals, supported accommodation, day-care centres, general practitioners' surgeries and other locations that such services users frequent. Other strategies to improve take-up include training ancillary workers, such as home helps or **community care** workers or family aides, so that they might become aware of potential problems of 'under-claiming'. Many agencies are systematically experimenting with outreach services to take advice services into communities through the use of communal facilities, mobile advice buses, or even door knocks to provide advice in people's communities or their own homes.

Targeting is a term originally borrowed from the world of advertising ('to target') by welfare rights workers to describe the intention to deliver information about particular benefits to those individuals or groups most likely to be eligible to claim them. Because of the plethora of under-claimed benefits (see *take-up*, above), each with its own set of rules, it is difficult in general campaigns to impart enough specific information to enable individuals to be sufficiently confident about their potential eligibility to make a claim. By finding ways of targeting information, it is possible to address the potential claimant more directly and to give fuller details to allow a more informed choice to be made. Examples of targeting information would include writing to people receiving domiciliary services about attendance allowance or **disability** living allowance, or writing to people who are registered blind about the lower-rate *mobility component* (**welfare rights 3**). Since the mid-1980s the word 'targeting' has been used by the government to justify an increased reliance on means-tested benefit – for example, 'targeting the most needy' – and to imply that universal provision is a waste of public expenditure. Thus a reduction in services may be described as 'better targeting'. In a way, welfare rights' work could be regarded as an industry that is built upon the failings of welfare agencies to reach the people their services are designed to support. But while the benefits system is so complex and while there are vulnerable people who cannot easily represent their own best interests, such an industry will be much needed.

welfare rights 2 *bereavement benefits* paid to men and women following the death of their spouses or civil partners, based on the contributions of the deceased person, unless he/she died in the course of an industrial accident or from a prescribed industrial disease, in which case it is payable *without* the need for national insurance contributions. Bereavement payments, widowed parents' allowance and bereavement allowance replaced widows' benefits from 9 April 2001. Bereavement benefits for widowers as well as widows were introduced in the UK as a response to European human rights legislation and a test case brought by the Campaign for Widows' and Fathers' Rights (*Willis and Others v United Kingdom* (1999)). In 2006 the benefits were extended to those in a civil **partnership**, but they are not payable to cohabiting **couple**s (see *Shakell v UK no. 45851/99, 27 April 2000*).

Bereavement payment: a tax-free one-off payment to meet the immediate costs of bereavement.

Widowed parent's allowance: payable to widows/widowers who are under pension age with dependent children. Widowed mother's allowance is still paid to surviving widows in respect of bereavement before April 2001.

Bereavement allowance: payable for a maximum period of 52 weeks to widows and widowers who are over 45 and under pension age, as long as they do not remarry, form a new civil **partnership**, or 'cohabit'.

welfare rights 3 *disability and carers' benefits* the several benefits that support those with a **disability** and their carers.

Attendance allowance: a benefit paid to people over the age of 65 with severe disabilities who need help looking after themselves or **supervision** to avoid danger. People under 65 claim *disability living allowance*. It is paid at two different rates depending on the level of care needed. The higher rate is paid to people who need frequent attention with bodily functions or continual **supervision** to avoid danger during the day and night. It is also paid to people who are terminally ill. The lower rate is paid to people needing frequent attention or continual **supervision** during the day or the night. Attendance allowance is a *non-contributory* and *non-means-tested benefit* (**welfare rights 1**). It is not taken into account as income for any means-tested benefits, but may act as a passport to extra benefits. Attendance allowance often provides extra income that enables **older people** to remain in their homes. Many **older people** in receipt of attendance allowance have been forced to spend the allowance on local authority home care charges, however, which has left many older people with income close to or below **poverty** levels. The report *Charging with Care*, published by the **Audit Commission** in May 2000, forced the government via the **Care Standards Act 2000** and associated statutory guidance to set out a broad framework to ensure that in future councils' charging policies are fair and operate consistently with their overall **social care** objectives. **Local authorities** should ensure that home care **service users** on a low income are no longer charged for services and that all those in receipt of attendance allowance or *disability living allowance* (see below) seeking support from home care services should have an **assessment** of income. They should also have an individual **assessment** of their disability-related expenditure.

   Care component: part of the *disability living allowance* (see below).

   Carer's allowance: formerly known as invalid care allowance, this is a benefit paid to someone who cares for a severely disabled person. The carer must spend at least 35 hours caring for someone who gets *attendance allowance* (see above) or *disability living allowance care component* (see below) at the higher or middle rate. Carer's allowance can be claimed from age 16, and there is no upper age limit. It cannot be paid if the carer earns above a prescribed amount (£95 a week in 2009–2010) or is in full-time education. *Take-up* (**welfare rights 1**) of the carer's allowance is thought to be low, and non-claimers who would gain include, for example, women with partners in full-time work. Although it is taken into account as income for means-tested benefits, it gives entitlement to a *carer's* premium, which increases the value of *income support* (**welfare rights 5**), *housing benefit* and *council tax benefit* (**welfare rights 6**), and *pension credit* (**welfare rights 8**). Carer's allowance overlaps with all income replacements benefits, including ESA and incapacity benefit, contributory *jobseeker's allowance* (**welfare rights 9**) and, most importantly, *retirement pension* (**welfare rights 8**). This means that many older carers may not actually be paid the carer's allowance although by claiming it they may qualify for extra means tested benefits.

   Constant attendance allowance: paid as part of the *industrial injuries scheme* (see below).

   Disability living allowance (DLA): a benefit paid to people with severe disabilities who need help looking after themselves or **supervision** to avoid danger, or who have difficulty with outdoor **mobility**. It includes a *care component*, paid at three different rates, and a *mobility component*, paid at two different rates. The benefit was introduced in 1992 for people aged under 65. People aged 65 or over must claim attendance allowance (which does not include a **mobility** element); however, an existing claim for DLA may continue after the age of 65 as long as the person remains eligible. Therefore, it is important, where possible, for people to have claimed before they reach 65, as the additional components and rates mean that a claim for DLA is more likely to succeed than one for attendance allowance. The higher-rate *care component* is paid to people who need frequent attention with bodily functions or continual **supervision** to avoid danger during the day and night. It is also paid to people who are terminally ill. The middle rate is paid to people needing frequent attention or continual supervision during the day or the night. The lower rate is paid to people needing attention for a significant part of the day or who are aged 16 or over but cannot prepare a cooked meal for themselves. The higher-rate *mobility component* is paid to people aged 3 or over who are physically disabled and unable or virtually unable to walk, or for whom the effort needed is likely to seriously affect their health. The lower rate is paid to people aged 5 or more who have a physical or mental disability and who need guidance or supervision from another person to get about out of doors. Disability living allowance is a *non-contributory* and *non-means tested benefit* (**welfare rights 1**). It acts as a passport to higher rates of *income support* (**welfare rights 5**) and *housing/council tax benefits* (**welfare rights 6**) but is not taken into account as income for any means-tested benefits. A claim for disability living allowance includes a long self-assessment form. This was envisaged as a great improvement on the previous, often unsatisfactory, medical examinations. In practice the form has proved contentious and difficult to use.

Exceptionally severe disablement allowance: benefit paid as part of the *industrial injuries scheme* (see below) to people needing personal care.

Industrial injuries benefits: benefits to employees who suffer personal injury through an accident arising out of and in the course of work, or who contract a prescribed disease or prescribed injury while working. The main benefit is *disablement benefit*, which is paid to compensate people who suffer as a result of an industrial accident or suffer from a prescribed disease involving '**loss** of physical or mental faculty'. This means it can take account of the effects of trauma and disfigurement as well as inability to do things. It is normally paid only if the disablement is assessed as 14 per cent or more. Disablement benefit awards are often provisional in the first place. Final awards may be for a fixed period or for life. If the disability increases, because of deterioration in the condition or because of the interaction of some other condition, an award can be reviewed on the grounds of unforeseen aggravation.

Reduced earnings allowance: can be claimed only if the accident happened or the disease began before October 1990, when it was abolished. Reduced earnings allowance is an extra benefit to provide some **compensation** for people who cannot earn as much as they could before the accident or disease. It can be paid provided that disablement is assessed at 1 per cent.

Retirement allowance: replaces reduced earnings allowance when people retire but is paid at a lower rate.

Mobility component: one of the two components of *disability living allowance* (see above).

Prescribed industrial disease: a disease that gives rise to benefits under the Industrial Injuries Scheme and is listed in detail in regulations showing the 'prescribed disease or injury' and the occupation that causes it.

welfare rights 4 benefits for children and young people

Child benefit: a benefit paid in respect of a child aged under 16, or under 19 (20 in some cases) and in full-time non-advanced education, to a person with whom the child lives or who contributes to the child's maintenance to the value of the benefit. Where two people would qualify for child benefit, rules dictate priority between claimants. HM Revenue and Customs administers child benefit (as well as *guardian's allowance*). It is a *non-means-tested, non-contributory benefit* (**welfare rights 1**) and is the best example of a universal benefit. People seeking to curtail public expenditure argue that child benefit is poorly targeted, because, with a take-up rate of nearly 100 per cent (unlike means-tested benefits), it is paid to all families regardless of need. Its defenders regard it, however, as an important expression of society's collective responsibility to maintain and encourage the family and see it as a way to support all children in low- and middle-income families.

Child tax credit (CTC): the CTC aims to create a seamless system of income-related support for families with children. It replaces the child-related elements formerly paid with benefits, and constitutes the payment for children for all means-tested and non-means-tested benefits, as well as for tax credits.

Education clothing grant: a discretionary scheme operated by some local education authorities to assist parents with the cost of school clothing. Although school 'uniform' cannot be a legal requirement, most schools and parents prefer to have a 'dress code' as a matter of local policy. Parents are generally expected to meet the cost of required clothing, including any sports or other specialist clothing, although many schools seek to keep their expectations as simple as possible. Financial assistance may be available directly from the school, especially secondary schools, or through a scheme administered by the local education authority, usually via the education **social work** (or education welfare) Service. Children should not be excluded from school for **breach**es of the school's uniform code unless the circumstances are exceptional, such as deliberate and persistent defiance.

Educational maintenance allowance (EMA): a discretionary cash payment that is made by local education authorities in England and Wales to young people who stay on in full-time education after Year 11 (post-16). Grants are usually small but more substantial schemes may be available in some areas such as Education Action Zones for deprived neighbourhoods.

Free school meals: an arrangement whereby children whose parents receive *income support,*(**welfare rights 5**), *income-related employment and support allowance, income-based jobseeker's allowance* (**welfare rights 9**) or *guarantee pension credit* (**welfare rights 8**) are entitled to a midday meal at school free of charge (Education Act 1980). Parents in receipt of *child tax credit* with income under a certain amount also qualify. Not all schools make a hot meal available under this arrangement, but they must provide a sandwich lunch as an alternative. Application needs to be made by the relevant parent through the local education authority's education **social work** or **education welfare service** and proof of entitlement must be produced. No cash alternative is available. The 1980 Act abolished the requirement to provide free milk, making it discretionary. Research carried out by the then Department of Employment and Education estimated that 1.8 million children were entitled to a free school meal although approximately 20 per cent did not take up their entitlement. **Social services department**s have the **power** to provide additional assistance in response to the particular nutritional needs and special diets of children, under their general powers in the **Children Act 1989**, section 17. When formal assessments are made of such needs, it is now recognized as essential that the needs of a child in relation to his or her religion, culture and **community** are addressed adequately, and, as with other aspects of support delivered through the **community care** system, consultation is vital: legal requirements can dictate that a failure to do so may render the **assessment** unlawful. Criticism of some social services departments' approaches to this important part of the **community care** system were made in influential reports in 2002 by Ayesha Vernon (*The User-Defined Outcomes of Community Care for Asian Disabled People*, Policy Press/J. Rowntree Foundation) and a study by the Leeds Involvement project, Joseph Rowntree Foundation, Joseph Rowntree Charitable Trust and the University of Leeds, *South Asian Disabled Young People and their Families* by Yasmin Hussain, Karl Atkin and Waqar Ahmad (Policy Press).

Guardian's allowance: a benefit paid to a person looking after a child who is effectively orphaned, that is, where both parents have died or one has died and the other is in **prison** or cannot be found. Guardian's allowance continues as an independent child-related benefit (together with *child benefit* – see above) following the introduction of the *child tax credit* (see above) in April 2002.

welfare rights 5 *means-tested benefits and the social fund*

Since 1988, the main means-tested benefit for those who have insufficient income to live on has been *income support*. In 1995, *income-based jobseekers allowance* (**welfare rights 9**) was introduced for those required to sign on for benefit, who had no other income. In 2003, *pension credit* (**welfare rights 8**) replaced income support for people of pension age. From 2008, those unable to work claim *income-related employment and support allowance* (**welfare rights 9**) instead of income support. At the same time, the government is reducing the qualifying age of children of lone parents, so that they are increasingly required to undergo job seeking activity in order to receive benefit. The government is seeking to simplify the benefits system, and has proposed abolishing income support in favour of jobseekers allowance for all those of working age who are not unable to do some paid work. This is causing concern for carers, the other group who currently claim income support. Critics argue that including such disparate groups as lone parents with young children and carers with other jobseekers will lead to a more complex system, as the job seeking requirements will be different for each group.

Applicable amount: the maximum amount of money that can be paid to people claiming means-tested benefits. It is made up of two elements: *personal, or basic, allowances*, set at fixed rates; *premiums, or additional amounts*, designed to provide extra money for particular groups of claimants, such as people with disabilities and carers. In addition, for *income support, pension credit, income-related ESA, and income-based JSA*, housing costs for home owners are included (see **welfare rights 6**). This consists of interest payments for mortgages and home improvement loans. The applicable amount is then compared with the income available (or treated as available) to the claimant, including income of a partner, and, if income is lower, the difference is paid to the claimant as benefit. Certain types of income are disregarded.

Earnings disregard: there are some circumstances where a person in receipt of a means-tested benefit can keep some of their earnings. The level of disregard varies according to the claimant's circumstances – for example, a carer, a person with disabilities, a lone parent and people in specified occupations (fire fighter, territorial army, coast guard) can earn up to £20 per week (in 2009) before benefit is reduced. In contrast, single people not in any of the above categories can earn only up to £5.

Income support: a *means-tested benefit* (**welfare rights 1**) available to those in a qualifying group who work for less than 16 hours a week (24 if it is a partner who works). Income support is mainly claimed by carers, or by lone parents with young children (youngest child must be under 10 from October 2009, and under 7 from October 2010). There is a capital limit, and some capital may be taken into account as **'tariff'** income. An individual's needs under income support are called the *applicable amount* (see above). Income support may be used to top up other benefits such as *carer's allowance* (**welfare rights 3**). Receipt of income support acts as a passport to health benefits, *housing benefit* and *council tax benefit* (**welfare rights 6**), *free school meals* (**welfare rights 4**) and access to funding from the community legal service fund. Income support claimants can also make claims on the *Social Fund* (see below).

Social Fund: a fund administered by the **Department for Work and Pensions** that provides lump-sum payments to people in need. The Social Fund consists of two different parts. The *Regulated Fund* provides the **Sure Start** *maternity grant* (see also **welfare rights 7**), *funeral expenses payments, cold weather payments* and *winter fuel payment* (see below) as of right but in closely defined circumstances. Appeals can be made to an independent **appeal tribunal**. The *Discretionary Fund* provides *community care grants, budgeting loans* and *crisis loans* (see below). Discretionary payments are made from a set budget allocated on a district basis so expenditure is therefore limited by its budget. The Discretionary Social Fund was introduced in 1988 along with *income support* (**welfare rights 5**). It replaced 'single payments' with a system of grants and repayable loans. The Discretionary Social Fund has been criticized on three main grounds: first, the budget limit which requires Social Fund officers to ration payments; second, the extensive use of discretion by fund officers; and third, the absence of an independent **appeal** mechanism. The law on the Discretionary Social Fund is provided by the Secretary of State's directions, which broadly outline the circumstances in which a payment can be made. Fund officers who make decisions must follow the directions and take account of guidance, local priorities and the local budget. Often, applications are refused, or only a partial award is granted. When this happens, an applicant may ask for an internal review; this may include an **interview** at the local office, at which a representative acting for the claimant may attend, but is often done over the phone.

A further review is provided by Social Fund inspectors at the Independent Review Service, but this is conducted in writing only. The inspectors check that previous decisions comply with the law, including the Secretary of State's directions. Frequently, the inspectors refer cases back for further consideration. This involves a lengthy process to deal with a claimant's needs, which are often immediate and essential.

The Regulated Social Fund: Cold weather payment: payments from the Regulated Social Fund to cover extra domestic heating costs during exceptionally cold weather. Cold weather payments can be made to certain people receiving *income support* (**welfare rights 5**), *income-related employment and support allowance* (**welfare rights 9**), or *income-based jobseeker's allowance* (**welfare rights 9**); also to those receiving *pension credit* (**welfare rights 8**), or *child tax credit* (**welfare rights 4**) which includes a **disability** element. Payment will be made for any period of seven consecutive days when the average of the mean daily temperature is freezing or below. A cold weather payment should be paid automatically when temperature conditions dictate.

Funeral expenses payment: a payment from the Regulated Social Fund to which there is a legal entitlement if the applicant is receiving specified means-tested benefits and *tax credits* (**welfare rights 9**) and has responsibility for a funeral held in the United Kingdom (there are special rules regarding the European Community). The regulations allow for the cost of a modest funeral. Costs are usually recovered from the deceased's estate.

Maternity payments: see **welfare rights 7** *Sure Start maternity grant.*

Winter fuel payment: a lump sum paid to households in which someone is aged 60 or over to help meet the costs of winter fuel payments. There is a higher rate for those aged 80 or over. It is generally paid automatically to people in receipt of retirement pension and most other social security benefits. Those not in receipt of benefits need to make a written claim.

The Discretionary Social Fund: Budgeting loan: a repayable loan from the Discretionary Social Fund that people can apply for if they have been claiming *income support* (**welfare rights 5**), *income-related employment and support allowance* (**welfare rights 9**), *income-based jobseeker's allowance* (**welfare rights 9**), or *pension credit* (**welfare rights 8**), for at least 26 weeks. Loans can be paid to assist with important intermittent expenses for which it is difficult to budget. Applications for budgeting loans are prioritized by weighting them against factual criteria laid down in the Social Fund directions. The maximum loan available is £1,000, but the amount that will be offered depends on the applicant's needs, budget and 'ability to repay' within 104 weeks. The loan is reduced by the value of any capital over £1,000 that the applicant has (or £2,000 if the person is aged over 60). In 2004/5, the average budgeting loan was £405.

Repayments can be deducted from most benefits. Repayments are recovered at a rate of between 5 and 20 per cent of the single person's *applicable amount* depending on other commitments. A second loan can be given before the first one is repaid, but the Social Fund officer will restrict the amount offered in line with the directions on the maximum amount of loan available to the claimant. No interest is charged on the loan.

Community care grant: a payment (not a loan) from the Social Fund that a person receiving *income support* (**welfare rights 5**), *income-related employment and support allowance* (**welfare rights 9**), *income-based jobseeker's allowance* (**welfare rights 9**), or *pension credit* (**welfare rights 8**), can apply for to help with a one-off expense. The law outlines six circumstances in which payment of a community care grant may be made, subject to the Social Fund's local budget:

1. to help a person re-establish himself or herself in the **community** following a stay in institutional or residential care;
2. to help a person remain in the community rather than enter institutional or residential care;
3. to help a person set up home in the community as part of a planned resettlement programme following a period when he or she has had an unsettled life;
4. to ease exceptional pressure on a person or his or her family;
5. to allow a person to care for a prisoner or young offender on home leave;
6. to pay travel expenses within the UK in specified circumstances, including visits to seriously ill relatives and attendance at funerals and to ease domestic crises.

These circumstances have the force of law. Guidance provided, although not legally binding on the Social Fund officer, lists 'priority groups' and 'priority items', concentrating on people defined vulnerable by age or ill-health; however, 'absence of guidance applying to a particular circumstance, item or service does not mean that help should be refused'. A community care grant will be reduced by the value of any capital over £500 (£1,000 if aged 60 or over) that the applicant has. In 2004/5, the average community care grant was £390. A substantial proportion of payments are made to families in order to ease exceptional pressure. However, pressure on the budget means that usually only high priority needs are met.

Crisis loan: repayable loans from the Social Fund towards expenses in an emergency if this is the only means to prevent serious damage or risk to health or safety. A claim may be made for an item or for living expenses. In 2004/5, the average crisis loan was £78. People can apply for a crisis loan, whether or not they receive benefits. Crisis loans must be applied for by phone, which can cause difficulties for applicants. They may need to attend an interview, and, although DWP should pay for any travel costs involved, the number of Jobcentre Plus offices is decreasing, making attendance difficult for many people.

welfare rights 6 *help with housing costs*

Council tax benefit: a benefit that provides help towards the payment of council tax. It is administered by the local authority charging the tax and is credited against the account of the person liable to pay. Council tax benefit can take two forms. *Main council tax benefit* depends on the income and circumstances of the person liable to pay council tax.

Second adult rebate depends only on the income and circumstances of other adults in the household. Only one of these will be paid, whichever is higher. Main council tax benefit cannot be paid to anyone who has more than £16,000 in capital (except for those on *guarantee pension credit* (**welfare rights 8**)). People receiving *income support* (**welfare rights 5**), *income-related employment and support allowance* (**welfare rights 9**), *income-based jobseeker's allowance* (**welfare rights 9**), or *guarantee pension credit* (**welfare rights 8**), get council tax benefit to cover the full liability unless non-dependant deductions apply, or the property is in council tax bands F–H when it is restricted to the maximum amount payable for a band E house.

Council tax benefit for people who have income above their *applicable amount* (**welfare rights 5**) is reduced at the rate of 20p in £1 (2009). The second adult rebate can be claimed where the liable person has no partner. If all the other adults are on a low income, the rebate given is of up to 25 per cent. People with a need for more room to accommodate a **disability** may have their council tax band lowered.

Discretionary housing payments: in large areas of the social security and community care services systems, decision-makers have 'discretion' rather than any clear statutory duty to meet people's welfare needs. Discretionary housing payments are payments that can be made by a local authority to help people to meet their rent or council tax liability or other exceptional housing costs – for example, if their housing benefit does not cover their rent. However, a payment will not be made for services to meet the costs of water and sewerage or ineligible services for *housing benefit* (see below). Payments are made from a cash-limited budget allocated to each local authority by central government, and requests should be made in writing.

Housing benefit: a benefit that provides help towards the payment of rent, administered by **local authorities**. *Rent allowance* is a cash payment to tenants of private landlords or registered social landlords; *rent rebate* is a credit against a local authority tenant's rent account. Housing benefit cannot be paid to anyone who has more than £16,000 in capital (except for those on *guarantee pension credit* (**welfare rights 8**). People receiving *income support* (**welfare rights 5**), *income-related employment and support allowance* (**welfare rights 9**), *income-based jobseeker's allowance* (**welfare rights 9**), or *guarantee pension credit* (**welfare rights 8**) get maximum housing benefit, less any reductions (see below). As income increases above this level, benefit is reduced at the rate of 65p per £1 (2009). For social tenants, the maximum housing benefit is equal to the claimant's full rent but subject to certain deductions, including deductions for heating charges and for non-dependent adults, who are expected to contribute towards housing costs. For private tenants, rent levels are determined by the Local Housing Allowance rules, and deductions apply as above. Under these rules, an allowance is determined each month by Rent Officers for different types of dwellings in 'Broad Rental Market Areas'. The size criteria will allocate numbers of bedrooms according to the make-up of the household. If the allowance is lower than the rent charged, then the tenant must find the difference. Where housing benefit does not meet the cost of rent, the person may be able to claim a *discretionary housing payment* (see above) to cover the cost of the shortfall. Benefit will normally be paid to the tenant, but **local authorities** have discretion to make payments to the landlord where the tenant is unlikely to pay, and must pay the landlord where there are 8 weeks rent arrears or where the landlord receives **direct payments** for arrears. In these situations, social workers can support a request that benefit be paid to the landlord.

Support for mortgage interest (SMI): a scheme enabling claimants of certain benefits to include the interest element of their mortgage costs in their *applicable amount* (**welfare benefits 5**). The interest is paid at a standard rate, which may be less than the rate being paid to a lender. Claimants who are over 60 receive help from the start of their benefit claim, but for others there is a waiting period. Normally, for a post-October 1995 mortgage, a claimant will have to wait 39 weeks before costs are paid (creating considerable arrears problems in situations like **loss** of employment, bereavement, assumption of carer responsibilities, and separation and **divorce**). For that reason, concessions are made to facilitate assistance. Specifically, help is brought forward in the cases of carers, partners going into **prison** on remand, people unable to access mortgage protection policies because of HIV, and those who have been 'abandoned' by a partner, leaving them responsible in the house for a child or young person. In these cases the 'wait' is reduced to eight weeks from the date of the income support claim, then 18 weeks at 50 per cent of eligible costs, and then 100 per cent of costs at the end of 26 weeks. In 2002 it was confirmed that a person who has been 'constructively' abandoned, for example by violent or unreasonable behaviour, which has prompted a partner to leave the house, can be assisted by the system. In addition, to cope with the exceptional financial situation in 2009, the usual 39 week wait was reduced to 13 weeks.

welfare rights 7 *maternity-related benefits*

Health in pregnancy grant: a one-off, non-means-tested grant for all women who are 25 weeks pregnant, and who are receiving antenatal care. Claim forms are available from the midwife or doctor.

Maternity allowance: an allowance paid to a woman off work while having a baby, payable for up to 26 weeks when *statutory maternity pay* (see below) is not available, for example to someone who is self-employed. The amount of maternity allowance payable depends on the level of a woman's earnings in the specified period before the baby is due. It is paid at a set weekly rate or 90 per cent of the mother's average weekly earnings, whichever is lower. The allowance can be claimed at any time after the 11th week before the expected confinement.

Milk tokens: free tokens that can be exchanged for milk, available to expectant mothers and children under 5 in families getting certain means-tested benefits.

Statutory adoption pay: a benefit payable during periods of **adoption**-related leave from work, as provided for by the Employment Act 2002.

Statutory maternity pay (SMP): a legal minimum rate of pay paid by employers during the maternity pay period (39 weeks in 2009), beginning between the 11th week before the expected week of confinement and the day after the birth. Many employers pay more than this statutory minimum. To be eligible, a woman must have been working for her employer for at least 26 weeks and have average earnings of at least the lower earnings limit. Women who have been dismissed or whose employment ended without their consent before they are due to take maternity leave are also eligible. For the first 6 weeks of maternity leave, statutory maternity pay is paid at the rate of 90 per cent of average earnings. For the remaining weeks it is either a set weekly amount or 90 per cent of the mother's average earnings whichever is lower. Women who do not qualify for SMP may be able to get *maternity allowance* (see above) from the DWP. Disputes over eligibility or non-payment can be referred to HMRC for determination, and decisions can be appealed. In some cases non-payment or payment at an inappropriate level may be a form of **discrimination** within the jurisdiction of the employment tribunal, as may other actions or omissions of employers prior to, during or after the maternity leave period.

Statutory paternity pay (SPP): a benefit payable to fathers during periods of paternity leave, as provided for by the Employment Act 2002.

Sure Start maternity grant: a payment made from the regulated *Social Fund* (**welfare rights 5**) to help meet the costs of a new baby. It is paid to an applicant who is in receipt of specified means-tested benefits or tax credits and has just had a child (including adopting a baby) or expects one within 11 weeks. The payment is worth £500 for each child.

welfare rights 8 *benefits for older people*

Attendance allowance: a benefit paid to people over the age of 65 with severe disabilities who need help looking after themselves or **supervision** to avoid danger (**welfare rights 3**).

Graduated pension: an additional pension paid with *state retirement pension* (see below). The scheme operated between 1961 and 1975 and pays limited benefits to people who contributed during that period.

Pension credit: a means-tested benefit for people of retirement age. There are two parts to the credit – a *guarantee credit* and a *savings credit*. The *guarantee credit* provides an income top-up to those currently aged 60 or over (in 2009/2010) but this lower age limit will rise in line with retirement age, so that by 2020 it will be 65 (and subsequently it may rise to 68). It works in the same way as *income support* (**welfare rights 5**), with similar capital rules. It tops up low income to a specified level, and includes additional amounts for people who are severely disabled and for carers.

There is also a *savings credit* for people aged 65 and over that provides extra money for people with incomes above the level of the basic state pension. However these payments are capped (see current benefit rates). Claims can be made online or by phone, and the Pension Service can calculate entitlement to the credit when an individual claims state retirement pension. Most people will have their credit reassessed every 5 years, and during this period most people will not be required to report changes of circumstances although they can ask for their credit to be reassessed if their income falls. In general, the government states that increases in income during this fixed period (known as the *assessed income period*) will be ignored.

Retirement age: the age at which state retirement pension (see below) is paid. For men this is 65 and for women this has been 60 up until April 2010 (recognized as *pensionable age*), but the retirement age for women will be gradually raised to 65 between 2010 and 2020. The government has announced that retirement age for everyone will rise further to 68.

Retirement allowance see **welfare rights 3** – *industrial injuries scheme.*

Stakeholder pension: schemes were introduced in April 2001 under the

Welfare Reform and Pensions Act 1999 and the Stakeholder Pension Schemes Regulations 2000, SI 2000 No. 1403 as a way of providing a highly regulated, low-cost pension, including a second-tier pension for those in employment, fixed-contract workers, the self-employed and people who are not actually working but can afford to make contributions. In many cases such people may or may not have a *state retirement pension* (see below) depending on their contributions record.

Most organizations are required by law to provide employees with access to a stakeholder pension – although they are not required to set up and run their own pension scheme. To qualify as a stakeholder pension the scheme must satisfy a number of criteria, including that it must be a money purchase arrangement and that management charges in each year must not exceed more than 1 per cent of the total value of the fund and are taken from the fund. The minimum contribution must not be set higher than £20. It is possible to contribute to someone else's stakeholder pension – for instance, someone can make contributions to a grandchild's or a non-working partner's stakeholder scheme on his or her behalf. Stakeholder pension schemes approved by HM Revenue and Customs are registered with Opra, the Occupational Pensions Regulatory Authority.

The performance of the stock market causes concerns that stakeholder pensions may not be able to deliver the benefit to retired people that was assumed when the government created them in 1999. This has not been helped by the way in which employers have started to retreat from occupational pension provision or imposing changes on pension schemes. This was the subject of a controversial report by Alan Pickering, *A Simpler Way to Better Pensions* (Alan Pickering, July 2002), which recommended deregulation of occupational pensions and the optional removal of guaranteed benefits, survivors' benefits, and other features of conventional pensions, as a means of giving employers incentives to maintain occupation pension provision. On publication, John Edmonds, General Secretary of the GMB union, reportedly said workers could be facing, by the end of 2002, 'the biggest pensions rip-off in history'.

State earnings-related pension scheme (Serps): a scheme providing an additional pension, based on individual contributions, that is paid to people claiming retirement. Since 2002, additional state pension has been built up under the State Second Pension (see below).

State retirement pension (SRP): the benefit payable to people over retirement age, which is 65 years for men, and up until april 2010 was 60 years for women; however, retirement age for women will be increased to 65, to be phased in between 2010 and 2020, affecting women born after April 1950. SRP can be paid even if a person continues to work. Alternatively, retirement can be deferred for up to 5 years when retirement age is reached. This increases the value of the pension when claimed. There are four types of retirement pension.

The *category A pension* is based on the claimant's contributions over his or her working life. From April 2010, the number of years needed to qualify for a basic state pension is 30. The *category B pension* is based on contributions paid by a spouse or civil partner: traditionally, it would be paid to a married woman who has either no or only reduced entitlement to a category A pension. It can only be paid once the contributor has reached retirement age. There is a non-contributory pension (**welfare rights 1**) for certain people age 80 or over.

State second pension (**S2P**): a pension introduced in April 2002 to replace the *state earnings-related pension scheme* (see above). It aims to provide a more generous additional state pension for low and moderate earners and certain carers and people with a long-term illness or **disability**. Research by the campaign group *Carers UK*, however, estimates that by 2050 even those who have spent the greater part of their working lifetime caring for others may receive only £50 per week extra on top of the basic state pension.

welfare rights 9 *working age benefits* benefits for people in work, people looking for work, and people unable to work through ill-health or **disability**.

(1) **benefits for those in work**

Child tax credit (see **welfare rights 4**)

Housing and council tax benefits (see **welfare rights 6**)

Working tax credit (WTC): a 'benefit' for parents, people with disabilities, and certain others to top up low earnings, administered by HMRC. Working tax credit, which replaced previous in-work benefits in 2003, is assessed on an annual basis, on gross earnings for the previous year. This method of administration inevitably causes both under and **overpayments**, which has led to substantial problems for many families, due largely to the way that overpayments have been recovered with little regard to claimants' financial circumstances. There has been widespread criticism of the scheme by **advice** organizations and the Parliamentary **Ombudsman**, and some changes have been made. However, the experience has deterred many people from claiming. Claimants may be able to offset up to 80 per cent of their childcare expenses (up to a maximum) which makes paid work more financially viable for many parents.

(2) **benefits for those seeking work**

Jobseeker's allowance (JSA): a benefit paid to a person who is unemployed, 'signing on' as available for work and actively seeking work. There are two types of JSA: *contribution-based JSA*, paid to claimants who have paid or have been credited with the required national insurance contributions, and *income-based JSA*, paid to claimants who satisfy the income and capital means test. Contribution-based JSA is an individual benefit that can be paid for a maximum of 26 weeks; income-based JSA can be paid to supplement contribution-based JSA, for example, to meet additional needs due to **disability**. It can be paid instead of contribution-based JSA to those who do not meet the national insurance contributions' conditions or who have exhausted their entitlement to the contribution-based benefit. Childless **couple**s over 18, where one or both partners were born after 28 October 1947, are required to make a joint claim for JSA. To claim jobseeker's allowance, all claimants must sign a *jobseeker's agreement* that specifies what steps they will take to find work and how they must demonstrate that they are 'available' for and are 'actively seeking' paid work. Those who do not comply with the regulations may be *sanctioned* (disqualified from benefit). Those who fail to comply with a direction to undertake job-search activity may be sanctioned for two or four weeks. Someone who is dismissed from his or her job for misconduct or leaves voluntarily without 'just cause' may be sanctioned for up to 26 weeks. Many cases of dismissal or of people leaving employment voluntarily include circumstances that justify only a short period of disqualification or none at all. In practice, a maximum disqualification is almost always imposed in the first instance, and claimants have to **appeal** to have their disqualification reviewed and to begin receiving their benefits. Jobseeker's allowance is not paid for any period covered by wages in lieu of notice. By contrast, redundancy payments do not affect entitlement. Income-based JSA operates like income support, and those in receipt of it are passported to other benefits such as free prescriptions.

(3) benefits for those unable to work due to sickness or disability
Employment and Support Allowance (ESA) replaced incapacity benefit on 27 October 2008, although existing claimants continue to claim incapacity benefit, or income support, until they are re-assessed and transferred to ESA. There are two types of ESA: *contribution-based ESA*, paid to claimants who have paid or have been credited with the required national insurance contributions (except for young people under the age of 20, or 25 if they have been in full-time education, who do not have to satisfy the national insurance contribution conditions), and *income-related ESA*, paid to claimants who have insufficient contributions, but who satisfy the income and capital means test. There are two phases to ESA: the **assessment** phase (the first 13 weeks, when benefit is equivalent to JSA), and the main phase (from week 14, when a higher rate of benefit is paid). During the **assessment** phase all claimants (except those who

are terminally ill) are assessed using the '*work capability assessment*'. Claimants may also be required to attend a work-focused interview.

Following the assessment phase, claimants who are eligible for ESA are put into two groups: the *Support Group* is for people who are not expected to be able to find or remain in work, and who are consequently not subject to any requirements to undertake work-related activity. The government expects only 10 per cent of claimants to fall in this category.

The *Work-related Activity Group* is for people who are expected to be able to return to work, and are required to attend work-focused interviews and undertake work-related activity. Benefit sanctions can be imposed if they fail to comply with requirements (although there is a right of appeal). The government expects 90 per cent of claimants to fall in this category.

The *Work Capability Assessment* (WCA) tests claimants for 'limited capability for work', and 'limited capability for work-related activity'. The first part of the test comprises a self-**assessment** questionnaire (form ESA50) which contains questions relating to both physical and **mental health** functions, and, along with information from health professionals and carers, provides the initial evidence that will determine whether the claimant is eligible for ESA. A small number of people may go straight into the support group, but most people will be sent for a face-to-face **assessment** by a 'healthcare professional' employed by the DWP.

Limited capability for work is assessed by descriptors for physical activities and for 'mental, cognitive and intellectual function', and claimants are given a score. Many features of the previous test (the PCA) were retained, although changes were made to the scoring system. The scope for **mental health** scoring was widened to take account of conditions such as **learning disability** and autistic spectrum disorder, and the scoring system includes the same range of levels of limitation as the physical descriptors. The government removed the differential between the scoring for physical and mental functions in the PCA in order to 'remove a bias against people with **mental health problems**'; with the PCA, people with mental health problems had to score on more descriptors than those with physical health problems. Assessors should take into account the person's ability to reliably repeat or sustain the activity, the effects of pain, fatigue or distress, and the detrimental effects of medication. Mental function should be considered even where it is not raised by the claimant.

Limited capability for work-related activity is also assessed by descriptors. If a claimant's condition means that at least one of these descriptors applies to them, then he/she is not required to undertake work-related activity as a condition of receiving ESA, and will go into the support group. All other claimants are assumed to have the ability to return to work at some point, and will go into the work-related activity group.

A *work focused health-related assessment* follows the WCA assessment, and is designed to gather information about the claimant's ability to undertake activity aimed at getting him/her back into work. A report is sent to a personal adviser who will use the information for work-focused interviews. Sanctions are imposed if a claimant fails to attend a health-related **assessment** without good cause.

Incapacity benefit: replaced on 27.10.08 by employment and support allowance (see above), but may still be paid to those whose claim began before that date. Assessment is based on the personal capability assessment, which formed the basis of the new *work capability assessment* for ESA.

Permitted Work: people on ESA (and incapacity benefit) can do some work and still receive benefit; there are various categories with earnings limits. Claimants may do voluntary work and claim reasonable expenses; there is no limit on hours, but an ability to **volunteer** 'full-time' may not be seen as consistent with 'limited capability for work'.

Statutory sick pay (SSP): a state benefit paid by an employer to those with 'employee' status earning above the lower earnings limit for national insurance contributions. A person who does not qualify can claim *employment and support allowance* (**welfare rights 9**). It is paid for the first 28 weeks of sickness. Some employers pay more or even full pay during the early weeks of sickness. It is no longer fully reimbursed, as in the past, which has tended to create problems of non-compliance by employers, in which case it may be necessary to refer disputes over non-payment to HMRC, which is ultimately responsible for paying SSP.

welfare state   the organizing, financing and provision of welfare benefits and services by government. The term 'welfare state' is used to describe the combination of benefits and services intended to provide citizens and residents with basic guarantees that their income, health and welfare will be provided for in the event that they cannot. The welfare state seeks to relieve **poverty** and reduce inequality by guaranteeing a minimum level of financial assistance through social security, unemployment benefit, family allowance and benefits related to inability to work. While state involvement in housing, education and social insurance occurred in Europe throughout the last half of the 19th century, the welfare state as it was constructed in Britain between 1944 and 1949 was unusually comprehensive and supported by a well-articulated philosophy that viewed it as a natural progression in social development. In Britain the welfare state became closely associated with the publicly funded, large organizations, such as the **National Health Service**, local authority council housing and state school systems.

For some 30 years after the Second World War, the continued expansion of the welfare state was taken for granted by a broad consensus across the political spectrum. Expenditure on services and benefits took a greater share of the gross national product each year until the mid-1970s, when the government came under pressure to limit the increasing costs of welfare. The architects of the welfare state had always linked its benefits and services to the presumption of full employment, for men if not for women. Most households, it was assumed, would have a relatively well-paid wage earner. In the mid-1970s the destabilizing effects of a sharp rise in the price of oil and the rapidly changing nature of the economy made full male employment difficult to sustain or achieve. Unemployment soared, as did inflation. At the same time, the broad consensus supporting the welfare state also began to weaken. Electorates became less willing to fund services and benefits through taxation, while politicians and commentators from the newly ascendant political right argued that welfare benefits were too generous and created a disincentive to work and a dependency on the state. Governments hostile to the welfare state as it took shape between 1945 and 1975 were elected in both the United States (1980) and Britain (1979). Sober assessment of the retrenchment of welfare policies that both these governments subsequently adopted, however, indicates that the welfare state has survived, if in a somewhat different form. Not until its second term did the Thatcher government attempt to cap social security spending by linking any increase in benefits to the cost of living (previously benefits had been up-rated with the increase in the national median wage, invariably a more generous calculation). Other reforms throughout the 1980s and 1990s changed the institutional arrangements of the welfare state by limiting the direct provision of welfare by state institutions, in particular those provided by the local authority such as housing and home care.

The **National Health Service and Community Care Act** of 1990 separated purchasers of services from the providers of those services encouraging a far greater role to private and voluntary organizations. At roughly the same time schools and hospitals were given greater powers to manage themselves rather than be managed by local or health authorities. In effect, this introduced competitive markets into some welfare provision, channelling public money into welfare services provided through an increasing number of private and voluntary organizations rather than by public institutions and **local authorities** as in the past. Alongside the arguments for greater efficiencies in the welfare provision by submitting them to market discipline other arguments from the conservative right were suggesting that the welfare state bred a sense of dependency and a reluctance to work by those receiving benefit. Many analysts have noted that, while the form of the welfare state changed, moving towards a greater role for private and voluntary organizations, government financing has not been cut as severely as first thought, and public support for the welfare state overall remains high. But whether it kept pace with the extent of need *as defined when the welfare state was in its infancy in the 1940s* is another, critical question but one with no clear answer. Council housing, once a well-supplied public sector resource for a mix of social classes including professionals, is now a residual service for only those on low incomes. A once generous home help service that provided domiciliary assistance for young mothers as well as for **older people** has been virtually eliminated. Child benefit is nothing like as generous now as when it was introduced as family allowance in 1945 and neither is the state pension. Equally welfare reform has tied the receipt of several key benefits to finding work or training by would-be recipients. As Britain has become a vastly more unequal society since 1980 the larger question concerning the current effectiveness of the welfare state remains. (See also **anti-poverty strategy**.)

Hills, J., Sefton, T. and Stewart, K. (2009) *Towards a More Equal Society? Poverty, inequality and policy since 1997*. Bristol: Policy Press.

wellbeing has different interpretations, referring to both a state of being (an individual's 'wellbeing') and a process. As such, it is multi-dimensional and highly complex. A person's wellbeing will change over time and their **life course**, and research suggests that wellbeing is closely linked to an individual's social, physical and cultural environment. Recent years have seen increased attention given to the concept of 'wellbeing', with many commentators relating this to significant social change; rapid globalization, increased individualism and consumerism, alongside a decline in collectivism, especially in advanced industrialized countries. In particular, questions are being asked as to how we might measure 'wellbeing', for example, in relation to levels of overall life satisfaction or the extent of our 'happiness'. Research has suggested that amongst affluent nations, increased economic growth does not seem to be resulting in increased wellbeing for that society as a whole. This has led many to question why this is the case, and moreover, to consider what needs to be implemented to improve citizens' wellbeing. There has therefore been increased attention to the area of 'wellbeing' both in policy and academic discussion. In academic debate, wellbeing is examined from various disciplinary perspectives, including economics, psychology, social policy and sociology.

As a general term, 'wellbeing' is often used alongside, or instead of 'health' (e.g. 'health and wellbeing centre'), however, there are many more dimensions of wellbeing; the most important being physical and **mental health**, close relationships, work satisfaction, trust in other citizens and activity within a faith **community**; as opposed to material circumstance. As a concept then, wellbeing is of great importance to both **social work** theory and practice, perhaps because social work '. . . involves a form of practice which aims to get people to feel better about themselves' (Jordan, 2007: vi). Indeed, the International Federation of Social workers (2001: 1) defined social work as a profession which '. . . promotes social change, problem solving in human relationships and the **empowerment** and liberation of people to enhance their wellbeing' (cited in Jordan, 2007: 1). However, despite this assertion, there remains debate (which lies at the heart of contemporary social work theory) about how this should be enacted by social work practitioners.

Jordan, B. (2007) *Social Work and Wellbeing*. Lyme Regis: Russell House Publishing.

Welsh Assembly responsibility for social services was transferred to the Welsh Office in 1971. This responsibility was linked to that for the health service in Wales in the Health and Social Work Department. As a result of this development, an attempt at establishing a coherent policy in respect of social services and health was embarked upon in 1976. The most notable success is the development of a fully evaluated 'all-Wales strategy' for people with learning disabilities. The existence of an integrated department for health and social services enabled the Welsh Office to overcome some of the departmentalism that has inhibited coordination of policies in England and Scotland. This integrated responsibility has been further enhanced through the creation of the Welsh Assembly. Devolution of powers to the elected Welsh Assembly has enabled local representatives to discuss provision of various services within the context of perceived Welsh needs. The Department for Health and Social Services advises the Welsh Assembly on setting policies for social care in Wales, including making legislation and providing funding, delivering and monitoring services.

whistleblowing a process of trying to make visible an abuse or misuse of **power** within an organization, usually by an employee of the organization, although the person may have a role other than a full-fledged employee, such as an agency worker or a student on placement working temporarily for an organization.

A number of public and internal enquiries within health and social welfare agencies over the past few decades have speculated about some employees' failure to report on perceived abuses in the behaviour of colleagues or about agencies' failures to respond to complaints about such abuses when they have been explicitly reported as abuses. The inability of workers to 'blow the whistle' and of agencies' unwillingness to respond to known abuses led to the devising of the Public Interest Disclosure Act 1998. This Act sought to provide protection for those who disclose abuses by discouraging employers from treating such employees in a 'detrimental manner'. Such measures included protection from unfair dismissal and other measures, such as a possible reduction in pay or failure to increase pay or failure to offer some benefit that might otherwise be provided.

The Act was designed to encourage a culture of openness. However, employers are not required to have a policy on disclosing abuses of **power** by their own employees, nor are there any rules about preventing employers refusing employment to an applicant on grounds that he or she was a whistleblower in a previous employment. Should an employee make a mistake, even in good faith, and an alleged abuse prove groundless or difficult to prove, then the whistleblower could find himself or herself in difficulty with a possible counterclaim of 'defamation'. These limitations have not brought about a fundamental change in the culture of health and social welfare agencies. Employees continue to feel the constraints of loyalty to colleagues or agency or a generalized wish 'not to rock the boat'. There may however be evidence of an increased use of anonymous complaints to the media or to agency **inspection** services or encouragement to **service user**s who wish to make formal complaints.

Students in training often have major problems in dealing with what they consider to be poor practice. They are obviously keen to pass their placements and prefer not to rock the boat perhaps until the placement is over and they have secured their pass grade. It is also possible that they do not feel safe to discuss any concerns with their practice teacher or a manager in the workplace. This has to be a matter of conscience for any student. In the first instance it may be possible to test out a practice teacher or workplace supervisor by enquiring, in a non-confrontational way, about their attitudes to practices perhaps close to the worrying issue in question. It will also be useful to consult a university tutor. Although it is difficult to 'blow the whistle' on poor practice, it is useful to remember that social workers are asked to encourage service users to confront oppression and to make complaints when services are poor or negligent. There are clear parallels because in both instances the relatively powerless are being asked to register a concern.

Brammer, A. (2006) *Social Work Law*. Harlow: Pearson/Longman.

whiteness refers to white ethnicities and the privileges associated with this. In recent years there has been increasing academic attention, both in Britain and in the United States, to the study of whiteness and the heterogeneity within white communities. The growth in post-structuralist thought has led to a plethora of literature on the subject of 'whiteness'. There is no consensus on what 'whiteness' is, nor a uniformity in theoretical approaches, rather its exploration seeks to further deconstruct the 'taken for granted' nature of racial and ethnic categories. The current interest in exploring 'whiteness' seeks to make it visible, yet also recognize its fragmented and heterogeneous nature. For example, studies of 'whiteness' can include the analysis of marginalized white working class communities, whilst also being about exploring minority white identities within the UK. Writers such as Anoop Nayak (2004) have focused attention on working class white youth culture and the performance of 'white' and 'English' identities. In Nayak's work, gender, class, sexuality, race and ethnicity intersect in the situational performance of whiteness, which also goes some way towards problematizing any simplistic notion of 'White on Black' **racism**. Nayak's work reflects the complex **power** relations at play in the performance of whiteness and thus highlights some of the more recent approaches to **anti-racism**. There has also been a revived discussion of white ethnicities within the political context in recent years, not least amongst political parties such as the BNP (British National Party), who are seeking to capitalize on insecurities relating to the changing nature of Britain.

Nayak, A. (2003) *Race, Place and Globalization: youth cultures in a changing world*. London: Berg Publishers.

Women's Aid a voluntary sector agency, established in 1975, concerned primarily with the problem of **domestic violence**. It is a campaigning organization run by women for women. It is also a source of **advice** and information for both women in abusive relationships (it runs a 24-hour helpline) as well as social welfare agencies seeking to identify relevant local resources. It is also essentially a **self-help** movement which supports a federation of **refuges** for women, and their children, seeking to leave or have respite from a violent partner. It is also active in **domestic violence forums** across the country.

In broad terms Women's Aid is prepared to accept any women experiencing difficulties with an abusive or violent partner. However there may be circumstances where a woman's behaviour, or that of her children, may **breach** refuge rules and she is asked to leave, often as a result of drug abuse or significant **mental health problems**. Women themselves define what they consider to be an unacceptable or intolerable situation; there is no 'objective test' set by the movement or any kind of defined threshold to meet. The joint aims for Women's Aid in relation to direct work are, first, to help women and children recover from trauma and, second, to encourage them to take control of their lives. The movement also has broad educational and campaigning aims in relation to social welfare and justice systems as well as the public. Campaigns are continuing to focus upon the problem that many women face in admitting that they have a problem. The current initiative is called ACT: A to admit that there is a problem; C call it by its name – **domestic violence**; and finally, T – talk to someone. Another campaign encourages women to talk to friends acknowledging that research has revealed that friends may be easier to talk to than family members or professionals in social welfare and justice agencies. Yet another current campaign is focused upon the idea of respect; both for oneself and for other people. The respect campaign is targeted especially upon young people in perhaps their first serious relationship.

Women's Aid has been instrumental in improving services for women in abusive relationships and there is no doubt that the problem has moved from being essentially a private problem to one that is now thought to be the responsibility of the state; that is, a public issue. However, the under-resourcing of **Women's Aid** in general and the erratic support of **local authorities** for refuges have dogged the movement and continue to make it vulnerable financially. Current provision is still far short of that recommended by the Domestic Violence Select Committee way back in 1975, although many would argue that much greater emphasis should be placed upon keeping women and children safe in their own homes and communities, rather than putting most resources into moving women into alien environments where there may be additional problems of adjustment. Women's Aid would, of course, advise that the woman should be able to chose the best and safest option.

Working Together the comprehensive guide to interagency working to safeguard and promote the welfare of children.

Originally published in 1999 the guide has undergone extensive revision in 2006 and then again in 2010 after lengthy consultation. It has been revised – and lengthened – in order to reflect a new conception of **safeguarding** children as well as to establish protocols for the coordination and integration of children's services shown to be lacking after the deaths of **Victoria Climbié** and **Baby P**. *Working Together* firmly establishes safeguarding children within the five **outcomes** of **Every Child Matters** and is now the responsibility of all agencies: health, schools, **early years, children's trust**s, voluntary sector and **youth justice**. Much of the document outlines the vast machinery that now must be engaged in safeguarding children. **Child and adolescent mental health services**, and family nurse **partnership**s have particular responsibilities as do sport, culture, leisure and youth services.

The coordinating task outlined is therefore immense and information sharing particularly through electronic **databases** such as **ContactPoint** is essential. Much of the volume is taken up with how to handle child protection investigations. This was central to earlier versions of *Working Together* and remains so with detail provided on constituting a core group for the protection of a specific child and the necessary components of a protection plan for that child.

workload management systems for determining and managing the quantity and quality of work of an individual worker and teams of workers. Two systems of workload management are typically used; the first rests upon estimates of time allocated to identified 'cases' and routine tasks or activities (for example, it is estimated that case A requires 5 hours a week, case B 10 hours, case C 8 hours, **group work** 6 hours, **team** meetings 3 hours, duty 7 hours, a training day 7 hours, and so on). Thus a worker might anticipate how work within the next month is to be spent. The second system is similar except that standard allowances (either points representing time or actual estimation of time) are given to, say, a **pre-sentence report**, a **supervision order**, a **child abuse** investigation, a day in court and other set pieces.

Systems vary in their complexity, depending upon their objectives. Some systems are also used to help management determine the range and duration of work. The principal objectives of effective workload management schemes are to help protect workers from overload, thereby sustaining quality in work, and to help management determine where resources are to be allocated. Workload management can also be an aid to **supervision** and, if information is shared, to **team** functioning. Unreasonable workload has been a feature of some cases where children have died, although this is not to suggest that such tragedies are all to be explained by this problem. In some of these cases the practice of some **local authorities** has been to allocate cases regardless of the workload already carried by some social workers. Although a social worker may nominally be responsible, they have, in practice, too little time to work effectively with families where there are complex problems and significant problems of risk. Sustained stress has featured in some of these well publicized tragedies, especially where there have been high levels of absenteeism and vacancies in children and families social work teams, notably in urban areas where there have been high levels of deprivation. The role of the **team** manager is crucial in these circumstances because they should be aware of the pressures already being experienced by **team** members and should be able to protect them as well as seeking to maintain high standards. Some team managers however may wish to be seen to manage their team without 'troubling' more senior managers.

written agreement a **statement** written and agreed jointly by **service user** and social worker, setting out the aims and tasks to be undertaken in any future work. Some prefer to use the term contract rather than written agreement. Written agreements or contracts are key tools in contemporary **social work**. They are designed to ensure that there is no misunderstanding over the scope and intention of any planned social work intervention and to highlight areas of cooperation between practitioner and service user. They should set out clearly what specific tasks are to be undertaken and by whom. The content of any written agreement should be arrived at by negotiation and always be framed in the service user's own words or in words that are readily understandable by all concerned, although this aspiration will be a challenge to some client groups where mental capacity may be an issue. When working with children and families, *Guidance to the Children Act* requires that a written agreement be drawn up before a child is placed in accommodation. In particular, such agreements will specify the length of time the child will spend in the 'care system', the frequency of **contact** between the child and his or her parents and the role the parents will play in the life of the child when he or she is accommodated.

Some commentators have argued that in practice written agreements or contracts cannot reflect an equal relationship between service user and social worker. The argument is that, in most cases, professional **power** will outweigh service user power, especially where social workers are gatekeepers to resources. Others have argued that social work must aspire to a 'needs led' practice and that service users and their **advocates** must be consulted to articulate needs even if resources cannot always meet them. This raises strategic issues about the use of scarce resources. If all the resources for a particular need are exhausted within a few months then managers need to make the case for additional resources. Failure to do so will mean that managers are content to ration resources regardless of need and, in effect, to find spurious technical solutions to what are essentially political and resource problems.

young offender institution (YOI) a secure institution for young
offenders serving **custodial sentences**, run by the **prison** service. They
house young offenders aged from 15 to 20 serving **detention and
training orders** and long-term **detention** under section 53 of the **Crime
and Disorder Act 1998** as well as **sentences** of **detention in a young
offender institution**, and comprise 84 per cent of the juvenile **secure
estate** (for which the **Youth Justice Board** bears responsibility). The
intended abolition of the **sentence** of **detention in a young offender
institution** would have meant that the juvenile **secure estate** was
reserved for offenders under 18, but with the delayed implementation
of this reform YOIs continue to cater for the 18–20 age group as well
as 15–17-year-olds.

young offenders see **youth justice**

youth conditional caution a measure similar to **conditional cautions**
for adults, whereby specific conditions can be attached to a **caution**
administered to a young offender. The youth conditional caution was
introduced by the **Criminal Justice and Immigration Act 2008**.
See also **final warning**.

youth court the **criminal court** responsible for young offenders aged
10 to 17 in England and Wales, which replaced the juvenile court in 1992.
It is a specialized version of the **magistrates' court**; youth court
magistrates are drawn from a special panel of local justices who have
particular experience and interest in work with young people. Proceedings
in the youth court are intended to be less formal than in an adult court.
The public is excluded, and the press may not normally report young
people's names and addresses, but in recent years there have been
attempts to 'open up' the court by encouraging greater **communication**
between magistrates, young offenders and their families and making the
courts more accessible to **victims**. The court is legally bound to have
regard to the welfare of the child, but the **sentences** available to it include

punishments such as **fines** and **custody** (in the form of the **detention and training order**) as well as measures such as the **youth rehabilitation order** and **reparation order**. Young offenders who are charged with certain 'grave crimes' (see section 53 of the **Crime and Disorder Act 1998**) may be tried in the adult **Crown Court** instead of the **youth court**. See also **youth justice**.

youth culture or subculture a system of values, attitudes and behaviours shared by a group of young people and different from those exhibited by other young people or people in general within a particular society.

Sociologists have examined the idea that there are youth subcultures in Britain. The characteristics thought by some to typify a youth subculture include a degree of classlessness, particularly in relation to leisure habits, a measure of opposition to adult values and behaviour and, most important, the replacement of the family by the peer group as the key set of social relationships. Critics of this analysis have argued that for most young people, class, race and gender continue to be the most important defining characteristics rather than age. They add that society is remarkably good at reproducing itself, and in this respect attitudes and values are frequently shared by generations. Where differences are discernible, they are thought, with some exceptions, to be transitory. Social workers and others working with adolescents and young people have it that particular peer groups can be extremely important influences upon the behaviour of individual young people. In practice, it may be difficult to distinguish between the influence of a youth culture as distinct from a more immediate peer group. It may be that a peer group is a subculture, but it is also possible, indeed usual, for the subculture to be much larger than the peer group. In some circumstances (with some offence behaviour, for example) social work with young people has to acknowledge the importance of the group in relation to an individual's behaviour and work with the group if particular problems are clearly rooted in group dynamics. Gangs, for example, can provide exclusive group membership with tightly prescribed roles and in some cases the expectation of very distinctive behaviour. Members of such groups may clearly be culturally different from other young people, but such all embracing social groupings are rare. The values and attitudes of particular youth groups may best be understood by reference to other social phenomena such as class or race. The class origins of rockers or skinheads, for example, may be a better explanation of their behaviour than intergenerational relations. Similarly, Rastafarianism among the young in Britain may, in part at least, be understood by examining racism and relations between ethnic groups rather than through age related explanations.

youth default order a court order (introduced by the **Criminal Justice**

and Immigration Act 2008) which imposes an **unpaid work** requirement, **curfew** requirement or **attendance centre** requirement on a young offender in lieu of an unpaid **fine**.

youth justice the criminal justice system as it applies to people under 18. Since the introduction of the **youth court** in England and Wales in 1992, the term 'youth justice' has replaced the previous 'juvenile justice'. From the middle of the 19th century there has been a recognition that young people cannot be held as fully responsible for their actions as adults, that it may be easier to change their behaviour than that of adults, and that they should be protected from the full force of adult punishment. At the same time, the fact that young people commit a large proportion of all crime suggests a need for an official response (but see **minimum intervention**). Since 1908, young offenders have been dealt with in a separate court that is closed to the public and where proceedings are meant to be less formal than in adult **criminal court**s. Special **sentences** and other measures (such as the **reprimand, final warning, youth conditional caution** and **youth rehabilitation order**) apply to **young offenders,** as do special **custodial sentences** such as the **detention and training order, detention in a young offender institution** and **detention** under section 53 of the **Crime and Disorder Act 1998**. The history of youth justice has been and remains one of tension between the **just deserts** model, the welfare model, in which the young person's welfare and **rehabilitation** are believed to be paramount, and the **minimum intervention** approach that seeks to avoid unnecessary **labelling** by managing the youth justice system in such a way as to divert young people away from it for as long as possible (see **labelling theory, systems management** and **diversion**). The **new youth justice** pursued under **New Labour** has emphasized holding young offenders more responsible for their actions than hitherto. However, the **youth court** retains its duty (under the **Children and Young Persons Act 1933**) to have regard to the welfare of the child, and the **new youth justice** also contains elements of **reparation** and **restorative justice**.

Youth Justice and Criminal Evidence Act 1999 a key piece of legislation with the objective of helping intimidated and **vulnerable witness**es give evidence in criminal proceedings in the most effective manner. The Act also is designed to enable witnesses to give evidence who might previously have been considered incompetent such as people with learning and physical disabilities. The Act allows witnesses to use a variety of special measures so as to enable them to give evidence without duress; such measures might include prior visits to courts to allow for familiarization of buildings, courts and procedures and video links to allow witnesses to be cross-examined 'from a distance' and, possibly, with the support of carers or other support staff who might offer 'emotional support' without any interference with what a witness might want to say. The measures described in the Act were thought likely to benefit complainants in relation to **domestic violence**, **service user**s where **racism** might have been a component and children and vulnerable adults where **abuse** is alleged to have taken place. In essence, the hope was to make the 'court experience' less traumatic and more likely to lead to just **outcomes**.

Youth Justice Board (YJB) a national body created by the **Crime and Disorder Act 1998** with responsibility for the management of the **secure estate** and for the implementation of government policy and good practice in the **youth justice** system, including advising on the content of the **National Standards for Youth Justice Services** and the regulation of **youth offending teams**. Board members are appointed jointly by the **Justice Secretary** and the Secretary of State for Children, Schools and Families. The Board has the **power** to monitor the operation of the system, to obtain and publish information for that purpose, to carry out and commission research and to advise the government on youth justice policy. While the board has been active in ensuring that **youth offending team**s are in a position to comply with national standards and to promote the defined aims of the youth justice system, it has been less successful in limiting the use of **custody** by the courts and in promoting consistency in sentencing between **youth courts**.

Youth Justice Plan an annual document prepared by **local authorities** in consultation with **youth offending teams** and other local agencies for the **Youth Justice Board**, setting out their progress against their objectives, their plans for the coming year and the funding arrangements for their work.

youth offender contract see youth offender panel

youth offender panel a local body which deals with a young offender under the age of 18 who is the subject of a **referral order** made by the **youth court**, placing the young person under the jurisdiction of the panel for between 3 and 12 months. The panel consists of a member of the local **youth offending team** and two lay members. It seeks to agree a 'youth offender contract' with the young person, a programme aimed at preventing re-offending. This programme can include **victim–offender mediation**, **reparation** by the offender, other elements of **restorative justice**, **unpaid work**, school attendance and other specified activities and conditions (but not **electronic monitoring**). The young person is then bound to abide by the terms of the contract, whose implementation is monitored by the panel. If a contract cannot be agreed, the panel must refer the offender back to court to be **sentenced**. Referral back to court for re-sentencing can also happen if the young offender is found to be in **breach** of the contract.

Newburn, T. *et al.* (2002) *The Introduction of Referral orders into the Youth Justice System: Final Report*, Research Study 242. London: Home Office.

youth offending team (YOT) a local interagency **team** responsible for the **supervision** of young offenders, advising **youth courts** on the sentencing of individual young people via **pre-sentence reports**, organizing and sitting on **youth offender panels**, making arrangements for **reparation**, **appropriate adult** schemes and remand management (see **bail**), and participating in **crime and disorder partnerships** and other **crime prevention** arrangements. Each **team** consists of at least one social worker, **probation officer, police** officer and representatives of the health and education services, and may also contain personnel from other agencies. YOTs were created in response to the criticisms of the **youth justice** system in the 1990s. The previous social services-run youth justice teams were seen by the government as overly concerned with the welfare of young offenders and insufficiently focused on carrying out the **sentences** imposed by courts. Youth offending teams, incorporating staff from a wider range of agencies, were seen as heralding a new culture of youth justice work, and as one component of a more accountable, efficient and consistent system. Numerically, however, the teams were predominantly made up of social workers from the previous youth justice teams, and most YOT members are still seconded from **social services departments**.

YOT workers supervise young people who are placed on **youth rehabilitation orders** and who are on **licence** following release from **custodial sentences** including **detention and training orders**. They are also responsible for **parenting orders, child safety orders** and **reparation orders**, and provide 'change programmes' linked to **final warnings** made by the **police**. The YOT also has an overall coordinating role in respect of youth justice services in its area. The detailed arrangements for funding and providing these services are agreed annually and included in a Youth Justice Plan submitted to the **Youth Justice Board**. YOTs are governed by the **National Standards for Youth Justice Services**. The YOT manager is directly accountable to the **local authority** chief executive and indirectly to the Youth Justice Board.

Holdaway, S. *et al.* (2001) *New Strategies to Address Youth Offending: the national evaluation of pilot youth offending teams*. London: Home Office.

youth rehabilitation order (YRO) a **community sentence** introduced by the **Criminal Justice and Immigration Act 2008**, similar to the adult

community order. A YRO may be passed on a convicted offender under the age of 18, and may contain one or any combination of 15 different requirements, including **unpaid work, supervision, activity, programme** and **curfew** and **exclusion requirements** enforced by **electronic monitoring**. The YRO replaced a number of separate **sentences** for young offenders including the community order (for 16–17-year-olds), **curfew order**, exclusion order, **attendance centre** order, **supervision order** and **action plan order**. (The **reparation order** for young offenders remains in existence, however.) YROs may also contain requirements for **intensive supervision and surveillance programmes** or for fostering.

youth work   a wide range of services concerned with children and young people roughly within the age range 10 to 21, focusing upon social, recreational and educational needs and the resolution of particular problems such as homelessness and unemployment.

Youth services witnessed rapid expansion in Britain in the 1960s in both the voluntary sector and the statutory sector. The core of these services was the youth club, offering mostly recreational provision. Clearly perceived by successive governments as a way of diverting potentially disaffected youth through constructive leisure, most localities had a youth club providing sports and leisure activities, with some weekend and holiday provision. Many clubs would additionally offer some kind of social education programme, especially the voluntary clubs located within churches. The content of social education would vary enormously depending upon the host organization, although all contended that preparation for citizenship and for adult roles was central to the task. Some youth workers were trained as social workers or had undertaken courses in teacher training colleges. A very large proportion, however, were volunteers or untrained sessional workers. An early innovation, in recognition of the fact that many young people did not attend clubs, was the unattached youth worker. Such workers were to engage with 'street-corner society', especially those young people considered to be 'at risk' of criminal activity or in moral danger. The major objective in this work was more closely akin to social work, that is, to identify problems, whether personal or in the neighbourhood, and to engage with the young people in solving them.

Over the past 20 years the youth club 'movement' has declined but not disappeared, largely because local authorities have been unable to maintain expenditure levels. Services for adolescents and young people have, however, developed in other ways to meet particular needs. Specialized work with young people who engage in antisocial behaviour and are at risk of being excluded from school is now more widely available in an effort to prevent them from offending (see **Crime and Disorder Act**). Other provision, much of it in the voluntary sector, focuses on homelessness (see **rough sleepers** and **foyers**). Young people who are looked after by the local authority have long been vulnerable to homelessness, poverty and offending. The **Children (Leaving Care) Act 2000** places particular responsibilities on local authorities to continue to support young people they have looked after until the age of 25. Similarly, substance misuse among young people has seen the development of advisory and counselling services, again mostly in the voluntary sector, but with limited statutory provision from health and social services. A similar picture exists in relation to pregnancy advisory services and gay and lesbian help lines. General youth counselling services are offered in some localities, but provision is uneven. At the direction of the **Department for Children, Schools and Families**, much attention has focused on schools and directed at young people at risk of truancy or exclusion from school. Pastoral support teams draw on a range of professionals including education social workers to help individual pupils while they complete studies for GCSEs or GNVQs. Building relationships with many marginalized young people is not straightforward because of negative past experiences and perhaps constricted opportunities for personal and social development. Sometimes unresponsive in conversation, erratic in time planning, acting on impulse – these are common habits among adolescents.

But practitioners should remember that despite the difficulties in the young person's interaction with parents, teachers, friends, mentors and social workers, relationships with adults are the crucial catalyst for marginalized young people overcoming those barriers and securing what they want. Much practice is directly or indirectly involved in creating and strengthening such bonds. For a practitioner working with young people to help sort out their feelings is an important objective. What they value above all is their relationship with the counsellor, social worker or youth worker who is attentive and available. This goes some way towards balancing previously hurtful, unsafe experiences with adults and gives the young person a broader emotional understanding for dealing with the dilemmas they face.

One of the hardest things for a young person to learn is to distinguish between 'what's me' and 'what's not me'. The practitioner's skill in 'reflecting back' – which means listening to what the young person has to say and then repeating it so that the young person can clarify what he or she actually feels – is an important tool. A social worker or counsellor should be warm but remain non-judgmental so that young people can begin to discover their own sense of good and bad.

A principal aim of youth work is to extend the effectiveness of a young person's network through which a young person can receive informal support, advice and help in finding job training or a place in higher education. This is often achieved through mentoring schemes; the government's **Connexions** aims to provide such support for all secondary school pupils. (See **teenage pregnancy, youth culture.**)

Jeffs, A & Smith, M (Eds), (2010), *Youth Work Practice*, Basingstoke, MacMillan

Z z

zero tolerance the notion that there should always be a firm
response to even minor offending and other **anti-social behaviour**
in order to 'nip it in the bud' and prevent it from leading to more
serious offences.

The theory was originally developed by the American criminologists
James Q. Wilson and George Kelling in their article 'Broken Windows'
(1982), referring to the idea that broken windows and graffiti in a
neighbourhood (if not swiftly fixed and removed) convey signals that
social authority and social norms no longer prevail in the area, leading
to further vandalism and a downward spiral. By extension it is argued
that the **police** should bear down on minor crime and 'incivilities' to
prevent the development of criminal neighbourhoods. The theory was
subsequently taken up by the New York Police Department in an
aggressive 'zero tolerance' campaign against minor crime and incivility,
which was widely claimed and believed to lead to a spectacular reduction
in the overall New York crime rate, although such claims are by their
nature difficult to prove or disprove any such causal link, and experience
in other American cities does not support it. Zero tolerance policing
has been criticized as leading to oppressive and discriminatory
police behaviour.

The more general belief that even minor rule-breaking, if it is not
challenged, is likely to lead on to more serious offending has been
highly influential in a number of spheres. It has been a significant
feature of the **new youth justice** pursued by **New Labour**, which
favours firm early intervention in response to minor offending by
young people. This approach is the diametric opposite of **minimum
intervention**, which contends that intervention which is too heavy or
too early is likely to provoke worse deviant behaviour by **labelling** and
stigmatizing young people who may only be going through a temporary
and self-limiting phase of minor misbehaviour which they will grow out

of if left alone. The **zero tolerance** approach has also been notably adopted by campaign groups concerned with the problem of **domestic violence**.

Wilson, J. and Kelling, G. (1982) Broken windows. *The Atlantic Monthly*, March.